6 sechs

A MODERN COURSE IN

German

C. R. GOEDSCHE *Northwestern University*

STEN FLYGT *Formerly Princeton University*

MENO SPANN *Northwestern University*

Houghton Mifflin Company

BOSTON NEW YORK CHICAGO DALLAS ATLANTA SAN FRANCISCO

The Riverside Press Cambridge

COPYRIGHT, 1947
BY C. R. GOEDSCHE, STEN G. FLYGT, AND MENO H. SPANN

ALL RIGHTS RESERVED INCLUDING THE RIGHT TO REPRODUCE
THIS BOOK OR PARTS THEREOF IN ANY FORM

The Riverside Press Cambridge
PRINTED IN THE U.S.A.

Preface

This book is intended for use in normally-paced courses which meet from three to five hours per week and also in intensive programs. It is even very suitable for independent study.

The text has been thoroughly tested by several people in many different situations: regular classes, semi-intensive classes, evening classes and private instruction. The results have been uniformly gratifying. As a matter of fact, it may be used in high schools as well as colleges. In subject matter the texts are sufficiently close to the student's own experience to give him pleasure while at the same time appealing to his imagination. The volume contains, in addition to an abundant variety of reading material, such comments on grammar as are necessary to a good understanding of the text, as well as a great deal of exercise and practice material. Subject matter, treatment of grammar, and exercises are completely integrated.

The writers of this book are convinced that a modern language course should not neglect any of the three important aspects of language competence: reading, speaking, and writing. They have therefore designed the book in such a way that the teacher, if he so desires, may use it for an aural-oral approach to reading proficiency. But the purpose of the book is to guide the student toward real independence in his use of the language.

Even from a casual examination it is apparent that this manual is very different from other language texts, that it employs a variety of techniques to achieve its aim, and that few of the techniques are traditional. Every innovation which now appears in this book has, however, been tested in average classes and found successful in achieving its purpose. It may be well to point out the main difference from conventional methods.

In the first place, the writers believe that the subject matter of the first stages of language learning should be as familiar to the student as possible. Obscurity or unfamiliarity of subject matter complicates language difficulties, because the student is never sure whether the combination of words he has before him means what it seems to mean. Therefore the basic situations in the early part of the book are extremely familiar, and only as the student's grasp of the language becomes more secure are new situations and ideas presented to him in German.

In the second place, English translations of the basic texts are an integral part of the plan. Among the advantages in using a translation in the beginning stages are the following:

1) When a translation is used it is not necessary to grade the vocabulary in the way that necessarily produces the painful "baby German" texts that are so well known, but it is possible from the very beginning to use texts which have greater maturity and interest.

2) The translation saves the student a great deal of time and energy usually expended on the completely unprofitable task of thumbing the pages of vocabularies, and allows him to devote this time and energy to building up a large stock of words and mastering difficulties of syntax.
3) The use of English translations makes possible the standard of complete perfection. The very lowest attainment required of the student is certainty of the meaning of every German word and sentence.
4) It cannot have escaped the observation of the teacher that language difficulty in a given sentence causes the student to forget in what logical relation that sentence stands to the rest of the text. The translation helps the student keep the continuity of thought constantly in mind, because he is not painfully groping from one obscure sentence to the next. Not only that, but it makes him carefully work out the relation of the individual words to the total meaning of a sentence and accustoms him to casting his translation in acceptable English form. One of the most important features of the technique of teaching by means of a translation as it is employed in this book is that it sharpens the student's sensitivity to the different genius of the two languages as no other method can. Even in the early lessons he is taught something about the art of translation. As an example let us take the sentence from Lesson Three: **Immer eins nach dem andern!** In the usual situation the beginner would look these words up in the vocabulary and learn that their transverbalization is *Always one thing after the other!* And, if he is not otherwise informed, he will render them thus or else he will guess at another meaning. If he is content to render them *Always one thing after the other* he shows that he hasn't understood the sentence. If he guesses at another meaning he is likely to guess wrong, because the English words suggest some idea like *If it isn't one thing, it's another* or *It's always one confounded thing after the other.* With this misconception in mind he goes on and he now has difficulty in connecting this idea with the context. But in the present text the sentence is first analyzed and then rendered in normal English idiom so that the student learns not only what the individual words mean but also that in this particular combination they mean "One thing at a time!" Thus from the very beginning he learns that the two languages frequently express similar ideas very differently, and he is trained in finding the most suitable and accurate English form to render a German sentence completely lucid to himself and others.

But, of course, not all of the work, and not even the bulk of it, consists of studying a translated text. When the student has thoroughly mastered a given text he goes on to practice and exercise material, which is a reworking of the words and constructions that the student already knows. If the student has worked through the basic text by means of the translation as he should, the practice and exercise material will cause him no difficulties. Although the practice and exercises are designed to drive home important principles, the read-

iness with which they can be done is a quick and sure test of whether the student has used the translation correctly. And it may be said here that the student should be warned about and guided in the correct use of the translation.

The "Practice" material, as distinguished from the "Exercise" material, consists of a great many variations of basic patterns which the student is expected to master. In so doing his efforts are directed to learning correct German, not to puzzling over mutilated words and sentences and trying to add endings to truncated forms, only to learn in class that most of his guesses were wrong anyway. The writers of this book believe that the student should not puzzle over incorrect and incomplete forms but should concentrate on learning patterns which he knows are right.

The "Exercise" material sets certain problems for the student to solve: — answering questions, translating new sentences, choosing the correct concluding clause, finding the sentence which applies to the key word, connecting dependent and independent clauses, and so on. Again, the student is not allowed to become uncertain about the correctness of forms and syntax, and the growing sureness of his **Sprachgefühl** is not confused by a multiplicity of possible incorrect choices. The tasks which he has to perform interest him because they have a purposiveness that derives from the subject matter, and in performing these tasks he learns correct expression, because the information for which he is called upon is evoked along established patterns.

Another innovation in this book is a feature called "Securing the Vocabulary." Certain words, especially elusive words like **doch, noch, sicher, denn, übrigens, ungefähr,** which experience has shown to be troublesome to the student and essential to a good knowledge of the language, are starred when they are first introduced. After that they are constantly and systematically reviewed by a device which focusses the student's attention upon them.

It should be a paramount aim of the instruction to give the student so secure a knowledge of all the words in the lesson as he goes along as to reduce to a minimum the need of using either a standard dictionary or the special vocabulary.

Suggestions for Using the Text

Of course, every teacher using this text will adapt it to his own needs and purposes, but even so it may be useful to know in some detail how the book has been used and what purposes are served by the various parts.

The first part of the book is built on the fiction that the students are reading some of the correspondence of a college freshman named Richard Neumann. This section is composed of sixteen chapters, the first fifteen of which follow the same plan.

At the beginning of each chapter comes a section known as Words and Phrases. This is the student's first contact with the material of the chapter and he must master it completely before going on.* In this section the sentences

* The writers believe that the students should learn pronunciation in class through direct imitation of the teacher. For the students' convenience, however, a section on pronunciation has been incorporated in the Appendix.

of the basic text are broken down and analyzed, one by one, and then reconstructed. It is the student's task to study the Words and Phrases, paying particular attention to the starred words until he knows the meaning of every word in the passage *out of context* and can easily and smoothly translate the Connected Text as it appears in the second section of the chapter. Indeed, he should know it so well that he can with his book closed translate accurately and unhesitatingly words, phrases, and sentences read to him by the teacher in random order. If the book is used in regular classes the Words and Phrases are assigned for home study, but if it is used in intensive or semi-intensive classes the Words and Phrases are repeated and drilled in the drill sections until mastery is complete. It cannot be over-emphasized that mastery must be *complete* so that it becomes unnecessary for the students repeatedly to look up words that they have had.

The third section of the chapter contains the Comments, to be taken up *after* the students know the text. The Comments are a discussion of certain matters of grammar which have occurred in the text and which the student needs to know for a better understanding of the text. The treatment of grammar is purely pragmatic, that is, only those features of grammar are commented upon which are useful to the student at the particular stage where he happens to be. For instance in the chapter where prepositions requiring the dative case are first discussed (Lesson Three), only those four prepositions are mentioned which have actually occurred in the texts. A complete list of these prepositions is, however, given in the Appendix in case the teacher wishes to supply the students with such an enumeration. The Comments are read aloud in class by the teacher or by various students, and the teacher makes sure that unfamiliar terms are explained and that the students understand what they have read. In the classes where the book has been used the students have liked to ask questions concerning other points of grammar and, of course, these questions are answered, but the teachers have had to curb a natural tendency to give a systematic account of whatever topic was under discussion. It was found to be unnecessary and, in the long run, confusing, to tell the student about things that he didn't need to know for his *immediate* purpose. One of the astonishing results of standard impartial tests was the demonstration that students who had been trained by this method, where they had never been called upon to give declension or conjugation, knew much more grammar than students at the same stage in other classes where the main business had been the learning of paradigms and the filling in of endings and such grammatical drill.

The fourth section of the chapter is called Practice. It consists of a number of variations of basic pattern sentences. It is through mastering the practice sentences that the students trained by this method develop a sensitivity to grammatical forms as part of their **Sprachgefühl.** The student is required to learn these variations so well that he not only knows the meaning of all the variations but also can easily and quickly give the correct response in German. The Practice is useful not only in teaching important language forms and syntax, since the sentences drill the points of grammar which have been explained, but

also in aiding the student to acquire some facility in self-expression. The variations are intended to suggest further new and original variations of familiar material and form the basis of composition and conversation. In semi-intensive classes they are drilled until letter perfect and then varied still further as the ingenuity of the teacher and the originality of the students suggest. In classes where reading proficiency is the main objective the Practice may be treated very cursorily or omitted altogether.

The Exercise material may be treated in a variety of ways. In semi-intensive classes, where much effort has been concentrated on the Practice, the Exercises can be done very quickly and chiefly by way of a final clinching of what the students have learned and by way of demonstrating that they have made definite progress. In regular classes the Exercises are assigned as homework and checked and tested in class. Certain portions of the Exercise material, namely those calling for answers to questions, correction of misinformation, and rearrangement of words and phrases to form sentences are usually assigned as written work.

The words which appear in the sixth section, Securing the Vocabulary, are assigned for study. The starred words from previous lessons are arranged in lists which serve two functions: They enable the student to check on his command of the vocabulary and they help him secure the meanings of words he has forgotten. The passing grade for tests based on the starred words should be no less than 96 per cent, and here it may be said parenthetically that since the use of English translation in the section called Words and Phrases makes it possible to set as the very lowest requirement certainty of the meaning of every German word and sentence, the passing grade on all tests may be made much higher than usual.

The second portion of the book is based on the fiction that the students are listening to radio programs and hear about a great variety of subjects from the merits of a marvelous brand of soap-flakes to a discussion of semantics. The basic design of the chapters is the same as in the first portion and therefore the chapters should be treated in substantially the same way as the Richard Neumann chapters.* Since, however, the sentences of the text are not broken down as much as were the sentences in those chapters, it is well for the drill master, where the book is used in semi-intensive courses, to isolate words in the German text and thus make sure that the student really knows the meaning of the words and does not simply recall the sense of the entire passage. Where the student is assigned the Words and Phrases for home study he must be checked in class on his knowledge of the words *out of context.* It is expected that the students will be required to learn the principal parts of the verbs as they occur and therefore the principal parts of all strong and irregular verbs are given for each lesson. There is one very important innovation in this portion of the book, however, and that is the Rewritten Text which concludes each chapter. This is a reading selection which uses no words or constructions which the student has

* Gothic type is introduced in this portion of the book (Lesson 17).

not already had. It is based on the original text of the chapter and is a reworking of that text, expressing new and different ideas without going outside the limits of what the student has had. Its purpose is to teach the student to read without having to translate, to grasp new ideas directly as they are expressed in familiar vocabulary. Incidentally, the Rewritten Text affords a convenient check on whether the student has properly mastered the first part of the lesson. If he has done so, the Rewritten Text will offer him little difficulty; if he has not done so, he will have to look up and verify words and constructions which he should already have learned.

The third portion of the book consists of a number of reading selections.* The first one, **"Die Geschichte von Walter Brooks,"** is a lively and entertaining story, meant to be read rapidly. For semi-intensive courses this story will be something in the nature of dessert at the end of the first year. In other courses, however, where less is required of the student in the way of aural comprehension, authenticity of pronunciation, progress towards self-expression, accurate knowledge of forms and syntax, there will be time left to read all or several of the stories following the story about Walter Brooks. New words, of course, occur and they should be studied and learned. More than that, certain idiomatic expressions, three or four to a page, are given separate explanation, and exercises based on them occur at the end of each story. The purpose of this section of the book is to build up the student's vocabulary very far beyond the range of the 1000 to 2000 words usually learned in the first year.

We gratefully acknowledge the tireless and invaluable secretarial assistance we received from Miss Lucie Schneiderbauer and Miss Monica Erlach.

C. R. G.
S. G. F.
M. H. S.

* **"Die Geschichte von Walter Brooks"** is original. **"Der Alchimist"** and **"Das Wirtshaus am Berge"** make use of old Novellenmotive. **"Der alte Dolch"** is a new version of a story by Arnold Ulitz called **"Der keltische Dolch,"** and **"Das Juwelenkästchen"** is a free version of E. T. A. Hoffmann's **"Das Fräulein von Scuderi."**

Contents

PREFACE

Section I

1. Der Held der nächsten vierzehn Aufgaben 3

1. *Capital Letters.* 2. *The Three Genders.* 3. *Inverted Word Order.* 4. *Formation of Questions.* 5. *Present Tense Forms.*

2. Was hat Richard an? 11

1. *Conventional Imperative.* 2. *Vowel Change* **a > ä, e > i.** 3. *Indefinite Article.* 4. *Adjective Endings after* **der** *and* **ein.**

3. Das hübsche Fräulein Anna 18

1. *Familiar Imperative.* 2. *Accusative and Dative Singular of Nouns.* 3. *The Dative as Indirect Object.* 4. *The Dative after Prepositions.* 5. *Definite and Indefinite Articles.* (*Summary*). 6. **Der-***Words:* **jeder.**

4. Eine lustige Szene 27

1. *Capital Letters.* 2. *Familiar Forms of the Personal Pronoun.* 3. *The Accusative after Prepositions.* 4. *Idiomatic Uses of the Accusative.*

5. Eine Überraschung 38

1. *Personal Pronouns.* 2. *Possessive Adjectives.*

6. Mach Dir keine Sorgen 48

1. *Reflexive Pronouns.* 2. *Separable Prefixes.*

7. Alles in bester Ordnung 58

1. *Formation of the Plural of Nouns.* 2. *Declension of the Plural of Nouns.*

8. Der Hedonist 69

1. *Adjective Declension.*

9. Der Tennismeister 79

1. *Present Perfect and Past Perfect Tenses.* 2. *Position of the Infinitive.*

10. Die Verkäuferin 91

1. *Prepositions.* 2. *Contractions of the Definite Article with Prepositions.* 3. **Da-** *and* **wo-***Compounds.* 4. *Transposed Word Order.*

11. Die Einladung 102

1. *The Genitive Case.* 2. *Declension of Nouns.* 3. *Passive Voice (present tense).* 4. *Dates.*

12. Eine gute Nachricht 113

1. *Future Tense.*

13. Zukunftsträume 123

1. *Modal Auxiliaries (present and simple past).* 2. **Wissen.**

14. Träumerei 135

1. *Subjunctive II.* 2. *Word Order in Conditional Clauses.*

15. Erfüllung 146

1. *Relative Pronouns.* 2. *Interrogative Pronouns.* 3. *Passive Voice (simple past and present perfect).*

16. Aus dem Leben Herbert Beckers. 157

Section II

17. Sender G F S 165

1. *Simple Past Tense of Weak Verbs.* 2. *Present and Past Participles.* 3. *Idiomatic Uses of* **lassen.**

18. Etwas Reklame 176

1. *Simple Past Tense of Strong Verbs.* 2. *Subordinating Conjunctions.*

19. Von einer Welle zur andern. 187

1. *Formation of the Imperative.* 2. *Present Subjunctive I.*

20. Doktor Allwissend 200

1. *Uses of the Infinitive.* 2. *Rules for Determining the Gender of Nouns.* 3. *The Long Attribute.*

21. Wie Sie wollen 213

1. *Adjectives with* **etwas, nichts** *and* **viel.** 2. *Rules for Determining the Plural of Nouns.* 3. *Passive Voice (future and past perfect).*

22. Die Großstadt spricht 227

1. *Variable Prefixes.* 2. *Idiomatic Use of the Past Participle.* 3. *Past Infinitive.* 4. *Modal Auxiliaries (compound tenses).* 5. *Double Infinitive with Modal Auxiliaries.* 6. *Double Infinitive with Other Verbs.*

23. Die Großstadt spricht (Schluß) 242

1. *Mixed Verbs.* 2. *The Future Perfect Tense.*

24. Frag mich was 257

1. *Comparison of Adjectives.* 2. *Inversion for Condition.* 3. *Indirect Statement.*

25. Frag mich was (*Rewritten*) 274

1. *The Long Attribute.*

Section III

26. Walter Brooks 283

27. Der alte Dolch 304

28. Der Alchimist 311

29. Das Wirtshaus am Berge 322

30. Das Juwelenkästchen 333

APPENDIX 359

VOCABULARY 383

INDEX 423

20. Doktor Allwissend 200

1. Uses of the Infinitive. 2. Rules for Determining the Gender of Nouns. 3. The Long Infinitive.

21. Wie Sie wollen 213

1. Adjectives with etwas, nichts and viel. 2. Rules for Determining the Plural of Nouns. 3. Passive Voice (Future and past perfect).

22. Die Großstadt spricht 227

1. Tuesday Evening. 2. Adjunctive (Use of the Past Participle). 3. Past Infinitive. 4. Model Auxiliaries (compound tenses). 5. Double Infinitive with Model Auxiliaries. 6. Double Infinitive with Other Verbs.

23. Die Großstadt spricht (Schluß) 242

1. Model Verbs. 2. The Future Perfect Tense.

24. Frau mich was 257

1. Comparisons of Adjectives. 2. Inversion for Condition. 3. Indirect Statement.

25. Frau mich was (Beschluß) 274

1. The Long Infinitive.

Section III

26. Walter Brooks 283

27. Der alte Dolch 301

28. Der Alchimist 311

29. Das Wirtshaus am Berge 322

30. Das Juwelenkästchen 333

APPENDIX 350

VOCABULARY 353

INDEX 423

Section One

Erste Aufgabe

* * * \

* nun	well then
hier	here
sein	(to) be
er ist	he is
Nun, hier ist er.	Well, here he is.

nett	nice
der Junge	the boy, fellow - der Knabe
ein netter Junge	a nice fellow
nicht wahr?	not true?
Ein netter Junge, nicht wahr?	A nice fellow, isn't he?

achtzehn	eighteen
das Jahr	the year
alt	old
achtzehn Jahre alt	eighteen years old
* gesund	healthy
intelligent′	intelligent
Er ist achtzehn Jahre alt, gesund und intelligent.	He is eighteen years old, healthy and intelligent.

sechs	six
der Fuß	the foot
* groß	large, big, tall
sechs Fuß groß	six feet tall
und	and
haben	(to) have
er hat	he has
breit	broad
die Schulter	the shoulder
breite Schultern	broad shoulders
Er ist sechs Fuß groß und hat breite Schultern.	He is six feet tall and has broad shoulders.

gut	good
der Schwimmer	the swimmer
ein guter Schwimmer	a good swimmer
* sehr	very
das Tennis	the tennis
der Spieler	the player

der Tennisspieler	the tennis player
ein sehr guter Tennisspieler	a very good tennis player
Er ist ein guter Schwimmer und ein sehr guter Tennisspieler.	He is a good swimmer and a very good tennis player.
* der Herbst	the autumn, fall
im Herbst	in the fall
gehen	(to) go
er geht	he goes
das College	the college
aufs College	to college
Im Herbst geht er aufs College.	He is going to college in the fall.
* warum′	why
sprechen	(to) speak
wir sprechen	we speak
von	about
Warum sprechen wir von Richard Neumann?	Why are we talking about Richard Neumann?
haben	(to) have
wir haben	we have
der Grund	the reason
Wir haben einen guten Grund.	We have a good reason.
Richard ist der Held der nächsten vierzehn Aufgaben.	Richard is the hero of the next fourteen lessons.

II. Text: *The following is the preceding passage in connected form. Read and translate.*

Lieber Student, liebe Studentin! Kennen Sie Richard Neumann? Nein? Nun, hier ist er. Ein netter Junge, nicht wahr? Er ist achtzehn Jahre alt, gesund und intelligent. Er ist sechs Fuß groß und hat breite Schultern. Er ist ein guter Schwimmer und ein sehr guter Tennisspieler. Im Herbst geht er aufs College. Warum sprechen wir von Richard Neumann? Wir haben einen guten Grund. Richard ist der Held der nächsten vierzehn Aufgaben.

III. Comments:

In these comments on each section of the German text we are going to take up only a few of the basic principles or striking features of the German language and ignore the rest for the time being. Don't expect a complete explanation of every principle that may be found in the text and if you wonder why you must say certain things that haven't been taken up, don't worry. Just accept the necessity of saying them. You will get the explanations in the course of time. Right now the important thing is to let a lot of vocabulary and language patterns soak in so that a full explanation of the basic principles will make good sense later on. If technical terms are used that you don't know, be sure to find out what they mean.

1. *Capital Letters:*

German differs from English in the use of capital letters in two important respects: (1) All nouns are capitalized; and (2) the word **Sie** meaning *you* is capitalized.

2. *The Three Genders:*

You will have noticed that the definite article (*the*) has three forms in German: **der, die, das.** **Der** is used with masculine nouns, **die** with feminine nouns, and **das** with neuter nouns. Generally speaking, the natural gender of living beings determines the grammatical gender of the designating noun: **der Student, die Studentin.** Noteworthy exceptions are **das Mädchen,** *girl;* **das Fräulein,** *Miss, young lady* whose neuter gender is determined by the suffixes **–chen** and **–lein.** Inanimate objects are either masculine, feminine or neuter. Consequently you must learn the definite article as part of the noun: **der Fuß, die Schulter, das Jahr.**

3. *Inverted Word Order:*

In German as well as in English the subject usually begins the sentence: **Richard ist ein guter Schwimmer.** When, however, a German sentence begins with an element that is not the subject, the subject follows the inflected verb. This is called *inverted order.*

Examples:

1. Hier ist er. *Here he is.*
2. Im Herbst geht er aufs College. *He is going to college in the fall.*

4. *Formation of Questions:*

In questions German does not use an auxiliary verb corresponding to the English verb *do* but simply uses the inverted order.

Example:

Kennen Sie Richard Neumann? *Do you know Richard Neumann?*

5. *Present Tense Forms:*

For your immediate needs you will have to know the following present tense forms:

ich kenne	*I know*	ich gehe	*I go*
er, sie, es kennt	*he, she, it knows*	er, sie, es geht	*he, she, it goes*
wir kennen	*we know*	wir gehen	*we go*
sie kennen	*they know*	sie gehen	*they go*
Sie kennen	*you know*	Sie gehen	*you go*
ich bin	*I am*	ich habe	*I have*
er, sie, es ist	*he, she, it is*	er, sie, es hat	*he, she, it has*
wir sind	*we are*	wir haben	*we have*
sie sind	*they are*	sie haben	*they have*
Sie sind	*you are*	Sie haben	*you have*

IV. Practice: *Master the following basic sentence patterns and their variations.*

1. Ich kenne Richard Neumann sehr gut.
   Der Student kennt
   Er
   Die Studentin
   Sie
   Der Student und ich kennen
   Wir
   Der Student und die Studentin
   Sie
   Kennen Sie Richard Neumann, Herr (*Mr.*) Weber?
   Fräulein (*Miss*) Schmidt?

2. Ich bin achtzehn Jahre alt.
   Richard Neumann ist
   Fräulein Schmidt
   Herr Neumann und ich sind
   Wir
   Herr Neumann und Fräulein Schmidt
   Sind Sie achtzehn Jahre alt, Herr Meier?
   Wie (*how*) alt sind Sie, Herr Weber?

3. Ich spreche von Wilhelm Weber.
   Elsa Schneider.
   Wir sprechen
   Sprechen Sie von Richard Neumann, Herr Jones?

4. Ich gehe im Herbst aufs College.
   Richard geht bald (*soon*)
   Elsa
   Elsa und ich gehen dann (*then*)
   Wir
   Elsa und Richard

5. Im Herbst gehe ich aufs College.
   Bald geht Richard
   Elsa
   Dann gehen Elsa und ich
   wir

6. Diesen (*this*) Herbst bin ich achtzehn Jahre alt.
   Sommer (*summer*) neunzehn (19)
   Winter (*winter*) zwanzig (20)
   Frühling (*spring*) einundzwanzig (21)

7. Gehen Sie		diesen Herbst	aufs College?
	Elsa und Wilhelm	Sommer	
Geht	Herr Weber	Winter	
	Fräulein Schneider	Frühling	

V. Exercises:

A. *Copy the German text under II. Check your copy carefully for mistakes.*

B. *Questions: Answer always in a complete sentence. Use the words, phrases and grammatical forms which the text provides, regardless of whether the question concerns the "story" of the text or not.*

1. Ist Richard Neumann ein Professor?
2. Wie (*how*) alt ist Richard?
3. Ist er acht Fuß groß?
4. Spielt er Tennis?
5. Schwimmt er?
6. Wann (*when*) geht er aufs College?
7. Warum sprechen wir von Richard Neumann?
8. Wer (*who*) ist der Held der nächsten vierzehn Aufgaben?

C. *Translate into English. Then reproduce the German sentences from the English.*

1. Hier ist der Held der nächsten vierzehn Aufgaben.
2. Richard Neumann ist ein netter Junge.
3. Der Held der nächsten vierzehn Aufgaben ist ein guter Schwimmer.
4. Der Student ist sechs Fuß groß und hat breite Schultern.
5. Die Studentin ist achtzehn Jahre alt, gesund und intelligent.
6. Im Herbst geht Richard aufs College.
7. Wir gehen im Herbst aufs College.
8. Gehen Sie im Herbst aufs College?

D. *The following sentences are grammatically correct but give wrong information. Change them so as to make them correct.*

1. Richard Neumann ist vierzehn Jahre alt.
2. Er ist fünf Fuß groß.
3. Er ist der Held der nächsten achtzehn Aufgaben.
4. Richard Neumann ist eine intelligente Studentin.
5. Im Sommer geht er aufs College.

VI. Securing the Vocabulary: *The plan of this section is as follows:*

Part A lists the words which appear marked with a star in Section I. Do not fail to learn these words perfectly. Beginning with the next lesson, Part B repeats se-

lected starred words from previous lessons in order to give you the chance to review their meanings at intervals.

A.	erst-	*first*	gesund	*healthy*
	nächst	*next*	groß	*large, big, tall*
	lieb	*dear*	sehr	*very*
	kennen	*(to) know*	warum	*why*
	nun	*well then*	der Herbst	*autumn, fall*

Zweite Aufgabe

* * * \

schön	beautiful, fine; very well
haben	(to) have
Richard hat	Richard has
braun	brown
das Haar	the hair
braunes Haar	brown hair
grau	gray
das Auge	the eye
graue Augen	gray eyes
Schön — Richard hat braunes Haar und graue Augen.	Very well then, Richard has brown hair and gray eyes.

* tragen	(to) carry; wear
er trägt	he wears
* meistens	mostly, generally
der Sport	the sport
der Anzug	the suit
der Sportanzug	the sport suit
Er trägt meistens einen Sportanzug.	Generally he wears a sport suit.

* heute	today
das Beispiel	the example
zum Beispiel	for example
grau	gray
die Hosen	the trousers
graue Hosen	gray trousers
er hat graue Hosen an	he has gray trousers on
weiß	white
das Hemd	the shirt
er hat ein weißes Hemd an	he has a white shirt on
braun	brown
der Rock	the coat, jacket, skirt
er hat einen braunen Rock an	he has a brown jacket on
Heute z.B. (zum Beispiel) hat er graue Hosen, ein weißes Hemd und einen braunen Rock an.	Today, for example, he is wearing gray trousers, a white shirt, and a brown jacket.

sein	his
der Schuh	the shoe
seine Schuhe	his shoes
Seine Schuhe sind weiß.	His shoes are white.

* nur	only
der Fehler	the mistake, fault
er hat nur einen Fehler	he has only one fault

* viel	much
nicht viel	not much
* das Geld	the money
nicht viel Geld	not much money
Er hat nur einen Fehler, er hat nicht viel Geld.	He has only one fault, he doesn't have much money.
jetzt	now
sein	(to) be
es ist	it is
aber	but, however
* die Zeit	the time
es ist Zeit	it is time
daß	that
ihn	him
das College	the college
zum College	to the college
* schicken	(to) send
wir schicken	we send
wir schicken ihn zum College	we send him off to college
Jetzt ist es aber Zeit, daß wir ihn zum College schicken.	But now it's time that we send him off to college.
der Vater	the father
geben	(to) give
er gibt	he gives
sein	his
der Junge	the boy, young man
seinem Jungen	to his boy
der Scheck	the check
er gibt seinem Jungen einen Scheck	he gives his boy a check
die Mutter	the mother
ihr	her
ihrem Jungen	to her boy
der Kuß	the kiss
sie gibt ihrem Jungen einen Kuß	she gives her boy a kiss
Fräulein Becker	Miss Becker
das Paket'	the package
ein kleines Paket	a small package
Vater Neumann gibt seinem Jungen einen Scheck, Mutter Neumann gibt ihrem Jungen einen Kuß, und Fräulein Becker gibt Richard ein kleines Paket.	Father Neumann gives his boy a check, Mother Neumann gives her boy a kiss, and Miss Becker gives Richard a small package.

II. Text:

Sie sagen jetzt wahrscheinlich: „Wir kennen Richard noch nicht gut genug. Erzählen Sie uns mehr von Richard!" Schön — Richard hat braunes Haar und graue Augen. Er trägt meistens einen Sportanzug. Heute z.B. (zum Beispiel) hat er graue Hosen, ein weißes Hemd und einen braunen Rock an. Seine Schuhe sind weiß. Er hat nur einen Fehler, er hat nicht viel Geld. Jetzt ist es aber Zeit, daß wir ihn zum College schicken. Vater Neumann gibt seinem Jungen einen Scheck, Mutter Neumann gibt ihrem Jungen einen Kuß, und Fräulein Becker gibt Richard ein kleines Paket.

III. Comments:

1. *Conventional Imperative:*

Polite form

Observe the two sentences:

Sprechen Sie von Richard Neumann? *Are you talking about Richard Neumann?*

Sprechen Sie von Richard Neumann! *Talk about Richard Neumann!*

The difference in tone of voice and punctuation makes the difference between a question and a command or request (imperative) in the above examples.

2. *Vowel Change* **a > ä** *and* **e > i:**

In some verbs there is a change of vowel in the present tense, *e.g.* **ich trage** — but — **er trägt,** and **ich spreche** — but — **er spricht,** which is somewhat like the change of vowel in the English *I do, he does,* and *I say, he says.*

3. *Indefinite Article:*

The masculine and neuter indefinite articles are identical in the nominative case, the case of the subject: **ein Paket, ein Scheck.** In the accusative case, the case of the direct object, the forms are: **ein Paket,** but **einen Scheck.** The feminine indefinite article is **eine** both in the nominative and the accusative.

Examples:

1. **Ein Hemd** ist in dem Paket. *A shirt is in the package.*
   Vater Neumann gibt Richard **ein Hemd.** *Father Neumann gives Richard a shirt.*
2. **Ein Sportanzug** ist in dem Paket. *A sport suit is in the package.*
   Vater Neumann gibt Richard **einen Sportanzug.** *Father Neumann gives Richard a sport suit.*
3. Martha Müller ist **eine** intelligente **Studentin.** *Martha Müller is an intelligent student.*
   Kennen Sie **eine Studentin** Martha Müller? *Do you know a student (by the name of) Martha Müller?*

4. *Adjective endings after* **der** *and* **ein:**

You have become aware that adjectives preceding nouns have various endings. For the time being it will suffice to learn that the ending of the adjective depends upon the noun it modifies and also upon the introductory word, as illustrated in the following examples:

M.	F.	N.
der gute Schwimmer	**die** intelligente Studentin	**das** graue Hemd
ein guter Schwimmer	**eine** intelligente Studentin	**ein** graues Hemd

IV. Practice:

1. a. Trägt Richard meistens einen Sportanzug?
   er
   Tragen Sie , Herr Neumann?
   b. Schickt Herr Neumann den Jungen zum College?
   Frau (*Mrs.*)
   Schicken Sie , Frau Neumann?
2. a. Geben Sie mir (*me*) einen Scheck, bitte (*please*)!
   Rock
   Anzug
   b. Geben Sie mir ein Hemd, bitte!
   Päckchen Zigaretten (*package of cigarettes*)
   c. Erzählen Sie uns mehr von Richard!
   Vater Neumann!
   Mutter Neumann!
   d. Bitte, schicken Sie dem Jungen ein Hemd!
   Päckchen Zigaretten!
   Paar (*pair*) weiße Hosen.

Bitte, schicken Sie dem Jungen einen Scheck!
Rock!
Sportanzug!

e. Sagen Sie mir, bitte, wie (*how*) alt Richard ist! dependent word
groß
intelligent
(verb at end)

f. Sagen Sie mir, bitte, wie alt Sie sind!

3. a. Heute hat Richard einen braunen Rock an.
in a question
grauen
weißen Anzug
blauen (*blue*)
schwarzen (*black*)

b. Heute hat er ein graues Hemd an.
weißes
blaues
braunes

c. Richard hat heute einen braunen Rock an, etc.
Er hat heute ein graues Hemd an, etc.

4. a. *Make questions based on the sentences in 3 above as follows:*
Haben Sie heute einen blauen Anzug an?
Hat Richard heute ein graues Hemd an?

V. Exercises:

A. *Copy the German text under II. Check your copy carefully for mistakes.*

B. *Questions:*

1. Kennen Sie Richard jetzt gut genug?
2. Hat Richard graues Haar?
3. Hat er braune Augen?
4. Was trägt er meistens?
5. Hat er heute braune Hosen an?
6. Sind seine Schuhe braun?
7. Was für einen (*what kind of a*) Fehler hat er?
8. Wer gibt Richard einen Scheck?
9. Was gibt Frau Neumann ihrem Jungen?
10. Gibt Fräulein Becker Richard ein großes Paket?

C. *Translate.*

1. Anna erzählt uns viel von Richard.
2. Ich habe nicht viel Geld.
3. Herr Neumann schickt seinen Jungen diesen Herbst aufs College.
4. Anna trägt meistens einen grauen Rock.
5. Ich gebe meiner Mutter einen Kuß.
6. Mein Vater hat graues Haar und blaue Augen.

7. Kennen Sie meine Mutter?
8. Erzählen Sie uns mehr von dem Helden der nächsten dreizehn Aufgaben.
9. Seine Schuhe sind braun und sein Hemd ist weiß.
10. Ich kenne eine intelligente Studentin.

D. *Correct the misinformation.*

1. Richard hat ein blaues Hemd an.
2. Er hat einen weißen Rock an.
3. Vater Neumann gibt seinem Jungen einen Kuß.
4. Mutter Neumann gibt ihrem Jungen ein kleines Paket.
5. Richards Schuhe sind braun.
6. Richard hat viel Geld.
7. Richard hat braune Augen.
8. Vater Neumann trägt meistens einen Sportanzug.
9. Vater Neumann gibt Richard einen Sportanzug.
10. Heute hat Richard schwarze (*black*) Schuhe an.

VI. Securing the Vocabulary:

vocabulary Test (erst) Friday June 15, 1950

A.

jetzt	*now*
wahrscheinlich	*probably*
noch	*still, yet*
noch nicht	*not yet*
genug	*enough*
erzählen	(*to*) *tell, narrate*
tragen	(*to*) *carry, wear*
meistens	*mostly, generally*
heute	*to-day*
nur	*only*
viel	*much*
die Zeit	*time*
schicken	(*to*) *send*
das Geld	*money*

B.

warum (4)	1. *well then*
der Herbst (7)	2. *dear*
nächst (5)	3. *healthy*
gesund (3)	4. *why*
lieb (2)	5. *next*
sehr (6)	6. *very*
nun (1)	7. *autumn*
erst (8)	8. *first*

Dritte Aufgabe

* * * \

* heißen	(to) be called
sie heißt	she is called
mit	with
der Vorname	the first name
mit Vornamen	by first name
sie heißt mit Vornamen	she is called by first name
Fräulein Becker heißt mit Vornamen Anna.	Miss Becker's first name is Anna.
die Schule	the school
die Kamera'din	the girl friend
die Schul'kamera'din	the schoolmate (feminine)
Sie ist Richards Schulkameradin.	She is Richard's schoolmate.
das Haar	the hair
blondes Haar	blond hair
das Auge	the eye
blaue Augen	blue eyes
Sie hat blondes Haar und blaue Augen.	She has blond hair and blue eyes.
schlank	slender
sehr	very
Sie ist schlank und sehr hübsch.	She is slender and very pretty.
tragen	(to) carry, wear
sie trägt	she wears
silbern	of silver
der Hals	the neck, the throat
das Band	the ribbon, band
das Halsband	the necklace
ein silbernes Halsband	a silver necklace
der Tag	the day
* jeder	each, every
jeden Tag	every day
das Kleid	the dress
zu jedem Kleid	with every dress
Sie trägt ein silbernes Halsband; sie trägt es jeden Tag und zu jedem Kleid.	She wears a silver necklace; she wears it every day and with every dress.
die Geburt	the birth
der Tag	the day
der Geburtstag	the birthday

* das Geschenk	the present
das Geburtstagsgeschenk	the birthday-present
Das Halsband ist ein Geburtstagsgeschenk.	The necklace is a birthday-present.
kochen	(to) cook
* gern	gladly
Anna kocht gern.	Anna likes to cook.
stellen	(to) put
sie stellt	she puts
die Frau	the woman; Mrs.
* die Frage	the question
Fragen	questions
* wie	how, as, like
essen	(to) eat
er ißt	he eats
er ißt gern	he likes to eat
Was ißt er gern?	What does he like to eat?
Anna kocht gern, und sie stellt Fragen wie: „Was ißt Richard gern?“	Anna likes to cook and she asks questions like: "What does Richard like to eat?"
bitte	please
das Rezept′	the recipe
für	for
der Apfel	the apple
der Strudel	the whirl-pool, swirl
der Apfelstrudel	the apfelstrudel
Geben Sie mir, bitte, das Rezept für Apfelstrudel!	Please give me the recipe for apfelstrudel!
Wien	Vienna
Wiener	of Vienna, Viennese
das Schnitzel	the cutlet
das Wiener Schnitzel	the breaded veal cutlet
Ißt Richard gern Wiener Schnitzel?	Does Richard like Wiener Schnitzel?
genug	enough
davon′	of it
genug davon	enough of it
* verstehen	(to) understand
Sie verstehen	you understand
mich	me
nicht wahr	isn't that so?
Genug davon. Sie verstehen mich, nicht wahr?	That's enough of that. You understand me, don't you?

auf	on, at, in
die Bahn	the train, track
* der Hof	the court, yard
* der Bahnhof	the railroad station
auf dem Bahnhof	at the railroad station
weinen	(to) weep, cry
sie weint	she cries
ein bißchen	a little, a bit
Auf dem Bahnhof weint Anna ein bißchen.	Anna cries a bit at the station.
ihr	her
letzt	last
das Wort	the word
ihre letzten Worte	her last words
schreiben	(to) write
schreib!	write!
* wenigstens	at least
zweimal	two times, twice
die Woche	the week
Ihre letzten Worte sind: „Schreib wenigstens zweimal die Woche!"	Her last words are, "Write at least twice a week!"
müssen	(to) have to
er muß	he has to
natür'lich	naturally, of course
die Eltern	the parents
seine Eltern	his parents
seinen Eltern	to his parents
* auch	also
schreiben	(to) write
Richard muß natürlich seinen Eltern auch schreiben.	Of course Richard has to write his parents, too.
interessieren	(to) interest
das interessiert Sie	that interests you
Das interessiert Sie nicht?	That doesn't interest you?
wie	how
schade	too bad
Wie schade!	What a pity!
* lesen	(to) read
Sie werden lesen	you will read

* der Brief	the letter
seine Briefe	his letters
Sie werden seine Briefe lesen	you are going to read his letters
In den nächsten zwölf Aufgaben werden Sie seine Briefe lesen.	In the next twelve lessons you are going to read his letters.

II. Text:

Sie fragen: „Was ist in dem Paket? — Wer ist Fräulein Becker?" Immer eins nach dem andern. In dem Paket sind Zigaretten und eine Tafel Schokolade. Fräulein Becker heißt mit Vornamen Anna. Sie ist Richards Schulkameradin. Sie hat blondes Haar und blaue Augen. Sie ist schlank und sehr hübsch. Sie trägt ein silbernes Halsband; sie trägt es jeden Tag und zu jedem Kleid. Das Halsband ist ein Geburtstagsgeschenk. Anna kocht gern, und sie stellt Fragen wie: „Was ißt Richard gern? — Geben Sie mir, bitte, das Rezept für Apfelstrudel! — Ißt Richard gern Wiener Schnitzel?" Genug davon. Sie verstehen mich, nicht wahr? Auf dem Bahnhof weint Anna ein bißchen. Ihre letzten Worte sind: „Schreib wenigstens zweimal die Woche!" Richard muß natürlich seinen Eltern auch schreiben. Das interessiert Sie nicht? — Wie schade! In den nächsten zwölf Aufgaben werden Sie seine Briefe lesen.

III. Comments:

1. *Familiar Imperative:*

You will notice that Anna says to Richard: **Schreib wenigstens zweimal die Woche!** meaning *Write at least twice a week.* She uses the form **schreib** instead of **schreiben Sie** because she and Richard are close friends. Schreiben Sie is the conventional imperative and **schreib** is the familiar imperative. Here are the familiar imperative forms of other verbs you have had: **schick, sag, erzähl, gib, sprich.**

2. *The Accusative and Dative Singular of Nouns:*

In the lists of words and phrases you have been given the nominative form of the definite article with each noun, *e.g.* **der Scheck, die Aufgabe, das Auge.** In the accusative form only the masculine definite article is different from the nominative, thus: **den Scheck, die Aufgabe, das Auge.** In the dative form, however, all three are different, thus: **dem Scheck, der Aufgabe, dem Auge.**

While most nouns remain unchanged in form in the accusative and dative cases, there is a group of masculines which end in **–n** or **–en** in every case but the nominative: N. **der Student,** A. **den Studenten,** D. **dem Studenten.**

3. *The Dative as Indirect Object:* (to, for) study all cases except genitive

The dative case is the case required for the indirect object.

Examples:

1. Vater Neumann gibt **dem Jungen** einen Scheck.
   Father Neumann gives the boy a check.
2. Richard gibt **der Schulkameradin** ein Halsband.
   Richard gives the (i.e. *his*) *schoolmate a necklace.*

4. *The Dative after Prepositions:*

The dative is also used after a number of prepositions of which you have had **mit** — *with;* **nach** — *after, towards;* **von** — *from, about;* **zu** — *to.* (For the complete list see Appendix.) aus, außer, bei, seit

Example:

Erzählen Sie mir mehr **von dem Tennisspieler!**
Tell me more about the tennis player!

Under certain circumstances, which will be defined later, the dative is used also after another group of prepositions of which you have had, **auf** — *on, at;* and **in** — *in:* **in dem Paket,** *in the package.* (For complete list see Appendix.)

5. *Definite and Indefinite Articles: Summary:*

Definite				Indefinite		
M.	F.	N.		M.	F.	N.
der	die	das	— Nom. —	ein	eine	ein
den	die	das	— Acc. —	einen	eine	ein
dem	der	dem	— Dat. —	einem	einer	einem

6. **Der-*Words:* Jeder:**

The word **jeder,** meaning *each, every,* belongs to a group of words called **der-words** (see Appendix). Their endings are almost identical with those of the definite article.

	M.	F.	N.
Nom.	jeder	jede	jedes
Acc.	jeden	jede	jedes
Dat.	jedem	jeder	jedem

IV. Practice:

1. a. Erzählen Sie uns mehr von Richard, Herr Professor!
   Erzähl uns mehr von Richard, Anna!
   b. Schicken Sie mir, bitte, einen Scheck, Herr Schmidt!
   Schick mir, bitte, einen Scheck, Vater!
   c. Geben Sie mir ein Päckchen Zigaretten, bitte!
   Gib mir ein Päckchen Zigaretten, Richard!

2. Erzählen Sie uns mehr von dem Jungen, bitte!
   Tennisspieler
   Bahnhof
   Brief
   Halsband
   Geburtstagsgeschenk
   Paket
   der Studentin
   Aufgabe
   Schulkameradin

3. Der Vater gibt dem Jungen den Anzug.
   Rock.
   Die Mutter Scheck.
   das Geld.
   Paket.
   Geschenk.
   Das Fräulein die Schokolade.
   Zigarette.

4. Der Junge gibt der Mutter einen Kuß.
   Schulkameradin ein Halsband.
   eine Zigarette.
   Tafel Schokolade.

5. Der Rock ist ein Geburtstagsgeschenk vom Vater.
   Scheck.
   Das Kleid von der Mutter.
   Geld
   Die Schokolade

6. Auf dem Bahnhof weint Anna ein bißchen.
   sagt Anna: „Sehreib wenigstens zweimal die Woche!"
   gibt der Vater dem Jungen einen Scheck.

7. In dem Paket ist ein Brief.
   Scheck.
   Halsband.
   Kleid.
   Geburtstagsgeschenk.
   eine Tafel Schokolade.

8. Richard sagt zum Vater: „Schick mir, bitte, einen Scheck!"
   zu Anna: „Weine jetzt nicht mehr!"
   zur Mutter: „Ich schreibe dir wenigstens einmal die Woche!"

9. Richard geht mit dem Vater zum Bahnhof.
   Fräulein
   der Mutter
   Schulkameradin

10. Ich esse gern Apfelstrudel.
    Wiener Schnitzel.
    Schokolade.
    rauche (*smoke*) gern Zigaretten.
    Zigarren. (*cigars*)
    Pfeife. (*pipe*)

11. a. Anna trägt jeden Tag ihr silbernes Halsband.
    ein schönes Kleid.
    b. Richard gibt seiner Schulkameradin jedes Jahr ein Geburtstagsgeschenk.
    c. Richard schreibt jede Woche einen Brief an (*to*) seinen Vater.
    an seine Mutter.
    d. Herr Neumann schickt seinem Jungen jede Woche einen Scheck.

12. Wie heißt der Held der nächsten zwölf Aufgaben?
    Er heißt Neumann.
    Wie heißt er mit Vornamen?
    Richard.
    Wie heißen Sie mit Vornamen, Herr Weber?
    Ich heiße Wilhelm.

V. Exercises:

A. *Questions:*

1. Was ist in dem Paket?
2. Wer ist Fräulein Becker?
3. Wie heißt Fräulein Becker mit Vornamen?
4. Hat Fräulein Becker braunes Haar?
5. Hat sie graue Augen?
6. Von wem hat sie das Halsband?

7. Kochen Sie gern?
8. Was ißt Richard gern?
9. Was waren Annas letzte Worte?
10. Wem (*to whom*) muß Richard schreiben?
11. Was werden Sie in den nächsten zwölf Aufgaben lesen?

B. *Translate and then learn to recall the German from the English:*

1. Richards Schulkameradin heißt mit Vornamen Anna.
2. Die Schokolade ist ein Geschenk von meinem Vater.
3. Das Halsband ist ein Geschenk von meiner Mutter.
4. Ich verstehe Sie nicht.
5. Das ist eine interessante Frage.
6. Auf dem Bahnhof weint Richards Mutter ein bißchen.
7. Kennen Sie Richard Neumann nicht? Wie schade!
8. Geben Sie mir eine Tafel Schokolade, bitte!
9. Ich lese einen Brief von meinem Vater.
10. Schreiben Sie wenigstens einmal die Woche!

C. *Correct the misinformation:*

1. Das Halsband ist ein Geschenk von Herrn Neumann.
2. Annas letzte Worte sind: „Schreib wenigstens einmal die Woche!"
3. Fräulein Becker hat schwarzes Haar und blaue Augen.
4. In den nächsten vierzehn Aufgaben werden wir Richards Briefe lesen.
5. Auf dem Bahnhof weint Richard.

VI. Securing the Vocabulary:

A.

fragen	(*to*) *ask*
wer	*who*
immer	*always*
nach	*after*
heißen	(*to*) *be called*
jeder	*every*
das Geschenk	*present*
gern	*gladly*
die Frage	*question*
wie	*how, as, like*
er ißt gern	*he likes to eat*
verstehen	(*to*) *understand*
der Hof	*court, yard*
der Bahnhof	*railroad station*
wenigstens	*at least*
auch	*also*
lesen	(*to*) *read*
der Brief	*letter*

B.

viel (3)	1. *mostly, generally*
noch nicht (8)	2. (*to*) *tell, narrate*
kennen (7)	3. *much*
groß (4)	4. *large, big, tall*
tragen (6)	5. *time*
meistens (1)	6. (*to*) *carry, wear*
die Zeit (5)	7. (*to*) *know*
erzählen (2)	8. *not yet*
erst (9)	9. *first*
der Herbst (4)	1. *healthy*
lieb (7)	2. *still, yet*
schicken (8)	3. *only*
nur (3)	4. *autumn, fall*
noch (2)	5. *probably*
jetzt (6)	6. *now*
gesund (1)	7. *dear*
nun (9)	8. (*to*) *send*
wahrscheinlich (5)	9. *well then*

Vierte Aufgabe

* * * \

der Name	the name
man schreibt seinen Namen	one writes his name
die Geburt	the birth
* der Ort	the place
der Geburtsort	the place of birth
die Heimat	the native-place, homeland
* die Stadt	the city
die Heimatstadt	the home town
weiter	on, farther
und so weiter	and so on
hundert	hundred
der Zettel	the piece of paper
antworten	(to) answer
man antwortet	one answers
die Frage	the question
man antwortet auf eine Frage	one answers a question

Man wartet den ganzen Tag und zwischendurch schreibt man seinen Namen, Geburtsort, Heimatstadt usw. (und so weiter) auf hundert Zettel und antwortet auf hundert Fragen.	You wait around all day and every now and then you write your name, place of birth, home address, etc. on a hundred slips of paper and answer a hundred questions.

* beschreiben	(to) describe
ich beschreibe	I describe
dir	for you, to you
eine lustige Szene	a funny scene
* einzig	single, only
die einzige lustige Szene	the only funny scene
ganz	entire; quite
der Tag	the day
des ganzen Tages	of the entire day

Ich beschreibe Dir die einzige lustige Szene des ganzen Tages.	I'll describe the only funny scene of the entire day for you.

unfreundlich	unfriendly
älter	older, elderly
der Herr	the gentleman
ein älterer Herr	an older gentleman
fragen	(to) ask
er fragt	he asks
mich	me
er fragt mich	he asks me

heißen	(to) be called, be named
wie heißen Sie?	what is your name?
Ein unfreundlicher, älterer Herr fragt mich: „Wie heißen Sie?“	A stern, elderly gentleman asks me, "What's your name?"
Ich: „Richard.“	I: "Richard."
* das Kind	the child
die Kinder	the children
der Garten	the garden
der Kindergarten	the kindergarten
im Kindergarten	in the kindergarten
Er: „Sie sind hier nicht im Kindergarten.	He: "You're not in kindergarten here.
* ich möchte	I would like to
die Fami'lię	the family
der Name	the name
der Fami'lięnna'me	the family name
* wissen	(to) know
ich möchte wissen	I would like to know
Ich möchte Ihren Familiennamen wissen.“	I would like to know your family name."
Ich: „Neumann, n wie in Napoleon.“	I: "Neumann, n as in Napoleon."
interessant'	interesting
Er: „Sehr interessant.	He: "Very interesting.
* wann	when
die Geburt	the birth
der Tag	the day
der Geburtstag	the birthday
Wann haben Sie Geburtstag?“	When is your birthday?"
der Montag	the Monday
nächsten Montag	next Monday
Ich: „Nächsten Montag.“	I: "Next Monday."
der Donner	the thunder
das Wetter	the weather
das Donnerwetter	the thunder-weather, thunderstorm
Zum Donnerwetter!	to the thunder-weather; Confound it!

machen	(to) make
machen Sie?	are you making?
sich	yourself
über	over, about, concerning
über mich	about me
lustig	merry, funny
machen Sie sich über mich lustig?	are you making yourself merry about me?
Er: „Zum Donnerwetter! Machen Sie sich über mich lustig?“	He: "Confound it! Are you making fun of me?"
Ich: „Nein.“	I: "No."
da	then
sagen	(to) say
einer sagt	someone says
mir	to me
das Ohr	the ear
ins Ohr	into the ear
einer sagt mir ins Ohr	somebody says to me into the ear
* die Vorsicht	the caution
* der Mensch	the human being, man
Vorsicht, Mensch!	Careful, bud!
der Dekan′	the dean
kommen	(to) come
der Dekan kommt	the dean comes
Da sagt mir einer ins Ohr: „Vorsicht, Mensch, der Dekan kommt!“	Then a fellow whispers into my ear, "Watch out, bud, the dean is coming!"
* übrigens	incidentally, by the way
der Dank	the thanks, gratitude
vielen Dank	much gratitude, many thanks
für	for
die Zigaret′te	the cigarette
die Zigaretten	the cigarettes
Übrigens, vielen Dank für die Schokolade und die Zigaretten.	Incidentally, thanks ever so much for the chocolate and the cigarettes.

war	was
lieb	dear, sweet, nice
von	about
von dir	of you
dein	your
deine Mutter	your mother
von deiner Mutter	of your mother
Das war lieb von Dir und Deiner Mutter.	That was sweet of you and your mother.

ihr	you (*pl.*)
sein	(to) be
ihr seid	you are
immer	always
nett	nice
zu mir	to me
Ihr seid immer so nett zu mir.	You are always so nice to me.

wie schade	what a pity
sein	(to) be
du bist	you are
Wie schade, daß Du nicht hier bist.	I am sorry you are not here.

denken	(to) think
ich denke	I think
oft	often
an	at, by, to, about
ich denke an dich	I think of you
Ich denke oft an Dich.	I think about you often.

* schon	already
* spät	late
es ist schon spät	it is already late
* müde	tired
Es ist schon spät, und ich bin müde.	It's already late and I'm tired.

treu	faithful, loyal
Dein treuer Richard	your devoted Richard
Dein treuer Richard.	Yours always, Richard.

II. Text:

Liebe Anna!

Endlich bin ich Student. So eine Immatrikulation ist schrecklich langweilig. Man wartet den ganzen Tag und zwischendurch schreibt man seinen Namen, Geburtsort, seine Heimatstadt usw. auf hundert Zettel und antwortet auf hundert Fragen. Ich beschreibe Dir die einzige lustige Szene des ganzen Tages. — Ein unfreundlicher, älterer Herr fragt mich: „Wie heißen Sie?" Ich: „Richard." Er: „Sie sind hier nicht im Kindergarten. Ich möchte Ihren Familiennamen wissen." Ich: „Neumann, n wie in Napoleon." Er: „Sehr interessant. Wann haben Sie Geburtstag?" Ich: „Nächsten Montag." Er: „Zum Donnerwetter, machen Sie sich über mich lustig?" Ich: „Nein." Da sagt mir einer ins Ohr: „Vorsicht Mensch, der Dekan kommt!"

Übrigens, vielen Dank für die Schokolade und die Zigaretten. Das war lieb von Dir und Deiner Mutter. Ihr seid immer so nett zu mir. Wie schade, daß Du nicht hier bist. Ich denke oft an Dich. Es ist schon spät, und ich bin müde.

Dein treuer Richard

III. Comments:

1. *Capital Letters:*

In a letter every pronoun and possessive adjective referring to the person addressed is capitalized.

2. *The Familiar Forms of the Personal Pronoun:*

There is in German a familiar verb form and the corresponding pronoun. The pronoun is **du** and the verb ending is **–st.** (Compare the obsolete English form *thou knowest.*) This form is used in addressing the deity, members of one's family, intimate friends, children, and animals. The plural of **du** is **ihr.** Here are present tense forms of a few verbs:

einsing e

ich schreibe	*I write*	ich antworte	*I answer*
du schreibst	*you write*	du antwortest	*you answer*
er, sie, es schreibt	*he, she, it writes*	er, sie, es antwortet	*he, she, it answers*
wir schreiben	*we write*	wir antworten	*we answer*
ihr schreibt	*you write*	ihr antwortet	*you answer*
sie schreiben	*they write*	sie antworten	*they answer*
Sie schreiben	*you write*	Sie antworten	*you answer*
ich gebe	*I give*	ich lese	*I read*
du gibst	*you give*	du liest	*you read*
er, sie, es gibt	*he, she, it gives*	er, sie, es liest	*he, she, it reads*
wir geben	*we give*	wir lesen	*we read*
ihr gebt	*you give*	ihr lest	*you read*
sie geben	*they give*	sie lesen	*they read*
Sie geben	*you give*	Sie lesen	*you read*
ich habe	*I have*	ich bin	*I am*
du hast	*you have*	du bist	*you are*
er, sie, es hat	*he, she, it has*	er, sie, es ist	*he, she, it is*
wir haben	*we have*	wir sind	*we are*
ihr habt	*you have*	ihr seid	*you are*
sie haben	*they have*	sie sind	*they are*
Sie haben	*you have*	Sie sind	*you are*

3. *The Accusative after Prepositions:*

The accusative case is the case required for the direct object and after a number of prepositions, the most frequent of which is **für.** (For complete list see Appendix.) bis, durch, für, ohne, um, gegen, wider

Examples:

1. Direct Object: Sie trägt **ein silbernes Halsband.**
   She wears a silver necklace.
2. Prepositional Object: Vielen Dank **für die Schokolade.**
   Thanks ever so much for the chocolate.

4. *Idiomatic Uses of the Accusative:*

There are other special uses of the accusative which are worth noting:

a. Stereotyped expressions for *Good morning, Good evening, Many thanks,* etc. are in the accusative.

Examples:

Guten Morgen	*Good morning*
Guten Tag	*Good day*
Guten Abend	*Good evening*
Gute Nacht	*Good night*
Vielen Dank	*Many thanks*

b. The accusative is used to express duration of time or definite time.

Examples:

den ganzen Tag	*the whole day*	nächsten Montag	*next Monday*
den ganzen Monat	*the whole month*	nächsten Monat	*next month*
das ganze Jahr	*the whole year*	nächstes Jahr	*next year*
die ganze Nacht	*the whole night*	nächste Woche	*next week*
die ganze Woche	*the whole week*		

IV. Practice:

1. Ich habe nächsten Montag Geburtstag.
   Dienstag
   Du hast Mittwoch
   Er hat Donnerstag
   Wir haben Freitag
   Sie Sonnabend
   Haben Sie nächsten Sonntag Geburtstag, Herr Jones?

2. Nächste Woche schickt Herr Neumann den Jungen zum College.
   Nächsten Monat
   Nächstes Jahr

3. Ich warte schon den ganzen Abend auf Sie, Herr Neumann.
   Morgen dich, Richard.
   Tag ihn.

4. Möchten Sie meinen Familiennamen wissen?
   Vornamen
   Geburtstag
   Geburtsort

5. Ich esse Wiener Schnitzel gern.
   Apfelstrudel
   Richard ißt Sauerkraut
   Wiener Wurst
   Wir essen Schinken (*ham*)
   Kalbfleisch (*veal*)
   Essen Sie Bratkartoffeln (*fried potatoes*) gern?

6. Vielen Dank für die Zigaretten. Bitte sehr. (*You're welcome.*)
Schokolade
das Geschenk
Paket
Hemd
den Scheck
Brief

7. a. Ich denke oft an Richard Neumann.
den Jungen.
die Schulkameradin.

b. Denken Sie oft an Richard Neumann? etc.
mich, Herr Jones?

Ja, ich denke oft an Sie.
Denkst du oft an mich, Richard?
Ja, ich denke jeden Tag an dich, Anna.

8. Wie heißen Sie?
Ich heiße Richard
Wie heißen Sie mit Familiennamen?
Neumann, mit zwei n.
Wo wohnen Sie?
Ich wohne in Newington.
Wann haben Sie Geburtstag?

V. Exercises:

A. *Questions:*

1. So eine Immatrikulation ist sehr interessant, nicht wahr?
2. Was schreiben die Studenten auf die Zettel?
3. Was beschreibt Richard in seinem ersten Brief?
4. Was fragt ihn der ältere, unfreundliche Herr?
5. Wie heißen Sie?
6. Wie heißt Richard mit Familiennamen?
7. Wie heißen Sie mit Vornamen?
8. Was sagt ihm der Student ins Ohr?
9. Denkt Richard an Anna?
10. Warum ist der erste Brief nicht lang?

B. *Memorize the names of the days of the week and the months of the year:*

1.	2.	
der Sonntag	der Januar	der Juli
Montag	Februar	August′
Dienstag	März	September
Mittwoch	April′	Oktober
Donnerstag	Mai	November
Freitag	Juni	Dezember
Sonnabend (Samstag)		

C. *Translate and learn to recall:*

1. Richard ist jetzt Student.
2. Wir beschreiben eine Immatrikulation.
3. Richard möchte wissen, wie das hübsche Fräulein heißt.
4. Sagen Sie mir, bitte, was Sie wissen möchten!
5. Ich denke oft an meinen Freund (meine Freundin).
6. Schreiben Sie Ihren Namen auf diesen Zettel, bitte!
7. Möchten Sie eine Zigarette oder eine Zigarre?
8. Es interessiert mich nicht, wann Sie Geburtstag haben.
9. Antworten Sie auf meine Frage, bitte!
10. Vielen Dank für den Scheck.

D. *Correct the misinformation:*

1. So eine Immatrikulation ist schrecklich lustig.
2. Ein älterer, freundlicher Herr fragt Richard: „Wie heißen Sie?"
3. Richard hat nächsten Monat Geburtstag.
4. Der Dekan möchte Richards Vornamen wissen.
5. Richard beschreibt Anna die einzige langweilige Szene des ganzen Tages.

E. *Learn the stereotyped expressions for* Good morning, etc. *and the expressions of time listed in the comments.*

VI. Securing the Vocabulary:

A.

endlich	*finally*
schrecklich	*frightful*
langweilig	*boring, dull*
man	*one, a person*
ganz	*entire, quite*
der Ort	*place*
die Stadt	*city*
beschreiben	*(to) describe*
einzig	*only, single*
das Kind	*child*
ich möchte	*I would like to*
wissen	*(to) know*
wann	*when*
die Vorsicht	*caution*
der Mensch	*human being, man*
übrigens	*incidentally, by the way*
schon	*already*
spät	*late*
müde	*tired*

B.

genug (5)	1. *(to) send*
noch (10)	2. *mostly, generally*
heute (3)	3. *today*
heißen (7)	4. *who*
schicken (1)	5. *enough*
die Zeit (9)	6. *every*
verstehen (8)	7. *(to) be called*
wer (4)	8. *(to) understand*
meistens (2)	9. *time*
jeder (6)	10. *still, yet*

tragen (8)	1. *railroad station*
das Geld (2)	2. *money*
wenigstens (9)	3. *why*
warum (3)	4. *next*
der Bahnhof (1)	5. *court, yard*
erzählen (10)	6. *(to) know*
nächst (4)	7. *after*
wissen (6)	8. *(to) carry; wear*
nach (7)	9. *at least*
der Hof (5)	10. *(to) tell, narrate*

jetzt (5)	1. *he likes to eat*
viel (4)	2. *(to) read*
er ißt gern (1)	3. *how, as, like*
wie (3)	4. *much*
wahrscheinlich (6)	5. *now*
lesen (2)	6. *probably*

Fünfte Aufgabe

* * * \

lachen	(to) laugh
wir lachen	we laugh
* jedesmal	every time
* wenn	when, whenever, if
* die Stelle	the place, passage, position

Mutter und ich lachen jedesmal, wenn wir die Stelle lesen: „Wann haben Sie Geburtstag?“ — „Nächsten Montag.“	Mother and I laugh every time that we read the passage, "When is your birthday?" — "Next Monday."

aber	but
übertrei′ben	(to) exaggerate
übertreib es nicht	don't exaggerate it
nur	only

Aber Richard, übertreib es nur nicht!	But Richard, just don't go too far!

wissen	(to) know
ich weiß	I know
der Humor′	the humor, sense of humor
meinen	(to) mean
* böse	bad, angry
der Profes′sor	the professor
die Professo′ren	the professors
* vielleicht′	perhaps

Ich weiß, Du hast Humor und meinst es nicht böse, aber Deine Professoren haben vielleicht keinen Humor.	I know you have a sense of humor and don't mean anything bad by it, but perhaps your professors don't have a sense of humor.

genug	enough
davon	of it, of that
Genug davon!	That's enough of that!

* etwas	something
neu	new
etwas Neues	something new
zu erzählen	(to) tell
Ich habe etwas Neues zu erzählen.	I have some news to tell.

setz dich hin	sit down
kommen	(to) come

groß	great, big
Setz Dich hin, hier kommt die große Überraschung.	Grab a chair, here comes the big surprise.
* arbeiten	(to) work
Ich arbeite.	I am working.
jawohl'	yes indeed
* verdienen	(to) earn
ich verdiene	I earn
das Geld	the money
Jawohl, und ich verdiene Geld.	Yes indeed, and I am earning money.
die Nummer	the number
achtundfünfzig	eight and fifty, 58
die Verkäuferin	the salesgirl
die Waren	the wares, goods
das Haus	the house
das Warenhaus	the department store
Ich bin Nummer achtundfünfzig, Verkäuferin in Webers Warenhaus.	I am number fifty-eight, salesgirl in Weber's department store.
* verkaufen	(to) sell
die Seide	the silk
der Strumpf	the stocking
der Seidenstrumpf	the silk stocking
die Seidenstrümpfe	the silk stockings
all	all
die Größe	the size
sieben	seven
* bis	until, to
elf	eleven
Ich verkaufe Seidenstrümpfe in allen Größen, von Größe sieben bis Größe elf.	I sell stockings in all sizes, from size seven to size eleven.
müssen	(to) have to
ich muß	I have to
* der Schluß	the end
ich mache Schluß	I make (an) end
Jetzt muß ich aber Schluß machen.	But now I have to close.
elf	eleven
*die Uhr	the watch, clock
elf Uhr	eleven o'clock

abends	in the evening
todmüde	dead tired
Es ist elf Uhr abends, und ich bin todmüde.	It's eleven at night and I am dead tired.
müssen	(to) have to
ich muß	I have to
morgen	tomorrow
früh	early
morgen früh	tomorrow morning
um	around, at
halb	half
acht	eight
halb acht	half past seven
*aufstehen	(to) get up
Ich muß morgen früh um halb acht aufstehen.	I have to get up tomorrow morning at half past seven.
* die Abtei'lung	the department
der Chef	the chief, head
der Abteilungschef	the head of the department
viel	much
* die Geduld	the patience
er hat Geduld mit mir	he has patience with me
haben	(to) have
es	it
gern	gladly
* er hat es gern	he likes it
wenn	if
zu	too
spät	late
kommen	(to) come
Mein Abteilungschef hat viel Geduld mit mir, aber er hat es nicht gern, wenn wir zu spät kommen.	My boss is very patient with me, but he doesn't like it if we come late.
die Liebe	the love
In Liebe — Anna.	Love, Anna.

II. Text:

Lieber Richard!

Dein erster Brief hat mir große Freude gemacht. Ich lese ihn immer wieder, morgens, mittags und abends, und Mutter liest ihn auch. Mutter und ich lachen jedesmal, wenn wir die Stelle lesen: „Wann haben Sie Geburtstag?"—„Nächsten Montag." Aber Richard, übertreib es nur nicht! Ich weiß, Du hast Humor und meinst es nicht böse, aber Deine Professoren haben vielleicht keinen Humor. Genug davon!

Ich habe etwas Neues zu erzählen. Setz Dich hin, hier kommt die große Überraschung. Ich arbeite. Jawohl, und ich verdiene Geld. Ich bin Nummer 58, Verkäuferin in Webers Warenhaus und verkaufe Seidenstrümpfe in allen Größen, von Größe sieben bis Größe elf.

Jetzt muß ich aber Schluß machen. Es ist elf Uhr abends, und ich bin todmüde. Ich muß morgen früh um halb acht aufstehen. Mein Abteilungschef hat viel Geduld mit mir, aber er hat es nicht gern, wenn wir zu spät kommen.

Dependent or transposed word order

In Liebe

Anna

III. Comments:

1. *Personal Pronouns:*

In German, as in English, pronouns are declined. Here are the nominative, accusative, and dative cases of the personal pronouns you have had:

Singular		*Plural*
N. ich — *I* A. mich D. mir	1. Person	wir — *we* uns uns
N. du — *you* A. dich D. dir	2. Person Familiar	ihr — *you* euch euch
N. er — *he* A. ihn D. ihm		
N. sie — *she* A. sie D. ihr	3. Person	sie — *they* sie ihnen
N. es — *it* A. es D. ihm		
N. Sie — *you* A. Sie D. Ihnen	2. Person Conventional	Sie — *you* Sie Ihnen

The three third person singular pronouns correspond to the three genders of nouns. The masculine pronoun is used to refer to a masculine noun, the feminine pronoun to a feminine noun, and the neuter pronoun to a neuter noun.

Examples:

1. Wo ist der Brief?	*Where is the letter?*
Er ist in meinem Rock.	*It is in my coat.*
2. Wo ist die Tafel Schokolade?	*Where is the chocolate bar?*
Sie ist in dem Paket.	*It is in the package.*
3. Wo ist das Halsband?	*Where is the necklace?*
Es ist in dem Paket.	*It is in the package.*

4. Wo sind die Zigaretten? *Where are the cigarettes?*
   Sie sind dort. *They are there.*

2. *Possessive Adjectives:*

The following are the possessive adjectives:

Singular		*Plural*	
mein	*my*	unser	*our*
dein	*your*	euer	*your*
sein	*his*	ihr	*their*
ihr	*her*		
sein	*its*		
Ihr	*your* Conventional form	Ihr	*your*

These possessives take endings depending upon the gender and case of the noun they modify.

	M.	F.	N.
N.	mein Geburtstag	meine Mutter	mein Geschenk
A.	meinen Geburtstag	meine Mutter	mein Geschenk
D.	meinem Geburtstag	meiner Mutter	meinem Geschenk

The possessive adjectives and **kein** (*no, not a*) are declined like the indefinite article **ein.**

	M.	F.	N.
N.	ein	eine	ein
A.	einen	eine	ein
D.	einem	einer	einem
G.	eines	einer	eines

Therefore, the possessive adjectives (**mein, dein, sein,** *etc.*) and **kein** are called **ein**-words.

IV. Practice:

1. a. Dein Brief macht mir große Freude.
   Sein
   Ihr (*three meanings*)

   b. Dein Geschenk macht mir große Freude.
   Sein
   Ihr

2. Kennen Sie meinen Professor? Ja, ich kenne ihn.
   seinen Vater?
   unseren Dekan?
   meine Mutter? Nein, ich kenne sie nicht.
   seine Schulkameradin?

3. a. Haben Sie meine Größe?
Was ist Ihre Größe, bitte? your (capital I)
Ich trage Größe neun.

b. Was ist deine Größe?
seine
ihre her, their

4. Haben Sie keine Strümpfe in meiner Größe?
seiner
ihrer

5. Geben Sie mir meinen Scheck, bitte! Jawohl, hier ist er.
Rock,
mein Halsband, Jawohl, hier ist es.
meine Schokolade, Jawohl, hier ist sie.
Uhr,

6. a. Was machen Sie da (*there*) mit meinem Brief?
Ich lese ihn zum zweiten Mal. (*I'm reading it for the second time.*)

b. Was machen Sie da mit meinem Rezept für Apfelstrudel?
Ich lese es zum zweiten Mal.

7. a. Ich habe etwas Neues zu erzählen. neuter
Interessantes (*interesting*)
Schönes
Lustiges
Schreckliches

b. Ich habe nichts (*nothing*) Neues zu erzählen, etc.

8. Wann stehen Sie auf, Herr Jones?
Ich stehe jeden Morgen um sieben Uhr auf.
Warum stehen Sie denn so früh (*early*) auf?
Mein Professor hat es nicht gern, wenn ich zu spät komme.

V. Exercises:

A. *Questions:*

1. Wann liest Anna Richards ersten Brief?
2. Ist Anna die einzige Leserin des Briefes?
3. Über welche (*which*) Stelle lachen Anna und Frau Becker?
4. Was ist die große Überraschung?
5. Wo (*where*) arbeitet Anna?
6. Wer ist Nummer achtundfünfzig in Webers Warenhaus?
7. Was verkauft Anna?
8. Welche Größen verkauft sie?
9. Warum muß Anna Schluß machen?
10. Wann muß Anna morgens aufstehen?
11. Was hat der Abteilungschef nicht gern?

B. *Translate:*

1. Anna lacht jedesmal, wenn sie die Stelle liest: „Wann haben Sie Geburtstag?"
2. Ich habe etwas Interessantes zu erzählen.
3. Gretel, es ist jetzt zehn Uhr. Du mußt Schluß machen.
4. Ich weiß, daß Sie Humor haben, Fräulein Haskell, aber der Dekan weiß das vielleicht nicht.
5. Lesen Sie Richards Brief schon zum zweiten Mal, Herr Noyes? Ja, er ist sehr interessant.
6. Paul ist Verkäufer in Webers Warenhaus und verkauft Tennisschuhe.
7. Nächsten Donnerstag hat meine Freundin Geburtstag, und ich möchte ihr etwas Schönes geben.
8. Sie müssen ihm erzählen, daß Sie Geld verdienen.
9. Kennen Sie meinen Professor? Nein, ich kenne ihn nicht.
10. Ich muß Ihnen etwas sagen, Fräulein Weaver: Ich habe es nicht gern, wenn Sie zu spät kommen.

C. *Correct the misinformation:*

1. Anna liest Richards Brief immer wieder und ihr Vater liest ihn auch.
2. Richard hat Humor und seine Professoren wissen das auch.
3. Anna arbeitet in Webers Warenhaus und ihre Nummer ist fünfundachtzig.
4. Anna muß morgens um halb sieben aufstehen.
5. Ihr Abteilungschef hat es gern, wenn sie zu spät kommt.

VI. Securing the Vocabulary:

A.

die Überraschung	*surprise*
die Freude	*joy, pleasure*
immer wieder	*again and again*
wieder	*again*
jedesmal	*every time*
wenn	*when, whenever, if*
die Stelle	*place, passage*
böse	*bad, angry*
vielleicht	*perhaps*
etwas	*something*
arbeiten	*(to) work*
verdienen	*(to) earn*
verkaufen	*(to) sell*
bis	*until, to*
der Schluß	*end*
die Uhr	*watch, clock*
aufstehen	*(to) get up*
die Abteilung	*department*
die Geduld	*patience*
er hat es gern	*he likes it*

B.

jeder (6)	1. *one, a person*
wer (7)	2. *mostly, generally*
nur (5)	3. *incidentally*
man (1)	4. *large, big, tall*
groß (4)	5. *only*
erst (9)	6. *every*
meistens (2)	7. *who*
heißen (10)	8. *already*
übrigens (3)	9. *first*
schon (8)	10. *(to) be called*
immer (4)	1. *tired*
schrecklich (8)	2. *also*
kennen (9)	3. *(to) send*
auch (2)	4. *always*
müde (1)	5. *time*
warum (7)	6. *at least*
die Zeit (5)	7. *why*
noch nicht (10)	8. *frightful*
wenigstens (6)	9. *(to) know*
schicken (3)	10. *not yet*

beschreiben (1)	1. *(to) describe*
ganz (5)	2. *when*
ich möchte (7)	3. *place*
die Vorsicht (9)	4. *city*
wahrscheinlich (8)	5. *entirely, quite*
die Stadt (4)	6. *how, as, like*
fragen (10)	7. *I would like to*
wie (6)	8. *probably*
wann (2)	9. *caution*
der Ort (3)	10. *(to) ask*

Zweite vocabulary test to hier - mostly on the viste und fünfte aufgabe - also know the imperatives and the days of the week and the months. Personal pronouns & possessive adjectives

Sechste Aufgabe

* * * \

arbeiten	(to) work
alle	all
wir arbeiten alle	we all work
viel	much
dann	then
wann	when
* dann und wann	now and then
das Kino	the movies
ins Kino	to the movies
Wir arbeiten alle viel und dann und wann gehen wir ins Kino.	We all work a lot and now and then we go to the movies.
beschreiben	(to) describe
ich beschreibe	I describe
dir	for you
typisch	typical
der Tag	the day
Ich beschreibe Dir einen typischen Tag.	I'll describe a typical day for you.
der Punkt	the point, dot
sieben	seven
Punkt sieben Uhr	at seven o'clock sharp
aufstehen	(to) get up
ich stehe auf	I get up
rasie'ren	(to) shave
ich rasiere mich	I shave myself
waschen	(to) wash
ich wasche mich	I wash myself
* anziehen	(to) dress
ich ziehe mich an	I dress myself
Punkt sieben Uhr stehe ich auf, rasiere mich, wasche mich und ziehe mich an.	At seven o'clock sharp I get up, shave, wash and dress.
dann	then
* das Zimmer	the room
der Genosse	the comrade
der Zimmergenosse	the roommate
frühstücken	(to) breakfast
Dann gehe ich mit meinem Zimmergenossen frühstücken.	Then I go to eat breakfast with my roommate.
trinken	(to) drink
die Milch	the milk
* manchmal	sometimes

die Tasse	the cup
der Kaffee	the coffee
Ich trinke meine Milch und manchmal eine Tasse Kaffee.	I drink my milk, and sometimes, a cup of coffee.
natür'lich	naturally, of course
Er ist natürlich nicht so gut wie Dein Kaffee.	Of course, it isn't as good as your coffee.
das Ei	the egg
die Eier	the eggs
der Speck	the bacon
die Minu'te	the minute
die Minuten	the minutes
der Weg	the road
auf dem Weg	on the way
die Klasse	the class
zur Klasse	to the class
Ich esse Eier mit Speck und zehn Minuten vor acht bin ich auf dem Weg zur Klasse.	I eat bacon and eggs and at ten minutes to eight I'm on my way to class.
kommen	(to) come
* nie	never
zu	too
spät	late
Ich komme nie zu spät.	I never come late.
der Punkt	the point
Punkt acht Uhr	at eight o'clock sharp
sitzen	(to) sit
der Platz	the place, seat
auf meinem Platz	at my place, in my seat
aufpassen	(to) pay attention
ich passe auf	I pay attention
Punkt acht Uhr sitze ich auf meinem Platz und passe gut auf.	At eight sharp I am sitting in my seat and listening carefully.
* die Stunde	the hour, class, lesson
der Plan	the plan
der Stundenplan	the class schedule
die Psychologie'	the psychology
anorganisch	inorganic
die Chemie'	the chemistry

Spanisch	Spanish
Englisch	English
Hier ist mein Stundenplan für Montag, Dienstag, Donnerstag und Freitag: Um acht Uhr Psychologie, um zehn anorganische Chemie, um elf Spanisch, um eins Englisch.	Here is my class schedule for Monday, Tuesday, Thursday and Friday: At eight o'clock psychology, at ten inorganic chemistry, at eleven Spanish, at one English.
der Nachmittag	the afternoon
nachmittags	in the afternoon, afternoons
zwei	two
chemisch	chemical
das Laborato′rium	the laboratory
Labor′	lab
Mittwoch nachmittags habe ich zwei Stunden chemisches Labor.	Wednesday afternoons I have two hours chem lab.
* außerdem	besides, in addition
aufhaben	(to) have assigned work to do
ich habe viel auf	I have much assigned work to do
Außerdem habe ich natürlich viel auf.	Of course, I have big assignments besides.
sehen	(to) see
du siehst	you see
die Zeit	the time
keine Zeit	no time
der Unfug	the mischief
treiben	(to) drive, carry on, perform
er treibt Unfug	he performs mischief
Du siehst, ich habe keine Zeit, Unfug zu treiben.	You see, I have no time to get into mischief.
die Wäsche	the laundry
das Paket′	the package
das Wäschepaket′	the laundry package
Am Sonnabend schicke ich Dir mein erstes Wäschepaket.	I'll send you my first laundry box Saturday.
spät	late
müde	tired
Es ist spät, und ich bin müde.	It's late and I'm tired.

das Mal	the time, occasion
das nächste Mal	the next time
mehr	more
Das nächste Mal mehr.	More next time.
alles	everything
gut	good
alles Gute	everything good, i.e. I wish you everything good
Alles Gute, liebe Mutter.	I wish all sorts of nice things for you, mother dear. (*literally*)
Dein Richard.	Your Richard.

II. Text:

Liebe Mutter!

Bitte, mach Dir keine Sorgen! Ich schlafe jede Nacht neun Stunden, ich esse gut, und die Studenten in unserem Haus sind ruhige Jungen. Wir arbeiten alle viel und dann und wann gehen wir ins Kino. Ich beschreibe Dir einen typischen Tag. Punkt sieben Uhr stehe ich auf, rasiere mich, wasche mich und ziehe mich an. Dann gehe ich mit meinem Zimmergenossen frühstücken. Ich trinke meine Milch und manchmal eine Tasse Kaffee. Er ist natürlich nicht so gut wie Dein Kaffee. Ich esse Eier mit Speck und zehn Minuten vor acht bin ich auf dem Weg zur Klasse. Ich komme nie zu spät. Punkt acht Uhr sitze ich auf meinem Platz und passe gut auf. Hier ist mein Stundenplan für Montag, Dienstag, Donnerstag und Freitag: Um acht Uhr Psychologie, um zehn anorganische Chemie, um elf Spanisch, um eins Englisch. Mittwoch nachmittags habe ich zwei Stunden chemisches Labor. Außerdem habe ich natürlich viel auf. Du siehst, ich habe keine Zeit, Unfug zu treiben. Am Sonnabend schicke ich Dir mein erstes Wäschepaket. Es ist spät, und ich bin müde. Das nächste Mal mehr. Alles Gute, liebe Mutter.

Dein Richard

III. Comments:

1. *Reflexive Pronouns:*

When the object of a verb, direct or indirect, refers to the subject of that verb, it is called a reflexive object. English reflexive pronouns end in *–self* or *–selves* e.g. *myself, themselves.* German uses personal pronouns as reflexives and has only one special reflexive form, **sich,** for the third person singular and plural and also for the conventional second person. The form **sich** functions as both direct and indirect object. Following are examples of verbs used with reflexive objects:

	Direct Object
ich ziehe mich an	*I dress myself*
du ziehst dich an	*you dress yourself*
er zieht sich an	*he dresses himself*
sie zieht sich an	*she dresses herself*
es zieht sich an	*it dresses itself*
wir ziehen uns an	*we dress ourselves*
ihr zieht euch an	*you dress yourselves*
sie ziehen sich an	*they dress themselves*
Sie ziehen sich an	*you dress yourself (–selves)*

Indirect Object

ich kaufe mir Schokolade	*I buy myself some chocolate*
du kaufst dir Schokolade	*you buy yourself some chocolate*
er kauft sich Schokolade	*he buys himself some chocolate*
sie kauft sich Schokolade	*she buys herself some chocolate*
es kauft sich Schokolade	*it buys itself some chocolate*
wir kaufen uns Schokolade	*we buy ourselves some chocolate*
ihr kauft euch Schokolade	*you buy yourselves some chocolate*
sie kaufen sich Schokolade	*they buy themselves some chocolate*
Sie kaufen sich Schokolade	*you buy yourself (–selves) some chocolate*

2. *Separable Prefixes:*

In English many adverbs and prepositions may be used in such close connection with a verb as to form a single verbal idea with it. Thus we say: *The earth turns on its axis* but *The cake turned out well; He turned up at twelve o'clock; We have to turn in at ten.* In German also there are very many instances of this sort. The German equivalent of our expression *get up* is **aufstehen.** Here the connection is felt to be so close that the modifying word **auf** is prefixed to the infinitive **stehen.** Similar verbs are **aufpassen** — *pay attention,* **anhaben** — *wear,* **anziehen** — *dress.* But in the present tense in independent clauses and in the imperative these prefixes are separated from the verb and come at the end of the clause.

Examples:

1. Ich stehe jeden Morgen um sieben Uhr auf. *I get up at seven every morning.*
2. Ziehe dich schnell an! *Get dressed quickly!*

Separable prefixes will be indicated in the lists of Words and Phrases as follows: **er steht . . . auf, ich habe . . . an.**

IV. Practice:

1. a. Ich mache mir keine Sorgen.
   viele Sorgen.

   b. Herr Schmidt macht sich keine Sorgen.
   Richard
   Frau Neumann
   Richard und Anna machen sich keine Sorgen.
   Richard und ich machen uns keine Sorgen.
   Machst du dir keine Sorgen, Richard?
   Machen Sie sich keine Sorgen, Herr Neumann?

   c. Substitute **viele Sorgen** and **viel Arbeit** for **keine Sorgen** in b. above.

2. a. Ich kaufe mir einen neuen Anzug.
   einen neuen Rock.
   ein neues Hemd.
   ein schönes Halsband.

b. Herr Neumann kauft sich einen neuen Anzug.
Richard
Kaufen Sie sich einen neuen Anzug, Herr Jones?

3. a. Ich wasche mich jeden Morgen um sieben Uhr.
Richard wäscht sich
Wir waschen uns
Richard und Wilhelm waschen sich
Sie waschen sich

b. Rasierst du dich jeden Morgen, Fritz?
Rasieren Sie sich jeden Morgen, Herr Spaeth?

4. a. Ich mache mich über meinen Zimmergenossen lustig.
meinen Professor
Er macht sich meinen Anzug
meine Schuhe

b. Richard macht sich über seinen Zimmergenossen lustig, etc.

c. Machen Sie sich nicht über mein Halsband lustig!
mein Kleid
meine Schulkameradin

5. a. Richard zieht sich jeden Morgen um sieben Uhr an.
halb sieben
acht Uhr
halb acht

b. Zieh dich an, Richard!
Ziehen Sie sich an, Herr Woodbridge!

6. a. Ich stehe jeden Montag um halb acht auf.
Anna steht
Wir stehen

b. Stehen Sie jetzt auf, Herr Webster!

7. a. Ich habe in Psychologie sehr viel auf.
Richard hat in Spanisch
Anna hat in Deutsch
Wir haben in Chemie
Sie haben in Physik
Er hat in Mathematik nur wenig (*only little*) auf.

b. Was haben wir in Geschichte (*history*) auf?
Das nächste Kapitel (*chapter*).

8. Passen Sie auf, jetzt kommt die große Überraschung.
jetzt erzähle ich Ihnen etwas über Anna.
jetzt beschreibe ich Ihnen einen typischen Tag.
jetzt gebe ich Ihnen die Aufgabe für Mittwoch.
(*now I'll give you the assignment for Wednesday.*)

9. Hören Sie gut zu (*listen carefully*), jetzt kommt die große Überraschung, *etc., etc.*

V. Exercises:

A. *Questions:*

1. Wie lange schläft Richard jede Nacht?
2. Arbeitet Richard jeden Abend?
3. Wann steht er morgens auf?
4. Rasiert sich Richard jeden Tag oder zweimal die Woche?
5. Was trinkt Richard morgens?
6. Was ißt er?
7. Wann beginnt Richards erste Klasse?
8. Wann hat Richard anorganische Chemie?
9. Was hat er um eins?
10. Wann hat er chemisches Labor?
11. Was schickt er seiner Mutter?
12. Hat er viel auf?

B. *Translate:*

1. Richard schreibt mir, er schläft jede Nacht neun Stunden.
2. Wir machen uns viele Sorgen.
3. Sie hat in Chemie sehr viel auf.
4. Passen Sie gut auf! Jetzt kommt die große Überraschung.
5. Stehen Sie jeden Morgen um halb sieben auf, Herr Noyes?
6. Das nächste Mal schreiben wir mehr.
7. Ich beschreibe Ihnen meinen Zimmergenossen.
8. Er ist ein ruhiger Junge, aber dann und wann treibt er gerne Unfug.
9. Robert hat heute einen braunen Anzug an.
10. Was ziehst du heute an?

C. *Learn the cardinal numerals 1–25:*

1. eins	6. sechs	11. elf	16. sechzehn
2. zwei	7. sieben	12. zwölf	17. siebzehn
3. drei	8. acht	13. dreizehn	18. achtzehn
4. vier	9. neun	14. vierzehn	19. neunzehn
5. fünf	10. zehn	15. fünfzehn	20. zwanzig

21. einundzwanzig
22. zweiundzwanzig
23. dreiundzwanzig
24. vierundzwanzig
25. fünfundzwanzig

D. *Correct the misinformation:*

1. Richard schläft jede Nacht acht Stunden.
2. Er geht jeden Abend ins Kino.
3. Er geht mit seinem Professor frühstücken.
4. Zehn Minuten nach acht ist er auf dem Weg zur Klasse.
5. Er hat viel Zeit, Unfug zu treiben.
6. Am Sonntag schickt er seiner Mutter sein erstes Wäschepaket.

VI. Securing the Vocabulary:

A.

die Sorge	*worry, care*
die Stunde	*hour, class, lesson*
ruhig	*quiet*
dann und wann	*now and then*
anziehen	*(to) dress*
das Zimmer	*room*
manchmal	*sometimes*
außerdem	*besides, in addition*
nie	*never*

B.

die Überraschung (4)	1. *human being, man*
noch (9)	2. *he likes it*
der Mensch (1)	3. *end*
lieb (7)	4. *surprise*
er hat es gern (2)	5. *only, single*
der Schluß (3)	6. *(to) be called*
sehr (10)	7. *dear*
einzig (5)	8. *again*
wieder (8)	9. *still, yet*
heißen (6)	10. *very*

erst (5)	1. *caution*
nach (6)	2. *child*
die Vorsicht (1)	3. *gladly*
das Geld (7)	4. *at least*
wenigstens (4)	5. *first*
der Brief (9)	6. *after*
gern (3)	7. *money*
vielleicht (10)	8. *incidentally*
das Kind (2)	9. *letter*
übrigens (8)	10. *perhaps*

ganz (4)	1. *place, passage*
die Frage (6)	2. *already*
verstehen (9)	3. *(to) earn*
die Stadt (5)	4. *entire, quite*
man (7)	5. *city*
schon (2)	6. *question*
endlich (10)	7. *one, a person*
die Stelle (1)	8. *every*
jeder (8)	9. *(to) understand*
verdienen (3)	10. *finally*

Siebente Aufgabe

* * * \

das Haus	the house
noch	still, yet
* ander	other
der Student′, die Studen′ten	the student, the students
Im selben Haus wohnen noch fünf andere Studenten.	Five other students are living in the same house.
der Osten	the east
vom Osten	from the east
* beide	both
der Süden	the south
* der Staat	the state
der Südstaat, die Südstaaten	the southern state, the southern states
Drei sind vom Osten, von Pennsylvanien und Neu York; die anderen beiden kommen aus den Südstaaten, aus Virginien und Nordkarolina.	Three are from the East, from Pennsylvania and New York; the other two come from the South, from Virginia and North Carolina.
die Stunde, die Stunden	the hour, class; the hours, classes
der Spaß	the joke, fun
das macht mir Spaß	that makes fun for me
Meine Stunden machen mir viel Spaß.	My classes are a lot of fun.
interessie′ren	(to) interest
das interessiert mich	that interests me
* besonders	especially
Psychologie interessiert mich besonders.	I'm especially interested in Psychology.
der Profes′sor	the professor
international′	international
die Autorität′	the authority
Unser Psychologieprofessor ist eine internationale Autorität.	Our psychology professor is an international authority.
spezial′	special
* das Gebiet	the territory, region
das Spezialgebiet, die Spezialgebiete	the special field, the special fields
die Rekla′me	the advertising
der Reklame	of advertising

das Kind, die Kinder	the child, the children
die Psychologie′	the psychology
die Kin′derpsychologie	the child psychology
Seine Spezialgebiete sind Psychologie der Reklame und Kinderpsychologie.	His special fields are the psychology of advertising and child psychology.

haben	(to) have
ich hatte	I had
länger	longer
* die Unterhal′tung	the conversation
über	over, about
solch	such
die Frage, die Fragen	the question, the questions
wie	how, as
warum′	why
* rauchen	(to) smoke
tanzen	(to) dance
gern(e)	gladly
wir tanzen gern	we like to dance
der Swing	the swing
Ich hatte eine längere Unterhaltung mit ihm über solche Fragen wie: Warum rauchen wir? Warum tanzen wir gerne Swing?	I had a rather long conversation with him about such questions as: Why do we smoke? Why do we like to dance swing?

* glauben	(to) believe
der Hedonist′	the hedonist
Er glaubt, ich bin Hedonist.	He thinks I'm a hedonist.

übrigens	by the way
das Buch, die Bücher	the book, the books
teuer	dear, expensive
Übrigens, meine Bücher sind sehr teuer.	By the way, my books are very expensive.

außerdem	besides
müssen	(to) have to
er muß	he has to
man	one (*i.e.* a person)
die Miete	the rent
der Monat	the month

voraus	ahead
* im voraus	in advance
* bezahlen – transitively	(to) pay
Außerdem muß man hier die Miete einen Monat im voraus bezahlen.	Besides, you have to pay the rent here a month in advance.
bitte	please
Bitte, schick mir einen Scheck mit dem nächsten Brief.	Please send me a check with your next letter.
* brauchen	(to) need
* weniger	less
das Geld	the money
Nächsten Monat brauche ich weniger Geld.	I'll need less money next month.
verstehen	(to) understand
all	all, every
der Anfang	the beginning
* schwer	difficult, heavy
Du verstehst, aller Anfang ist schwer.	You understand, it isn't so easy to get started.
* bald	soon
lang	long
Bitte, schreib mir bald einen langen Brief.	Please write me a long letter soon.
viel	much
viele	many
der Klient', die Klien'ten	the client, the clients
Hast Du viele Klienten?	Do you have many clients?
zahlen – either transitively oder intransitively	(to) pay
* die Rechnung, die Rechnungen	the bill, the bills
Zahlen sie ihre Rechnungen?	Do they pay their bills?
erkältet	ill with a cold
Ist Mutter noch erkältet?	Does Mother still have a cold?
hoffentlich	it is to be hoped
die Sorge, die Sorgen	the care, worry; the worries
Hoffentlich macht sie sich keine Sorgen um mich.	I hope she doesn't worry about me.

immer	always
noch	yet
* immer noch	still, after all this time
* traurig	sad
* weil	because
fort	gone, away

Ist Prinz immer noch traurig, weil ich fort bin?	Is Prince still sad because I'm away?

vergessen	(to) forget
vergiß!	forget!
das Gold	the gold
der Fisch	the fish
der Goldfisch, die Goldfische	the goldfish
füttern	(to) feed

Vergiß nicht, die Goldfische zu füttern!	Don't forget to feed the goldfish!

* schließen	(to) close
die Zeit	the time
die Klasse	the class

Ich schließe jetzt; es ist Zeit, zur Klasse zu gehen.	I'll close now; it's time to go to class.

die Mutter	the mother
herzlichst	heartiest
der Gruß, die Grüße	the greeting, the greetings

Dir und Mutter die herzlichsten Grüße.	My best to you and Mother.
Dein Richard.	Yours, Richard.

P.S. (Post Scriptum)	P.S.
der Schläger	the racquet
der Tennisschläger	the tennis racquet
der Schuh	the shoe
der Tennisschuh, die Tennisschuhe	the tennis shoe, the tennis shoes

P.S. Bitte, schick mir meinen Tennisschläger und die Tennisschuhe.	P.S. Please send me my tennis racquet and tennis shoes.

* sonst	otherwise
* nichts	nothing

Sonst habe ich nichts vergessen.	I haven't forgotten anything else.

II. Text:

Lieber Vater!

Ich bin schon seit acht Tagen hier, und alles ist in bester Ordnung. Ich wohne bei einer netten Familie. Im selben Haus wohnen noch fünf andere Studenten. Drei sind vom Osten, von Pennsylvanien und Neu York; die anderen beiden kommen aus den Südstaaten, aus Virginien und Nordkarolina. Meine Stunden machen mir viel Spaß. Psychologie interessiert mich besonders. Unser Psychologieprofessor ist eine internationale Autorität. Seine Spezialgebiete sind Psychologie der Reklame und Kinderpsychologie. Ich hatte eine längere Unterhaltung mit ihm über solche Fragen wie: Warum rauchen wir? Warum tanzen wir gerne Swing? Er glaubt, ich bin Hedonist. Übrigens, meine Bücher sind sehr teuer. Außerdem muß man hier die Miete einen Monat im voraus bezahlen. Bitte, schick mir einen Scheck mit dem nächsten Brief. Nächsten Monat

no umlaut – be careful of pronunciation
also line 2, next page

brauche ich weniger Geld. Du verstehst, aller Anfang ist schwer. Bitte, schreib mir bald einen langen Brief. Hast Du viele Klienten? Zahlen sie ihre Rechnungen? Ist Mutter noch erkältet? Hoffentlich macht sie sich keine Sorgen um mich. Ist Prinz immer noch traurig, weil ich fort bin? Vergiß nicht, die Goldfische zu füttern! Ich schließe jetzt; es ist Zeit, zur Klasse zu gehen. Dir und Mutter die herzlichsten Grüße.

Dein Richard

P.S. Bitte, schick mir meinen Tennisschläger und die Tennisschuhe. Sonst habe ich nichts vergessen.

III. Comments:

1. *Formation of the Plural of Nouns:*

Nouns themselves are made plural by the addition of endings to the nominative singular form, *e.g.* **das Kleid, die Kleider**; by the modification of the stem vowel, **der Garten, die Gärten**; or by both at once, **der Gruß, die Grüße.**

On the basis of their endings or the absence of endings in the plural, nouns may be classified into five groups: 1) no ending; 2) ending **–e**; 3) ending **–er**; 4) ending **–n**; 5) ending **–s**. Nearly all German nouns belong to the first four groups. A few but rather common nouns belong to the fifth group and may be considered exceptions to the general classification. Examples of each group follow. Note that the definite article in the plural is the same for the three genders.

	Singular	*Plural*
1. No ending	der Fehler	die Fehler
	der Vater	die Väter
	der Garten	die Gärten
	die Mutter	die Mütter
2. Ending **–e**	der Tag	die Tage
	der Brief	die Briefe
	der Strumpf	die Strümpfe
3. Ending **–er**	das Kleid	die Kleider
	das Buch	die Bücher
	das Haus	die Häuser
4. Ending **–(e)n**	der Student	die Studenten
	die Rechnung	die Rechnungen
	die Klasse	die Klassen
	die Sorge	die Sorgen
5. Ending **–s**	der Scheck	die Schecks
	der Chef	die Chefs
	das Auto	die Autos
	das Radio	die Radios

2. *Declension of the Plural of Nouns:*

In the plural the same declensional pattern is followed by the definite article and the **der-** and **ein-**words. Nouns belonging to groups 1 to 3 add the case ending **–n** in the dative plural, unless they already end in **–n** in the singular, *e.g.* **der Garten.**

N. die, solche, unsere Fehler, Briefe, Bücher
A. die, solche, unsere Fehler, Briefe, Bücher
D. den, solchen, unseren Fehlern, Briefen, Büchern

Nouns of group 4 and 5 do not add an **–n** in the dative.

N. die Studenten, Autos
A. die Studenten, Autos
D. den Studenten, Autos

Plurals will be indicated in the lists of Words and Phrases as follows: **der Fehler, —; der Vater, ¨; der Tag, –e; der Gruß, ¨e; das Kleid, –er; das Buch, ¨er; der Student, –en; die Klasse, –n; das Auto, –s.**

IV. Practice:

A. *Make a list of the nouns in this lesson and the following lessons as they are taken up, classifying them according to the plural endings.*

B. *Practice until mastered:*

1. a. Ich bin nur einen Tag hier.
einen Monat
ein Jahr
eine Woche

b. Ich bin seit vier Tagen hier.
zwei Monaten
drei Jahren
fünf Wochen

2. a. Im selben Haus wohnt ein Student aus Neu York.
ein Professor Kalifornien.

b. Im selben Haus wohnen drei Studenten vom Norden. (*north*)
zwei Professoren Westen. (*west*)

3. a. Unser Professor ist eine internationale Autorität.
ein guter Tennisspieler.
ein guter Schwimmer.

b. Unsere Professoren sind internationale Autoritäten.
gute Tennisspieler.
gute Schwimmer.

4. a. Richard hat nur ein Radio.
ein Auto.
eine Klasse.
einen Tennisschläger.

b. Herr Weber hat drei Radios.
zwei Autos.
fünf Klassen.
keine Tennisschläger.

5. a. Sehen Sie das Buch dort (*there*)?
das Haus
das Halsband
den Brief
den Schuh
den Goldfisch
den Studenten
die Studentin

b. Sehen Sie die Bücher dort?
Häuser
Halsbänder
Briefe
Schuhe
Goldfische
Studenten
Studentinnen

6. Ich hatte eine längere Unterhaltung mit ihm über meine Klassen.
seine Patienten.
die Südstaaten.
seine Spezialgebiete.
die Colleges im Osten.

after {weil / wenn} the verb comes at end of sentence
dependent word order

V. Exercises:

A. *Questions:*

1. Seit wann ist Richard in der Universitätsstadt?
2. Wo wohnt Richard?
3. Wie viele Studenten in seinem Haus kommen aus Virginien?
4. Was interessiert Richard besonders?
5. Was sind die Spezialgebiete des Psychologieprofessors?
6. Mit wem hatte Richard eine längere Unterhaltung?
7. Warum ist Prinz traurig?
8. Wer füttert die Goldfische?
9. Warum braucht Richard mehr Geld?
10. Warum hat Richard keine Zeit, einen längeren Brief zu schreiben?

B. *Translate:*

1. Wohnen Sie bei einer netten Familie?
2. Anna schreibt, ihre Klassen machen ihr viel Spaß.
3. Sie interessiert sich besonders für Chemie. — in chemistry
4. Ich glaube, sie kommt aus Oklahoma.

5. Ich habe nur einen Tennisschläger. Wie viele Tennisschläger haben Sie?
6. Herr Doktor Neumann hat zwei Autos.
7. Es ist Zeit, die Goldfische zu füttern. → infinitive used dependently.
8. Richard unterhält sich gern mit seinen Professoren.
9. Die Fragen interessieren mich besonders.
10. Du verstehst, ich brauche nächsten Monat mehr Geld.
11. Es ist Zeit aufzustehen. → infinitive used dependently.
12. Bitte, schick mir einen langen Brief mit dem nächsten Scheck. | separable
13. Wie viele Patienten hast du jetzt? → particle – no translation | prefix
14. Ich bin schon seit Montag erkältet. → have a cold
15. Das ist ein sehr interessantes Buch.

C. *Learn the cardinal numerals 26–150:*

26. sechsundzwanzig	31. einunddreißig	80. achtzig
27. siebenundzwanzig	40. vierzig	90. neunzig
28. achtundzwanzig	50. fünfzig	100. hundert
29. neunundzwanzig	60. sechzig	101. hunderteins
30. dreißig	70. siebzig	150. hundertfünfzig

D. *Correct the misinformation:*

1. Richard ist seit acht Wochen hier.
2. Im selben Hause wohnen noch zehn andere Studenten.
3. Seine Klassen machen ihm viel Spaß. Chemie interessiert ihn besonders.
4. Richard braucht diesen Monat weniger Geld.
5. Prinz macht sich Sorgen um Richard.

E. *Rearrange the following words and groups of words to make a correct sentence. Translate your sentence:*

1. bei einer netten Familie, wohnt, seit acht Tagen, Richard.
2. wohnen, aus den Südstaaten, fünf Studenten, im selben Haus.
3. er, die Miete, eine Woche im voraus, muß, bezahlen.
4. über viele interessante Fragen, mit ihm, hatte, eine längere Unterhaltung, er.
5. ich, jetzt, muß, gehen, zur Klasse.

VI. Securing the Vocabulary:

A.

seit	*since*	die Unterhaltung	*conversation*
wohnen	*(to) live, dwell*		
bei	*at, with, near, at the house of*	rauchen	*(to) smoke*
		glauben	*(to) believe*
ander	*other*	im voraus	*in advance*
beide	*both*	bezahlen	*(to) pay*
der Staat	*state*	brauchen	*(to) need*
besonders	*especially*	weniger	*less*
das Gebiet	*territory, region, special field*	schwer	*heavy, difficult*
		bald	*soon*

immer noch	*still, after all this time*	schließen	*(to) close*
		die Rechnung	*bill*
traurig	*sad*	sonst	*otherwise*
weil	*because*	nichts	*nothing*

B.

die Geduld (2)	1. *always*	fragen (8)	1. *(to) know*
kennen (9)	2. *patience*	noch nicht (6)	2. *surprise*
der Ort (6)	3. *sometimes*	wahrscheinlich (9)	3. *only*
auch (8)	4. *something*	heute (10)	4. *quiet*
immer (1)	5. *frightful*	nur (3)	5. *(to) get up*
etwas (4)	6. *place*	ruhig (4)	6. *not yet*
spät (10)	7. *when, whenever, if*	die Überraschung (2)	7. *every time*
manchmal (3)	8. *also*	aufstehen (5)	8. *(to) ask*
wenn (7)	9. *(to) know*	wissen (1)	9. *probably*
schrecklich (5)	10. *late*	jedesmal (7)	10. *today*

außerdem (8)	1. *(to) carry*
verdienen (10)	2. *(to) sell*
endlich (12)	3. *boring, dull*
der Schluß (5)	4. *hour, class, lesson*
die Abteilung (9)	5. *end*
langweilig (3)	6. *I would like to*
die Stunde (4)	7. *never*
tragen (1)	8. *besides, in addition*
die Uhr (11)	9. *department*
verkaufen (2)	10. *(to) earn*
ich möchte (6)	11. *watch, clock*
nie (7)	12. *finally*

Achte Aufgabe

* * * \

verkaufen	(to) sell
du wirst verkaufen	you will sell
Mit Seidenstrümpfen fängst Du an, aber bald wirst Du Pelzmäntel verkaufen.	You start with silk stockings, but soon you will be selling fur coats.
heute	today
haben	(to) have
ich hatte	I had
* schlecht	bad
Heute hatte ich einen schlechten Tag.	I had a tough day today.
fragen	(to) ask
er fragt	he asks
rauchen	(to) smoke
In Psychologie fragt mich Professor Berg: „Herr Neumann, rauchen Sie?“	In psychology Professor Berg asked me: "Mr. Neumann, do you smoke?"
antworten	(to) answer
ich antworte	I answer
der Liebling, –e	the darling, favorite
die Marke, –n	the brand
die Lieblingsmarke, –n	the favorite brand
Ich antworte: „Ja. Meine Lieblingsmarke ist —.“	I answered: "Yes, my favorite brand is —."
wollen	(to) want to
ich will	I want to
wissen	(to) know
warum	why
„Das will ich nicht wissen. Warum rauchen Sie?“	"I don't want to know that. Why do you smoke?"
sagen	(to) say
ich sage	I say
* schnell	quickly
Ich sage schnell: „Es macht mir Spaß.“	I said quickly: "I enjoy it."
schön	beautiful, fine
sehr	very
intelligent′	intelligent
originell′	original
die Antwort, –en	the answer
„Schön,“ sagt Berg, „eine sehr intelligente und originelle Antwort.	"Fine," said Berg, "A very intelligent and original answer.

die Welt, –en	the world
die Anschauung, –en	the view
die Weltanschauung, –en	the view of the world, philosophy of life
Sie haben eine Weltanschauung, Sie sind Hedonist.“	You have a philosophy of life, you are a hedonist.”
das Fräulein, —	the young lady
hübsch	pretty
* schwarz	black
* der Kopf, ¨e	the head
der Schwarzkopf, ¨e	the brunette
die Reihe, –n	the row
Dann fragt er Fräulein Blake, einen hübschen Schwarzkopf in der ersten Reihe: „Fräulein Blake, tanzen Sie Swing?“	Then he asked Miss Blake, a pretty brunette in the first row: “Miss Blake, do you dance swing?”
lachen	(to) laugh
ein bißchen	a bit, a little
sehr gerne	very gladly
Fräulein Blake lacht ein bißchen und sagt: „Sehr gerne.“	Miss Blake laughed a bit and said: “I love to.”
die Tänzerin, –nen	the dancer (*feminine*)
der Campus, –se	the campus
man sagt	one says, it is said
Fräulein Blake ist die beste Tänzerin auf dem Campus, sagt man.	They say Miss Blake is the best dancer on the campus.
schlank	slender
mittelgroß	medium tall
Sie ist schlank und mittelgroß.	She is slender and not very tall.
die Psychologie′stun′de, –n	the psychology class
anorganisch	inorganic
die Chemie′	the chemistry
Nach meiner Psychologiestunde hatte ich anorganische Chemie.	After my psychology class I had inorganic chemistry.
kommen	(to) come
spät	late
zu spät	too late
sarka′stisch	sarcastic
das Kino, –s	the movie

jung	young
der Mann, ¨er	the man
Ich komme zu spät, und der Professor sagt sarkastisch: „Das ist hier kein Kino, junger Mann.	I came late and the professor said sarcastically: "This is not a movie, young man.
rechtzeitig	on time
* gar nicht	not at all
Kommen Sie bitte rechtzeitig oder gar nicht."	Please come on time or not at all."
wahrschein'lich	probably
das Militär'	the military, service
Der Mann war wahrscheinlich beim Militär.	The fellow probably used to be in the service.
außerdem	besides
können	(to) be able to
ich kann	I can, am able to
fünfmal	five times
schwänzen	cut class
wenn	if
wollen	(to) want to
ich will	I want to
Außerdem kann ich fünfmal schwänzen, wenn ich will.	Besides, I can cut five times if I want to.
können	(to) be able to
du kannst	you are able to
natür'lich	naturally, of course
so	thus, so
* arm	poor
Du kannst natürlich nicht so schwänzen, arme Anna.	Poor Anna, of course, you can't simply cut.
verdienen	(to) earn, deserve
die Arbeit, –en	the work
ausgeben	(to) spend
ich gebe . . . aus	I spend
Aber Du verdienst Geld für Deine Arbeit, und ich gebe Geld aus für meine Arbeit.	But you earn money for your work and I spend money for my work.
Schreib bald!	Write soon!
treu	loyal, faithful
Dein treuer Richard	Ever yours, Richard

omit def. article before titles.

II. Text:

Liebe Anna!

Das ist allerdings eine Überraschung. Anna Becker ist also Verkäuferin in Webers Warenhaus! Das kann ich mir kaum vorstellen. Aber hab nur Geduld! Mit Seidenstrümpfen fängst Du an, aber bald wirst Du Pelzmäntel verkaufen.

Heute hatte ich einen schlechten Tag. In Psychologie fragt mich Professor Berg: „Herr Neumann, rauchen Sie?" Ich antworte: „Ja. Meine Lieblingsmarke ist —." „Das will ich nicht wissen. Warum rauchen Sie?" Ich sage schnell: „Es macht mir Spaß." „Schön," sagt Berg, „eine sehr intelligente und originelle Antwort. Sie haben eine Weltanschauung. Sie sind Hedonist." Dann fragt er Fräulein Blake, einen hübschen Schwarzkopf in der ersten Reihe: „Fräulein Blake, tanzen Sie Swing?" Fräulein Blake lacht ein bißchen und sagt: „Sehr gerne." Fräulein Blake ist die beste Tänzerin auf dem Campus, sagt man. Sie ist schlank und mittelgroß. Nach meiner Psychologiestunde hatte ich anorganische Chemie. Ich komme zu spät, und der Professor sagt sarkastisch: „Das ist hier kein Kino, junger Mann. Kommen Sie bitte rechtzeitig oder gar nicht!" Der Mann war wahrscheinlich beim Militär. Außerdem kann ich fünfmal schwänzen, wenn ich will. Du kannst natürlich nicht so schwänzen, arme Anna. Aber du verdienst Geld für Deine Arbeit, und ich gebe Geld aus für meine Arbeit. Schreib bald!

Dein treuer Richard

	M.	F.	N.	Pl.
N.	e	e	e	en
A.	en	e	e	en
D.	en	en	en	en

III. Comments:

1. *Adjective Declension:* strong endings are same as der declension.

The seeming complexity of adjective endings in German can be systematized and mastered rather easily. In Lesson 2 you observed that an adjective preceded by the definite article or a **der**-word in the nominative case always has the ending **–e;** if preceded by **ein** or an **ein**-word it has **–er** for the masculine, **–e** for the feminine, **–es** for the neuter. Since, for the feminine and neuter, the accusative case of these introductory words is the same as the nominative, the adjective endings are also the same in the accusative as in the nominative. In all other cases the adjective has the ending **–en,** if preceded by an inflected form of **der** or **ein** or of a **der**-word or an **ein**-word. By all other cases, of course, is meant the accusative singular of the masculine, the dative and genitive * singular of all three genders, and all plural forms. The following patterns sum up this rule:

der words & inflected ein-words – weak endings.
no word or uninflected ein-word – strong endings.

* N.	der **–e** Mann	ein **–er** Mann
N. & A.	die **–e** Frau	eine **–e** Frau
N. & A.	das **–e** Mädchen	ein **–es** Mädchen
	All other cases **–en**	

If the adjective is not preceded by a **der-** or **ein**-word, it has the endings of the **der**-words, which you already know: masculine: **–er, –en, –em;** feminine: **–e, –e, –er;** neuter: **–es, –es, –em;** plural: **–e, –e, –en.**

So the phrases for *black coffee, sweet milk, hot water,* and *fresh eggs* are declined as follows:

	Masculine	*Feminine*	*Neuter*	*Plural*
N.	schwarzer Kaffee	süße Milch	heißes Wasser	frische Eier
A.	schwarzen Kaffee	süße Milch	heißes Wasser	frische Eier
D.	schwarzem Kaffee	süßer Milch	heißem Wasser	frischen Eiern

The predicate adjective, that is, the adjective which "belongs" to the verb and not to the noun, has no endings. Contrast: **Unser Professor ist sarkastisch** with **unser sarkastischer Professor** and **Die Antwort ist intelligent** with **eine intelligente Antwort.**

IV. Practice:

1. Memorize the following phrases:

strong endings
weak endings

a.	ein junger Freund	eine junge Freundin	ein junges Kind
	mein lieber Freund	meine liebe Freundin	mein liebes Kind
	kein guter Freund	keine gute Freundin	kein gutes Kind
b.	der junge Freund	die junge Freundin	das junge Kind
	der liebe Freund	die liebe Freundin	das liebe Kind
	der gute Freund	die gute Freundin	das gute Kind

* The genitive case will be discussed in Lesson 11.

Learn

2. a. Richard ist ein intelligenter junger Mann.
   origineller
   lustiger
   Richards Mutter ist eine ruhige ältere Frau.
   mittelgroße
   Anna ist ein hübsches junges Fräulein.
   interessantes

more than one adjective modifying a noun all take the same endings.

   b. Richard ist der einzige intelligente junge Mann in der Klasse.
   originelle
   lustige
   Anna ist das einzige hübsche junge Fräulein in der Klasse.
   interessante

3. Heute hatte ich einen schlechten Tag.
   Gestern (*yesterday*)
   Vorgestern (*day before yesterday*) hatte ich einen guten Tag.

4. Richard hat einen sarkastischen Professor.
   guten Vater.
   eine hübsche Freundin. (*girl friend*)
   liebe Mutter.
   ein schönes Zimmer.
   interessantes Buch.

5. In der ersten Reihe sitzt ein hübscher Schwarzkopf.
   eine hübsche Blondine. (*blonde*)
   zweiten ein guter Student.
   dritten ein ruhiges Mädchen.
   vierten ein guter Freund von Richard.
   fünften eine gute Freundin von mir.

6. a. Richard spricht gerade mit der besten Tänzerin in der Schule.
   Studentin Klasse.
   dem besten Studenten
   den besten Studenten

   nom.

   b. Wer spricht gerade mit der besten Tänzerin in der Schule?
   Mit wem spricht Richard?

   dat.

7. Marie und Elsa sind die besten Tänzerinnen in der Schule.
   Richard und Wilhelm sind die besten Tennisspieler in der Schule.

8. a. Richard hat seinen neuen Anzug an.
   seinen braunen Rock
   sein graues Hemd
   seine weißen Schuhe
   Anna hat ihr neues Kleid an.
   ihre braunen Schuhe an.

   b. Haben Sie Ihren neuen Anzug an, Herr Jones?
   Ja, ich habe meinen neuen Anzug an, etc.

9. Nach der Psychologiestunde habe ich organische Chemie.
europäische Geschichte.
(*European history*)
moderne Philosophie.
(*modern philosophy*)
deutsche Konversation.
(*German conversation*)

V. Exercises:

A. *Questions:*

1. Was wird Anna bald verkaufen?
2. Hatte Richard heute einen guten Tag?
3. Raucht er?
4. Was raucht er?
5. Warum raucht er?
6. Hat er eine pessimistische Weltanschauung?
7. Wo sitzt Fräulein Blake?
8. Wer ist die beste Tänzerin auf dem Campus?
9. Was ist Ihr Lieblingstanz? Rhumba? Tango? Fox Trott? Walzer?
10. Wie oft kann Richard schwänzen? → infinitive at the end.
11. Warum kann Anna nicht schwänzen? with auxiliary (kann)

B. *Translate:*

1. Richard hat eine hedonistische Weltanschauung.
2. Dann fragt er mich: „Tanzen Sie gern?"
3. Haben Sie einen sarkastischen Professor, Fräulein Haskell?
4. Anna Becker ist ein hübsches junges Fräulein.
5. Richard hat seine weißen Schuhe an.
6. Er verdient viel Geld für seine Arbeit.
7. Das ist die beste Antwort auf diese Frage.
8. Er ist eine weltbekannte Autorität.
9. Sie schreibt immer interessante Briefe an ihre Freunde.
10. Passen Sie gut auf, junger Mann!

C. *Correct the misinformation:*

1. Heute hatte Richard einen guten Tag.
2. Professor Berg hat eine hedonistische Weltanschauung.
3. Fräulein Blake ist eine hübsche Blondine.
4. Anna Becker ist die beste Tänzerin auf dem Campus.
5. Fräulein Blake sitzt in der dritten Reihe.
6. Nach der Psychologiestunde hatte Richard organische Chemie.
7. Richards Chemieprofessor ist ein freundlicher Mann.
8. Anna gibt Geld aus für ihre Arbeit.

D. *Rearrange the following words and groups of words to make correct sentences and translate:*

1. nur dreimal, arme Marie, schwänzen, kannst, du.
2. er, nach der Philosophiestunde, hatte, europäische Geschichte.
3. heute, sie, ein neues Kleid, hat . . . an.
4. zur Klasse, können Sie, kommen, nicht rechtzeitig?
5. Richard und ich, uns, über unsere Stunden, unterhalten.
6. das kleine Paket, von seiner Mutter, ist, ein Geschenk.
7. die beiden Mädchen, um halb elf, haben, deutsche Konversation.

VI. Securing the Vocabulary:

A.

allerdings	*indeed, to be sure*
also	*well then, and so, therefore*
können	*(to) be able to*
kaum	*hardly, scarcely*
anfangen	*(to) begin*
schlecht	*bad*
schnell	*quickly*
schwarz	*black*
der Kopf	*head*
arm	*poor*
gar nicht	*not at all*

B.

das Zimmer (4)	1. *much*
sehr (6)	2. *hour, class, lesson*
die Freude (7)	3. *still, after all this time*
viel (1)	4. *room*
die Stunde (2)	5. *(to) work*
immer noch (3)	6. *very*
immer (10)	7. *joy, pleasure*
arbeiten (5)	8. *never*
traurig (11)	9. *perhaps*
vielleicht (9)	10. *always*
nie (8)	11. *sad*

übrigens (5)	1. *until*
wenn (8)	2. *since*
der Mensch (10)	3. *railroad station*
das Geschenk (7)	4. *at, with, near, at the house of*
der Bahnhof (3)	5. *incidentally*
bis (1)	6. *how, as, like*
lesen (11)	7. *present*
bei (4)	8. *when, whenever, if*
seit (2)	9. *nothing*
wie (6)	10. *human being, man*
nichts (9)	11. *(to) read*

schon (4)	1. *bad*
anziehen (8)	2. *(to) need*
schwer (9)	3. *(to) get up*
aufstehen (3)	4. *already*
brauchen (2)	5. *state*
böse (1)	6. *because*

immer wieder (10)	7. *now and then*
dann und wann (7)	8. *(to) dress*
der Staat (5)	9. *heavy, difficult*
wieder (11)	10. *again and again*
weil (6)	11. *again*

July 11, 1950
Start here & learn
the forms of the verbs.

Neunte Aufgabe

* * * \

* vor	before
die Meisterschaft, –en	the championship, championship games
* der Fremde, –n	the stranger
ein Fremder	a stranger
der Platz, ¨e	the place, square
der Tennisplatz, ¨e	the tennis court
kommen	(to) come
ich bin gekommen	I have come
fragen	(to) ask
ich habe gefragt	I have asked
Am Tage vor der Meisterschaft ist ein Fremder zu mir auf den Tennisplatz gekommen und hat mich gefragt:	On the day before the championship games a stranger came out on the tennis court to me and asked me:
der Winter, —	the winter
letzten Winter	last winter
* verschieden	different, various
die Stadt, ¨e	the city
* spielen	(to) play
ich habe gespielt	I have played
nicht wahr?	isn't that so?
„Sie haben letzten Winter in verschiedenen Städten Floridas gespielt, nicht wahr?	"You played last winter in various Florida cities, didn't you?
sein	(to) be
Sie waren	you were
der Lehrer, —	the teacher
der Tennislehrer, —	the tennis coach
das Hotel', –s	the hotel
Sie waren Tennislehrer für vier Hotels in Kalifornien, nicht wahr?	You were a tennis coach for four hotels in California, weren't you?
* der Beruf, –e	the vocation, profession
der Spieler, —	the player
der Berufsspieler, —	the professional player
Sie sind Berufsspieler.	You're a professional.
wissen	(to) know
können	(to) be able

als	as
der Amateur′, –e	the amateur
Sie wissen, Sie können nicht als Amateur spielen.“	You know you can't play as an amateur.”
erst	first, at first
können	(to) be able
ich konnte nicht	I was not able
vor	before
das Erstaunen	the amazement
vor Erstaunen	because of amazement
* reden	(to) speak
dann	then
der Mann, ¨er	the man
* gründlich	thorough, thoroughly
* die Meinung, –en	the opinion
sagen	(to) say
ich habe gesagt	I have said
Erst konnte ich vor Erstaunen nicht reden; dann habe ich dem Mann aber gründlich meine Meinung gesagt.	At first I couldn't talk, I was so flabbergasted; but then I really gave the fellow a piece of my mind.
* verwechseln	(to) confuse
ich habe verwechselt	I have confused
Er hat mich mit dem Berufsspieler Richard Niemann verwechselt.	He took me for the professional Richard Niemann.
so	such
der Esel, —	the donkey
So ein Esel!	What a dope!
die Meisterschaft, –en	the championship
der Kampf, ¨e	the fight, contest
der Meisterschaftskampf, ¨e	the championship contest
sein	(to) be
ich war	I was
nie	never
Ich war nie in Kalifornien.	I have never been in California.
schwer	heavy, difficult
Der Meisterschaftskampf war schwer.	The final match was tough.

einzeln	single, individual
das Spiel, –e	the game
das Einzelspiel, –e	the game of singles
der Satz, ⸗e	set
verlieren	(to) lose
ich habe verloren	I have lost
Ich habe im Einzelspiel einen Satz verloren.	I lost one set in the singles.

das Ende	the end
das Resultat′, –e	the result
die Null, –en	the zero
Das Endresultat war: sechs zu vier, null zu sechs, zehn zu acht.	The final score was six-four, love-six, ten-eight.

der Gegner, —	the opponent
ganz	entire
das Jahr, –e	the year
trainie′ren	(to) train
ich hatte trainiert	I had trained
Mein Gegner hatte das ganze Jahr trainiert; er kommt aus Kalifornien.	My opponent had been training all year; he comes from California.

* eben	just, just now
das Glück	the luck, happiness, fortune
haben	(to) have
ich habe gehabt	I have had
Er hat sehr gut gespielt, aber ich habe eben Glück gehabt.	He played very well but I was just lucky.

übrigens	by the way
finden	(to) find
ich habe gefunden	I have found
Hat Mutter übrigens meinen alten Tennisschläger gefunden?	By the way, has Mother found my old tennis racquet?

so	thus, so, as
wie	how, as
so . . . wie	as . . . as
* so bald wie	as soon as
möglich	possible
Schicke ihn, bitte, so bald wie möglich!	Please send it as soon as possible.

immer	always
hinten	at the rear
rechts	to the right
der Schrank, ¨e	the closet
im Schrank	in the closet
stehen	(to) stand
ich habe gestanden	I have stood
Er hat immer hinten rechts im Schrank gestanden.	It always used to stand at the back of the closet to the right.

vielleicht′	perhaps
das Packen	the packing
beim Packen	in packing, during packing
verlegen	(to) mislay
ich habe verlegt	I have mislaid
Vielleicht habe ich ihn beim Packen verlegt.	Perhaps I mislaid it when I was packing.

müssen	(to) have to
ich muß	I have to
das Bett, –en	the bed
gehen	(to) go
Jetzt muß ich aber zu Bett gehen.	But now I must go to bed.

heute	today
* früh	early
* heute früh	this morning
sehr	very
aufstehen	(to) get up
ich bin aufgestanden	I got up
Ich bin heute sehr früh aufgestanden.	I got up very early this morning.

* berühmt	famous
der Sohn, ¨e	the son
Dein berühmter Sohn Richard.	Your famous son Richard.

II. Text:

Lieber Vater!

Hast Du es in der Zeitung gelesen? Hast Du es schon gehört? Also, ich habe die Tennismeisterschaft der Freshman-Klasse gewonnen. Stell Dir vor! Am Tage vor der Meisterschaft ist ein Fremder zu mir auf den Tennisplatz gekommen und hat mich gefragt: „Sie haben letzten Winter in verschiedenen Städten Floridas gespielt, nicht wahr? Sie waren Tennislehrer für vier Hotels in Kalifornien, nicht wahr? Sie sind Berufsspieler. Sie wissen, Sie können nicht als Amateur spielen." Erst konnte ich vor Erstaunen nicht reden; dann habe ich dem Mann aber gründlich meine Meinung gesagt. Er hat mich mit dem Berufsspieler Richard Niemann verwechselt. So ein Esel! Ich war nie in Kalifornien.

Der Meisterschaftskampf war schwer. Ich habe im Einzelspiel einen Satz verloren. Das Endresultat war: sechs zu vier, null zu sechs, zehn zu acht. Mein Gegner hatte das ganze Jahr trainiert; er kommt aus Kalifornien. Er hat sehr gut gespielt, aber ich habe eben Glück gehabt.

Hat Mutter übrigens meinen alten Tennisschläger gefunden? Schicke ihn, bitte, so bald wie möglich! Er hat immer hinten rechts im Schrank gestanden. Vielleicht habe ich ihn beim Packen verlegt. Jetzt muß ich aber zu Bett gehen. Ich bin heute sehr früh aufgestanden.

Dein berühmter Sohn
Richard

III. Comments:

1. *Present Perfect and Past Perfect Tenses:*

The present forms of **haben** are used as tense auxiliaries with the past participle of most verbs to form their present perfect tense. Hence: **ich habe gemacht,** *I have made.* However, German commonly uses the present perfect tense to express simple past action; thus **ich habe gemacht** can also mean *I made.* However, the verbs **sein** and **haben** themselves frequently use the simple past tense forms to express past action: **ich war** — *I was;* **ich hatte** — *I had.*

all weak verbs

Learn

ich habe gemacht	*I have made, I made*
du hast gemacht	*you have made, you made*
er, sie, es hat gemacht	*he, she, it has made, he, she, it made*
wir haben gemacht	*we have made, we made*
ihr habt gemacht	*you have made, you made*
sie haben gemacht	*they have made, they made*
Sie haben gemacht	*you have made, you made*

strong verbs

ich habe gefunden	*I have found, I found*
du hast gefunden	*you have found, you found*
er, sie, es hat gefunden	*he, she, it has found, he, she, it found*
wir haben gefunden	*we have found, we found*
ihr habt gefunden	*you have found, you found*
sie haben gefunden	*they have found, they found*
Sie haben gefunden	*you have found, you found*

The simple past tense forms of **haben** (**hatte,** *etc.*) are used as tense auxiliaries with the past participle of most verbs to form their past perfect tense.

Learn

ich hatte gemacht	*I had made*
du hattest gemacht	*you had made*
er, sie, es hatte gemacht	*he, she, it had made*
wir hatten gemacht	*we had made*
ihr hattet gemacht	*you had made*
sie hatten gemacht	*they had made*
Sie hatten gemacht	*you had made*

ich hatte gefunden	*I had found*
du hattest gefunden	*you had found*
er, sie, es hatte gefunden	*he, she, it had found*
wir hatten gefunden	*we had found*
ihr hattet gefunden	*you had found*
sie hatten gefunden	*they had found*
Sie hatten gefunden	*you had found*

intransitive verbs denoting change of position or condition of the subject

Under certain circumstances, however, the auxiliary **sein** is employed in the formation of the present and past perfect: **ich bin gekommen,** *I have come, I came;* **ich war gekommen,** *I had come.* Similarly, in older English and in elevated style, you sometimes see such sentences as *Christ is risen* and *I am come to pronounce judgment* instead of *Christ has risen* and *I have come.* This mode of forming the perfect tense is very common in German and follows a definite rule: If a verb is intransitive, that is, if it cannot take an accusative object, and if it also signifies a change of position or condition, it requires the use of **sein** as tense auxiliary. In addition, **sein** and **werden** use **sein** as tense auxiliary. Thus: **ich bin gewesen,** *I have been;* **ich bin geworden,** *I have become.*

Examples:

Learn

ich bin gekommen	*I have come, I came*
du bist gekommen	*you have come, you came*
er, sie, es ist gekommen	*he, she, it has come, he, she, it came*
wir sind gekommen	*we have come, we came*
ihr seid gekommen	*you have come, you came*
sie sind gekommen	*they have come, they came*
Sie sind gekommen	*you have come, you came*
ich war gekommen	*I had come*
du warst gekommen	*you had come*
er, sie, es war gekommen	*he, she, it had come*
wir waren gekommen	*we had come*
ihr wart gekommen	*you had come*
sie waren gekommen	*they had come*
Sie waren gekommen	*you had come*

An important fact about the compound tenses in German is that the past participle comes at the end of the clause. The first sentence in Richard's letter to his father is: **Hast Du es in der Zeitung gelesen?** This is as if we were to say, *Have you it in the paper read?* instead of *Have you read it in the paper?* Compare the past participles of basic verbs and verbal compounds: **stehen — gestanden** and **aufstehen — aufgestanden; geben — gegeben** and **ausgeben — ausgegeben.**

Example: Ich bin heute sehr früh aufgestanden.
I got up very early this morning.

From now on the lists of Words and Phrases will indicate what the present perfect tense of a verb is, as follows: **fragen, ich habe gefragt; aufstehen, ich bin aufgestanden; verstehen, ich habe verstanden.** Notice that the form of the present perfect tense also indicates whether or not a verb prefix is separable.

2. *Position of Infinitive:*

So far you have learned two elements that must come at the end of an independent clause: the separable prefix and the past participle. The third element that comes at the end of an independent clause is the infinitive.

Examples:

Sie können nicht als Amateur spielen.
You can't play as an amateur.

Jetzt muß ich aber zu Bett gehen.
But now I have to go to bed.

IV. Practice:

Learn

1. Hast du es schon gehört?
   Haben Sie gelesen?
   Hat er gesagt?
   gefunden?

2. Am Tage vor der Meisterschaft ist ein Fremder zu mir gekommen.
   mein Gegner
   ein Tennislehrer

3. Ich habe letzten Winter in Florida gespielt.
   Sommer in Kalifornien trainiert.
   Er hat Herbst in Iowa Geld verdient.
   Frühling in Illinois gearbeitet.

4. Das kann ich mir gar nicht vorstellen.
   kannst du dir
   kann er sich
   können wir uns
   können Sie sich

5. Das habe ich mir nie so vorgestellt.
   hast du dir
   etc.

6. a. Ich habe dem Mann meine Meinung gesagt.
   Richard hat seine
   Anna hat der Frau ihre
   Haben Sie dem Dekan Ihre Meinung gesagt, Herr Jones?

   b. Wer hat dem Mann seine Meinung gesagt?
   Wem haben Sie Ihre Meinung gesagt? etc., etc.

7. a. Ich habe meine Uhr verloren.
   mein Buch

   b. Was haben Sie verloren?
   hat Richard
   Wer hat seinen Tennisschläger verloren?

8. a. Frau Neumann hat den alten Tennisschläger im Schrank gefunden.
   die Tennisschuhe
   Herr Neumann ein kleines Paket
   Fräulein Schmidt hat ein schönes Geschenk

b. Was hat Frau Neumann im Schrank gefunden?
Wer hat den alten Tennisschläger im Schrank gefunden?
Wo hat Frau Neumann den alten Tennisschläger gefunden? etc.

9. a. Ich muß jetzt zu Bett gehen.
morgen sehr früh aufstehen.
jeden Morgen sehr früh aufstehen.
um halb sieben aufstehen.

b. Müssen Sie jetzt zu Bett gehen, Herr Jones?
Stehen Sie jeden Morgen um halb sieben auf, Herr Fischer?

10. a. Ich bin heute sehr früh aufgestanden.
Richard ist gestern
Wilhelm ist vorgestern

b. Sind Sie heute sehr früh aufgestanden, Herr Jones?
Warum ist Wilhelm sehr früh aufgestanden?

11. a. Gestern früh bin ich um halb sieben aufgestanden.
Heute früh sechs Uhr
Aber morgen früh stehe ich erst (*not until*) um neun Uhr auf.

b. Warum sind Sie um halb neun aufgestanden?
Warum stehen Sie erst um neun Uhr auf?

V. Exercises:

A. *Questions:*

1. Was kann man in der Zeitung über Richard lesen?
2. Wer hat in verschiedenen Städten Floridas gespielt?
3. Wo war Richard Niemann Tennislehrer?
4. Ist Herr Niemann ein Amateur?
5. Mit wem hat der Fremde den Amateur Richard Neumann verwechselt?
6. War Richard einmal in Kalifornien?
7. Welchen Satz hat Richard sechs zu vier gewonnen?
8. Warum kann Richards Gegner das ganze Jahr trainieren?
9. Wo hat der alte Tennisschläger gestanden?
10. Warum kann Frau Neumann Richards alten Tennisschläger nicht finden?
11. Warum muß Richard jetzt schon zu Bett gehen?

B. *Translate:*

1. Er hatte schon einen Satz verloren.
2. Er hat dem Fremden seine Meinung gesagt.
3. Ich kann mich nicht für Mathematik interessieren.
4. Was für ein Halsband haben Sie verloren?
5. Ich habe Richards letzten Brief an mich verlegt.
6. Können Sie sich das vorstellen?
7. Waren Sie letzten Winter in Kalifornien?
8. Ich bin gestern zu spät zur Stunde gekommen.

9. Er konnte sich das gar nicht vorstellen.
10. Was für Zigaretten möchten Sie?
11. Der Fremde hat sie mit Fräulein Jones verwechselt.
12. Jetzt mußt du zu Bett gehen. Hast du mich verstanden?
13. Wo hat Frau Neumann den alten Tennisschläger gefunden?
14. Unsere Gegner hatten den ganzen Winter trainiert.
15. Wissen Sie nicht, daß Sie als Amateur nicht spielen können?

C. *Rearrange:*

1. in verschiedenen Städten Floridas, er, letzten Winter, hat . . . gespielt.
2. dem Dekan, sie, ihre Meinung, hat . . . gesagt.
3. ihn, hat . . . verwechselt, der Professor, mit dem bekannten Tennisspieler.
4. bin . . . gegangen, zu Bett, ich, gestern, sehr spät.
5. um halb elf, ich muß, zu Bett gehen, jeden Abend.
6. ich, das, konnte, nicht, mir, vorstellen.
7. mein Freund, letzten Montag, zu mir, ist . . . gekommen, auf mein Zimmer.
8. sind . . . gegangen, gestern abend, wir, ins Theater.

D. *Correct the misinformation:*

1. Am Tage vor der Meisterschaft ist ein Berufsspieler zu Richard auf den Tennisplatz gekommen.
2. Richard Niemann hat letzten Sommer in verschiedenen Städten Floridas gespielt.
3. Er war Tennislehrer für fünf Hotels in Kalifornien.
4. Richard hat keinen einzigen (*single*) Satz verloren.
5. Sein Gegner hatte nicht gut trainiert.
6. Richard hat kein Glück gehabt.
7. Richards alter Tennisschläger hat immer hinten links im Schrank gestanden.
8. Richard ist heute sehr spät aufgestanden.

VI. Securing the Vocabulary:

A.

die Zeitung	*newspaper*	die Meinung	*opinion*
gewinnen	(*to*) *win*	verwechseln	(*to*) *confuse*
der Fremde	*stranger*	eben	*just*
verschieden	*different, various*	so bald wie	*as soon as*
spielen	(*to*) *play*	möglich	*possible*
der Beruf	*vocation, profession*	früh	*early*
vor	*before*	heute früh	*this morning*
reden	(*to*) *speak*	berühmt	*famous*
gründlich	*thorough*		

B.

seit (4)	1. *especially*
die Stelle (9)	2. *room*
arm (6)	3. *black*
das Zimmer (2)	4. *since*
besonders (1)	5. *head*
schwarz (3)	6. *poor*
die Rechnung (10)	7. *soon*
der Kopf (5)	8. *(to) close*
schließen (8)	9. *place, passage*
bald (7)	10. *bill*

schlecht (9)	1. *because*
wer (10)	2. *besides, in addition*
etwas (8)	3. *frightful*
außerdem (2)	4. *less*
die Unterhaltung (6)	5. *watch, clock*
das Gebiet (7)	6. *conversation*
die Uhr (5)	7. *territory, region, special field*
weil (1)	8. *something*
schrecklich (3)	9. *bad*
weniger (4)	10. *who*

nun (3)	1. *at, with, near, at the house of*
tragen (11)	2. *letter*
schnell (6)	3. *well then*
der Brief (2)	4. *(to) pay*
die Sorge (8)	5. *quiet*
bei (1)	6. *quickly*
kennen (10)	7. *in advance*
ruhig (5)	8. *worry, care*
bezahlen (4)	9. *(to) sell*
im voraus (7)	10. *(to) know*
verkaufen (9)	11. *(to) carry, wear*
gar nicht (12)	12. *not at all*

Zehnte Aufgabe

* *

Die Verkäuferin

I. Words and Phrases:

Zehnte Aufgabe.	Tenth lesson.
die Verkäuferin, –nen	the salesgirl
Lieber Richard!	Dear Richard,
glänzend	shining, brilliant
* die Zukunft	the future
prophezei'en	(to) prophesy, predict
Vielen Dank für Deinen letzten Brief, in dem Du mir eine glänzende Zukunft in Webers Warenhaus prophezeist.	Many thanks for your last letter, in which you predict a brilliant future in Weber's department store for me.
* leider	unfortunately
* es gibt	there is (are), there exists (exist)
* so etwas	such a thing
das Märchen, —	the fairy-tale
der Film, –e	the motion picture, film
Leider gibt es so etwas nur in Märchen oder im Film.	Unfortunately things like that happen only in fairy-tales or in the movies.
nun	well then
komisch	comical
die Idee', –n	the idea
lachen, ich habe gelacht	(to) laugh
die Abwechslung	the change
Nun, ich habe über Deine komischen Ideen gelacht; jetzt kannst Du zur Abwechslung über mich lachen.	Well, I have laughed at your funny ideas, now you can laugh at me for a change.

der Laden, ¨	the store
der Tisch, –e	the table
der Ladentisch, –e	the counter
* gleich	directly, immediately
der Eingang, ¨e	the entrance
Mein Ladentisch ist gleich beim Eingang.	My counter is right at the entrance.
wer	who, whoever
etwas	something
wissen, ich habe gewußt	(to) know
wollen, ich habe gewollt	(to) want to
er will	he wants to
* gewöhnlich	usually
* zuerst′	at first
Wer etwas wissen will, kommt gewöhnlich zuerst zu mir.	Anybody who wants information usually comes to me first.
täglich	daily
allerlei	all sorts of
antworten, ich habe geantwortet	(to) answer
auf eine Frage antworten	(to) answer a question
mancher (manche, manches)	many a
manche (*plural*)	some
* merkwürdig	remarkable
Täglich muß ich auf allerlei Fragen antworten, und manche dieser Fragen sind sehr merkwürdig.	I have to answer all sorts of questions every day and some of these questions are very peculiar.
ein paar	a few
die Probe, –n	the sample
Hier sind ein paar Proben.	Here are a few samples.
* entschuldigen, ich habe entschuldigt	(to) excuse
das Fräulein, —	the young lady, Miss
halten, ich habe gehalten	(to) hold, stop
der Autobus, –se	the bus
„Entschuldigen Sie, Fräulein, wo hält Autobus drei?“	"Excuse me, Miss, where does the number three bus stop?"
links	to the left
die Ecke, –n	the corner
„Gleich hier links an der Ecke.“	"Right here on the corner to the left."
die Socke, –n	the sock
die Tasche, –n	the pocket

das Tuch, ⸗er	the cloth
das Taschentuch, ⸗er	the handkerchief
* kaufen, ich habe gekauft	(to) buy
„Können Sie mir sagen, wo ich Socken und Taschentücher kaufen kann?“	"Can you tell me where I can buy socks and handkerchiefs?"
der Stock, —werke	the floor
im dritten Stock	on the fourth floor
* fahren, ich bin gefahren	(to) travel, ride
der Stuhl, ⸗e	the chair
der Fahrstuhl, ⸗e	the elevator
da	there
drüben	yonder
* da drüben	over there
„Im dritten Stock; der Fahrstuhl ist da drüben.“	"On the fourth floor; the elevator is over there."
wo	where
* vorig	previous, preceding
der Sommer, —	the summer
die Hand, ⸗e	the hand
die Tasche, -n	the pocket, bag
die Handtasche, -n	the hand-bag
der Schmuck	the adornment
der Arti'kel —	the article
der Schmuck'arti'kel, —	the decorative article
verkaufen	(to) sell
„Wo ist das Fräulein, das im vorigen Sommer hier Handtaschen und Schmuckartikel verkaufte?“	"Where is the salesgirl who sold handbags and costume jewelry here last summer?"
* sich verheiraten, ich habe mich verheiratet	(to) get married
„Sie hat sich vor einer Woche verheiratet.“	"She got married a week ago."
* schlimm	bad
am schlimmsten	worst
aufgeregt	excited
die Dame, -n	the lady
sich beschweren, ich habe mich beschwert	(to) complain
Am schlimmsten sind die aufgeregten alten Damen, die sich bei mir beschweren:	Worst of all are the excited old ladies who make complaints to me.

kennen, ich habe gekannt	(to) be acquainted with
die Marke, –n	the brand
* der Frühling, –e	the spring
der Traum, ¨e	the dream
der Frühlingstraum, ¨e	the spring dream
„Sie verkaufen Seidenstrümpfe und kennen die Marke ‚Frühlingstraum' nicht?"	"You sell silk stockings and don't know the brand 'Spring Dream'?"
tun, ich habe getan	(to) do
das Leid	the sorrow
* es tut mir leid	it causes me sorrow, I'm sorry
* wirklich	really
furchtbar	awful, terrible
„Es tut mir wirklich furchtbar leid."	"I'm really awfully sorry."
sich ansehen, ich habe mir angesehn	(to) look at
ich sehe mir etwas an	I look at something
„Sehen Sie sich diesen Strumpf an, Fräulein!	"Take a look at this stocking, Miss!"
zweimal	twice
waschen, ich habe gewaschen	(to) wash
* laufen, ich bin gelaufen	(to) run
die Masche, –n	the stitch, mesh
die Laufmasche, –n	the run
Ich habe ihn zweimal gewaschen, und schon hat er eine Laufmasche."	"I have washed it twice and it has a run already."
* sicher	sure, certain
das Waschen	the (*act of*) washing
„Sind Sie sicher, daß die Laufmasche nicht schon vor dem Waschen im Strumpf war?"	"Are you sure that the run wasn't already in the stocking before you washed it?"
lesen, ich habe gelesen	(to) read
eben	just now
die Zeitung, –en	the newspaper
das College, –s	the college
das Jahr, –e	the year
das Hundert, –e	the hundred
das Jahrhundert, –e	the century

die Feier, –n	the celebration
die Jahrhundertfeier, –n	the centennial celebration
Richard, ich habe eben in der Zeitung gelesen, daß Dein College im November Jahrhundertfeier hat.	Richard, I have just read in the newspaper that your college is going to have its centennial celebration in November.
überra'schen, ich habe überrascht'	(to) surprise
Das hat mich sehr überrascht.	That surprised me very much.
wissen, ich habe gewußt	(to) know
gar nicht	not at all
ich wußte gar nicht	I didn't know at all
schon	already
Ich wußte gar nicht, daß Dein College schon so alt ist.	I had no idea that your college is so old.
füllen, ich habe gefüllt	(to) fill
die Feder, –n	the feather, pen
die Füllfeder, –n	the fountain pen
*leer	empty
außerdem	besides, in addition
* heute abend	this evening
das Geschirr	the table utensils
spülen, ich habe gespült	(to) rinse
Meine Füllfeder ist leer, und außerdem muß ich heute abend das Geschirr spülen.	My fountain pen is dry and besides, I have to do the dishes tonight.
Schreib bald!	Write soon!
In Liebe — Anna	With love, Anna
übrigens	incidentally
die Weltanschauung, –en	the world-view
gefallen, es hat gefallen	(to) please
es hat mir gefallen	it pleased me, I liked it
Übrigens, was Professor Berg über Deine Weltanschauung sagte, hat mir gar nicht gefallen.	Incidentally, I didn't at all like what Professor Berg said about your philosophy of life.

II. Text:

Lieber Richard!

Vielen Dank für Deinen letzten Brief, in dem Du mir eine glänzende Zukunft in Webers Warenhaus prophezeist. Leider gibt es so etwas nur in Märchen oder im Film. Nun, ich habe über Deine komischen Ideen gelacht; jetzt kannst Du zur Abwechslung über mich lachen. Mein Ladentisch ist gleich beim Eingang. Wer etwas wissen will, kommt gewöhnlich zuerst zu mir. Täglich muß ich auf allerlei Fragen antworten, und manche dieser Fragen sind sehr merkwürdig. Hier sind ein paar Proben: „Entschuldigen Sie, Fräulein, wo hält Autobus drei?" — „Gleich hier links an der Ecke." — „Können Sie mir sagen, wo ich Socken und Taschentücher kaufen kann?" — „Im dritten Stock, der Fahrstuhl ist da drüben." — „Wo ist das Fräulein, das hier im vorigen Sommer Handtaschen und Schmuckartikel verkaufte?" — „Sie hat sich vor einer Woche verheiratet." Am schlimmsten sind die aufgeregten alten Damen, die sich bei mir beschweren: „Sie verkaufen Seidenstrümpfe und kennen die Marke ‚Frühlingstraum' nicht?" — „Es tut mir wirklich furchtbar leid . . ." — „Sehen Sie sich diesen Strumpf an, Fräulein! Ich habe ihn zweimal gewaschen, und schon hat er eine Laufmasche." — „Sind Sie sicher, daß die Laufmasche nicht schon vor dem Waschen im Strumpf war?"

Richard, ich habe eben in der Zeitung gelesen, daß Dein College im November Jahrhundertfeier hat. Das hat mich sehr überrascht. Ich wußte gar nicht, daß Dein College schon so alt ist.

Meine Füllfeder ist leer, und außerdem muß ich heute abend das Geschirr spülen. Schreib bald!

In Liebe

Anna

Übrigens, was Professor Berg über Deine Weltanschauung sagte, hat mir gar nicht gefallen.

III. Comments:

1. *Prepositions:*

It is important to realize that the meaning of a preposition is very hard to define and that you must not expect a preposition always to mean one or two specific things and to have one or two specific uses. Think of the widely differing meanings of the English preposition *for* in the sentences: *Please do it for me, I'll be gone for ten days, Let's go for a walk.* Thus, any meanings which are attached to the German prepositions in this unit are meant simply to indicate their more common use or merely the meanings which they tend to have.

Some prepositions always require the dative case. The most common ones are: **aus** — *out of;* **außer** — *besides, in addition to;* **bei** — *with, at the house of;* **mit** — *with;* **nach** — *after, to(wards);* **seit** — *since;* **von** — *of, from;* **zu** — *to.*

Some prepositions always require the accusative case. The most common ones are: **durch** — *through;* **für** — *for;* **gegen** — *against;* **ohne** — *without;* **um** — *around, about.*

A third group of prepositions requires sometimes the dative and sometimes the accusative case. These prepositions are: **an** — *at, to;* **auf** — *on;* **hinter** — *behind;* **in** — *in;* **neben** — *next to;* **über** — *over;* **unter** — *under;* **vor** — *before;* **zwischen** — *between.*

When one of the prepositions in the third group is used with the accusative, the idea is that of motion toward a goal or limit, *e.g.* **Ein Fremder kommt auf den Tennisplatz.** *A stranger is coming out onto the tennis court.* When one of these prepositions is used with the dative however, the idea is that of locality or station: **Mein Ladentisch ist neben dem Eingang.** *My counter is at the entrance.* **Der Autobus hält an der Ecke.** *The bus stops at the corner.* The prepositions **an, auf** and **über** are used with the accusative also in a figurative sense: **Ich habe über deine Ideen gelacht.** *I laughed at your ideas.*

2. *Contractions of Definite Article with Prepositions:*

Some of the prepositions form contractions with the following article. Thus **bei dem** becomes **beim, von dem — vom, zu dem — zum, zu der — zur, durch das — durchs, für das — fürs, um das — ums, an dem — am, in dem — im, in das — ins.**

3. **Da** *and* **wo** *Compounds:*

In English it is possible, and in legal language customary, to replace a preposition and its pronoun object such as *with it* and *with what* by the compound forms *therewith* and *wherewith.* German regularly employs such compounds composed of the particles **da** and **wo** (**dar-** and **wor-** before vowels) plus the preposition. Thus: *with it* — **damit,** *with what* — **womit,** *in it* — **darin,** *in what* — **worin.**

4. *Transposed Word Order:*

In subordinate clauses the inflected verb stands at the end. This is called transposed word order. There are three types of subordinate clauses in German:

wenn, weil

1. A clause introduced by a conjunction: Ich höre, **daß** dein College Jahrhundertfeier **hat.** *I hear that your college has its centennial celebration.* (For complete list of subordinating conjunctions, see Appendix.)

2. A clause introduced by a relative pronoun: Vielen Dank für Deinen Brief, **in dem** Du mir eine glänzende Zukunft **prophezeist.** *Many thanks for your letter in which you predict a brilliant future for me.*

3. A clause introduced by an interrogative, *i.e.* an indirect question: Können Sie mir sagen, **wo** ich Taschentücher kaufen **kann?**

IV. Practice:

I am just going —

1. Ich gehe gerade ins Kino.
   Theater.
   zur Klasse.
   Deutschstunde.
   Bank (*bank*).
   *auf die Post (*post-office*).
   in die Stadt (*downtown*).
   *nach Hause (*home*). zu Hause – at home

use right preposition

2. Was du über deine Professoren sagst, hat mir gar nicht gefallen.
   Klassen
   Was Sie über Ihre Weltanschauung schreiben, hat mir sehr gut gefallen.
   Arbeit

3. Mein Tisch ist gleich links beim Eingang. – from gehen, ging, gegangen
   out ← Ausgang.
   Fahrstuhl.
   bei der Tür (*door*).

4. Wer etwas wissen will, kommt gewöhnlich zuerst zu mir.
   an meinen Tisch.
   zum Abteilungschef.
   Professor.

5. Sind Sie sicher, daß die Laufmasche nicht schon vor dem Waschen im Strumpf war?
   Autobus drei an der Ecke hält?
   das Fräulein sich verheiratet hat?
   Sie meine Füllfeder nicht gesehen haben?

6. Wissen Sie, wer hier im vorigen Frühjahr Handtaschen verkauft hat?
   wann die junge Dame sich verheiratet hat?
   ob (*whether*) Autobus drei an der nächsten Ecke hält?
   wofür Ihre Freundin sich besonders interessiert?

7. Es tut mir leid, daß Sie sich über die Strümpfe beschweren müssen.
   schon nach Hause gehen müssen.
   Ihre neue Füllfeder verloren haben.

8. Mein Freund hat sich vor einer Woche verheiratet.
   einem Monat
   Jahr
   zwei Jahren
   sechs Monaten
   zehn Wochen

9. Ich sehe mir diese schönen Taschentücher an.
   grauen Hemden
   Richard sieht sich einen neuen Tennisschläger an.
   das kleine Paket

V. Exercises:

A. *Questions:*

1. In welchem Brief hat Richard Anna eine glänzende Zukunft prophezeit?
2. Wo ist Annas Ladentisch?
3. Wo hält Autobus drei?
4. Was kann man in Webers Warenhaus im dritten Stock kaufen?
5. Wer hat sich vor einer Woche verheiratet?
6. Warum war die alte Dame so aufgeregt?
7. Welche Marke Seidenstrümpfe gibt es in Webers Warenhaus nicht?
8. Wie oft hat die alte Dame den Strumpf mit der Laufmasche gewaschen?
9. Wann hat Richards College Jahrhundertfeier?
10. Was hat Anna in Richards letztem Brief gar nicht gefallen?

B. *Translate:*

1. Heute mußte ich auf eine merkwürdige Frage antworten.
2. Sind Sie sicher, daß das Fräulein sich vor einem Jahr verheiratet hat?
3. Hat er wirklich so etwas gesagt?
4. Ich mußte über die komische Antwort lachen, und er mußte auch darüber lachen.
5. Sehen Sie sich diese schöne Handtasche an!

6. Ich konnte auf die merkwürdige Frage nicht antworten.
7. Mein Freund ist vor zehn Minuten nach Hause gegangen.
8. Können Sie mir sagen, warum sie sich so aufgeregt hat?
9. Sind Sie sicher, daß es ihm gefallen hat?
10. Ich habe zweimal die Woche chemisches Labor.
11. In dem kleinen Paket hat Richard Socken und Taschentücher gefunden.
12. Ich lese eben in der Zeitung, daß Willi Meyer die Tennismeisterschaft gewonnen hat.
13. Ich möchte mir das Buch hier ansehen.
14. Was du über die anderen Studenten in deinem Hause schreibst, hat mir sehr gut gefallen.
15. Möchten Sie heute abend mit mir ins Theater gehen?

C. *Rearrange:*

1. über den aufgeregten Abteilungschef, hat . . . gelacht, er.
2. sie, im vorigen Winter, hat . . . verkauft, hier, Schmuckartikel.
3. sind Sie sicher, es, in diesem Geschäft, daß, gibt, einen Fahrstuhl?
4. was, schreibst, über deine Professoren, du, hat . . . gefallen, mir, sehr gut.
5. täglich, auf allerlei komische Fragen, muß, sie, antworten.
6. über die Verkäuferin, hat sich . . . beschwert, die aufgeregte Dame.
7. vor drei Monaten, hat sich . . . verheiratet, er.
8. eine Füllfeder, ich, und ein silbernes Halsband, kaufen, mir, möchte.
9. sie möchte wissen, wo, Taschentücher, sie kann, kaufen.
10. haben Sie . . . gelesen, in der Zeitung, das?

subject of dependent clause.

D. *Correct the misinformation:*

1. Richards letzter Brief hat Anna sehr gut gefallen.
2. Annas Ladentisch ist gleich beim Fahrstuhl.
3. Wer etwas wissen will, geht gewöhnlich zuletzt zu ihr.
4. Autobus drei hält gleich rechts an der Ecke.
5. Man kann Socken und Taschentücher im vierten Stock kaufen.
6. Es gibt keinen Fahrstuhl im Geschäft.
7. Anna hat sich vor einer Woche verheiratet.
8. Die aufgeregte Dame sagt, daß sie den Strumpf nur einmal gewaschen hat.
9. Richard hat Anna geschrieben, daß sein College im November Jahrhundertfeier hat.
10. Anna muß morgen früh das Geschirr spülen.

VI. Securing the Vocabulary:

A.

die Zukunft	*future*	gleich	*directly, immediately*
leider	*unfortunately*		
es gibt	*there is (are), there exists (exist)*	gewöhnlich	*usually*
		zuerst	*at first*
so etwas	*such a thing*	merkwürdig	*remarkable*

entschuldigen	*(to) excuse*	der Frühling	*spring*
kaufen	*(to) buy*	es tut mir leid	*I am sorry*
fahren	*(to) travel, ride*	wirklich	*really*
da drüben	*over there*	laufen	*(to) run*
vorig	*previous, preceding*	sicher	*sure, certain*
sich verheiraten	*(to) get married*	leer	*empty*
schlimm	*bad*	heute abend	*this evening*

B.

auch (6)	1. *I would like to*	der Beruf (7)	1. *place*
schlecht (2)	2. *bad*	vielleicht (10)	2. *because*
früh (11)	3. *(to) confuse*	wohnen (4)	3. *in advance*
traurig (5)	4. *both*	weil (2)	4. *(to) live, dwell*
beide (4)	5. *sad*	im voraus (3)	5. *opinion*
ich möchte (1)	6. *also*	ander (9)	6. *indeed, to be sure*
schwarz (10)	7. *time*	die Meinung (5)	7. *vocation, profession*
die Zeit (7)	8. *never*	der Ort (1)	8. *place, passage*
verwechseln (3)	9. *to begin*	allerdings (6)	9. *other*
anfangen (9)	10. *black*	die Stelle (8)	10. *perhaps*
nie (8)	11. *early*	sonst (11)	11. *otherwise*

also (4)	1. *(to) speak*
vor (6)	2. *as soon as*
möglich (8)	3. *at least*
so bald wie (2)	4. *well then, and so, therefore*
reden (1)	5. *(to) need*
heute früh (9)	6. *before, ago*
spielen (10)	7. *incidentally*
dann und wann (11)	8. *possible*
übrigens (7)	9. *this morning*
wenigstens (3)	10. *(to) play*
brauchen (5)	11. *now and then*

Lesson IX & X pp. 89-90 & 100-101

Verbs in X lesson 91 → (acc.- extent of time)

Er hat vier Jahre im Warenhaus gearbeitet.

Er arbeitet seit vier Jahren in dem Warenhaus.

He has been working in the department store for four years.

Er hat vor vier Jahren in dem Warenhaus gearbeitet.

He worked in the department store four years ago.

Elfte Aufgabe

* * * \

der Ersatz	the substitute, replacement
die Ersatzblume, –n	the substitute for a flower
„O nein, keine Ersatzblumen.	"Oh no, no substitutes.
unbedingt	absolute
frisch	fresh
Ich muß unbedingt frische Blumen haben."	I simply have to have fresh flowers."
dann	then
schon	already
die Blume, –n	the flower
* das Geschäft, –e	the business, store
das Blumengeschäft, –e	the flower store
„Ja, dann müssen Sie schon in ein Blumengeschäft gehen."	"Well, then you'll have to go to a flower store."
liebenswürdig	charming, kind
„Sie sind sehr liebenswürdig, Fräulein.	"You are very kind, Miss.
sagen, ich habe gesagt	(to) say, tell
würden Sie sagen	would you say
vielleicht′	perhaps
auch	also
noch	still, yet, in addition
nächst	nearest
Würden Sie mir vielleicht auch noch sagen, wo das nächste Blumengeschäft ist?"	Perhaps you would also tell me where the nearest flower store is?"
* ziemlich	rather
* weit	far
„Das nächste Blumengeschäft ist ziemlich weit von hier.	"The nearest flower store is rather far from here.
* lieber	rather, preferably
* der Schutz	the protection
der Mann, ⸗er	the man
der Schutzmann, Schutzleute	the policeman
Fragen Sie lieber einen Schutzmann!"	You had better ask a policeman."
also	well then
* erraten, ich habe erraten	(to) guess correctly
Also, mein liebes Fräulein Becker, Sie haben es wohl schon erraten. Die Blumen sind natürlich für Sie.	Well, my dear Miss Becker, you have probably already guessed it. Of course the flowers are for you.

hiermit	herewith
der Galaball, ¨e	the gala ball
geliebt	beloved
die Alma Mater	the Alma Mater
der Alma Mater	of the Alma Mater
einladen, ich habe eingeladen	(to) invite
Sie werden eingeladen	you are invited

Sie werden hiermit zum großen Galaball unserer geliebten Alma Mater eingeladen.	You are hereby invited to the great gala ball of our beloved Alma Mater.

dreißig	thirty
der dreißigste	the thirtieth
das College, –s	the college
hundert	hundred
das Jahr, –e	the year
der Abend, –e	the evening
* wichtig	important
der Tag, –e	the day
dieses Tages	of this day

Am 30. (dreißigsten) November wird unser berühmtes College hundert Jahre alt, und am Abend dieses wichtigen Tages haben wir einen großen Ball.	On November thirtieth, our famous college will be one hundred years old and on the evening of this important day we will have a great ball.

der Tanz, ¨e	the dance
beginnen, ich habe begonnen	(to) begin
* ungefähr	approximately
enden, ich habe geendet	(to) end
der Punkt, –e	the point, dot, period

Der Tanz beginnt ungefähr um zehn Uhr und endet Punkt eins.	The dance will begin at approximately ten o'clock and will end at one o'clock sharp.

* stattfinden, es hat stattgefunden	(to) take place
* die Gesellschaft, –en	the society, company
der Raum, ¨e	the room
der Gesellschaftsraum, ¨e	the social room
* das Gebäude, —	the building
des Gebäudes	of the building

Er findet in den Gesellschaftsräumen des Wilby Gebäudes statt.	It will take place in the social rooms of Wilby Hall.

die Kapel'le, –n	the chapel, band
der Pirat', –en	the pirate
die Musik'	the music
die Tanz'musik'	the dance music
liefern, ich habe geliefert	(to) deliver
wird liefern	will furnish
man	one, a person
nördlich	northerly, north

Die berühmte Kapelle, Toni und seine Piraten, wird die beste Tanzmusik liefern, die man nördlich des Rio Grande hören kann.

The famous band, Toni and his Pirates, will play the best dance music that you can hear north of the Rio Grande.

* während	during
der Aufenthalt	the stay
des Aufenthaltes	of the stay
während Ihres Aufenthaltes	during your stay
der Gast, ¨e	the guest
erstklassig	first-class
das Hotel, –s	the hotel
des Hotels	of the hotel
eines erstklassigen Hotels	of a first-class hotel
sein	(to) be
Sie werden sein	you will be

Während Ihres Aufenthaltes werden Sie der Gast eines erstklassigen Hotels sein.

During your stay you will be the guest of a first-class hotel.

die Zeit, –en	the time
die Lust	the pleasure, desire
Haben Sie Lust?	Have you the desire? Do you want to?

Haben Sie Zeit, haben Sie Lust?

Do you have the time, do you have the inclination?

baldig	prompt, early
die Antwort, –en	the answer
erwarten, ich habe erwartet	(to) expect, await
die Antwort wird erwartet	the answer is expected

Eine baldige Antwort wird erwartet.

An early reply is expected.

hoch	high
die Achtung	esteem
voll	full
hochachtungsvoll	respectfully

II. Text:

„Verzeihung, ich habe mich verlaufen. Ich möchte Blumen für eine junge Dame kaufen. Das ist wohl nicht der richtige Ort? Natürlich nicht, ich sehe, hier werden Seidenstrümpfe verkauft.“ — „Wünschen Sie künstliche Blumen?“ — „Oh nein, keine Ersatzblumen! Ich muß unbedingt frische Blumen haben.“ — „Ja, dann müssen Sie schon in ein Blumengeschäft gehen.“ — „Sie sind sehr liebenswürdig, Fräulein. Würden Sie mir vielleicht auch noch sagen, wo das nächste Blumengeschäft ist?“ — „Das nächste Blumengeschäft ist ziemlich weit von hier. Fragen Sie lieber einen Schutzmann!“

Also, mein liebes Fräulein Becker, Sie haben es wohl schon erraten. Die Blumen sind natürlich für Sie. Sie werden hiermit zum großen Galaball unserer geliebten Alma Mater eingeladen. Am 30. (dreißigsten) November wird unser berühmtes College hundert Jahre alt, und am Abend dieses wichtigen Tages haben wir einen großen Ball. Der Tanz beginnt ungefähr um zehn Uhr und

endet Punkt eins. Er findet in den Gesellschaftsräumen des Wilby Gebäudes statt. Die berühmte Kapelle, Toni und seine Piraten, wird die beste Tanzmusik liefern, die man nördlich des Rio Grande hören kann. Während Ihres Aufenthaltes werden Sie der Gast eines erstklassigen Hotels sein. Haben Sie Zeit, haben Sie Lust?

Eine baldige Antwort wird erwartet.

Hochachtungsvoll

Richard Neumann

III. Comments:

1. *The Genitive Case:*

The fourth case of German substantives is known as the genitive. In a general way it corresponds to the English possessive case as in *father's car*. The genitive form of the article is **des** for the masculine and neuter singular and **der** for the feminine singular and for the plural. The **der**-words and **ein**-words take corresponding endings:

Masculine	*Feminine*	*Neuter*
des	der	des
keines	keiner	keines

Plural

der
keiner

In the genitive singular all neuter nouns (except **das Herz,** the genitive case of which is **des Herzens**) and most masculines end in **–s** or **–es,** but some masculines end in **–n** or **–en.** (Those that take **–n** or **–en** retain this ending through the rest of the singular and the plural). Feminine nouns are unchanged in the singular. Here are examples of the genitive singular masculine, feminine and neuter, and of the plural.

Masculine	*Feminine*	*Neuter*
des Mannes	der Dame	des Gebäudes
meines Studenten	meiner Klasse	meines Zimmers

Plural

der Männer, Damen, Gebäude
meiner Studenten, Klassen, Zimmer

The genitive case is also used after a number of prepositions, such as **während: während Ihres Aufenthaltes,** during your stay. (For complete list see Appendix)

From now on the lists of Words and Phrases will indicate the principal parts of nouns (the nominative and genitive singular, and the nominative plural) as follows: **der Mann, –es, ¨er; die Dame, —, –n; das Gebäude, –s, —.**

2. *Declension of Nouns:*

In the following are given the complete declensions of representative nouns together with the definite and indefinite articles:

	Masculine	*Feminine*
N.	der (ein) Mann, Student	die (eine) Nacht, Dame
A.	den (einen) Mann, Studenten	die (eine) Nacht, Dame
D.	dem (einem) Mann(e), Studenten	der (einer) Nacht, Dame
G.	des (eines) Mannes, Studenten	der (einer) Nacht, Dame

Neuter

das (ein) Gebäude
das (ein) Gebäude
dem (einem) Gebäude
des (eines) Gebäudes

Plural

die (keine) Männer, Studenten; Nächte, Damen; Gebäude
die (keine) Männer, Studenten; Nächte, Damen; Gebäude
den (keinen) Männern, Studenten; Nächten, Damen; Gebäuden
der (keiner) Männer, Studenten; Nächte, Damen; Gebäude

3. *Passive Voice (Present Tense):*

In the text of this lesson there are three examples of the passive voice: **Sie werden verkauft.** *They are sold;* **Sie werden hiermit zum großen Galaball eingeladen.** *You are hereby invited to the great galaball;* **Eine baldige Antwort wird erwartet.** *A speedy answer is expected.* Here is the complete present tense of a passive sentence:

Ich werde um acht Uhr erwartet.	*I am expected at eight o'clock.*
Du wirst um acht Uhr erwartet.	*You are expected at eight o'clock.*
Er, sie, es wird um acht Uhr erwartet.	*He, she, it is expected at eight o'clock.*
Wir werden um acht Uhr erwartet.	*We are expected at eight o'clock.*
Ihr werdet um acht Uhr erwartet.	*You are expected at eight o'clock.*
Sie werden um acht Uhr erwartet.	*They are expected at eight o'clock.*
Sie werden um acht Uhr erwartet.	*You are expected at eight o'clock.*

If you analyze these sentences you will see that the forms of **werden** are used as auxiliaries with the past participle of a verb to form its passive voice. The past participle comes in its normal position, the end of the clause.

4. *Dates:*

The following patterns represent the most common expressions for dates:

1. **Am 30. (dreißigsten) November** — *On the 30th of November.* **Heute ist der 30. (dreißigste) November.** — *Today is the 30th of November.*
2. The accusative of time is used in dating letters: **Berlin, den 1.** (*read:* **den ersten) Dezember.**

IV. Practice:

1. Richard hat sich verlaufen.
   Anna
   Anna und ich haben uns verlaufen.
   Hast du dich verlaufen, Richard?
   Haben Sie sich verlaufen, Herr Jones?
   Wer hat sich verlaufen?

2. In der Mitte (*middle*) des Ladentisches sehen wir viele Seidenstrümpfe.
   In der Mitte des Raumes sehen wir viele schöne Handtaschen.
   einen großen Ladentisch.
   die berühmte Kapelle.

3. a. Auf der anderen Seite der Straße ist ein großes Blumengeschäft.
   das bekannte Warenhaus von Weber.
   des Geschäftes ist Fräulein Beckers Ladentisch.
   b. Das College liegt am anderen Ende der Stadt.
   Der Bahnhof

4. a. Richard Neumann wird sehr leicht mit Richard Niemann verwechselt.
   Ich werde sehr leicht mit Richard Niemann verwechselt.
   b. Wirst du oft mit deinem Bruder (*brother*) verwechselt, Richard?
   Werden Sie oft mit Ihrer Schwester (*sister*) verwechselt, Fräulein Becker?

5. An diesem Tisch wird keine Butter verkauft.
   kein Kaffee
   kein Fleisch (*meat*)
   werden keine Eier
   keine Blumen
   keine Schmuckartikel

6. a. Fräulein Becker wird von Richard zum großen Tanz eingeladen.
   Ich werde von Richard zum großen Tanz eingeladen.
   Wir werden
   b. Du wirst hiermit zum Tanz eingeladen.
   Sie werden

7. Der Tanz findet in den Gesellschaftsräumen des Wilby Gebäudes statt.
   Die Vorstellung (*performance*) findet in der großen Halle (*hall*) des Theaters statt.
   Die Sitzung (*meeting*) findet in den Zimmern der Deutschen Gesellschaft statt.

8. Er ist der Freund des berühmten Tennisspielers, Richard Niemann.
   großen Schauspielers (*actor*), Heinrich George.
   Sie ist die Freundin der großen Schauspielerin (*actress*), Elizabeth Bergner.
   kleinen Verkäuferin im Blumengeschäft an der Ecke.

V. Exercises:

A. *Questions:*

1. Was möchte der junge Mann kaufen?
2. Für wen (*whom*) möchte er Blumen kaufen?
3. Wo kauft man Blumen?
4. Wo ist das nächste Blumengeschäft?
5. Wen fragt man, wenn man nicht weiß, wo eine Straße oder ein Geschäft ist?
6. Zu welchem Ball wird Anna eingeladen?
7. Wann beginnt der Tanz?
8. Wann endet der Tanz?
9. Wo findet der Tanz statt?
10. Wo kann Anna während ihres Aufenthaltes in der Universitätsstadt wohnen?
11. Wer wird die Tanzmusik liefern?

B. *Translate:*

1. Ich lade dich hiermit zum großen Tanz ein.
2. Otto wird auch eingeladen.
3. Das College ist ziemlich weit von hier, am anderen Ende der Stadt.
4. Ich bin sicher, daß hier Schmuckartikel verkauft werden.
5. Wirst du oft mit deinem Bruder verwechselt, Hans?
6. Ich werde nächsten Montag neunzehn Jahre alt.
7. In der Mitte des Gesellschaftsraumes steht der berühmte Tennisspieler.
8. Die Vorstellung (*performance*) beginnt Punkt acht Uhr und endet ungefähr um halb elf.
9. Haben Sie Lust, morgen mit mir Tennis zu spielen?
10. Haben wir Zeit, eine Zigarette zu rauchen?

C. *Rearrange:*

1. Zigarren, kaufen, ich, für meinen Vater, möchte.
2. des Geschäfts, auf der anderen Seite, werden . . . verkauft, am Ladentisch, Handtaschen.
3. gehen, wir, in ein Blumengeschäft, müssen, schon.
4. lieber, den Abteilungschef, fragen Sie!
5. können Sie mir sagen, wo, stattfindet, der große Tanz?
6. im Großen Theater, findet . . . statt, heute abend, die Vorstellung.
7. hiermit, wirst . . . eingeladen, zum großen Tanz, du.
8. wird . . . verwechselt, er, oft, mit seinem Bruder.
9. meine kleine Schwester, am zwanzigsten Juni, wird, zehn Jahre alt.
10. sind Sie sicher, daß, im Blumengeschäft, Fräulein Becker, arbeitet, an der Ecke?

D. *Correct the misinformation:*

1. Richard will künstliche Blumen für Anna kaufen.
2. Er kann Seidenstrümpfe in einem Blumengeschäft kaufen.
3. Wenn er Blumen kaufen will, muß er schon in ein Warenhaus gehen.
4. In einem Warenhaus werden frische Blumen verkauft.
5. Der Schutzmann kann ihm nicht sagen, wo das Blumengeschäft ist.
6. Anna kann nicht erraten, für wen Richard Blumen kaufen möchte.
7. Anna wird zum großen Tanz am zwanzigsten November eingeladen.
8. Richard ladet Anna zum großen Tanz am einunddreißigsten November ein.
9. Richards geliebte Alma Mater wird am dreißigsten Oktober hundert Jahre alt.
10. Der Tanz beginnt Punkt halb zehn Uhr und endet ungefähr um ein Uhr.
11. Er findet in den Gesellschaftsräumen des Warenhauses statt.
12. Toni und seine Piraten werden die beste Tanzmusik liefern, die man südlich des Rio Grande hören kann.

VI. Securing the Vocabulary:

A.

die Verzeihung	*pardon*	erraten	*(to) guess correctly*
mögen	*(to) like to*	einladen	*(to) invite*
wohl	*probably, no doubt*	wichtig	*important*
das Geschäft	*business, store*	ungefähr	*approximately*
ziemlich	*rather*	stattfinden	*(to) take place*
weit	*far*	die Gesellschaft	*society, company*
lieber	*rather, preferably*	das Gebäude	*building*
der Schutz	*protection*	während	*during*

B.

können (6)	1. *different, various*	außerdem (7)	1. *joy, pleasure*
gern (5)	2. *soon*	sich verheiraten (8)	2. *just*
bald (2)	3. *(to) work*	die Freude (1)	3. *especially*
verschieden (1)	4. *there is (are), there exists (exist)*	eben (2)	4. *nothing*
die Zukunft (8)	5. *gladly*	besonders (3)	5. *(to) excuse*
schnell (9)	6. *(to) be able*	laufen (10)	6. *directly, immediately*
arbeiten (3)	7. *now*	auch (11)	7. *besides, in addition*
jetzt (7)	8. *future*	entschuldigen (5)	8. *(to) get married*
gar nicht (10)	9. *quickly*	gleich (6)	9. *frightful*
es gibt (4)	10. *not at all*	schrecklich (9)	10. *(to) run*
		nichts (4)	11. *also*

übrigens (4)	1. *until*
der Fremde (9)	2. *poor*
brauchen (8)	3. (*to*) *ask*
wirklich (6)	4. *incidentally*
die Abteilung (7)	5. *boring, dull*
arm (2)	6. *really*
fragen (3)	7. *department*
heute abend (11)	8. (*to*) *need*
bis (1)	9. *stranger*
gewinnen (12)	10. (*to*) *buy*
kaufen (10)	11. *this evening*
langweilig (5)	12. (*to*) *win*

Zwölfte Aufgabe

* * * \

übrigens	incidentally, by the way
gleich	immediately
fragen, ich habe gefragt	(to) ask
der Schutzmann, –es, Schutzleute	the policeman
Warum haben Sie übrigens nicht gleich einen Schutzmann gefragt?	Incidentally, why didn't you ask a policeman right away?
wollen, ich habe gewollt	(to) want to
Sie wollten	you wanted to
wohl	probably, no doubt
gern	gladly
ein bißchen	a little
plaudern, ich habe geplaudert	(to) chat
Sie wollten wohl gern ein bißchen mit dem Fräulein im Warenhaus plaudern?	No doubt, you wanted to chat a bit with the girl in the store?
noch	yet, still, in addition
eins	one, one thing
* noch eins	one more, one thing more
Noch eins, Herr Neumann.	One thing more, Mr. Neumann.
leben, ich habe gelebt	(to) live
teuer	dear, expensive
die Zeit, —, –en	the time, era, epoch
Wir leben in teuren Zeiten.	These are hard times we are living in.
machen, ich habe gemacht	(to) make, do
die Unkosten (pl.)	the expenses
Sie machen sich Unkosten	you are making expenses for yourself
Machen Sie sich keine Unkosten!	Don't go to any expense!
überzeugt′	convinced
das Herz, –ens, –en	the heart
die Dame, —, –n	the lady
die Herzensdame, —, –n	the lady of one's heart
gern haben, ich habe gern gehabt	(to) be fond of, like
auch	also
die Garde′nię, —, –n	the gardenia
die Orchidee′, —, –n	the orchid
Ich bin überzeugt, Ihre Herzensdame hat Sie sehr gern, auch ohne Gardenien und Orchideen.	I am convinced the lady of your heart is very fond of you even without gardenias and orchids.

all	all
der Ernst, –es no plural	the seriousness
der Liebling, –s, –e	the darling
furchtbar	awful, terrible
die Freude, —, –n	the joy, happiness
es macht mir Freude	it gives me pleasure
In allem Ernst, Liebling, Du hast mir eine furchtbar große Freude gemacht.	Seriously, darling, you made me awfully happy.
tausend	thousand
Tausend Dank!	A thousand thanks.
können, ich habe gekonnt	(to) be able to
du kannst	you can
gar nicht	not at all
sich vorstellen, ich habe mir vorgestellt	(to) imagine
* einsam	lonesome
langweilig	dull, boring
fort	away, gone
Du kannst Dir gar nicht vorstellen, wie einsam ich hier bin, und wie langweilig es ist, seit Du fort bist.	You simply can't imagine how lonely I am here and how dull it is since you have been away.
* die Nachricht, —, –en	the news
Ich habe auch eine gute Nachricht für Dich.	I have some good news for you too.
der Chef, –s, –s	the chief, boss
lassen, ich habe gelassen	(to) let, permit
er läßt	he permits
der Donnerstag, –s, –e	the Thursday
der Nachmittag, –s, –e	the afternoon
Donnerstag nachmittag	Thursday afternoon
gehen, ich bin gegangen	(to) go, walk
brauchen, ich habe gebraucht	(to) need
der Dienstag, –s, –e	the Tuesday
* zurück′	back
sein, ich bin gewesen	(to) be
Mein Chef läßt mich schon Donnerstag nachmittag gehen, und ich brauche vor Dienstag nicht zurück zu sein.	My boss is going to let me go Thursday afternoon and I don't have to be back before Tuesday.
wunderbar	wonderful
Ist das nicht wunderbar?	Isn't that wonderful?

noch nicht	not yet
alles	everything
Das ist aber noch nicht alles.	But that isn't everything.
das Auto, –s, –s	the automobile
* mitnehmen, ich habe mitgenommen	(to) take along
sie wird mich mitnehmen	she will take me along
Gretel wird mich in ihrem Auto mitnehmen.	Gretel is going to take me in the car.
vergessen, ich habe vergessen	(to) forget
Natürlich hast Du vergessen, wer Gretel ist.	Of course, you have forgotten who Gretel is.
die Frau, —, –en	the woman, wife
der Bruder, –s, ¨	the brother
Sie ist die Frau meines Bruders Robert.	She is my brother Robert's wife.
jetzt	now
Robert ist jetzt in Mexiko.	Robert is in Mexico now.
arbeiten, ich habe gearbeitet	(to) work
als	as
der Ingenieur′, –s, –e	the engineer
* schwierig	difficult
die Strecke, —, –n	the stretch
panamerika′nisch	Pan-American
das Auto, –s, –s	the automobile
die Straße, —, –n	the street
die Autostraße, —, –n	the highway
Er arbeitet als Ingenieur an einer schwierigen Strecke der panamerikanischen Autostraße.	He is an engineer on a difficult section of the Pan-American highway.
die Weihnachten (pl.)	the Christmas
das Haus, –es, ¨er	the house,
nach Hause	to home, home
kommen, ich bin gekommen	(to) come
er wird kommen	he will come
nur	only
* kurz	short
auf kurze Zeit	for a short time
Vor Weihnachten wird er nicht nach Hause kommen und dann auch nur auf kurze Zeit.	He won't come home before Christmas and then it will be only for a short time.

wollen, ich habe gewollt	(to) want to
sie will	she wants to
der Einkauf, –s, ¨e	the purchase
ich mache Einkäufe	I make purchases, I go shopping
*verwandt	related
der Verwandte, –n, –n	the male relative
die Verwandte, –n, –n	the female relative
Verwandte	relatives
* besuchen, ich habe besucht	(to) visit
Gretel will mit mir Einkäufe machen und Verwandte besuchen.	Gretel wants to go shopping with me and visit relatives.
wieder	again
zurück'fah'ren; ich bin zurück'gefah'ren	(to) drive back, ride back
Montag nachmittag werden wir wieder zurückfahren.	We are going to drive back on Monday afternoon.
* zählen, ich habe gezählt	(to) count
der Tag, –s, –e	the day
Ich zähle die Tage bis zum Freitag.	I'm counting the days until Friday.
das Wiedersehen	the seeing again, reunion
Auf Wiedersehen	to seeing (each other) again, goodbye
Auf baldiges Wiedersehen	to seeing each other again soon
Auf baldiges Wiedersehen — Deine Anna.	I'll be seeing you soon, Yours, Anna.

II. Text:

Lieber Herr Neumann!

Es tut mir schrecklich leid, daß Sie solche Schwierigkeiten hatten, das Blumengeschäft zu finden. Das Ladenfräulein hat Ihnen außerdem keine gute Auskunft gegeben. In derselben Straße, in der Webers Warenhaus ist, drei Straßen entfernt, ist ein kleines Blumengeschäft. Warum haben Sie übrigens nicht gleich einen Schutzmann gefragt? Sie wollten wohl gern ein bißchen mit dem Fräulein im Warenhaus plaudern? — Noch eins, Herr Neumann. Wir leben in teuren Zeiten. Machen Sie sich keine Unkosten. Ich bin überzeugt, Ihre Herzensdame hat Sie sehr gern, auch ohne Gardenien und Orchideen.

In allem Ernst, Liebling, Du hast mir eine furchtbar große Freude gemacht. Tausend Dank! Du kannst Dir gar nicht vorstellen, wie einsam ich hier bin, und wie langweilig es ist, seit Du fort bist. Ich habe auch eine gute Nachricht für Dich. Mein Chef läßt mich schon Donnerstag nachmittag gehen, und ich brauche vor Dienstag nicht zurück zu sein. Ist das nicht wunderbar? Das ist aber noch nicht alles. Gretel wird mich in ihrem Auto mitnehmen. Natürlich hast Du vergessen, wer Gretel ist. Sie ist die Frau meines Bruders Robert. Robert ist jetzt in Mexiko. Er arbeitet als Ingenieur an einer schwierigen Strecke der panamerikanischen Autostraße. Vor Weihnachten wird er nicht nach Hause kommen und dann auch nur auf kurze Zeit. Gretel will mit mir Einkäufe machen und Verwandte besuchen. Montag nachmittag werden wir wieder zurückfahren.

Ich zähle die Tage bis zum Freitag. Auf baldiges Wiedersehen

Deine Anna

III. Comments:

1. *Future Tense:*

As you have noticed, the present tense in German is very frequently used with a future meaning. This is especially true when the idea of future time is expressed by some adverbial word or phrase. At times, however, it is necessary to express the idea of future time in the verb itself. This is done, as it is done in English, by using the form of the future tense auxiliary with the infinitive of a verb. The auxiliary of the future in German is **werden.** Thus:

ich werde arbeiten	*I will work* (shall)
du wirst arbeiten	*you will work*
er, sie, es wird arbeiten	*he, she, it will work*
wir werden arbeiten	*we will work* (shall)
ihr werdet arbeiten	*you will work*
sie werden arbeiten	*they will work*
Sie werden arbeiten	*you will work*

The infinitive, of course, stands at the end of the clause: **Ich werde in der Psychologieklasse gut aufpassen.** Notice carefully the difference between these two sentences:

Richard **wird** Anna zum Galaball **einladen.** (future tense)
Richard will invite Anna to the galaball.

Anna **wird** von Richard zum Galaball **eingeladen.** (passive voice)
Anna is invited to the gala ball by Richard.

IV. Practice:

1. Es tut mir leid, daß Sie sich solche Unkosten machen.
   Sorgen
   Schwierigkeiten
2. Fragen Sie das Ladenfräulein; sie wird Ihnen Auskunft geben.
   den Schutzmann; er wird Ihnen sagen, wo die Post ist.
   die Verkäuferin; sie wird Ihnen sagen, wo Sie Blumen kaufen können.
   den Professor; er wird Ihnen gern helfen. (*help*)
   den Tennislehrer; er wird es Ihnen erklären. (*explain*)
3. Das wird dem Professor eine große Freude machen.
   meinem Bruder
   seinem Freund
   seiner Schwester
   Ihrer Mutter
   unseren Verwandten
4. Du kannst dir gar nicht vorstellen, wie einsam ich hier bin.
   wie wunderbar das sein wird.
   Sie können sich wie interessant das ist.
   Ich kann mir wie das möglich ist.

5. Ich habe eine gute Nachricht für dich: Gretel wird mich im Auto mitnehmen.
Sie: Robert wird bald nach Hause kommen.
Sie: Wir haben im Spanischen nichts auf.
Sie: Sie haben in Chemie ein A bekommen (*got*).

6. Richard wird Anna einladen, und Sie werden natürlich auch eingeladen.
Ich werde Rita Anna wird
Wilhelm wird Sie wir werden

7. a. Gretel nimmt mich in ihrem Auto mit.
Hans seinem
Ich nehme Sie in meinem
Wir nehmen in unsrem

b. Gretel wird mich in ihrem Auto mitnehmen.
Hans seinem
Ich werde Sie in meinem
Wir werden Sie in unsrem

8. Wann werden Sie wieder nach Hause kommen?
Mexiko fahren?
zurückfahren müssen?
Ihre Verwandten in Iowa besuchen?

9. Haben Sie schon vergessen, wer Gretel ist?
was für Blumen Sie kaufen wollten?
für wen Sie Blumen kaufen wollten?
um wieviel Uhr der Tanz beginnt?
wann Ihre Freundin Geburtstag hat?

10. Ich werde den Tag nie vergessen.
meinen alten Professor nie vergessen.
das kleine Blumengeschäft an der Ecke nie vergessen.
diese teuren Zeiten nie vergessen.

V. Exercises:

A. *Questions:*

1. Wie weit ist das nächste Blumengeschäft von Webers Warenhaus entfernt?
2. Warum hat der junge Mann nicht gleich einen Schutzmann gefragt?
3. Warum sagt Anna: „Machen Sie sich keine Unkosten!"
4. Muß Richard seiner Herzensdame Orchideen kaufen?
5. Warum findet Anna es langweilig in ihrer Heimatstadt?
6. Wann läßt der Abteilungschef Anna gehen?
7. Wann muß Anna wieder zurück sein?
8. Wer ist Gretel?
9. Wie verdient Robert sein Geld?
10. Wann wird Robert nach Hause kommen?
11. Was will Gretel in der Universitätsstadt tun?

B. *Translate:*

1. Ich bin überzeugt, er wird vor Weihnachten nach Hause kommen.
2. Wie lange wird Robert in Mexiko arbeiten?
3. Es tut mir leid, daß sie nicht kommen wird.
4. Morgen früh werde ich Einkäufe machen.
5. Es wird hier furchtbar langweilig sein, wenn du fort bist.
6. Es tut mir schrecklich leid, daß Robert mit seinem Auto Schwierigkeiten hat.
7. Sie brauchen sich keine Unkosten zu machen.
8. Der Schutzmann wird ihn gleich mitnehmen.
9. Sind Sie sicher, daß das Blumengeschäft am anderen Ende der Stadt ist?
10. Dein letzter Brief hat mir große Freude gemacht.

C. *Rearrange:*

1. es tut mir leid, daß, vor Weihnachten, er, nach Hause, kommen wird, nicht.
2. mit dem Schutzmann, Sie, plaudern, wollten, gern, wohl, ein bißchen.
3. auch, er, für, hat, Sie, gute Nachrichten.
4. gern, hat, Richard, sie.
5. morgen früh, Einkäufe, wird . . . machen, mit, Gretel, mir.
6. kann, geben, gute Auskunft, der Ingenieur, Ihnen.
7. als Schutzmann, Willi, jetzt, in einer kleinen Stadt, arbeitet, in Oklahoma.
8. ihr, die Nachricht, große Freude, wird . . . machen.
9. sich, große Unkosten, Richard, macht.
10. den Professor, nicht gleich, du, warum, hast . . . gefragt?

D. *Correct the misinformation:*

1. Es tut Anna schrecklich leid, daß er sie zum Tanz eingeladen hat.
2. Es macht Richard große Freude, daß Anna schon am Sonntag zurückfahren wird.
3. Annas Bruder Robert wird bald auf lange Zeit nach Hause kommen.
4. Robert arbeitet als Schutzmann an einer schwierigen Strecke der panamerikanischen Autostraße.
5. Montag früh fahren Anna und Gretel wieder zurück.
6. Anna hat es sehr gern, daß Richard fort ist.
7. Der Chef läßt Anna schon Donnerstag früh gehen.
8. Anna hat natürlich vergessen, wer Robert ist.
9. Annas Verwandte wollen sie besuchen.

VI. Securing the Vocabulary:

A.

die Schwierigkeit	*difficulty*
entfernt	*distant, removed*
noch eins	*one more, one thing more*
einsam	*lonesome*
die Nachricht	*news*

zurück	*back*
mitnehmen	*(to) take along*
schwierig	*difficult*
kurz	*short*
verwandt	*related*
besuchen	*(to) visit*
zählen	*(to) count*

B.

das Geschenk (2)	1. *(to) believe*
vorig (6)	2. *present*
glauben (1)	3. *unfortunately*
schlimm (10)	4. *such a thing*
bei (8)	5. *as soon as*
so etwas (4)	6. *previous*
leider (3)	7. *vocation, profession*
so bald wie (5)	8. *at, with, near, at the house of*
der Beruf (7)	9. *future*
die Zukunft (9)	10. *bad*

ziemlich (8)	1. *empty*
sicher (6)	2. *usually*
es tut mir leid (10)	3. *bad*
allerdings (9)	4. *(to) dress*
das Geld (7)	5. *well then, and so, therefore*
anziehen (4)	6. *sure, certain*
böse (3)	7. *money*
gewöhnlich (2)	8. *rather*
leer (1)	9. *indeed, to be sure*
also (5)	10. *I am sorry*

die Rechnung (6)	1. *(to) like to*
die Zeitung (7)	2. *spring*
da drüben (5)	3. *(to) pay*
der Frühling (2)	4. *famous*
bezahlen (3)	5. *over there*
berühmt (4)	6. *bill*
mögen (1)	7. *newspaper*
nie (8)	8. *never*

schicken (1)	1. *(to) send*
laufen (5)	2. *(to) begin*
merkwürdig (4)	3. *(to) invite*
anfangen (2)	4. *remarkable*
die Stelle (7)	5. *(to) run*
einladen (3)	6. *thorough*
wichtig (8)	7. *place, passage*
gründlich (6)	8. *important*

Dreizehnte Aufgabe

* * * \

nachdenken, ich habe nachgedacht	(to) reflect, ponder, think
ich habe darüber nachgedacht	I have thought about it
* werden, ich bin geworden	(to) become
mögen, ich habe gemocht	(to) like to
ich möchte Ingenieur werden	I would like to become an engineer
glauben, ich habe geglaubt	(to) believe
immer noch	still
die Lust, —	the pleasure, joy, desire
ich habe Lust, Ingenieur′ zu werden	I have a desire to become an engineer
Ich habe lange darüber nachgedacht, was ich werden möchte und ich glaube, ich habe immer noch große Lust, Ingenieur zu werden.	I have thought a long time about what I would like to be and I think I still want very much to become an engineer.
* bekommen, ich habe bekommen	(to) receive
* dauernd	continuous, constant
* trotzdem	although; in spite of it
* streng	strict
In Chemie bekomme ich dauernd ein A, trotzdem unser Professor sehr streng ist.	I always get an A in chemistry even though our professor is very strict.
die Zensur′, —, -en	the grade
Auch im Spanischen sind meine Zensuren gut.	My grades are good in Spanish too.
* einmal	once, sometime
die Stelle, —, -n	the place, passage, position
Süd′ame′rika	South America
* deshalb	for that reason
studie′ren, ich habe studiert′	(to) study
der Eifer, -s	the zeal, enthusiasm
Ich möchte auch gerne einmal eine Stelle in Südamerika bekommen, deshalb studiere ich Spanisch mit großem Eifer.	I would like to get a job sometime in South America too, that's why I am studying Spanish hard.
die Idee′, —, -n	the idea
halten, ich habe gehalten	(to) hold, consider
was halten Sie von der Idee	what do you think about the idea

werden, ich bin geworden	(to) become
Schreib mir, was Du von meiner Idee hältst, Ingenieur zu werden.	Write me what you think about my idea of becoming an engineer.
schon wieder	again already
sich erkälten, ich habe mich erkältet	(to) catch cold
Es tut mir furchtbar leid, daß Mutter sich schon wieder erkältet hat.	I'm terribly sorry that Mother has caught cold again.
* reisen, ich bin gereist	(to) travel
Wie schön, daß sie nach Kalifornien reisen konnte.	How nice, that she was able to go to California.
wunderbar	wonderful
das Klima, –s	the climate
dort	there
tun, ich habe getan	(to) do
es tut mir gut	it does me good
es wird ihr gut tun	it will do her good
Das wunderbare Klima dort wird ihr gut tun.	The wonderful climate there will be good for her.
Ich habe schon einen Brief an sie geschrieben.	I have already written her a letter.
wissen, ich habe gewußt	(to) know
ich weiß	I know
* sich freuen, ich habe mich gefreut	(to) be happy
gleich	immediately
die Ankunft, —	the arrival
gleich bei ihrer Ankunft	immediately upon her arrival
Ich weiß, sie freut sich, wenn sie gleich bei ihrer Ankunft einen Brief von mir bekommt.	I know she will be happy if she gets a letter from me as soon as she arrives.

böse	bad
der Schnupfen, –s, —	the head cold
den	whom, that, which
gar nicht	not at all
los	free, rid
ich werde los	I get rid of
ich werde meinen Schnupfen los	I get rid of my cold
können, ich habe gekonnt	(to) be able
ich kann	I am able
Ich habe übrigens auch einen bösen Schnupfen, den ich gar nicht los werden kann.	By the way, I have a bad cold in the head too, that I simply can't get rid of.
doch	(*adds to the urgency of the request*)
mal (*shortened from* einmal)	once
fragen Sie mal!	go ahead and ask
frag doch mal!	I wish you would ask
* dagegen	against it
* sollen, ich habe gesollt	(to) be supposed to
ich soll	I am supposed to
Frag doch mal Dr. Jones, was ich dagegen tun soll.	I wish you would ask Dr. Jones what to do for it.
bevor	before
O ja, bevor ich es vergesse: Ich habe Anna zu unserem Jubiläumsball eingeladen.	Oh yes, before I forget it! I've invited Anna to our anniversary ball.
ein bißchen	a little, a bit
mehr	more
kosten, es hat gekostet	(to) cost
* anfangs	at first
denken, ich habe gedacht	(to) think
ich dachte	I thought
Dieser Ball wird mich ein bißchen mehr kosten, als ich anfangs dachte.	This ball is going to cost me a bit more than I thought at first.
verstehen, ich habe verstanden	(to) understand
das Restaurant′, –s, –s	the restaurant
die Rechnung, —, –en	the bill
die Restaurantrechnung, —, –en	the restaurant check

das Geld, –es, –er	the money
das Taxi, –s, –s	the taxi
usw. (und so weiter)	and so on
Du verstehst: Gardenien, Restaurantrechnungen, Geld für Taxis, usw.	You understand: gardenias, restaurant checks, money for taxis and so on.
können, ich habe gekonnt	(to) be able
könntest du	could you
vielleicht′	perhaps
der Vorschuß, –es, ⸗e	the advance
schicken, ich habe geschickt	(to) send
Könntest Du mir vielleicht einen kleinen Vorschuß schicken?	Perhaps you could send me a small advance?
müssen, ich habe gemußt	(to) have to
du mußt	you must
beide	both
abziehen, ich habe abgezogen	(to) pull off, deduct
Du mußt ihn aber von meinen nächsten beiden Schecks abziehen.	But you must deduct it from my next two checks.
wollen, ich habe gewollt	(to) want to
* einfach	simple
das Geschenk, –es, –e	the present
* annehmen, ich habe angenommen	(to) accept
Ich will das Geld nicht einfach als Geschenk annehmen.	I don't want to simply accept the money as a gift.
im voraus	in advance
Vielen Dank im voraus.	Many thanks in advance.
Dein Richard	Your Richard

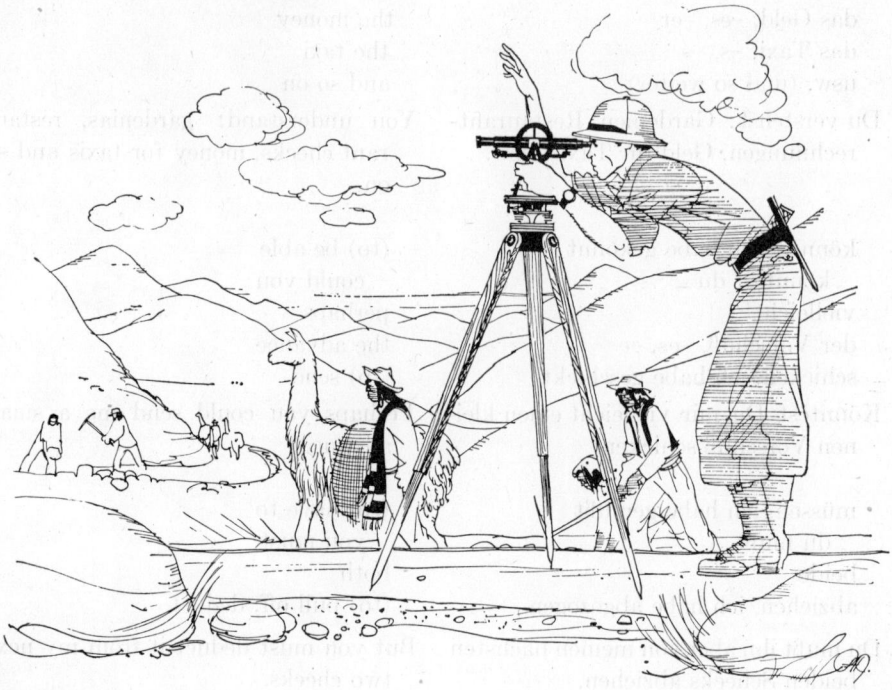

II. Text:

Lieber Vater!

Vor einigen Tagen schrieb mir Anna von ihrem Bruder, der in Mexiko als Ingenieur am Bau der panamerikanischen Autostraße arbeitet. Ich habe lange darüber nachgedacht, was ich werden möchte, und ich glaube, ich habe immer noch große Lust, Ingenieur zu werden. In Chemie bekomme ich dauernd ein A, trotzdem unser Professor sehr streng ist. Auch im Spanischen sind meine Zensuren gut. Ich möchte auch gerne einmal eine Stelle in Südamerika bekommen, deshalb studiere ich Spanisch mit großem Eifer. Schreib mir, was Du von meiner Idee hältst, Ingenieur zu werden.

Es tut mir furchtbar leid, daß Mutter sich schon wieder erkältet hat. Wie schön, daß sie nach Kalifornien reisen konnte. Das wunderbare Klima dort wird ihr gut tun. Ich habe schon einen Brief an sie geschrieben. Ich weiß, sie freut sich, wenn sie gleich bei ihrer Ankunft einen Brief von mir bekommt. Ich habe übrigens auch einen bösen Schnupfen, den ich gar nicht loswerden kann. Frag doch mal Dr. Jones, was ich dagegen tun soll.

O ja, bevor ich es vergesse: Ich habe Anna zu unserem Jubiläumsball eingeladen. Dieser Ball wird mich ein bißchen mehr kosten, als ich anfangs dachte. Du verstehst: Gardenien, Restaurantrechnungen, Geld für Taxis usw. Könntest Du mir vielleicht einen kleinen Vorschuß schicken? Du mußt ihn aber von meinen beiden nächsten Schecks abziehen. Ich will das Geld nicht einfach als Geschenk annehmen.

Vielen Dank im voraus.

Dein Richard

III. Comments:

1. *Modal Auxiliaries (present and simple past):*

We have discussed certain verbs called tense auxiliaries because they are used to express distinctions in the time of action. For example, **wird arbeiten** — *will work* and **hat gearbeitet** — *has worked.* There are certain other auxiliary verbs, called modal auxiliaries because they are used to express distinctions in the mode of action. In English *may work, can work, should work,* are phrases employing such modal auxiliaries.

There are six modal auxiliaries in German. They are, with their basic meanings: **dürfen** — *(to) be-allowed-to;* **können** — *(to) be-able-to, can;* **mögen** — *(to) like to;* **müssen** — *(to) have-to, must;* **sollen** — *(to) be-supposed-to;* **wollen** — *(to) want-to.* Their complementary infinitive comes at the end of the clause, as you would expect. Example:

Du mußt ihn von meinen beiden nächsten Schecks abziehen.
You have to deduct it from my next two checks.

The modal auxiliaries are irregular in the formation of tenses. The present tense forms are:

ich darf	*I am permitted to*
du darfst	*you are permitted to*
er, sie, es darf	*he, she, it is permitted to*
wir dürfen	*we are permitted to*
ihr dürft	*you are permitted to*
sie dürfen	*they are permitted to*
Sie dürfen	*you are permitted to*

ich kann	*I am able to*
du kannst	*you are able to*
er, sie, es kann	*he, she, it is able to*
wir können	*we are able to*
ihr könnt	*you are able to*
sie können	*they are able to*
Sie können	*you are able to*

ich mag	*I like to*	ich muß	*I have to*
du magst	*etc.*	du mußt	*etc.*
er, sie, es mag		er, sie, es muß	
wir mögen		wir müssen	
ihr mögt		ihr müßt	
sie mögen		sie müssen	
Sie mögen		Sie müssen	

ich soll	*I am supposed to*	ich will	*I want to*
du sollst	*etc.*	du willst	*etc.*
er, sie, es soll		er, sie, es will	

wir sollen	wir wollen
ihr sollt	ihr wollt
sie sollen	sie wollen
Sie sollen	Sie wollen

The commonly used past tense of the modals is the simple past. These forms are:

ich durfte	*I was allowed to*	ich konnte	*I was able to*
du durftest	*etc.*	du konntest	*etc.*
er, sie, es durfte		er, sie, es konnte	
wir durften		wir konnten	
ihr durftet		ihr konntet	
sie durften		sie konnten	
Sie durften		Sie konnten	
ich mochte	*I liked to*	ich mußte	*I had to*
etc.		*etc.*	
ich sollte	*I was supposed to*	ich wollte	*I wanted to*
etc.		*etc.*	

Certain subjunctive forms of the modals are used very frequently. These forms have the endings: **–e, –est, –e, –en, –et, –en, –en,** which are identical with the endings of the simple past indicative. Here are the subjunctive forms with their most common meanings:

ich dürfte	*I might*
du dürftest	*you might*
er dürfte	*he might*
wir dürften	*we might*
ihr dürftet	*you might*
sie dürften	*they might*
Sie dürften	*you might*
ich könnte	*I could*
etc.	
ich möchte	*I would like to*
etc.	
ich müßte	*I would have to*
etc.	
ich sollte	*I ought to, I should*
etc.	
ich wollte	*I would want to*
etc.	

You will notice that these subjunctive forms of the modal auxiliaries **dürfen, können, mögen,** and **müssen** differ from the simple past indicative only in the fact

that they have a modified vowel. But the subjunctive forms of **sollen** and **wollen** are identical with the simple past indicative forms and can be distinguished only by their use and context. Examples:

Indicative: **Anna sollte ursprünglich mit dem Nachmittagszug ankommen.**
Anna was originally supposed to come on the afternoon train.

Subjunctive: **Sie sollten etwas gegen Ihren Schnupfen tun.**
You ought to do something about your cold.

2. **Wissen:**

The verb **wissen** — (*to*) *know* is similar in form to the modals:

ich weiß	*I know*	ich wußte	*I knew*
du weißt	*etc.*	du wußtest	*etc.*
er, sie, es weiß		er, sie, es wußte	
wir wissen		wir wußten	
ihr wißt		ihr wußtet	
sie wissen		sie wußten	
Sie wissen		Sie wußten	

IV. Practice:

1. Denken Sie darüber nach, was Sie werden möchten!
   was Sie studieren möchten!
   was Sie dagegen tun sollten!
   was Sie damit machen könnten!

2. a. Richard hat große Lust, Ingenieur zu werden.
   Wilhelm — Professor
   Arzt (*physician*)
   Rechtsanwalt (*lawyer*)
   Geschäftsmann (*business man*)
   Musiker (*musician*)

   b. Richard möchte gern Ingenieur werden.
   Wilhelm — Professor
   etc.

3. Richard will auch einmal nach Mexiko fahren.
   Ich — Schweden
   Wir wollen — Deutschland
   Wollen Sie auch einmal nach Frankreich fahren, Herr Jones?
   Willst du — England — fahren, Willi?

4. Ich kann diesen Winter nicht nach Kalifornien reisen.
   Sie — Florida
   Wir können — Honolulu
   Können Sie diesen Sommer nach der Schweiz reisen?
   Kannst du — Herbst — Norwegen

think
ponder
consider

5. a. Ich mußte lange darüber nachdenken, was ich meinem Vater als Geschenk geben sollte.
Ich mußte lange darüber nachdenken, was ich meiner Mutter davon sagen könnte. could tell
Ich mußte lange darüber nachdenken, wie ich meinem Professor antworten sollte.

b. Du mußtest lange darüber nachdenken, was du deinem Vater als Geschenk geben solltest.
etc.

6. a. Ich freue mich sehr, daß Sie kommen wollen. want to
können. can
werden. will
dürfen. are allowed

b. Richard freut sich, daß wir kommen wollen.
du kommen kannst.
ich kommen werde. shall
Anna kommen darf.

7. a. Richard weiß, daß die Reise nach Kalifornien seiner Mutter gut tun wird.
daß sein Vater ihm einen kleinen Vorschuß schicken wird.

b. Ich weiß nicht, was ich gegen meinen Schnupfen tun soll. cold
ob ich das Geld annehmen darf.

c. Wissen Sie, was für eine Zensur Richard im Spanischen bekommen hat?
wo Omnibus drei hält?

8. Ich möchte das Geld nicht einfach als Geschenk annehmen. simply accept
kann
könnte
will
sollte
darf

I must not (not müssen) Ich darf nicht

V. Exercises:

A. *Questions:*

1. Wo ist die schwierige Strecke der panamerikanischen Autostraße, an der Robert arbeitet?
2. Worüber (*about what*) hat Richard lange nachgedacht?
3. Was möchte Richard werden?
4. Warum lernt Richard Spanisch?
5. Warum wird das kalifornische Klima Frau Neumann gut tun?
6. Warum hat Richard einen Brief im voraus geschrieben?
7. Was soll Herr Neumann Dr. Jones fragen?
8. Welche Unkosten hat Richard durch den Ball?
9. Wie kann Richard Geld für die vielen Rechnungen bekommen?
10. Wird der Vorschuß ein Geschenk sein?

B. *Translate:*

1. Ich muß Herrn Dr. Jones fragen, was ich dagegen tun soll.
2. Müssen Sie wirklich schon am Montag zurückfahren?
3. Ich kann das Geld nicht einfach als Geschenk annehmen.
4. Du mußt gleich bei deiner Ankunft einen Brief an deine Mutter schreiben.
5. Ich bin meinen Schnupfen jetzt wieder los.
6. Ich kann leider nicht zum großen Tanz gehen.
7. Ich weiß nicht, ob ich das Geld annehmen darf.
8. Richard freut sich, daß Anna zum Tanz kommen darf.
9. Können Sie mich verstehen, oder muß ich lauter sprechen?
10. Ich freue mich sehr, daß Sie kommen können.
11. Er konnte das Geld nicht einfach als Geschenk annehmen.
12. Ich möchte Musiker werden.
13. Ich darf nicht rauchen, bis ich zwanzig Jahre alt bin.
14. Er wird einmal eine Stellung in Kalifornien bekommen.
15. Richard weiß, daß die Reise nach Kalifornien seiner Mutter gut tun wird.
16. Haben Sie Lust, heute abend mit mir ins Kino zu gehen?

C. *Rearrange:*

1. von ihrem Bruder, mir, schrieb, vor einigen Tagen, Anna.
2. er, als Ingenieur, an einer schwierigen Strecke, der panamerikanischen Autostraße, arbeitet.
3. hast du, zu werden, immer noch, große Lust, Ingenieur?
4. Richard möchte . . . bekommen, gerne, in Südamerika, eine Stellung, als Ingenieur.
5. daß, ich, erkältet habe, ich, dir, schon wieder, mich, schrieb.
6. das, in Kalifornien, Klima, wunderbare, Mutter, wird . . . gut tun.
7. Mutter, wird . . . sich freuen, wenn, sie, gleich bei ihrer Ankunft, Brief, bekommt, von mir, einen.
8. loswerden, meinen, ich kann, bösen, gar nicht, Schnupfen.
9. der Jubiläumsball, wird . . . kosten, mich, ein bißchen, als, dachte, mehr, ich, anfangs.
10. Zieh . . . ab, von meinen beiden, Schecks, nächsten, den Vorschuß.

D. *Correct the misinformation:*

1. Annas Bruder arbeitet in Kalifornien am Bau einer Autostraße.
2. Richard denkt, daß er Musiker werden will.
3. In Chemie bekommt er dauernd ein A, weil der Professor nicht sehr streng ist.
4. Er will einmal eine Stellung in Kalifornien bekommen.
5. Weil Richards Mutter sich erkältet hatte, mußte sie nach Pennsylvanien reisen.
6. Richard hat noch keinen Brief an sie geschrieben.
7. Richard ist seinen bösen Schnupfen losgeworden.
8. Er hat fast vergessen, seinen Vater um Geld zu bitten.

9. Er will, daß sein Vater ihm das Geld als Geschenk schickt.
10. Er braucht nicht so viel Geld für Gardenien, Restaurantrechnungen usw. auszugeben, als er anfangs dachte.

VI. Securing the Vocabulary:

Kapitel 11 & 12 vocabulary on Mittwoch.

A.

der Bau	*construction*	deshalb	*for that reason*
darüber	*about it*	reisen	*(to) travel*
werden	*(to) become*	sich freuen	*(to) be happy*
bekommen	*(to) receive*	dagegen	*against it*
dauernd	*continuous, constant*	sollen	*(to) be supposed to*
trotzdem	*in spite of it, although*	vor einigen Tagen	*a few days ago*
einige	*a few, several*	anfangs	*at first*
streng	*strict*	einfach	*simple*
einmal	*once, some time*	annehmen	*(to) accept*

B.

traurig (8)	1. *just*	zuerst (10)	1. *entire*
zurück (10)	2. *rather, preferably*	viel (8)	2. *(to) visit*
eben (1)		stattfinden (6)	3. *also*
weit (3)	3. *far*	bis (9)	4. *(to) buy*
ander (7)	4. *(to) travel, ride*	ganz (1)	5. *distant, removed*
fahren (4)	5. *(to) need*	besuchen (2)	
lieber (2)	6. *difficult*	auch (3)	6. *(to) take place*
brauchen (5)	7. *other*	erraten (7)	7. *(to) guess correctly*
schwierig (6)	8. *sad*	entfernt (5)	
der Schutz (9)	9. *protection*	kaufen (4)	8. *much*
	10. *back*		9. *until*
			10. *at first*

die Sorge (5)	1. *only, single*	wohl (1)	1. *both*
lieb (3)	2. *quiet*	beide (1)	2. *every time*
arbeiten (4)	3. *dear*	verwandt (8)	3. *late*
einzig (1)	4. *(to) work*	nie (9)	4. *probably, no doubt*
es gibt (6)	5. *worry, care*	jedesmal (2)	
das Geschäft (7)	6. *there is (are); there exists (exist)*	spät (3)	5. *pardon*
ungefähr (8)		die Verzeihung (5)	6. *well then, and so, therefore*
ruhig (2)		zählen (7)	
	7. *business, store*	also (6)	7. *(to) count*
	8. *approximately*		8. *related*
			9. *never*

Vierzehnte Aufgabe

***

ich bin noch auf	I am still up
anstellen, ich habe angestellt	(to) turn on
ganz	entire, quite, very
* leise	soft, quiet
Ich bin noch auf und habe das Radio angestellt, natürlich nur ganz leise.	I am still up and have turned on the radio, of course only very soft.
jedesmal	every time
* das Stück, –es, –e	the piece
ein Stück, zu dem wir getanzt haben	a piece to which we have danced
die Woche, —, –n	the week
das Ende, –s, –n	the end
das Wochenende, –s, –n	the week-end
Eine Tanzkapelle spielt, und jedesmal, wenn ich ein Stück höre, zu dem wir getanzt haben, muß ich an unser schönes Wochenende denken.	A dance band is playing and every time I hear a piece that we danced to, I have to think of our wonderful week-end.
sein	(to) be
ich wäre	I would be
wissen	(to) know
wenn ich wüßte	if I knew
nach Hause	home
Ich wäre sehr traurig, wenn ich nicht wüßte, daß Du bald nach Hause kommst.	I would be very sad, if I didn't know that you will soon be coming home.
können, ich habe gekonnt	(to) be able
ich kann	I am able
denken, ich habe gedacht	(to) think
ich kann mir gar nicht denken	I absolutely cannot think to myself
vor drei Tagen	three days ago
* zusammen	together
Ich kann mir gar nicht denken, daß wir vor drei Tagen zusammen getanzt haben.	I simply can't believe that we were dancing together three days ago.
vorkommen, es ist vorgekommen	(to) occur, happen
es kommt mir vor	it seems to me
* vor einem Monat	a month ago

sein, ich bin gewesen	(to) be
als wäre es vor einem Monat gewesen	as if it had been a month ago
Es kommt mir vor, als wäre es vor einem Monat gewesen.	It seems to me as if it had been a month ago.
eben	just now
Eben kommt Mutter ins Zimmer.	Mother is just coming into the room.
sollen, ich habe gesollt	(to) be supposed to
ich soll ihr sagen	I am supposed to tell her
wer	who
an wen	to whom
* als ob	as though
wissen, ich habe gewußt	(to) know
als ob sie das nicht wüßte	as though she didn't know that
Ich soll ihr sagen, an wen ich schreibe — als ob sie das nicht wüßte.	She wants me to tell her whom I am writing to — as though she didn't know that.
mögen, ich habe gemocht	(to) like
sie mag dich sehr gern	she likes you very much
das Heim, –s, –e	the home
die Reise, —, –n	the trip
die Heimreise, —, –n	the trip home
sprechen, ich habe gesprochen	(to) speak
Gretel mag Dich sehr gern und hat auf der Heimreise viel von Dir gesprochen.	Gretel is very fond of you and spoke a lot about you on the way home.
* äußerst	extremely
lieb	dear, sweet
liebenswürdig	charming, gracious
Du warst aber auch äußerst lieb zu mir und sehr liebenswürdig zu ihr.	But you really were awfully sweet to me and very nice to her.
die Sorge, —, –n	the care, the worry
Gretel hat auch ihre Sorgen.	Gretel has her troubles too.
furchtbar	terrible, frightful
der Mann, –es, ⸗er	the man, the husband

fahren, ich bin gefahren	(to) ride, drive
Sie möchte furchtbar gerne zu ihrem Mann nach Mexiko fahren.	She would like terribly much to go to Mexico to her husband.
nun	well then
* trösten, ich habe getröstet	(to) console
wir trösten uns	we console each other
gegenseitig	reciprocal
Nun, wir trösten uns gegenseitig.	Well, we console each other.
das Ausland, –s	the foreign country
ich gehe ins Ausland	I am going abroad
gehen, ich bin gegangen	(to) go
wenn du ins Ausland gingest	if you went abroad
* der Erfolg, –s, –e	the success
du hast Erfolg	you have success
haben, ich habe gehabt	(to) have
du würdest großen Erfolg haben	you would be very successful
Richard, ich glaube, wenn Du ins Ausland gingest, würdest Du großen Erfolg haben.	Richard, I think if you were to go abroad, you would be very successful.
sagen, ich habe gesagt	(to) say
ich habe Gretel gesagt	I have said to Gretel
sollen, ich habe gesollt	(to) be supposed to
sie soll ihrem Mann schreiben	she is to write to her husband
das Interes'se, –s, –n	the interest
ich habe Interes'se für	I am interested in
der Ingenieur', –s, –e	the engineer
das Wesen, –s, —	the being
das Ingenieur'we'sen, –s	the engineering
arbeiten, ich habe gearbeitet	(to) work
du würdest gern im Ausland arbeiten	you would like to work abroad
bekommen, ich habe bekommen	(to) receive
Ich habe Gretel gesagt, sie soll ihrem Mann schreiben, daß Du großes Interesse für das Ingenieurwesen hast und auch gerne im Ausland arbeiten würdest und daß Du ein A im Spanischen bekommen hast.	I have told Gretel to write her husband that you are very much interested in engineering and would like to have a job abroad and that you have got an A in Spanish.

das Verhältnis, -ses, -se	the relationship, condition
Zentral'ame'rika	Central America
Süd'ame'rika	South America
Er kennt die Verhältnisse in Zentral- und Südamerika.	He knows conditions in Central and South America.
* vor einiger Zeit	some time ago
der Balkan	the Balkan countries
brauchen, ich habe gebraucht	(to) need
Ingenieu're werden gebraucht	engineers are needed
Er schrieb Gretel vor einiger Zeit, daß amerikanische Ingenieure auch im Balkan gebraucht werden.	He wrote Gretel some time ago, that American engineers are needed in the Balkan countries too.
die Sekretä'rin, —, -nen	the secretary (*feminine*)
Nun, wo Ingenieure gebraucht werden, braucht man auch Sekretärinnen, nicht wahr?	Well, where engineers are needed they'll need secretaries too, don't you think?
zählen, ich habe gezählt	(to) count
bis	until
Weihnachten (*pl.*)	Christmas
Jetzt zähle ich die Tage bis Weihnachten.	Now I'm counting the days until Christmas.
hoffentlich	it is to be hoped for
fliegen, ich bin geflogen	(to) fly
während	during
* die Fe'riĕn (*pl.*)	the vacation
die Weih'nachtsfe'rien	the Christmas vacation
verfliegen, es ist verflogen	(to) fly away, vanish
Hoffentlich fliegt die Zeit nicht so schnell während der Weihnachtsferien, wie sie während des Wochenendes verflogen ist.	I hope time won't fly as fast during the Christmas holidays as it did during the week-end.
treu	true, faithful
In treuer Liebe — Anna.	Lots of love, Anna.

II. Text:

Lieber Richard!

Es war gut, daß ich mit Gretel nach Hause fahren konnte, ich wäre sonst sehr traurig gewesen. Jetzt bin ich wieder bei der Arbeit, und alles ist beim Alten. Es ist schon elf Uhr, und das Haus ist ruhig. Ich bin noch auf und habe das Radio angestellt, natürlich nur ganz leise. Eine Tanzkapelle spielt, und jedesmal, wenn ich ein Stück höre, zu dem wir getanzt haben, muß ich an unser schönes Wochenende denken. Ich wäre sehr traurig, wenn ich nicht wüßte, daß Du bald nach Hause kommst. Ich kann mir gar nicht denken, daß wir vor drei Tagen zusammen getanzt haben. Es kommt mir vor, als wäre es vor einem Monat gewesen. Eben kommt Mutter ins Zimmer. Ich soll ihr sagen, an wen ich schreibe — als ob sie das nicht wüßte! Gretel mag Dich sehr gern und hat auf der Heimreise viel von Dir gesprochen. Du warst aber auch äußerst lieb zu mir und sehr liebenswürdig zu ihr. Gretel hat auch ihre Sorgen. Sie möchte furchtbar gerne zu ihrem Mann nach Mexiko fahren. Nun, wir trösten uns gegenseitig.

Richard, ich glaube, wenn Du ins Ausland gingest, würdest Du großen Erfolg haben. Ich habe Gretel gesagt, sie soll ihrem Mann schreiben, daß Du großes Interesse für das Ingenieurwesen hast und auch gerne im Ausland arbeiten würdest und daß Du ein A im Spanischen bekommen hast. Er kennt die Verhältnisse in Zentral- und Südamerika. Er schrieb Gretel vor einiger Zeit, daß amerikanische Ingenieure auch im Balkan gebraucht werden. Nun, wo Ingenieure gebraucht werden, braucht man auch Sekretärinnen, nicht wahr?

Ich bin geworden

Jetzt zähle ich die Tage bis Weihnachten. Hoffentlich fliegt die Zeit nicht so schnell während der Weihnachtsferien, wie sie während des Wochenendes verflogen ist.

In treuer Liebe
Anna 5

III. Comments:

1. *Subjunctive II.*

Among the functions of the subjunctive mood in German is that of expressing certain kinds of conditions, known as conditions contrary to fact. An example of such a condition is: **Ich wäre sehr traurig, wenn ich das nicht wüßte.** *I would be very sad if I did not know that.* Often either the conditional clause or the conclusion of such a sentence is used independently with a somewhat different meaning. Thus: **Ich wäre sonst sehr traurig.** *Otherwise I would be very sad,* and **Wenn ich das nur wüßte!** *If I only knew that!* And, of course, the subjunctive is used in such clauses as: **Als ob sie das nicht wüßte.** *As if she did not know that,* which can also be expressed **Als wüßte sie das nicht.**

Let us call the type of subjunctive we are here discussing subjunctive II. Subjunctive I will be taken up later.

As you have learned in connection with the modal auxiliaries, there is only one set of subjunctive endings: **–e, –est, –e, –en, –et, –en.** Here are examples of the subjunctive II of **sein, haben, werden, gehen, glauben,** and **wissen:**

Present II:

ich wäre hätte würde ginge glaubte wüßte

Past II:

ich wäre gewesen, hätte gehabt, wäre geworden, wäre gegangen, hätte geglaubt, hätte gewußt

Future II:

ich würde sein, würde haben, würde werden, würde gehen, würde glauben, würde wissen

The forms of the present subjunctive II are used to express present or future time; the past forms, to express past time; and the future forms to express present or future time. This means, practically speaking, that the forms of the present subjunctive II and of the future subjunctive II are interchangeable. Illustrations:

Pres. II: Wenn du jetzt ins Ausland gingest — *If you went abroad now.*
Wenn du später ins Ausland gingest — *If you went abroad later.*

Past II: Wenn du ins Ausland gegangen wärest — *If you had gone abroad.*

Fut. II: Wenn du jetzt ins Ausland gehen würdest — *If you were to go abroad now.*
Wenn du später ins Ausland gehen würdest — *If you were to go abroad later.*

2. *Word Order in Conditional Clauses:*

Conditional clauses, of course, use transposed order in the dependent clause: Wenn du nicht hier **wärest;** als ob sie das nicht **wüßte.**

Frequently **als** is used instead of **als ob** to mean *as if.* In that case inverted order is used: Als **wüßte** sie das nicht; als **wäre** es vor einem Monat gewesen. Remember then: **Als** followed immediately by a verb means *as if.*

IV. Practice:

1. Ich wäre sonst sehr traurig gewesen.
   Du wärest einsam
   Er wäre glücklich (*happy*)
   Wir wären optimistisch

2. Wenn du nicht hier wärest, würde ich sehr traurig sein.
   unglücklich
   einsam

It seems to me

3. a. Es kommt mir vor, als ob ich das Stück gehört hätte. Transposed
   den Film gesehen hätte.
   das in der Zeitung gelesen hätte.

   b. Es kommt mir vor, als hätte ich das Stück gehört. Inverted
   etc.

myself

4. Wenn ich es nicht selbst gesehen hätte, würde ich es nicht glauben.
   gehört
   gelesen
   gesagt
   geschrieben

5. Wenn Mutter jetzt ins Zimmer käme, würde sie mich fragen, an wen ich schreibe.
   , würde sie wissen wollen, an wen ich schreibe.
   , würde ich es ihr sagen müssen.

success

6. a. Wenn du ins Ausland gingest, würdest du großen Erfolg haben.
   schwer arbeiten müssen.
   deine alten Freunde vermissen.
   eine Sekretärin brauchen.

   b. Wenn Sie ins Ausland gingen, würden Sie großen Erfolg haben.
   etc.

7. Sie würden großen Erfolg haben, wenn Sie ins Ausland gingen.
   wenn Sie mehr arbeiteten.
   wenn Sie besser aufpaßten.

8. Wenn Robert nicht Ingenieur geworden wäre, wäre er jetzt nicht in Mexiko.
   Wenn Wilhelm nicht Tennisspieler geworden wäre, wäre er jetzt nicht in Florida.

If I were in your place—(if I were you)—

9. Ich würde an Ihrer Stelle zu einem Arzt gehen.
   sehr gut aufpassen.
   nach Kalifornien fahren.

V. Exercises:

A. *Questions:*

1. Warum war es gut, daß Anna mit Gretel nach Hause fahren konnte?
2. Warum hat Anna das Radio nur ganz leise angestellt?
3. Was tut Anna, wenn sie ein Stück hört, zu dem sie mit Richard getanzt hat?
4. Wann war sie in der Universitätsstadt?
5. Welche Frage stellt die Mutter?
6. Warum mag Gretel Richard sehr gern?
7. Was für Sorgen hat Gretel?
8. Wo, sagt Anna, würde Richard großen Erfolg haben?
9. Was soll Gretel ihrem Mann über Richard schreiben?
10. Warum, denkt Anna, würde Richard in Zentral- oder Südamerika Erfolg haben?
11. Wie viele Tage sind es noch bis Weihnachten?

B. *Translate:*

1. Wie könnte ich ihn vergessen?
2. Sie würde gern als Verkäuferin in Webers Warenhaus arbeiten.
3. Sie würden großen Erfolg haben, wenn Sie besser aufpassen würden.
4. Wann könnten Sie nach Neu York kommen?
5. Sie hätte ihn geheiratet, wenn er nicht ins Ausland gegangen wäre.
6. Ich habe ihr geschrieben, daß du nächste Woche nach Hause kommen würdest.
7. Wenn er wirklich (really) so lange in Südamerika gewesen wäre, würde er die Verhältnisse dort besser kennen. (conditions)
8. Du könntest auf der Heimreise durch Mexiko fahren und Robert besuchen.
9. Ich möchte furchtbar gerne einmal ins Ausland gehen.
10. Könnten Sie uns schreiben, wieviel amerikanische Ingenieure für dies Projekt gebraucht werden?

C. *Rearrange:*

1. noch, auf, Anna, ist, und, das Radio, hat . . . angestellt.
2. mir, ich, gar nicht, denken, kann, daß, zurückfahren kann, nach Hause, nächste Woche, ich.
3. als, sie, wüßte, nicht, das!

time before place

4. meinem Bruder, habe . . . geschrieben, ich, daß, im Ausland, gerne, arbeiten würdest, du.
5. in Europa, gute Ingenieure, werden . . . gebraucht.
6. kommt . . . vor, es, mir, als ob, gewesen wäre, vor einem Monat, es.
7. gesehen hätte, nicht selbst, er, es, wenn, er, nicht, es, würde . . . glauben.
8. was, an meiner Stelle, Sie, würden . . . tun?
9. das Radio, wir, nicht, wenn, angestellt hätten, wir, die guten Nachrichten, hätten . . . gehört, nicht.
10. in Hollywood, du, großen Erfolg, würdest . . . haben.

D. *Correct the misinformation:*

1. Wenn Anna nicht mit Gretel nach Hause gefahren wäre, wäre sie sehr froh gewesen.
2. Das Haus ist sehr ruhig, denn alle sind zu Bett gegangen.
3. Auf der Heimreise hat Gretel fast gar nicht von Richard gesprochen.
4. Wenn Richard ins Ausland gehen würde, würde Anna nicht gerne mitgehen.
5. Wo Ingenieure gebraucht werden, werden keine Sekretärinnen gebraucht.

VI. Securing the Vocabulary:

A.

leise	*soft, quiet*	äußerst	*extremely*
das Stück	*piece*	trösten	*(to) console*
zusammen	*together*	der Erfolg	*success*
vor einem Monat	*a month ago*	vor einiger Zeit	*some time ago*
als ob	*as though*	die Ferien	*vacation*

B.

streng (7)	1. *(to) visit*	bekommen (2)	1. *(to) invite*
reisen (9)	2. *construction*	zurück (5)	2. *(to) receive*
besuchen (1)	3. *(to) understand*	wahrscheinlich (4)	3. *in spite of it, although*
berühmt (6)	4. *once, some time*	sich freuen (8)	4. *probably*
der Bau (2)	5. *future*	außerdem (7)	5. *back*
einmal (4)	6. *famous*	trotzdem (3)	6. *(to) accept*
verstehen (3)	7. *strict*	einsam (10)	7. *besides, in addition*
kaum (10)	8. *indeed, to be sure*	annehmen (6)	8. *(to) be happy*
allerdings (8)	9. *(to) travel*	einladen (1)	9. *child*
die Zukunft (5)	10. *hardly, scarcely*	das Kind (9)	10. *lonesome*

ungefähr (6)	1. *continuous, constant*
die Nachricht (3)	2. *short*
dauernd (1)	3. *information*
dagegen (4)	4. *against it*
also (7)	5. *(to) play*
kurz (2)	6. *approximately*
spielen (5)	7. *well then, and so, therefore*
verschieden (9)	8. *a few, some*
einige (8)	9. *different, various*
nichts (10)	10. *nothing*

verwandt (3)	1. *simple*
die Schwierigkeit (4)	2. *about it*
die Geduld (6)	3. *related*
darüber (2)	4. *difficulty*
einfach (1)	5. *probably, no doubt*
zuerst (7)	6. *patience*
werden (8)	7. *at first*
wohl (5)	8. *(to) become*
sonst (9)	9. *otherwise*

Fünfzehnte Aufgabe

* * * \

brauchen, ich habe gebraucht	(to) need
man brauchte	one needed
verstehen, ich habe verstanden	(to) understand
der Chef, –s, –s	the chief
der Ingenieur′, –s, –e	the engineer
der Chef′ingenieur′, –s, –e	the chief engineer

Für die Arbeit im Balkan brauchte man einen Ingenieur, der Deutsch versteht, und so bin ich jetzt der Chefingenieur.	For the work in the Balkans an engineer was needed who understands German and so I am the chief engineer now.

fahren, ich bin gefahren	(to) ride, travel
das Komitee′, –s, –s	the committee
die Küste, —, –n	the coast
* die Leute (*pl.*)	the people
der Bau, –s	the construction
die Kosten (*pl.*)	the cost
die Baukosten (*pl.*)	the construction cost
der Flug, –s, ¨e	the flight
der Hafen, –s, ¨	the harbor
der Flughafen, –s, ¨	the airport
* um . . . zu	in order to
* besprechen, ich habe besprochen	(to) discuss

Morgen fahre ich mit einem Komitee an die Küste, um mit den Leuten die Baukosten eines Flughafens zu besprechen.	Tomorrow I am going to the coast with a committee in order to discuss the construction costs of an airport with them.

bis auf weiteres	until further notice
postlagernd	stored in the post office

Du kannst mir Deine Briefe bis auf weiteres postlagernd nach Athen, schicken.	Until further notice you can send me your letters to Athens in care of general delivery.

schon wieder	already again
es macht mir Sorge	it causes me worry

Daß Ännchen schon wieder Schnupfen hat, macht mir Sorge.	It worries me that Ännchen has another cold.

gehen, ich bin gegangen	(to) go
geh!	go!
doch	(*stresses the urgency of the request.*)
mal (*for* einmal)	once (*not translated*)
geh doch mal zu Dr. Jones	do go to Dr. Jones
mit ihr	with her
Geh doch mal zu Dr. Jones mit ihr!	Why don't you take her to Dr. Jones?
die Leber	the liver
der Tran, –s	the fish oil
der Lebertran, –s	the liver oil
Vielleicht braucht sie nur mehr Lebertran.	Maybe she only needs more cod liver oil.
hübsch	pretty
hübschest	prettiest
die Puppe, —, –n	the doll
* die Sammlung, —, –en	the collection
finden, ich habe gefunden	(to) find
Sag ihr, daß ich die hübschesten Puppen für ihre Sammlung gekauft habe, die ich finden konnte.	Tell her that I have bought the prettiest dolls which I could find for her collection.
mitbringen, ich habe mitgebracht	(to) bring along
* dürfen, ich habe gedurft	(to) be permitted
ich darf nicht	I must not
das Geheimnis, –ses, –se	secret
* denn	for (*conjunction*)
* verraten, ich habe verraten	(to) betray
sie werden verraten	they are betrayed
Ich werde auch Roberts Weihnachtsgeschenk für Gretel mitbringen, aber ich darf nicht sagen, was es ist, denn er will nicht, daß seine Geheimnisse verraten werden.	I am also going to bring along Robert's Christmas present for Gretel, but I mustn't tell what it is, for he doesn't want his secrets to be betrayed.
der Papa, –s, –s	the daddy
der Kerl, –s, –e	the fellow
das Kerlchen, –s, —	the little rascal (chen *is a diminutive ending which also signifies tenderness*)
Weihnachten (*pl.*)	Christmas
der Mann, –s, ¨er	the man
der Weihnachtsmann, –s, ¨er	the Christmas man
fliegen, ich bin geflogen	(to) fly

die Schwester, —, -n	the sister
etwas Schönes	something beautiful
mitbringen, ich habe mitgebracht	(to) bring along
Wenn Philipp wieder fragt, wann Papa nach Hause kommt, sag dem kleinen Kerlchen, daß ich mit dem Weihnachtsmann nach Hause fliegen werde, und daß der Weihnachtsmann ihm und seiner kleinen Schwester etwas Schönes mitbringen wird.	If Philip asks again when Daddy is coming home, tell the little rascal that I will be flying home with Santa Claus, and that Santa Claus will bring something nice for him and his little sister.
* überra'schen, ich habe überrascht	(to) surprise
Überrascht Dich das?	Does that surprise you?
wohl	probably, no doubt
kaum	scarcely
Wohl kaum.	Probably not very much.
wetten, ich habe gewettet	(to) bet, wager
die ganze Zeit	all the time
der Urlaub, -s	the furlough, leave of absence
bekommen, ich habe bekommen	(to) get, receive
ich würde bekommen	I would get
Ich wette, Du hast die ganze Zeit gewußt, daß ich Weihnachten Urlaub bekommen würde.	I'll bet you knew all the time that I would get a leave at Christmas.
die Villa, —, Villen	the villa
in der wir wohnen	in which we live
* herrlich	glorious, splendid
Die kleine Villa, in der wir Ingenieure seit einer Woche wohnen, hat eine herrliche Lage.	The little villa that we engineers have been living in for a week has a wonderful location.
wollen, ich habe gewollt	(to) want to
ich wollte (*subjunctive*)	I would want, I wish
können, ich habe gekonnt	(to) be able to
du könntest	you would be able to, you could

* die Aussicht, —	the view
die Terras'se, —, –n	the terrace
Ich wollte, Du könntest die Aussicht sehen, die wir von unserer Terrasse haben.	I wish you could see the view we have from our terrace.
wahrschein'lich	probably
immer noch	still
wir haben zu tun	we have to do
Im nächsten Jahr werden wir wahrscheinlich immer noch im Balkan zu tun haben.	Next year we will probably still have things to do in the Balkans.
das Kind, –es, –er	the child
während	during
die Fe'rič̌n (*pl.*)	the vacation
nachkommen, ich bin nachgekommen	(to) follow after
Du kannst dann mit den Kindern während der Ferien nachkommen.	Then you can come after me with the children during vacation.
* ein paar	a few
mittel (*used in compounds*)	middle
* das Meer, –s, –e	the ocean, sea
das Mittelmeer, –s	the Mediterranean
Ein paar Monate am Mittelmeer werden Ännchen gut tun.	A couple of months on the Mediterranean will be good for Ännchen.
Auf Wiedersehen Weihnachten.	I'll see you Christmas.
In Liebe — Dein Richard.	Love, Richard.

II. Text:

Dies ist der letzte Brief. Der Leser sollte wissen, daß er zwölf Jahre nach dem Universitätsjubiläum und im Balkan geschrieben wurde. Wenn der Leser dies nicht wüßte, würde er sich wundern.

Liebe Anna!

Zuerst — ich bin befördert worden. Für die Arbeit im Balkan brauchte man einen Ingenieur, der Deutsch versteht, und so bin ich jetzt der Chefingenieur. Morgen fahre ich mit einem Komitee an die Küste, um mit den Leuten die Baukosten eines Flughafens zu besprechen. Du kannst mir Deine Briefe bis auf weiteres postlagernd nach Athen schicken.

Daß Ännchen schon wieder Schnupfen hat, macht mir Sorge. Geh doch mal zu Dr. Jones mit ihr! Vielleicht braucht sie nur mehr Lebertran. Sag ihr, daß ich die hübschesten Puppen für ihre Sammlung gekauft habe, die ich finden konnte. Ich werde auch Roberts Weihnachtsgeschenk für Gretel mitbringen, aber ich darf nicht sagen, was es ist, denn er will nicht, daß seine Geheimnisse verraten werden. Wenn Philipp wieder fragt, wann Papa nach Hause kommt, sag dem kleinen Kerlchen, daß ich mit dem Weihnachtsmann nach Hause fliegen werde, und daß der Weihnachtsmann ihm und seiner kleinen Schwester etwas Schönes mitbringen wird. Überrascht Dich das? Wohl kaum. Ich wette, Du hast die ganze Zeit gewußt, daß ich Weihnachten Urlaub bekommen würde.

Die kleine Villa, in der wir Ingenieure seit einer Woche wohnen, hat eine herrliche Lage. Ich wollte, du könntest die Aussicht sehen, die wir von unserer Terrasse haben! Im nächsten Jahr werden wir wahrscheinlich immer noch im Balkan zu tun haben. Du kannst dann mit den Kindern während der Ferien nachkommen. Ein paar Monate am Mittelmeer werden Ännchen gut tun.

Auf Wiedersehen Weihnachten.

In Liebe
Dein Richard

III. Comments:

1. *Relative Pronouns:* intro. a clause & refers back to something gone bef

follows comma & has no kown following it

The relative pronouns are very similar in form to the definite article.

Examples:

Sie brauchten einen Ingenieur, **der** Deutsch versteht.
They needed an engineer who understands German.

Die Aussicht, **die** wir von unserer Terrasse haben, ist herrlich.
The view which we have from our terrace is magnificent.

Since relative clauses are subordinate clauses the inflected verb stands at the end of a relative clause. This results in the practical rule: When you find a form of **der, die, das** without a noun following it and the verb is postponed, you are dealing with a relative clause and the form which looks like a definite article means *who* or *whom, which* or *that.* The relatives have long forms in certain cases as indicated in the following paradigms:

	M.	*F.*	*N.*	*Plural*
N.	der	die	das	die
A.	den	die	das	die
D.	dem	der	dem	denen
G.	dessen	deren	dessen	deren

2. *Interrogative Pronouns:*

The interrogative pronouns are **wer** — *who* and **was** — *what.* They are declined as follows:

	M. & F.	*N.*
N.	wer	was
A.	wen	was
D.	wem	—
G.	wessen	(wessen)

You will notice that there is no plural, that the genitive case of the neuter is enclosed in parentheses to indicate that it is rarely used, and that the dative case of the neuter is missing, being replaced by compounds of **wo-** plus a preposition *e.g.* **womit** — *with what, wherewith,* **wozu** — *to what, whereto,* **woraus** — *out of what.* The forms of **wer** and **was,** of course, introduce indirect questions as well as direct: **Sie wissen doch sicher, an wen ich eben schreibe.** *But surely you know to whom I am writing just now.*

3. *Passive Voice (Simple Past and Present Perfect):*

As stated in Lesson 11 forms of **werden** are used as auxiliaries with the past participle of a verb to form the passive voice. An example of the passive voice in the simple past tense is **ich wurde befördert,** etc. and in the present perfect, **ich bin befördert worden,** etc. (*For complete conjugation see Appendix.*)

IV. Practice:

1. Ich würde mich wundern, wenn ich das nicht wüßte.
   er ins Ausland ginge.
   Sie großen Erfolg hätten.
   sie sich verheiraten würde.

2. Ich bin vor drei Wochen befördert worden.
   zum Tanz eingeladen worden.
   oft mit meinem Freund verwechselt worden.
   Wir sind vor drei Wochen zum Tanz eingeladen worden.
   Sind Sie schon befördert worden, Herr Jones?

3. Er wäre schon befördert worden, wenn er fleißiger gearbeitet hätte.
   wenn er großen Erfolg gehabt hätte.
   wenn er mehr Glück gehabt hätte.

4. Herr Neubauer ist der Ingenieur, der schon zweimal befördert worden ist.
   dessen Arbeit in Brasilien so gelobt wurde.
   mit dem wir die Baukosten des Flughafens besprechen werden.
   den wir vor zwei Jahren nach Mexiko geschickt haben.

5. Wo ist das Komitee, das morgen an die Küste fährt?
   mit dem wir die Baukosten des Flughafens besprechen werden?
   dessen Mitglieder (*members*) alle Ingenieure sind?

6. Die Villa, in der wir wohnen, hat eine herrliche Lage.
   die wir kaufen möchten,
   die übrigens nur zwei Jahre alt ist,

7. Die Ingenieure, deren Chef übrigens Deutsch versteht, kommen alle aus Amerika.
   mit denen wir die Baukosten besprechen werden, sind hier.

8. Haben Sie die ganze Zeit gewußt, daß ich bald Urlaub bekommen würde?
   daß ich bald nach Hause kommen würde?
   daß Richard im Balkan arbeiten würde?
   daß er sich mit Anna verheiraten würde?

9. Ich wollte, Sie könnten die Aussicht sehen, die wir von der Terrasse haben!
während der Ferien nachkommen!
wir hätten ein neues Auto!
ich wäre jetzt am Mittelmeer! (zu Hause, in Honolulu, etc.)

10. Fräulein Becker wurde immer zu jedem Tanz eingeladen.
Ich wurde
Wir wurden
Sind Sie zu jedem Tanz eingeladen worden, Fräulein Wright?

V. Exercises:

A. *Questions:*

1. Warum sollte der Leser wissen, daß dieser letzte Brief zwölf Jahre nach den anderen geschrieben wurde?
2. Wo wurde dieser Brief geschrieben?
3. Hat Richard seiner Frau etwas Neues zu erzählen?
4. Warum ist Richard befördert worden?
5. Warum muß er an die Küste fahren?
6. Was ist bis auf weiteres Richards Adresse?
7. Was soll Frau Neumann mit Ännchen tun, die schon wieder Schnupfen hat?
8. Was für ein Weihnachtsgeschenk wird Richard seiner Tochter mitbringen?
9. Wann wird Richard Urlaub bekommen?
10. Wie lange wohnen die Ingenieure schon in der kleinen Villa?
11. Von wo hat man die beste Aussicht?
12. Was wird Ännchen, die sich zu oft und zu leicht erkältet, gut tun?

B. *Translate:*

1. Ich wollte, du könntest während der Ferien nachkommen.
2. Wofür interessierst du dich besonders?
3. An wen schreiben Sie so oft Briefe?
4. Deine Briefe werden weitergeschickt.
5. Für wen arbeiten Sie jetzt?
6. Mit wem spielen Sie heute Tennis?
7. Die Leute, mit denen ich das besprechen werde, sind Ingenieure.
8. Das Geschenk, das ich Ännchen mitbringe, wird ihr sicher große Freude machen.
9. Es ist nicht alles wahr, was in der Zeitung steht.
10. Er ist vor einem Jahr befördert worden.

C. *Rearrange:*

1. er, wüßte, wenn, das, nicht, ich, würde . . . mich wundern.
2. das schönste Halsband, ich, ihr, habe . . . gekauft, das, finden konnte, ich.

3. würde mich wundern, ich, wenn, keinen, hätten, großen Erfolg, damit, Sie.
4. sie, die ganze Zeit, hat . . . gewußt, daß, bekommen würde, er, Urlaub, Weihnachten.
5. eine herrliche Lage, in der, wohnen, wir, hat, die kleine Stadt.

D. *Correct the misinformation:*

1. Anna soll ihre Briefe an Richard postlagernd nach dem Balkan schicken.
2. In seinem Brief hat Richard Anna gesagt, daß er im Sommer Urlaub bekommen wird.
3. Richard wohnt seit einem Monat in einer kleinen Villa, die eine herrliche Lage hat.
4. Richard kommt Weihnachten nach Hause, weil er im Balkan nichts mehr zu tun hat.
5. Im nächsten Jahr wird Richard wahrscheinlich immer noch in Mexiko zu tun haben.

VI. Securing the Vocabulary:

13, 14, 15 Kapitel vocabulary test Fri 21 July 1950

A.

die Leute	*people*
besprechen	*(to) discuss*
die Sammlung	*collection*
dürfen	*(to) be permitted*
denn	*for*
verraten	*(to) betray*
überraschen	*(to) surprise*
herrlich	*glorious, splendid*
um . . . zu	*in order to*
die Aussicht	*view*
ein paar	*a few*
das Meer	*ocean, sea*

B.

immer (4)	1. *besides, in addition*
wohl (9)	2. *probably*
außerdem (1)	3. *already*
wahrscheinlich (2)	4. *always*
nur (8)	5. *for that reason*
ziemlich (10)	6. *enough*
deshalb (5)	7. *(to) receive*
schon (3)	8. *only*
genug (6)	9. *probably, no doubt*
bekommen (7)	10. *rather*

wer (10)	1. *how, as, like*
wie (1)	2. *approximately*
zusammen (7)	3. *well then*
viel (8)	4. *incidentally*
nun (3)	5. *to be sure*
übrigens (4)	6. *usually*
ungefähr (2)	7. *together*
kaum (9)	8. *much*
allerdings (5)	9. *hardly, scarcely*
gewöhnlich (6)	10. *who*
nie (11)	11. *never*

eben (4)	1. *a month ago*
ganz (8)	2. *perhaps*
auch (12)	3. *well then, and so, therefore*
sonst (9)	4. *just*
vielleicht (2)	5. *nothing*
leider (10)	6. *for*
also (3)	7. *at least*
vor einem Monat (1)	8. *entire, quite*
zurück (11)	9. *otherwise*
wenigstens (7)	10. *unfortunately*
denn (6)	11. *back*
nichts (5)	12. *also*

noch (6)	1. *there is (are), there exists (exist)*
besonders (3)	2. *soon*
vor einiger Zeit (5)	3. *especially*
es gibt (1)	4. *in spite of it, although*
gar nicht (11)	5. *some time ago*
bald (2)	6. *still, yet*
äußerst (10)	7. *(to) become*
bis (12)	8. *a few, some*
trotzdem (4)	9. *in order to*
werden (7)	10. *extremely*
einige (8)	11. *not at all*
um . . . zu (9)	12. *until*

Sechzehnte Aufgabe

* * * \

Der Brief ist an eine Freundin in der Heimatstadt dieser Studentin geschrieben, die so freundlich war, ihn uns für Herberts Biographie zu geben. „O Roberta, Du kannst Dir gar nicht vorstellen, wie schön der Galaball zum hundertjährigen Jubiläum unserer Alma Mater war. Daß die Musik wunderbar war, wirst Du verstehen, wenn ich Dir schreibe, daß Toni und seine Piraten für uns spielten. Das Schönste am ganzen Abend waren aber meine zwei Tänze mit Herbert. Herbert ist wunderbar! Er hat große braune Augen und außerdem ist er ein wunderbarer Tänzer. . . .“ Das zweite Dokument, das wir Ihnen geben, um Herberts Biographie authentischer zu machen, ist ein Artikel aus der Studentenzeitung ‚Der Grislybär.‘ „Auch ein Skeptiker von Beruf muß nach diesem Meisterschaftskampf von der Klasse Herbert Beckers überzeugt sein. Dieser Wilkins aus Kalifornien und unser Herbert Becker haben wie Berufsspieler gespielt. Es ist schwer zu sagen, wer von den beiden die bessere Technik hat. Vielleicht spielt Becker etwas besser am Netz als der Mann aus dem Orangenstaat. Das ist aber sicher: Becker hat gewonnen, weil er die besseren Nerven hat und nie aufgeregt wurde.“ . . . Dieses Tennismatch war am 29. Mai. Am 25. Dezember treffen wir unseren Helden wieder im Elternhause in Neu York.

Die Familie Becker, d.h. Herr und Frau Becker, Herbert und seine Schwester Elisabeth, sitzt am Eßtisch und wartet auf das gute Essen, das Mama Becker für sie gekocht hat. Mama Becker kocht wie der beste Koch eines internationalen Hotels und sie weiß außerdem, was ihr Herbert gern ißt. Die Mutter ihres Mannes war als junge Frau von Wien nach den Vereinigten Staaten gekommen und Frau Becker hat viele Wiener Rezepte von ihr gelernt. Ihre Wiener Schnitzel und Apfelstrudel z.B sind bei den Verwandten und Freunden der Familie Becker berühmt. Wie gesagt, die Familie Becker sitzt am Eßtisch und wartet. Frau Becker unterhält sich mit Elisabeth über einen Pelzmantel, den sie in einem Warenhaus am Broadway gesehen hat, als sie ihre Weihnachtseinkäufe machte. Elisabeth ist zwei Jahre älter als ihr Bruder Herbert. Sie hat eine Stelle als Sekretärin in einem Neu Yorker Geschäft. Die Damen unterhalten sich über den Pelzmantel, und Herr Becker erzählt seinem Sohn eine aufregende Geschichte aus den Tagen, als er für Zürich College Fußball spielte.

Nun will Herbert eine Fußballgeschichte vom letzten Herbst erzählen, aber da kommt das Mädchen, die Mutter Becker beim Kochen und Geschirrspülen hilft, und bringt das Essen.

Wenn Herbert ißt, hat er längere Unterhaltungen nicht gern. Jetzt interessiert er sich mehr für die Meisterwerke seiner Mutter als für Fußball.

Dann serviert das Mädchen Herberts Lieblingsdessert, Apfelstrudel, und Papa erklärt, daß er sich wieder erkältet hätte und seine Pillen haben wollte, die ihm Dr. Jones gegen Schnupfen und Erkältung gegeben hätte. Herbert geht aus dem Zimmer und bringt seinem Vater die Pillen. Dann setzt er sich wieder an den Tisch, um noch eine Portion Apfelstrudel zu essen. Da sieht er ein Stück Papier und er sieht auch, daß dieses Stück Papier ein Scheck über sechshundert Dollar ist. Die sechshundert Dollar sind Papa Beckers Weihnachtsgeschenk für seinen Sohn. Herr Becker will, daß sein Junge mit diesem Geld während der Sommerferien nach Deutschland fährt.

Sieben Monate später treffen wir die Familie Becker auf einem Pier des Norddeutschen Lloyd in Neu York. Herbert will mit der ‚Europa' nach Deutschland fahren. Die ‚Europa' liegt am Pier, und Herberts Eltern gehen mit ihrem Sohn an Bord, denn die Passagiere dürfen Gäste mitbringen. Erika geht natürlich auch an Bord. Wer ist Erika? Aber lieber Leser, liebe Leserin, muß ich Ihnen alles erklären? Erika wohnt auch in Neu York, sie wohnt auch in der zweiundachtzigsten Straße, nur drei Häuser und eine Garage von Herbert entfernt. Sie macht sich Sorgen, weil bald der breite Atlantische Ozean zwischen der zweiundachtzigsten Straße und Herbert liegen wird. Herberts Schwester ist nicht an Bord, denn sie hat sich im Frühling verheiratet und ist jetzt mit ihrem Mann in Detroit, wo er Abteilungschef eines Detroiter Warenhauses ist.

Herbert, Herberts Eltern und Erika gehen also mit anderen Passagieren und Gästen durchs ganze Schiff. Sie sehen sich den Maschinenraum, den Damensalon, das Sportdeck und auch ein paar Kabinen erster Klasse an. Die Stewards und Schiffsoffiziere geben über alles Auskunft.

Herberts Kabine ist eine Kabine dritter Klasse für zwei Passagiere, und die Frau Becker will natürlich sehen, wo Herbert die nächste Woche wohnen wird. Sie sitzen alle in Herberts Kabine, und Mama Becker sagt allerlei. Sie sagt ihrem Sohn, was er in Deutschland tun soll. „Laß dir rechtzeitig die Hemden und die Socken waschen! Trink genug Milch! Schreib wenigstens zweimal die Woche! Iß nur in guten Restaurants! Treib keinen Unfug! Vergiß nicht, daß wir in Berlin Verwandte haben. Ich weiß, Onkel Anton wird sich schrecklich freuen, wenn du ihn in Berlin besuchst. Ich habe Tante Ida nichts von deiner Reise geschrieben. Wenn du nach Hannover kommst, mußt du sie überraschen. Tante Ida liebt Überraschungen!" Mama Becker möchte gerne noch etwas länger mit ihrem Sohn plaudern, aber das Lautsprechersystem des Schiffes macht bekannt, daß alle, die nicht nach Deutschland, England oder Frankreich fahren wollen, jetzt von Bord gehen müssen. Frau Becker weint ein bißchen, und Herbert sagt: „Aber Mama, warum bist du traurig? Ich reise doch nur nach Deutschland, um Deutsch zu lernen. Die ‚Europa' ist doch kein Truppenschiff!" (Herbert wußte nicht, was er da sagte. Sechs Jahre später brachte die ‚Europa' als Truppenschiff der Vereinigten Staaten Tausende amerikanischer Soldaten nach Hause zurück.)

Nun gibt Mutter Becker ihrem Jungen einen Kuß und Erika gibt ihm ein Buch, das er auf der Reise lesen soll, und ein paar Minuten später stehen Herberts Eltern und Erika wieder auf dem Pier. Sie hören die Schiffssirene und sehen, wie das große Schiff in den Hudson hinausfährt.

Herbert steht an der Reling und sieht die elektrischen Lichter von Coney Island durch die Nacht blinken. Bald wird es kälter, und Herbert geht in seine Kabine, denn er hat nur einen Sommeranzug an. Er wäscht sich und geht zu Bett. Da er nicht sehr müde ist, liest er das Buch, das ihm Erika geschenkt hat. Es heißt ‚Das Geheimnis der Villa' und beginnt sehr interessant: „Auf der Terrasse einer kleinen Villa, von der man eine herrliche Aussicht auf das Mittelmeer hat, sitzt Clancy Wuthermore und frühstückt. Clancy frühstückt, weil er sehr hungrig ist, aber er weiß nicht, wer ihm das Frühstück gebracht hat. Er weiß

auch nicht, warum er in dieser Villa ist und wie der kleine Ort heißt, den er von der Terrasse sehen kann. Clancy weiß nur, daß er gestern in Athen einen Brief bekommen hat, in dem ein Freund seines Vaters schrieb, er sollte ihn in der Stadionstraße besuchen. Als er in das Hotelzimmer kam, sah er nicht den Freund seines Vaters sondern drei Fremde, die ihm mit Revolvern in der Hand sagten, er müsse ruhig sein und mit ihnen kommen. Die drei Männer hatten den armen Clancy, der vor Erstaunen nicht reden konnte, in ihre Mitte genommen, und bevor er es wußte, hatten sie ihn in ihrem Auto. Die drei Fremden hatten Clancy in diese Villa gebracht, in der er die ganze Nacht darüber nachgedacht hatte, was man von ihm wollte. Darüber dachte er auch jetzt nach, als er sein Frühstück aß!"

An dieser interessanten Stelle kommt der zweite Passagier in die Kabine und sagt: „Verzeihung, daß ich so spät komme. Ich sehe, Sie sind schon zu Bett gegangen. Ich hatte mich verlaufen und war im Gesellschaftsraum der zweiten Klasse gelandet, wo es ein kleines Konzert gab. Ich heiße Albert Niemeier und bin Mechaniker. Ich arbeite in Detroit in einer Autofabrik."

Herbert und der Mechaniker unterhalten sich nun eine Weile über Neu York, das Schiff und Detroit, aber sie sind beide sehr müde und nach ein paar Minuten Unterhaltung schlafen sie schon. Herbert hat einen merkwürdigen Traum. Er träumt, er spielt Fußball gegen Notre Dame. Er trägt den Ball und im nächsten Moment liegt er auf dem Ball und drei schwere Spieler von Notre Dame sitzen auf ihm. Der Ball rollt unter ihm hin und her. In diesem kritischen Moment wacht er auf und sieht nach der Uhr. Es ist acht Uhr. Der junge Mechaniker sagt leise: „Hören Sie etwas?" Ja, Herbert hört etwas. Er hört, wie die Wasser des Atlantischen Ozeans gegen die Seite des Schiffes donnern, auf der sein Bett ist, und er sagt: „Wir müssen Sturm haben!" Der junge Mechaniker sagt nichts. Er liegt im Bett und hält sich den Kopf mit beiden Händen.

Herbert ist ein Held, er steht auf, wäscht sich und zehn Minuten später hat er Hose und Hemd an. Mehr kann er nicht tun. Der Zimmersteward kommt in die Kabine und sagt: „Warum so still, meine Herren? Wollen Sie nicht frühstücken? Es gibt guten frischen Kaffee, Eier mit Speck, frische Orangen, alles, was Sie haben wollen." Herbert verliert die Geduld. „Zum Donnerwetter," sagt er, „wollen Sie sich über uns lustig machen?" „Aber Herr Becker," antwortet der Zimmersteward, „natürlich mache ich mich nicht über Sie lustig. Ich wollte die Herren nur auf andere Gedanken bringen. Warten Sie hier, ich gehe zum Schiffsdoktor und werde den Herren ein paar Pillen mitbringen."

Der Zimmersteward geht, und Herbert will eine Unterhaltung mit dem jungen Mechaniker beginnen, aber der junge Mann aus Detroit sagt nichts. Er sieht Herbert nur mit müden, traurigen Augen an. Herbert versteht und ist still. Der Zimmersteward kommt zurück und sagt: „Wir haben einen schlechten Tag, der Sturm kommt von der Seite, aber machen Sie sich keine Sorgen, hier sind Ihre Pillen."

Herbert gibt dem Mechaniker zwei Pillen in einem Glas Wasser und fragt ihn: „Kann ich Ihnen Frühstück mitbringen? Haben Sie auf etwas Appetit?" Der junge Mann von Detroit antwortet leise: „Das ist sehr liebenswürdig von Ihnen, aber sprechen Sie bitte nicht von Essen, wenn Sie hier in der Kabine sind."

Herbert geht an Deck und sieht den wilden, grauen Atlantischen Ozean. Er hat genug gesehen und geht wieder unter Deck, um etwas zu essen. In der großen Halle sitzen nur ein paar Leute an den Tischen und frühstücken. Herbert trinkt eine Tasse Tee und ißt etwas Toast. Auf der anderen Seite des Tisches sitzt eine junge Dame, die auch wenig Appetit hat. Herbert beginnt eine Unterhaltung mit ihr und sagt liebenswürdig: „. . .

Section Two

Siebzehnte Aufgabe

* * * \

* leicht	light, easy
leichter	easier
Was ist leichter als sich einzubilden, daß man knallende Revol'ver oder quietschende Autobremsen hört?	What is easier than to imagine that one is hearing revolver shots or squeaking automobile brakes?
Denken Sie einmal an die * Zuschauer in einem Thea'ter zur Zeit Shakespeares!	Just think of the spectators in a theater in Shakespeare's time!
von denen	of these
* verlangen, ich habe verlangt	(to) demand
man verlangte	one demanded
Von denen verlangte man sehr viel Phantasie'.	A great deal of imagination was demanded of them.
Ein Busch auf der * Bühne bedeutete damals einen Wald, ein paar Bänke einen Thronsaal usw. (und so weiter)	A bush on the stage at that time signified a forest, a few benches, a throne-room, and so on.
Jungen in Frauenkleidern spielten die * reizende Ophelia oder rezitierten die * Zeilen:	Boys in women's clothes played the charming Ophelia or declaimed the lines:
was uns Rose heißt	what is called a rose to us
wie es auch hieße	however it might be called
Was ist ein Name? Was uns Rose heißt,	What is a name? What we call a rose,
Wie es auch hieße, würde lieblich duften.	no matter what its name might be, would smell sweet. (*cf. "Romeo & Juliet," Act II, sc. II, ll. 43–44.*)
Außerdem waren Shakespeares Römer, Griechen, Schotten und Venezia'ner * genau so angezogen wie die großen Herren zur Zeit der Königin Elisabeth.	Besides, Shakespeare's Romans, Greeks, Scots, and Venetians were dressed exactly as the great lords at the time of Queen Elizabeth.
* damals	at that time
ersetzen, ich habe ersetzt	(to) replace, substitute
er ersetzte	he replaced
noch kein Verständnis	still no understanding
Damals hatte das Theaterpublikum noch kein * Verständnis für histo'-	The audience of that time had not yet developed an understanding of his-

risches Kostüm′ und Bühnenbild entwickelt und ersetzte durch Phantasie′, was das Theater dem Auge nicht * zeigen konnte.	torical costuming and staging and by imagination made up for what the theater could not show.
Noch eins!	One thing more!
Wenn Sie wollen, können Sie natür′lich Sen′destation′ spielen.	If you wish, you can, of course, play broadcasting station.
schauspielerisch	theatrical
Mit etwas schauspielerischem Talent′ können Sie die folgenden Aufgaben so vorlesen, daß Ihre Klassengenossen glauben werden, sie hören * die Stimme eines Ansagers, eines Bandi′ten, eines poli′tischen Redners u. dgl. m. (und derglei′chen mehr)	With some acting ability you can read the following chapters in such a way that your classmates will believe they are listening to the voice of an announcer, a bandit, a political speaker, and the like.
Oder lassen Sie Ihre Klassengenossen die verschiedenen Rollen spielen!	Or have your classmates play the various parts!
* nachmachen, ich habe nachgemacht das Geräusch läßt sich nachmachen	(to) imitate the noise lets itself be imitated
Viele drama′tische Geräusche lassen sich * sogar′ im Klassenzimmer ohne komplizierte Appara′te nachmachen, wie z.B. der zischende Dampf einer abfahrenden Lokomoti′ve, das Galoppieren eines Pferdes, eine Autohupe, ein Revol′verschuß, das Quietschen einer rostigen Tür usw.	Many dramatic sound effects can be imitated even in the classroom without complicated apparatus, as, for example, the hissing steam of a departing locomotive, the gallop of a horse, an automobile horn, a revolver shot, the creaking of a rusty door and so on.
Dramatisieren Sie alles, was Sie dramatisieren können!	Dramatize everything that you can dramatize!
Es macht * Spaß!	It's fun!

II. Text*:

Sender GFS

In den folgenden Aufgaben müssen Sie sich vorstellen, Sie haben einen Radioapparat und hören deutsche Programme. Wir erwarten allerdings von Ihnen, daß Sie Ihrer Einbildungskraft freien Lauf lassen. Wenn es heißt: Die Kapelle spielt einen Wiener Walzer, dann müssen Sie eben „An der schönen, blauen Donau" oder „Geschichten aus dem Wiener Wald" mit dem geistigen Ohre hören. Wie mit der Musik, so machen Sie es auch mit den Geräuschen! Was ist leichter als sich einzubilden, daß man knallende Revolver oder quietschende Autobremsen hört?

Denken Sie einmal an die Zuschauer in einem Theater zur Zeit Shakespeares! Von denen verlangte man sehr viel Phantasie. Ein Busch auf der Bühne bedeutete

* See Appendix paragraph 2 for the alphabet in Gothic type.

damals einen Wald, ein paar Bänke einen Thronsaal usw. (und so weiter). Jungen in Frauenkleidern spielten die reizende Ophelia oder rezitierten die Zeilen:

Was ist ein Name? Was uns Rose heißt,
Wie es auch hieße, würde lieblich duften.

Außerdem waren Shakespeares Römer, Griechen, Schotten und Venezianer genau so angezogen wie die großen Herren zur Zeit der Königin Elisabeth. Damals hatte das Theaterpublikum noch kein Verständnis für historisches Kostüm und Bühnenbild entwickelt und ersetzte durch Phantasie, was das Theater dem Auge nicht zeigen konnte.

Noch eins! Wenn Sie wollen, können Sie natürlich Sendestation spielen. Mit etwas schauspielerischem Talent können Sie die folgenden Aufgaben so vorlesen, daß Ihre Klassengenossen glauben werden, sie hören die Stimme eines Ansagers, eines Banditen, eines politischen Redners u. dgl. m. (und dergleichen mehr). Oder lassen Sie Ihre Klassengenossen die verschiedenen Rollen spielen! Viele dramatische Geräusche lassen sich sogar im Klassenzimmer ohne komplizierte Apparate nachmachen, wie z.B. der zischende Dampf einer abfahrenden Lokomotive, das Galoppieren eines Pferdes, eine Autohupe, ein Revolverschuß, das Quietschen einer rostigen Tür usw. Dramatisieren Sie alles, was Sie dramatisieren können! Es macht Spaß!

III. Comments:

1. *Simple Past Tense of Weak Verbs:*

So far we have taken up the simple past tense of only a few verbs, such as sein, haben, and the modal auxiliaries. The reason for this was that the simple past tense is much less generally used than the present perfect tense in colloquial language or in unconnected sentences. But now we are going to encounter passages of connected narrative or exposition in the past time and for this purpose German employs the simple past tense.

By far the larger number of German verbs belong to a group known as weak verbs. The English verbs *walk, walked, walked* and *play, played, played* are of this type. In German, the simple past tense of weak verbs is formed by adding to the infinitive stem the tense sign –t– plus personal endings. Thus, the infinitive stem of spielen is spiel– plus tense sign –t– = spielt– plus personal endings = spielte, spieltest, spielten, etc. Here are the simple past tense forms of the verbs verlangen and erwarten. Notice that the vowel –e– must be inserted between the final –t of the stem erwart– and of the tense sign –t– in order to facilitate pronunciation.

ich verlangte — I demanded, I was demanding, etc.	ich erwartete — I expected, I was expecting, etc.
du verlangtest	du erwartetest
er verlangte	er erwartete
wir verlangten	wir erwarteten

ihr verlangtet	ihr erwartetet
sie verlangten	sie erwarteten
Sie verlangten	Sie erwarteten

2. *Present and Past Participles:*

The present participle of a verb is formed by the addition of -end to the present infinitive stem. Thus: verlang-end, *demanding;* erwart-end, *expecting;* spiel-end, *playing.* The past participle of a verb is its third principal part. In the case of a weak verb it is formed by the addition of -t to the stem and, in most instances, by the prefixing of ge-: gespielt — *played,* gemacht — *made,* geglaubt — *believed.* The past participles of the so-called strong verbs (to be discussed in the next unit) all end in -en: geheißen — *called,* gelesen — *read.* But if the first syllable of a verb does *not* bear the main stress ge is not prefixed: entwickelt — *developed,* kompliziert — *complicated,* erwartet — *expected.*

Participles are adjectives and have the normal adjective declension: die folgende Aufgabe, *the following lesson;* eine quietschende Autobremse, *a squeaking automobile brake;* das galoppierende Pferd, *the galloping horse;* komplizierte Apparate, *complicated apparatus.*

3. *Idiomatic Uses of* lassen:

The verb lassen means *let, allow, permit.* But in the sentence Lassen Sie Ihre Klassengenossen die verschiedenen Rollen spielen! it is used as English uses the verb *have* in the sense of *cause to, order to: Have your classmates play the various parts.*

Another use of lassen is with a complementary infinitive and reflexive object. A literal translation of the sentence: Dieses Geräusch läßt sich leicht nachmachen would be, *This sound lets itself be imitated easily.* Of course, English usage requires the translation, *This sound can easily be imitated.*

IV. Practice:

1. Sie müssen sich vorstellen, Sie hören knallende Revolver.
   quietschende Autobremsen.
   eine zischende Lokomotive.
   ein galoppierendes Pferd.
   die reizende Ophelia.

   Sie müssen sich vorstellen, daß Sie dramatisierte Theaterstücke hören.

2. Von dem Theaterpublikum zur Zeit Shakespeares verlangte man viel Einbildungskraft.

3. a Ein Busch auf der Bühne bedeutete damals einen Wald.
   Eine Bank — einen Thronsaal.

   b. Ein paar Büsche auf der Bühne bedeuteten damals einen Wald.
   Bänke — einen Thronsaal.

4. Ein Junge in Frauenkleidern spielte die Julia.
   Will Kemp — die komischen Rollen.

   Shakespeare spielte verschiedene Rollen in seinen Dramen.

5. Lassen Sie Fräulein O'Brien die Julia spielen!
   Herrn Murphy den Banditen
   den Professor den Ansager

6. Die Geräusche lassen sich sehr leicht nachmachen.
   Die Aufgaben dramatisch vorlesen.
   Die Geschichten sehr gut dramatisieren.

7. a Die Zuschauer hatten viel Einbildungskraft.
   Die Zuschauer mußten ihrer Einbildungskraft freien Lauf lassen.
   b. Man erwartete etwas.
   von den Zuschauern.
   c. Man erwartete von den Zuschauern, daß sie ihrer Einbildungskraft freien Lauf ließen.

8. a. Die Kapelle spielt.
   einen Wiener Walzer.
   übers Radio.
   b. Das müssen Sie sich vorstellen.
   c. Sie müssen sich vorstellen, daß die Kapelle einen Wiener Walzer übers Radio spielt.

9. a. Die Lokomotive fährt ab.
   Eine abfahrende Lokomotive
   b. Der Dampf zischt.
   Der zischende Dampf
   einer abfahrenden Lokomotive.
   c. Das Geräusch läßt sich nachmachen.
   Ein Geräusch, das sich leicht nachmachen läßt.
   d. Der zischende Dampf einer abfahrenden Lokomotive ist ein Geräusch, das sich leicht nachmachen läßt.

V. Exercises:

A. *Questions:*

1. Was wird in den folgenden Aufgaben von Ihnen erwartet?
2. Wie heißen zwei berühmte Wiener Walzer?
3. Wie kann man das Geräusch galoppierender Pferde nachmachen?
4. Wer war Englands Königin zur Zeit Shakespeares?
5. Was bedeutete zu Shakespeares Zeit einen Thronsaal?
6. Was bedeutete ein Busch auf der Bühne?
7. Wer spielte damals die Frauenrollen?
8. Trug Julius Caesar auf Shakespeares Bühne ein römisches Kostüm?
9. Was zeigt die moderne Bühne dem Zuschauer, das man zu Shakespeares Zeit nicht zeigte?
10. Was hört man, wenn eine Lokomotive abfährt?

B. *Translate:*

1. Sie müssen sich vorstellen, Sie hören eine Kapelle schöne Walzer spielen.
2. Sie müssen die Stimme der Schauspieler mit dem geistigen Ohre hören.
3. Er war immer wie ein großer Herr angezogen.
4. Sie zeigte kein Verständnis für Musik.
5. Lassen Sie Herrn Murphy den Banditen spielen!
6. Sie hatte ein gut entwickeltes schauspielerisches Talent.
7. Das kann man sich sehr leicht vorstellen.
8. Sie ist ein reizendes Mädchen.
9. Er hat eine sehr komplizierte Rolle.
10. Wir hatten eben das Radio angestellt und wollten Tanzmusik hören, als Autobremsen vor unserem Hause quietschten.

C. *Rearrange and translate:*

1. sehr gut, die folgenden Aufgaben, dramatisch, sich, lassen, vorlesen.
2. eben, einen Tango, spielte, die Kapelle, als, man, eines Pferdes, hörte, das Galoppieren.
3. Sendestation, gestern, wir, spielten.
4. die Geschichte, dramatisch, lesen Sie . . . vor!
5. sich einbilden, Sie, müssen, Sie, knallende Revolverschüsse, hören.

D. *Correct the misinformation:*

1. Von Ihnen wird erwartet, daß Sie sich vorstellen, Sie wären Zuschauer in einem Theater zur Zeit Shakespeares.
2. Zur Zeit Shakespeares hatten die Zuschauer ein gut entwickeltes Verständnis für historisches Kostüm und Bühnenbild.
3. Shakespeares Römer waren genau so angezogen wie die großen Herren zur Zeit Julius Cäsars.
4. Das heutige Radiopublikum muß sich einbilden, daß es quietschende Autobremsen hört.
5. Im heutigen Theater sieht man Jungen in Frauenkleidern, die die reizende Ophelia spielen.

E. *Make a sentence by combining the first clause or phrase in each group with that one of the other clauses which best completes the sense of the first clause, and translate your sentence. Thus in the first group clause,* c *best completes the sentence.*

1. Wenn Sie Ihrer Einbildungskraft freien Lauf lassen,
   a. können Sie die reizende Ophelia hören.
   b. hören Sie die Stimme des Ansagers.
   c. können Sie die Musik mit dem geistigen Ohre hören.
2. Zur Zeit Shakespeares mußten Jungen in Frauenkleidern die Rollen der Frauen spielen,
   a. weil das Theaterpublikum noch kein Verständnis für historisches Kostüm entwickelt hatte.

b. weil Frauen sich nicht auf der Bühne zeigen durften.
c. weil sie ihrer Einbildungskraft freien Lauf lassen konnten.

3. Von Ihnen wird erwartet, daß Sie mit Phantasie ersetzen,
a. was Sie in den folgenden Aufgaben lesen werden.
b. was Sie auf der Bühne sehen.
c. was Sie im Klassenzimmer nicht nachmachen können.

4. Mit etwas schauspielerischem Talent
a. können Sie die folgenden Aufgaben dramatisch vorlesen.
b. werden Sie die Kapelle spielen hören.
c. denken Sie an die Zuschauer zur Zeit Shakespeares.

VI. Principal Parts: *Below are given the principal parts of strong and mixed verbs and of nouns appearing in this lesson. (For Ablaut classes see Appendix, § 35). Weak verbs and proper nouns are omitted.*

anziehen,	zog . . . an,	ich habe angezogen	dress
vorlesen,	las . . . vor,	ich habe vorgelesen	read aloud
abfahren,	fuhr . . . ab,	ich bin abgefahren	depart
lassen,	ließ,	ich habe gelassen	let, allow
heißen,	hieß,	ich habe geheißen	be named
sein,	war,	ich bin gewesen	be
müssen,	mußte,	ich habe gemußt	must, have to
können,	konnte,	ich habe gekonnt	be able
wollen,	wollte,	ich habe gewollt	want to
denken,	dachte,	ich habe gedacht	think

der Zuschauer, –s, —	spectator	die Bank, —, ¨e	bench
der Walzer, –s, —	waltz	das Pferd, –es, –e	horse
der Römer, –s, —	Roman	das Beispiel, –s, –e	example
der Revolver, –s, —	revolver	das Gefühl, –es, –e	feeling
der Ansager, –s, —	announcer	das Geräusch, –es, –e	noise, sound effect
der Redner, –s, —	speaker		
das Klassenzimmer, –s, —	classroom	das Talent, –s, –e	talent, ability
das Theater, –s, —	theater		
der Lauf, –es, ¨e	course, run	das Programm, –s, –e	program
der Dampf, –es, ¨e	steam	das Vorwort, –s, –e	foreword, preface
der Busch, –es, ¨e	bush		
der Thronsaal, –es,...säle	throne-room	das Kostüm, –s, –e	costume, costuming
der Spaß, –es, ¨e	fun		
der Revolverschuß, –es, ¨e	revolver shot	der Wald, –es, ¨er	woods, forest
der Regenschirm, –es, –e	umbrella	das Bühnenbild, –s, –er	scenery, staging
der Apparat, –s, –e	apparatus		

die Autobremse, —, –n	automobile brake	die Zeile, —, –n	line
die Autohupe, —, –n	automobile horn	die Königin, —, –nen	queen
die Bühne, —, –n	stage	die Tür, —, –en	door
die Geschichte, —, –n	history; story, tale	die Sendestation, —, –en	broadcasting station
die Kapelle, —, –n	orchestra	der Klassengenosse, –n, –n	classmate
die Lokomotive, —, –n	locomotive	der Junge, –n, –n	boy
die Rolle, —, –n	rôle, part	der Herr, –n, –en	Mr., gentleman, lord
die Rose, —, –n	rose	der Bandit, –en, –en	bandit
die Stimme, —, –n	voice	das Ohr, –es, –en	ear
		der Name, –ns, –n	name

VII. Securing the Vocabulary:

A.

sich vorstellen	(to) imagine	die Zeile	line
die Einbildungskraft	imagination	genau	exactly
das Geräusch	noise	damals	at that time
leicht	light, easy	das Verständnis	understanding
der Zuschauer	spectator	zeigen	(to) show
verlangen	(to) demand	die Stimme	voice
die Bühne	stage	nachmachen	(to) imitate
reizend	charming	sogar	even
		der Spaß	fun

B.

genug (9)	1. little, few	vielleicht (10)	6. first, only, not until
gewöhnlich (3)	2. soft, quiet	endlich (4)	7. late
brauchen (5)	3. usually	leise (2)	8. until, to
spät (7)	4. finally	erst (6)	9. enough
wenig (1)	5. need	bis (8)	10. perhaps

VIII. Sender G F S:

The rewritten texts contain nothing new in vocabulary and grammar. They are meant to be read rapidly.

Die Schauspieler, die zur Zeit Shakespeares den Venezianer Antonio oder den römischen Diktator Julius Cäsar spielten, waren angezogen wie Sir Walter Raleigh, Lord Essex und andere große Herren zur Zeit der Königin Elisabeth. Die damaligen Theaterdirektoren erwarteten sehr viel von der Phantasie ihres Publikums. Ein Busch auf der Bühne bedeutete einen Wald, und ein paar Bänke einen Thronsaal. Eine Frau spielt heute manchmal die Rolle eines jungen Mannes; aber was würden

moderne Zuschauer denken, wenn ein Junge in Julias Kleide rezitieren würde:

Was ist ein Name? Was uns Rose heißt,
Wie es auch hieße, würde lieblich duften.

Wir verlangen nicht zu viel von Ihnen, wenn Sie sich vorstellen müssen: Die Kapelle spielt einen argentinischen Tango; zwei Revolverschüsse knallen durch die Nacht; eine alte, rostige Tür quietscht; eine Frauenstimme singt „Stille Nacht, Heilige Nacht!" u. dgl. m.

Noch eins! Es wird Ihnen Spaß machen, die Radioprogramme zu dramatisieren, d.h. wenn Sie schauspielerisches Talent haben, werden Ihre Klassengenossen glauben, daß sie in einer Sendestation sind oder ein Radio hören. Sie brauchen keine komplizierten Apparate. Mit der Stimme, den Händen und Füßen kann man viele Geräusche nachmachen. Trommeln Sie z.B. auf einem Buch, und jeder kann sich vorstellen, daß er das Galoppieren eines Pferdes hört. Wenn Ihr Publikum etwas guten Willen zeigt, können Sie alles dramatisieren, was Sie in den folgenden Aufgaben lesen werden.

Achtzehnte Aufgabe

* * * \

finden, fand, ich habe gefunden	(to) find
* werfen, warf, ich habe geworfen	(to) throw
wollen, wollte, ich habe gewollt	(to) want to
Finden Sie abends die Briefe in der * Tasche, die Sie morgens in den Briefkasten werfen wollten?	In the evening do you find those letters in your pocket that you intended to put in the mail-box in the morning?
In dem * Fall wird Ihnen der Doktor vielleicht sagen, daß Sie nervös′ sind und Ruhe brauchen.	In that case perhaps the doctor will tell you that you are nervous and need rest.
Wahrschein′lich schlafen Sie nicht genug.	Probably you are not sleeping enough.
* Untersu′chen Sie einmal Ihre Matrat′ze!	Just examine your mattress!
Wahrschein′lich ist sie zu hart.	Probably it is too hard.
* nötig haben	(to) have need of
sie haben Schlaf nötig	they need sleep
Ein Mann, der so viel arbeitet wie Sie, eine Hausfrau, die den ganzen Tag auf den Beinen ist, ein junges Mädchen, das acht Stunden im Geschäft hinter dem Ladentisch steht oder im Büro′ hinter der Schreibmaschine sitzt, alle diese Leute haben viel Schlaf nötig.	A man who works as much as you, a housewife who is on her feet all day, a young girl who stands for eight hours behind the counter in a store or sits at a typewriter in the office, all these people need a great deal of sleep.
* Versuchen Sie einmal unsere Traumulus Matrat′ze!	Just try our Traumulus Mattress!
liegen, lag, ich habe gelegen	(to) lie, recline
Sie liegen wie auf einer * weichen Wolke.	You will rest as though on a soft cloud.
Vergessen Sie nicht!	Don't forget!
Kein wirklich tiefer Schlaf ohne Traumulus Matrat′ze!	No really sound sleep without a Traumulus Mattress!
* bestehen, bestand, es hat bestanden	(to) consist
die Federn bestehen aus Stahl	the springs consist of steel
* Trotz aller Vorzüge und trotz des erstklassigen Stahles, aus dem die	In spite of all the excellences and in spite of the first-class steel the nu-

* zahlreichen Federn bestehen, ist eine Traumulus Matrat'ze kein Lu'xusarti'kel.	merous springs are made of, a Traumulus Mattress is no luxury article.
klein	small, little
der kleine Mann	the little man
Auch der kleine Mann kann sich einen tiefen, ruhigen Schlaf leisten.	Even the man on the street can afford a sound, restful sleep.
Traumulus Matrat'zen können Sie in * irgendeinem Möbelgeschäft kaufen.	You can buy Traumulus Mattresses in any furniture store.
der Reim, -es, -e	rhyme, jingle
Denken Sie an den Reim: Schlafen Sie auf Traumulus, Ist der Schlaf ein Hochgenuß.	Think of the jingle: If you sleep on Traumulus, sleep is a rare delight.
Die Musik' beginnt, leise und innig ein Schlummerlied zu spielen.	The music begins to play a lullaby softly and tenderly.
* Während die Musik' noch spielt, hört man ein furchtbares Gehuste.	While the music is still playing a terrific outburst of coughing is heard.
als ob	as if
Es * klingt, als ob ein hungriger Seehund seinen Wärter anbellt.	It sounds as though a hungry seal is barking at its keeper.
Dann hört man die * ärgerliche Stimme einer Dame:	Then one hears the irritated voice of a lady:
„Da hustet Onkel Julius wieder und weckt die ganze Fami'lie auf.	"There Uncle Julius is coughing again and he'll wake up the whole family.
* nehmen, nahm, ich habe genommen	(to) take
er nimmt	he takes
Warum nimmt er nicht Bron'chophil' Hustenbonbons?	Why doesn't he take Bronchophil cough drops?
Bron'chophil' Hu'stenbonbons' sind so preiswert!	Bronchophil cough drops are so reasonable!
Eine ganze Schachtel mit fünfzig Hu'stenbonbons' kostet nur fünfundzwanzig Cent!	A whole box of fifty cough drops costs only twenty-five cents!
Ich werde ihm eine Schachtel kaufen und neben das Bett legen."	I am going to buy him a box and put it beside his bed."

II. Text:

Etwas Reklame

Eine begeisterte, energische Stimme: Ein zerstreuter Professor lief auf der Straße gegen einen kleinen Jungen. Der Junge fiel hin und fing an zu weinen. Der gutmütige Professor hob das Kind auf, streichelte ihm die Backen und fragte: „Wie heißt du, Kleiner?" Der Kleine hörte auf zu weinen und sagte erstaunt: „Aber Papa, kennst du mich denn nicht?" — Sind Sie auch zerstreut? Vergessen Sie Ihren Regenschirm? Öffnen Sie die Haustür, wenn Ihr Telephon klingelt? Finden Sie abends die Briefe in der Tasche, die Sie morgens in den Briefkasten werfen wollten? In dem Fall wird Ihnen der Doktor vielleicht sagen, daß Sie nervös sind und Ruhe brauchen. Wahrscheinlich schlafen Sie nicht genug. Untersuchen Sie einmal Ihre Matratze! Wahrscheinlich ist sie zu hart. Ein Mann, der so viel arbeitet wie Sie, eine Hausfrau, die den ganzen Tag auf den Beinen ist, ein junges Mädchen, das acht Stunden im Geschäft hinter dem Ladentisch steht oder im Büro hinter der Schreibmaschine sitzt, alle diese Leute haben viel Schlaf nötig. Versuchen Sie einmal unsere Traumulus Matratze! Sie liegen wie auf einer weichen Wolke. Vergessen Sie nicht! Kein wirklich tiefer Schlaf ohne Traumulus Matratze! Trotz aller Vorzüge und trotz des erstklassigen Stahles, aus dem die zahlreichen Federn bestehen, ist eine Traumulus Matratze kein Luxusartikel. Auch der kleine Mann kann

sich einen tiefen, ruhigen Schlaf leisten. Traumulus Matratzen können Sie in irgendeinem Möbelgeschäft kaufen. Denken Sie an den Reim:

Schlafen Sie auf Traumulus,
Ist der Schlaf ein Hochgenuß.

Die Musik beginnt, leise und innig ein Schlummerlied zu spielen. Während die Musik noch spielt, hört man ein furchtbares Gehuste. Es klingt, als ob ein hungriger Seehund seinen Wärter anbellt. Dann hört man die ärgerliche Stimme einer Dame: „Da hustet Onkel Julius wieder und weckt die ganze Familie auf. Warum nimmt er nicht Bronchophil Hustenbonbons? Bronchophil Hustenbonbons sind so preiswert! Eine ganze Schachtel mit fünfzig Hustenbonbons kostet nur fünfundzwanzig Cent! Ich werde ihm eine Schachtel kaufen und neben das Bett legen."

III. Comments:

1. *The Simple Past Tense of Strong Verbs:*

In the preceding unit we took up the simple past tense of weak verbs, a very large group whose important characteristic is the use of the tense sign –t– in the formation of the simple past tense and the perfect participle.

A much smaller but very important group of verbs is known as strong verbs. Their important characteristic is that they change the vowel of the stem in the formation of the simple past tense and the past participle. Thus: springen, sprang, gesprungen; sprechen, sprach, gesprochen. This change of vowel, known as Ablaut, is the characteristic feature of the English strong verb as: *speak, spoke, spoken; begin, began, begun.* (*For German Ablaut classes see Appendix* § 35)

An additional characteristic, with which you are already familiar, is the modification of the stem vowel of some verbs in the second and third persons singular of the present tense and in the singular imperative. Thus: ich spreche, du sprichst, er spricht; sprich! The principal parts of strong verbs will therefore include the present tense third person singular: springen, sprang, ich bin gesprungen, er springt; sprechen, sprach, ich habe gesprochen, er spricht.

All strong verbs end in the simple past tense as does the following verb:

ich sprach	I spoke, I was speaking
du sprachst	*etc.*
er, sie, es sprach	
wir sprachen	
ihr sprach	
sie sprachen	
Sie sprachen	

2. *Subordinating Conjunctions:*

Subordinating conjunctions introduce dependent clauses and require transposed word order; *i.e.* the inflected part of the verb goes to the end. Example: Sie schlafen nicht gut, weil Ihre Matratze zu hart ist. *You don't sleep well because your mattress is too hard.*

So far you have had the following subordinating conjunctions: als — *when;* bevor — *before;* da — *since (causal);* daß — *that;* trotzdem — *in spite of the fact that;* während — *while;* weil — *because;* wenn — *if; when, whenever.* (*For complete list see Appendix* § 7)

IV. Practice:

1. a. Ein zerstreuter Professor läuft gegen eine Bank.
   Radioansager
   Schauspieler einen Jungen.
   b. Ein zerstreuter Professor lief gegen eine Bank.
   etc.

2. a. Der Junge, der hingefallen ist, fängt an zu weinen.
   Der Kleine
   Das Mädchen, das
   Die Kleine, die
   b. Der Junge, der hingefallen war, fing an zu weinen.
   etc.

3. a. Sehen Sie nur, wie schnell unser Freund läuft!
   der Fußballspieler
   der kleine Junge
   b. Ich sah, wie schnell unser Freund lief.
   etc.

4. Mein Freund und ich gingen immer zusammen zur Universität.
   sprachen immer viel über das Theater.
   fingen an, ärgerlich zu werden.
   Mein Freund und ich hoben den kleinen Jungen auf, der eben hingefallen war.

5. Die Aufgaben ließen sich dramatisch vorlesen.
   Geschichten sehr gut dramatisieren.

6. a. Sie arbeiten
   den ganzen Tag.
   im Geschäft.
   oder im Büro.
   b. Sie haben Schlaf nötig.
   tiefen und ruhigen Schlaf nötig.
   jede Nacht tiefen und ruhigen Schlaf nötig.
   c. Wenn Sie den ganzen Tag im Geschäft oder im Büro arbeiten, haben Sie jede Nacht tiefen und ruhigen Schlaf nötig.

7. a. Die Federn bestehen aus Stahl.
   Die vielen Federn bestehen aus erstklassigem Stahl.
   Die vielen Federn der Traumulus Matratze bestehen aus erstklassigem Stahl.
   b. Sie können sich eine Traumulus Matratze leisten.
   c. Obwohl die vielen Federn der Traumulus Matratze aus erstklassigem Stahl bestehen, können Sie sich eine Traumulus Matratze leisten.

8. a. Versuchen Sie einmal Bronchophil!
die preiswerten Hustenbonbons!
Versuchen Sie einmal eine Schachtel Bronchophil, die preiswerten Hustenbonbons!

b. Sie husten wieder.
wie ein hungriger Seehund.
Sie husten wieder wie ein hungriger Seehund und wecken die ganze Familie auf.

c. Wenn Sie eine Schachtel Bronchophil, die preiswerten Hustenbonbons, versuchen, werden Sie nie wieder wie ein hungriger Seehund husten und die ganze Familie aufwecken.

9. a. Die Musik spielt.
leise und innig.
das bekannte Schlummerlied.
Die Musik spielt leise und innig das bekannte Schlummerlied von Brahms.

b. Man hört zwei Revolverschüsse.
knallende Revolverschüsse.

c. Während die Musik leise und innig das bekannte Schlummerlied von Brahms spielt, hört man zwei knallende Revolverschüsse.

V. Exercises:

A. *Questions:*

1. Warum weinte der Kleine?
2. Was tat der Professor, um das Kind zu trösten?
3. Wer war der Kleine?
4. Wer legt den Regenschirm ins Bett und stellt sich in die Ecke?
5. Was sollte man mit Briefen tun, die man morgens in die Tasche steckt?
6. Warum sind viele Leute so nervös?
7. Welchen Fehler haben viele Matratzen?
8. Wie schläft man auf einer Traumulusmatratze?
9. Aus welchem Material bestehen die Federn der Matratze?
10. Welchen Fehler hat Onkel Julius?
11. Was tut ein Seehund, wenn er den Wärter mit den Fischen kommen sieht?

B. *Translate:*

1. Er untersuchte die Schreibmaschine, konnte aber nichts finden.
2. Die Musik begann, leise und innig das bekannte Schlummerlied von Brahms zu spielen.
3. Er schlief jede Nacht neun Stunden.
4. Als das Drama begann, stand der nervöse Schauspieler auf der Bühne und wußte nicht, was die ersten Worte seiner Rolle waren.
5. Traumulus Matratzen werden in jedem Möbelgeschäft verkauft.
6. Es klingt, als ob ein kleines Kind weint.
7. Der Doktor sagte mir, daß ich jede Nacht neun Stunden schlafen sollte.
8. Obgleich der zerstreute Professor seinen Regenschirm vergessen hatte, lief er durch den Regen zur Klasse.

C. *Rearrange and translate:*

1. ein Mann, der, arbeitet, im Büro, den ganzen Tag, viel Schlaf, hat, nötig.
2. meinen Regenschirm, im Büro, ich, vergessen, habe.
3. wenn, auf Traumulus, Sie, schlafen, der Schlaf, ein Hochgenuß, ist.
4. Bronchophil Hustenbonbons, in jeder Drogerie, Sie, kaufen, können.
5. als, aufhob, das Kind, der gutmütige Onkel Julius, es, hörte — auf, zu weinen.
6. während, das bekannte Schlummerlied, die Musik, spielte, er, schlief, wie auf einer weichen Wolke.
7. nervös, Sie, sind, weil, nicht genug, schlafen, Sie.
8. klingt, das, ein hustender Seehund, wie.

D. *Correct the misinformation:*

1. Ein zerstreuter Theaterdirektor lief auf der Straße gegen einen kleinen Jungen.
2. Die Kleine sagte erstaunt: „Aber Papa, kennst du mich denn nicht?"
3. Wenn Sie jeden Tag acht Stunden arbeiten, haben Sie wenig Schlaf nötig.
4. Die Musik begann, leise und innig ein Liebeslied zu spielen.
5. Während die Musik noch spielte, hörte man die ärgerliche Stimme des Ansagers.

E. *Complete the following sentences by means of the suitable clause or phrase:*

1. Der Junge fing an zu weinen,
   a. weil er nervös war und Ruhe brauchte.
   b. weil Bronchophil Hustenbonbons so preiswert sind.
   c. obgleich er im Möbelgeschäft arbeitete.
2. Wenn Sie acht Stunden im Büro hinter der Schreibmaschine sitzen,
   a. wird von Ihnen verlangt, daß Sie Ihrer Einbildungskraft freien Lauf lassen.
   b. entwickeln Sie ein Gefühl für historisches Kostüm.
   c. werden Sie leicht nervös.
3. Wenn Sie Bronchophil Hustenbonbons versuchen,
   a. werden Sie eine Schachtel in jedem größeren Geschäft kaufen können.
   b werden Sie nie wieder wie ein hungriger Seehund husten.
   c hört man furchtbares Gehuste.
4. Während ich noch schlief,
   a war die Traumulus Matratze ein Luxusartikel.
   b. arbeitete ich acht Stunden im Geschäft.
   c. fuhr die Lokomotive zischend ab.
5. Nachdem sie den ganzen Tag hinter dem Ladentisch gestanden hatte,
   a. wollte sie nicht nach Hause und zu Bett gehen.
   b. ging sie ins Theater und sah sich das berühmte Drama von Schiller an, das eben im Kleinen Theater spielte.

F. *Connect the following pairs of sentences by means of the conjunction indicated and translate:*

1. (da) since

   Wir stellen das Radio an.
   Wir wollen deutsche Programme hören.

Write out

2. (wenn)

Sie wollen wie auf einer weichen Wolke schlafen.
Sie müssen in ein Möbelgeschäft gehen und sich eine Traumulus Matratze kaufen.

3. (während)

Ich sah den Banditen mit dem Direktor sprechen.
Ich saß im Büro hinter der Schreibmaschine.

4. (als)

Ich war vor zwei Jahren in Chicago.
Ich wurde einem berühmten Professor vorgestellt.

5. (obgleich)

Dieses erstklassige Produkt hat viele Vorzüge.
Es ist sehr preiswert.

VI. Principal Parts: *In this and the following lessons the principal parts of all strong and mixed verbs appearing in the lesson are given; however, only those nouns are listed whose principal parts have not been listed in previous lessons.*

aufheben,	hob . . . auf,	ich habe aufgehoben,	er hebt . . . auf	pick up
finden,	fand,	ich habe gefunden,	er findet	find
klingen,	klang,	ich habe geklungen,	er klingt	sound
werfen,	warf,	ich habe geworfen,	er wirft	throw
nehmen,	nahm,	ich habe genommen,	er nimmt	take
beginnen,	begann,	ich habe begonnen,	er beginnt	begin
vergessen,	vergaß,	ich habe vergessen,	er vergißt	forget
liegen,	lag,	ich habe gelegen,	er liegt	lie, recline
anfangen,	fing . . . an,	ich habe angefangen,	er fängt . . . an	begin
hinfallen,	fiel . . . hin,	ich bin hingefallen,	er fällt . . . hin	fall down
laufen,	lief,	ich bin gelaufen,	er läuft	run
heißen,	hieß,	ich habe geheißen,	er heißt	be named, be called
stehen,	stand,	ich habe gestanden,	er steht	stand
bestehen,	bestand,	es hat bestanden,	es besteht	consist, exist
sein,	war,	ich bin gewesen,	er ist	be
können,	konnte,	ich habe gekonnt,	er kann	can, be able
wollen,	wollte,	ich habe gewollt,	er will	want to
kennen,	kannte,	ich habe gekannt,	er kennt	know
denken,	dachte,	ich habe gedacht,	er denkt	think

der Briefkasten, –s, ¨	mail-box	das Gehuste, –s	coughing
der Garten, –s, ¨	garden	der Fall, –es, ¨e	case
der Onkel, –s, —	uncle	der Reim, –es, –e	rhyme
der Wärter, –s, —	keeper, guard	der Seehund, –es, –e	seal
		der Ladentisch, –es, –e	counter

der Beruf, –es, –e	occupation	die Matratze, —, –n	mattress
der Vorzug, –es, ⸗e	excellence	die Stunde, —, –n	hour
das Bein, –es, –e	leg	die Tasche, —, –n	pocket
das Geschäft, –es, –e	store	die Wolke, —, –n	cloud
das Möbelgeschäft, –es, –e	furniture store	die Schachtel, —, –n	box
		die Feder, —, –n	pen, spring
das Haus, –es, ⸗er	house	die Haustür, —, –en	front door
das Kind, –es, –er	child	die Hausfrau, —, –en	housewife
das Schlummerlied, –es, –er	lullaby	der Doktor, –s, –en	doctor
		der Professor, –s, –en	professor
die Backe, —, –n	cheek	das Interesse, –s, –n	interest
die Reklame, —, –n	advertisement	der Cent, –s, –s	cent
		das Büro, –s, –s	office
die Schreibmaschine, —, –n	typewriter	der Papa, –s, –s	papa
die Straße, —, –n	street		

VII. Securing the Vocabulary: 17, 18, 19 vocabulary test

A.

begeistert	enthusiastic	versuchen	(to) try
aufheben	(to) pick up	weich	soft
aufhören	(to) stop	bestehen	(to) consist, exist
klingeln	(to) ring	trotz	in spite of
werfen	(to) throw	zahlreich	numerous
die Tasche	pocket	irgendein	any
der Fall	case	während (*conj.*)	while
untersuchen	(to) examine	(*prep.*)	during
nötig haben	(to) need	ärgerlich	angry, irritable
nehmen	(to) take	klingen	(to) sound

B.

das Geräusch (1)	1. noise	verlangen (4)	1. show
leicht (3)	2. even	zeigen (1)	2. line
sogar (2)	3. light, easy	jetzt (8)	3. imagine
die Bühne (5)	4. fun	sich vorstellen (3)	4. demand
die Stimme (9)	5. stage	die Zeile (2)	5. today
die Einbildungskraft (7)	6. imitate	besonders (7)	6. every time
		heute (5)	7. especially
der Spaß (4)	7. imagination	jedesmal (6)	8. now
damals (10)	8. charming	kaufen (10)	9. spectator
nachmachen (6)	9. voice	der Zuschauer (9)	10. buy
reizend (8)	10. at that time		

VIII. Etwas Reklame: *(Rewritten)*

Sie kennen die Geschichte vom zerstreuten Professor, der sich in die Ecke stellte und seinen Regenschirm ins Bett legte. Die folgende Anekdote aber kennen Sie wahrscheinlich nicht: Professor Goodrich hatte in seinem alten Anzug im Garten gearbeitet und kam zu seinem Hause zurück. Vor der Haustür stand ein Herr, der den Professor nicht kannte, und sagte: „Herr Goodrich ist nicht zu Hause. Ich habe schon zweimal geklingelt." „Professor Goodrich ist nicht zu Hause?" sagte der Professor erstaunt. „Ja, dann müssen wir warten." Mit diesen Worten hob er die Zeitung auf, die vor der Haustür lag, und begann sie mit Interesse zu lesen.

Sie sind kein Professor und können sich wahrscheinlich so eine Zerstreutheit nicht leisten. Ihre Zerstreutheit ist Nervosität, und Sie sind nervös, weil Sie nicht genug schlafen. Sie sitzen acht Stunden im Büro, Sie arbeiten in einem Geschäft, vielleicht sind Sie Hausfrau und sind den ganzen Tag auf den Beinen, vielleicht sind Sie Bürofräulein und sitzen den ganzen Tag hinter einer Schreibmaschine. — In all diesen Fällen haben Sie viel Schlaf nötig. Auf einer harten Matratze können Sie aber nicht so gut schlafen wie auf einer weichen. Nur eine weiche Matratze gibt Ihnen den wirklich tiefen Schlaf, den Sie brauchen. Eine wirklich weiche Matratze ist nun die Traumulus Matratze. Dieses erstklassige Produkt hat viele Vorzüge. Die zahlreichen Federn z.B. bestehen aus feinstem Stahl. Gehen Sie in irgendein Möbelgeschäft und fragen Sie nach dem Preis unserer Matratzen! Sie werden erstaunt sein, wie wenig Sie zu zahlen brauchen. Vergessen Sie nicht: „Wie man sein Bett macht, so schläft man."

(Ein Schlummerlied wird leise und innig gespielt, dann hört man ein furchtbares Gehuste.) Das war kein hungriger Seehund, der seinen Wärter anbellt, das war Onkel Julius, der die ganze Familie mit seinem Husten aufweckt. Onkel Julius ist ein gutmütiger Mann. Wenn ein kleines Kind auf der Straße hinfällt, hebt er es auf, streichelt ihm die Backen und gibt ihm Schokolade. Trotzdem ist aber die ganze Familie ärgerlich auf Onkel Julius. Die Familie Meier arbeitet den ganzen Tag und braucht viel Schlaf. Warum hat Onkel Julius keine Bronchophil Hustenbonbons neben dem Bette? Eine Schachtel Hustenbonbons ist wirklich so preiswert! Sogar Onkel Julius könnte sie sich leisten.

Neunzehnte Aufgabe

* * * \

aufsteigen, stieg . . . auf, es ist aufgestiegen, es steigt . . . auf	(to) rise
Eine furchtbare Angst steigt in ihm auf.	A horrible fear rises in him.
* ähnlich	similar
sehen, sah, ich habe gesehen, er sieht	(to) see
er sieht ihm ähnlich	he resembles him
Die Schrift auf dem Zettel ist nicht die Handschrift seiner Frau; sie sieht ihr nur ähnlich.	The writing on the note is not his wife's handwriting; it only resembles it.
Er läuft ins Schlafzimmer, er sieht unter die Betten, unter die Kommo'de; er läuft in die Küche und da, unter dem Küchentisch . . .	He runs into the bedroom, he looks under the beds, under the dresser; he runs into the kitchen and there, under the kitchen table . . .
. . . bericht für morgen.	. . . report for tomorrow.
Im südlichen * Teil des Staates wärmer und Regen.	In the southern part of the state, warmer and rain.
Im Norden kühler, * teilweise bewölkt, leichter Schnee.	In the north, cooler, partly cloudy, light snow.
Dieser Wetterbericht . . .	This weather report . . .
. . . keine Seife.	. . . no soap.
auffallen, fiel . . . auf, ist aufgefallen, er fällt . . . auf	(to) strike the attention
es fällt mir auf	it strikes my attention
welcher, welche, welches	which, what
der Wert, –es, –e	the worth, value
legen, legte, ich habe gelegt, er legt	(to) lay, place
er legt Wert auf schöne Hände	he values lovely hands
Ist es Ihnen * schon einmal aufgefallen, welchen Wert Männer auf schöne, gepflegte Frauenhände legen?	Have you ever noticed how much men admire lovely, well-cared-for women's hands?
Wir wissen, Sie müssen täglich das Geschirr spülen, die Treppe fegen, Kartof'feln schälen und all die anderen Hausarbeiten tun.	We know you have to wash the dishes every day, sweep the stairs, peel potatoes, and do all the other housework.

aussehen, sah . . . aus, ich habe ausgesehen, er sieht . . . aus	(to) look, appear
Sehen Ihre Hände rot aus?	Do your hands look red?
Verlieren Sie nicht den * Mut!	Don't lose courage!
* Der Unterschied zwischen Schneewittchen Schönheitskrem und gewöhnlicher Hautkrem . . .	The difference between Snow White Beauty Cream and ordinary skin cream . . .
eingebaut	built-in
Lügen Sie nicht! Wir wissen, daß Ihr Mann hier * irgendwo im Hause einen eingebauten Geldschrank hat, in dem große Geldsummen sind.	Don't lie! We know that your husband has a wall-safe here somewhere in the house, in which are large sums of money.
(Eine weinerliche Frauenstimme)	(*A weepy woman's voice*)
Martern Sie mich, tun Sie, was Sie wollen, Sie * feiger Tunichtgut!	Torture me, do what you like, you cowardly good-for-nothing!
Wie recht mein Mann hatte, daß er Sie aus seiner Bank gejagt hat!	How right my husband was to throw you out of his bank!
Reden Sie keinen Unsinn! Sie machen sich * lächerlich mit Ihrem Herois'mus. Wir haben andere Mittel.	Don't talk nonsense! You are making yourself ridiculous with your heroism. We have other means.
. . . Neu Yorker Börse.	. . . New York Stock Exchange.
Versuchen wir festzustellen, warum die Preise für Schweinefleisch in den letzten Monaten um zehn Prozent' gefallen sind. Wir müssen * zunächst' * annehmen, . . .	Let us try to determine why the price of pork has fallen by ten percent in the last months. We must first of all assume . . .
(Ein Tenor' singt zärtlich)	(*A tenor sings tenderly*)
der Schatz, –es, ¨e	treasure; sweetheart
Umarm' mich, du süßer umarm'barer Schatz;	Embrace me, you sweet embraceable sweetheart;
Umarm' mich, du Süße, für die kein Ersatz!	embrace me, you sweet girl, for whom there is no substitute.

. . . eben Mozarts „Eine kleine Nacht'-musik'" gehört.	. . . just heard Mozart's "A Little Serenade."
Nun bringen wir Ihnen Tanz'musik' der Unsterblichen.	Now we will bring you Dance Music of the Immortals.
Wir spielen zuerst' den berühmten Walzer von Strauß „An der schönen, blauen Donau" . . .	We will first play the famous waltz by Strauss "On the beautiful blue Danube" . . .
hereinkommen, kam . . . herein, ich bin hereingekommen, er kommt . . . herein	(to) come in
er komme herein!	let him come in!
„Er komme herein!" sagte der König und stand vom Throne auf.	"Let him come in!" said the king and got up from his throne.
. . . und wißt ihr, was der große Teddybär zu dem kleinen Teddybär sagte?	. . . and do you know what the big Teddy Bear said to the little Teddy Bear?
Das werden wir euch morgen erzählen, Kinder, und wenn ihr recht artig seid, wird Mama . . .	We'll tell you that tomorrow, children, and if you are real good, Mother will . . .

II. Text:

Von einer Welle zur andern

... zurück zu unserer Geschichte „Der Mann ohne Seele" — Percy Flaggins, einer der Verkäufer des Möbelgeschäfts „Henning und Noyes" steht in seinem Wohnzimmer vor dem Schreibtisch und liest einen Zettel, auf dem steht: „Wenn Du mich wiedersehen willst, mußt Du mir erklären, woher all das Geld kam, das Du beim Pferderennen verloren hast, während ich mir ein Radio auf Abzahlung kaufen mußte. Wenn Du wissen willst, wo ich bin, schreib Mutter in Kalifornien. Noch besser wäre es, wenn ..." Percy liest nicht weiter. Eine furchtbare Angst steigt in ihm auf. Die Schrift auf dem Zettel ist nicht die Handschrift seiner Frau; sie sieht ihr nur ähnlich. Er läuft ins Schlafzimmer, er sieht unter die Betten, unter die Kommode; er läuft in die Küche, und da, unter dem Küchentisch ..... bericht für morgen. Im südlichen Teil des Staates wärmer und Regen. Im Norden kühler, teilweise bewölkt, leichter Schnee. Dieser Wetterbericht...

... keine Seife. Ist es Ihnen schon einmal aufgefallen, welchen Wert Männer auf schöne, gepflegte Frauenhände legen? Wir wissen, Sie müssen täglich das Geschirr spülen, die Treppe fegen, Kartoffeln schälen und all die anderen Hausarbeiten

tun. Sehen Ihre Hände rot aus? Verlieren Sie nicht den Mut! Der Unterschied zwischen Schneewittchen Schönheitskrem und gewöhnlicher Hautkrem. . .

Lügen Sie nicht! Wir wissen, daß Ihr Mann hier irgendwo im Hause einen eingebauten Geldschrank hat, in dem große Geldsummen sind. (Eine weinerliche Frauenstimme). Martern Sie mich, tun Sie, was Sie wollen, Sie feiger Tunichtgut! Wie recht mein Mann hatte, daß er Sie aus seiner Bank gejagt hat! — Reden Sie keinen Unsinn! Sie machen sich lächerlich mit Ihrem Heroismus. Wir haben andere Mittel.

. . . Neu Yorker Börse. Versuchen wir festzustellen, warum die Preise für Schweinefleisch in den letzten Monaten um zehn Prozent gefallen sind. Wir müssen zunächst annehmen, . . .

(Ein Tenor singt zärtlich)

Umarm mich, du süßer, umarmbarer Schatz;
Umarm mich, du Süße, für die kein Ersatz.

. . . eben Mozarts „Eine kleine Nachtmusik" gehört. Nun bringen wir Ihnen Tanzmusik der Unsterblichen. Wir spielen zuerst den berühmten Walzer von Strauß „An der schönen, blauen Donau" . . .

„Er komme herein!" sagte der König und stand vom Throne auf.

. . . und wißt ihr, was der große Teddybär zu dem kleinen Teddybär sagte? Das werden wir euch morgen erzählen, Kinder, und wenn ihr recht artig seid, wird Mama . . .

III. Comments:

1. *Formation of the Imperative:*

The familiar plural imperative is the same as the familiar plural present indicative. Notice that those strong verbs which change e to i or ie in the second and third persons singular of the present indicative retain this change in the familiar singular imperative. Thus the complete imperative paradigms of the verbs sein, haben, werden, arbeiten, fallen, gehen, sehen, and geben are:

command or request

Familiar singular	*Familiar plural*	*Conventional singular and plural*
sei!	seid!	seien Sie!
habe!	habt!	haben Sie!
werde!	werdet!	werden Sie!
arbeite!	arbeitet!	arbeiten Sie!
falle!	fallt!	fallen Sie!
geh!	geht!	gehen Sie!
sieh!	seht!	sehen Sie!
gib!	gebt!	geben Sie!

used with those with whom you are on intimate terms

don't use pronoun

2. *Present Subjunctive I:* Indirect discourse usually.

In lesson XIV you learned that there are two types of subjunctives which we call subjunctive I and subjunctive II. And you have also learned some of the uses of subjunctive II. The use of the present subjunctive I in direct discourse is restricted very largely to a few pious formulas and to imperatives in the third person singular and first person plural in formal language. For example: Gott sei Dank! *Thanks be to God!* Er komme herein! *Let him come in!* Versuchen wir festzustellen, warum die Preise gefallen sind! *Let us try to determine why the prices have fallen.*

present stem. with usual subjunctive endings: -e, est, e, en, et, en.

IV. Practice:

1. a. Ich lese gerade den Wetterbericht in der Zeitung.
   Er liest
   Wir lesen

   b. Ich las gerade den Wetterbericht in der Zeitung.
   Er las
   Wir lasen

2. Stellen wir zuerst fest, warum die Preise um fünf Prozent gefallen sind!
   wieviel Geld er schon verloren hat!
   welchen Wert das Radiopublikum auf gute Musik legt!

3. a. Verstehst du, was der Ansager sagt?
   was der Tenor singt?
   warum die Preise gefallen sind?

   b. Versteht ihr, was der Ansager sagt?

4. Ist es Ihnen schon einmal aufgefallen, wie oft dieser Walzer gespielt wird?
   Ist es dir
   Ist es euch

5. Schält zuerst Kartoffeln und dann fegt die Treppe, Kinder! sweep
   Spült zuerst das Geschirr und dann tut die anderen Hausarbeiten, Kinder!

6. Gott sei Dank, daß es endlich kühler wird!
   wärmer

7. Wißt ihr, was der große Teddybär zum kleinen Teddybär sagte?
   Könnt ihr mir erzählen, . . .
   Wollt ihr wissen, . . .
   Habt ihr gelesen, . . .

8. a. Nehmen wir an, daß die Preise um zehn Prozent gefallen sind.
   Nehmen wir an, daß die Frage beantwortet werden kann.
   das Barometer noch immer fällt.
   Nehmen wir an, daß AB eine Seite des Vierecks (*quadrangle*) ABCD ist.

   b. AB sei die Seite eines Vierecks ABCD!

9. a. Der große Teddybär untersuchte die Matratze.
   Der große Teddybär untersuchte die Matratze und fand Goldhaar in seinem Bett.
   b. Das erzählen wir euch morgen.
   c. Morgen werden wir euch erzählen, wie der große Teddybär die Matratze untersuchte und Goldhaar in seinem Bett fand.
10. a. Ich laufe aus der Küche ins Schlafzimmer.
   Er läuft
   Ihr lauft
   b. Ich lief aus der Küche ins Schlafzimmer.
   Er lief
   Ihr lieft
11. Hast du beim Pferderennen viel Geld verloren?
   Habt ihr
   Haben Sie

V. Exercises:

A. *Questions:*

1. Was hat Percy Flaggins seiner Frau nie erklärt?
2. Wie kann das Publikum wissen, daß er seiner Frau nicht viel Geld gibt?
3. Wie kann Percy Flaggins die Adresse seiner Frau bekommen?
4. Warum steigt eine furchtbare Angst in Percy auf?
5. Was für Möbel stehen in einem Schlafzimmer?
6. Was für Wetter haben wir heute?
7. Was für Hausarbeiten muß eine Hausfrau tun?
8. Um wieviel sind die Preise für Schweinefleisch in den letzten Monaten gefallen?
9. Zu welcher Komposition kann man besser tanzen: „Eine kleine Nachtmusik" oder „An der schönen blauen Donau"?
10. Was ist ein gutes Weihnachtsgeschenk für einen kleinen Jungen, der etwa drei Jahre alt ist?

B. *Translate:*

1. Ist es euch schon einmal aufgefallen, wie oft dieser Walzer gespielt wird?
2. Sie legt viel Wert darauf, daß ihre Kinder all die Hausarbeiten tun können.
3. „Er komme!", sagte der alte Sioux und hob seinen Tomahawk auf.
4. Wenn er den Mut nicht verloren hätte, so hätte er sicher gewonnen.
5. Wißt ihr, was der Unterschied zwischen Schneewittchen Schönheitskrem und gewöhnlicher Hautkrem ist?
6. Wenn ihr artiger wäret, würde euch Mama das erzählen, Kinder.
7. Der Bandit stand vor dem Geldschrank und zog den Revolver.
8. Der Verkäufer sah todmüde aus.

C. *Rearrange and translate:*

1. sich vorstellen, müssen, Sie, daß, ein alter Bankdirektor, ist, Herr Wilhite.
2. mir, ansehen, möchte, ich, dieses Bild.
3. verloren . . . hätte, so viel Geld, wenn, beim Pferderennen, er, nicht, so, wäre . . . gereist, vor drei Wochen, er, nach Schweden.
4. wenn, wäre, ein Mann, er, so, seine Freunde, er, hätte . . . verraten, nicht.
5. wenn, könnten, verstehen, wir, nur, was, sagt, der Ansager!
6. wissen Sie, warum, in den letzten Tagen, gestiegen sind, für Schweinefleisch, die Preise?
7. Sie, Schneewittchen Seife, gebrauchen, wenn, Ihre Hände, werden, aussehen, schön und gepflegt.

D. *Correct the misinformation:*

1. Eine furchtbare Angst stieg in Percy Flaggins auf. Die Schrift auf dem Zettel war die Handschrift seiner Frau.
2. Ein furchtbares Husten macht es beinah unmöglich zu verstehen, was der Ansager über Schneewittchen Schönheitskrem sagt.
3. Die Frau des Bankdirektors zeigt den Banditen den Geldschrank.
4. Die Preise für Schweinefleisch sind in den letzten Monaten um zehn Prozent gefallen.
5. Ein Tenor singt zärtlich: „Schlafen Sie auf Traumulus, ist der Schlaf ein Hochgenuß."

E. *Complete by means of the suitable clause or phrase. Translate:*

1. Während Fräulein Erlach die Treppe fegte,
   a. schälte sie Kartoffeln.
   b. fielen die Preise für Schweinefleisch um zehn Prozent.
   c. sang sie begeistert: „Umarm mich, du süßer umarmbarer Schatz."
2. Man kann den Ansager nicht verstehen,
   a. weil die Kapelle einen Wiener Walzer spielt.
   b. trotzdem er täglich das Geschirr spülen muß.
   c. obgleich er sehr begeistert und energisch spricht.
3. Der kleine Teddybär weinte,
   a. als er Goldhaar in seinem Bett fand.
   b. weil er täglich das Geschirr spülen mußte.
   c. trotzdem er auf seinen Wärter ärgerlich war.
4. Sie machen sich lächerlich,
   a. obgleich die Kapelle die Ouvertüre von Mozarts „Zauberflöte" spielt.
   b. da Sie gepflegte Hände haben.
   c. wenn Sie uns nicht sagen, wo der Geldschrank ist.
5. Wenn ihr gut aufpaßt,
   a. werdet ihr verstehen, was der Ansager sagt.

b. hört ihr eine weinerliche Frauenstimme.
c. versteht ihr, wie recht er hatte.

6. Wenn ihr mich nicht aus eurer Bank gejagt hättet,
a. würde euch Mama erzählen, was der große Teddybär zu Goldhaar sagte.
b. könnte ich mir einen Geldschrank leisten.
c. hätte ich euch nie verraten.

F. *Connect by means of the conjunction indicated and translate:*

1. (obgleich)
Sie müssen täglich das Geschirr spülen und all die anderen Hausarbeiten tun.
Ihre Hände können schön und gepflegt aussehen.

2. (nachdem)
Sie spielte einen von den bekannten Wiener Walzern.
Die Kapelle hatte Mozarts „Eine kleine Nachtmusik" gespielt.

3. (da)
Ihr wart den ganzen Tag so artig.
Ich werde euch eine Geschichte erzählen.

4. (daß)
Es wird endlich kühler.
Gott sei Dank!

5. (daß)
Die Frage kann beantwortet werden.
Es kann sein.

VI. Principal Parts:

Study verbs

aufsteigen	stieg . . . auf	es ist aufgestiegen	es steigt . . . auf	rise
schreiben	schrieb	ich habe geschrieben	er schreibt	write
verlieren	verlor	ich habe verloren	er verliert	lose
lügen	log	ich habe gelogen	er lügt	lie
singen	sang	ich habe gesungen	er singt	sing
annehmen	nahm . . . an	ich habe angenommen	er nimmt . . . an	assume
kommen	kam	ich bin gekommen	er kommt	come
lesen	las	ich habe gelesen	er liest	read
sehen	sah	ich habe gesehen	er sieht	see
aussehen	sah . . . aus	ich habe ausgesehen	er sieht . . . aus	look, appear
wiedersehen	sah . . . wieder	ich habe wiedergesehen	er sieht . . . wieder	see again
fallen	fiel	ich bin gefallen	er fällt	fall
auffallen	fiel . . . auf	ich bin aufgefallen	er fällt . . . auf	strike the attention
laufen	lief	ich bin gelaufen	er läuft	run
sein	war	ich bin gewesen	er ist	be
stehen	stand	ich habe gestanden	er steht	stand
tun	tat	ich habe getan	er tut	do

müssen	mußte	ich habe gemußt	er muß	must
wollen	wollte	ich habe gewollt	er will	want to
bringen	brachte	ich habe gebracht	er bringt	bring
wissen	wußte	ich habe gewußt	er weiß	know

+ = omit for time being

B. *Nouns:*

der Verkäufer, –s, —	salesman	die Welle, —, –n	wave, wave length
der Zettel, –s, —	slip of paper	die Treppe, —, –n	stairs
die Mutter, —, ¨	mother	die Seife, —, –n	soap
das Mittel, –s, —	means	die Seele, —, –n	soul
das Wohnzimmer, –s, —	living room	die Pfeife, —, –n	pipe
das Schlafzimmer, –s, —	bed room	die Küche, —, –n	kitchen
+ das Pferderennen, –s, —	horse race	die Frage, —, –n	question
der Preis, –es, –e	price	die Börse, —, –n	stock exchange
der Schatz, –es, ¨e	treasure; sweetheart	die Frauenstimme, —, –n	woman's voice
der Strumpf, –es, ¨e	stocking	die Geldsumme, —, –n	sum of money
der Wert, –es, –e	worth, value	die Kommode, —, –n	dresser
der Freund, –es, –e	friend	die Kartoffel, —, –n	potato
+ der Geldschrank, –es, ¨e	safe	die Zeitung, —, –en	newspaper
der Küchentisch, –es, –e	kitchen table	die Abzahlung, —, –en	instalment
der Schreibtisch, –es, –e	desk	die Hausarbeit, —, –en	housework
der Unterschied, –es, –e	difference	die Sekretärin, —, –nen	secretary
der Monat, –es, –e	month	die Bank, —, –en	bank
der Bericht, –es, –e	report	die Frau, —, –en	woman, wife, Mrs.
+ der Tunichtgut, –es, –e	good-for-nothing	die Schrift, —, –en	writing
der Tenor, –s, –e	tenor	die Zeit, —, –en	time
die Hand, —, ¨e	hand	der Unsterbliche, –n, –n	immortal
die Frauenhand, —, ¨e	woman's hand	+ der Teddybär, –en –en	Teddy Bear
das Jahr, –es, –e	year	der Staat, –es, –en	state
der Mann, –es, ¨er	man	das Bett, –es, –en	bed
das Haus, –es, ¨er	house	das Radio, –s, –s	radio
das Geld, –es, –er	money		

VII. Securing the Vocabulary:

A.

die Geschichte	story	der Unterschied	difference
ohne	without	irgendwo	somewhere
ähnlich	similar	lächerlich	ridiculous

der Teil	part	zunächst	first of all
teilweise	partly	annehmen	(to) assume
schon einmal	(*in question*) ever	feig(e)	cowardly
der Mut	courage		

B.

leicht (1)	1. light, easy	untersuchen (3)	1. try
nötig haben (3)	2. even	verlangen (4)	2. throw
aufheben (4)	3. need	versuchen (1)	3. examine
reizend (5)	4. pick up	werfen (2)	4. demand
sogar (2)	5. charming	die Tasche (9)	5. imagine
die Stimme (9)	6. at that time	sich vorstellen (5)	6. understanding
damals (6)	7. fun	zeigen (8)	7. in spite of
der Spaß (7)	8. take	das Verständnis (6)	8. show
nehmen (8)	9. voice	während (10)	9. pocket
genau (10)	10. exactly	trotz (7)	10. while, during

VIII. Von einer Welle zur andern: (*Rewritten*)

. . . auf Abzahlung. Aber Gretel, weißt du nicht, daß du all das bei Henning und Noyes kaufen kannst? Willst du einen neuen Küchentisch, eine größere Kommode, willst du Möbel für ein modernes Schlafzimmer? Geh heute noch zu Henning und Noyes. Wir können uns das alles leisten. Bei Henning und Noyes kannst du solche Möbel auf Abzahlung kaufen. — Ja, Herr Schmidt hat recht. Henning und Noyes machen es für alle möglich, schöne, moderne Möbel zu haben. — Doch zurück zu unserer Geschichte „Die Handschrift seiner Frau." Harold Lang hatte also dreitausend Dollar beim Pferderennen verloren. Es war nur eine Frage der Zeit, bis er die dreitausend Dollar in den Geldschrank seiner Bank zurücklegen mußte. Harold sitzt vor seinem Schreibtisch und spielt mit der Pistole. (Die Stimme einer jungen Frau) Harold, warum kommst du nicht zum Essen? Alles wird kalt, und außerdem macht es Mutter ärgerlich, wenn du. . . .

Das Barometer fällt noch immer. Leichter Schnee im Westen; im Osten warm und etwas bewölkt. . . .

Aber Schatz, sieh dir mal deine Hände an! Du solltest wirklich etwas für deine Hände tun! — Da kritisierst du mich schon wieder. Ja, du sitzt den ganzen Tag im Büro und diktierst hübschen Sekretärinnen Briefe. Aber ich muß den ganzen Tag mit den Händen arbeiten, ich muß Geschirr spülen, Kartoffeln schälen, die Treppe fegen. — Ich weiß, aber es ist trotzdem nicht nötig, daß deine Hände rot aussehen. Gebrauche Schneewittchen Schönheitskrem, und deine Hände werden schön und gepflegt aussehen! Solche Hände . . .

Der alte Sioux nahm die Pfeife aus dem Mund und sagte: „Der weiße Mann sage uns, wo seine Freunde sind, und wir lassen ihn leben. Wenn er es nicht sagt, so martern wir ihn, und bevor der Präriehund bellt, wird seine Seele zu seinen Vätern

gehen." Nick Buster sagte nur: „Laufender Bär ist ein großer Sioux. Soll ich feige meine Freunde verraten?" Laufender Bär stand auf und nahm seinen Tomahawk in die Hand. In diesem Moment hörte Nick Buster ein Geräusch hinter sich, zwei Pistolenschüsse knallten, und . . .

Sind Sie ein Mann, der sein Geld unter die Matratze legt? Das wäre lächerlich, denn heute gibt es Banken, die . . . 5

Wissen Sie, wieviel ein Pfund Schweinefleisch im Jahre 1934 gekostet hat? Können Sie uns sagen, wie schnell eine Lichtwelle ist? Solche Fragen . . .

Zwanzigste Aufgabe

* * * \

Stammt Ihre Fami'lie aus Deutschland?"	Does your family come from Germany?"
„Nein, aus Österreich."	"No, from Austria."
„Ihre Adres'se, Fräulein Schröder?"	"Your address, Miss Schröder?"
„Washingtonstraße vierundfünfzig."	"Fifty-four Washington Street."
woher	whence, from where
„Fräulein Schröder, woher habe ich meinen Radionamen?	"Miss Schröder, where did I get my radio name?
stehen, stand, ich habe gestanden, er steht	stand
In welchem litera'rischen Werk steht der Name Dr. Allwissend?"	In what literary work does the name Dr. Know-it-all occur?"
„In Goethes ‚Faust'."	"In Goethe's 'Faust'."
*„Wie schade! Leider haben Sie nicht recht.	"Too bad! Unfortunately you are not right.
das Märchen, –s, — Kinder- und Hausmärchen der Brüder Grimm	the fairy-tale fairy-tales for children and home of the Grimm brothers
Dr. Allwissend ist der Titel eines Märchens in den Kinder- und Hausmärchen der Brüder Grimm.	Dr. Know-it-all is the title of a fairy-tale in Grimms' Fairy Tales.
Sie bekommen aber eine Schachtel Seife, Fräulein Schröder."	But you get a box of soap, Miss Schröder."
„Herr Doktor, wir haben einen Herrn für Sie."	"Doctor, we have a gentleman for you."
„Gut. Wie heißen Sie?"	"Good. What's your name?"
„Albert Heinke, Lincolnallee hundertfünfundsechzig."	"Albert Heinke, one hundred sixty-five Lincoln Avenue."
* der Roman', –s, –e die Wort'zusam'menset'zung, —, –en drei mit ‚Roman' gebildete Wortzusammensetzungen	the novel the word-compound three compounds made with the word 'novel'
„Herr Heinke, wir geben Ihnen acht Silberdollar, wenn Sie uns drei mit ‚Roman" gebildete Wort'zusam'menset'zungen nennen können, wie zum Beispiel Kriminal'roman'.	"Mr. Heinke, we will give you eight silver dollars, if you can mention three compounds made with the word 'Roman' (novel), as, for example, Kriminalroman (crime novel)
Nicht vorsagen, bitte!"	No prompting, please."

Lie'besroman' Bil'dungsroman'	love novel novel of personality development
„Liebesroman, Bildungsroman, Geschichtsroman."	"Love novel, novel of development, historical novel."
„Gut, ich gratuliere. Acht Silberdollar für Herrn Heinke.	"Good, congratulations. Eight silver dollars for Mr. Heinke.
Nun kommen wir zu unserer großen biogra'phischen Frage.	Now we come to our great biographical question.
Wir beginnen mit zweihundertachtzig Dollar."	We'll begin with two hundred eighty dollars."
„Herr Doktor, wir haben einen Herrn für Sie, Herrn Friedrich Lenz, Ashlandstraße siebenundachtzig."	"Doctor, we have a gentleman for you, Mr. Friedrich Lenz, eighty seven Ashland Street."
„Herr Lenz, wer wurde am achtundzwanzigsten August' siebzehnhundertneunundvierzig geboren?	"Mr. Lenz, who was born August twenty eighth, 1749?
(Tiefes *Schweigen)	(*Deep silence*)
Ihre Zeit ist um.	Your time is up.
Jetzt sind es zweihundertfünfzig Dollar.	Now it's two hundred fifty dollars.
Wer studierte siebzehnhundertsiebzig die Rechte an der Straßburger Universität?	Who studied law at the University of Strassburg in 1770?
(Tiefes Schweigen)	(*Deep silence*)
Jetzt sind es noch zweihundertzwanzig Dollar.	Now there are two hundred twenty dollars left.
* holen, holte, ich habe geholt, er holt	(to) fetch, get
Von wem nahmen zwei französ'ische O'pernkomponi'sten den Stoff für ihre Opern, die denselben Namen im Titel haben und in denen ein Universitäts'profes'sor vom Teufel geholt wird?"	From whom did two French opera composers take the material for their operas which have the same name in their titles and in which a university professor is carried off by the devil?"

„Goethe, Johann Wolfgang Goethe.

"Goethe, Johann Wolfgang Goethe.

Es sind Gounods und Berlioz' Faust-Opern."

They are Gounod's and Berlioz' Faust operas."

„Ich gratuliere, Sie haben meine Frage richtig beantwortet.

"Congratulations, you have answered my question correctly.

Herr Lenz erhält zweihundertzwanzig Dollar.

Mr. Lenz gets two hundred twenty dollars.

Auch Sie können sich von zehn bis hundert Dollar verdienen, wenn Sie uns Fragen einschicken, die wir gebrauchen können.

You too, can earn from ten to one hundred dollars if you send questions to us that we can use.

die Packung
gewickelt
die gewickelte Packung
die um jedes Stück Kirschblütenseife gewickelte Packung

the wrapper
wrapped
the wrapped wrapper
the wrapper which is wrapped around every piece of Cherry Blossom Soap.

Schicken Sie mit jeder Frage eine der um jedes Stück Kirschblütenseife gewickelten Packungen und schreiben Sie den Namen und die Adresse des Absenders auf die Innenseite!"

With every question send the wrapper from a bar of Cherry Blossom Soap and write the name and address of the sender on the inside."

Das Programm' beginnt uns zu langweilen.

The program is beginning to bore us.

Wir wollen Musik' hören und einen *Augenblick später haben wir eine Station' eingestellt, die die Ouvertü're von Mozarts „Zauberflöte' sendet.

We want to listen to music and a moment later we have turned on a station which is playing the overture to Mozart's 'Zauberflöte' (Magic Flute).

II. Text:

Doktor Allwissend

Eine begeisterte, lebhafte Stimme spricht rasch, aber verständlich. „Kirschblüte, die leicht parfümierte Seife, reinigt die Hände des Mechanikers wie auch die Hände der Dame. Feine Wäsche, die blütenweiß war und schmutzig geworden ist, wird wieder blütenweiß, wenn sie mit Kirschblütenseifenflocken gewaschen wird. Kirschblütenseife hat eine zauberhafte Wirkung. Wir geben jetzt Herrn Doktor Allwissend das Mikrophon."

Eine freundliche, gepflegte Stimme spricht: „Guten Abend, meine Damen und Herren. Wir beginnen unser Programm mit einer Zwanzig-Dollar-Frage." ... „Doktor Allwissend, eine Dame hat sich gemeldet." ... „Schön. Wie heißen Sie?" ... „Emma Schröder." ... „Das ist ein deutscher Name. Stammt Ihre Familie aus Deutschland?" ... „Nein, aus Österreich." ... „Ihre Adresse, Fräulein Schröder?" ... „Washingtonstraße vierundfünfzig." ... „Fräulein Schröder,

woher habe ich meinen Radionamen? In welchem literarischen Werk steht der Name Dr. Allwissend?" ... „In Goethes ‚Faust'." ... „Wie schade! Leider haben Sie nicht recht. Dr. Allwissend ist der Titel eines Märchens in den Kinder- und Hausmärchen der Brüder Grimm. Sie bekommen aber eine Schachtel Seife, Fräulein Schröder."

„Herr Doktor, wir haben einen Herrn für Sie." ... „Gut. Wie heißen Sie?"... „Albert Heinke, Lincolnallee hundertfünfundsechzig." ... „Herr Heinke, wir geben Ihnen acht Silberdollar, wenn Sie uns drei mit Roman gebildete Wortzusammensetzungen nennen können, wie zum Beispiel Kriminalroman. Nicht vorsagen, bitte!" ... „Liebesroman, Bildungsroman, Geschichtsroman." ... „Gut, ich gratuliere. Acht Silberdollar für Herrn Heinke.

Nun kommen wir zu unserer großen biographischen Frage. Wir beginnen mit zweihundertachtzig Dollar." ... „Herr Doktor, wir haben einen Herrn für Sie, Herrn Friedrich Lenz, Ashlandstraße siebenundachtzig." ... „Herr Lenz, wer wurde am achtundzwanzigsten August siebzehnhundertneunundvierzig geboren? (Tiefes Schweigen) Ihre Zeit ist um. Jetzt sind es zweihundertfünfzig Dollar. Wer studierte siebzehnhundertsiebzig die Rechte an der Straßburger Universität? (Tiefes Schweigen) Jetzt sind es noch zweihundertzwanzig Dollar. Von wem nahmen zwei französische Opernkomponisten den Stoff für ihre Opern, die denselben Namen im Titel haben, und in denen ein Universitätsprofessor vom Teufel geholt wird?" ... „Goethe, Johann Wolfgang Goethe. Es sind Gounods und Berlioz' Faust-Opern." ... „Ich gratuliere, Sie haben meine Frage richtig beantwortet. Herr Lenz erhält zweihundertzwanzig Dollar.

Auch Sie können sich von zehn bis hundert Dollar verdienen, wenn Sie uns Fragen einschicken, die wir gebrauchen können. Schicken Sie mit jeder Frage eine der um jedes Stück Kirschblütenseife gewickelten Packungen und schreiben Sie den Namen und die Adresse des Absenders auf die Innenseite!"

Das Programm beginnt uns zu langweilen. Wir wollen Musik hören und einen Augenblick später haben wir eine Station eingestellt, die die Ouvertüre von Mozarts „Zauberflöte" sendet.

III. Comments:

1. *Uses of the Infinitive:*

The infinitive of a verb is often used as an imperative without reference to person or number. Thus: Nicht vorsagen, bitte! — *No prompting, please!* Nicht hinauslehnen! — *Do not lean out (of the window)!* Nicht auf den Fußboden spucken! — *Do not spit on the floor!*

The infinitive is also frequently used as a noun. It is then, of course, capitalized and it is always neuter. Examples: das Schweigen, *the silence;* das Können, *the ability;* das Schreiben, *the writing;* ein Kommen und Gehen, *a coming and going.*

2. *Rules for Determining the Gender of Nouns:*

As you have found out, the best way to master the gender of nouns is to learn the definite article with each noun, since no rules can be given which will cover all nouns. But there are certain noun endings which indicate gender with almost complete regularity.

1. Masculine are: nouns ending in –er signifying agency (der Mechaniker, *the mechanic;* der Arbeiter, *the worker;* der Ansager, *the announcer*).

2. Neuter are: infinitives used as nouns (das Schweigen, *the silence*), nouns ending in the diminutive suffixes –chen and –lein (das Mädchen, *the girl;* das Kätzchen, *the kitty;* das Fräulein, *the young lady*), nouns ending in –tum (das Königtum, *the kingship;* das Christentum, *the Christianity*). There are two exceptions to the last rule: der Reichtum, *the riches*, der Irrtum, *the error*.

3. Feminine are: nouns ending in –ei, –in, –heit, –keit, –schaft, –ung (die Malerei, *the art of painting;* die Freundin, *the girl friend;* die Schönheit, *the beauty;* die Geschwindigkeit, *the speed;* die Mannschaft, *the team;* die Packung, *the wrapping.*)

3. *The Long Attribute:*

A striking feature of German, especially in formal and technical style, is the long attribute. In its simple forms it is readily intelligible to people who know English, e.g. die nur sehr leicht parfümierte Seife — *the only very gently perfumed soap.* Notice how far the article has been removed from its noun by the interpolation of a series of modifiers, each restricting the one it precedes. But the literal translation of the phrase die um jedes Stück Seife gewickelte Packung would be *the around every piece of soap wrapped wrapper*, which is exceedingly awkward English. This type of construction is frequently best translated by a relative clause, as for example, *the wrapper which is wrapped around every piece of soap.*

The example quoted above could be made more complex: die um jedes mit Kirschblüten parfümierte Stück Seife gewickelte Packung — *the wrapper wrapped around every piece of soap which has been perfumed with cherry blossoms.*

In this chapter and the chapters immediately following there are some simple examples of this construction which you will need to study in order to acquire a feeling for it in preparation for the fuller discussion to be found in Lesson XXV.

IV. Practice:

1. a. Die Wäsche ist schmutzig geworden.
wird wieder blütenweiß.
wird mit Kirschblütenseifenflocken gewaschen.

b. Schmutzig gewordene Wäsche.
wird wieder blütenweiß.

Schmutzig gewordene Wäsche wird wieder blütenweiß, wenn sie mit Kirschblütenseifenflocken gewaschen wird.

2. a. Schröder ist der Name einer bekannten Familie.
aus Österreich.

b. Die Familie stammt aus Österreich.

c. Schröder ist der Name einer bekannten Familie, die aus Österreich stammt.

3. Kirschblütenseifenflocken ist eine Wortzusammensetzung.
Kirschblütenseifenflocken ist eine mit Flocke gebildete Wortzusammensetzung.
formed

4. a. Der Universitätsprofessor wird vom Teufel geholt.
Der Universitätsprofessor wird in den beiden Opern vom Teufel geholt.

b. Der Universitätsprofessor heißt Faust.

c. Der Universitätsprofessor, der in den beiden Opern vom Teufel geholt wird, heißt Faust.

5. Sie haben meine Frage richtig beantwortet.
Sie erhalten zwanzig Dollar.
Für jede richtig beantwortete Frage erhalten Sie zwanzig Dollar.

6. Für jede richtig beantwortete Frage erhält er siebenundzwanzig Dollar.
erhielt
hat erhalten.

7. Wenn ich mich gemeldet hätte, so hätte ich den ersten Preis gewonnen.
die Frage richtig beantwortet.
eine Schachtel Seife bekommen.

8. Wenn das Hemd nur mit Kirschblütenseifenflocken gewaschen worden wäre,
könntest du es immer noch tragen.
brauchtest du dir jetzt kein neues Hemd zu kaufen.
würde es blütenweiß aussehen.

9. Das Programm beginnt immer mit einer Fünfzehn-Dollar-Frage.
begann Fünfzig-
hat Sechzig- begonnen.

10. Wenn der Absender seinen Namen und seine Adresse auf die Innenseite der Packung geschrieben hätte, so könnten wir die Frage gebrauchen.
würden wir an ihn schreiben können.
hätte er den dritten Preis gewonnen.

V. Exercises:

A. *Questions:*

hat kind of

1. Was ist die zauberhafte Wirkung der Kirschblütenseife?
2. Was für eine Stimme hat Dr. Allwissend?
3. Was ist die Zwanzig-Dollar-Frage?
4. Woher stammt Fräulein Schröders Familie?
5. In welchem literarischen Werk steht der Name „Allwissend"?
6. Wer hat den „Faust" geschrieben?
7. Ist Scott's „Ivanhoe" ein Bildungs-, Liebes- oder Geschichtsroman?
8. Wer wurde am 28. August 1749 geboren?
9. An welcher Universität studierte Goethe die Rechte?
10. Welcher „Faust" ist älter, Gounods oder Goethes „Faust"?
11. Wie heißt der Teufel in der Faust-Oper?

B. *Translate:*

1. Können Sie uns zwei mit ‚weiß' gebildete Wortzusammensetzungen nennen?
2. Vergessen Sie nicht, Ihren Namen und Ihre Adresse auf die Innenseite der Packung zu schreiben!
3. Wenn ich mich gemeldet hätte, hätte ich zweihundert Dollar gewonnen.
4. Können Sie mir sagen, wann Johann Wolfgang Goethe geboren wurde?
5. Die Frage wurde von einem sechsjährigen Jungen beantwortet.
6. Wenn ich eine gute Frage eingeschickt hätte, hätte ich mir dreihundert Dollar verdient.
7. Ja, Sie haben recht. „Faust" ist der Titel einer von Gounod komponierten Oper.
8. Ich würde mich melden, wenn ich die Frage beantworten könnte.

C. *Correct the misinformation:*

1. Das heutige Programm beginnt mit einer Dreißig-Dollar-Frage.
2. Dr. Allwissend ist der Name eines Universitätsprofessors, den der Teufel holt.
3. Gounods „Faust" ist ein bekannter Liebesroman.
4. „Die Zauberflöte" ist der Titel einer von Berlioz komponierten Oper.
5. Jakob Grimm studierte siebzehnhundertsiebzig die Rechte an der Straßburger Universität.
6. Wilhelm Grimm wurde am achtundzwanzigsten August siebzehnhundertneunundvierzig geboren.
7. Gounod und Berlioz nahmen den Stoff für ihre Opern aus den Kinder- und Hausmärchen der Brüder Grimm.
8. Man kann sich zehn bis hundert Dollar verdienen, wenn man seinen Namen und seine Adresse auf die Innenseite der Packung schreibt und diese Packung ohne Frage an Doktor Allwissend einschickt.
9. Die eben eingestellte Station sendet die Ouvertüre von Mozarts „Don Juan."

D. *Rearrange:*

1. „Figaros Hochzeit," der Titel, einer von Mozart komponierten Oper, ist.
2. in welchem literarischen Werk, der Teufel, Mephistopheles, heißt?
3. leider, wir, die Frage, können, annehmen, nicht.
4. wenn, mit Kirschblütenseife, Sie, die Hände, sich, waschen, werden . . . aussehen, schön und gepflegt, sie.
5. sich, kann, zweihundert Dollar, verdienen, man, wenn, eine brauchbare Frage, einschickt, man.
6. der Universitätsprofessor, der, geholt wurde, vom Teufel, Faust, hieß.
7. Herr Lenz, uns, eine interessante Frage, hat . . . eingeschickt, über das Theater.
8. hat . . . genannt, Fräulein Niemeier, uns, eine mit Roman gebildete Wortzusammensetzung.

E. *Complete by means of the suitable clause or phrase and translate:*

1. Wir erhalten täglich Briefe,
   a. weil der Absender vergessen hat, seinen Namen auf die Innenseite der Packung zu schreiben.

b. in denen gute Fragen eingeschickt werden.
c. in denen der Titel dieses berühmten Märchens steht.

2. Auch Sie können sich hundert Dollar verdienen,
a. wenn Sie uns eine Frage einschicken, die wir gebrauchen können.
b. wenn Sie Ihren Namen auf die Packung schreiben und diese Packung dann mit einer Frage einschicken.
c. obgleich wir die Frage nicht gebrauchen können.

3. Schmutzig gewordene Wäsche wird wieder schneeweiß,
a. wenn Sie sie mit Kirschblütenseife waschen.
b. trotzdem sie mit Kirschblütenseife gewaschen wird.
c. weil Kirschblütenseife nur sehr leicht parfümiert ist.

4. Wenn ich mich gemeldet hätte,
a. würde ich die Rechte studieren.
b. hätte ich zweihundert Dollar gewonnen.
c. könnten Sie die Frage gebrauchen.

5. Faust war der Name eines Universitätsprofessors,
a. der vom Teufel geholt wurde.
b. der Kindermärchen schrieb.
c. von dem zwei französische Opernkomponisten den Stoff für ihre Opern nahmen.

6. „Die Zauberflöte" ist der Titel
a. eines Liebesromans, den Milton geschrieben hat.
b. eines Musikinstrumentes.
c. einer von Mozart komponierten Oper.

F. *Connect by means of the conjunction indicated. Translate:*

1. (wenn)
Ich würde das wissen.
Ich hätte Goethes „Faust" gelesen.

2. (obgleich)
Wir können die Frage nicht gebrauchen.
Der Absender hat seinen Namen und seine Adresse auf die Innenseite der Packung geschrieben.

3. (da)
Das Programm beginnt uns zu langweilen.
Wir stellen eine andere Station ein.

4. (weil)
Ihre Hände sehen schön und gepflegt aus.
Sie gebraucht Kirschblütenseife, wenn sie sich die Hände wäscht.

learn

VI. Principal Parts:

schreiben	schrieb	ich habe geschrieben	er schreibt	write
beginnen	begann	ich habe begonnen	er beginnt	begin
—sprechen	sprach	ich habe gesprochen	er spricht	speak
nehmen	nahm	ich habe genommen	er nimmt	take
kommen	kam	ich bin gekommen	er kommt	come
—bekommen	bekam	ich habe bekommen	er bekommt	get, receive
—geben	gab	ich habe gegeben	er gibt	give
—waschen	wusch	ich habe gewaschen	er wäscht	wash
—erhalten	erhielt	ich habe erhalten	er erhält	get, receive
heißen	hieß	ich habe geheißen	er heißt	be called, named
sein	war	ich bin gewesen	er ist	be
stehen	stand	ich habe gestanden	er steht	stand
können	konnte	ich habe gekonnt	er kann	be able
wollen	wollte	ich habe gewollt	er will	want to
—werden	wurde	ich bin geworden	er wird	become, get
—nennen	nannte	ich habe genannt	er nennt	name
—senden	sandte	ich habe gesandt	er sendet	send

der Absender, –s, — sender
der Bruder, –s, ¨ brother
der Mechaniker, –s, — mechanic
der Teufel, –s, — devil
der Titel, –s, — title
der Dollar, –s, — dollar
das Märchen, –s, — fairy tale
das Fräulein, –s, — Miss, young lady
der Augenblick, –s, –e moment
der Stoff, –es, –e material
der Abend, –s, –e evening
der Roman, –s, –e novel
das Recht, –es, –e law
das Stück, –es, –e piece
das Werk, –es, –e work
das Mikrophon, –s, –e microphone
die Adresse, —, –n address
die Dame, —, –n lady
die Familie, —, –n family
die Ouvertüre, —, –n overture
die Zwanzig-Dollar-Frage, —, –n twenty dollar question
die Packung, —, –en wrapper
die Wirkung, —, –en effect
die Wortzusammensetzung, —, –en word compound
die Oper, —, –n opera
die Station, —, –en station
die Universität, —, –en university
der Opernkomponist, –en, –en opera composer
der Universitätsprofessor, –s, –en university professor
der Radioname, –ns, –n radio name

VII. Securing the Vocabulary:

A.

rasch	rapidly	das Schweigen	silence
schmutzig	dirty, soiled	der Stoff	material
wie schade	too bad	holen	fetch, get, carry off
der Roman	novel	der Augenblick	moment

B.

begeistert (3)	1. imitate	der Fall (7)	6. stop
nachmachen (1)	2. without	sogar (4)	7. case
rasch (5)	3. enthusiastic	ähnlich (10)	8. consist, exist
ohne (2)	4. even	schon einmal (*in question*) (9)	9. ever
aufhören (6)	5. rapidly	bestehen (8)	10. similar

irgendein (2)	1. ridiculous	die Stimme (4)	1. in spite of
der Unterschied (8)	2. any	trotz (1)	2. try
lächerlich (1)	3. too bad	die Zeile (6)	3. spectator
der Mut (4)	4. courage	der Zuschauer (3)	4. voice
wie schade (3)	5. pocket	versuchen (2)	5. material
werfen (10)	6. need	zunächst (7)	6. line
brauchen (6)	7. soft	der Stoff (5)	7. at first
die Tasche (5)	8. difference	teilweise (9)	8. numerous
weich (7)	9. while; during	schnell (10)	9. partly
während (9)	10. throw	zahlreich (8)	10. fast, quick

VIII. Doktor Allwissend (*Rewritten*)

Sind Sie Mechaniker, sind Sie ein Doktor der Rechte? Gebrauchen Sie das nächste Mal, wenn Sie sich die Hände waschen, Kirschblüte! Auch die feinste Wäsche wird wieder weiß, wenn sie mit Kirschblütenseifenflocken gewaschen wird. Und jetzt, meine Damen und Herren, Dr. Allwissend!

„Zwanzig Dollar für den, der unsere erste Frage beantworten kann." „Dr. Allwissend, wir haben einen Herrn für Sie, Friedrich Schröder, Bahnhofsplatz siebzehn." „Herr Schröder: Wie heißt der Teufel in den folgenden drei Werken der Weltliteratur: In Miltons ‚Verlorenem Paradies', in Dantes ‚Göttlicher Komödie', in Goethes ‚Faust'? „Satan, Dis, Mephistopheles." „Richtig, zwanzig Dollar für Herrn Schröder.

Wir haben heute dreihundert Dollar für Fragen aus der Biographie eines berühmten Mannes." „Dr. Allwissend, eine Dame hat sich gemeldet." . . . „Ihren Namen und Ihre Adresse, bitte?" . . . „Elisabeth Bauer, Marktstraße zwölf." . . . „Wer wurde am siebenundzwanzigsten Januar siebzehnhundertsechsundfünfzig in Salzburg, Österreich, geboren? (Schweigen) Jetzt sind es noch zweihundertfünfzig

Dollar. Wie hieß das sechsjährige Kind, das in Wien und Paris durch Konzerte Geld verdiente? (Schweigen) Zweihundert Dollar, wenn Sie mir sagen können, wer siebzehnhunderteinundneunzig eine Oper schrieb, deren Titel der Name eines Musikinstrumentes ist." ... „Wolfgang Amadeus Mozart. Die Oper heißt ‚Die Zauberflöte'." ... „Fräulein Bauer, Sie haben sich Ihre zweihundert Dollar verdient.

Wir erhalten täglich Briefe, in denen gute Fragen eingeschickt werden, die wir leider nicht annehmen können, weil der Absender vergessen hat, seinen Namen und seine Adresse auf die Innenseite der um Kirschblütenseife gewickelten Packung zu schreiben.

Wir haben acht Silberdollar für die nächste richtige Antwort." ... „Fräulein Niemeier." ... „Nennen Sie mir einen Roman, der eine Wortzusammensetzung mit ‚Zauber' im Titel hat." ... „Thomas Manns ‚Zauberberg'." ... „Ich gratuliere, Sie haben recht." ... „Wenn Sie schmutzige Hände haben, versuchen Sie Kirschblüte ..."

Einundzwanzigste Aufgabe

* *

Wie Sie wollen

I. Words and Phrases:

Wie Sie wollen.	As you wish.
„Also, meine Damen und Herren, Sie kennen die * Bedingungen.	"Well then Ladies and Gentlemen, you know the conditions.
Hier an der Tafel sehen Sie die Nummern, die die verschiedenen Interes'sengebie'te * bezeichnen.	Here on the board you see the numbers which designate the various fields of interest.
das ausgesuchte Gebiet	the chosen field
Sie * wählen eine Nummer, und ich stelle Ihnen Fragen aus dem von Ihnen ausgesuchten Gebiet.	You choose a number and I will put questions to you from the field which you have selected.
bis dahin	up to that time
der bis dahin gewonnene Preis	the prize won up to that time
Jedesmal, wenn Sie eine Frage richtig beantworten, wird der bis dahin gewonnene Preis verdoppelt.	Every time you answer a question correctly the prize won up to that time will be doubled.
Bei der ersten falschen Antwort verlieren Sie alles, was Sie gewonnen haben.	With the first wrong answer you will lose everything that you have won.
Sie können * jederzeit aufhören, sogar nachdem Sie nur einen Dollar gewonnen haben.	You can stop at any time, even after you have only won one dollar.
Ich * wiederho'le meine Bitte ans Publikum: Bitte, nicht vorsagen!	I'll repeat my request to the audience: Please, no prompting!
losgehen, ging . . . los, ist losgegangen, geht . . . los	(to) commence, begin
es geht los	things are commencing
So, jetzt kann's losgehen.	So, now we can start.

Sie sind an der Reihe	you are at the (head of the) line
Sie sind zuerst' an der Reihe.	It's your turn first.
Wie heißen Sie, Fräulein?"	What's your name, Miss?"
„Rita Müller."	"Rita Müller."
„Ich sehe auf diesem Zettel, daß Sie auf dem Gebiet des Kinos bewandert sind.	"I see on this slip of paper that you are well-versed in the movies.
Stimmt das?"	Is that correct?"
„Ja."	"Yes."
„Schön! Welche amerika'nische Filmschauspielerin deutscher * Abstammung kennen Sie?	"Fine! What American movie actress of German descent do you know?"
„Marlene Dietrich."	"Marlene Dietrich."
„Gut, Sie haben einen Dollar gewonnen.	"Good, you have won a dollar.
Wollen Sie noch eine Frage?	Do you wish another question?
Sie * nicken, Sie haben Mut.	You're nodding, you have courage.
gehen, ging, ich bin gegangen, er geht	(to) go
es geht	it goes
es geht um zwei Dollar	it goes about two dollars, i.e. two dollars are at stake
Jetzt geht es um zwei Dollar.	Now two dollars are at stake.
Nennen Sie mir einen Film, in dem Marlene Dietrich die * weibliche Hauptrolle gespielt hat."	Name a film in which Marlene Dietrich played the feminine lead."
„Kismet."	"Kismet."
„Schön! Jetzt kommt die Vier-Dollar-Frage.	"Fine! Now comes the four dollar question.
In welchem Film wird der Held bei dem Versuch, einen Schmetterling zu fangen, erschossen?	In what film is the hero shot to death in the attempt to catch a butterfly?
Sie haben noch fünfzehn Sekun'den."	You have fifteen seconds left."
„Sieben Gräber bis Kairo."	"Seven Graves to Cairo."
„O, das tut mir leid.	"Oh, I'm sorry.
Das stimmt leider nicht.	Unfortunately, that isn't correct.

im Weſten nichts Neues	in the west nothing new
* Erinnern Sie ſich an die Verfilmung des Kriegsromans ‚Im Weſten nichts Neues' von Remarque?	Do you remember the film version of the war novel by Remarque, 'All Quiet on the Western Front?'
Der Held wird von einem franzö'ſiſchen Solda'ten erſchoſſen, als er aus dem Schützengraben kriecht, um einen Schmetterling zu * fangen.	The hero is shot and killed by a French soldier as he creeps out of the trench in order to catch a butterfly.
er kommt an die Reihe	he comes to the (head of the) line
Jetzt kommt ein Herr an die Reihe.	Now it's a gentleman's turn.
ich bin Verkäufer von Beruf	I am a salesman by occupation
Herr Schönfeld, was ſind Sie von Beruf?"	Mr. Schönfeld, what is your occupation?"
„Verkäufer in der Abtei'lung für Pelzmäntel in Webers Warenhaus."	"A salesman in the fur coat department of Weber's department store."
„O, Sie ſind es, der meiner Frau den teuren Pelzmantel verkauft hat.	"Oh, it's you who sold my wife that expensive fur coat.
Nun, machen Sie ſich keine Sorgen. Ich bin Ihnen nicht * böſe.	Well, don't worry. I'm not angry with you.
Zum * Beweis gebe ich Ihnen eine überra'ſchend leichte Frage.	As proof I'll give you a surprisingly easy question.
Sie haben die Oper als Ihr Gebiet angegeben.	You have given the opera as your field.
Welche Tetralogie hat den Namen eines Schmuckſtückes im Titel?"	Which tetralogy has the name of a piece of jewelry in its title?"
„Der Ring des Nibelungen."	"The Ring of the Nibelung."
„Richtig. Soll ich weiterfragen?"	"Right, shall I keep on asking?"
„Bitte."	"Yes, please."
„Wer war der erſte Beſitzer des Ringes?"	"Who was the first owner of the ring?"
„Es war der Zwerg Alberich, der den Rheintöchtern das Gold geſtohlen hatte."	"It was the dwarf Alberich who had stolen the gold from the daughters of the Rhine."
„Gut, können Sie mir jetzt für vier Dollar die vier Opern nennen, aus denen die Tetralogie' beſteht?"	"Good, now for four dollars, can you name the four operas of which the tetralogy consists?"
„Das Rheingold, Die Walküre, Siegfried, Götterdämmerung."	"Das Rheingold (the Rhine Gold), Die Walküre, Siegfried, Götterdämmerung (Twilight of the Gods)."

* „Ausgezeichnet! Wollen Sie jetzt acht Dollar riskieren? — Gut.

"Excellent! Do you want to risk eight dollars now? — Good.

Nennen Sie einen Riesen, einen König und einen Gott aus dem ‚Ring'."

Name a giant, a king, and a god from the 'Ring'."

„Fafner war ein * Riese, der in der Gestalt eines Drachen den Nibelungenhort bewachte und von Siegfried mit dem Schwert * erschlagen wurde.

"Fafner was a giant, who in the shape of a dragon, guarded the Nibelungen treasure and was slain by Siegfried with his sword.

Wotan war der Gott, der den Ring * besitzen wollte, und Gunther war der König, dessen Schwester Siegfried heiratete."

Wotan was the god, who wished to possess the treasure and Gunther was the king whose sister Siegfried married."

„Es * überrascht' mich nicht, daß Sie nicht aufhören wollen.

"It doesn't surprise me that you don't want to stop.

Können Sie ein Motiv' oder ein Lied aus dem ‚Ring' singen oder pfeifen?"

Can you sing or whistle a motif or song from the 'Ring'?"

(Herr Schönfeld singt mit einer Stimme, die * hauptsächlich in der Badewanne ausgebildet worden ist, eine Zeile aus der ‚Walküre': „Winterstürme wichen dem Wonnemond.")

(*With a voice which has been trained chiefly in the bath tub, Mr. Schönfeld sings a line from "Die Walküre":* "Winterstürme wichen dem Wonnemond" [Winter storms gave way to the moon of bliss]).

„Herr Schönfeld, Sie stehen dicht vor dem * Sieg.

"Mr. Schönfeld, you are close to victory.

Hier ist die letzte Frage: Welche Zauberkraft hatte der Nibelungenring?"

Here is the last question: What magic power had the Nibelungenring?"

„Er gab dem Träger Macht über Menschen und Götter."

"It gave its wearer power over men and gods."

„Sie haben sich Ihr Geld verdient.

"You have earned your money.

Wie kommt es, daß Sie so gut Bescheid wissen?"

How does it happen, that you are so well informed?"

„Ich bin * eigentlich Musik'leh'rer.

"I'm really a music teacher.

Verkäufer ist nur mein Nebenberuf."

Salesman is only my secondary occupation."

II. Text:

Wie Sie wollen

„Also, meine Damen und Herren, Sie kennen die Bedingungen. Hier an der Tafel sehen Sie die Nummern, die die verschiedenen Interessengebiete bezeichnen. Sie wählen eine Nummer, und ich stelle Ihnen Fragen aus dem von Ihnen ausgesuchten Gebiet. Jedesmal, wenn Sie eine Frage richtig beantworten, wird der bis dahin gewonnene Preis verdoppelt. Bei der ersten falschen Antwort verlieren Sie alles, was Sie gewonnen haben. Sie können jederzeit aufhören, sogar nachdem Sie nur einen Dollar gewonnen haben. Ich wiederhole meine Bitte ans Publikum: Bitte, nicht vorsagen! So, jetzt kann's losgehen.

Sie sind zuerst an der Reihe. Wie heißen Sie, Fräulein?" „Rita Müller." „Ich sehe auf diesem Zettel, daß Sie auf dem Gebiet des Kinos bewandert sind. Stimmt das?" ... „Ja." ... „Schön! Welche amerikanische Filmschauspielerin deutscher Abstammung kennen Sie?" ... „Marlene Dietrich." ... „Gut, Sie haben einen Dollar gewonnen. Wollen Sie noch eine Frage? Sie nicken, Sie haben Mut. Jetzt geht es um zwei Dollar. Nennen Sie mir einen Film, in dem Marlene

Dietrich die weibliche Hauptrolle gespielt hat." ... „Kismet." ... „Schön! Jetzt kommt die Vier-Dollar-Frage! In welchem Film wird der Held bei dem Versuch, einen Schmetterling zu fangen, erschossen? Sie haben noch fünfzehn Sekunden." ... „Sieben Gräber bis Kairo." ... „O, das tut mir leid. Das stimmt leider nicht. Erinnern Sie sich an die Verfilmung des Kriegsromans ‚Im Westen nichts Neues' von Remarque? Der Held wird von einem französischen Soldaten erschossen, als er aus dem Schützengraben kriecht, um einen Schmetterling zu fangen.

Jetzt kommt ein Herr an die Reihe. Herr Schönfeld, was sind Sie von Beruf?" ... „Verkäufer in der Abteilung für Pelzmäntel in Webers Warenhaus." ... „O, Sie sind es, der meiner Frau den teuren Pelzmantel verkauft hat. Nun, machen Sie sich keine Sorgen. Ich bin Ihnen nicht böse. Zum Beweis gebe ich Ihnen eine überraschend leichte Frage. Sie haben die Oper als ihr Gebiet angegeben. Welche Tetralogie hat den Namen eines Schmuckstückes im Titel?" ... „Der Ring des Nibelungen." ... „Richtig. Soll ich weiterfragen?" ... „Bitte." ... „Wer war der erste Besitzer des Ringes?" ... „Es war der Zwerg Alberich, der den Rheintöchtern das Gold gestohlen hatte." ... „Gut. Können Sie mir jetzt für vier Dollar die vier Opern nennen, aus denen die Tetralogie besteht?" ... „Das Rheingold, Die Walküre, Siegfried, Götterdämmerung." ... „Ausgezeichnet! Wollen Sie jetzt acht Dollar riskieren? — Gut. Nennen Sie einen Riesen, einen König und einen Gott aus dem ‚Ring'!" ... „Fafner war ein Riese, der in der Gestalt eines Drachen den Nibelungenhort bewachte und von Siegfried mit dem Schwert erschlagen wurde. Wotan war der Gott, der den Ring besitzen wollte, und Gunther war der König, dessen Schwester Siegfried heiratete." ... „Es überrascht mich nicht, daß Sie nicht aufhören wollen. Können Sie ein Motiv oder ein Lied aus dem ‚Ring' singen oder pfeifen?" (Herr Schönfeld singt mit einer Stimme, die hauptsächlich in der Badewanne ausgebildet worden ist, eine Zeile aus der ‚Walküre': ‚Winterstürme wichen dem Wonnemond'.) „Herr Schönfeld, Sie stehen dicht vor dem Sieg. Hier ist die letzte Frage: Welche Zauberkraft hatte der Nibelungenring?" ... „Er gab dem Träger Macht über Menschen und Götter." ... „Sie haben sich Ihr Geld verdient. Wie kommt es, daß Sie so gut Bescheid wissen?" ... „Ich bin eigentlich Musiklehrer. Verkäufer ist nur mein Nebenberuf."

III. Comments:

1. *Adjectives with* etwas, nichts *and* viel:

Adjectives are often used together with the words etwas, nichts and viel to express ideas such as something beautiful, nothing new, much that is interesting. The adjective is then capitalized and given the neuter ending –es. Thus: etwas Schönes, *something beautiful;* nichts Neues, *nothing new;* viel Interessantes, *many interesting things.*

2. *Rules for determining the plural of nouns:*

The only sure way to know the declension of a noun is to learn its principal parts, that is, the nominative and genitive singular and the nominative plural.

These three forms indicate what all the other forms are. But there are certain general rules which may be helpful in determining to what declensional group a noun belongs.

1. Masculine and neuter nouns ending in –el, –en, –er belong to Group I. (*See Lesson 7, Comments, to refresh your memory on the classification of nouns and Lesson 11 for their declension.*) Examples: der Garten, –s, ¨ *the garden;* der Tennisspieler, –s, — *the tennis player.*

2. Neuter nouns with the prefix Ge– and the ending –e belong to Group I. Examples: das Gebäude, –s, — *the building;* das Gebirge, –s, — *the mountain range.*

3. Neuter nouns with the diminutive endings –chen and –lein belong to Group I. Examples: das Mädchen, –s, — *the girl;* das Fräulein, –s, — *the young lady.*

4. Masculine nouns ending in –ich, –ig, –ing, –ling belong to Group II. Examples: der König, –s, –e *the king;* der Liebling, –s, –e *the darling.*

5. A great many masculines of one syllable belong to Group II. Examples: der Arm, –es, –e *the arm;* der Baum, –es, ¨e *the tree.*

6. The most common neuter monosyllables belong to Group III. These nouns always umlaut the stem vowels a, o, u, au in the plural. Examples: das Haus, –es, ¨er *the house;* das Blatt, –es, ¨er *the leaf.*

7. Words ending in –tum belong to Group III. The u is always umlauted. Examples: das Königtum, –s, ¨er *the kingdom;* der Reichtum, –s, ¨er *the wealth.*

8. Masculine nouns ending in –e and denoting living beings belong to Group IV. Examples: der Knabe, –n, –n *the lad;* der Löwe, –n, –n *the lion.*

9. Feminine nouns of more than one syllable belong to Group IV. Examples: die Rose, —, –n *the rose;* die Freundin, —, –nen *the girl friend;* die Mannschaft, —, –en *the team.*

10. Feminine nouns of one syllable belong either to Group II or to Group IV. Examples: die Stadt, —, ¨e *the city;* die Uhr, —, –en *the time piece.*

3. *Passive Voice: Future and Past Perfect:*

You are already familiar with the present, simple past, and present perfect indicative of the passive voice. The future passive employs the future tense of werden. Thus, *I will be surprised, etc.*

ich werde überrascht werden	ich werde eingeladen werden
du wirst überrascht werden	du wirst eingeladen werden
er wird überrascht werden	er wird eingeladen werden
wir werden überrascht werden	wir werden eingeladen werden
ihr werdet überrascht werden	ihr werdet eingeladen werden
sie werden überrascht werden	sie werden eingeladen werden
Sie werden überrascht werden	Sie werden eingeladen werden

The past perfect passive requires the past perfect tense of werden, but the past participle geworden appears in the form worden. Thus, *I had been surprised, etc.*

ich war überrascht worden	ich war eingeladen worden
du warst überrascht worden	du warst eingeladen worden
er war überrascht worden	er war eingeladen worden
wir waren überrascht worden	wir waren eingeladen worden
ihr wart überrascht worden	ihr wart eingeladen worden
sie waren überrascht worden	sie waren eingeladen worden
Sie waren überrascht worden	Sie waren eingeladen worden

IV. Practice:

1. Die verschiedenen Interessengebiete werden durch die Nummern an der Tafel bezeichnet. pres. passiv
   Die verschiedenen Interessengebiete werden bezeichnet werden. future passive
   Die verschiedenen Interessengebiete waren bezeichnet worden. past perf. passive

2. a. Der bis dahin gewonnene Preis wird verdoppelt.
   wurde
   wird werden.
   ist worden. pres. perf. passive
   war

   b. Die Frage wird richtig beantwortet.
   wurde
   wird werden.
   ist worden.
   war

   c. Jedesmal, wenn die Frage richtig beantwortet wird, wird der bis dahin gewonnene Preis verdoppelt. etc.

3. a. Die Bitte wird wiederholt.
   zu Anfang jedes Programmes wiederholt.

   b. Die Bitte wurde wiederholt. etc.

4. Jetzt geht es um zwei Dollar.
   den großen Preis.
   ums Leben.

5. a. Der Held wird erschossen.
   gegen Ende des Films erschossen.
   Der Held wird gegen Ende des Films von einem französischen Soldaten erschossen. the agent english by

   b. Der Held wurde erschossen. etc.

   c. Der Held wird erschossen werden. etc.

   d. Der Held ist erschossen worden. etc.

   e. Der Held war erschossen worden. etc.

synopsis passive voice

6. Die weibliche Hauptrolle wird von Marlene Dietrich gespielt. pres. passive
wurde past passive
ist worden. pres. perf. passive
war worden. past perf. passive
wird werden. fut. passive

7. Die beiden Romane werden viel gelesen. etc.

8. Die aus vier Musikdramen bestehende Tetralogie wird oft in Amerika gespielt.
Der aus vier Opern bestehende Zyklus wird oft in Amerika gespielt.

9. Fragen Sie mich etwas Leichtes, bitte!
Interessantes,
Lustiges,

10. Ich habe nichts Neues von ihm gehört.
Gutes
viel Interessantes

V. Exercises:

A. *Questions:*

1. Was bezeichnen die Nummern an der Tafel?
2. Wann wird der bis dahin gewonnene Preis verdoppelt?
3. Kennen Sie eine Oper, in der ein deutscher Professor die Hauptrolle spielt?
4. Von welchem deutschen Roman stammt der Stoff des amerikanischen Filmes „All Quiet on the Western Front?"
5. Wie wird der Held des amerikanischen Filmes „Im Westen nichts Neues" erschossen?
6. Was für einen Beruf hat Herr Schönfeld?
7. Welche Verfilmungen von deutschen Literaturwerken kennen Sie?
8. Welche deutsche Oper hat den Namen eines Musikinstrumentes im Titel?
9. Wie heißt die erste Oper in Wagners Tetralogie „Der Ring des Nibelungen"?
10. Wen heiratet Siegfried in Wagners Oper „Götterdämmerung"?
11. Wer bewacht den Nibelungenhort in Wagners Oper „Siegfried"?
12. Wo singen viele Leute laut und begeistert?
13. Was ist der eigentliche Beruf des Mannes, der die 64-Dollar-Frage gewann?

B. *Translate:*

1. Er wird nicht gerne daran erinnert.
2. Er hat sich eine andere Nummer gewählt.
3. Wenn Sie mich etwas Leichtes fragen, kann ich Ihnen die richtige Antwort geben.
4. Zu Shakespeares Zeit wurden die weiblichen Rollen von Jungen in Frauenkleidern gespielt.
5. Bei der ersten falschen Antwort verlieren Sie den bis dahin gewonnenen Preis.
6. Er hat sich etwas Gutes ausgesucht.
7. Das Gold wurde von Siegfried gefunden.
8. Der Riese, dessen Bruder den Nibelungenhort bewacht, heißt Fasolt.

C. *Correct the misinformation:*

1. Fräulein Müller weiß auf dem Gebiet der Oper gut Bescheid.
2. Der erste Besitzer des Nibelungenringes war ein Riese namens Alberich.
3. „Die Zauberflöte" ist eine deutsche Oper, die den Namen eines Schmuckstücks im Titel hat.
4. Fafner war ein König, dessen Schwester Siegfried heiratete.
5. „Winterstürme wichen dem Wonnemond" ist eine Arie aus dem „Rheingold."
6. Wotan war ein Zwerg, der in der Gestalt eines Drachen den Nibelungenhort bewachte.
7. Gunther war der Name eines Königs, der von Siegfried mit dem Schwert erschlagen wurde.
8. Das Schwert des Nibelungen gab dem Besitzer Macht über Menschen und Götter.
9. In dem Film „Im Westen nichts Neues" wird ein Schmetterling vom Helden gefangen.
10. Herrn Schönfelds Beruf ist eigentlich Verkäufer.

D. *Rearrange:*

1. von Marlene Dietrich, ist . . . gespielt worden, die weibliche Hauptrolle.
2. einen teuren Pelzmantel, Herr Schönfeld, der Frau des Ansagers, hat . . . verkauft.
3. als mein Gebiet, das Theater, habe . . . angegeben, ich.
4. wird . . . erschossen, im letzten Akt, der Held, des Dramas.
5. wurde . . . gespielt, die männliche Hauptrolle, von einem amerikanischen Schauspieler.
6. von einem Mann, wurde . . . gewonnen, der Preis, der, arbeitet, in Webers Warenhaus, als Verkäufer.

E. *Complete by means of the suitable clause or phrase. Translate:*

1. Hier an der Tafel sehen Sie die Nummern,
   a. nachdem Sie einen Dollar gewonnen haben.
   b. die die verschiedenen Interessengebiete bezeichnen.
   c. die verdoppelt werden, wenn Sie die Frage richtig beantworten.

2. Auf dem Zettel steht,
   a. daß Fräulein Müller auf dem Gebiet des Kinos bewandert ist.
   b. daß Marlene Dietrich die Hauptrolle in „Kismet" gespielt hat.
   c. daß es jetzt um zwei Dollar geht.

3. Wotan ist der Name eines Gottes,
   a. der den Riesen Fafner mit dem Schwert erschlägt.
   b. dessen Schwester Siegfried heiratet.
   c. der den Nibelungenring besitzen will.

4. Herr Schönfeld wußte auf dem Gebiet der Oper so gut Bescheid,
   a. weil er dicht vor dem Sieg stand.
   b. während er die Arie „Winterstürme wichen dem Wonnemond" sang.
   c. da er Musiklehrer war.
5. Fafner war ein Riese,
   a. der Siegfried erschlug.
   b. der den Nibelungenhort bewachte.
   c. der von Siegfried erschossen wurde.
6. Im Kriegsfilm „Im Westen nichts Neues" wird der Held erschossen,
   a. nachdem er einen Schmetterling gefangen hat.
   b. als er versucht, einen Schmetterling zu fangen.
   c. ehe er aus dem Schützengraben kriecht, um einen Schmetterling zu fangen.
7. Wenn Marlene Dietrich die weibliche Hauptrolle gespielt hätte,
   a. würde ich mich sicher an den Film erinnern.
   b. würde die Frage richtig beantwortet werden.
   c. würden wir die Bedingungen kennen.
8. Wenn ich die Frage richtig beantwortet hätte,
   a. könnte ich mir jetzt einen schönen Pelzmantel leisten.
   b. hätte Siegfried den Riesen nie erschlagen.
   c. würde die Tetralogie aus vier Opern bestehen.

study F. *Connect by means of the conjunction indicated and translate:*

1. (als)
   Fafner wurde von Siegfried erschlagen.
   when Er bewachte den Nibelungenhort in Gestalt eines Drachen.
2. (obgleich)
   although Der Nibelungenring gab seinem Träger Macht über Menschen und Götter.
   Alle Besitzer des Ringes wurden erschlagen.
3. (wenn)
   if Er würde nicht aufhören wollen.
   Er könnte die Frage leicht beantworten.
4. (ob)
   whether Er will die acht Dollar riskieren.
   Er denkt darüber nach.

VI. Principal Parts:

learn

—pfeifen	pfiff	ich habe gepfiffen	er pfeift	whistle
—weichen	wich	ich bin gewichen	er weicht	give way
— kriechen	kroch	ich bin gekrochen	er kriecht	creep
— erschießen	erschoß	ich habe erschossen	er erschießt	shoot
verlieren	verlor	ich habe verloren	er verliert	lose

ſingen	ſang	ich habe geſungen	er ſingt	sing
—gewinnen	gewann	ich habe gewonnen	er gewinnt	win
kommen	kam	ich bin gekommen	er kommt	come
—ſtehlen	ſtahl	ich habe geſtohlen	er ſtiehlt	steal
geben	gab	ich habe gegeben	er gibt	give
ſehen	ſah	ich habe geſehen	er ſieht	see
— beſitzen	beſaß	ich habe beſeſſen	er beſitzt	possess
—erſchlagen	erſchlug	ich habe erſchlagen	er erſchlägt	slay
— fangen	fing	ich habe gefangen	er fängt	catch
heißen	hieß	ich habe geheißen	er heißt	be called, be named
ſein	war	ich bin geweſen	er iſt	be
—gehen	ging	ich bin gegangen	er geht	go
ſtehen	ſtand	ich habe geſtanden	er ſteht	stand
beſtehen	beſtand	es hat beſtanden	es beſteht	consist
tun	tat	ich habe getan	er tut	do
können	konnte	ich habe gekonnt	er kann	be able, can
— ſollen	ſollte	ich habe geſollt	er ſoll	shall, be supposed to
wollen	wollte	ich habe gewollt	er will	want to
kennen	kannte	ich habe gekannt	er kennt	know
nennen	nannte	ich habe genannt	er nennt	name
wiſſen	wußte	ich habe gewußt	er weiß	know

der Beſitzer, –s, — owner
der Muſiklehrer, –s, — music teacher
der Pelzmantel, –s, ¨ fur coat
der Schützengraben, –s, ¨ trench
der Träger, –s, — wearer
der Beruf, –s, –e occupation
der Beweis, –es, –e proof
der Film, –es, –e film
der König, –s, –e king
der Kriegsroman, –s, –e war novel
der Nebenberuf, –s, –e secondary occupation
der Ring, –es, –e ring
der Schmetterling, –s, –e butterfly
der Sieg, –es, –e victory
der Verſuch, –s, –e attempt
der Winterſturm, –s, ¨e winter storm
der Zwerg, –es, –e dwarf
die Macht, —, ¨e power
die Zauberkraft, —, ¨e magic power
das Schmuckſtück, –s, –e piece of jewelry
das Motiv, –s, –e motif
das Gebiet, –es, –e field (of interest)
das Grab, –es, ¨er grave
das Lied, –es, –er song
das Schwert, –es, –er sword
das Warenhaus, –es, ¨er department store
der Gott, –es, ¨er god
die Badewanne, —, –n bath tub
die Bitte, —, –n request
die Hauptrolle, —, –n lead
die Reihe, —, –n row, line
die Sekunde, —, –n second
die Sorge, —, –n worry
die Filmſchauſpielerin, —, –nen movie actress
die Abteilung, —, –en department
die Bedingung, —, –en condition

die Verfilmung, —, -en	film version	der Drache, -n, -n	dragon
die Gestalt, —, -en	shape	der Riese, -n, -n	giant
die Antwort, —, -en	answer	der Held, -en, -en	hero
die Nummer, —, -n	number	der Mensch, -en, -en	human being
die Schwester, —, -n	sister	der Soldat, -en, -en	soldier
die Tafel, —, -n	board	das Kino, -s, -s	movies

VII. Securing the Vocabulary:

A.

die Bedingung	condition	böse sein	(to) be angry
bezeichnen	(to) designate	der Beweis	proof
wählen	(to) choose, elect	ausgezeichnet	excellent
jederzeit	at any time	der Riese	giant
wiederholen	(to) repeat	die Gestalt	form, shape, stature
die Abstammung	descent	erschlagen	(to) slay
nicken	(to) nod	besitzen	(to) possess, own
weiblich	feminine, female	sich erinnern	(to) remember
überraschen	(to) surprise	hauptsächlich	chiefly
fangen	(to) catch	der Sieg	victory
		eigentlich	really

B.

holen (4)	1. need	die Geschichte (3)	1. courage
ärgerlich (2)	2. angry, irritated	der Teil (6)	2. silence
klingeln (6)	3. ever	der Stoff (4)	3. story; history
klingen (7)	4. fetch, get	das Schweigen (2)	4. material
schon einmal (*in question*) (3)	5. assume	zahlreich (8)	5. novel
	6. ring	der Mut (1)	6. part
nötig haben (1)	7. sound	der Roman (5)	7. without
annehmen (5)	8. in spite of	der Fall (10)	8. numerous
damals (10)	9. moment	ohne (7)	9. somewhere
trotz (8)	10. at that time	irgendwo (9)	10. case
der Augenblick (9)			

VIII. Wie Sie wollen: (*Rewritten*)

„Herr Schröder, Sie stehen dicht vor dem Sieg. Wie heißt der amerikanische Filmschauspieler österreichischer Abstammung, der in dem Film ‚Sieben Gräber bis Kairo' die Hauptrolle, die Rolle des Feldmarschalls Rommel, gespielt hat?" . . . „Erich von Strohheim." . . . „Gut. Jetzt kommt der große Moment, jetzt geht es ums Ganze. Herr Schröder, in welcher amerikanischen Verfilmung eines deutschen Dramas wird der Held erschossen?" . . . „In ‚Juarez und Maximilian'. Es ist eine Verfilmung eines Dramas von Werfel. Der Kaiser von Mexiko, Maximilian, wird von Soldaten des mexikanischen Präsidenten Juarez bei Queretaro erschossen." . . . „Bravo, Sie haben sich Ihre vierundsechzig Dollar verdient."

„Nun, Fräulein Wendell, welche Nummer haben Sie gewählt? Dreiundvierzig? Dann sind Sie also auf dem Gebiet der Musik bewandert. Fräulein Wendell, die Musik ist aber ein weites Gebiet. Welches Spezialgebiet in der Musik möchten Sie sich aussuchen?" ... „Die Oper." ... „Gut. Hier ist die erste Frage. Welche Rolle spielt Siegfried in der Geschichte der Oper?" ... „Er ist der Held in Wagners Oper ‚Siegfried'." ... „Gut. Wollen Sie sich zwei Dollar verdienen?" ... „Ja." ... „‚Siegfried' ist die dritte Oper in der Tetralogie ‚Der Ring des Nibelungen'; wie heißen die anderen drei Opern?" ... „Die erste Oper heißt ‚Rheingold', dann kommt ‚Die Walküre', dann ‚Siegfried', und die letzte Oper, die am vierten Tag gespielt wird, ist ‚Götterdämmerung.'" ... „Ich glaube, Sie wollen Ihren bis jetzt gewonnenen Preis verdoppeln. Habe ich recht? Sie nicken, das dachte ich mir. Können Sie mir drei Motive aus dem ‚Ring' nennen?" ... „Das Ringmotiv, das Schwertmotiv, das Liebesmotiv." ... „Ich wiederhole die Bedingungen unseres Frage- und Antwortspieles. Bei der ersten falschen Antwort verlieren Sie alles. Wollen Sie jetzt aufhören oder haben Sie genug Mut, Ihre vier Dollar zu riskieren?" ... „Ich riskiere." ... „Herrlich! Wie heißen die beiden Riesen, die im ‚Ring' eine Rolle spielen?" ... „Fafner und Fasolt. Fragen Sie mich weiter!" ... „Sagen Sie mir, bitte, für sechzehn Dollar, welche Zauberkraft der Nibelungenring hat." ... „Er gibt seinem Besitzer Macht über Götter und Menschen." ... „Sie wissen Bescheid wie ein Musikprofessor. Ich kann mir denken, daß Sie nicht aufhören wollen. Soll ich weiterfragen?" ... „Bitte." ... „Wie heißen die Besitzer des Nibelungenringes?" ... „Der erste Besitzer war der Zwerg Alberich. Der nächste Besitzer des Ringes war Wotan, aber Wotan muß ihn den Riesen Fafner und Fasolt geben. Fafner erschlägt seinen Bruder und bewacht den Ring in Gestalt eines Drachen. Siegfried erschlägt Fafner und nimmt sich den Ring; Siegfried heiratet Gunthers Schwester Gudrun und wird von seinen Verwandten erschlagen. Die Götterdämmerung beginnt, und die Rheintöchter bekommen den Ring." ... „Das ist mehr als wir erwartet haben. Fräulein Wendell, Sie haben bis jetzt zweiunddreißig Dollar gewonnen. Wollen Sie dicht vor dem Sieg Schluß machen? Soll ich weiterfragen? Soll ich aufhören?"

Während Fräulein Wendell nachdenkt, stellt ein Besucher eine andere Station ein. ... „Ist Ihre Frau böse, weil sie keinen Pelzmantel hat? Sie glauben, Sie können sich diesen Luxus nicht leisten. Kommen Sie mit Ihrer Frau zu Webers Warenhaus und sehen Sie selbst, wie überraschend preiswert unsere wirklich eleganten Pelzmäntel sind."

Zweiundzwanzigste Aufgabe

* * * \

Er ist * etwas lauter als gewöhnlich vielleicht', denn es ist Viertel nach fünf, und viele Leute kommen jetzt von ihrer Arbeit, aus Fabri'ken, aus Büros', aus Geschäften.	It is somewhat louder than usual perhaps, for it is quarter past five and many people are coming from their work now, from factories, from offices, from stores.
Aus diesem Verkehrsstrom werde ich mir ein paar Opfer für mein Interview herausfischen.	I'm going to fish a couple of victims for my interview out of this stream of traffic.
... O, o! ich muß etwas falsch gemacht haben, da kommt ein Schutzmann auf mich zu, er sieht mich an, er meint mich, hier ist er."	... Oh, oh! I must have done something wrong, there's a cop coming up to me, he is looking at me, he means me, here he is."
(Eine * grobe, * kräftige Stimme, die Stimme des Schutzmanns.)	(*A rough, powerful voice, the voice of the policeman*).
„Sie, junger Mann, * treten Sie ein bißchen zurück', Sie versperren hier den Weg.	"You, young man, step back a bit, you are blocking the way here.
der Kinobesucher, -s, —	the person at the movies
* der Durchgang muß frei * bleiben.	the passage must remain open
Der Durchgang für die Kinobesucher muß frei bleiben."	Give the people room to get in and out of the movies."
der Wachtmeister, -s, —	the sergeant, policeman
„Jawohl, Herr Wachtmeister! Ist es so besser?"	"Yes, Officer! Is that better?"
was wollen Sie hier machen?	what do you intend to do here?
„Ja. Was wollen Sie hier machen?	"Yes, what are you doing here?
* Gehören Sie zu einer Rekla'mefir'ma?"	Do you belong to an advertising company?"
„Nein, ich bin Ra'diointerview'er; ich will mich nur mit den Fußgängern vor dem Mikrophon' unterhal'ten, so wie ich mich jetzt mit Ihnen unterhal'te."	"No, I am a radio interviewer; I simply want to converse with the passers-by in front of the microphone, just as I am conversing with you now."
„O, deshalb halten Sie mir das Mikrophon' so * dicht unter die Nase.	"Oh, so that's why you're holding the microphone so close up under my nose.
Dann bin ich wohl Ihr erstes * Opfer?"	Then I suppose I am your first victim?"

* raten, riet, ich habe geraten, er rät	(to) guess
„Gut geraten, Herr Wachtmeister, aber können Sie nicht noch einen Augenblick hier bleiben?	"You've guessed it, Officer, but can't you stay here a minute longer?
Ich möchte gerne ein paar Fragen an Sie stellen."	I would like to ask you some questions."
es ist mir recht es soll mir recht sein	it's all right with me I'll agree to it.
„Na, wenn es nicht zu lange * dauert, soll's mir recht sein. Schießen Sie los!"	"Well, if it doesn't take too long, it will be all right with me. Fire away!"
„Wie heißen Sie, Herr Wachtmeister?"	"What's your name, Officer?"
„Peter McGuire."	"Peter McGuire."
„Jetzt werden Sie glauben, ich mache mich über Sie lustig.	"Now you will think I am making fun of you.
McGuire war der Mädchenname meiner Mutter.	McGuire was my mother's maiden name.
Ich bin, wie Sie sehen, halbirisch.	As you see, I'm half Irish.
Herr Wachtmeister, in Ihrem Beruf erleben Sie viele aufregende Dinge.	Officer, in your profession you have many exciting experiences.
Was war der interessan'teste Fall, den Sie * erlebt haben?"	What was the most interesting case that you have experienced?"
„Das war vor drei Jahren.	"That was three years ago.
* fertig	finished, ready
Ich war * gerade mit dem Dienst fertig und wollte nach Hause gehen, als mein Freund Gus Carlson auf mich zukam und sagte: ‚Peter, komm mit!	I was just coming off duty and was intending to go home, when my friend Gus Carlson came up to me and said, 'Peter, come along!
Hier hast du eine Zigar're; du ißt heute mit mir Abendbrot!'	Here is a cigar for you; you're having supper with me today!'
Ich sage: ‚Also ein Junge! Na, da gratuliere ich, Gus.	I said: 'So it's a boy! Well, congratulations, Gus.
Wo sollen wir hingehen?'	Where shall we go?'
Gus sagt: ‚In Bauers Bierstube.	Gus said, 'To Bauer's tavern.
Bei Bauer gibt es heute Sauerkraut und Schweinsfüße; das ißt du doch gern?'	They have sauerkraut and pigs' feet at Bauer's place today; you like that, don't you?'
Bauers Restaurant ist heute im Norden bei der Zugbrücke, damals war es aber noch in der Kanal'stra'ße.	Today Bauer's restaurant is up north, near the draw-bridge, but at that time it was still on Canal Street.

Es war ſchon ſpät, und wir wollten gerade bei der Kanal'ſtra'ße um die Ecke * biegen, als ich einen Schuß hörte.	It was already late and we were just about to turn the corner at Canal Street when I heard a shot.
herunter, runter contraction	downward
Im nächſten Augenblick rannte * jemand aus einer Kneipe und wollte an uns vorbei' zum Fluß runter.	The next moment somebody ran out of a beer joint and wanted to go past us down to the river.
Dann kamen Leute gelaufen; die ſchrien: ‚Haltet ihn! Haltet ihn!'	Then people came running; they screamed 'Stop him! Stop him!'
Ich wartete natür'lich nicht, * ſondern jagte hinter dem Kerl her, ſo ſchnell ich konnte.	Of course, I didn't wait, but chased after the fellow as fast as I could.
* Plötzlich ſprang er hinter einen Later'nenpfahl' und ſchoß.	Suddenly he jumped behind a lamp post and shot.
Ich drückte mich in eine Türöffnung und ſchoß zurück.	I squeezed myself into the opening of a door and shot back at him.
Wir * wechſelten noch ein paar Schüſſe, dann ſprang der Kerl hinter der Later'ne hervor' und rannte über einen Bauplatz.	We exchanged a few more shots, then the fellow jumped out from behind the lamp post and ran across a building lot.
Er mußte wohl gedacht haben, ich hätte meine Munition' verſchoſſen.	He must have thought I had used up my ammunition.
Da hatte er ſich aber geirrt.	But there he had made a mistake.
Ich * zielte * ſorgfältig und traf ihn ins * Bein.	I aimed carefully and hit him in the leg.
Die Jagd war zu Ende.	The chase was over.
Das war mein erſter Fang.	That was my first catch.
Natür'lich ein ſeit langem geſuchter Verbrecher: Diebſtähle, Einbrüche und dergglei'chen mehr. (u. dgl. m.)	Of course, a criminal who had long been wanted: theft, burglary, and so on.
Na, heute ſitzt er immer noch, wie Sie ſich denken können.	Well, he is still in jail even to this day, as you can imagine.
Jetzt muß ich aber gehen, ſonſt ſchimpft meine Frau.	But now I have to go, otherwise my wife will bawl me out.
Verheiratet bin ich nämlich auch."	You see, I am married too."
„Danke ſchön, Herr Wachtmeiſter, das war ſehr intereſſant', und ich weiß, Ihre drama'tiſche Beſchreibung hat unſeren Hörern * gefallen."	Thank you very much, Officer, that was very interesting and I know our listeners liked your dramatic description."
(Schluß folgt.)	(Conclusion follows.)

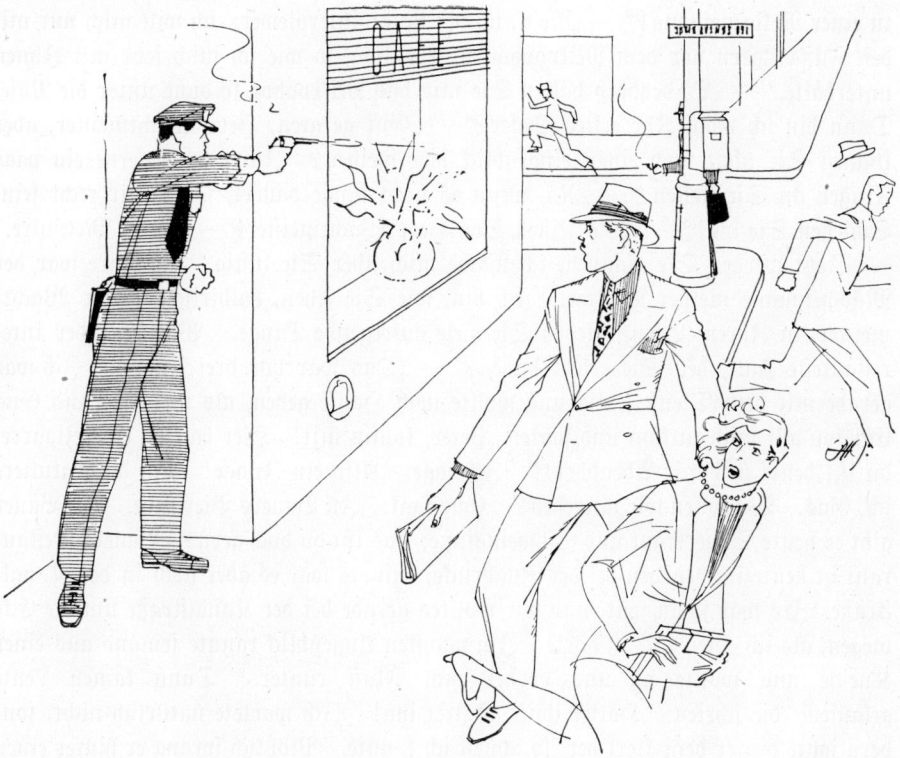

II. Text:

Die Großstadt spricht

(Stimme des Ansagers) Wir bringen jetzt unser Programm „Die Großstadt spricht." Sie werden gleich Herrn Baumers Stimme hören, der irgendwo in unserer Stadt die Leute auf der Straße interviewen wird.

„Ich stehe in der Hauptstraße vor dem Palastkino; ich halte das Mikrophon in die Straße, um Ihnen ein Klangbild, eine akustische Photographie, zu geben. (Man hört ratternde und klingelnde Straßenbahnen, ungeduldige Autohupen, eine vorbeidonnernde Hochbahn und die Rufe der Zeitungsverkäufer.) Ja, meine Hörer, das klingt sonderbar, wenn man es nicht sehen kann, das klingt wie Dschungelgeräusche, aber es ist echter Straßenlärm. Er ist etwas lauter als gewöhnlich vielleicht, denn es ist Viertel nach fünf, und viele Leute kommen jetzt von ihrer Arbeit, aus Fabriken, aus Büros, aus Geschäften. Aus diesem Verkehrsstrom werde ich mir ein paar Opfer für mein Interview herausfischen . . . O, o, ich muß etwas falsch gemacht haben, da kommt ein Schutzmann auf mich zu, er sieht mich an, er meint mich, hier ist er."

(Eine grobe, kräftige Stimme, die Stimme des Schutzmanns.)

„Sie, junger Mann, treten Sie ein bißchen zurück, Sie versperren hier den Weg. Der Durchgang für die Kinobesucher muß frei bleiben." — „Jawohl, Herr Wachtmeister! Ist es so besser?" — „Ja. Was wollen Sie hier machen? Gehören Sie

zu einer Reklamefirma?" — „Nein, ich bin Radiointerviewer; ich will mich nur mit den Fußgängern vor dem Mikrophon unterhalten, so wie ich mich jetzt mit Ihnen unterhalte." — „O, deshalb halten Sie mir das Mikrophon so dicht unter die Nase. Dann bin ich wohl Ihr erstes Opfer?" — „Gut geraten, Herr Wachtmeister, aber können Sie nicht noch einen Augenblick hier bleiben? Ich möchte gerne ein paar Fragen an Sie stellen." — „Na, wenn es nicht lange dauert, soll's mir recht sein. Schießen Sie los!" — „Wie heißen Sie, Herr Wachtmeister? — „Peter McGuire." — „Jetzt werden Sie glauben, ich mache mich über Sie lustig. McGuire war der Mädchenname meiner Mutter. Ich bin, wie Sie sehen, halbirisch. Herr Wachtmeister, in Ihrem Beruf erleben Sie viele aufregende Dinge. Was war der interessanteste Fall, den Sie erlebt haben?" — „Das war vor drei Jahren. Ich war gerade mit dem Dienst fertig und wollte nach Hause gehen, als mein Freund Gus Carlson auf mich zu kam und sagte: ‚Peter, komm mit! Hier hast du eine Zigarre; du ißt heute mit mir Abendbrot!' Ich sage: ‚Also ein Junge! Na, da gratuliere ich, Gus. Wo sollen wir hingehen?' Gus sagt: ‚In Bauers Bierstube. Bei Bauer gibt es heute Sauerkraut und Schweinsfüße; das ißt du doch gern?' Bauers Restaurant ist heute im Norden bei der Zugbrücke, damals war es aber noch in der Kanalstraße. Es war schon spät, und wir wollten gerade bei der Kanalstraße um die Ecke biegen, als ich einen Schuß hörte. Im nächsten Augenblick rannte jemand aus einer Kneipe und wollte an uns vorbei zum Fluß runter. Dann kamen Leute gelaufen; die schrien: ‚Haltet ihn! Haltet ihn!' Ich wartete natürlich nicht, sondern jagte hinter dem Kerl her, so schnell ich konnte. Plötzlich sprang er hinter einen Laternenpfahl und schoß. Ich drückte mich in eine Türöffnung und schoß zurück. Wir wechselten noch ein paar Schüsse, dann sprang der Kerl hinter der Laterne hervor und rannte über einen Bauplatz. Er mußte wohl gedacht haben, ich hätte meine Munition verschossen. Da hatte er sich aber geirrt. Ich zielte sorgfältig und traf ihn ins Bein. Die Jagd war zu Ende. Das war mein erster Fang. Natürlich ein seit langem gesuchter Verbrecher: Diebstähle, Einbrüche und dergleichen mehr. (u. dgl. m.) Na, heute sitzt er immer noch, wie Sie sich denken können. Jetzt muß ich aber gehen, sonst schimpft meine Frau. Verheiratet bin ich nämlich auch." — „Danke schön, Herr Wachtmeister, das war sehr interessant, und ich weiß, Ihre dramatische Beschreibung hat unseren Hörern gefallen."

Schluß folgt.

III. Comments:

1. *Variable Prefixes:*

There are three kinds of verb prefixes in German. The prefixes which are always inseparable are be–, ge–, emp–, ent–, er–, ver–, zer–. Examples: bekommen (*obtain*), bekam, ich habe bekommen, er bekommt; gestatten (*permit*), gestattete, ich habe gestattet, er gestattet. The separable prefixes, of which there are a great many, are prepositions and adverbs which enter into close association with verbs. Verbs with separable prefixes that you have had are: anfangen, anziehen, aufstehen,

ausgeben, aufpassen, einladen, stattfinden, herankommen. Examples of the principal parts of two such separable compounds are: wie'derbringen (*bring back*), brachte . . . wieder, ich habe wiedergebracht, er bringt . . . wieder; un'terkommen (*find lodgings*), kam . . . unter, ich bin untergekommen, er kommt . . . unter.

But a certain number of prefixes are variable, that is, they may form either separable or inseparable compounds with verbs. The variable prefixes are durch, über, um, unter, wieder. The verbs wie'derbringen and un'terkommen above are separable compounds of the prefixes wieder and unter. Inseparable compounds of these prefixes are: wiederho'len (*repeat*), wiederholte, ich habe wiederholt, er wiederholt; unterhal'ten (*entertain*), unterhielt, ich habe unterhalten, er unterhält.

You see that in separable compounds the prefix bears the main stress and the perfect participle shows a ge- inserted between the separable prefix and the verb as in wiedergebracht, untergekommen. But in inseparable compounds the verb bears the main stress and there is no ge- in the perfect participle as in wiederholt, unterhalten. This means that the variable prefixes bear the stress in separable compounds but lose it in inseparable compounds.

2. *Idiomatic Use of the Past Participle:*

The past participle is used with kommen where English speakers would expect the present participle: er kam gelaufen — *he came running*, es kommt geflogen — *it comes flying*.

3. *Past Infinitive:*

You are already familiar with the present infinitive from the principal parts of verbs. The past infinitive of a verb is made up of its past participle and the infinitive of its tense auxiliary: bekommen haben — (*to*) *have obtained*, gesagt haben — (*to*) *have said*, gekommen sein — (*to*) *have come*, hinausgegangen sein — (*to*) *have gone out*. The chief use of the perfect infinitive is as a complement to a modal auxiliary: Ich muß etwas falsch gemacht haben — *I must have done something wrong;* Er kann das nicht gesagt haben — *He can't have said that.*

4. *Modal Auxiliaries: Compound Tenses.*

So far you have had the present and simple past tenses of the modal auxiliaries. The future tense forms are:

ich werde dürfen du wirst dürfen er wird dürfen wir werden dürfen ihr werdet dürfen sie werden dürfen Sie werden dürfen	I will be permitted to, *etc.*	ich werde können du wirst können er wird können wir werden können ihr werdet können sie werden können Sie werden können	I will be able to, *etc.*
ich werde mögen	I will like to, *etc.*	ich werde müssen	I will have to, *etc.*
ich werde sollen	I will be supposed to, *etc.*	ich werde wollen	I will want to, *etc.*

The present perfect and past perfect tenses of the modals, when they have no complementary infinitive, are:

ich habe gedurft du haſt gedurft er hat gedurft wir haben gedurft ihr habt gedurft ſie haben gedurft Sie haben gedurft	I have been allowed to, *etc.*	ich hatte gedurft du hatteſt gedurft er hatte gedurft wir hatten gedurft ihr hattet gedurft ſie hatten gedurft Sie hatten gedurft	I had been allowed to, *etc.*
ich habe gekonnt	I have been able to, *etc.*	ich hatte gekonnt	I had been able to, *etc.*
ich habe gemocht	I have liked to, *etc.*	ich hatte gemocht	I had liked to, *etc.*
ich habe gemußt	I have had to, *etc.*	ich hatte gemußt	I had had to, *etc.*
ich habe geſollt	I have been supposed to, *etc.*	ich hatte geſollt	I had been supposed to, *etc.*
ich habe gewollt	I have wanted to, *etc.*	ich hatte gewollt	I had wanted to, *etc.*

5. *Double Infinitive with Modal Auxiliaries:*

When a complementary infinitive is used with the modal auxiliaries in the perfect tenses, however, the past participle of the modal appears in a form which is identical with its present infinitive. Thus:

ich habe gehen dürfen	I have been (was) allowed to go *etc.*
ich habe kommen können	I have been (was) able to come *etc.*
ich hatte arbeiten müſſen	I had had to work *etc.*
ich hatte ſpielen wollen	I had wanted to play *etc.*

Such combinations as kommen können, arbeiten müſſen are known as the double infinitive. The double infinitive always comes last in a clause.

6. *Double Infinitive with other Verbs.*

Certain other verbs, the most common being helfen, hören, ſehen, and laſſen also take the double infinitive construction: Ich habe ihn kommen ſehen. *I saw him come;* Er hatte den Schlüſſel ſtecken laſſen. *He had left the key inserted;* Wir haben ihn ſpielen hören. *We have heard him play.*

IV. Practice:

1. a. Da kommt eben ein Schutzmann auf uns zu.
über die Straße und auf uns zu.

b. Wir müssen etwas falsch gemacht haben.

c. Wir müssen etwas falsch gemacht haben, denn da kommt ein Schutzmann über die Straße und auf uns zu.

2. a. Wir haben den Weg versperrt.
den Kinobesuchern den Weg versperrt.

b. Wir haben ein bißchen zurücktreten müssen.

c. Wir haben ein bißchen zurücktreten müssen, weil wir den Kinobesuchern den Weg versperrten.

3. a. Ich unterhalte mich mit dem Schutzmann.
Ich unterhalte mich mit dem Schutzmann über seine aufregenden Erlebnisse.

b. Ich habe mich mit dem Schutzmann unterhalten.
Ich habe mich mit dem Schutzmann über seine aufregenden Erlebnisse unterhalten.

c. Er hat sich mit dem Schutzmann unterhalten. etc.

4. Der Verbrecher rannte an der Türöffnung vorbei.
Kneipe
am Restaurant
Kino

5. a. Sie versperrt den Weg.
versperrte
hat versperrt.

b. Sie tritt ein bißchen zurück.
trat
ist zurückgetreten.

c. Sie trat ein bißchen zurück, denn sie versperrte den Weg.

6. a. Herr Schröder ißt bei Bauer Sauerkraut und Schweinsfüße.
aß

b. Ein Kerl kommt auf ihn zu und hält ihm einen Revolver unter die Nase.
kam hielt

c. Als Herr Schröder bei Bauer Sauerkraut und Schweinsfüße aß, kam ein Kerl auf ihn zu und hielt ihm einen Revolver unter die Nase.

7. a. Wachtmeister McGuires dramatische Beschreibung seines ersten Fanges gefällt uns.
gefiel unseren Hörern.

b. Das können Sie sich denken.

c. Sie können sich denken, wie Wachtmeister McGuires dramatische Beschreibung seines ersten Fanges uns gefällt.

8. Jemand ist an uns vorbeigerannt.
Es muß der Verbrecher gewesen sein.
Es muß der Verbrecher gewesen sein, der an uns vorbeigerannt ist.

9. Ein Polizist erlebt viel.
   hat erlebt.
   muß erlebt haben.

10. a. Es dauert nicht lange.
   dauerte
   hat gedauert.

   b. Der Kerl springt hinter dem Laternenpfahl hervor.
   sprang
   ist hervorgesprungen.

   c. Es dauert nicht lange, bis der Kerl hinter dem Laternenpfahl hervorspringt.
   usw.

V. Exercises:

A. *Questions:*

1. Wo finden die Interviews für das Programm „Die Großstadt spricht" statt?
2. Warum ist der Lärm der Hauptstraße um Viertel nach fünf ein bißchen stärker als gewöhnlich?
3. Warum muß der Interviewer zurücktreten?
4. Warum hält der Interviewer dem Schutzmann das Mikrophon unter die Nase?
5. Welche von den interviewten Personen hat die aufregendsten Dinge erlebt?
6. Wo ist Bauers Restaurant zur Zeit dieses Interviews?
7. Wie konnte der Wachtmeister wissen, daß der Mann, der aus der Kneipe lief, ein Verbrecher war?
8. Erschoß der Wachtmeister den Verbrecher?
9. Wer war der erste Fang des Wachtmeisters?
10. Warum muß der Wachtmeister schließlich gehen?

B. *Translate:*

1. Er muß etwas falsch gemacht haben, denn ein Schutzmann kommt auf ihn zu.
2. Wie lange sitzt der Verbrecher schon?
3. Wir wollten gerade ins Kino gehen, als ein Polizist auf uns zukam.
4. Er wollte eben zum Fluß hinunter rennen, als ihn ein Schuß ins Bein traf.
5. Hätte ich ihn nur sehen können!
6. Ich unterhielt mich mit dem berühmten Schauspieler, Heinrich George.
7. Er lief aus dem Haus, um nachzusehen, wen oder was sein Hund so ärgerlich anbellte.
8. Ich möchte mir den Film noch einmal ansehen.
9. Das kann nur Tarzan getan haben.
10. Er muß schon nach Hause gegangen sein.

C. *Rearrange:*

1. hat . . . stellen wollen, ein paar Fragen, er, an der Ecke, an die Dame.
2. ich, wenn, etwas, nicht, hätte, gemacht, so, der Schutzmann, auf mich zu, nicht, falsch, wäre . . . gekommen.

3. wollte, sich, die alte Dame, unterhalten, mit mir, über einen interessanten Kriminalfilm.
4. vor fünf Jahren, jeden Tag, es, Schweinsfüße und Sauerkraut, bei Bauer, gab.
5. dachte, ich, hätte . . . verschossen, meine Munition, der Kerl. normal word order no daß (conj.)

D. *Complete by means of the suitable clause or phrase. Translate:*

1. Nachdem sie ein paar Schüsse gewechselt hatten,
   a. lief der Verbrecher davon.
   b. kam er tief in Gedanken aus dem Kino.
   c. wollte er sich die interessante Photographie ansehen.
2. Ich habe mir den anderen Film ansehen müssen,
   a. obgleich ich das nicht wollte.
   b. trotzdem er eben gezeigt wurde.
   c. und rannte deshalb an dem Kino vorbei.
3. Er hat sich immer wieder fragen müssen,
   a. weil er bei Bauer Sauerkraut und Schweinsfüße aß.
   b. was er seiner Frau sagen sollte.
   c. obgleich der Mann ein seit langem gesuchter Verbrecher war.
4. Hätte der Schutzmann seine Munition verschossen,
   a. als der Bandit hinter den Laternenpfahl sprang.
   b. und der Bandit konnte zum Fluß hinunter laufen.
   c. so hätte er den Banditen nicht fangen können.
5. Während ich vor dem Kino stand und auf meinen Freund wartete,
   a. will sie sich mit mir unterhalten.
   b. donnerte eine Straßenbahn vorbei.
   c. kann ich ungeduldige Autohupen hören.

E. *Correct the misinformation:*

1. Der Straßenlärm ist um zwei Uhr laut, denn viele Leute wollen nach Hause.
2. Herr Baumer will den Leuten auf der Straße eine akustische Photographie geben.
3. Der Schutzmann wollte seinem Freund Carlson eine Zigarre geben.
4. Wachtmeister McGuire hat seine Munition verschossen.
5. Der Schutzmann hat eine schöne, klangvolle Stimme.
6. McGuire jagte an dem Verbrecher vorbei und an den Fluß hinunter.
7. Der Wachtmeister zielte sorgfältig und traf den Kerl in den Arm.

F. *Connect by means of the conjunction indicated and translate:*

1. (da)
   Er hörte zwei durch die Stille knallende Revolverschüsse.
   Er lief schnell um die Ecke um nachzusehen, was los war.
2. (aber)
   Vor dem Schaufenster standen viele Leute, die ihr den Weg versperrten.
   Sie wollte sich die Pelzmäntel ansehen.

3. (wenn)
Seine Frau wird schimpfen.
Er geht jetzt nicht nach Hause.

4. (nachdem)
Sie hatten ein paar Schüsse gewechselt.
Der Bandit sprang ins Auto hinein und fuhr davon.

VI. Principal Parts:

heißen	hieß	ich habe geheißen	er heißt	be called
—*bleiben	blieb	ich bin geblieben	er bleibt	remain
—schreien	schrie	ich habe geschrien	er schreit	scream
—biegen	bog	ich habe gebogen	er biegt	bend, turn
schießen	schoß	es hat geschossen	es schießt	shoot
klingen	klang	ich habe geklungen	er klingt	sound
—springen	sprang	ich bin gesprungen	er springt	jump
sprechen	sprach	ich habe gesprochen	er spricht	speak
—treffen	traf	ich habe getroffen	er trifft	hit
kommen	kam	ich bin gekommen	er kommt	come
—essen	aß	ich habe gegessen	er ißt	eat
geben	gab	ich habe gegeben	er gibt	give
sehen	sah	ich habe gesehen	er sieht	see
—zurücktreten	trat . . . zurück	ich bin zurückgetreten	er tritt . . . zurück	step back
—sitzen	saß	ich habe gesessen	er sitzt	sit
—gefallen	gefiel	ich habe gefallen	er gefällt	like
halten	hielt	ich habe gehalten	er hält	hold
—raten	riet	ich habe geraten	er rät	guess
laufen	lief	ich bin gelaufen	er läuft	run
stehen	stand	ich habe gestanden	er steht	stand
können	konnte	ich habe gekonnt	er kann	can, be able
müssen	mußte	ich habe gemußt	er muß	must, have to
sollen	sollte	ich habe gesollt	er soll	shall
wollen	wollte	ich habe gewollt	er will	want to
denken	dachte	ich habe gedacht	er denkt	think
—rennen	rannte	ich bin gerannt	er rennt	run
—bringen	brachte	ich habe gebracht	er bringt	bring
wissen	wußte	ich habe gewußt	er weiß	know

der Fußgänger, –s, —	pedestrian	der Verbrecher, –s, —	criminal
der Hörer, –s, —	listener	der Wachtmeister, –s, —	officer
der Kinobesucher, –s, —	moviegoer	der Zeitungsverkäufer, –s, —	newspaper vendor
der Radiointerviewer, –s, —	radio interviewer	das Opfer, –s, —	victim

das Viertel, –s, —	quarter
der Bauplatz, –es, ⸗e	building lot
der Diebstahl, –s, ⸗e	theft
der Dienst, –es, –e	duty
der Durchgang, –s, ⸗e	passage
der Einbruch, –s, ⸗e	burglary
der Fang, –es, ⸗e	catch
der Fluß, –es, ⸗e	river
der Kerl, –es, –e	fellow
der Laternenpfahl, –s, ⸗e	lamp post
der Ruf, –es, –e	reputation
der Schuß, –es, ⸗e	shot
der Schweinsfuß, –es, ⸗e	pig's foot
der Verkehrsstrom, –s, ⸗e	stream of traffic
der Weg, –es, –e	way
die Stadt, —, ⸗e	city
das Abendbrot, –s	supper
das Dschungelgeräusch, –es, –e	jungle noise
das Ding, –es, –e	thing
das Klangbild, –es, –er	sound picture
der Schutzmann, –s, ...leute	policeman
die Bierstube, —, –n	tavern
die Hauptstraße, —, –n	main street
die Kneipe, —, –n	beer joint
die Laterne, —, –n	lamp post
die Nase, —, –n	nose
die Photographie, —, –n	photograph
die Zigarre, —, –n	cigar
die Zugbrücke, —, –n	draw bridge
die Beschreibung, —, –en	description
die Fortsetzung, —, –en	continuation
die Türöffnung, —, –en	doorway
die Hochbahn, —, –en	elevated train
die Jagd, —, –en	chase
die Straßenbahn, —, –en	streetcar
die Arbeit, —, –en	work
die Fabrik, —, –en	factory
die Reklamefirma, —, ...firmen	advertising company
das Interview, –s, –s	interview
das Restaurant, –s, –s	restaurant

VII. Securing the Vocabulary:

20, 21, 22 vocabulary test

A.

echt	genuine	dauern	(to) last, take
der Lärm	noise	erleben	(to) experience
sonderbar	strange, odd	gerade	just
etwas	something, somewhat	fertig	finished, ready
grob	rough	biegen	(to) bend, turn
kräftig	strong, powerful	sondern	but
treten	step	plötzlich	suddenly
der Durchgang	passage	wechseln	(to) change, exchange
bleiben	(to) remain	zielen	(to) aim
gehören	(to) belong	sorgfältig	carefully
dicht	close	das Bein	leg
das Opfer	victim	gefallen	(to) like
raten	(to) guess	jemand	somebody

B.

feig(e) (1)	1. cowardly	hauptsächlich (5)	6. charming
die Gestalt (3)	2. stop	reizend (6)	7. take
aufhören (2)	3. form, shape	ausgezeichnet (4)	8. designate
der Sieg (9)	4. excellent	bezeichnen (8)	9. victory
ähnlich (10)	5. chiefly	nehmen (7)	10. similar

besitzen (2)	1. somewhere	überraschen (4)	6. remember
irgendwo (1)	2. possess, own	die Bedingung (3)	7. while, during
während (7)	3. condition	der Riese (8)	8. giant
der Teil (5)	4. surprise	eigentlich (10)	9. partly
sich erinnern (6)	5. part	teilweise (9)	10. really

der Unterschied (3)	1. imagine	wählen (2)	4. first of all
sich vorstellen (1)	2. choose, elect	die Tasche (6)	5. show
zunächst (4)	3. difference	zeigen (5)	6. pocket

Study

VIII. Die Großstadt spricht: (*Rewritten*)

„Gleich werden Sie ein sehr sonderbares Konzert hören. (Man hört etwas, das wie Dschungelgeräusche oder ultramoderne Musik klingt.) Ja, meine Hörer, das ist der Verkehrslärm, den Sie jeden Abend kurz nach fünf auf unserer Hauptstraße hören können. Ich stehe mit dem Mikrophon vor dem Palastkino. — Hören Sie den Donner? — Das war eine Hochbahn. — Diese Straßenbahn, die Sie gerade vorbeirattern hörten und die so ungeduldig klingelte, war, wie Sie sich denken können, ein sehr altes Modell. — Können Sie den Jungen verstehen? — Es ist ein Zeitungsverkäufer, und er hat eine Stimme wie eine Trompete.

Nun ist es aber Zeit, daß ich mit meinen Interviews beginne. Wer wird das erste Opfer sein? Da kommt eine ältere Dame, mit der ich mich unterhalten möchte. (Man hört den Interviewer rufen.) Einen Augenblick bitte — Ja, ich meine Sie." (Man hört eine ältere Frau lachen). „Ha, ha, ha, ich kann nicht singen." — „Aber wir wollen wirklich nicht, daß Sie singen, wir wollen uns nur ein bißchen mit Ihnen unterhalten. Tausende von Frauen wie Sie sitzen jetzt zu Hause oder besser, sind bei der Hausarbeit und haben unsere Station eingestellt. Diese Frauen interessieren sich dafür, wer Sie sind und was Sie tun. Können Sie einen Augenblick hier bleiben? Ich möchte gerne ein paar einfache Fragen an Sie stellen." — „Na, wenn es nicht lange dauert, soll's mir recht sein. Ich muß nämlich um sechs Uhr zu Hause sein, sonst schimpft mein Mann. Wir haben heute sein Lieblingsessen, Schweinsfüße und Sauerkraut." + „Ihr Mann kann nicht lange ärgerlich sein, wenn er sein Lieblingsessen auf dem Tisch stehen sieht." — „Ha, ha, ha. Sie kennen meinen Mann nicht. Wenn er von der Arbeit nach Hause kommt, schimpft er immer. Sie wollen wissen, wie ich heiße. Ich heiße McGuire, mein Mädchenname war McAllister." + „Jetzt werden Sie glauben, daß ich mich über Sie lustig mache, aber der Mädchenname meiner Mutter war auch McAllister. Frau McGuire, woher kommen Sie gerade?" — „Ich komme von Webers Warenhaus, ich habe mir einen automatischen Toaster gekauft. Mein Mann schimpft immer, wenn sein Toast schwarz ist, besonders wenn er morgens keine Zeit hat. Er muß nämlich jeden Morgen sehr früh ins Büro gehen. Er arbeitet für eine Reklamefirma. Vor einem Jahr hat er in Detjens Radiogeschäft als Verkäufer gearbeitet, aber die Büroarbeit ge-

fällt ihm besser. Er kann nämlich nicht lange auf den Füßen stehen. Er hat" — „Frau McGuire, das war sehr interessant, aber ich muß mit meinem Mikrophon weitergehen, ich sehe, ich versperre hier den Durchgang für die Kinobesucher.

Ah, dort sehe ich Wachtmeister Blackwell. Viele unserer Hörer werden wissen, daß Wachtmeister Blackwell vor zwei Wochen bei der Zugbrücke einen Mann herausgefischt hat, der mit seinem Auto in den Fluß gefallen war. Ohne Wachtmeister Blackwell hätten wir ein Verkehrsopfer mehr gehabt. — Wachtmeister Blackwell, haben Sie einen Augenblick Zeit? — Wir möchten Sie interviewen. Wir möchten von Ihnen hören, was der interessanteste Fall in Ihrem aufregenden Beruf war. Können Sie uns etwas von Verbrechen, Einbrüchen, Diebstählen u. dgl. m. erzählen, mit denen Sie zu tun hatten?" — „Sie wissen, ich bin jetzt Verkehrsschutzmann und erlebe nicht viel Aufregendes. Aber als ich im Norden bei der Kanalstraße Dienst hatte, da habe ich viel erlebt." — „Wachtmeister Blackwell, was war Ihr erster Fang? Wer war der erste Verbrecher, den Sie gefangen haben?" — „Hm, das war vor zehn Jahren. Es war kein Berufsverbrecher, nur ein Amateur, ein junger Kerl. Der dachte, es wäre leichter, den Leuten einen Revolver unter die Nase zu halten als zu arbeiten. Der Mann hieß — hm, ich habe den Namen vergessen." — „Können Sie uns beschreiben, wie Sie den Mann fingen?" — „Ja, das werde ich nie vergessen. Ich war damals noch nicht verheiratet und aß oft in Fritz Bauers Restaurant Abendbrot. Fritz Bauer hatte damals ein Restaurant mit einer Bierstube in der Kanalstraße. Die Bierstube war neben dem Restaurant. Ich war gerade mit dem Essen fertig, als jemand in der Bierstube sagte: ‚Hände hoch, oder ich schieße!' Durch die Türöffnung sah ich, wie ein junger Kerl mit einem Revolver vor Fritz stand. Ich wollte gerade in die Bierstube laufen, da sah mich Fritz und schrie ‚Hilfe'. Der Bandit sprang aus der Tür und lief auf die Straße. Ich wartete nicht und rannte hinter ihm her. Das hatte ich falsch gemacht. Als ich auf die Straße kam, stand der Bandit hinter einer Laterne und schoß. Ich drückte mich in die Türöffnung und schoß zurück. Wir wechselten noch ein paar Schüsse. Als der Bandit seine Munition verschossen hatte, rannte er über einen Bauplatz, aber da kam Wachtmeister Lennert gelaufen. Lennert hatte das Schießen gehört, und als der Bandit an ihm vorbei zum Fluß rennen wollte, schoß er ihn in die Schulter. Jetzt erst sah ich, daß der erste Schuß des Banditen gut gezielt war. Er hatte mich ins rechte Bein getroffen." — „Danke schön, Herr Wachtmeister. Ihre dramatische Beschreibung war sehr interessant. Ich danke Ihnen auch im Namen meiner Hörer."

Dreiundzwanzigste Aufgabe

* * * \

Laſſen Sie mich mal nachdenken.

Let me think about it.

Vor vielen Jahren, es muß gleich nach dem erſten Weltkrieg geweſen ſein, da kam ein Mann zu mir, der wollte ſeine Heimatſtadt photographiert haben.

Many years ago, it must have been right after the first World War, a man came to me, he wanted to have his home town photographed.

Seine Heimatſtadt war irgendein kleines * Städtchen in den Südſtaaten.

His home town was some tiny little place in the South.

Den Namen hab ich vergeſſen; ich glaube, es war irgendwo in Georgia.

I have forgotten the name; I think it was somewhere in Georgia.

wie ſtellt er ſich das vor?

how does he imagine that?

Ich fragte ihn, wie er ſich das vorſtellte.

I asked him what he had in mind.

Der Mann wollte eine Art Panora'ma haben.

The man wanted to have a kind of panorama.

Ich mußte auf verſchiedene * Dächer klettern und von da Aufnahmen machen.

I had to climb up on different roofs and take pictures from there.

Die Reiſekoſten hat er mir natür'lich bezahlt.

Of course, he paid my traveling expenses.

Ältere Damen wollen ihre Tierlieblinge, Hunde, Katzen, Kana'riĕnvö'gel, Papagei'en photographiert haben.

Older ladies want to have pictures taken of their animal pets, dogs, cats, canaries, parrots.

Und wenn die Tiere * krank ſind, fragen ſie mich oft auch noch um * Rat: ‚Ich glaube mein Fifi hat Lungenentzündung; glauben Sie, daß Prinz Fieber hat?'

And when the animals are sick they even often ask me for advice as well: ‚I believe my Fifi has pneumonia; do you think Prince has a fever?'

Als * ob ich ein * Tierarzt wäre!"

As if I were a veterinary!"

„Was für Aufnahmen machen Sie am liebſten?"

"What kind of pictures do you like to take best?"

die Perſo'nenauf'nahme, —, -n

the picture of a person or persons

„Perſo'nenauf'nahmen, ältere Leute.

"Human subjects, older people.

wenn es nötig iſt

when it's necessary

Die beißen nicht, ſitzen ſtill und * lächeln, wenn es nötig iſt."

They don't bite, sit still and smile when it's necessary."

„Was für Perſonenaufnahmen machen Sie nur ungern?"

"What kind of pictures of human subjects don't you like to take?"

„Gruppenaufnahmen. Da iſt immer einer in der Gruppe, der im letzten Augenblick einen * Witz macht oder eine * unvernünftige Frage ſtellt.

"Group pictures. There is always somebody in the group who makes a joke at the last moment or asks a senseless question.

stecken lassen	(to) leave sticking
Oder wenn ich alles eingestellt habe, erinnert sich plötzlich einer, daß er seine * Schlüssel im Auto hat stecken lassen, und läuft auf die Straße, um nachzusehen, und so weiter (usw.)."	Or when I have focussed everything, somebody suddenly remembers that he has left his keys in the car and runs out into the street to look after it, and so on."
„Woher kommen Sie gerade, Herr Schröder?"	"Where are you just coming from, Mr. Schröder?"
das Essen, –s	the eating, meal
„Ich komme gerade vom Essen."	"I have just had something to eat."
„Wohin gehen Sie?"	"Where are you going?"
„Ich gehe ins Kino."	"I'm going to the movies."
„Welchen Film haben Sie sich ausgesucht?"	"What picture have you decided on?"
„Es ist ein alter Film im Kino an der Ecke: ‚Bring sie leben'dig zurück'.	"It's an old film in the movie theater on the corner: 'Bring Them Back Alive'.
Ich sehe Tierfilme am liebsten."	I like animal pictures best."
„Das glaube ich.	"I can believe that.
Sie sind * Fachmann und kennen die Schwierigkeiten bei Tieraufnahmen."	You are an expert and know the difficulties in taking pictures of animals."
„Na, da ist ein Unterschied.	"Well, there is a difference.
Tiger und Riesenschlangen sind * schließlich doch schwerer zu photographieren als ein bellendes Schoßhündchen oder ein alter, verbitterter Kater, der beißt und kratzt, wenn man ihn in Photographierstellung bringen will."	After all, tigers and pythons are harder to photograph than a barking lap dog or a nasty old tomcat that bites and scratches when you want to pose him."
„Nun, glauben Sie nicht, daß die Wildtieraufnahmen schließlich auch Gewohnheitssache werden?"	"Well, don't you think that wild animal shots finally become a matter of routine too?"
„Nein, das glaube ich nicht."	"No, I don't think so."
„Wir danken Ihnen, Herr Schröder. Es war sehr interessant'. Guten Abend."	"We thank you, Mr. Schröder. That was very interesting. Good evening."
„Guten Abend."	"Good evening."
„Da kommt ein Mann tief in Gedanken aus dem Kino. Hallo!	"There's a man coming out of the movies lost in thought. Oh say!

Ja, Sie; würden Sie mir einen * Gefallen tun?	Yes, you; would you do me a favor?
Kommen Sie doch bitte hierher zum Mikrophon'!	Please come over here to the microphone.
Wir wollen nur ein paar harmlose Fragen stellen.	We just want to ask a few innocent questions.
Unsere Hörer wollen gerne * erfahren, was ihre Mitbürger tun, denken, lieben und hoffen.	Our listeners are very much interested to find out what their fellow citizens do, think, love, and hope.
Sie waren gerade im Kino.	You have just been in the movies.
Welchen Film haben Sie eben gesehen?"	What picture have you just seen?"
„‚Tarzan entrinnt'."	"'Tarzan Escapes'."
„Sehen Sie Tarzanfilme gerne?"	"Do you like Tarzan pictures?"
„Nein."	"No."
„Das ist interessant', Herr . . . Sehen Sie, jetzt habe ich vergessen, Sie nach Ihrem Namen zu fragen.	"That's interesting, Mr. . . . you see, now I have forgotten to ask you your name.
Wie heißen Sie?"	What's your name?"
„Aloysius Xavier Baumgartner."	"Aloysius Xavier Baumgartner."
„Herr Baumgartner, woher kommt Ihre Fami'lie?"	"Mr. Baumgartner, where does your family come from?"
„Aus Bubikon."	"From Bubikon."
„O, wo ist denn das?"	"Oh; well, where is that?"
„Das ist doch in der Schweiz.	"That's in Switzerland, of course.
Bubikon ist doch nicht weit vom Züricher See!"	Why, Bubikon isn't far from Lake Zürich."
„Ja, natür'lich. Wie dumm von mir, nicht zu wissen, wo Bubikon ist.	"Yes, of course. How stupid of me not to know where Bubikon is.
Herr Bubikon, ha, ha, entschuldigen Sie, Herr Baumgartner, Sie sagten eben, daß Sie sich nicht für Tarzanfilme interessieren.	Mr. Bubikon, ha, ha, excuse me, Mr. Baumgartner, you said just now that you don't care for Tarzan pictures.
Warum haben Sie sich ‚Tarzan entrinnt' angesehen?"	Why did you see 'Tarzan Escapes'?

„Ich habe den Tarzanfilm doch gar nicht sehen wollen.

"But I didn't want to see the Tarzan picture at all.

Ich habe doch *‚Das Geheimnis des schwarzen * Schlosses' sehen wollen."

What I wanted to see was 'The Secret of the Black Castle'."

„Hat es Ihnen gut gefallen?"

"Did you like it?"

„Ja, sehen Sie, der Fremde war ein Detektiv', und wissen Sie, wer die schwarze Maske war?"

"Yes, you see, the stranger was a detective and do you know who the Black Mask was?"

„Nein, ich habe den Film leider nicht gesehen."

"No, I'm sorry but I haven't seen the picture."

„Das war der Briefträger * unten aus dem Dorf.

"That was the postman from down in the village.

Der hat all die Leute umgebracht.

He was the one that killed all the people.

Er hat die Briefe gelesen und wußte immer, wer Geld kriegte."

He read the letters and always knew who got money."

„Na, das war alles sehr interessant'. Wir danken Ihnen, Herr Baumgartner.

"Well, that was all very interesting. Thank you, Mr. Baumgartner.

Da kommt ein Fräulein mit einer Fasa'nenfe'der am Hut.

There comes a young lady with a pheasant feather on her hat.

O Fräulein, kommen Sie doch bitte einen Augenblick her! (Man hört einen angstvollen Schrei.)

Oh Miss, please come here a moment! (*One hears a frightened scream.*)

Das tut mir leid, sie ist uns davon'gelau'fen.

I'm sorry, she ran away from us.

* schaden, schadete, es hat geschadet

(to) harm

Aber das schadet nichts. Unsere Zeit ist sowieso schon um, und wir müssen jetzt Schluß machen.

But that makes no difference. Our time is up now anyway and we have to stop now.

II. Text:

Die Großstadt spricht (Schluß)

„Hoffentlich haben wir mit unserem nächsten Opfer auch Glück. Ein älterer Herr, er hat es nicht eilig, er steht vor einem Schaufenster. Entschuldigen Sie, dürften wir für unsere Hörer ein paar Fragen an Sie stellen?" — „Fragen Sie, ich werde antworten, wenn ich kann. Mein Name ist Henry Schröder, ich bin Photograph, sechsundfünfzig Jahre alt und unverheiratet." — „Das spart uns Zeit, Herr Schröder. Sind Sie Portraitphotograph?" — „Ja, aber ich photographiere auch andere Dinge und manchmal sehr seltsame." — „So? Können Sie uns ein bißchen mehr von diesen seltsamen Dingen erzählen, die man von Ihnen photographiert haben will?" — „O, ich weiß gar nicht, wo ich da anfangen soll. Lassen Sie mich mal nachdenken. Vor vielen Jahren, es muß gleich nach dem ersten Weltkrieg gewesen sein, da kam ein Mann zu mir, der wollte seine Heimatstadt photographiert haben. Seine Heimatstadt war irgendein kleines Städtchen in den Südstaaten. Den Namen hab ich vergessen; ich glaube, es war irgendwo in Georgia. Ich fragte ihn, wie er sich das vorstellte. Der Mann wollte eine Art Panorama haben. Ich mußte auf verschiedene Dächer klettern und von da Aufnahmen machen. Die Reisekosten hat er mir natürlich bezahlt. Ältere Damen wollen ihre Tierlieblinge, Hunde, Katzen,

Kanarienvögel, Papageien photographiert haben. Und wenn die Tiere krank sind, fragen sie mich oft auch noch um Rat: ‚Ich glaube, mein Fifi hat Lungenentzündung; glauben Sie, daß Prinz Fieber hat?‘ Als ob ich ein Tierarzt wäre!“ — „Was für Aufnahmen machen Sie am liebsten?“ — „Personenaufnahmen, ältere Leute. Die beißen nicht, sitzen still und lächeln, wenn es nötig ist.“ — „Was für Personenaufnahmen machen Sie nur ungern?“ — „Gruppenaufnahmen. Da ist immer einer in der Gruppe, der im letzten Augenblick einen Witz macht oder eine unvernünftige Frage stellt. Oder wenn ich alles eingestellt habe, erinnert sich plötzlich einer, daß er seine Schlüssel im Auto hat stecken lassen, und läuft auf die Straße, um nachzusehen, und so weiter (usw.).“ — „Woher kommen Sie gerade, Herr Schröder?“ — „Ich komme gerade vom Essen.“ — „Wohin gehen Sie?“ — „Ich gehe ins Kino.“ — „Welchen Film haben Sie sich ausgesucht?“ — „Es ist ein alter Film im Kino an der Ecke: ‚Bring sie lebendig zurück‘. Ich sehe Tierfilme am liebsten.“ — „Das glaube ich. Sie sind Fachmann und kennen die Schwierigkeiten bei Tieraufnahmen.“ — „Na, da ist ein Unterschied. Tiger und Riesenschlangen sind schließlich doch schwerer zu photographieren als ein bellendes Schoßhündchen oder ein alter verbitterter Kater, der beißt und kratzt, wenn man ihn in Photographierstellung bringen will.“ — „Nun, glauben Sie nicht, daß die Wildtieraufnahmen schließlich auch Gewohnheitssache werden?“ — „Nein, das glaube ich nicht.“ — „Wir danken Ihnen, Herr Schröder. Es war sehr interessant. Guten Abend.“ — „Guten Abend.“

„Da kommt ein Mann tief in Gedanken aus dem Kino. Hallo! Ja, Sie; würden Sie mir einen Gefallen tun? Kommen Sie doch bitte hierher zum Mikrophon! Wir wollen nur ein paar harmlose Fragen stellen. Unsere Hörer wollen gerne erfahren, was ihre Mitbürger tun, denken, lieben und hoffen. Sie waren gerade im Kino. Welchen Film haben Sie eben gesehen?“ — „‚Tarzan entrinnt.‘“ — „Sehen Sie Tarzanfilme gerne?“ — „Nein.“ „Das ist interessant, Herr . . . Sehen Sie, jetzt habe ich vergessen, Sie nach Ihrem Namen zu fragen. Wie heißen Sie?“ — „Aloysius Xavier Baumgartner.“ — „Herr Baumgartner, woher kommt Ihre Familie?“ — „Aus Bubikon.“ — „O, wo ist denn das?“ — „Das ist doch in der Schweiz. Bubikon ist doch nicht weit vom Züricher See!“ — „Ja, natürlich. Wie dumm von mir, nicht zu wissen, wo Bubikon ist. Herr Bubikon, ha, ha, entschuldigen Sie, Herr Baumgartner, Sie sagten eben, daß Sie sich nicht für Tarzanfilme interessieren. Warum haben Sie sich ‚Tarzan entrinnt‘ angesehen?“ — „Ich habe den Tarzanfilm doch gar nicht sehen wollen. Ich habe doch ‚Das Geheimnis des schwarzen Schlosses‘ sehen wollen.“ — „Hat es Ihnen gut gefallen?“ — „Ja, sehen Sie, der Fremde war ein Detektiv, und wissen Sie, wer die schwarze Maske war?“ — „Nein, ich habe den Film leider nicht gesehen.“ — „Das war der Briefträger unten aus dem Dorf. Der hat all die Leute umgebracht. Er hat die Briefe gelesen und wußte immer, wer Geld kriegte.“ — „Na, das war alles sehr interessant. Wir danken Ihnen, Herr Baumgartner.“

„Da kommt ein Fräulein mit einer Fasanenfeder am Hut. O Fräulein, kommen

Sie doch bitte einen Augenblick her! (Man hört einen angstvollen Schrei.) Das tut mir leid, sie ist uns davongelaufen. Aber das schadet nichts. Unsere Zeit ist sowieso schon um, und wir müssen jetzt Schluß machen.

III. Comments:

1. *Mixed verbs:*

As you already know, a weak verb is one which forms its simple past tense and past participle by adding the tense sign –t– to the infinitive stem: sagen (*say*), sagte, ich habe gesagt. And a strong verb is one which forms its simple past tense and past participle by a change of vowel in the stem: treten (*step*), trat, ich bin getreten. There are also a number of mixed verbs which both add the tense sign –t– and change the stem vowel: rennen (*run*), rannte, ich bin gerannt. The mixed verbs are:

brennen	(burn)	brannte	es hat gebrannt	es brennt
bringen	(bring)	brachte	ich habe gebracht	er bringt
denken	(think)	dachte	ich habe gedacht	er denkt
kennen	(know)	kannte	ich habe gekannt	er kennt
nennen	(name)	nannte	ich habe genannt	er nennt
rennen	(run)	rannte	ich bin gerannt	er rennt
senden	(send)	sandte (sendete)	ich habe gesandt (gesendet)	er sendet
wenden	(turn)	wandte (wendete)	ich habe gewandt (gewendet)	er wendet
wissen	(know)	wußte	ich habe gewußt	er weiß

2. *The Future Perfect Tense:*

The indicative mood is the mood of fact. It has six tenses, of which you have studied five, or all but the future perfect tense, which is not frequently used. The tense auxiliary werden is used with the past infinitive of a verb to form its future perfect tense: ich werde gesagt haben — *I will have said* and ich werde gekommen sein — *I will have come.* (*For complete paradigms see Appendix* §§ 32–33)

Pres. Past. Infin.

ich werde gesagt haben	ich werde gekommen sein
du wirst gesagt haben	du wirst gekommen sein
er, sie, es wird gesagt haben	er, sie, es wird gekommen sein
wir werden gesagt haben	wir werden gekommen sein
ihr werdet gesagt haben	ihr werdet gekommen sein
sie werden gesagt haben	sie werden gekommen sein
Sie werden gesagt haben	Sie werden gekommen sein

IV. Practice:

1. a. Herr Schröder muß nachdenken.
darüber nachdenken, was er erzählen soll.

b. Herr Schröder hat nachdenken müssen. pres. perf.
Herr Schröder hat darüber nachdenken müssen, was er erzählen sollte.

2. a. Herr Pechvogel ließ seine Schlüssel im Auto stecken.
hat lassen.

b. Herr Pechvogel lief auf die Straße.
ist gelaufen.

c. Herr Pechvogel ist auf die Straße gelaufen, um nachzusehen, ob er seine Schlüssel im Auto hat stecken lassen.

3. a. Herr Baumgartner sieht sich die interessante Photographie an.
hat angesehen.

b. Herr Baumgartner will sich die interessante Aufnahme ansehen.
hat wollen.

4. a. Er will nur den Tarzanfilm sehen.
Er will nur den Tarzanfilm sehen, aber er muß sich auch den andern Film ansehen.
Er wollte nur den Tarzanfilm sehen, aber er hat sich auch den andern Film ansehen müssen.

b. Er kommt eben aus dem Kino an der Ecke, wo der Tarzanfilm spielt.

c. Er muß den Tarzanfilm gesehen haben, denn er kommt eben aus dem Kino an der Ecke, wo dieser Film spielt.

5. a. Er rennt auf die Straße.
rannte
ist gerannt.

b. Er will nachsehen, ob er sein Auto vor dem Hause hat stehen lassen.
Er wollte hatte

c. Er rennt auf die Straße, um nachzusehen, ob er sein Auto vor dem Hause hat stehen lassen.

6. a. Er weiß, wer die schwarze Maske ist.
Er wußte, war.

b. Er hat die ganze Zeit gewußt, daß die schwarze Maske die Leute aus dem Dorf umgebracht hat.

7. a. Ich kenne ihn, aber ich kann mich nicht an seinen Namen erinnern.
Er kennt er sich
Wir kennen wir können uns

b. Ich kannte ihn, aber ich konnte mich nicht an seinen Namen erinnern.
Er er sich
Wir kannten wir konnten uns

8. Herr Schröder interessiert sich am meisten für Tierfilme, denn er weiß, wie schwierig es ist, gute Tieraufnahmen zu machen.
Herr Schröder interessiert sich am meisten für Tierfilme, denn er kennt die Schwierigkeiten bei Tieraufnahmen.

9. Sieh mal bitte nach, ob die Katze immer noch auf dem Dach sitzt!
der Tarzanfilm im Kino an der Ecke spielt!
alles fertig ist!
ready

V. Exercises:

A. *Questions:*

1. Was wollte der Interviewer von dem Photographen Schröder erzählt haben?
2. Was war eine der seltsamsten Aufnahmen, die Schröder machen mußte?
3. Hatte Schröder Unkosten, als er das Panorama des Städtchens photographierte?
4. Was mußte Herr Schröder tun, um diese Aufnahmen machen zu können?
5. Zu wem sollte man mit kranken Hunden oder Katzen gehen?
6. Warum macht Herr Schröder nur ungern Gruppenaufnahmen?
7. Warum photographiert er am liebsten ältere Leute?
8. Wie erklärt der Interviewer, daß Herr Schröder Tierfilme am liebsten sieht?
9. Wo liegt das Städtchen Bubikon?
10. Warum hat der Briefträger all die Leute umgebracht?
11. Warum kann der Interviewer das Fräulein mit der Fasanenfeder am Hut nicht interviewen?

B. *Translate:*

1. Haben Sie es wirklich so eilig, daß Sie schon gehen müssen?
2. Sie interessiert sich besonders für die Riesenschlangen in den Tierfilmen.
3. Der verbitterte alte Schoßhund hat ihn ins linke Bein gebissen.
4. Er ist Fachmann und deshalb interessiert er sich besonders für diesen Fall.
5. Sie würden mir damit einen großen Gefallen tun.

C. *Rearrange and translate:*

1. auf verschiedene Dächer, klettern, er, mußte, um . . . zu photographieren, das Dorf.
2. der Verkehrsschutzmann, hat . . . gebracht, den unvernünftigen Autofahrer, aufs Polizeibüro.
3. der kleine Hund, an Lungenentzündung, ist . . . gestorben, obgleich, kam, der berühmte Tierarzt, Doktor Lyon, gleich.
4. kam . . . vor, ihm, es, als, der Film, hätte . . . gedauert, schon lange.
5. vor vielen Jahren, habe . . . gelesen, ich, einen Kriminalroman, in dem, umgebracht hat, der Detektiv, all die Leute.

D. *In the following exercise are a number of words or phrases, each followed by three statements. Determine which statement is in some way associated with the key word:*

1. **der Radiointerviewer**
   a. Er hat uns drei mit Fall gebildete Wortzusammensetzungen genannt.
   b. Er interessiert sich am meisten für die Tiger in den Tierfilmen.
   c. Er hat schon sein erstes Opfer aus dem Verkehrsstrom herausgefischt.
2. **die Hauptstraße**
   a. Die Hochbahn donnerte eben vorbei.
   b. Der Verbrecher hat die Frage falsch beantwortet.
   c. Es ist immer sehr ruhig dort.

3. **das Polizeibüro**
   a. Ich aß gerade Schweinsfüße mit Sauerkraut.
   b. Wenn ich nicht so schnell gefahren wäre, wäre ich jetzt nicht hier.
   c. Dort stand eine Frau, die sich die eleganten Pelzmäntel im Schaufenster ansah.
4. **die Gewohnheitssache**
   a. Die junge Dame, die der Ansager eben interviewen wollte, ist davongelaufen.
   b. Ich habe diesen Film schon einmal gesehen, aber das schadet nichts, denn ich würde ihn mir ganz gerne noch einmal ansehen.
   c. Seit vierzehn Jahren bringt uns derselbe alte Briefträger die Post.

E. *Correct the misinformation:*

1. Die Dame mit der Fasanenfeder am Hut sieht aus, als hätte sie es sehr eilig.
2. Herr Schröder will den Leuten auf der Straße ein Klangbild oder eine akustische Photographie geben.
3. Herr Baumgartner hat sich ‚Das Geheimnis des schwarzen Schlosses' ansehen müssen.
4. Herr Schröder macht Gruppenaufnahmen gerne.
5. Der Mann aus Georgia wollte seine Tierlieblinge photographiert haben.

F. *Connect by means of the conjunction indicated and translate:*

1. (nachdem) after
   Der Kater hatte den Tierarzt in den Finger gebissen.
   Er kletterte aufs Dach.
2. (weil) because
   Er hatte die Briefe gelesen.
   Der Briefträger wußte immer, wer Geld bekam.
3. (als) when
   Wir mußten alle über den Witz lachen, den Herr Baumgartner machte.
   Der Photograph hatte alles eingestellt.
4. (ob) whether
   Die Katze sitzt noch immer auf dem Dach.
   Sieh mal bitte nach!

VI. Principal Parts:

beißen	biß	ich habe gebissen	er beißt	bite
sprechen	sprach	ich habe gesprochen	er spricht	speak
entrinnen	entrann	ich bin entronnen	er entrinnt	escape
kommen	kam	ich bin gekommen	er kommt	come
lesen	las	ich habe gelesen	er liest	read
sehen	sah	ich habe gesehen	er sieht	see
nachsehen	sah . . . nach	ich habe nachgesehen	er sieht . . . nach	look
vergessen	vergaß	ich habe vergessen	er vergißt	forget
sitzen	saß	ich habe gesessen	er sitzt	sit
erfahren	erfuhr	ich habe erfahren	er erfährt	find out

gefallen	gefiel	ich habe gefallen	er gefällt	please
laufen	lief	ich bin gelaufen	er läuft	run
davonlaufen	lief . . . davon	ich bin davongelaufen	er läuft . . . davon	run away
anfangen	fing . . . an	ich habe angefangen	er fängt . . . an	begin
lassen	ließ	ich habe gelassen	er läßt	let
heißen	hieß	ich habe geheißen	er heißt	be called
sein	war	ich bin gewesen	er ist	be
gehen	ging	ich bin gegangen	er geht	go
stehen	stand	ich habe gestanden	er steht	stand
tun	tat	ich habe getan	er tut	do
dürfen	durfte	ich habe gedurft	er darf	may, be permitted
müssen	mußte	ich habe gemußt	er muß	must, have to
können	konnte	ich habe gekonnt	er kann	can, be able
sollen	sollte	ich habe gesollt	er soll	shall
wollen	wollte	ich habe gewollt	er will	want to
denken	dachte	ich habe gedacht	er denkt	think
nachdenken	dachte . . . nach	ich habe nachgedacht	er denkt . . . nach	think about
kennen	kannte	ich habe gekannt	er kennt	know
bringen	brachte	ich habe gebracht	er bringt	bring
umbringen	brachte . . . um	ich habe umgebracht	er bringt . . . um	kill
zurückbringen	brachte . . . zurück	ich habe zurückgebracht	er bringt . . . zurück	bring back

Class I

der Briefträger, –s, — postman
der Gefallen, –s, — favor
der Kanarienvogel, –s, ¨ canary
der Kater, –s, — tomcat
der Mitbürger, –s, — fellow citizen
der Schlüssel, –s, — key
der Tiger, –s, — tiger
das Schaufenster, –s, — show window
das Schoßhündchen, –s, — lap dog
das Städtchen, –s, — small town
der Detektiv, –s, –e detective
der Hund, –es, –e dog
der Hut, –es, ¨e hat
der Rat, –es, ¨e advice

Class II

der Schluß, –es, ¨e end, conclusion
der Schrei, –s, –e scream
der Tierarzt, –es, ¨e veterinary
der Tierfilm, –s, –e animal film
der Tierliebling, –s, –e animal pet
der Weltkrieg, –es, –e World War
der Witz, –es, –e joke
das Geheimnis, . . .nisses, . . .nisse secret
das Tier, –es, –e animal
das Dach, –es, ¨er roof
das Dorf, –es, ¨er village
das Schloß, –es, ¨er castle
der Fachmann, –s, . . .leute expert

die Gewohnheitssache, —, –n	matter of routine	die Schwierigkeit, —, –en	difficulty
die Gruppe, —, –n	group	die Fasanenfeder, —, –n	pheasant feather
die Gruppenaufnahme, —, –n	group picture	die Art, —, –en	kind
die Katze, —, –n	cat	der Fremde, –n, –n	stranger
die Maske, —, –n	mask	der Photograph, –en, –en	photographer
die Personenaufnahme, —, –n	picture of a person or persons	der See, –s, –n	lake
		der Südstaat, –es, –en	southern state
		der Gedanke, –ns, –n	thought
		das Auto, –s, –s	auto, car
die Riesenschlange, —, –n	python	das Panorama, –s, –s	panorama

VII. Securing the Vocabulary:

A.

es eilig haben	(to) be in a hurry	der Witz	joke
seltsam	strange, odd	unvernünftig	unreasonable, senseless
das Städtchen	small town	der Schlüssel	key
das Dach	roof	der Fachmann	expert
krank	sick	schließlich	finally, after all
der Rat	advice	der Gefallen	favor
ob	if, whether	das Geheimnis	secret
das Tier	animal	das Schloß	castle
der Arzt	doctor, physician	unten	below, down
der Tierarzt	veterinary	schaden	(to) harm
lächeln	smile	erfahren	(to) find out
sparen	(to) save		

B.

die Einbildungskraft (6)	1. please	echt (3)	1. really
	2. angry, irritated	gehören (5)	2. consist, exist
gefallen (1)	3. descent	bestehen (2)	3. genuine
der Lärm (10)	4. assume	während (6)	4. remain
aufheben (5)	5. pick up	bleiben (4)	5. belong
holen (9)	6. imagination	eigentlich (1)	6. while, during
annehmen (4)	7. bend, turn	böse sein (9)	7. catch
die Abstammung (3)	8. strange, odd	fangen (7)	8. close, dense
biegen (7)	9. fetch, get	gerade (10)	9. be angry
ärgerlich (2)	10. noise	dicht (8)	10. just
sonderbar (8)			

die Geschichte (4)	1. but	brauchen (5)	6. exchange
raten (2)	2. guess	wechseln (6)	7. victim
sondern (1)	3. careful	das Opfer (7)	8. step
sorgfältig (3)	4. story; history	treten (8)	9. at any time
zielen (10)	5. need	jederzeit (9)	10. aim

VIII. Die Großstadt spricht: (*Rewritten*)

„Da kommt ein freundlicher älterer Herr, der kann uns sicher etwas Interessantes erzählen. O, haben Sie einen Augenblick Zeit, wir . . ." — „O, ein Radiointerview? Wenn es nicht zu lange dauert, antworte ich Ihnen gerne." — „Sehr freundlich. Wen darf ich unseren Hörern vorstellen?" — „Dr. Watson, Tierarzt." — „O, Dr. Watson, ich habe von Ihnen gehört. Sie haben die große Tierklinik in der Südstadt, nicht wahr? Ich las vor ein paar Tagen einen Artikel in der Zeitung über Ihre Tierklinik. Dr. Watson, es ist immer interessant zu erfahren, warum jemand seinen Beruf gewählt hat. Wie sind Sie auf den Gedanken gekommen, Tierarzt zu werden?" — „Nun, ich habe Tiere gerne; ich habe sie immer gerne gehabt. Schon als kleiner Junge habe ich immer Katzen, Hunde, Kanarienvögel, Papageien und dergleichen um mich gehabt." — „Ich wette, Ihre Mutter war eine geduldige Frau." — „Gut geraten! Geduldig mußte sie schon sein. Das Haus war immer voller Tiere. Mein Vater war Arzt, und so ist es wohl verständlich, daß ich Tierarzt geworden bin." — „Dr. Watson, können Sie uns ein paar seltsame Fälle aus Ihrer Praxis erzählen?" — „Es war vor ein paar Jahren. Unser zoologischer Garten hatte einen kleinen einjährigen Gorilla. Manche Ihrer Hörer werden sich noch an ihn erinnern. Der Winter kam, und der kleine Gorilla wurde krank, Lungenentzündung. Ich wurde geholt, aber es war schon zu spät. Ich konnte dem Tier nur den Tod leichter machen. Es dauerte ein paar Tage. Der kleine Gorilla kannte mich und hat mich oft angesehen wie ein krankes Kind. Als er dann schließlich starb, kam es mir vor, als ob ein menschlicher Patient gestorben wäre." — „Haben Sie oft Schwierigkeiten mit Ihren Tierpatienten?" — „Nicht oft, aber manchmal. Dann wird man gekratzt oder gebissen." — „Was für Tierpatienten haben Sie am liebsten?" — „Hunde, denn Hunde habe ich am liebsten von allen Tieren. Außerdem sind sie meistens sehr gute Patienten, oft viel vernünftiger als ihre Herren." — „Ha! Ha! das glaube ich." — „Nun muß ich aber gehen, sonst schimpft meine Frau." — „Das kenne ich, Herr Doktor, ich bin nämlich auch verheiratet." — „Guten Abend." — „Guten Abend."

„Dort kommt ein Herr aus dem Kino. Verzeihung, falls Sie einen Augenblick Zeit haben, möchten wir gerne von Ihnen hören, wie Ihnen der Film gefallen hat. Was wurde gezeigt?" — „Frank Buck: ‚Bring sie lebendig zurück'!" — „Mögen Sie Tierfilme gern?" — „Ja." — „Wie hat Ihnen dieser Frank Buck Film gefallen?" — „Gut." — „Schön, was gefällt Ihnen am besten in einem Frank Buck Film, die Kämpfe der Tiere, seine Fangtechnik, die Naturszenen?" — „Die Dschungelgeräusche." — „O ja, dürften wir Sie um Ihren Namen bitten?" — „Smith." — „Herr Smith, was sind Sie von Beruf?" — „Privatdetektiv." — „Das ist interessant. Da sehen Sie sicher viele interessante Fälle und Dinge, die wir nur in Kriminalromanen lesen?" — „Nein." — „Sie meinen, die wirklichen Fälle sind nicht so interessant wie die Kriminalgeschichten?" — „Ja." — „Aber interessant ist Ihr Beruf, nicht wahr?" — „Nein." — „Warum nicht?" — „Es wird Gewohnheitssache. Jetzt muß ich gehen. Guten Abend."

Ich glaube, ich sehe unser nächstes Opfer. Es ist eine junge Dame mit einer Fasanenfeder am Hute. Sie scheint es nicht eilig zu haben. Sie steht vor dem Schaufenster von Cooks Reisebüro und sieht sich etwas sehr interessiert an. Jetzt kommt sie auf mich zu. O, entschuldigen Sie. Dürfte ich für unsere Radiohörer ein paar Fragen an Sie stellen. Ja? Dann tun Sie mir den Gefallen und sprechen Sie ins Mikrophon. Wie heißen Sie?" — „Martha Baumgartner." — „Fräulein Baumgartner, was haben Sie sich in dem Schaufenster so interessiert angesehen?" — „Eine große Photographie des Züricher Sees, auf der ich mein Heimatstädtchen erkennen konnte." — „Kommen Sie aus der Schweiz, Fräulein Baumgartner?" — „Ja, ich bin aber schon als kleines Kind nach den Vereinigten Staaten gekommen. Ich wollte nach der Schweiz fahren, um meine Heimatstadt zu sehen, aber da kam der Weltkrieg, und das war das Ende meiner Reisepläne. Jetzt muß ich aber gehen! Mutter erwartet mich zum Abendbrot." — „Danke, Fräulein Baumgartner. Hoffentlich können Sie recht bald eine Schweizer Reise machen."

Vierundzwanzigste Aufgabe

* * * \

Die Germa'nen waren eine Völkergruppe, über deren Herkunft wir * wenig wissen.

The Teutons were a group of people about whose origin we know little.

Eins aber ist sicher:

But one thing is certain:

Zur Zeit Cäsars waren die Germa'nen in drei Untergruppen aufgeteilt: Nord'germa'nen, Ost'germa'nen und West'germa'nen.

In Caesar's day the Teutons were divided into three sub-groups: the North Teutons, the East Teutons, and the West Teutons.

Die Nordgermanen wohnten zur Zeit Cäsars im südlichen Skandinavien, die Ostgermanen wohnten an den Ufern der Ostsee, und die * Grenzen des westgermanischen Gebietes waren Rhein, Donau, Elbe und Nordsee.

In Caesar's day the North Teutons lived in southern Scandinavia, the East Teutons lived on the shores of the Baltic, and the boundaries of West Teuton territory were the Rhine, the Danube, the Elbe, and the North Sea.

Die Nordgermanen schickten Schiffe und kleine Flotten bis nach Island, nach Amerika, nach Grönland, an die Küsten des Mittelmeeres, ja bis ins Schwarze Meer, um Beute zu machen oder Länder zu erobern.

The North Teutons sent ships and small fleets to Iceland, America, Greenland, to the shores of the Mediterranean, yes, into the Black Sea, in order to get booty or to conquer territory.

Das waren die Wikingerzüge, deren einzige bleibende * Folge die Besiedlung Islands mit Nordmännern war.

Those were the Viking expeditions, whose only lasting consequence was the colonization of Iceland by Norsemen.

Die Wikinger wurden * überall gefürchtet und hatten den wohlverdienten Ruf, unbesiegbare Krieger zu sein.

The Vikings were feared everywhere and had the well-deserved reputation of being invincible warriors.

Sie gründeten in Frankreich das Norman'nenreich' (die heutige Normandie'), das aber von der roma'nischen Kultur' absorbiert' wurde.

In France they founded the Norman Kingdom (present-day Normandy), which, however, was absorbed by Romanic culture.

Die ostgermanischen Stämme der Goten, Vanda'len und Burgun'der wanderten nach Süden und Westen.

The East Teutonic tribes of the Goths, Vandals, and Burgundians migrated south and west.

Sie stießen überall mit den Römern zusam'men, die sie in langen Kriegen besiegten.

Everywhere they clashed with the Romans, whom they defeated in long wars.

Mit der Eroberung Roms durch Germanenstämme endete das alte römische Reich.

The ancient Roman Empire ended with the conquest of Rome by Teutonic (Germanic) tribes.

Die neuen Reiche, die den Ostgermanen ihren *Ursprung verdankten, dauerten aber nicht lange.

The new empires which owed their origin to the East Teutons did not last long, however.

Die Burgun'der, Vanda'len und Goten kamen in den Kriegen der Völkerwanderungszeit um oder gingen in dem Völkermeer des *ehemaligen römischen Reiches unter.

The Burgundians, Vandals, and Goths perished in the wars of the era of the tribal migrations or were submerged in the sea of nations of the former Roman Empire.

Außerdem war die römische Kultur' älter und der jungen primiti'ven Kultur der Eroberer *überle'gen.

Besides, the Roman culture was older and superior to the young primitive culture of the conquerors.

Die Westgermanen hatten mehr Glück.

The West Teutons had better luck.

Die Reiche, die sie gründeten, bestehen noch heute.

The empires which they founded exist even to-day.

Die Angeln und Sachsen, beides westgermanische Stämme, eroberten die römische Provinz' Britan'nien.

The Angles and Saxons, both West Germanic (Teutonic) tribes, conquered the Roman province of Britain.

Das ist der Beginn der englischen Geschichte.

That is the beginning of English history.

Die Stämme, die zu Hause oder doch wenigstens in Mitteleuropa geblieben waren, entwickelten sich *langsam zu den Natio'nen, die wir heute unter den Namen Holland, Deutschland und Österreich kennen.

The tribes that had stayed at home or, at any rate, in central Europe, evolved gradually into the nations, which we know today under the names of Holland, Germany, and Austria.

Nun können wir die Frage, die uns gestellt wurde, einfach beantworten.

Now we can give a simple answer to the question that was put to us.

Die Germanen sind die Vorfahren der heutigen Deutschen, Skandina'vier, Isländer, Engländer und Niederländer.

The Teutons are the ancestors of the present-day Germans, Scandinavians, Icelanders, Englishmen, and Netherlanders.

Ein Farmer aus Cedar Rapids, Iowa, fragt uns: „Welches ist das stärkste Tier?"

A farmer from Cedar Rapids, Iowa, asks us: "Which animal is the strongest?"

Die Frage ist in der Form, in der sie gestellt ist, unbeantwortbar.

In the form in which it is asked, the question is unanswerable.

Sie ist unbeantwortbar, weil das Wort „stark", genau so wie das Wort „strong" in der englischen * Sprache, viele * Bedeutungen hat.

It is unanswerable, because the word "stark" just as the word "strong" in the English language, has many meanings.

In den Unterhal'tungen des täglichen Lebens sind wir uns * durchaus nicht immer klar darüber, welche Bedeutung eines Wortes wir im Augenblick meinen.

In the conversations of daily life we are by no means always clear about what meaning of a word we intend at the moment.

Aus dem Zusam'menhang' gerissen, kann das Wort „stark" aber so viele Bedeutungen haben, daß **eine** Antwort auf die Frage unmöglich ist.

Torn out of context, however, the word "strong" can have so many meanings that a single answer to the question is impossible.

Natür'lich kennen wir die Tiere unseres Erdballes genügend, um sie unter irgendeinem * Gesichtspunkt zu * vergleichen.

Of course, we know the animals of our globe sufficiently to compare them from any point of view at all.

das kommt in Frage

that comes into question

Zuerst' müssen wir aber wissen, welcher Gesichtspunkt in Frage kommt.

But first we must know what point of view is to be adopted.

Die Schwierigkeit bei der Beantwortung dieser Frage ist also nicht eine zoolo'gische sondern eine seman'tische.

The difficulty in answering this question is therefore not one of zoology but one of semantics.

in denen wir täglich denken

in which we think every day

Die Seman'tik befaßt sich mit der Bedeutung der Wörter und zeigt uns, wie unklar, vieldeutig oder auch widerspre'chend die Bedeutungen der Wörter sind, in denen wir täglich denken.

Semantics is concerned with the meaning of words and shows us how obscure, ambiguous, or even contradictory are the meanings of the words which we use in our daily thinking.

ſich denken, dachte ſich, ich habe mir gedacht, er denkt ſich	(to) think to oneself, imagine
Die Seman'tik zeigt uns, daß wir erſt wiſſen müſſen, was wir uns bei einem Wort denken, * ehe wir anfangen dürfen, unſere * Urteile und Meinungen in Wörter zu kleiden, die der Welt um uns Sinn und Wert geben ſollen.	Semantics shows us that we must first know what we intend by a word before we may begin to clothe our judgments and opinions in words which are to give meaning and value to the world about us.
Um bei unſerer Frage zu bleiben: Es iſt genau ſo richtig zu behaupten, der Löwe wäre ſtärker als das Pferd, wie, * das Pferd wäre ſtärker als der Löwe.	To stay with our question: it is just as correct to say 'the lion is stronger than the horse' as 'the horse is stronger than the lion.'
Ein Löwe, der in der Wildnis aufgewachſen, alſo in vollem Beſitz ſeiner Kampfkraft iſt (nicht ein Zirkuslöwe oder ein in der Gefangenſchaft geborener Löwe eines zoolo'giſchen Gartens), würde in wenigen Minu'ten den ſtärkſten und wildeſten Hengſt töten.	A lion that has grown up in the wilderness, and therefore is in full possession of its fighting strength (not a circus lion or a lion born in the captivity of a zoological garden), would kill the strongest and wildest stallion in a few minutes.
* Dage'gen kann ein altes Bauernpferd Laſten tragen, die einen Löwen erdrücken würden.	On the other hand, an old farm horse can carry burdens that would crush a lion.
anbetreffen, anbetraf, anbetroffen, anbetrifft	(to) concern, refer to
Was Zugkraft anbetrifft, wird wohl ein ſchwerer belgiſcher Hengſt mehr * ziehen können als zehn Löwen.	As far as tractive power is concerned, a heavy Belgian stallion can probably pull more than ten lions.
Man muß alſo bei unſerer Frage zuerſt' eine Gegenfrage ſtellen: Was heißt „ſtark"?	So in the case of our question we must first ask a counterquestion: What is the meaning of "strong"?
Wenn in unſerem Falle die * geſamte Zugkraft der Muskeln eines Tieres gemeint iſt, dann iſt das Pferd, wie geſagt, dem Löwen an Stärke weit überle'gen.	If in our case the total tractive force of an animal's muscles is intended, then, as has been said, the horse is far superior to the lion in strength.
Ein belgiſcher Hengſt wiegt viermal ſo viel wie ein ausgewachſener männlicher Löwe, deſſen Durchſchnittsgewicht fünfhundert Pfund * beträgt.	A Belgian stallion weighs four times as much as a full-grown male lion, the average weight of which amounts to five hundred pounds.

In dem Falle wird wohl der Walfisch, das schwerste aller lebenden Tiere, auch das stärkste Tier sein, und von den Landtieren ist dann der Elefant' der König der Tiere.

In that case the whale, the heaviest of all living animals, is probably the strongest animal, too, and of the terrestrial animals the elephant is then king of beasts.

Meinen wir mit „stark" die Kampfkraft eines Tieres, also seine Fähigkeit, andere Tiere umzubringen, dann ist der Löwe stärker als das Pferd.

But if by "strong" we mean an animal's fighting strength, that is, his ability to kill other animals, then the lion is stronger than the horse.

Dann müssen wir aber der Tierfabel und der litera'rischen Überlie'ferung widerspre'chen, die den Löwen von jeher für den König der Tiere gehalten hat.

But then we have to contradict the animal fable and literary tradition, which has always considered the lion king of beasts.

Den Ehrentitel „stärkstes Lebewesen" müßten wir in dem Fall wahrscheinlich einer besonders gefährlichen Mikro'be geben, die Walfische, Löwen, Pferde und Goril'las in kurzer Zeit umbringen könnte.

In that case we would probably have to give the honorary title "strongest living being" to an especially dangerous microbe which could kill whales, lions, horses, and gorillas in a short time.

Einige Leute definieren das Wort „stark" noch anders.

Some people define the word "strong" in a still different way.

Sie sagen: Stark ist, wer den Kampf ums Dasein mit anderen Organis'men am besten erträgt.

They say, whoever best endures the struggle for existence with other organisms is strong.

Der Organis'mus ist der stärkste, der dem Wetter, Krankheiten, kurz, den täglichen Angriffen auf sein Wohlergehen am besten widersteht'.

That organism is the strongest which best resists weather, illness, in short, the daily attacks upon its welfare.

In dem Falle wäre zum Beispiel ein Straßenköter stärker als ein Rennpferd.

In that case, a street-cur, for example would be stronger than a race horse.

Ein Straßenköter kann Abfall fressen und bei Wind und Wetter * draußen sein.

A cur can eat refuse and be outside in bad weather.

sorgfältig

careful

Ein Rennpferd dage'gen muß sorgfältig gepflegt werden und würde in der freien Natur' sehr bald umkommen.

A race-horse, on the other hand, must be given good care and would soon perish in the wild state.

II. Text:

Frag mich was!

Wer uns eine Frage einschickt, die wir gebrauchen können, erhält zehn Dollar. Wir können nur solche Fragen annehmen, die von Interesse für die Allgemeinheit sind. Falls Sie Ihre Fragen zurückhaben wollen, müssen Sie einen frankierten und adressierten Briefumschlag mitschicken.

Herr Klein aus Brooklyn fragt uns: „Was ist der Unterschied zwischen Deutschen und Germanen?"

Man liest immer wieder in amerikanischen Zeitungen, aber auch in Aufsätzen, deren Verfasser besser informiert sein sollten, Ausdrücke wie The Teutons, wo der Autor die Deutschen meint. Andrerseits liest man oft den Ausdruck The Old Germans, wo es hätte heißen sollen The Old Teutons.

Die Germanen waren eine Völkergruppe, über deren Herkunft wir wenig wissen. Eins aber ist sicher: Zur Zeit Cäsars waren die Germanen in drei Untergruppen aufgeteilt: Nordgermanen, Ostgermanen und Westgermanen. Die Nordgermanen wohnten zur Zeit Cäsars im südlichen Skandinavien, die Ostgermanen wohnten an den Ufern der Ostsee, und die Grenzen des westgermanischen Gebietes waren Rhein, Donau, Elbe und Nordsee. Die Nordgermanen schickten Schiffe und kleine Flotten bis nach Island, nach Amerika, nach Grönland, an die Küsten des Mittelmeeres, ja bis ins Schwarze Meer, um Beute zu machen oder Länder zu erobern. Das waren die Wikingerzüge, deren einzige bleibende Folge die Besiedlung Islands mit Nordmännern war. Die Wikinger wurden überall gefürchtet und hatten den wohlverdienten Ruf, unbesiegbare Krieger zu sein. Sie gründeten in Frankreich das Normannenreich (die heutige Normandie), das aber von der romanischen Kultur absorbiert wurde. Die ostgermanischen Stämme der Goten, Vandalen und Burgunder wanderten nach Süden und Westen. Sie stießen überall mit den Römern zusammen, die sie in langen Kriegen besiegten. Mit der Eroberung Roms durch Germanenstämme endete das alte römische Reich. Die neuen Reiche, die den Ostgermanen ihren Ursprung verdankten, dauerten aber nicht lange. Die Burgunder, Vandalen und Goten kamen in den Kriegen der Völkerwanderungszeit um oder gingen in dem Völkermeer des ehemaligen römischen Reiches unter. Außerdem war die römische Kultur älter und der jungen primitiven Kultur der Eroberer überlegen. Die Westgermanen hatten mehr Glück. Die Reiche, die sie gründeten, bestehen noch heute. Die Angeln und Sachsen, beides westgermanische Stämme, eroberten die römische Provinz Britannien. Das ist der Beginn der englischen Geschichte. Die Stämme, die zu Hause oder doch wenigstens in Mitteleuropa geblieben waren, entwickelten sich langsam zu den Nationen, die wir heute unter den Namen Holland, Deutschland und Österreich kennen. Nun können wir die Frage, die uns gestellt wurde, einfach beantworten. Die Germanen sind die Vorfahren der heutigen Deutschen, Skandinavier, Isländer, Engländer und Niederländer.

Wer ist am stärksten?

Ein Farmer aus Cedar Rapids, Iowa, fragt uns: „Welches ist das stärkste Tier?"

Die Frage ist in der Form, in der sie gestellt ist, unbeantwortbar. Sie ist unbeantwortbar, weil das Wort „stark", genau so wie das Wort „strong" in der englischen Sprache, viele Bedeutungen hat. In den Unterhaltungen des täglichen Lebens sind wir uns durchaus nicht immer klar darüber, welche Bedeutung eines Wortes wir im Augenblick meinen. Aus dem Zusammenhang gerissen, kann das Wort „stark" aber so viele Bedeutungen haben, daß **eine** Antwort auf die Frage unmöglich ist. Natürlich kennen wir die Tiere unseres Erdballes genügend, um sie unter irgendeinem Gesichtspunkt zu vergleichen. Zuerst müssen wir aber wissen, welcher Gesichtspunkt in Frage kommt. Die Schwierigkeit bei der Beantwortung dieser Frage ist also nicht eine zoologische sondern eine semantische. Die Semantik befaßt sich mit der Bedeutung der Wörter und zeigt uns, wie unklar, vieldeutig oder auch widersprechend die Bedeutungen der Wörter sind, in denen wir täglich denken. Die Semantik zeigt uns, daß wir erst wissen müssen, was wir uns bei einem Wort denken, ehe wir anfangen dürfen, unsere Urteile und Meinungen in Wörter zu kleiden, die der Welt um uns Sinn und Wert geben sollen. Um bei unserer Frage zu bleiben: Es ist genau so richtig zu behaupten, der Löwe wäre

ſtärker als das Pferd, wie, das Pferd wäre ſtärker als der Löwe. Ein Löwe, der in der Wildnis aufgewachſen, alſo in vollem Beſitz ſeiner Kampfkraft iſt (nicht ein Zirkuslöwe oder ein in der Gefangenſchaft geborener Löwe eines zoologiſchen Gartens), würde in wenigen Minuten den ſtärkſten und wildeſten Hengſt töten. Dagegen kann ein altes Bauernpferd Laſten tragen, die einen Löwen erdrücken würden. Was Zugkraft anbetrifft, wird wohl ein ſchwerer belgiſcher Hengſt mehr ziehen können als zehn Löwen.

Man muß alſo bei unſerer Frage zuerſt eine Gegenfrage ſtellen: Was heißt „ſtark"? Wenn in unſerem Falle die geſamte Zugkraft der Muskeln eines Tieres gemeint iſt, dann iſt das Pferd, wie geſagt, dem Löwen an Stärke weit überlegen. Ein belgiſcher Hengſt wiegt viermal ſo viel wie ein ausgewachſener männlicher Löwe, deſſen Durchſchnittsgewicht fünfhundert Pfund beträgt. In dem Falle wird wohl der Walfiſch, das ſchwerſte aller lebenden Tiere, auch das ſtärkſte Tier ſein, und von den Landtieren iſt dann der Elefant der König der Tiere. Meinen wir mit „ſtark" die Kampfkraft eines Tieres, alſo ſeine Fähigkeit, andere Tiere umzubringen, dann iſt der Löwe ſtärker als das Pferd. Dann müſſen wir aber der Tierfabel und der literariſchen Überlieferung widerſprechen, die den Löwen von jeher für den König der Tiere gehalten hat. Den Ehrentitel „ſtärkſtes Lebewesen" müßten wir in dem Fall wahrſcheinlich einer beſonders gefährlichen Mikrobe geben, die Walfiſche, Löwen, Pferde und Gorillas in kurzer Zeit umbringen könnte. Einige Leute definieren das Wort „ſtark" noch anders. Sie ſagen: Stark iſt, wer den Kampf ums Daſein mit anderen Organismen am beſten erträgt. Der Organismus iſt der ſtärkſte, der dem Wetter, Krankheiten, kurz, den täglichen Angriffen auf ſein Wohlergehen am beſten widerſteht. In dem Falle wäre zum Beiſpiel ein Straßenköter ſtärker als ein Rennpferd. Ein Straßenköter kann Abfall freſſen und bei Wind und Wetter draußen ſein. Ein Rennpferd dagegen muß ſorgfältig gepflegt werden und würde in der freien Natur ſehr bald umkommen.

III. Comments:

1. *Comparison of Adjectives:*

The comparison of adjectives in German is very much like the comparison of adjectives in English. The comparative adds –er to the stem of the positive and the superlative adds –ſt or –eſt: gefährlich, gefährlicher, gefährlichſt–; wild, wilder, wildeſt–. Many monosyllabic adjectives with the stem vowels a, o, u modify these vowels in the comparative and superlative: ſtark, ſtärker, ſtärkſt–. Two very common adjectives have an irregular comparison: gut (*good*), beſſer, beſt–; viel (*much*), mehr, meiſt–.

The comparative and superlative degrees of an adjective are used with nouns just as is the positive degree and the usual declensional endings are added to them; das ſtarke Tier *the strong animal*, das ſtärkere Tier *the stronger animal*, das ſtärkſte Tier *the strongest animal*.

2. *Inversion for condition:*

In English the sentence, *If I had known that, I would have come,* can also be expressed, *Had I known that, I would have come.* That is, the inversion of subject and object makes the clause a condition. This construction, which in English is frequent but restricted to a few stereotyped expressions, is very common in German. Examples:

Wenn wir mit „stark" die Kampfkraft eines Tieres meinen = Meinen wir mit „stark" die Kampfkraft eines Tieres = If by "strong" we mean the animal's fighting strength.

3. *Indirect statement:*

As you know, the subjunctive mood has two basic types, subjunctive I and II. But the endings are the same for all time distinctions in both types. These endings are: –e, –est, –e, –en, –et, –en. A partial exception to this statement is the present subjunctive I of sein which you can compare with the present subjunctive I of a number of other words in the following paradigms:

ich **sei**	habe	werde	arbeite	falle	sehe
du **seiest**	**habest**	**werdest**	arbeitest	**fallest**	**sehest**
er **sei**	**habe**	**werde**	**arbeite**	**falle**	**sehe**
wir **seien**	haben	werden	arbeiten	fallen	sehen
ihr **seiet**	habet	werdet	arbeitet	fallet	sehet
sie **seien**	haben	werden	arbeiten	fallen	sehen
Sie **seien**	haben	werden	arbeiten	fallen	sehen

If you will compare the subjunctive forms of these verbs with their present indicative forms you will see that many of them are very similar to or even identical with the indicative forms. In the above paradigms those forms which are unmistakably subjunctive are printed in boldface. As you learned in Lesson 19 their chief use in direct statement is in certain formulas or formal expressions like: Gott sei Dank! Versuchen wir festzustellen, warum die Preise gefallen sind!

In this unit you will learn something about the use of the subjunctive in indirect statement. Imagine a conversation between Oskar, Anna, and Richard:

Oskar: The horse is stronger than the lion.
Richard: What is he saying?
Anna: He says that the horse is stronger than the lion.

What Oskar says is a direct statement, but when Anna reports it to Richard it becomes an indirect statement. This dialogue may appear in German as:

Oskar: Das Pferd ist stärker als der Löwe.
Richard: Was sagt er?
Anna: Er sagt, das Pferd ist stärker als der Löwe.

Anna, reporting to Richard what Oskar says, uses the indicative mood, thus indicating that she sees no reason to question Oskar's statement. But if Anna felt

the statement to be open to question, she would use the subjunctive mood in reporting it and the conversation would run:

Oskar: Das Pferd ist stärker als der Löwe.
Richard: Was sagt er?
Anna: Er sagt, das Pferd wäre stärker als der Löwe.

Therefore, in indirect discourse in colloquial speech, subjunctive II is used when the person reporting a statement wishes to indicate that he believes the statement open to question. In more formal or literary style subjunctive I would be used under the same circumstances and then Anna's line would read:

Er sagt, das Pferd sei stärker als der Löwe.

Now let us imagine another short conversation between Oskar, Richard and Anna:

Oskar: Ein Hund kann Abfall fressen, ohne krank zu werden.
(*A dog can eat refuse without getting sick.*)
Richard: Was sagt er?
Anna: Er sagt, ein Hund kann Abfall fressen, ohne krank zu werden.

Again, if Anna wanted to indicate her belief that the statement is open to question she would use the subjunctive, type II in colloquial style; type I in a more formal statement:

Type II Er sagt, ein Hund könnte Abfall fressen, ohne krank zu werden.
Type I Er sagt, daß ein Hund Abfall fressen könne, ohne krank zu werden.

But now suppose that Oskar uses the plural and says: Hunde können Abfall fressen, ohne krank zu werden. Again, to indicate a belief that the statement is open to question Anna would use the subjunctive Type II: Er sagt, daß Hunde Abfall fressen könnten, ohne krank zu werden. It would not be possible to use present subjunctive I here, since the third person plural subjunctive I of können is one of the forms that is identical with an indicative and the sentence, Er sagt, daß Hunde Abfall fressen können, ohne krank zu werden will necessarily be taken as an indicative sentence, implying that the person reporting what has been said sees no reason to question the statement. This means that even in literary or formal style, subjunctive II forms must be used when subjunctive I forms are identical with indicative forms.

IV. Practice:

1. a. Wir können die Frage gebrauchen.
,die Sie uns einschicken, gebrauchen.
b. Sie erhalten zehn Dollar.
c. Wenn wir die Frage, die Sie uns einschicken, gebrauchen können, erhalten Sie zehn Dollar.
Können wir die Frage, die Sie uns einschicken, gebrauchen, so erhalten Sie zehn Dollar.

2. Der Verfasser dieses Artikels ist gut informiert.
author
besser informiert als ich.
am besten informiert.

3. Die römische Kultur war alt.
älter als die Kultur der Germanen.
älter als die Kultur der primitiven germanischen Stämme.

4. Die germanischen Stämme hatten eine junge und primitive Kultur.
eine jüngere und primitivere Kultur als die Römer.

5. a. Ein starkes Pferd kann viel ziehen.
mehr ziehen als zehn Löwen.

b. Herr Schmidt glaubt, daß ein starkes Pferd mehr ziehen könnte als zehn Löwen.

6. a. Wir sind uns klar darüber, welcher Gesichtspunkt in Frage kommt.
welche Bedeutung des Wortes wir meinen.
daß die Schwierigkeit eine semantische ist.

b. Wir können die Frage beantworten, wenn wir uns klar darüber sind, welcher Gesichtspunkt in Frage kommt.
etc.

c. Sind wir uns darüber klar, welcher Gesichtspunkt in Frage kommt, dann können wir die Frage beantworten.
Sind wir uns darüber klar, welche Bedeutung des Wortes wir meinen, dann können wir die Frage beantworten.
Sind wir uns darüber klar, daß die Schwierigkeit eine semantische ist, dann können wir die Frage beantworten.

concern

7. a. Wir befassen uns mit der Semantik.
Zoologie.
Geschichte der germanischen Stämme.

vorsitze

b. Befassen wir uns mit der Semantik, so werden wir uns klar darüber, wie vieldeutig die Bedeutungen der Wörter sind.
Befassen wir uns mit der Zoologie, so werden wir uns darüber klar, daß ein Straßenköter den täglichen Angriffen auf sein Wohlergehen besser widersteht als ein Rennpferd.

attacks wellbeing withstands

8. a. Der Löwe ist ein gefährliches Tier.
Die Klapperschlange (*rattlesnake*) ist ein gefährlicheres Tier als der Löwe.
Der Bazillus ist das gefährlichste Lebewesen.

b. Richard hat eben gesagt, daß der Löwe ein gefährliches Tier ist.
daß die Klapperschlange gefährlicher als der Löwe wäre.
daß der Bazillus das gefährlichste Lebewesen wäre.

9. a. Ein Bauernpferd kann den Kampf ums Dasein gut ertragen.
Ein Straßenköter besser ertragen als ein Rennpferd.

Dependent (Transposed) Word Order

b. Oskar sagt, daß ein Bauernpferd den Kampf ums Dasein gut ertragen kann.
Oskar sagt, daß ein Straßenköter den Kampf ums Dasein besser ertragen kann als ein Rennpferd.
Oskar sagt, daß ein Löwe den Kampf ums Dasein besser ertragen kann als ein Gorilla.

c. Weißt du, was Oskar sagt? Er meint, ein Straßenköter könnte den Kampf ums Dasein besser ertragen als ein Rennpferd.
Weißt du, was Oskar sagt? Er meint, ein Löwe könnte den Kampf ums Dasein besser ertragen als ein Gorilla.

d. Der berühmte Zoologe, Professor Reinhold, schreibt in seinem neusten Buch, daß ein Straßenköter den Kampf ums Dasein besser ertragen könne als ein Rennpferd.

V. Exercises:

A. *Questions:*

1. Was für Fragen werden angenommen?
2. Unter welcher Bedingung bekommt man seine Fragen zurück?
3. Ist die Geschichte der Deutschen älter als die Geschichte der Germanen?
4. Wie heißen die drei Untergruppen der Germanen?
5. Zu welcher Germanengruppe gehören die Engländer?
6. Zu welcher Germanengruppe gehörten die Wikinger?
7. Woher kamen die Goten?
8. Welche germanischen Nationen entwickelten sich aus den westgermanischen Stämmen?
9. Welches Tier hält die Tierfabel für den König aller Tiere?
10. Welches Tier muß mehr gepflegt werden, ein Bauernpferd oder ein Rennpferd?
11. Welches Landtier ist das stärkste, was Zugkraft anbetrifft?

B. *Translate:*

1. Wie würde England heute aussehen, wenn die Angeln und Sachsen zu Hause geblieben wären?
2. Wenn die Schwierigkeit nur eine zoologische wäre, könnten wir die Frage leicht beantworten.
3. Die germanischen Stämme widerstanden den Angriffen der Römer auf ihre Selbständigkeit. (*independence*).
4. Ein weniger widerstandsfähiges Tier käme sehr bald um.
5. Werden wir uns darüber klar, daß ein Straßenköter den täglichen Angriffen auf sein Wohlergehen besser widersteht als ein Rennpferd.
6. Im Jahre eintausendsechsundsechzig wurde England von Nordgermanen erobert, deren Vorfahren ungefähr hundert Jahre früher in Frankreich das Normannenreich gegründet hatten.
7. Die älteste Demokratie der Welt hat Island; sie besteht seit dem Jahre neunhundertdreißig.
8. Er befaßt sich jetzt mit bakteriologischen Studien.
9. Die Isländer haben eine reiche literarische Überlieferung.
10. Die isländischen Sagas gehören zu den größten Literaturdenkmälern der Welt.

C. *Rearrange:*

1. eine besonders gefährliche Mikrobe, in dem Falle, wird wohl . . . sein, das stärkste Lebewesen.
2. große Schwierigkeiten, er, hatte, zu beantworten, die Frage.
3. den Löwen, das Pferd, und, hat . . . verglichen, der Muskelkraft, unter dem Gesichtspunkt, er.
4. ist, der Durchschnittsmensch, sich oft nicht darüber klar, welche Bedeutung, im Augenblick, eines Wortes, meint, er.
5. im Kampf, die Burgunder, kamen, ums Dasein, um.
6. konnte, der Germanenstämme, das alte Römische Reich, widerstehen, den Angriffen, nicht.

D. *Complete by means of the suitable clause or phrase and translate:*

1. Es ist richtig zu behaupten,
   a. die Germanen wären die heutigen Deutschen.
   b. die Isländer verdankten den Ostgermanen ihren Ursprung.
   c. die heutigen Engländer stammten von verschiedenen germanischen Stämmen ab.
2. Die Semantik zeigt uns,
   a. welcher Gesichtspunkt bei der Lösung eines Problems in Frage kommt.
   b. welche Bedeutung eines Wortes wir im Augenblick meinen.
   c. wie vieldeutig die Wörter sind, die wir in den Unterhaltungen des täglichen Lebens gebrauchen.
3. Wären wir uns immer klar darüber, welche Bedeutung eines Wortes wir im Augenblick meinen,
   a. könnten wir alle Probleme ohne Schwierigkeit lösen.
   b. würden unsere Freunde uns nie widersprechen.
   c. könnten wir unsere Meinungen über verschiedene Probleme besser vergleichen.
4. Die westgermanischen Stämme, die in Mitteleuropa geblieben waren,
   a. kamen in den Kriegen der Völkerwanderungszeit um.
   b. entwickelten sich langsam zu modernen europäischen Nationen.
   c. waren den römischen Eroberern an Kultur überlegen.

E. *Examine the sentences in each group to see which sentence is associated with the preceding word:*

1. **die Völkerwanderung**
   a. Viele Stämme kamen in langen Kriegen um.
   b. Die Deutschen gründeten ein Reich in Mitteleuropa.
   c. Die Engländer besiegten die Deutschen in langen Kriegen.
2. **die Nordgermanen**
   a. Die Grenzen ihres Gebietes waren Rhein, Donau, Elbe und Nordsee.
   b. Sie entwickelten eine reiche Literatur.
   c. Sie gründeten in Mitteleuropa Reiche, die noch heute bestehen.
3. **das Urteil**
   a. Würden Sie mir bitte erklären, wer die Ostgermanen waren?

b. Er hat Löwen und Elefanten in Afrika gejagt.
c. Der Löwe ist dem Pferd an Kampfkraft überlegen.

4. **die Überlieferung**
a. Was diese Frage anbetrifft, haben sie fast genau denselben Gesichtspunkt wie ihre Vorfahren.
b. Wir wollen jetzt die Bedeutungen dieser Wörter vergleichen.
c. Wir müssen zuerst eine Gegenfrage stellen.

VI. Principal parts:

bleiben	blieb	ich bin geblieben	er bleibt	remain, stay
reißen	riß	ich habe gerissen	er reißt	tear
vergleichen	verglich	ich habe verglichen	er vergleicht	compare
wiegen	wog	ich habe gewogen	er wiegt	weigh
annehmen	nahm . . . an	ich habe angenommen	er nimmt . . . an	accept
widersprechen	widersprach	ich habe widersprochen	er widerspricht	contradict
kommen	kam	ich bin gekommen	er kommt	come
umkommen	kam . . . um	ich bin umgekommen	er kommt . . . um	perish
fressen	fraß	ich habe gefressen	er frißt	eat (*said of animals*)
geben	gab	ich habe gegeben	er gibt	give
lesen	las	ich habe gelesen	er liest	read
halten	hielt	ich habe gehalten	er hält	hold
erhalten	erhielt	ich habe erhalten	er erhält	receive
anfangen	fing . . . an	ich habe angefangen	er fängt . . . an	begin
tragen	trug	ich habe getragen	er trägt	carry
betragen	betrug	es hat betragen	es beträgt	amount to
ertragen	ertrug	ich habe ertragen	er erträgt	endure
aufwachsen	wuchs . . . auf	ich bin aufgewachsen	er wächst . . . auf	grow up
zusammenstoßen	stieß . . . zusammen	ich bin zusammengestoßen	er stößt . . . zusammen	clash
heißen	hieß	ich habe geheißen	er heißt	be called
bestehen	bestand	es hat bestanden	es besteht	exist
widerstehen	widerstand	ich habe widerstanden	er widersteht	resist
untergehen	ging . . . unter	ich bin untergegangen	er geht . . . unter	be submerged
dürfen	durfte	ich habe gedurft	er darf	may, be permitted
müssen	mußte	ich habe gemußt	er muß	have to
können	konnte	ich habe gekonnt	er kann	be able
sollen	sollte	ich habe gesollt	er soll	should
wollen	wollte	ich habe gewollt	er will	want to

sich denken	dachte sich	ich habe mir gedacht	er denkt sich	imagine
kennen	kannte	ich habe gekannt	er kennt	know
umbringen	brachte . . . um	ich habe umgebracht	er bringt . . . um	kill
wissen	wußte	ich habe gewußt	er weiß	know

der Engländer, –s, — Englishman
der Eroberer, –s, — conqueror
der Farmer, –s, — farmer
der Krieger, –s, — warrior
der Straßenköter, –s, — street cur
der Verfasser, –s, — author
der Ehrentitel, –s, — honorary title
das Lebewesen, –s, — living being
das Ufer, –s, — shore
der Abfall, –s, ¨e refuse
der Angriff, –s, –e attack
der Aufsatz, –es, ¨e article
der Ausdruck, –s, ¨e expression
der Besitz, –es, –e possession
der Briefumschlag, –s, ¨e envelop
der Gesichtspunkt, –s, –e point of view
der Hengst, –es, –e stallion
der Kampf, –es, ¨e struggle, fight
der Krieg, –s, –e war
der Sinn, –es, –e meaning
der Stamm, –es, ¨e tribe
der Ursprung, –s, ¨e origin
der Walfisch, –es, –e whale
der Wetterbericht, –s, –e weather report
der Wikingerzug, –s, ¨e Viking expedition
der Wind, –es, –e wind
die Zugkraft, — tractive power
das Landtier, –s, –e terrestrial animal
das Pfund, –es, –e pound
das Schiff, –es, –e ship
das Reich, –es, –e empire
das Rennpferd, –es, –e race horse
das Urteil, –s, –e judgment
das Land, –es, ¨er land
das Wort, –es, ¨er *or* –e word
die Gegenfrage, —, –n counterquestion

die Beute, — booty
die Grenze, —, –n boundary
die Folge, —, –n consequence
die Flotte, —, –n fleet
die Küste, —, –n coast
die Mikrobe, —, –n microbe
die Minute, —, –n minute
die Sprache, —, –n language
die Stärke, — strength
die Völkergruppe, —, –n group of people
die Bedeutung, —, –en meaning
die Besiedlung, —, –en population, colonization
die Eroberung, —, –en conquest
die Meinung, —, –en opinion
die Überlieferung, —, –en tradition
die Unterhaltung, —, –en conversation
die Allgemeinheit, — general public
die Krankheit, —, –en illness
die Fähigkeit, —, –en ability
die Muskel, —, –n muscle
die Tierfabel, —, –n animal fable
die Form, —, –en form
die Last, —, –en load
die Welt, —, –en world
die Kultur, —, –en culture
die Natur, —, –en nature
die Nation, —, –en nation
die Provinz, —, –en province
der Deutsche, –n, –n German
der Löwe, –n, –n lion
der Vorfahr, –en, –en ancestor
der Elefant, –en, –en elephant
der Autor, –s, –en author
der Gorilla, –s, –s gorilla
der Organismus, . . .muses, . . .men organism

VII. Securing the Vocabulary:

A.

erhalten	(to) receive	die Grenze	boundary
annehmen	(to) accept, assume	erobern	(to) conquer
der Aufsatz	article	die Folge	consequence
der Ausdruck	expression	überall	everywhere
wenig	little	der Ursprung	origin
ehemalig	former	das Urteil	judgment
überlegen	superior	das Pferd	horse
langsam	slowly, gradually	dagegen	against it; on the other hand
die Bedeutung	meaning		
durchaus	absolutely, by all means	ziehen	(to) pull
		gesamt	whole, total
der Gesichtspunkt	point of view	betragen	(to) amount to
vergleichen	(to) compare	draußen	outside
ehe	before	die Sprache	language

B.

eigentlich (2)	1. similar	etwas (2)	1. just
der Augenblick (7)	2. really	gerade (1)	2. something
gehören (6)	3. passage	die Bedingung (5)	3. suddenly
der Durchgang (3)	4. finished, ready	sondern (7)	4. possess, own
fertig (4)	5. doctor, physician	besitzen (4)	5. condition
hauptsächlich (8)		plötzlich (3)	6. roof
der Rat (9)	6. belong	das Dach (6)	7. but
kräftig (10)	7. moment	der Beweis (10)	8. last, take
ähnlich (1)	8. chiefly	dauern (8)	9. remain
der Arzt (5)	9. advice	bleiben (9)	10. proof
	10. strong, powerful		

schließlich (4)	1. pocket	erleben (3)	1. somebody
das Tier (6)	2. below, down	jemand (1)	2. rough
die Tasche (1)	3. find out	grob (2)	3. experience
trotz (7)	4. finally, after all	seltsam (5)	4. harm
der Spaß (10)	5. unreasonable, senseless	schaden (4)	5. strange, odd
unvernünftig (5)		ob (7)	6. small city
erfahren (3)	6. animal	die Folge (8)	7. if, whether
unten (2)	7. in spite of	das Städtchen (6)	8. consequence
der Schlüssel (8)	8. key	sogar (10)	9. smile
treten (9)	9. step	lächeln (9)	10. even
	10. fun		

Fünfundzwanzigste Aufgabe

Frag mich was! *(Rewritten)*

Wollen Sie sich zehn Dollar verdienen? Dann schicken Sie uns eine für die Allgemeinheit interessante Frage ein, (send us a question which is interesting to the general public) d.h. eine Frage, die nicht nur von Spezialisten verstanden wird.

das heißt → that is

Herr Klein aus Brooklyn sendet uns eine historische Frage: „Was war die Völkerwanderung und was war ihre Bedeutung?"

Im vierten Jahrhundert nach Christus begannen germanische Stämme nach Süden und Westen auszuwandern. Bei diesen Wanderungen stießen sie mit den Römern zusammen, die in langen Kriegen schließlich von den Germanen besiegt wurden. Die Eroberung Roms durch die Westgoten bedeutete das Ende des alten römischen Reiches. Als diese Wanderungen in der Mitte des sechsten Jahrhunderts aufhörten, waren in dem von Römern jahrhundertelang beherrschten Gebiet (in the territory which had been ruled by Romans for centuries) neue germanische Reiche entstanden. Die westgermanischen Angeln und Sachsen hatten die römische Provinz Britannien erobert und dort ein germanisches Reich, England, gegründet. Die von den ostgermanischen Goten in Italien und Spanien gegründeten Reiche (the empires founded by the East Germanic Goths in Italy and Spain) verloren bald ihren germanischen Charakter, da die germanischen Eroberer durch dauernde Kriege untergingen. In Italien und Spanien werden heute also keine germanischen sondern romanische Sprachen gesprochen. Ein Reich, das die Vandalen in Afrika gründeten, dauerte nur zwei Generationen. Die Vandalen eroberten Rom auf ihren langen Wanderungen, die sie auch durch Italien führten. Die Einwohner der italienischen Halbinsel hatten große Angst vor den wilden Leuten aus dem Norden, die aber nicht schlimmer waren als andere Eroberer zu dieser Zeit. Die Vandalen verdienen in Wirklichkeit nicht ihren durch das Wort „Vandalismus" entstandenen schlechten Ruf (their bad reputation which came into being through the word "vandalism"). Die Franken, der mächtigste westgermanische Stamm, gingen über den Rhein und gründeten das berühmte Frankenreich. Drei Jahrhunderte später eroberten die Nordmänner, die von ganz Europa wegen ihrer Wildheit gefürchteten Wikinger (the Vikings feared by all of Europe on

account of their ferocity), den nördlichen, heute nach ihnen Normandie genannten Teil des Frankenreiches (the northern part of the Frankish empire which today is called Normandy after them). Heute sind Frankreich und seine nördliche Provinz, die Normandie, aber rein romanisch. Die einzige germanisch gebliebene Wikingersiedlung (the only Viking settlement which remained Germanic) ist Island. Die westgermanischen Stämme, die während der Völkerwanderung zu Hause, d.h. in dem zwischen Rhein und Elbe, Nordsee und Donau gelegenen Gebiet (in the territory situated between the Rhine and the Elbe, the North Sea and the Danube) geblieben waren, entwickelten sich im Laufe der auf die Völkerwanderung folgenden Jahrhunderte (of the centuries following the migration of tribes) zu den heute Deutschland, Österreich und die Deutschschweiz genannten Ländern und Gebieten (into the countries and territories which are called today . . .). Herrn Kleins Frage nach der Bedeutung der Völkerwanderung können wir jetzt einfach beantworten: Man kann mit Recht behaupten, daß das heutige Europa durch die Völkerwanderung gegründet wurde.

Fräulein Jean Schröder aus Virginien möchte wissen, was Semantik ist.

Das Wort Semantik kommt aus dem Griechischen. Sema ist Griechisch für Zeichen (sign, symbol). Die Semantik sieht in den Wörtern nur Zeichen für Bedeutungen, Zeichen, die wir oft nicht richtig verstehen, da diese Zeichen oft vieldeutig und unklar sind. Immer wieder werden Wörter und ihre Bedeutungen miteinander verwechselt. Das mag in der täglichen Unterhaltung kein Unglück sein. Wenn wir aber Urteile und Meinungen ausdrücken wollen, dürfen wir keine Wörter gebrauchen, die vieldeutig sind oder deren Bedeutung uns nicht klar ist.

Ein Franzose hat einmal gesagt: Es ist immer die Seele, die jedem Ding seinen Wert gibt. Ein einfaches Beispiel kann uns das klar machen. Was für den einen Menschen nichts weiter ist als ein Straßenköter, ist für einen kleinen Jungen der wertvollste Besitz, den er hat. Nicht nur einzelne Menschen, sondern auch ganze Menschengruppen geben den Dingen ihren Wert. Verschiedene Zeiten, verschiedene Gesellschaftsklassen haben den Dingen ihren Sinn, ihren Wert gegeben, und in den für diese Dinge gebrauchten Wörtern (and in the words used for these objects) leben solche Werte noch heute weiter.

Ein ganz einfaches Beispiel: In Wörtern wie „Herr" und gentleman lebt noch der alte, mit dem Wort Edelmann am besten bezeichnete aristokratische Begriff (the old aristocratic concept best signified by the word nobleman). Daß diese Wörter unserem von demokratischen Ideen beherrschten Denken (our thinking which is dominated by democratic thoughts) widersprechen und oft falsch gebraucht werden, ist bekannt.

Ein gutes Beispiel für widersprechende, durch ein einziges Wort ausgedrückte Begriffe (for contradictory concepts expressed by a single word) ist das Wort „gut". Was bedeutet das Wort „gut" in den folgenden Sätzen? Ein guter Mensch tut so etwas nicht. Ein guter Boxer hat Kampfkraft und Kampfwillen. Das Essen war gut. Das war ein wirklich guter Witz. Sie hat ein gutes Herz. Die Butter ist nicht gut. Heute haben wir gutes Wetter. Ich lese gerne ein gutes Buch. Ein gutes Rennpferd kostet viel Geld. Haben Sie keine Angst, das ist ein gutes Pferd, Sie werden nicht fallen. Der Zirkusdirektor sagte, Goliath wäre der einzige gute Löwe in der Gruppe.

Was ist die Bedeutung von „stark"? Wenn wir einen Organismus stark nennen, weil er im Kampf ums Dasein, im Kampf mit Bazillen, Krankheiten, dem Wetter u. dgl. siegt, dann ist die Frau stärker als der Mann. Die Frauen widerstehen den täglichen Angriffen auf ihr Wohlergehen besser als die Männer. Dann ist auch der Mensch stärker als der Gorilla und eine gefährliche Mikrobe vielleicht stärker als der Mensch. Die Semantik zeigt uns, wie sinnlos viele Debatten sind, wie z.B.: Ist der Mann ein besserer Mensch als die Frau? Ist die europäische Kultur besser als die amerikanische? In diesen und ähnlichen Debatten, die oft bitter und erfolglos sind, gebraucht jeder der Debattierenden die wichtigen Wörter, mit denen oder um die debattiert wird, in ganz subjektivem Sinne. Am Ende solcher Debatten glaubt dann

jeder, daß er recht hat, und ist ärgerlich, weil der andere ihn nicht versteht oder ihn nicht verstehen will.

In solchen Fällen würde die Semantik es für beide Parteien klar machen, daß sie nicht dasselbe meinen und sich deshalb nicht verstehen können. Die Semantik kann natürlich keine Antwort auf die großen Denkprobleme der Menschheit geben; sie kann aber das sein, was die Philosophen „hygienische Polizei" im Reich des Denkens nennen.

II. Comments:

1. The Long Attribute:

The long attribute constructions, first introduced in Lesson 20, were comparatively simple so that a word by word translation could reveal their meaning. The long attribute constructions of this lesson, however, are more complex and need special attention. *Example:* Die von ganz Europa wegen ihrer Wildheit gefürchteten Wikinger (*The Vikings feared by all Europe because of their ferocity*).

The following rules will show you how to deal with these trouble makers which are common in formal and technical style. Study the following paragraph carefully to understand first of all the "loading" of an attribute in the German fashion.

Introductory word		*Key word*	*Noun*
The		feared	Vikings
The	by all of Europe	feared	Vikings
The	by all of Europe because of their ferocity	feared	Vikings
Die	von ganz Europa wegen ihrer Wildheit	gefürchteten	Wikinger

This jumble of words can be put into correct English in two different ways:

1) The Vikings **feared** by all of Europe because of their ferocity.
2) The Vikings **who were feared** by all of Europe because of their ferocity.

Before you can start translating a long attribute you must first of all be aware that you have encountered such a construction. The long attribute starts with a combination of words which cannot stand together in English. We call this impossible combination the "clash". In the above example the words Die von (*the by*) constitute the "clash".

Once you have noticed the clash, you break up the long attribute as indicated:

Die von ganz Europa wegen ihrer Wildheit gefürchteten Wikinger
1 4 3 2

The first task is to combine the introductory word Die (1) with the noun to which it belongs and from which it has been separated by the long attribute. The best way to find this noun (2) is to find the keyword(s) which is either a participial or a plain adjective. The following rules will be of help: A) If the introductory word is ein or an uninflected ein-word, the keyword will end in either -er or -es. B) If the introductory word is der, die, das, dieser, eine, eines etc., if it is, in other words, a definite article, der-word, or inflected ein-word, the ending of the

keyword will be -e or -en. C) If the introductory word is an adjective, the keyword will have the same ending as the adjective.

Thus in the above example the introductory word Die (1) leads you to the keyword gefürchteten (3) after which you find the noun Wikinger which has to be number 2 in your translation. The remaining words of the construction constitute part 4. You translate in the order 1, 2, 3, 4.

1 The
2 Vikings
3 feared
4 by all of Europe because of their ferocity

Note: Instead of translating the keyword as a participle or adjective, it will often be advisable to use a relative construction. Instead of saying *The Vikings* ***feared*** *by all* etc. you may say: *The Vikings* ***who were feared*** *by all Europe because of their ferocity.*

If more than one adjective precedes the noun (2), only the first will be the keyword (3). The other or others must be translated with the noun (2).

Example:

Die von ganz Europa wegen ihrer Wildheit gefürchteten skandinavischen Wikinger
1 4 3 2

The Scandinavian Vikings feared by all Europe because of their ferocity
1 2 3 4

Now study the additional examples in the light of the rules given above:

1. In dem von Römern jahrhundertelang beherrschten Gebiet
1 4 3 2

2. Eine für die Allgemeinheit interessante Frage
1 4 3 2

3. Der alte, mit dem Wort Edelmann am besten bezeichnete aristokratische Begriff.
1 4 3 2

III. Exercises:

Translate:

1. Die Kapelle spielte einen uns allen unbekannten Walzer.
2. Zu Shakespeares Zeit spielten siebzehnjährige, wie Frauen angezogene Jungen die weiblichen Rollen.
3. Die aus erstklassigem Stahle bestehenden Federn der Traumulusmatratze garantieren Ihnen einen ruhigen Schlaf.
4. Dr. Berg untersuchte die der Handschrift des Bankräubers sehr ähnliche Schrift auf dem in der Küche gefundenen Zettel.
5. Auf dieser Tafel sehen Sie die die verschiedenen Interessengebiete bezeichnenden Nummern.
6. Wissen Sie, in welchem von Orson Welles produzierten Film Joan Fontaine die weibliche Hauptrolle spielte?

7. Eine in diesem Augenblick über die Brücke ratternde Straßenbahn machte es uns unmöglich, die Stimme des die Leute auf der Brücke interviewenden Herrn Braun zu verstehen.
8. Er versuchte, sein durch den Lärm wild gewordenes Pferd in Photographierstellung zu bringen.
9. Die von vielen mit Unrecht für wilde Barbaren gehaltenen Vandalen waren in Wirklichkeit nicht schlimmer — vielleicht sogar besser — als ihre sie so grimmig hassenden Feinde, die Römer.
10. Eine bessere Kenntnis der semantischen Probleme würde das Ende vieler in allen wesentlichen Punkten sinnloser Debatten bedeuten.
11. Wir müssen der Tierfabel widersprechen, die den Löwen wegen seiner Stärke zum König der Tiere macht, denn es gibt wilde, dem Löwen an Kampfkraft überlegene Tiere wie z.B. den Tiger, die Riesenschlange, den Grislybären usw.

Section Three

Sechsundzwanzigste Aufgabe

Walter Brooks

Unsere Geschichte beginnt an der Ecke der Universitätsstraße an einem Oktobermorgen. Es hatte die ganze Nacht geregnet, und die Leute, die sich in Büros und Geschäften trafen, um die Arbeit des Tages zu beginnen, erzählten sich, was der Regen und der Sturm der letzten Nacht mit Bäumen,[1] Garagendächern, offenen [2] Fenstern,[3] und dergleichen gemacht hatte, daß sie nicht gut geschlafen hätten, und dann sagten sie gewöhnlich noch ein paar philosophische aber unfreundliche Dinge über das Wetter dieses Herbstes. Auch die Studenten, die mit Sorgen im Herzen in ihre acht Uhr Stunden eilten,[4] kritisierten das Wetter und wünschten, sie lägen noch zu Hause im warmen Bett oder säßen am Frühstückstisch und tränken noch eine Tasse Kaffee.

Wir sagten, unsere Geschichte beginne an der Ecke der Universitätsstraße. Das war aber nicht ganz richtig. Sie beginnt, um es ganz genau zu sagen, in einem kleinen See von Regenwasser, der sich an dieser Ecke gebildet [5] hat. An diesem kleinen See steht Sylvia Wendel und möchte über die Straße gehen, aber trotz ihrer Überschuhe scheint [6] es ihr zu gefährlich zu sein, in den kleinen See zu treten.[7] Häuserdächer, die Bäume und Sylvia spiegeln sich [8] in dem dunklen [9] Regenwasser, aber Sylvia hat im Augenblick wenig Interesse dafür,[10] wie hübsch ihr Spiegelbild [11] im Wasser aussieht, denn es ist schon ein bißchen spät, und Wilby Hall, wo sie ihre erste Stunde hat, ist am anderen Ende des Campus. Sylvia hatte kein Interesse für ihr Spiegelbild, aber Walter Brooks interessierte sich sehr für das Original. Walter Brooks fährt langsam in seinem alten Ford auf die Ecke der Universitätsstraße zu. Er fährt langsam, weil er langsam fahren muß, denn sein Ford ist so alt wie er — zwanzig Jahre.

In these footnotes new words are given and idioms are explained. Do not fail to learn perfectly the words marked with a star.

*[1] der Baum, –es, ⸗e, *tree.* *[2] offen, *open.* *[3] das Fenster, –s, —, *window.* *[4] eilen, *hurry.* *[5] bilden, *form.* *[6] scheinen, ie, ie, *seem.* *[7] treten, a, e (ist), *step.* [8] sich spiegeln, *be reflected.* *[9] dunkel, *dark.* [10] dafür, *in.* From the point of view of English dafür seems unnecessary but it is necessary in German, much as the words *to it* are necessary in such English expressions as *See to it that you come home early.* Actually da in dafür functions as object for the preposition für, which cannot modify a clause in German; da (*it*) anticipates the following clause and is not translated. [11] das Spiegelbild, –es, –er, *reflection.*

Walter wiegt genau hundertſiebzig Pfund, ſein Ford wiegt eintauſend ſechshundertvierundachtzig Pfund. Hinten im Ford liegt ein großes Bücherpaket — die Bücher will Walter in Chicago verkaufen — und dieſes Bücherpaket wiegt vierzig Pfund. Das Geſamtgewicht [1] von eintauſend achthundertvierundneunzig Pfund trifft das Waſſer mit einer Geſchwindigkeit [2] von zwanzig Meilen die Stunde. Ein Phyſiker hätte uns genau ſagen können, wie hoch [3] und wie weit das Waſſer aus dem kleinen See geſpritzt [4] war. Das brauchen wir aber nicht ſo genau zu wiſſen. Es genügt zu wiſſen, daß etwas Regenwaſſer in Sylvias Haar und Geſicht,[5] das meiſte [6] aber auf ihren Sweater und Rock ſpritzte. Man kann verſtehen, daß dieſe Kataſtrophe Walters Nervenreflexe einen Augenblick lang [7] lähmte.[8] Man kann auch verſtehen, daß er nicht gleich ſah, daß das grüne Licht vor ihm rot geworden war. Der Fahrer des Buick, der vor Walter an die Ecke gekommen war, hatte das auch erſt [9] im letzten Augenblick geſehen, denn er hielt ſo plötzlich, daß die Bremſen quietſchten. Der arme alte Ford Walters hatte natürlich nicht ſo gute Bremſen wie der neue Buick vor ihm und ſo fuhr der kleine Ford in den großen Buick hinein. 2.

Dieſer kleine Zuſammenſtoß ſah ſehr luſtig aus. Man hätte meinen können, der kleine Ford wolle den großen Buick rammen, nichts lag aber unſerem armen Walter ferner,[10] der langſam und traurig aus ſeinem Wagen [11] kam. Die Stoßſtange [12] des Ford hatte ſich über die des Buick gelegt und das Vorderende des Ford hing deshalb an dem größeren Auto. Der Herr des Buick und Sylvia begannen zur gleichen Zeit zu ſprechen. Der Herr des Buick zeigte auf das hintere Ende ſeines Autos, Sylvia zeigte auf die Flecke,[13] die das Regenwaſſer auf ihren weißen Rock gemacht hatte. Walter verſtand kein Wort, denn beide ſprachen ſehr ſchnell, aber er konnte ſich vorſtellen, wovon [14] ſie ſprachen. Endlich ging der Herr des Buick zu ſeinem Wagen zurück und unterſuchte die Stelle, wo Walters Ford den Buick gerammt hatte. Dieſe Stelle ſah er lange und traurig an, wie ein Arzt, der einen ſchwerkranken Patienten unterſucht. Während dies geſchah,[15] konnte Sylvia dem Herrn des Ford ſagen, was ſie von ihm und ſeinem alten Wagen dachte. Sie ſagte: „Schlafen Sie, wenn Sie fahren? Wiſſen Sie vielleicht nicht, daß ein Fußgänger genau ſo viel Recht hat wie ein Autofahrer? Warum kaufen Sie ſich nicht ein richtiges Auto, wenn Sie nicht zu Fuß gehen wollen? Jetzt muß ich nach Hauſe gehen und ein anderes Kleid anziehen. Wir haben heute ein Examen in Geſchichte. Wenn ich meinem Geſchichtsprofeſſor erzähle, was Sie gemacht haben, wird er es nicht glauben. Kein Menſch wird mir das glauben, denn kein Menſch kann ſich vorſtellen, daß jemand mit fünfzig Meilen Geſchwindigkeit in einen See von Regenwaſſer fährt." 3. In

[1] das Geſamtgewicht, –es, *total weight.* *[2] die Geſchwindigkeit, —, *speed.* *[3] hoch, *high.* [4] ſpritzen, *splash.* *[5] das Geſicht, –es, –er, *face.* *[6] das meiſte, *most of it.* *[7] einen Augenblick lang, *for a moment.* The word lang following nouns denoting lapse of time does not mean *long*, but it is used to express the idea of duration. Thus: drei Jahre lang, *for three years.* [8] lähmen, *paralyze.* *[9] erſt im letzten Augenblick, *only at the last moment.* In expressions of time erſt means *not until* or, less often, *only.* *[10] nichts lag aber unſerem armen Walter ferner, *nothing, however, was further from Walter's mind.* *[11] der Wagen, –s, —, *car.* [12] die Stoßſtange, —, –n, *bumper.* [13] der Fleck, –es, –e, *spot.* *[14] wovon, *about what.* *[15] geſchehen, a, e (iſt), *happen.*

dieſem Augenblick mußte die wütende [1] Sylvia Luft holen,[2] und der arme Walter konnte etwas ſagen. Er ſagte mit leiſer Stimme: „Fünfzig Meilen? So ſchnell kann mein alter Ford nicht einmal [3] bergab [4] fahren!" Sylvia wollte antworten, aber der Herr des Buick war inzwiſchen [5] mit ſeiner Unterſuchung fertig geworden und kam wieder auf Walter zu. Er war ein älterer Herr, mit grauen Haaren und einem kurzen grauen Schnurrbart.[6] Er hatte ein ſehr energiſches, beinah [7] brutales Geſicht und ſehr breite Schultern. Der Herr des Buick hielt ein Stück Papier in der einen Hand und einen Bleiſtift [8] in der anderen. Er ſah Walter nicht an, ſondern ſagte, während er Zahlen [9] auf das Papier ſchrieb: „Wie heißen Sie? Sie wiſſen wohl nicht, wo die Bremſe in Ihrem Auto iſt? Das Auto gehört Ihnen vielleicht nicht? Was? Wie heißen Sie? Soll ich dem Präſidenten Ihrer Univerſität erzählen, daß Sie wie ein Betrunkener [10] anderen Leuten ins Auto fahren? Zeigen Sie mir Ihre Papiere, falls Sie Papiere haben!" Walter hatte ein paar Mal während dieſer langen Rede ſeinen Namen genannt, aber der aufgeregte breitſchultrige Herr des Buick hatte ihn nicht gehört. Jetzt gab ihm Walter ſeine Papiere, und der Breitſchultrige ſchrieb ſich alles auf, was er wiſſen wollte. Während er noch ſchrieb, ſagte Walter: „Geben Sie mir bitte auch Ihren Namen!" Der Breitſchultrige blickte auf [11] und wurde rot im Geſicht. „Wer iſt wem ins Auto gefahren?" brüllte [12] er. „Sie haben hier nichts zu wünſchen und zu ſagen, verſtehen Sie? Sie wollen meinen Namen wiſſen, ſo eine Frechheit!" [13] Er ſchwieg [14] einen Augenblick, dann ſagte er mit ruhiger Stimme: „Na ja, Sie ſind noch ſehr grün. Ich will Ihnen eine Chance geben. Die Reparatur meines Autos wird über fünfzig Dollar koſten. Ich verliere Zeit, und Zeit iſt Geld für mich. Wenn Sie mir fünfzig Dollar geben, vergeſſe ich die ganze Sache,[15] und alles iſt in Ordnung." „Fünfzig Dollar!" ſagte Walter angſtvoll. „Soviel Geld kann ich Ihnen nicht geben. Von fünfzig Dollar lebe ich einen ganzen Monat." Der Herr des Buick dachte einen Augenblick nach, dann ſagte er: „Gut, dann leihen [16] Sie ſich das Geld von Ihren Freunden. Ich werde hier bei Ihrem Ford auf Sie warten." Walter mußte ein bißchen lachen. „Wenn ich Glück habe, kann ich mir fünf Dollar von meinen Freunden leihen, mehr haben die armen Kerle nicht. Nein, das kann ich wirklich nicht tun." Walter trat an den Buick heran und beugte ſich [17] über die Stelle, an der ſein Ford das andere Auto getroffen hatte. „Ich kann wirklich nicht ſehen, warum die Reparatur fünfzig Dollar koſten ſoll. Hier iſt ein bißchen Farbe [18] weg [19] und hier iſt . . . ." „Laß die Finger von meinem Wagen!" brüllte der grauhaarige Herr und wurde rot im Geſicht. „Meine Verſicherung [20] weiß, was ſie mit Kerlen wie dir zu tun hat." Bei dieſen

*1 wütend, *furious.* 2 Luft holen, literally *fetch air*, here *gasp for breath.* *3 nicht einmal, *not even.* 4 bergab, *downhill.* *5 inzwiſchen, *meanwhile.* 6 der Schnurrbart, –es, ¨–e, *mustache.* *7 beinah, *almost.* *8 der Bleiſtift, –es, –e, *pencil.* *9 die Zahl, —, –en, *number; figure.* 10 ein Betrunkener, *a drunk.* *11 aufblicken, *look up.* 12 brüllen, *roar, bellow.* 13 die Frechheit, —, *impertinence.* *14 ſchweigen, ie, ie, *be silent.* *15 die Sache, —, –n, *thing, matter.* *16 leihen, ie, ie, *lend, borrow.* *17 ſich beugen, *bend.* *18 die Farbe, —, –n, *color.* 19 weg, *gone.* 20 die Verſicherung, —, *insurance company.*

Worten ſprang er in ſein Auto, der Motor ſtartete, der Buick fuhr ab, der kleine Ford fiel auf ſeine Vorderräder [1] zurück, und die Stoßſtange fiel auf die Erde.[2]

Walter hob die Stoßſtange auf und legte ſie hinten ins Auto neben das Bücherpaket. Sylvia hatte die ganze Zeit dageſtanden, ohne [3] ein Wort zu ſagen. Sie hatte ſich Walters Autonummer aber auch die Nummer des Buick aufgeſchrieben.[4] Als der Buick um die Ecke gefahren war, ſagte ſie: „So eine Frechheit von dem alten Kerl. So etwas [5] habe ich noch nicht erlebt. Ich habe es mit meinen eigenen [6] Augen geſehen, daß er zu plötzlich gehalten hat." Walter ſagte nur: „Ja, das wird mir wenig helfen,[7] denn ich bin in ihn hineingefahren, ſoviel iſt ſicher. Mein Name iſt Brooks, Walter Brooks. Ich ſehe, Sie haben ſich meine Autonummer ſchon aufgeſchrieben. Ich werde Ihnen noch meine Adreſſe und Telefonnummer geben." Er ſchrieb beides auf ein Stück Papier. „Laſſen Sie ſich Ihr Kleid auf meine Koſten reinigen [8] und ſchicken Sie mir die Rechnung, oder telefonieren Sie, und ich werde Ihnen das Geld ſofort [9] ſchicken." Sylvia nahm das Stück Papier und ſagte lächelnd [10]: „Machen Sie ſich keine Sorgen. Meinen Sweater waſche ich ſelbſt, und das Reinigen meines Rockes wird nicht viel koſten." Sie ſchwieg einen Augenblick; dann ſagte ſie: „Ich glaube auch nicht, daß Sie mit fünfzig Meilen Geſchwindigkeit gefahren ſind." Walter lächelte ſchwach [11]: „Dreißig Meilen iſt die Höchſtgeſchwindigkeit [12] für mein altes Wägelchen. Wenn Ihnen das nicht zu langſam iſt, fahre ich Sie nach Hauſe." Sylvia ſah ihn einen Augenblick an und in dieſem Augenblick ſah ſie wieder, was ſie ſchon vorher geſehen hatte, daß dieſer Herr Brooks mit ſeinen grauen, ernſten Augen und ſeinem blonden Haar ſehr gut ausſah, und daß er wirklich ein ſehr netter junger Mann zu ſein ſchien. Sie ſtieg [13] in den Ford und ſagte: „Ich heiße Sylvia Wendel und wohne bei meinen Eltern, dreihundertfünfundſiebzig Linden, das iſt die Weſtſeite der Lindenavenue." Walter ſetzte ſich neben ſie, der Motor ſtartete, huſtete ein bißchen, und dann fuhr der kleine Ford mit zwanzig Meilen Geſchwindigkeit von der Unglücksſtelle [14] fort.

Vor der Tür des Elternhauſes wiederholte Sylvia ihre tröſtenden Worte, daß Walter ſich wegen [15] ihres Rocks und Sweaters keine Sorgen machen ſollte. Dann ſtiegen die beiden aus,[16] und Walter ſah zum erſten Mal, daß Sylvias Familie ſehr viel Geld haben mußte, denn ſie wohnte in einem ſchönen großen Hauſe im Kolonialſtil, und hinter dem Haus war ein richtiger Park. An der Tür drehte ſich Sylvia noch einmal [17] um.[18] „Machen Sie ſich keine Sorgen wegen des Buick! Der Mann mit den grauen Haaren hat viel zu plötzlich gehalten, das habe ich geſehen." Walter

[1] das Vorderrad, –es, ⸗er, *front wheel.* *[2] die Erde, —, *earth; ground.* *[3] ohne zu ſagen, *without saying.* The infinitive phrase zu ſagen is the object of the preposition ohne. This infinitive is best translated by a verbal noun in *–ing.* [4] aufſchreiben, ie, ie, *write down.* *[5] ſo etwas, *such a thing.* *[6] eigen, *own.* *[7] helfen, a, o, *help.* *[8] Laſſen Sie ſich Ihr Kleid reinigen! *Have your dress cleaned.* This use of laſſen in the sense of *cause to have done* is very frequent and important. *[9] ſofort, *at once.* [10] lächeln, *smile.* *[11] ſchwach, *weakly.* [12] die Höchſtgeſchwindigkeit, —, *top speed.* *[13] ſteigen, ie, ie (iſt), *climb.* [14] die Unglücksſtelle, —, –n, *place of the accident.* *[15] wegen, *because of.* *[16] ausſteigen, ie, ie (iſt), *get out.* *[17] noch einmal, *once more.* *[18] ſich umdrehen, *turn around.*

lächelte. „Ich wollte, ich hätte den grauhaarigen Mann mit Regenwaſſer vollgeſpritzt und wäre in Ihren Buick hineingefahren.“ „Das iſt leider nicht möglich,“ ſagte Sylvia, „denn ich habe keinen Buick.“ Walter wollte ſeinen Wunſch [1] ſorgfältig erklären, aber Sylvia lachte und ſagte: „Ich verſtehe ganz gut, wie Sie es meinen. Auf Wiederſehen.“ Sie lächelte ihn noch einmal freundlich an und dann war ſie ins Haus verſchwunden.[2] Walter ging langſam zu ſeinem Auto zurück und dachte über dieſes Lächeln und den Ton von Sylvias Stimme nach, in dem ſie „Auf Wiederſehen“ geſagt hatte.

Walter kam ungefähr fünf Minuten zu ſpät zu ſeiner zweiten Stunde. Profeſſor Wilmore, bei dem er in dieſer Stunde engliſche Literatur hatte, war ein ſehr nervöſer Herr, und wenn Studenten zu ſpät in ſeine Stunde kamen, machte ihn das ganz beſonders nervös. Als Walter die Tür öffnete und leiſe an ſeinen Platz ging, hörte Profeſſor Wilmore auf zu reden. Er trat ans Fenſter und trommelte [3] mit den Fingern die Marſeillaiſe ans Fenſterglas. Warum er immer die Marſeillaiſe trommelte, wenn er nervös wurde, wußte niemand,[4] trotzdem Generationen von Studenten verſucht hatten, eine Erklärung dafür zu finden. Er trommelte diesmal, bis er an die Stelle kam „Aux armes citoyens (Zu den Waffen,[5] Bürger)“, dann drehte er ſich um und ſagte zu Walter mit ruhiger Stimme: — ſeine ganze Aufregung hatte er ausgetrommelt — „Herr Brooks, Sie ſind hier nicht im Kino, nicht wahr? Kommen Sie bitte rechtzeitig oder gar nicht!“ Dann huſtete er und ſagte mit etwas trauriger Stimme: „Wie ich eben ſagte, ehe wir von Herrn Brooks unterbrochen [6] wurden, viele Situationen in Shakeſpeares Dramen ſind auch in unſerer Zeit möglich. Um beim „Kaufmann von Venedig“ zu bleiben, Sie brauchen ſich Antonio nicht im Koſtüm eines Venezianers zur Zeit der Renaiſſance vorzuſtellen. Jeder moderne Menſch kann ſich denken, welche Sorgen ſich der arme Antonio macht. Dreitauſend Dukaten ſoll er zahlen und er hat nichts. Und Shylock? Auch im modernen Leben können wir Shylock leicht wiederfinden. Laſſen Sie Ihrer Einbildungskraft freien Lauf! Jeder Menſch, der einen anderen Menſchen in ſeiner Gewalt [7] hat und ſein „Pfund Fleiſch“ will, iſt Shylock. Aber zurück zum Rialto und zum Venezianer Antonio. In welcher ſchwierigen Lage [8] befindet ſich Antonio? Erklären Sie uns das bitte, Herr Aſhton!“ „Fehlt“ [9] ſagten drei oder vier männlich robuſte Stimmen. Profeſſor Wilmore ſeufzte [10] tief, ſah in ſein kleines Büchlein und rief Fräulein Bandelow auf.[11] Fräulein Bandelow rollte ihre Augen etwas, und dann ging es los: „Profeſſor Wilmore, ich dachte, wir ſollten für heute nur den erſten Akt leſen, ich dachte Sie hätten das geſagt. Ich kenne die Geſchichte vom Kaufmann von Venedig. Ich habe zu Hauſe eine Sammlung „Die Klaſſiker der Weltliteratur.“ Da wird die Geſchichte vom Kaufmann von Venedig erzählt und da habe ich geleſen, daß . . .“ „Nein, nein Fräulein Bandelow,“ unterbrach Profeſſor

*1 der Wunſch, –es, ¨–e, *wish.* *2 verſchwinden, a, u (iſt), *disappear.* 3 trommeln, *drum, tap.* *4 niemand, *nobody.* 5 die Waffen (pl.), *arms.* *6 unterbrechen, a, o, *interrupt.* *7 die Gewalt, —, *force, power.* *8 die Lage, —, –n, *situation.* *9 fehlen, *be absent.* 10 ſeufzen, *sigh.* 11 aufrufen, ie, u, *call on.*

Wilmore. „Was man nicht im Original lieſt, kennt man nur halb oder gar nicht.“ Er blickte wieder in ſein Büchlein, huſtete und ſagte: „Herr Brooks.“ Walter erſchrak,[1] aber er konnte ſeine Aufgabe. Nur ſeine Stimme klang ein bißchen träumeriſch,[2] — er hatte an die fünfzig Dollar für die Buickreparatur gedacht — als er begann: „Antonio hat ſich dreitauſend Dukaten von Shylock geliehen. Wenn er das Geld in drei Monaten nicht zurückgeben kann, hat Shylock das Recht, ihm ein Pfund Fleiſch aus der Bruſt zu ſchneiden. Antonio hat Unglück [3]; er verliert ſeine Schiffe, und ſo kann er die fünfzig Dollar — “ die Klaſſe lachte laut, und Profeſſor Wilmore trommelte „Allons enfants de la patrie (Auf! Kinder des Vaterlands)“, und alle wurden ſtill. „Er kann die dreitauſend Dukaten nicht zurückgeben, und Shylock verlangt ſein Pfund Fleiſch aus Antonios Bruſt. Der Richter [4] Bellario verſucht Shylock zu überreden,[5] Mitleid [6] mit Antonio zu haben.“ „Wer war dieſer Richter Bellario?“ unterbrach Profeſſor Wilmore. „Das war natürlich Sylvia, o, ich wollte ſagen, Portia.“ Wieder lachte die Klaſſe brüllend, denn Sylvia war der Name der Heldin eines Filmes, der gerade im Varſity-Kino ſpielte, was Walter übrigens nicht wußte. Profeſſor Wilmore trommelte diesmal nicht. Er ſeufzte tief und ſagte: „Ich verſtehe Sie nicht. Wenn Sie die wirklich luſtigen Witze von Shakeſpeares Narren leſen, dann lachen Sie nie. Wenn aber unſer junger Freund hier ſtatt [7] dreitauſend Dukaten fünfzig Dollar ſagt, dann gibt es ein brüllendes Gelächter. Nun, ich kann nur ſagen, daß ich perſönlich Shakeſpeares dreihundertfünfzig Jahre alte Witze viel luſtiger finde als dieſe modernen, darf ich ſagen, etwas grünen Witze.“ Walter war wieder allein mit ſeinen Gedanken, während Profeſſor Wilmore der Klaſſe erklärte, daß Shylock zu Shakeſpeares Zeit eine Art Clown war, über den man lachen konnte und ſollte, daß er aber für unſeren modernen Geſchmack [8] ein tragiſcher Charakter iſt. Walter dachte gerade darüber [9] nach, ob wohl der breitſchultrige Herr des Buick auch ein tragiſcher Charakter wäre. Da klingelte es, die Stunde war um. In der Pauſe rannte Walter ſchnell zum Parkplatz, um ſeinen Ford noch einmal zu unterſuchen. Es war, wie er es ſich gedacht hatte. Die letzte Kataſtrophe war zu viel für den linken Vorderreifen [10] geweſen. Schon von weitem ſah er, wie ſein alter Ford nach links hing. Eine Reparatur war diesmal unmöglich, und ſo ging Walter mit einer neuen Geldſorge im Herzen zur Univerſität zurück. Die nächſten beiden Stunden waren nicht gefährlich, denn die Profeſſoren hielten Vorträge,[12] und Walter konnte träumen und ſpekulieren, ſo viel er wollte.

Es wurde Mittag, und er war noch immer tief in Gedanken. In was für Gedanken? — Nun, er dachte über zwei ganz verſchiedene Dinge nach: Wie er die fünfzig Dollar zuſammenbringen könnte und ob und wann er Sylvia wiederſehen würde. Mechaniſch ging er in die Studentenkafeteria und ließ ſich [13] in der langen

*1 erſchrecken, a, o (iſt), *be startled.* [2] träumeriſch, *dreamy.* *3 das Unglück, *bad luck, misfortune.* [4] der Richter, –s, —, *judge.* *5 überreden, *persuade.* *6 das Mitleid, *pity.* *7 ſtatt, *instead of.* *8 der Geſchmack, *taste.* [9] darüber (*See Note 10, page 283*). [10] der Vorderreifen, –s, —, *front tire,* [11] hängen, i, a, *hang, dangle.* [12] einen Vortrag halten, ie, a, *deliver a lecture.* *13 ließ ſich ſchieben. *let himself be shoved.* The German active infinitive (ſchieben) with laſſen must often be translated by the English passive infinitive.

Reihe der Wartenden bis an die Stelle ſchieben, wo eine ſtattliche Matrone in Weiß die Teller [1] der Hungrigen mit allerlei [2] guten Dingen füllte. Walter war ſo zerſtreut, daß er nicht einmal ſah, daß es heute Wiener Schnitzel und auch Apfelſtrudel gab, — und er aß Wiener Schnitzel und Apfelſtrudel ſo gerne! Als er an die Reihe kam, ſich etwas auszuſuchen, wußte er nicht, was er nehmen ſollte. Er zeigte deshalb auf das, was ihm zuerſt ins Auge fiel, und ſo hatte er bald, was er nicht wollte, nämlich, Kartoffelſuppe, Sauerkraut, Frankfurter Würſtchen und Reispudding. Das deprimierte ihn natürlich noch mehr, und ſo ging er durch den Speiſeſaal,[3] an deſſen einem Ende er ein paar Tiſche geſehen hatte, an denen niemand ſaß. Dort, ſo dachte er, würde er alleine ſein, um ſich Sorgen zu machen und ſein uninteressantes Sauerkraut uſw. in Frieden [4] zu eſſen. Es kommt oft aber ganz anders als man denkt. Auf halbem Wege fühlte Walter einen ſchweren Schlag [5] auf die Schulter, ſo daß er beinah ſein Tablett [6] fallen ließ. Tennisſpieler haben aber gute Reflexe, und Walter war nicht nur ein guter Tennisſpieler ſondern ſogar Tennismeiſter ſeiner Alma Mater. Er hielt ſein Tablett feſt,[7] und ſo ſpritzte nur etwas Kartoffelſuppe in den Kaffee und etwas Kaffee auf den Reispudding. Ohne ſich umzudrehen, wußte Walter, wer ihn auf die Schulter geſchlagen [8] hatte. Hans Lübke, der rieſige Tackle, Hans Lübke, der Mann der Superlative, hatte Walter wieder einmal gezeigt, daß er, Lübke, ſein guter Freund war. Lübkes mächtige Hand lag noch immer auf Walters Schulter und führte ihn in die Mitte des Speiſeſaales zurück,[9] wo der Lärm am größten war. Dort ſetzte ſich Lübke an ſeinen Tiſch, und Walter ſetzte ſich mit einem Seufzer neben ihn.

Niemand konnte lange auf Lübke ärgerlich ſein trotz ſolcher koloſſalen Witze, denn er war, was man in der deutſchen Studentenſprache „ein gutes altes Haus" nennt. (In der amerikaniſchen Studentenſprache wäre Lübke a good egg.) Auch Walter war nicht lange ärgerlich, denn er hatte Lübke gern. Natürlich wäre er gerade heute lieber alleine geweſen. Wir nannten Lübke den Mann der Superlative, und das war keine Übertreibung. Er war ohne Zweifel [10] der ſtärkſte Mann auf dem Campus. Bei einem Studentenkarnival z.B. hatte er ein Brett [11] auf den Füßen balanziert, auf dem drei Sophomores und ein Laboratoriumsaſſiſtent ſaßen. Außerdem beſaß er die größten Hände und Füße, die die Verkäufer von Schuhen und Handſchuhen je [12] geſehen hatten, und das kann man verſtehen, denn er wog in ſeiner Fußballuniform zwiſchen zweihundertſechzig und zweihundertſiebzig Pfund.

In dieſem Semeſter hatte Lübke allerdings keine Gelegenheit,[13] ſeine Fußballuniform anzuziehen. Warum? Nun, er ſelber [14] ſagte, daß er genug für ſeine Alma Mater im Fußballſtadion getan hätte, und daß er jetzt ganz ſeinen Studien leben werde. Da ſei beſonders Spaniſch, eine Sprache, die ihn ganz beſonders intereſſiere, da [15] er ſpäter Südamerika und Mexiko beſuchen werde. Dann wolle er

*1 der Teller, –s, —, *plate.* *2 allerlei, *all sorts of.* 3 der Speiſeſaal, –es, ...ſäle, *dining room.* *4 der Frieden, –s, *peace.* 5 der Schlag, –es, ¨–e, *blow, slap.* 6 das Tablett, –es, –e, *tray.* *7 feſt, *firmly.* *8 ſchlagen, u, a, *hit, strike.* 9 zurückführen, *lead back.* *10 der Zweifel, –s, —, *doubt.* 11 das Brett, –es, –er, *board.* *12 je, *ever.* *13 die Gelegenheit, —, –en, *opportunity.* *14 ſelber, *himself.* *15 da, *since.*

nicht in ſeinem Auto irgendwo auf der panamerikaniſchen Autoſtraße vor einer Tankſtelle halten und kein Benzin kaufen können, weil man ihn nicht verſtehe. Er kenne die Verhältniſſe in Süd- und Zentralamerika! Außerdem ſei da die Phyſik, eine ſehr wichtige Wiſſenſchaft [1] für einen Mann wie ihn, der ſich fürs Ingenieurweſen intereſſiere. Er könne nicht dauernd ein D in Phyſik bekommen. Außerdem ſei er im Engliſchen etwas ſchwach, oder beſſer, ſeine engliſchen Aufſätze ſeien früher zu kurz geweſen. Dies und Ähnliches hatte Lübke zu ſagen, wenn man ihn fragte, warum er in dieſem Semeſter nicht Fußball ſpiele. Leider ſagte er all dies auch, wenn man ihn nicht fragte. Walter z.B. hatte ihn nicht gefragt, denn Walter kannte Lübkes Lebensgeſchichte und alle Gründe, warum Lübke in dieſem Semeſter nicht ſpielte. Trotzdem mußte er aber doch Lübkes langem Vortrag zuhören. Lübke war heute beſonders aufgeregt über ſein Unglück, denn heute war der Sonnabend, an dem ſeine Mannſchaft gegen die Silberlöwen [2] von Weſt College ſpielen mußte. Der Kampf mit den Silberlöwen gehörte zur Tradition der Univerſität, die in den letzten zehn Jahren jedes Spiel [3] gewonnen hatte. Wir können natürlich verſtehen, daß Lübke ſich dieſes Spiel wenigſtens anſehen wollte.

Da Lübke ſehr aufgeregt war und viel und laut ſprach, brauchte Walter nur mit einem Ohr zuzuhören, um von Zeit zu Zeit an der richtigen Stelle „ja, natürlich" oder „natürlich nicht" ſagen zu können. Dabei [4] erinnerte er ſich, daß er heute für fünfzig Cent gegeſſen hatte, und daß er für fünfzig Dollar hundertmal zu Mittag eſſen könnte, und daß er außerdem noch einen neuen Reifen kaufen mußte. Plötzlich ſagte Lübke: „Walter, Menſch, wir müſſen gehen, ſonſt kommen wir zu ſpät zum Spiel," und da erſt [5] erinnerte ſich Walter, daß ja heute ſeine Alma Mater im eigenen Stadion gegen die Silberlöwen ſpielte. Er war froh, ſeine Sorgen auf ein paar Stunden vergeſſen zu können, und ſo machte er ſich mit Lübke auf den Weg zum Fußballſtadion.

Es war richtiges Fußballwetter. Der Regen hatte ſchon am Morgen aufgehört, und die warme Sonne lachte vom blauen Himmel.[6] Trotzdem die Luft kühl war, konnte man aber ohne Mantel [7] im Freien [8] ſitzen. Das rieſige Fußballſtadion war ſchon voll, als Lübke mit Walter erſchien.[9] Das Publikum war in beſter Stimmung,[10] und ſogar Walter vergaß ſeine Geldſorgen, als die Univerſitätskapelle in die Arena marſchiert kam und das Lied der Alma Mater ſpielte.

Er und die Tauſende um ihn ſchrien ſo laut ſie konnten: „Hurra, hurra, ſchlagt die Sil-ber-lö-wen!"

Die Fußballmannſchaften erſchienen auf dem Spielfeld, liefen ein bißchen hin und her, warfen, fingen und traten [11] ein paar Fußbälle, und dann ging es los. Peter

*1 die Wiſſenſchaft, —, -en, *science.* [2] der Silberlöwe, -n, -n, (*silver lion*) *cougar.* *3 das Spiel, -es, -e, *game.* *4 dabei, in doing so, at the same time. *5 da erſt, *only then.* In expressions of time erſt means *not until* or, less often, *only.* Compare erſt um 10 Uhr, *not until 10 o'clock.* *6 der Himmel, -s, *sky, heaven.* *7 der Mantel, -s, ¨, *topcoat.* *8 im Freien, *in the open.* *9 erſcheinen, ie, ie (iſt), *appear.* [10] die Stimmung, —, -en, *mood.* *11 **treten, a, e,** here: *kick;* usually: *step.*

Molechalski trat den Ball, der hoch in die Luft flog und dreißig Meter vor dem Tor von einem der Silberlöwen, Michael O'Meara, gefangen wurde. Michael galoppierte vorwärts, aber trotz aller Seitensprünge wurde er in der Mitte des Spielfeldes gestoppt. Beim Hinfallen fiel ihm der Ball aus der Hand.[1] Peter Molechalski hob den rollenden Ball auf und . . . Was dann geschah, konnte Walter nicht sehen, denn Lübke stand auf, um einer Studentin Platz zu machen, die sich auf den leeren Platz an Walters linker Seite setzte, und nun sah Walter, daß er das Mädchen kannte. Sie war eine junge Kanadierin, die im Chemielaboratorium an dem Tisch hinter ihm experimentierte oder besser, Gläser zerbrach [2] und sich die Finger an dem Bunsenbrenner verbrannte.[3] Sie war sehr schwach in Chemie, aber eine ausgezeichnete Tänzerin und eine reizende Blondine. Walter hatte sie bei dem Maskenball kennengelernt,[4] bei dem Lübke als „Kraftmensch" [5] drei Sophomores und einen Chemieassistenten auf einem Brett balanziert hatte. Auf diesem Ball war Fräulein Ruth Wilberton — so hieß die junge Dame — mit einem Studenten der Medizin erschienen, der ein ausgezeichneter Tennisspieler war und mit dem Walter deshalb oft spielte. Walter sprach ein paar Worte mit Ruth, als Lübke plötzlich den Mund [6] aufmachte [7]: „Ich habe Sie auch auf dem Ball gesehen, von dem Walter spricht. Ich hatte die Balanziernummer auf dem Programm. Außerdem spiele ich hier manchmal Fußball, aber . . ." „Entschuldige Hans," sagte Walter, „daß ich dich unterbreche. Fräulein Wilberton war nach Hause gegangen, ehe deine Nummer an die Reihe kam. Ruth, dieser Herr ist Hans Lübke; er war im vorigen Jahr unser bester Tackle. Hans, diese Dame ist Ruth Wilberton aus Kanada, die beste Tänzerin auf dem Campus. Ihr beide solltet euch gut verstehen. Hans lernt nämlich im Augenblick tanzen. Er hat in der Hochbahn eine Reklame gelesen: ‚Weller Tanzinstitut. Wenn Sie gehen können, lehren [8] wir Sie tanzen.' Nun, Hans kann nicht nur gehen, er kann sogar laufen und zwar hundert Meter in 12,5 Sekunden, was für einen Mann von seinem Gewicht eine kolossale Leistung [9] ist." Lübke lächelte, sah seine riesigen Hände an und sagte schließlich: „Sie kennen meinen armen Freund Walter nicht, er hat im letzten Sommer zu viel in der heißen Sonne Tennis gespielt, er ist aber ganz harmlos. Sie kommen aus Kanada? Das ist ja äußerst interessant. — Entschuldige, Walter!" Ehe Walter etwas sagen konnte, hatte Lübke sich an Fräulein Wilbertons Seite gesetzt. Walter wollte protestieren, aber plötzlich verlor er alles Interesse am Spiel und an Fräulein Wilberton. Lübkes Bemerkung [10] „mein armer Freund" hatte ihn an den Zusammenstoß mit dem Buick erinnert,[11] und nun saß er da und dachte darüber nach, wie er schnell fünfzig Dollar verdienen könnte. Leider war der Kampf der Mannschaften in der Arena nicht sehr aufregend. Die Kampffronten gingen vorwärts [12] und rückwärts.[13] Der Ball wanderte von der Mannschaft

*[1] ihm aus der Hand, *from his hand.* The idea of possession with reference to parts of the body and articles of clothing is expressed in German by the dative case. *[2] zerbrechen, a, o, *break.* *[3] verbrennen, verbrannte, verbrannt, *burn.* *[4] kennenlernen, *become acquainted, meet.* [5] der Kraftmensch, –en, –en, *strong man.* *[6] der Mund, –es, ¨–er, *mouth.* *[7] aufmachen, *open.* *[8] lehren, *teach.* *[9] die Leistung, —, –en, *achievement.* [10] die Bemerkung, —, –en, *remark.* *[11] erinnern, *remind.* [12] vorwärts, *forward.* [13] rückwärts, *backward.*

der Alma Mater zur Mannschaft der Besucher, aber nichts Dramatisches geschah. Als die Halbzeit herankam,[1] stand das Spiel sechs zu sechs. Lübke hatte sich während der ganzen Zeit sehr interessiert mit Fräulein Wilberton unterhalten. Er hatte viele intelligente Fragen gestellt wie z.B.: ob das Wetter in Kanada besser wäre als in den Vereinigten Staaten; was die Haupterportartikel Kanadas wären; ob Fräulein Wilberton die kanadischen Rockies kenne; u. dgl. m. Als der Pistolenschuß die erste Hälfte des Spieles beendete, sagte Lübke: „Gestatten Sie,[2] Fräulein Wilberton, daß ich Sie zu einer Tasse Kaffee und einem warmen Würstchen einlade. Willst du auch mitkommen, Walter?" Walter war so tief in Gedanken, daß er die Frage nicht richtig verstand. Er sagte: „Ja, schön, das glaube ich auch." Lübke schüttelte[3] den Kopf und sah Fräulein Wilberton lächelnd an. Ruth Wilberton hatte sich etwas über Walter geärgert.[4] Sie wollte sich eigentlich mit ihm unterhalten, aber Walter zeigte gar kein Interesse für sie sondern starrte nur vor sich hin.[5] So sagte Fräulein Wilberton mit künstlichem Lächeln zu ihrem neuen Kavalier Herrn Lübke: „Das ist eine ausgezeichnete Idee, Hans. Gehen wir! Herr Brooks scheint wichtigere Dinge zu tun zu haben als mit uns Kaffee zu trinken." „O nein, nein," protestierte Walter, ohne viel Nachdruck[6] in seine Worte zu legen. Schweigend ging Walter mit den beiden zu einer der improvisierten Bars, wo Kaffee und Frankfurter Würstchen verkauft wurden.

Die zweite Hälfte des Spieles war interessanter als die erste. Es war klar, daß der Coach den Grislybären — so hieß die Fußballmannschaft der Alma Mater — dies und das gesagt hatte. Sie spielten in schnellerem Tempo und viel besser. Schon nach ein paar Minuten gab es einen hochdramatischen Augenblick. Bob Miller, genannt „der fliegende Holländer," lief etwa zehn Meter hinter die eigene Spielfront zurück, blickte einen Augenblick suchend über das Spielfeld, bis er in etwa dreißig Meter Entfernung seinen Mitspieler Peter Molechalski rennen sah. Molechalski lief in einer Diagonale von der Seitenlinie ins Spielfeld, und Bob Miller warf ihm den Ball zu.

Was in den nächsten Sekunden geschah, wurde noch nach Tagen von den Studenten diskutiert und war der Beginn einer langen Reihe von Briefen, die aufgeregte Sportsenthusiasten und Freunde Bob Millers an den „Campus-Herold" schrieben. Schließlich, und das interessiert uns hier am meisten, war es für Walter Brooks die Lösung[7] seines Problems und außerdem eines der wichtigsten Ereignisse[8] seines Lebens. Woher wir das wissen? Lieber Leser, ein Autor weiß alles, was das zukünftige Leben seines Helden betrifft.[9] Wir kommen aber vom Thema ab.[10] Was war geschehen?

Molechalski lief diagonal über das Spielfeld, und Bob Miller hatte den Ball hoch in die Luft geworfen. Zwanzigtausend Augen sahen, wie der Ball sich in einer

[1] herankommen, a, o (ist), *approach.* [2] Gestatten Sie, daß . . . , *Permit me to . . .* [3] schütteln, *shake.* *[4] sich ärgern, *be annoyed by.* *[5] starrte vor sich hin, *stared in front of himself*, i.e. *into space.* [6] der Nachdruck, -es, *emphasis.* [7] die Lösung, —, -en, *solution.* *[8] das Ereignis, . . .nisses, . . .nisse, *event.* *[9] was . . . betrifft, *as far as . . . is concerned.* [10] abkommen, a, o (ist), *deviate, get away.*

ſchönen Kurve durch die Luft bewegte,[1] genau auf den galoppierenden Molechalski zu. Nicht ganz genau, das war es, was der Campus-Herold ſagte. Der Ball bewegte ſich genau auf Molechalski zu, aber Molechalski änderte [2] plötzlich ſein Tempo und lief zu langſam: Das war es, was die aufgeregten Briefe behaupteten.

Jedenfalls [3] mußte Molechalski hoch in die Luft ſpringen, um den Ball zu fangen; er fing ihn aber nicht, ſondern ſtieß [4] mit der Hand gegen ihn, ſodaß er in die erſten Reihen der Zuſchauer flog. Ein breitſchultriger Mann mit grauen Haaren ſprang auf, fing den Ball und warf ihn ins Spielfeld zurück, während die Umſitzenden lachten und applaudierten.

Walter ſtarrte den breiten Rücken vor ſich an, als ob er Bankos Geiſt [5] geſehen hätte. Ja, darüber konnte er nicht im Zweifel ſein. Etwa zehn Reihen vor und unter ihm ſaß der Herr des Buick. Als er ſich von ſeiner erſten Überraſchung erholt [6] hatte, ſah er, daß der Herr des Buick nicht alleine ſaß. Er unterhielt ſich mit einer Dame in einem ſchönen Pelzmantel, der ſoviel wert zu ſein ſchien wie ein Buick. Die Dame intereſſierte Walter aber nicht ſo ſehr wie der Mann, der links neben dem Breitſchultrigen ſaß. Es war ein kleiner, ſchwächlicher [7] Mann von ungefähr vierzig Jahren. Wenn er mit ſeinem Begleiter [8] ſprechen wollte, legte er ihm jedesmal die Hand auf die Schulter, und der Herr des Buick zog jedesmal die Schulter zurück. Gute Freunde waren die beiden ſicher nicht, das konnte Walter ſehen. Der Kleine wollte ſich eine Zigarette anzünden,[9] aber ſeine Hände zitterten [10] ſo ſtark, daß er das Streichholz [11] nicht ſtill halten konnte. Der Herr des Buick ſchien ärgerlich zu werden. Er faßte [12] den Arm, mit dem der kleine Mann die Zigarette hielt, und gab ihm Feuer. Dann ſagte er ihm etwas ins Ohr, ſicherlich [13] nichts Freundliches. Wenn Walter etwas von medizinischer Pſychologie verſtanden hätte, wäre es ihm ſofort klar geweſen, daß der kleine Mann außer [14] Eſſen und Trinken auch Morphium oder Kokain brauchte, um am Leben zu bleiben. Walter wunderte ſich über die ſonderbaren Drei, dann machte er ſich aber wieder ſeine alten Geldſorgen. Er beſchloß,[15] dem Breitſchultrigen zum Parkplatz zu folgen, um ſich den Schaden [16] noch einmal anzuſehen. Er konnte noch immer [17] nicht verſtehen, wie der kleine Zuſammenſtoß den Buick ſo hatte beſchädigen [18] können, daß die Reparatur fünfzig Dollar koſten ſollte. „Walter," ſagte Ruth Wilberton plötzlich, „das iſt wirklich ein ſchöner Pelzmantel!" „Wer iſt das?" ſagte Walter. „Weſſen Pelz iſt das?" Ruth lachte und Lübke, der auch nicht verſtand, was Ruth geſagt hatte, ſagte: „Armer Freund!"

Als der Piſtolenſchuß das Spiel beendete, ſtand das Spiel trotz allem, was der Coach ſeiner Mannſchaft in der Halbzeit geſagt hatte, immer noch ſechs zu ſechs. Die Menge [19] begann aus dem Stadion zu ſtrömen, und Walter wollte den Herrn

*1 ſich bewegen, *move.* *2 ändern, *change.* *3 jedenfalls, *at any rate.* 4 ſtoßen, ie, o, *hit, knock.* 5 der Geiſt, –es, –er, *ghost.* 6 ſich erholen, *recover.* 7 ſchwächlich, *weakly, sickly.* 8 der Begleiter, –s, —, *companion.* 9 anzünden, *light.* *10 zittern, *tremble, shake.* 11 das Streichholz, –es, ¨er, *match.* 12 faſſen, *grasp.* *13 ſicherlich, *undoubtedly.* 14 außer, *besides.* *15 beſchließen, o, o, *decide.* *16 der Schaden, –s, ¨, *damage.* *17 noch immer or immer noch, *still.* 18 beſchädigen, *damage.* *19 die Menge, —, *crowd.*

des Buick nicht aus den Augen verlieren. Er legte die Hand auf Lübkes Gorillaarm und ſagte mit verlegenem [1] Lächeln: „Lieber Hans, liebe Ruth, ihr müßt mich wirklich entſchuldigen — ich muß, — ich möchte, — ich muß einen Mann unten ſprechen, ich erkläre das ſpäter.“ Ruths Lächeln war nicht verlegen ſondern leicht ironiſch. „Wäre es vielleicht möglich,“ ſagte ſie, „daß der Mann einen Pelzmantel trägt? Nun, viel Glück! Montag im Labor werde ich dich wiederſehen. Sollen wir gehen?“ [2] Die beiden verſchwanden und Walter lief ſo ſchnell er konnte durch die Menge, bis er dicht hinter dem Herrn des Buick war. Er ſah ſofort, daß die Dame im Pelzmantel mit ihren beiden Begleitern ſtritt.[3] Sie ſprach ſehr laut, dann drehte ſie den beiden den Rücken [4] und ging raſch davon. Die beiden Männer ſahen ihr einen Augenblick nach, dann gingen ſie weiter. Walter folgte ihnen ungeſehen, was leicht war, ſolange er inmitten der aus dem Stadion ſtrömenden Menſchenmenge ging. Auf dem Parkplatz begannen die Schwierigkeiten, aber hinter jedem Auto Deckung [5] ſuchend, kam er ganz [6] nahe an die beiden Männer heran, die langſam ans andere Ende des Parkplatzes gingen. Der kleine nervöſe Mann blieb plötzlich ſtehen [7] und faßte den Arm ſeines Begleiters. „Gilbert,“ ſagte er mit einem ſüdländiſchen Akzent, „ich brauche das Geld, gib mir wenigſtens ein paar Hundert.“ Der Herr des Buick, deſſen Namen wir jetzt kennen, aber ſchrie: „Zum Donnerwetter, Menſch, woher ſoll ich ein paar hundert Dollar nehmen?“ Dann wurde ſeine Stimme ruhiger, und er fuhr fort [8]: „Wir müſſen alle warten. Louis kommt Ende der nächſten Woche wieder. Ich hab' dir geſagt, er muß den Dampfer [9] nach Key Weſt nehmen. Im Flugzeug kann er nicht genug Papiergeld von Havannah mitbringen. Größere Scheine [10] als Zehndollarſcheine ſoll er nicht mitnehmen. Jetzt ſei ſtill, ich geb' dir ein paar Gramm, wenn wir wieder im Hotel ſind.“ Schweigend gingen die beiden weiter. Vor dem Buick blieben ſie ſtehen, und Walter, halb unter einem Ford liegend, betrachtete [11] ſich das Hinterende des Wagens. Leider konnte er nicht viel ſehen, denn Gilbert fuhr ſein Auto ſchnell und ſicher aus den Wagenreihen heraus und auf die Straße, wo Walter es bald in der langen Prozeſſion der heimwärts fahrenden Automobile aus den Augen verlor.

Walters Wirtin,[12] Frau Eliſe Wetzel, eine typiſche Studentenmutter, hatte ihre Freundin, Frau Finnegan, zu Beſuch. Es war ungefähr neun Uhr abends, die beiden alten Damen hatten ſich eine Taſſe Kaffee gekocht und ſaßen zuſammen auf dem Plüſchſofa unter dem Bilde [13] des verſtorbenen [14] Herrn Wetzel und unterhielten ſich. Frau Finnegan ſah die Decke [15] an. „Was iſt denn mit dem Herrn da oben [16] los? [17] Warum geht er dauernd hin und her? Du ſollteſt an die Decke klopfen,[18]

[1] verlegen, *embarrassed.* *[2] Sollen wir gehen? *Let's go!* The expression *let's* is usually rendered in German by the verbs ſollen or wollen used in the form of a question. [3] ſtreiten, i, i, *quarrel.* *[4] der Rücken, –s, —, *back.* [5] die Deckung, —, *cover.* *[6] ganz, *very.* *[7] ſtehen bleiben, ie, ie (iſt). Sometimes ſtehen bleiben means *remain standing*, but more often it means *stop* or *come to a halt.* [8] fortfahren, u, a, *continue.* [9] der Dampfer, –s, —, *steamer.* [10] der Schein, –es, –e, *bill.* *[11] ſich betrachten, *look at.* [12] die Wirtin, —, –nen, *landlady.* *[13] das Bild, –es, –er, *picture.* [14] verſtorben, *deceased, late.* *[15] die Decke, —, –n, *ceiling.* [16] da oben, *up there.* *[17] Was iſt denn los? *What's the matter?* *[18] klopfen, *knock.*

damit [1] er weiß, daß er uns stört." [2] „Ach nein," sagte Frau Wetzel, „das werde ich nicht tun. Walter ist mein bester Mieter. So ein stiller, lieber Junge, und seine Miete bezahlt er immer im voraus! Dabei [3] hat er viel weniger Geld als meine anderen Mieter. Oft arbeitet er in der Stadt, in der Fordgarage, um sich ein paar Extradollar zu verdienen. Wenn er dann nach Hause kommt, muß der arme Kerl oft bis spät in die Nacht aufsitzen, um seine Schularbeiten zu machen. Seine Familie hat Unglück gehabt. Der Vater war Arzt, hat aber bei einem Autounfall [4] den rechten Arm verloren. Die Familie hat natürlich nicht viel Geld, und Walter weiß, wie schwierig es für seinen Vater ist, ihn auf die Universität zu schicken. Heute abend war Walter so nervös und sah besorgt [5] aus. Ich mache mir Sorgen um den Jungen, denn der [6] sagt nichts, wenn ihm etwas fehlt.[7] Vielleicht hat er schlechte Nachrichten von zu Hause bekommen. Ich muß ihn morgen fragen." In diesem Augenblick klingelte das Telephon. Frau Wetzel ging hinaus, und im nächsten Augenblick hörte Frau Finnegan sie rufen [8]: „Walter, komm runter,[9] es ist für dich!" Frau Wetzel kam wieder ins Zimmer, sie schloß aber die Tür nicht ganz, denn sie interessierte sich, wie das bei Wirtinnen oft der Fall ist, für das Privatleben ihrer Mieter. Frau Wetzel schwieg, und auch Frau Finnegan, die bis jetzt sehr viel und sehr schnell geredet hatte, sagte kein Wort. So verstanden die beiden Damen alles, was Walter sagte. „Walter Brooks . . . Entschuldigen Sie, ich habe den Namen nicht genau verstanden . . . O, Fräulein Wendel . . . Das ist eine Überraschung . . . O, das freut mich . . . Ich wette aber, Sie haben eine halbe Stunde daran waschen müssen . . . O nein, Sie müssen mir die Rechnung schicken . . . Aber Fräulein Wendel, es war doch meine Schuld [10] . . . Sie haben doch aber selber gesagt, daß ich schlief, als es geschah. . . . Wollen Sie mir glauben, daß ich in Wirklichkeit beide Augen weit auf hatte . . . Das müssen Sie raten . . . Um noch einmal von Ihrem grauen Rock zu sprechen . . . Also schön,[11] der Rock ist nicht grau, er ist weiß. . . . Schön, wenn Sie es so energisch verlangen, muß ich wohl davon still sein . . . Jetzt verlange ich aber auch etwas. Ich verlange, daß Sie mir erlauben,[12] Sie für morgen abend zum Abendessen einzuladen . . . Ist es Ihnen recht um sechs Uhr? . . . Wie wäre es mit drei Viertel sieben? . . . Und hinterher [13] gehen wir natürlich ins Kino. . . . Ach, das ist doch gar nicht so schwer. Ich habe den alten Knaben [14] voriges Jahr gehabt. Ich weiß, was er will. Ich helfe Ihnen am Dienstag. . . . Nein, ich habe noch nichts von Gilbert gehört . . . O, so heißt der Mann, das erkläre ich Ihnen morgen, das ist eine sehr interessante und sehr mysteriöse Geschichte. . . . Ja, das stimmt, er wollte fünfzig Dollar haben. Wahrscheinlich wird die Versicherung aber mehr

*1 damit, *so that.* *2 stören, *disturb.* *3 dabei, *moreover.* 4 der Autounfall, -es, ¨-e, *auto accident.* 5 besorgt, *worried.* *6 der, *he.* The forms of der are used as demonstrative pronouns. A simple practical suggestion is: When a form of der is used without a noun, notice the position of the inflected verb. If the verb is in normal or inverted order, the form of der is a demonstrative pronoun, meaning *he, she, it,* etc. If the verb is in transposed order, the form of der is a relative pronoun and means *who, which, that,* etc. *7 ihm fehlt etwas, *something is wrong with him.* *8 rufen, ie, u, *call.* 9 runter, short for herunter, *downstairs.* 10 die Schuld, *fault.* *11 also schön, *all right then.* *12 erlauben, *permit.* 13 hinterher, *afterwards.* *14 der Knabe, -n, -n, *boy.*

verlangen. Aber sprechen wir lieber von etwas Angenehmem! [1] Sie kommen also wirklich mit? Ich hole Sie um drei Viertel sieben zu Hause ab . . . Gute Nacht, Fräulein Wendel." Walter hängte das Telephon ein, pfiff ein paar Noten [2] von „Du mein süßer umarmbarer Schatz," hörte aber sogleich [3] wieder auf und sprang die Treppe hinauf. Die beiden Damen hörten, wie er oben in seinem Zimmer laleralerala und titerateteritera sang. Frau Finnegan hatte schon das Telephonbuch vom Korridor geholt, sie schlug unter W auf [4] und murmelte [5] „Weiß, Welch, Welles, Wendel." Dann mit lauter Stimme: „O, es gibt so viele Wendel. Könnte es vielleicht Juwelier Wendel sein?" „Aber Hannchen," lachte Frau Wetzel. „Du bist schon zwanzig Jahre hier und weißt noch immer nicht, daß Juwelier Wendel ein unverheirateter Sechziger ist! Nein, in der Familie gibt es kein Fräulein Wendel." Die beiden Damen rieten noch ein bißchen und gaben es dann auf in der Hoffnung, daß sie in der nahen [6] Zukunft mehr von diesem mysteriösen Fräulein Wendel hören und sie vielleicht eines schönen Tages [7] auch sehen würden. Um unsere Leser nicht zu sehr aufzuregen, sei es hier gesagt, daß die Hoffnung der beiden Damen in Erfüllung ging. Sie wollen auch wissen, wer der „alte Knabe" war, von dem Walter sprach? Das war Professor Hostett, eine international bekannte Autorität auf dem Gebiet der Psychologie der Reklame.

Walter war mäuschenstill [8] geworden, denn er saß an seinem Studiertisch und las in Hostetts Buch „Psychologie und Volkswirtschaft" [9], um sich auf seine Rolle als Sylvias Helfer vorzubereiten. Wir lassen ihn auf seinem Zimmer und beobachten [10] die anderen Charaktere, die an diesem Sonnabend in Walters Leben eine Rolle gespielt haben.

Wo sind z.B. Ruth und Lübke, der Tackle? Sie sitzen im Kino. Ruth sitzt links von Lübke und ärgert sich. Sie ärgert sich, weil Lübke eingeschlafen ist.[11] Sie faßt seine Hand und schüttelt sie, um ihn aufzuwecken, aber da macht Lübke grunzende [12] Geräusche. Nun ärgert sie sich noch ein bißchen mehr. Ein Schuljunge, der rechts von Lübke sitzt, fühlt sich bedroht,[13] da der Tackle sich jetzt nach rechts lehnt.[14] Er stößt den Koloß mit der Schulter, und Lübke grunzt noch einmal, diesmal etwas lauter. Die Umsitzenden kichern,[15] und Ruth ärgert sich noch etwas mehr.

Und wo ist Gilbert, der breitschultrige Gilbert? Er sitzt in einem Hotelzimmer und schreibt einen Brief. In dem Zimmer sind zwei Betten, und auf dem einen Bett liegt der Morphinist und raucht eine Zigarette. Gilbert sieht nicht, daß der kleine Morphinist ihn in seinem hilflosen, kalten Haß [16] anstarrt.[17]

Sylvia sitzt im Schlafzimmer oder besser im Boudoir ihrer Mutter — die Wendels haben Geld — und unterhält sich mit ihrer Mutter. „Das graue,

*1 angenehm, *pleasant, agreeable.* [2] die Note, —, -n, *measure.* *3 sogleich, *at once.* [4] aufschlagen, u, a, *open.* [5] murmeln, *mumble, mutter.* *6 nah, *near.* *7 eines schönen Tages, *one day, some day.* The genitive is frequently used to denote indefinite time. [8] mäuschenstill, literally *quiet like a little mouse, absolutely quiet.* [9] die Volkswirtschaft, —, *economics.* *10 beobachten, *watch, observe.* *11 einschlafen, ie, a (ist), *fall asleep.* [12] grunzen, *grunt.* [13] bedrohen, *threaten.* [14] lehnen, *lean.* [15] kichern, *giggle.* [16] der Haß, *hatred.* [17] anstarren, *stare at.*

Mama? Ach nein, ich glaube, ich ziehe morgen mein hellblaues Kleid an. Dann ſieht er wenigſtens, daß ich ſchwarze Haare habe." „Aber Sylvia, der Junge iſt doch nicht blind! Nach allem, was du mir erzählt haſt, hat er ganz gut geſehen, wie du ausſiehſt." „Na ja, Mama, du haſt recht. Ich glaube aber, das hellblaue wird ihm am beſten gefallen. Du hätteſt ihn ſehen ſollen, Mama, wie er da vor mir ſtand. Er hat ein ſehr ſenſitives Geſicht, und ſeine Augen ſahen ſo traurig aus, daß ich nur die Hälfte von all dem ſagen konnte, was ich ihm ſagen wollte. Schließlich tat er mir ſo leid, daß ich auf den Kerl wütend wurde, dem er in den Wagen gefahren war. Kann Papa ſich nicht um dieſe Sache kümmern? [1] Der Mann hat ſo plötzlich gehalten, daß Walter ihn rammen mußte. Der Mann hat Geld; warum ſoll der einem armen Studenten das Geld aus der Taſche ziehen?" „Ja Kind, du weißt doch, wieviel Papa zu tun hat. Solange er mit dem Prozeß [2] gegen Webers Warenhaus beſchäftigt [3] iſt, kann man ſowieſo nicht mit ihm reden. Ich werde es aber verſuchen. Na, ich bin neugierig,[4] was für ein junger Mann dieſer Walter iſt. Guten Geſchmack haſt du ja,[5] das muß ich ſagen. Na, wir werden ſehen."

Zurück zu Walter! Wir kommen ein bißchen zu ſpät. Walter hat beſchloſſen,[6] zu Bett zu gehen, und wie er ſo friedlich daliegt, denken wir an das ſchöne Wort Shakeſpeares vom Schlaf: „Sleep that knits up the ravell'd sleave of care."

Ganz ſo ſorglos war allerdings ſein Schlaf nicht. Walter hatte einen ſonderbaren Traum. In dieſem Traum warf er Lübke einen Fußball zu, den Lübke nicht fangen konnte. Der Fußball flog über Lübkes Kopf auf die Straße, wo er ein Auto traf, das er vollkommen [7] zerſchmetterte.[8] Aus dem zerſchmetterten Auto ſtieg Profeſſor Wilmore, der Shakeſpearespezialiſt, aber eigentlich war es nicht Profeſſor Wilmore ſondern Gilbert, und ſchrie ſo laut er konnte: „Ein Pfund Fleiſch für fünfzig Dollar, fünfzig Dollar für ein Pfund Fleiſch!" Das ſchien Walter eine ſehr gefährliche Situation zu ſein, deshalb lief er ſo ſchnell er konnte fort über den Rialto, denn jetzt war er plötzlich auf dem Rialto. Aber wartete nicht Shylock auf ihn auf dem Rialto? Er ſprang in das Waſſer des Kanals, und Sylvia ruderte [9] eine Gondel [10] auf ihn zu. Er ſtieg in die Gondel, und ſie fuhren über das blaue Meer, bis ſie an eine Inſel [11] kamen; die [12] war wie eine Inſel des Paradieſes. Er nahm Sylvia bei der Hand und wanderte mit ihr unter den Bäumen dahin und erzählte ihr, daß er alles wüßte, was in Profeſſor Hoſtetts Buch ſtünde.[13] Da ſtand plötzlich der breitſchultrige Gilbert vor ihm und hatte den Fußball in der Hand, den Lübke nicht gefangen hatte. Gilbert hielt Walter den Fußball unter die Naſe, was in Walters Traum ſoviel bedeutete wie: „Dieſer Fußball iſt der Beweis,

*1 ſich kümmern um, *concern oneself with.* [2] der Prozeß, –es, –e, *law suit.* *3 beſchäftigt, *occupied, busy.* *4 neugierig, *curious.* *5 ja. This particle is frequently employed to give the sentence an affirmative complexion. The meaning *indeed*, which seems to be foremost in the student's mind, does not lend itself to a good translation. Here simply stress the English auxiliary: *you do have.* *6 beſchließen, o, o, *decide.* *7 vollkommen, *completely.* [8] zerſchmettern, *smash.* [9] rudern, *row.* [10] die Gondel, —, –n, *gondola.* [11] die Inſel, —, –n, *island.* [12] die, (see 6, p. 295). [13] ſtünde, *was printed or written.* Literally, of course, the word ſtünde (ſtehen) means *stood*, in the sense of *stood printed.* Thus, Es ſteht in der Bibel means *It says so in the Bible.*

daß du mein Auto zerſchmettert haſt!" Und wie es eben in Träumen geht — plötzlich ſchien es Walter, als ob er auch für den Pelzmantel bezahlen ſollte und er ſchrie: „Nein, nein!" Davon wachte er auf. Nun lag er lange wach und wußte nicht, ob er ſich wegen der Geſchichte mit dem Buick Sorgen machen ſollte oder ob er ſich auf den Abend mit Sylvia freuen [1] ſollte. Er beſchloß, das letztere zu tun und während er ſich überlegte,[2] was er ihr ſagen wollte, wenn er ſie träfe, und während er ſich einen Dialog mit ihr ausdachte, ſchlief er wieder ein.

Den Dialog und den Beginn des Abends hatte ſich Walter gut ausgedacht. Punkt drei Viertel ſieben würde er an der Haustür des Wendelſchen Hauſes erſcheinen und klingeln. Wahrſcheinlich würde das Mädchen aufmachen — Wendels haben, wie ſchon erwähnt,[3] viel Geld — und er würde ſagen: „Mein Name iſt Walter Brooks, dürfte ich Fräulein Sylvia Wendel ſprechen?" Dann würde er eine Weile im Wohnzimmer warten, dann würde Sylvia fünf Minuten ſpäter erſcheinen und ſich entſchuldigen, daß ſie ſich etwas verſpätet [4] hatte, und er würde etwa [5] ſagen, daß ihr die kleine Unpünktlichkeit genau ſo gut ſtehe [6] wie ihr ſchönes Kleid. Dann würde er wahrſcheinlich der Frau Mama vorgeſtellt [7] werden. Und er hatte ſich auch für ſie ein paar liebenswürdige Worte ausgedacht.

In Wirklichkeit kam aber alles ziemlich anders. Um pünktlich zu ſein, fuhr Walter ſchon kurz nach ſechs von Hauſe fort. Er wollte in der Fordgarage tanken.[8] Jedermann [9] in der Garage kannte ihn, und er erzählte in ein paar Worten ſeinen Zuſammenſtoß mit dem Buick. Erich, einer der Mechaniker, unterbrach ihn und fragte ihn, ob der Buick ſchwarz geweſen wäre. Auf Walters bejahende [10] Antwort zeigte Erich in eine Ecke der Garage und ſagte: „Da ſteht der Buick, in den du gefahren biſt." Walter ſtieg aus ſeinem Auto und folgte Erich. Der Mechaniker hatte recht, es war der Buick, den Walter gerammt hatte. Erich hatte am Mittag dem breitſchultrigen Gilbert Benzin verkauft und dabei bemerkt,[11] daß der Brennſtoffbehälter [12] beſchädigt war. Als guter Geſchäftsmann [13] hatte er ſofort ſeine Hilfe angeboten [14] und außerdem auch verſprochen,[15] die anderen beſchädigten Stellen zu reparieren. Walter begann nachzudenken. Offenbar [16] hatte Gilbert kein Intereſſe daran, ſeiner Verſicherung etwas von der Sache zu ſagen, und erwartete außerdem gar kein Geld von ihm. Warum aber nicht? Erich war wieder vor die Garage gegangen, um einem neuen Kunden [17] Benzin zu verkaufen. So hatte Walter Zeit, ſich den Buick gut anzuſehen. Er öffnete die Motorhaube,[18] als ob Gilberts Geheimniſſe unter der Motorhaube wären, aber er ſah nichts als einen ſtarken achtzylindrigen Buickmotor. Er öffnete die Tür zum Hinterſitz. Auch hier gab es offenbar keine

*1 ſich freuen auf, *look forward to.* *2 ſich überlegen, *think out, figure out.* *3 erwähnen, *mention.* 4 ſich verſpäten, *come late.* *5 etwa, *perhaps.* *6 die Unpünktlichkeit ſteht ihr, *the unpunctuality is becoming to her.* *7 vorſtellen, *introduce.* 8 tanken, *buy gasoline.* *9 jedermann, *everybody.* 10 bejahend, *affirmative.* *11 bemerken, *notice.* 12 der Brennſtoffbehälter, –s, —, *fuel tank.* 13 der Geſchäftsmann, –es, . . .leute, *business man.* *14 anbieten, o, o, *offer.* *15 verſprechen, a, o, *promise.* *16 offenbar, *apparently.* 17 der Kunde, –n, –n, *customer.* 18 die Motorhaube, —, –n, *motor hood.*

Geheimniſſe. Eben wollte er die Wagentür ſchließen, da ſah er im Schein[1] des elektriſchen Deckenlichtes etwas Glänzendes am Boden des Wagens liegen. Er blickte genauer hin[2] und ſah, daß es eine ziemlich große Patrone[3] war. Walter begann zu ſpekulieren. Wenn Gilbert ein Jäger war, dann mußte ſein Wild[4] ziemlich groß ſein, denn mit dieſem Kaliber hätte er Nashörner[5] ſchießen können und vielleicht auch das gefährlichſte Wild von allen — Menſchen! Walter ſteckte die Patrone, um ſie ſpäter genauer zu unterſuchen, in die Taſche. Glücklicherweiſe[6] hatte er genug Gangſterfilme geſehen und genug Kriminalgeſchichten geleſen, um zu wiſſen, wie man ein Auto unterſucht. Er öffnete die Tür zum Führerſitz, zog den Sitz halb heraus und ließ ſeine Hand umherwandern. Schon wollte er den Sitz wieder zurückſchieben, als er etwas ſah, das wie ein künſtlicher Schnurrbart ausſah. Er war grau, grau wie der kurz geſchnittene Schnurrbart und das Kopfhaar des Banditen Gilbert, denn daß Gilbert ein Bandit war, daran zweifelte Walter nicht mehr. Er ſteckte den künſtlichen Bart in einen leeren Briefumſchlag,[7] den er in der Taſche hatte, und richtete ſich auf.[8] Es ſchien ihm, als[9] ſähe er jemand aus der Garage laufen, aber das war wohl ſeine aufgeregte Phantaſie. Als er Erich draußen fragte, ſagte der ihm, daß er niemanden geſehen hätte, und Walter lachte über ſeine Nervoſität. Er war ein ſchöner Privatdetektiv!

Er ſtieg wieder in ſeinen Ford und ſah auf ſeine Armbanduhr. „Zum Donnerwetter," ſchrie er laut. Es war beinah drei Viertel ſieben, außerdem waren ſeine Hände ſchmutzig, und er hatte einen Ölfleck auf ſeinem weißen Hemd. Er wußte nicht, wie der Ölfleck auf ſein neues Hemd gekommen war. Er wußte aber, daß er nicht zu ſpät kommen wollte. Einen Augenblick überlegte er ſich, ob er ſich nicht erſt die Hände waſchen ſollte, aber er zog es vor,[10] rechtzeitig und mit ſchmutzigen Händen zu erſcheinen. Er war etwa drei Minuten gefahren, da begann ſein Motor zu ſpucken,[11] und im nächſten Augenblick ſtand der Wagen ſtill. Walter verſtand das nicht. Er hatte doch eben Benzin gekauft. Sollte ſein Tank vielleicht auch beſchädigt ſein? Aus einem Auto hinter ihm ſtieg ein Mann aus, er ſah es nicht. Er bückte[12] ſich über ſeinen Benzintank. Aha, da war etwas nicht in Ordnung, der Tank war naß[13] und tropfte[14] noch, jemand mußte . . .

Sylvia wartete bis ſieben Uhr. Dann wurde ſie ärgerlich; um Viertel nach ſieben wurde ſie wütend. Sie fragte ihre Mutter: „Glaubſt du, er hat es vergeſſen, Mama?" „Frag mich nicht, Kind," antwortete Mama freundlich. „Ich verſtehe euch junge Leute von heute manchmal nicht. Du ſagteſt mir zwar,[15] der junge Mann hätte gute Manieren,[16] aber vielleicht iſt es modern, unpünktlich zu ſein oder Verab-

[1] der Schein, –es, *shine, light.* [2] hinblicken, *look.* [3] die Patrone, —, –n, *cartridge.* [4] das Wild, –es, *game.* [5] das Nashorn, –s, ⸗er, *rhinoceros.* *[6] glücklicherweiſe, *fortunately.* [7] der Briefumſchlag, –es, ⸗e, *envelope.* [8] ſich aufrichten, *straighten up.* *[9] als ſähe er, as if he saw. Als at the beginning of a clause and immediately followed by the verb means *as if;* als with the verb at the end of the clause means *when, as.* *[10] vorziehen, o, o, *prefer.* [11] ſpucken, *spit.* [12] ſich bücken, *bend.* [13] naß, *wet.* [14] tropfen, *drip.* *[15] zwar, *to be sure, of course.* [16] die Manieren (pl.), *manners.*

redungen[1] zu vergessen." „Nein, Mama, es ist nicht möglich. Walter ist so ein liebenswürdiger Junge und er schien sich so darauf zu freuen, mit mir heute abend auszugehen; da ist etwas nicht in Ordnung. Mama, ich werde telephonieren." „Aber Sylvia, du machst dich lächerlich. Wenn er es nun vergessen hat, was soll er von dir denken?" „Das Risiko[2] nehme ich auf mich," sagte Sylvia und ging zum Telephon.

Wer wagt[3] es, sich über die Intuition der Frauen lustig zu machen? Die innere Stimme sagte ihr, daß Walter in Gefahr war. Das Telephon klingelte eine ganze Weile, ehe die aufgeregte Stimme der Studentenmutter, Frau Elise Wetzel, antwortete: „Wen? Was? O Gott, unseren armen Walter wollen Sie sprechen? Wer sind Sie?" Eine männliche Stimme unterbrach sie. „Hier Wachtmeister Wilken, wer dort?" Sylvia erschrak und gab ihren Namen, Telephonnummer und Adresse. Der Wachtmeister wollte auch wissen, warum sie diesen Walter Brooks angerufen[4] hätte. Als sie alles genügend erklärt hatte, erzählte ihr der Wachtmeister, daß man guten Grund habe anzunehmen, daß Walter entweder[5] umgebracht oder entführt[6] worden sei. Man habe sein Auto bei einem Hydranten stehen gefunden, der Brennstoffbehälter sei durchlöchert[7] gewesen, offenbar ein Trick der Verbrecher, um ihn zum Halten zu zwingen,[8] das Schlimmste aber sei, man habe Blutflecken am Tank und auf der Straße gefunden. Die Polizei wisse nur, daß er in der Fordgarage getankt hätte.

Das erste, was Walter nach der schwarzen Nacht wieder fühlte, war kühle Luft, ein dumpfer[9] Schmerz[10] am Hinterkopf und der Geschmack von Blut auf der Zunge.[11] Er öffnete die Augen und sah, daß er hinten in einem Auto auf dem Boden lag. Das Auto hielt, die Vordertür war offen, er hörte die Schritte[12] eines Mannes, der auf das Auto zukam. „Wir sind auf dem richtigen Wege, Nummer fünfundachtzig, wie ich dir sagte," das war der südländische Akzent und die Stimme des Morphinisten. Gilberts Stimme antwortete: „Ist er noch nicht zu sich gekommen?[13] Sieh mal nach!" Walter schloß die Augen und atmete[14] kaum. Der Morphinist faßte ihm ins Gesicht und legte die Hand auf seine Brust. „Ich glaube, er kommt bald zu sich," sagte der Morphinist. Wäre es nicht besser, wenn ich ihn erledigte?"[15] „Du bist wohl verrückt!"[16] antwortete Gilbert. „Ich will kein Blut im Auto haben, und der Schuß könnte gehört werden. Setz dich hin und rede keinen Unsinn! Es sind nur noch drei Meilen bis zum Kanal. Wenn er vorher aufwacht, gebe ich ihm noch eins."[17]

Walter hatte genug gehört, er wußte von Kriminalgeschichten und Gangsterfilmen, daß die Verbrecher ihn mit Eisenstücken[18] an den Beinen ins Wasser werfen

[1] die Verabredung, —, –en, *appointment.* [2] das Risiko, –s –s, *risk.* [3] wagen, *dare.* [4] anrufen, ie, u, *call up.* *[5] entweder . . . oder, *either . . . or.* [6] entführen, *kidnap.* [7] durchlöchern, *perforate.* [8] zwingen, a, u, *force.* [9] dumpf, *dull.* *[10] der Schmerz, –ens, –en, *pain.* *[11] die Zunge, —, –n, *tongue.* *[12] der Schritt, –es, –e, *footstep.* [13] zu sich kommen, a, o (ist), *regain consciousness.* *[14] atmen, *breathe.* [15] erledigen, *finish.* [16] verrückt, *crazy.* *[17] noch eins, literally *still one thing;* here *another blow.* [18] das Eisenstück, –s, –e, *piece of iron.*

wollten. Er vergaß seinen schmerzenden [1] Kopf, er fühlte nichts, als den Willen zu leben und einen brennenden Haß für die beiden, die ihn ermorden wollten. In dem kleinen Spiegel [2] über dem Führersitz sah er das Licht von Scheinwerfern,[3] hin und wieder [4] begegneten [5] sie einem anderen Auto, es gab also Verkehr auf dieser Straße. In der Ferne [6] hörte er einen Zug.[7] Das Geräusch wurde lauter. Jetzt fuhr das Auto unter einer Eisenbahnbrücke [8] durch im gleichen Augenblick, in dem der Zug über die Brücke donnerte. Walter wußte: Jetzt oder nie! Er sprang auf, warf die Decke,[9] unter der er gelegen hatte, über Gilberts Kopf und hielt sich mit aller Kraft an seinem Halse fest,[10] während er den Morphinisten wegstieß, der das Steuerrad [11] fassen wollte. Der Kampf war kurz. Trotzdem Gilbert auf die Fußbremse trat und die Handbremse zog, fuhr das Auto in einer scharfen Kurve von der rechten Seite der Straße auf die linke und im nächsten Augenblick in den Straßengraben,[12] in dem es sich überschlug.[13]

Zwei Autos hielten bald an der Unglücksstelle. Der eine Fahrer parkte sein Auto so, daß das Licht der Scheinwerfer auf den Graben fiel, in dem der Buick, Räder [14] in der Luft, auf dem Dach lag. Autos kamen von der anderen Richtung und hielten auch. Mehrere [15] Männer waren inzwischen in den Straßengraben gestiegen und nahmen das zerbrochene Glas aus den Fenstern, denn die Türen ließen sich nicht öffnen.[16] Zuerst zogen sie den Morphinisten heraus, dann Walter und schließlich Gilbert. Ein Arzt war in der Gruppe, der die Drei sofort untersuchte. Das Resultat der Untersuchung war das folgende: Der Morphinist war tot, er hatte sich das Genick [17] gebrochen, und Gilbert hatte schwere innere Verletzungen.[18] Die frische Nachtluft brachte Walter wieder zum Bewußtsein,[19] er wollte aufspringen, aber der Doktor verhinderte [20] das. „Vorsicht, junger Mann," sagte er, „seien Sie nicht ungeduldig, wir möchten erst ein paar Röntgenaufnahmen [21] von Ihnen machen, ehe wir Sie weglaufen lassen. Außerdem möchte ich dies Stück Holz [22] als Schiene [23] für Ihren gebrochenen Arm benutzen." [24] Jetzt erst fühlte Walter, was der Arzt meinte, und er fühlte es stark. Ein Motorrad hielt, ein Polizist schob sich durch die Menge. Von dem Arm des Doktors gestützt,[25] erzählte Walter dem Polizisten alles, was geschehen war. — B.

Hier sollte unsere Geschichte enden, aber, da es eine Art modernes Märchen ist, ist sie noch nicht ganz zu Ende. Die Bösen haben ihre Strafe,[26] aber die Guten sind

[1] schmerzend, *aching.* [2] der Spiegel, –s, —, *mirror.* [3] der Scheinwerfer, –s, —, *head light.* *[4] hin und wieder, *occasionally, now and then.* *[5] begegnen (ist), *meet.* *[6] die Ferne, *distance.* *[7] der Zug, –es, ⸗e, *train.* [8] die Eisenbahnbrücke, —, –n, *rail-road bridge.* [9] die Decke, —, –n, *cover, blanket.* [10] sich festhalten, ie, a, *hang on, cling.* [11] das Steuerrad, –es, ⸗er, *steering wheel.* [12] der Straßengraben, –s, ⸗, *ditch.* [13] sich überschlagen, u, a, *somersault.* *[14] das Rad, –es, ⸗er, *wheel.* *[15] mehrere, *several.* *[16] ließen sich nicht öffnen, *could not be opened.* The active infinitive (öffnen) with lassen must be translated by the English passive infinitive. Literally: *did not allow themselves to be opened.* [17] das Genick, –s, –e, *neck.* [18] die Verletzung, —, –en, *injury.* *[19] das Bewußtsein, –s, *consciousness.* [20] verhindern, *prevent.* [21] die Röntgenaufnahme, —, –n, *X-ray photograph.* *[22] das Holz, –es, *wood.* [23] die Schiene, —, –n, *splint.* *[24] benutzen, *use.* [25] stützen, *support.* *[26] die Strafe, —, *punishment.*

noch nicht belohnt.[1] Im Märchen heiratet der Held die Prinzessin und bekommt ein Königreich. Die Analogie zur Prinzessin ist leicht zu sehen, wie steht [2] es aber mit dem Königreich?

Gilbert und der Morphinist waren beide Verbrecher, die die Polizei schon seit langem suchte. Gilbert war erst achtundzwanzig Jahre alt. Die grauen Haare waren natürlich künstlich. Gilbert mußte sich etwas maskieren, denn in jedem größeren Postamt konnte man sein Bild sehen. Unter diesen Bildern stand, daß Gilbert als Führer einer Bande [3] in verschiedenen Städten die Postämter beraubt habe. Deshalb wolle die Regierung [4] demjenigen [5] zweitausend Dollar geben, der ihn tot oder lebendig fange oder beim Einfangen dieses Verbrechers mithelfe.

Gilberts Kamerad, der Morphinist, war nicht so wertvoll. Er hatte die Post benutzt, um größere Mengen [6] Morphium in die Staaten zu schmuggeln. Außerdem hatte er einen Briefträger ermordet. Als der arme Mann auf dem Wege zu einem Dorf den Vorderreifen an seinem kleinen Ford wechselte, hatte ihn der feige Morphinist in den Rücken geschossen, um das Auto stehlen zu können, das er zur Flucht [7] in einen anderen Staat brauchte. Für ihn wollte die Regierung tausend Dollar bezahlen. Walter bekam also dreitausend Dollar.

Soviel vom „Königreich." Nun zurück zur „Prinzessin." Ein paar Wochen nach diesem ereignisreichen [8] Sonntag war Walter bei Wendels zum Abendessen eingeladen. Herr Wendel hatte eine wichtige Sitzung [9] aufgegeben, um den jetzt berühmten Freund seiner Tochter persönlich kennenzulernen. Er ließ sich die ganze Geschichte von Anfang bis zu Ende noch einmal erzählen, trotzdem er das alles in den Zeitungen gelesen hatte. Frau Wendel lächelte den erzählenden Walter mütterlich an, während Sylvia das Fleisch auf seinem Teller zerschnitt,[10] denn sein rechter Arm war noch bis zur Schulter im Gipsverband.[11] Jetzt ist es aber genug. Falls Sie noch mehr wissen wollen, sehen Sie sich ein paar Filme an und achten Sie darauf,[12] wie sie enden.

A. Practice Sentences:

Translate the following sentences which are based on the idioms explained in the footnotes:

1. Sie war vier Monate lang in Südamerika.
2. Herr Lübke hat ein ganzes Jahr lang nicht Fußball gespielt.
3. Der Dampfer kommt erst nächsten Montag zurück.
4. Ich weiß nicht, worüber sie sprachen.
5. Worauf saßen die vier Personen, die Lübke balanzierte?
6. Lassen Sie sich nicht überreden!
7. Der Herr ließ sich den Schaden bezahlen.
8. Der Professor sprach noch immer vor sich hin.
9. Wo haben Sie so etwas gelesen? Es steht in der Zeitung.

*1 belohnen, *reward.* [2] wie steht es mit, *what about.* [3] die Bande, —, –n, *gang.* *4 die Regierung, —, –en, *government.* *5 demjenigen . . . der, *to him who.* *6 die Menge, —, –n, *quantity.* [7] die Flucht, —, *escape.* *8 ereignisreich, *eventful.* [9] die Sitzung, —, –en, *conference.* *10 zerschneiden, i, i, *cut up.* [11] der Gipsverband, –es, ⸗e, *plaster cast.* *12 achten auf, *pay attention to.*

10. Der weiß das nicht einmal!
11. Sein Begleiter blieb stehen, während die anderen Zuschauer sich setzten.
12. Er blieb stehen, nahm das Geld aus der Tasche und warf es, ohne ein Wort zu sagen, auf den Tisch.
13. Er starrte vor sich hin, als hätte er einen Geist gesehen.
14. Sie ließen sich das Geld zurückgeben.
15. Auf einmal hörte der Richter auf zu sprechen.

B. Securing the Vocabulary:

In Part B of each lesson associated words already used in preceding texts are grouped together. It is expected that this grouping will give the student an insight into certain principles of word formation, thereby enabling him not only to fix the meaning of old words more firmly, but also to recognize new words more readily.

1. antworten
   die Antwort
   beantworten
   die Beantwortung
2. anfangen
   der Anfang
   anfangs
3. kaufen
   der Einkauf
   verkaufen
   der Verkäufer
   die Verkäuferin
4. liegen
   die Lage
5. gründen
   der Grund
   gründlich
6. der Brief
   der Briefkasten
   der Briefträger
   der Briefumschlag
7. früh
   früher
   das Frühjahr
   der Frühling
   der Frühlingstraum
   das Frühstück
   frühstücken
8. bilden
   das Bild
   die Bildung
   der Bildungsroman
   ausbilden
   sich einbilden
   die Einbildungskraft
9. rufen
   der Ruf
   der Beruf
   der Berufsspieler
   anrufen
   aufrufen
10. schreiben
    die Schreibmaschine
    der Schreibtisch
    beschreiben
    die Beschreibung
    aufschreiben
    die Schrift

Siebenundzwanzigste Aufgabe

Der alte Dolch[1]

Erſt gegen [2] zehn Uhr verließ [3] Walter Kollmann in ſchlechter Laune [4] das Bett, denn er hatte keinerlei [5] Grund, ſich auf den kommenden Tag zu freuen. Die Büros, wo er ſich täglich mit fünftauſend anderen Arbeitslosen [6] der mittelgroßen Induſtrieſtadt nach Stellungen [7] erkundigte,[8] waren geſchloſſen, denn heute war Sonntag. „Hurra," ſagte er laut in ſein kleines, kaltes Zimmer hinein. „Heute hat Herr Kollmann Ferien, er braucht ſich heute um nichts zu kümmern. Was kann Herr Kollmann mit all der freien Zeit anfangen? [9] — Wie wäre es, wenn wir das Muſeum beſuchten? Da iſt es ſchön warm, und außerdem iſt der Eintritt [10] heute frei, was für Herrn Kollmann nicht ganz unwichtig iſt. Die Arbeitsloſigkeit hat doch wirklich auch ihre guten Seiten. Man kultiviert ſich aus Langweile."

Er ſtellte ſich vor den Spiegel und betrachtete ſich ernſt und lange. Seine Geſichtsfarbe war ungeſund, und außerdem hatte er einen zwei Tage alten Bart. Er rieb [11] ſich das Kinn [12] und ſprach wieder laut mit ſich ſelbſt. „Walter, du mußt dich raſieren, ſonſt laſſen dich die Muſeumsdiener nicht ins Muſeum. Die Muſeumsdiener werden deinen alten blauen Anzug nicht mögen. Die Muſeumsdiener werden die Köpfe zuſammenſtecken und ſagen: ‚Aha, da iſt ſchon wieder ſo ein Arbeitsloſer,[13] der ſich wärmen will. Warum haben wir keine öffentlichen [14] Wärmehallen, ſo daß dieſe Leute nicht in die Muſeen und die öffentlichen Gebäude gelaufen kommen?'

Die Muſeumsdiener ſteckten die Köpfe nicht zuſammen, als Walter eintrat.[15] Sie unterbrachen nicht einmal ihre Unterhaltung, ſo daß er ganz ſich ſelbſt überlaſſen war.

Ziellos [16] wanderte er durch die großen Säle [17] voller griechiſcher Athleten, ägyptiſcher Prieſter und mittelalterlicher [18] Madonnen. Die wenigen Beſucher, die an dieſem kalten Wintermorgen gekommen waren, ſahen klein und unbedeutend [19] aus

[1] der Dolch, –es, –e, *dagger*. *[2] erſt gegen, *not until around*. In expressions of time erſt means *not until* or *only*. The preposition gegen, which usually means *against*, is used in expressions of time to mean *toward, close to, around*. *[3] verlaſſen, ie, a, leave. *[4] die Laune, —, *humor*. *[5] keinerlei, *no . . . whatsoever*. [6] der Arbeitsloſe, –n, –n, *unemployed*. *[7] die Stellung, —, –en, *position*. [8] ſich erkundigen, *inquire*. *[9] anfangen, i, a, *do*. *[10] der Eintritt, –es, *entrance*. [11] reiben, ie, ie, *rub*. [12] das Kinn, –es, –e, *chin*. *[13] ſchon wieder ſo ein Arbeitsloſer, *another one of those unemployed*. Literally *already again such an . . .* **Note:** ſchon wieder *again so soon*, and ſo ein *such a*. [14] öffentlich, *public*. *[15] eintreten, a, e (iſt), *enter*. *[16] ziellos, *aimlessly*. [17] der Saal, –e, Säle, *hall, room*. [18] mittelalterlich, *medieval*. *[19] unbedeutend, *insignificant*.

neben den Riesen aus Stein [1] und Bronze. Walter Kollmann hörte bald auf, an seinen alten Anzug zu denken und begann, die Dinge um sich mit Interesse zu betrachten.

Er war in den Waffensaal [2] gekommen, wo er eine Weile stehen blieb, um sich zu orientieren. Er sah die lange Reihe von Schwertern, Speeren und Panzern [3] und entdeckte,[4] daß sie in der tiefen Stille des Museums fast friedlich aussahen. Jetzt entdeckte Walter auch, daß der Wärter dieses Saales ihn aufmerksam [5] betrachtete. Es war ein alter Mann mit schneeweißem Haar und Schnurrbart und einem etwas roten Gesicht. In dem roten, einfachen Gesicht konnte Walter lesen, daß dieser Mann über ihn Bescheid wußte. ‚Wieder so ein armer Kerl, dem es zu Hause zu kalt ist.' Das ärgerte ihn etwas, und er beschloß, den Alten zum besten zu haben.[6]

Erst wollte er ihn in ausländischem Akzent um Auskunft bitten, aber den Gedanken gab er gleich auf, denn selbst für einen sehr exzentrischen Ausländer war er zu schlecht angezogen. So beschloß er denn, den interessierten Kenner [7] zu spielen. Er sah sich langsam im Kreise [8] um und ging dann rasch auf einen Glaskasten [9] zu, vor dem er interessiert stehen blieb. Der Kasten enthielt [10] eine Sammlung von Dolchen aus der Zeit der Renaissance. Walter Kollmann spielte seine Rolle gut. Er beugte sich tief über die Glasplatte [11] und rieb sich mit der Hand nachdenklich [12] das Kinn. Dann trat er einen Schritt zurück, zog ein Notizbuch und einen Bleistift aus der Tasche und begann, einen der Dolche abzuzeichnen.[13] Das mußte dem alten Mann imponieren.[14]

Während er den Dolch abzeichnete, vergaß er aber bald seine Kennerrolle, steckte Bleistift und Notizbuch wieder in die Tasche und lehnte sich mit beiden Händen auf das Glas, um die kleine Waffe genau ansehen zu können.

Der Dolch war aus der Scheide [15] gezogen, die aus massivem Gold gearbeitet war. Der Griff [16] des Dolches bestand aus einer goldenen Schlange,[17] die einen Edelstein [18] im Maul [19] hielt.

Walters Blicke wanderten von der Scheide und dem Griff zur Klinge.[20] Es war ihm, als sähe er Blut daran.

Es war ein kleiner praktischer Dolch, so recht dazu geeignet,[21] versteckt [22] getragen zu werden, um dann in kleinen Gassen,[23] dunklen Korridoren oder festlichen [24] Sälen seine blutige Arbeit schnell und sicher zu verrichten.[25] „Du bist das Symbol der Renaissance," dachte Walter höhnisch,[26] „brutale Gewalt unter goldener Hülle.[27] Nur der Renaissance? Was war Kultur anders als eine schöne Maske, hinter der sich der brutale Wille zur Macht versteckte. So war es damals zur Zeit der Medici,

*1 der Stein, –es, –e, *stone.* 2 der Waffensaal, –es, . . .säle, *weapon room.* 3 der Panzer, –s, —, *coat of mail.* *4 entdecken, *discover.* *5 aufmerksam, *attentively.* 6 den Alten zum besten zu haben, *to fool the old man.* 7 der Kenner, –s, —, *connoisseur, expert.* 8 der Kreis, –es, –e, *circle.* 9 der Glaskasten, –s, ¨, *showcase.* *10 enthalten, ie, a, *contain.* 11 die Glasplatte, —, –n, *glass top.* *12 nachdenklich, *reflecting.* 13 abzeichnen, *sketch.* 14 imponieren, *impress.* 15 die Scheide, —, –n, *sheath.* 16 der Griff, –es, –e, *hilt.* 17 die Schlange, —, –n, *snake.* 18 der Edelstein, –es, –e, *precious stone.* 19 das Maul, –es, ¨er, *mouth.* 20 die Klinge, —, –n, *blade.* 21 dazu geeignet, getragen zu werden, *suitable to be carried.* *22 verstecken, *hide.* 23 die Gasse, —, –n, *side street.* *24 festlich, *festive.* 25 verrichten, *perform, accomplish.* 26 höhnisch, *sarcastic.* 27 die Hülle, *cover.*

so ist es heute zur Zeit der Industriebarone. Ja, die Macht ist wirklich, alles andere ist nur Schein [1] oder Lüge."

„Bitte nicht auflehnen!",[2] sagte der Museumsdiener mit nicht unfreundlicher Stimme und zeigte zugleich [3] auf das Schildchen,[4] das über dem Glaskasten hing. Erschrocken las Walter, was auf dem Schildchen stand. Er murmelte eine verlegene Entschuldigung und lächelte den Wärter schwach an. Sein Trotz [5] war plötzlich gebrochen, es kam ihm vor, als habe er etwas sehr Böses getan. Er konnte die linke Hand nicht sofort vom Glas nehmen, denn ein Knopf [6] seines Jackenärmels [7] war in der schmalen [8] Öffnung zwischen dem Holzrahmen [9] der Glasplatte und der Seite des Glaskastens stecken geblieben.[10] Der Wärter sah, wie verlegen der junge Mann war, und ging weg, zufrieden [11] seine Pflicht [12] getan und soviel Eindruck [13] auf ihn gemacht zu haben.

Walter zog vorsichtig den Knopf heraus und bemerkte dabei,[14] daß sich die Glasplatte ein wenig hob.[15]

Der Museumswärter patrouillierte schon wieder an den Fenstern entlang. Walter stand vor dem Glaskasten, ohne sich zu rühren,[16] und folgte dem Wärter mit den Augen. Der war vor einem der ziemlich schmutzigen Fenster stehen geblieben und sah auf die Straße hinaus, wo er etwas Interessanteres entdeckt zu haben schien als diesen fanatischen Waffenfachmann. Walter starrte auf den Rücken des Alten und tastete [17] mit den Fingern nach dem Glasdeckel. Ja, er hob sich. Der Kasten war nicht verschlossen.[18] Vorsichtig ließ er den Deckel wieder sinken.[19]

Er ging zum Nachbarkasten [20] und zum nächsten und zum übernächsten. Er ging in den Nachbarsaal und stand lange vor einem mittelalterlichen Panzer. Er war voll Unruhe und Angst aber gleichzeitig [21] spürte [22] er eine gewisse erwartungsvolle [23] Aufgeregtheit.[24]

Er hörte den Wärter auf sich zukommen, und kalter Schweiß [25] brach auf seiner Stirn [26] aus. „Ja, ja, so ist das Leben," sagte die Stimme des Alten neben ihm. „Dieser Panzer gehörte einem Grafen [27] von Schöneberg, der im Jahre 1568 von einem Fußsoldaten erschossen wurde. Die Kugel . . ." Walter hörte nicht mehr zu. Er starrte auf das Loch [28] im Panzer und dachte an Schmidtchen, an seinen guten Freund, den Infanteristen [29] Peter Schmidt. Ein Jahr lang waren sie zusammen an der Westfront gewesen, bis zu dem Sonntag, an dem Schmidtchen mit drei anderen

[1] der Schein, *illusion.* *[2] Nicht auflehnen! *Do not lean!* The infinitive is used to express an impersonal, general command. Compare: Nicht vorsagen! *No prompting!* *[3] zugleich, *at the same time.* [4] das Schildchen, –s, —, *small sign.* *[5] der Trotz, *defiance.* *[6] der Knopf, –es, ⸗e, *button.* [7] der Jackenärmel, –s, —, *coat sleeve.* *[8] schmal, *narrow.* [9] der Holzrahmen, –s, —, *wooden frame.* [10] stecken bleiben, ie, ie (ist), *stick fast.* *[11] zufrieden, *satisfied.* *[12] die Pflicht, —, –en, *duty.* *[13] der Eindruck, –s, ⸗e, *impression.* *[14] dabei, *in doing so.* [15] sich heben, o, o, *can be raised.* [16] sich rühren, *move.* [17] tasten, *grope.* *[18] verschließen, o, o, *lock.* [19] ließ sinken, *lowered.* [20] Nachbarkasten, –s, ⸗, *adjoining case.* *[21] gleichzeitig, *simultaneously.* *[22] spüren, *feel, experience.* *[23] erwartungsvoll, *full of expectation.* *[24] die Aufgeregtheit, —, *excitement.* [25] der Schweiß, –es, *perspiration.* *[26] die Stirn, —, –en, *forehead.* [27] der Graf, –en, –en, *count.* *[28] das Loch, –es, ⸗er, *hole.* [29] der Infanterist, –en, –en, *infantry man.*

auf Patrouille gegangen war. Peter Schmidt kam von dieser Patrouille nicht mehr zurück. Am nächsten Morgen ging der Feind [1] zurück, und sie konnten ihn suchen. Er lag mit dem Gesicht nach unten im Schnee. Als sie ihn umdrehten, sah Walter das Loch in Peters Brust.

Was für ein feiner Kerl das kleine Schmidtchen gewesen war! Wie oft hatte er ein freundliches Wort für ihn, wenn er, Unteroffizier [2] Walter Kollmann, die endlosen Märsche, den Krieg und das Soldatenleben verfluchte.[3] Doch wenn auch Schmidtchen oft selber nahe am Zusammenbrechen war, verlor er doch nie den Mut. Er pflegte [4] dann zu sagen: „Kopf hoch, Walter, das Schlimmste ist vorüber!"

Jetzt erst bemerkte Walter, daß der Wärter aufgehört hatte zu sprechen und ihn verwundert [5] ansah. Walter bewegte die Lippen. „Da hinten ist ein Kasten nicht verschlossen worden," wollte er sagen, aber etwas ganz anderes kam heraus: „Der elende [6] Krieg, — es ist mir nicht immer so schlecht gegangen."

Der Alte verstand, er blickte über den alten Anzug, sah die alten Schuhe und sagte mitleidig: „Tja, ja."

Hier brach die Unterhaltung ab, denn Walter fühlte, er werde ein längeres Gespräch [7] nicht aushalten [8] können, ohne sein aufregendes Geheimnis zu verraten. Er murmelte etwas Unverständliches und begann mit verlegenem Lächeln weiterzuwandern. Er senkte [9] beim Gehen den Kopf auf die Brust, als wolle er dem Blick des alten Wärters entgehen.[10] Der sah aber schon wieder zu einem der Fenster hinaus und dachte sorgenvoll an seine Tochter, die gern bald heiraten wollte, und deren Verlobter [11] ein Arbeitsloser war, wie der Herr da in dem alten blauen Anzug, dem es nicht immer so schlecht gegangen war und der jetzt so viel Zeit hatte. — So ist das Leben — Tja, ja.

Walter Kollmann war in den Nachbarsaal getreten und versuchte die Glasdeckel [12] der Kästen zu heben. Sie waren alle fest verschlossen. Es konnte unmöglich schwer sein, den kleinen goldenen Dolch mitzunehmen. Er versuchte zu lächeln, um sich selber zu beweisen, die ganze Sache sei nur ein Spaß und nicht die erste richtige Versuchung [13] in seinem Leben, etwas zu stehlen.

Es gelang [14] ihm nicht, an diese Lüge zu glauben. Natürlich hatte er daran [15] gedacht, den alten Dolch zu stehlen. Die goldene Scheide und der Edelstein waren mindestens [16] tausend Mark wert. Hatte er Glück, so konnte er die Waffe einem Sammler [17] verkaufen.

Walter Kollmann war also ein Dieb,[18] oder besser, er war im Begriff,[19] einer zu

*1 der Feind, –es, –e, *enemy*. 2 der Unteroffizier, –s, –e, *corporal*. 3 verfluchen, *curse*. *4 pflegen, (with zu and infinitive) *be in the habit of*. *5 verwundert, *surprised*. *6 elend, *miserable*. *7 das Gespräch, –s, –e, *conversation*. 8 aushalten, ie, a, *bear, stand*. 9 senken, *lower*. *10 entgehen, entging, ist entgangen, *escape*. 11 der Verlobte, –n, –n, *fiancé*. 12 der Glasdeckel, –s, —, *glass-lid*. *13 die Versuchung, —, –en, *temptation*. *14 Es gelang ihm nicht, *He did not succeed*. The verb gelingen (*succeed*) requires an impersonal subject. *Thus* es gelingt mir means *it succeeds for me* or *I succeed*. *15 er hatte daran gedacht zu stehlen, *he had thought of stealing*. The word daran (*of it*) anticipates the following phrase. *16 mindestens, *at least*. 17 der Sammler, –s, —, *collector*. *18 der Dieb, –es, –e, *thief*. *19 er war im Begriff einer zu werden, *he was on the point of becoming one*. Im Begriff sein is often used to mean *to be in the act or process* or *on the point of*.

werden. Er dachte an ſeinen Vater, der an einem Winterabend bei einem Autounfall das Leben verloren hatte, als er ſpät abends zu einem ſeiner armen Bauernpatienten[1] fuhr, die ihre Rechnung nie bezahlen konnten, aber trotzdem oft krank wurden. Das Verſicherungsgeld hatte kaum gereicht,[2] die hinterlaſſenen Schulden[3] zu bezahlen. Vater war ein guter Landarzt aber ein ſchlechter Geſchäftsmann geweſen. Mutter hatte ihr ganzes Leben lang gearbeitet und geſpart. Nun wohnte ſie bei ihrer verheirateten Tochter.

Kollmann lachte bitter. Unteroffizier Kollmann, der eine Medaille und zwei Schrapnellkugeln aus dem Krieg mitgebracht hat, Walter Kollmann, Sohn ehrlicher[4] Eltern, geht ins Muſeum und beginnt die Verbrecherlaufbahn,[5] indem[6] er einen Dolch ſtiehlt.

Schön,[7] dann war er eben ein Dieb. — Und was ſchadete es denn, wenn ein goldener Dolch aus dem Muſeum verſchwand? Das Muſeum gehörte dem Staate, und der Staat hatte Walter Kollmann ſchlecht genug behandelt.[8] Zwei Jahre an der Front, einmal ſchwer verwundet,[9] und nun konnte er ſich ſeine Arbeitsloſenunterſtützung[10] abholen[11] und ſich von Muſeumswärtern bemitleiden[12] laſſen.

Er ſchüttelte den Kopf. „So ein Unſinn!" dachte er. Sollte er vielleicht den alten ehrlichen Wärter ins Unglück bringen, der doch für unverſchloſſene Glaskäſten verantwortlich[13] war? Das Beſte wäre wohl, ſchnellſtens nach Hauſe zu gehen und die ganze Sache zu vergeſſen.

„Wie ſpät[14] war es eigentlich?" Er zog ſeine Uhr aus der Taſche, eine altmodiſche[15] Uhr, die er von ſeinem Vater hatte. Oft genug war er verſucht geweſen, ſie zu verkaufen, aber bis jetzt hatte er es nicht getan. Er hielt die Uhr in der Hand und wie er das tat, fühlte er plötzlich eine unwiderſtehliche[16] Begierde,[17] das andere, den Dolch, auch ſo in der Hand zu haben. Mit zitternden Fingern ſteckte er die Uhr in die Taſche zurück und ging ſchnell auf den unverſchloſſenen Glaskaſten zu.

Mit geſenktem Kopf ſah er ſich vorſichtig um. Der alte Wärter war im Nachbarſaal, kein anderer Beſucher war zu ſehen.[18] Schnell hob er den Glasdeckel auf, ſchob den Dolch in die Scheide und ſteckte ihn in die Hoſentaſche.

Er wollte gehen, aber er konnte nicht. Schatten[19] ſchwammen ihm vor den Augen, und in ſeinen Ohren rauſchte[20] es. Er lehnte ſich ſchwer auf die Glasplatte. Wie im Traum hörte er den Wärter herankommen.

[1] der Bauernpatient, -en, -en, *farmer patient.* *[2] reichen, *be sufficient.* *[3] die Schulden (pl.), *debts.* *[4] ehrlich, *honest, honorable.* [5] die Verbrecherlaufbahn, *career of a criminal.* *[6] indem er einen Dolch ſtiehlt, *by stealing a dagger.* When the subject of the subordinate clause introduced by the conjunction indem refers to the same thing as does the subject of the main clause, the most satisfactory way of rendering the subordinate clause usually is to translate the finite verb of the clause as a verbal noun after the preposition *by,* as shown in the instance above. [7] ſchön, here: *all right.* *[8] behandeln, *treat.* [9] ſchwer verwundet, *seriously wounded.* [10] die Arbeitsloſenunterſtützung, *unemployment compensation.* *[11] abholen, *call for.* *[12] bemitleiden, *pity.* *[13] verantwortlich, *responsible.* *[14] Wie ſpät iſt es? *What time is it?* [15] altmodiſch, *old-fashioned.* [16] unwiderſtehlich, *irresistible.* [17] die Begierde, *desire.* *[18] war zu ſehen, *was to be seen,* or *could be seen.* Frequently a German active infinitive must be translated by an English passive infinitive. [19] der Schatten, -s, —, *shadow.* *[20] rauſchen, *roar.*

„Aber Sie ſollen ſich doch nicht auflehnen!" Das klang, als ob es von weit käme. Er richtete ſich auf und ließ die Hände von der Glasplatte ſinken. „Aber um Himmelswillen,[1] was iſt Ihnen?"[2] fragte der alte Mann beſorgt. „Sie ſind ja blaß[3] wie der Tod!" „Ich . . . mir iſt ſchlecht," flüſterte[4] Walter.

„Und wir haben nicht einen einzigen Stuhl in dieſem Saal. — Ich hole Ihnen ein Glas Waſſer."

„Nein, bemühen[5] Sie ſich nicht, ich werde hinausgehen. In der friſchen Luft werde ich mich beſſer fühlen."

Mit unſicheren Schritten ging er fort. Der alte Wärter ſah ihm nach. „Der hat lange nichts zu eſſen gehabt. Das iſt die ganze Krankheit. Tja, ja." Er ging ans Fenſter und patrouillierte wieder langſam auf und ab.[6]

Als Walter aus dem Muſeum heraustrat, mußte er einen Augenblick lang die Augen ſchließen. Die ſtrahlende[7] Winterſonne auf dem Schnee blendete[8] ihn. Langſam ging er die breite Freitreppe[9] hinab. Unten an der Treppe blieb er wieder einen Augenblick ſtehen. Er mußte warten, bis der Schwächeanfall[10] vorüber war. Es war kein Wunder. Seit Tagen keine anſtändige[11] Mahlzeit,[12] heute kein Frühſtück und nun dies!

Er nahm ſich zuſammen[13] und wollte gerade über den Muſeumsplatz, als er auf der anderen Seite der Straße einen Soldaten gehen ſah. Er ſtarrte ihn wie eine Geiſtererſcheinung[14] an. Der ging ja[15] wie Schmidtchen! Der ſah ja wie Schmidtchen aus! Erſchüttert[16] blieb Walter Kollmann ſtehen und ſtarrte den Mann an. Dann ſah er, daß es ein Fremder war. Trotzdem aber ſah er ihm nach, bis er um die Ecke verſchwunden war. In ſeinen Ohren aber klang des Freundes Stimme: „Kopf hoch, Walter, das Schlimmſte iſt vorüber!"

Ohne recht zu wiſſen, was er tat, drehte er ſich um und ging ins Muſeum zurück. Der alte Wärter ſtand an ſeinem Lieblingsfenſter und träumte. Walter faßte ihn ſanft[17] am Arm. „Kommen Sie bitte mit, ich will Ihnen etwas zeigen, was für Sie ſehr wichtig iſt." Sprachlos vor Erſtaunen folgte ihm der alte Mann.

Vor dem unverſchloſſenen Glaskaſten blieb Walter ſtehen. Auf der roten Sammetdecke konnte man deutlich[18] ſehen, wo der geſtohlene Dolch gelegen hatte. Walter hob den Glasdeckel auf, legte Dolch und Scheide genau dorthin,[19] wo ſie gelegen hatten, und machte den Glasdeckel wieder zu.[20]

„Sehen Sie, ſo einfach iſt das," ſagte er lächelnd zu dem erſchrockenen Muſeumswärter, der immer noch verwirrt[21] den zurückgebrachten Dolch anſtarrte, als Walter ſchon wieder im Freien war, in der ſtrahlenden Winterſonne.

[1] um Himmels willen, *for heaven's sake.* [2] was iſt Ihnen? *what is the matter with you?* *[3] blaß, *pale.* *[4] flüſtern, *whisper.* *[5] ſich bemühen, *trouble oneself.* *[6] auf und ab, *up and down.* *[7] ſtrahlen, *beam.* [8] blenden, *blind.* [9] die Freitreppe, —, -n, *outside staircase.* [10] der Schwächeanfall, -s, ¨-e, *spell of dizziness.* *[11] anſtändig, *decent.* *[12] die Mahlzeit, —, -en, *meal.* [13] ſich zuſammennehmen, a, o, *pull oneself together.* [14] die Geiſtererſcheinung, —, -en, *apparition.* [15] Der ging ja! *Why, he walked!* [16] erſchüttert, *deeply moved.* *[17] ſanft, *gently.* *[18] deutlich, *clearly.* *[19] dorthin, *there* or omit. The words hin and her are used with adverbs of place (wo, dort, hier, etc.) if such words are used with verbs of motion to denote that the motion described proceeds away from (hin) or toward (her) the speaker. *[20] zumachen, *close.* *[21] verwirrt, *bewildered.*

A. Practice Sentences:

1. Einen Augenblick lang dachte er daran, den Dolch in den Glaskasten zurückzulegen.
2. Nicht einmal der alte Wärter war in dem großen Saal zu sehen.
3. Mit so einem wertvollen Dolch könnte er allerlei anfangen.
4. Walter war im Begriff, dorthin zu gehen.
5. Er bleibt auf der großen Treppe stehen.
6. Gelingt ihm der Diebstahl, so kann er wenigstens ein paar Monate lang gut leben.
7. „Nicht vor dem Eingang stehenbleiben!" sagte der Polizist, indem er auf ein Schild über der Tür zeigte.
8. Vielleicht wird es ihm morgen gelingen, eine Stellung zu bekommen.
9. Der Fremde sah wie Schmidtchen aus, aber der war ja lange tot.
10. Vielleicht wollte der alte Wärter ihn nur zum besten haben.
11. Es steht ja in allen Zeitungen, daß ein alter Dolch gestohlen worden ist.
12. Er hatte eben seine Uhr aus der Tasche gezogen, um nachzusehen, wie spät es war.
13. Walter zog den Dolch aus der Scheide und merkte dabei, daß der Griff aus Gold war.
14. Der Wärter tat seine Pflicht, indem er den Besucher beobachtete.
15. Im Nachbarsaal sind keine Waffen zu sehen.

B. Securing the Vocabulary:

1. bedeuten
   die Bedeutung
   deutlich
   undeutlich
2. halten
   die Haltestelle
   erhalten
   enthalten
   aushalten
3. enden
   das Ende
   endlich
   endlos
4. denken
   der Gedanke
   ausdenken
   nachdenken
   nachdenklich
5. sprechen
   die Sprache
   sprachlos
   besprechen
   versprechen
   das Gespräch
6. stellen
   die Stelle
   die Stellung
   anstellen
   (sich) vorstellen
7. lieben
   die Liebe
   lieb
   lieblich
   der Liebling
   liebhaben
   liebenswürdig
   der Liebesroman
8. gehen
   entgehen
   fortgehen
   weggehen
   der Eingang
9. (sich) setzen
   der Satz
   ersetzen
   der Ersatz
   die Ersatzblume
10. das Blut
    blutig

Achtundzwanzigste Aufgabe

* * * \

auf dem mit allerlei ſonderbaren Inſtrumenten bedeckten [1] Tiſche hatte er ein ſehr altes Buch, den „Codicillus" des ſpaniſchen Meiſters Raimundus Lullus, das ſchon ſein Großvater für ſeine Experimente gebraucht hatte.

Bertram hatte es ſchon lange aufgegeben, Gold gewinnen [2] zu wollen, denn die Experimente der Goldgewinnung waren zu teuer. Er hoffte aber beſtimmt, eines Tages künſtliches Silber produzieren zu können, denn zu dieſen Experimenten hatte er trotz des Widerſtandes [3] ſeiner Frau genug Geld.

Gerade an dieſem Abend hoffte er auf Erfolg, denn geſtern abend [4] ſchien der Mond,[5] und ſein ſilbernes Licht, ſo ſtand es in dem „Codicillus," war günſtig [6] für die Kunſt [7] des Silbermachens.

Er blickte von ſeinem Buche auf, in dem er das magiſche Zeichen [8] des Silbers, die Mondſichel, angeſtarrt hatte, und jetzt erſt merkte [9] er, wie finſter [10] es draußen war. Er trat an die Tür und ſah, daß dunkle Wolken den ganzen Himmel bedeckten. Ein ſtarker Wind wehte,[11] und die erſten Tropfen ſchlugen gegen das Fenſter. Er horchte [12] auf das Rollen des Donners, das immer näher [13] kam.

Gerade wollte [14] er wieder ins Haus treten, als er einen ſchwachen Hilferuf hörte, und im Lichte eines fernen Blitzes [15] ſah er einen alten Mann, der an der Wand [16] des gegenüberliegenden Hauſes zuſammengebrochen war. Bertram lief über die Straße, hob den Alten auf und trug ihn in ſein Haus.

In der Apotheke hatte er für die Kranken, die manchmal zu ihm anſtatt [17] zum Doktor gingen, ein Ruhebett, auf das er nun den alten Mann legte. Er kannte ihn; es war der Wucherer [18] Grimaldi, der nur einige Straßen von ihm entfernt in einem elenden Häuschen wohnte, trotzdem er einer der reichſten Bürger der Stadt Augsburg war. Das geübte [19] Auge des Apothekers erkannte [20] ſofort, daß er hier nicht viel helfen konnte. Grimaldi hatte einen Schlaganfall,[21] und während er ihm das Hemd am Halſe öffnete, ſeufzte der Alte tief und hatte ſeinen letzten Atemzug getan.[22]

Bertram legte das Ohr an die Bruſt des alten Mannes, aber das Herz ſchlug nicht mehr. Er wollte ihm das Hemd wieder ſchließen, als er einen Schlüſſelring [23] mit einigen Schlüſſeln entdeckte, den der alte Wucherer an einem Lederband [24] unter dem Hemd trug.

Faſt [25] ohne zu wiſſen, was er tat, nahm Bertram den Schlüſſelring von dem Lederband ab. Dann ſtand er lange Zeit vor dem Toten, in Gedanken verſunken.[26]

*1 bedecken, *cover*. *2 gewinnen, a, o, *win, produce*. 3 der Widerſtand, –s, *opposition*. *4 geſtern abend, *last night*. 5 der Mond, –s, *moon*. *6 günſtig, *favorable*. *7 die Kunſt, —, ¨–e, *art*. *8 das Zeichen, –s, —, *sign*. *9 merken, *notice*. *10 finſter, *dark*. 11 wehen, *blow*. *12 horchen, *listen*. *13 immer näher, *closer and closer*. This is a regular use of immer when used with the comparative degree of an adjective or adverb. *14 Gerade wollte er wieder ins Haus treten. *He was just about to step into the house again*. Wollen, especially when used with the adverb gerade, very frequently conveys the meaning of *being on the point of* or *just about to*. *15 der Blitz, –es, –e, *lightning*. *16 die Wand, —, ¨–e, *wall*. *17 anſtatt, *instead of*. 18 der Wucherer, –s, —, *usurer*. 19 geübt, *trained*. *20 erkennen, *recognize*. 21 der Schlaganfall, –s, ¨–e, *stroke*. 22 hatte ſeinen letzten Atemzug getan, *had taken his last breath*. The verb tun is used in a variety of meanings besides the standard meaning *do*. 23 der Schlüſſelring, –es, –e, *key-ring*. 24 das Lederband, –es, ¨–er, *leather cord*. *25 faſt, *almost*. 26 in Gedanken verſunken, *lost* or *absorbed in thoughts*.

Solange er zurückdenken konnte, hatte er Grimaldi als ein altes Männchen gekannt, der ohne Frau und Kinder in ſeinem kleinen Häuschen wohnte, das er nur ſelten verließ. Grimaldi brauchte nicht viel auszugehen, denn die Leute kamen zu ihm. Sie kamen zu ihm, um ſich Geld zu leihen, um ihre Zinſen [1] zu bezahlen oder um ihn zu bitten, noch einen Monat auf ſein Geld zu warten.

Grimaldi war nicht der Schlimmſte unter den Wucherern, aber er war ein unfreundlicher Menſch, der in ſeinem Leben weder [2] Freundſchaft noch Liebe nötig [3] hatte und offenbar zu ſeinen Mitmenſchen [4] nur in geſchäftlichen Beziehungen [5] ſtehen wollte. Bertram erinnerte ſich daran,[6] daß ſein Vater ihm einſt [7] geſagt hatte, Grimaldi ſei von politiſchen Feinden aus Italien vertrieben [8] worden und habe in Augsburg lange Zeit als Juwelier gelebt, ehe er Wucherer geworden war.

Wie oft hatte er ſich gewundert, warum der kinderloſe Mann reich ſein wollte. Wem half der Reichtum dieſes Wucherers? Nicht einmal ihm ſelbſt, denn er führte das Leben eines armen Mannes.

Das Gewitter hatte ſeinen Höhepunkt [9] erreicht.[10] Es donnerte faſt ununterbrochen, und der Regen ſtrömte [11] aus den niedrig [12] hängenden Wolken. Ein Windſtoß [13] warf die Tür, die Bertram nicht feſt geſchloſſen hatte, mit einem lauten Knall [14] gegen die Wand. Er erſchrak und blickte auf die Straße hinaus. Man konnte nicht die Hand vor den Augen ſehen, denn es hatte aufgehört zu blitzen.

Einen Augenblick lang horchte er hinaus — nichts als das Geräuſch des Regens auf den Steinen und das Heulen [15] des Sturmes war zu hören. Da ſteckte er die Schlüſſel in die Taſche, nahm eine Laterne vom Tiſch, über die er ein Tuch warf, und ging aus dem Hauſe, die Tür ſorgfältig hinter ſich zuſchließend.

Der ſtrömende Regen und die Dunkelheit machten es unmöglich, einen Schritt weit zu ſehen, aber er verlor den Mut nicht. Bald fand er das Haus Grimaldis. Mit dem größten Schlüſſel öffnete er die ſchwere Haustür und trat in das Haus. Er ſah, daß alle Fenſter verhängt [16] waren, und ſo nahm er das Tuch von ſeiner Laterne und durchſuchte alle Räume. Er wußte, daß er nicht viel finden werde, denn der alte Geizhals [17] war nicht ſo dumm, ſein Geld in einem Hauſe liegen zu laſſen, in dem er alleine wohnte. Trotzdem mußte er irgendwo Bargeld [18] verſteckt haben, denn es verging [19] faſt kein Tag, an dem er nicht Geld erhielt oder auslieh. Aber es war zu gefährlich, hier lange herumzuſuchen; der tote Grimaldi lag in ſeiner Apotheke, und irgendjemand, der vor Zahnſchmerzen [20] nicht ſchlafen konnte oder das Opfer einer

[1] die Zinſen (pl.), *interest.* *[2] weder . . . noch, *neither . . . nor.* *[3] nötig hatte, *had need of.* [4] die Mitmenſchen (pl.), *fellow-men.* [5] die Beziehung, —, -en, *relation(ship).* *[6] Bertram erinnerte ſich daran, *Bertram remembered.* Erinnern means *to remind;* ſich erinnern, *to remind oneself* or *to remember.* The word daran anticipates the clause which follows. *[7] einſt, *once, one day.* [8] vertreiben, ie, ie, *banish.* [9] der Höhepunkt, -s, -e, *climax.* *[10] erreichen, *reach.* [11] ſtrömen, *pour.* *[12] niedrig, *low.* [13] der Windſtoß, -es, ¨-e, *gust of wind.* [14] der Knall, -s, ¨-e, *bang.* [15] das Heulen, -s, *howling.* [16] verhängen, *cover with a curtain.* [17] der Geizhals, es, ¨-e, *miser.* [18] das Bargeld, -s, *cash(-money).* *[19] vergehen, verging, iſt vergangen, *pass.* [20] die Zahnſchmerzen (pl.), *toothache.*

Schlägerei [1] war, mochte an ſeine Tür klopfen. Es war aber doch zu ſchade,[2] daß er mit leeren Händen gehen mußte. Vielleicht hatte der Alte Geld in der Matratze verſteckt. Er beugte ſich gerade über das Bett, als er auf dem Fußboden [3] ein metalliſches Geräuſch hörte. Erſchrocken ſtellte er die Lampe hin und trat leiſe in eine dunkle Ecke des Zimmers. Wieder hörte er das metalliſche Geräuſch und ein leiſes Kratzen.[4] Er hielt den Atem an [5] — unter dem Bett bewegte ſich etwas — jetzt ſah er es und er lachte laut, es war eine junge Katze, die mit irgendetwas geſpielt hatte. Trotzdem ſah er unter das Bett. Im Licht der Laterne, die er auf den Boden geſtellt hatte, entdeckte er einen eiſernen [6] Ring.

Schnell ſchob er das Bett auf die Seite und nun ſah er, daß der Ring zu einer Falltür [7] gehörte. Vorſichtig zog er an dem Ring, und die Falltür öffnete ſich über einem Raum, in den einige Stufen [8] hinabführten. Er hielt die Laterne hinab und ſah, daß der Raum voller Käſten war. Nun ſtieg er hinab und nach einigem Suchen fand er die richtigen Schlüſſel, mit denen er die Käſten aufſchließen konnte. Sie waren voller Schmuckſachen,[9] und in einigen war auch Geld.

Er trug einen Holzkaſten, in dem fünf Geldſäcke mit Goldmünzen [10] lagen, in das Schlafzimmer Grimaldis. Sorgfältig ſchob er das Bett genau auf den gleichen Platz, auf dem es geſtanden hatte, ſchloß alle Türen zu und trug den Kaſten aus dem Hauſe.

Es war eine ſchwere Laſt, aber der Apotheker war ſtark, und die Angſt, entdeckt zu werden, gab ihm die nötige Kraft, in kürzeſter Zeit die koſtbare [11] Laſt in ſein eigenes Haus zu tragen.

Sobald [12] er in ſein Laboratorium kam, warf er ſich auf den Fußboden und lag dort ſtöhnend [13] und nach Atem ringend,[14] während er ſich überlegte, was nun zu tun ſei.

Zunächſt mußte er den toten Grimaldi loswerden.[15] Nach kurzer Raſt ſtand er auf, trat zu dem Toten und band [16] die Schlüſſel wieder an das Lederband. Dann hob er den toten Grimaldi auf ſeine Schulter und ging mit ihm durch den ſtrömenden Regen ans Ende der Straße, wo er ihn an einer Gartenmauer auf die Erde legte.

Nach Hauſe zurückgekehrt,[17] verſteckte er die Geldſäcke auf dem Boden [18] ſeines Hauſes an Stellen, die nur ihm bekannt waren, und wo er alchimiſtiſche Materialien vor ſeiner Frau verſteckt hielt. Den Kaſten vergrub [19] er in einer Ecke des Kellers,[20] in der ein Haufen [21] Steine lag, die er ſorgfältig wieder auf dieſelbe Stelle legte.

Als er alles in Ordnung gebracht hatte, war es Morgen geworden. Es hatte zu regnen aufgehört, und der Himmel war wieder blau. Eben wollte er in ſeine Küche gehen, um zu frühſtücken, als heftig an ſeine Tür geklopft wurde.[22] Sein Herz ſtand

[1] die Schlägerei, —, –en, *fight(ing)*. [2] es war aber doch zu ſchade, *but it really was too great a pity*. *[3] der Fußboden, –s, ¨, *floor*. [4] das Kratzen, –s, *scratching*. *[5] anhalten, ie, a, *stop*. [6] eiſern, *iron*. [7] die Falltür, —, –en, *trap-door*. *[8] die Stufe, —, –n, *step*. [9] die Schmuckſachen (pl.), *jewels*. [10] die Goldmünze, —, –n, *gold coin*. *[11] koſtbar, *valuable*. *[12] ſobald, *as soon as*. [13] ſtöhnen, *groan*. [14] nach Atem ringend, *gasping for breath*. [15] er mußte Grimaldi loswerden, *he had to get rid of Grimaldi*. *[16] binden, a, u, *bind, tie*. *[17] zurückkehren (iſt), *return*. [18] der Boden, –s, ¨, *attic*. [19] vergraben, u, a, *hide in the ground, bury*. *[20] der Keller, –s, —, *cellar*. [21] der Haufen, –s, —, *pile*. *[22] als heftig an ſeine Tür geklopft wurde, *when there was a violent pounding on his door*. The passive voice is often used in an impersonal construction without a subject. Such a clause can be rendered in English only by a complete recasting such as is suggested above.

einen Augenblick ſtill. Aber das war doch [1] unmöglich. Er hatte keinen Fehler gemacht, keine Spur [2] hinterlaſſen. Wie gelähmt ſtand er in der Küche. Das Klopfen wurde lauter, ungeduldiger, und nun hörte er die Stimme ſeines Nachbars, des Bäckermeiſters, der ihn laut bei Namen rief. Mit einem Seufzer der Erleichterung [3] öffnete er die Tür.

Der dicke [4] Bäckermeiſter ſetzte ſich auf einen Stuhl; er war rot im Geſicht vor Aufregung. „Bertram, der alte Grimaldi — der Wucherer — mein Geſelle [5] hat es heute morgen ſelber geſehen — ſie haben ihn tot auf der Straße gefunden, auf unſerer Straße." Dann ſagte er ruhiger: „Nicht einmal in ſeinem Bett iſt der Alte geſtorben.[6] Was macht er nun mit ſeinem Geld! Mitnehmen kann er es nicht, haha!" Er lachte laut und ſchlug auf den Tiſch. Jetzt erſt ſah er, wie blaß der Apotheker ausſah. „Komm mit, Bertram," ſagte er gutmütig, „meine Frau hat Frühſtück fertig, iß mit uns." Und Bertram aß mit gutem Appetit.

Die Leute, die während dieſes Tages in ſeinen Laden kamen, erzählten ihm, daß die Polizei das ganze Haus durchſucht [7] und dabei einen Schatz gefunden hätte, den der alte Grimaldi in einem geheimen Raum ſeines Hauſes verſteckt gehalten hätte.

Nach einigen Tagen hatte die Polizei und die neugierige Stadt alles erfahren, was ſie erfahren wollten. Ein reicher Kaufmann [8] berichtete, daß der Wucherer am Tage ſeines Todes bei ihm Abendbrot gegeſſen und ſich dann mit ihm über geſchäftliche Dinge unterhalten hätte. Der Kaufmann ſagte, der Alte hätte ſchlecht ausgeſehen und auch hin und wieder darüber geklagt,[9] daß er ſich nicht wohl fühle. Er habe ihn darauf eingeladen, die Nacht in ſeinem Hauſe zu bleiben, aber Grimaldi hätte dieſe Einladung nicht angenommen, da er nie über Nacht wegblieb. Das Gewitter hätte ihn ſicherlich auf dem Wege nach Hauſe überraſcht, und wahrſcheinlich wäre er durch einen plötzlichen Blitz erſchreckt worden und hätte einen Schlaganfall gehabt.

Wochen waren vergangen, und der Apotheker lebte glücklich [10] und zufrieden mit ſeiner Frau und ſeinen Kindern, ohne von dem Golde Grimaldis den geringſten [11] Gebrauch zu machen. Aber ſchließlich hatte er ſich einen guten Plan ausgedacht, das Geld zu gebrauchen, ohne den Verdacht [12] ſeiner Mitmenſchen zu erregen.[13]

Als Apotheker mußte er kleinere Mengen Silber für ſeine Arzeneien [14] kaufen, und ſo war es leicht für ihn, etwas mehr Silber zu kaufen, als er für ſeine Apotheke brauchte.

Zu gleicher Zeit [15] arbeitete er viel in ſeinem Laboratorium und erzählte ſeiner Frau und ſeinen Freunden, daß er kurz vor einer großen Entdeckung ſtände. Seine Freunde lachten, ſeine Frau war beſorgt; ſie kannte dieſe großen „Entdeckungen."

Der Alchimiſt Bertram hatte aber das Silber, das er für ſeine alchimiſtiſche Küche gekauft hatte, mit anderen Metallen legiert [16] und ſo eine ſilberhaltige [17] Miſchung hergeſtellt, die er in eine Barre [18] goß.

*1 doch, *surely*. [2] die Spur, —, -en, *trace, clue*. [3] die Erleichterung, —, *relief*. *4 dick, *big, fat*. [5] der Geſelle, -n -n, *helper*. *6 ſterben, a, o (iſt), *die*. [7] durchſuchen, *search*. *8 der Kaufmann, -es, ...leute, *merchant*. *9 klagen, *complain*. *10 glücklich, *happy*. *11 geringſt-, *least, slightest*. [12] der Verdacht, -s, *suspicion*. [13] erregen, *arouse*. [14] die Arzenei, —, -en, *medicine*. *15 zu gleicher Zeit, *at the same time*. [16] legieren, *alloy*. [17] ſilberhaltig, *containing silver, argental*. [18] die Barre, —, -n, *bar*.

Nun lud er ſeine Freunde ein und zeigte ihnen die Barre. Sie lachten. „Das iſt ſchlechtes Silber, guter Bertram," ſagten ſie. „Haſt du wie die Kaiſerin Barbara Kupfer und Arſenik zuſammengeſchmolzen [1] und willſt jetzt Münzen aus dem weißen Metall machen laſſen?" [2]

Bertram hörte geduldig zu. Dann nahm er die Barre Metall in die Hand und ſagte: „Liebe Freunde, liebe Frau, ihr habt recht.[3] Ich würde ein Narr ſein, wenn ich Nacht für Nacht hier gearbeitet hätte, um euch mit dieſer Silberbarre zum beſten zu haben. Ich bin kein Narr. Hier in dieſer Barre liegt mein zukünftiges Vermögen,[4] und um es aus der Barre herauszudeſtillieren,[5] brauche ich keine alchimiſtiſche Kunſt. Eine Reiſe nach Paris wird dieſe Barre weiches Silber in ein paar tauſend Silbertaler [6] verwandeln.[7] Ich ſelber kann in meiner kleinen alchimiſtiſchen Küche nicht genug ſolcher Barren herſtellen,[8] um Geld damit zu verdienen. Ich kenne aber Alchimiſten in Paris, die reiche Gönner [9] haben und als Fachleute gelten.[10] Die könnten ſolche Barren in ſolchen Mengen herſtellen, daß ſich ein großes Vermögen damit verdienen ließe.[11] Sie könnten es, wenn ſie mein geheimes Verfahren [12] kennten. Ich werde nach Paris gehen und ihnen mein Geheimnis für ein paar tauſend Taler verkaufen. Das iſt mein Entſchluß,[13] und nun ſagt, was ihr wollt, ich ändere ihn nicht."

Erſt lachten die Freunde des Alchimiſten, dann verſuchten ſie ihn davon zu überzeugen,[14] daß ſo eine Reiſe Wahnſinn [15] wäre, denn niemand würde ihm einen Pfennig für ſeine Erfindung [16] geben. Seine Frau ſaß in der Ecke des Zimmers und weinte.

Sie weinte den ganzen Abend, ſie weinte während der Nacht und am nächſten Tag ſah ſie krank und blaß aus. Bertram liebte ſeine Frau und konnte ſie nicht leiden ſehen; er wollte ihr aber nicht die ganze Wahrheit [17] ſagen, damit ſie nicht ſchlecht von ihm denke. Als ſie am nächſten Abend zu Bett gegangen war, ſtieg er auf den Boden hinauf und holte leiſe den kleinſten der Geldſäcke aus dem Verſteck. Er leerte [18] den Sack auf dem Küchentiſch aus, ſchob die Münzen zu einem Haufen zuſammen und rief ſeine Frau.

Die arme Frau weinte ſchon wieder,[19] denn ſie dachte, ihr Mann werde wieder von der Reiſe ſprechen. Als ſie den Haufen Goldmünzen ſah, ſtand ſie erſchrocken ſtill. „Setz dich," ſagte Bertram, „und laß dir mein Geheimnis erzählen.[20] Ich war der

[1] zuſammenſchmelzen, o, o, *alloy*. *[2] willſt du jetzt Münzen machen laſſen? *do you intend to have coins made?* Where in English we speak of *having something done*, in German we speak of *letting something be done*. *[3] ihr habt recht, *you are right*. [4] das Vermögen, –s, *wealth, fortune*. [5] herausdeſtillieren, *distil (out)*. [6] der Silbertaler, –s, —, *silver taler*. *[7] verwandeln, *change, transform*. [8] herſtellen, *produce*. [9] der Gönner, –s, —, *benefactor*. *[10] als Fachleute gelten, *are considered experts*. *[11] daß ſich ein großes Vermögen damit verdienen ließe, *that a great fortune could be earned in that way*. [12] das Verfahren, –s, *process, method*. *[13] der Entſchluß, –es, ¨–e, *decision*. *[14] überzeugen, *convince*. [15] der Wahnſinn, –s, *insanity, madness*. *[16] die Erfindung, —, –en, *invention, discovery*. *[17] die Wahrheit, *truth*. *[18] leeren, *empty*. *[19] die arme Frau weinte ſchon wieder, *the poor woman was weeping again*. The phrase ſchon wieder stresses the idea of repetition more than the word wieder by itself would do. *[20] laß dir mein Geheimnis erzählen, *let me tell you my secret*. More literally, of course, the words mean: *let my secret be told you*. This is another instance of the active infinitive in German where English requires the passive.

erſte, der den toten Grimaldi auf der Straße fand. Er lag beinah vor unſerer Tür. Dieſen Geldbeutel [1] hielt er noch im Tode unter den Arm gepreßt. Sollte ich einen anderen das Gold finden laſſen? Sollte die Stadt es bekommen, wie ſie alles andere übernommen hat, was Grimaldi gehörte? Die Nacht war dunkel, und der Regen ſtrömte. Ich brachte das Geld ins Haus und trug Grimaldi die Straße hinab zu der Stelle, wo ihn der Nachtwächter [2] fand. Du verſtehſt, daß du niemandem ein Wort von dieſem Geheimnis ſagen darfſt." Sie küßte und umarmte ihn und war außer ſich vor Freude über das Geld. Sie ſchwor beim Leben ihrer Kinder, das Geheimnis niemandem zu verraten.

Als er nun nach Paris fuhr, tat [3] ſie, als ob ihr vor Schmerz das Herz bräche. Sie weinte und ſchrie, daß man es drei Häuſer weit hörte, und als ihr Mann gegangen war, ging ſie, wie es ſchien, äußerſt betrübt [4] zu ihrem Vater aufs Land.

Bertram reiſte mit zwei Geldbeuteln, die er in einem Koffer [5] mit falſchem Boden [6] transportierte, nach Paris und zahlte das Geld nach zwei Wochen in eine Bank ein [7] und ließ ſich einen Kreditbrief an eine Augsburger Bank geben. Dann beſuchte er die Alchimiſten in Paris, erzählte ihnen von ſeinen Verſuchen, Silber herzuſtellen, die keinen Erfolg gehabt hätten, und ſie erzählten ihm von ihren Verſuchen, Gold herzuſtellen, die bis jetzt zwar erfolglos geblieben ſeien, aber bald zu Ergebniſſen [8] führen müßten. Er hatte einen langen Brief an ſeine Frau geſchrieben, in dem er ihr die freudige [9] Nachricht ſchickte, daß verſchiedene Pariſer Alchimiſten, deren Namen ein Geheimnis bleiben müſſe, von dem Erfolg ſeines Verfahrens ſo überzeugt ſeien, daß ſie die Formel für dreitauſend Taler gekauft hätten.

Als er nach etwa [10] einem Monat wieder nach Augsburg zurückkehrte, empfingen [11] ihn ſeine Freunde mit Freude und Bewunderung.[12] Er war auf einmal [13] in ſeiner Vaterſtadt berühmt geworden. Reiche Kaufleute wollten von ſeinen Experimenten hören, aber er lächelte nur und ſagte, daß er ſeinen Pariſer Kollegen das Geheimnis verkauft hätte, da ſich niemand in ſeiner Heimatſtadt dafür intereſſiert hätte.

Hatte er auch in der Alchimie keinen Erfolg gehabt,[14] ſo hatte er jetzt um ſo mehr [15] Erfolg mit ſeinem kleinen Kapital. Er kaufte Land und einen Bauernhof [16]; das ausgegebene Geld kam reichlich [17] wieder zurück, ſo daß er im Laufe weniger Jahre durch Landkäufe und Geldſpekulationen zu einem reichen Manne wurde.[18]

Trotz allem Reichtum gab er aber die Alchimie nicht auf. Im Gegenteil,[19] jetzt hatte er Zeit und Geld genug, die kompliziertesten und teuerſten Experimente zur

[1] der Geldbeutel, –s, —, *money-bag.* [2] der Nachtwächter, –s, —, *night-watchman.* *[3] tat ſie, *she acted.* Tun followed by an als ob clause means *act* or *pretend.* *[4] betrübt, *grieved, depressed.* [5] der Koffer, –s, —, *trunk.* *[6] der Boden, –s, —, *bottom.* [7] einzahlen, *pay in, deposit.* *[8] das Ergebnis, ...niſſes, ...niſſe, *result.* *[9] freudig, *joyous, cheerful.* *[10] etwa, *approximately.* *[11] empfangen, i, a, *receive.* *[12] die Bewunderung, *admiration.* *[13] auf einmal, *suddenly.* *[14] hatte er auch keinen Erfolg gehabt, *even though he had had no success.* If the verb is used in inverted word order and is followed by auch, begin with *even though* or *even if.* *[15] um ſo mehr, *all the more.* [16] der Bauernhof, –es, ¨–e, *farm.* [17] reichlich, *abundantly.* [18] zu einem reichen Manne wurde, *became a rich man.* This construction, *i.e.* zu etwas werden, regularly signifies *to turn into something.* *[19] im Gegenteil, *on the contrary.*

Gewinnung von Gold zu machen. Am liebſten war er in dem kleinen Häuschen, in dem er als Apotheker gewohnt hatte und das er nun vollkommen in ein alchimiſtiſches Laboratorium umgebaut [1] hatte. Dort konnte man ihn oft tagelang und halbe Nächte lang über ſeine Retorten gebückt ſehen.

Er hatte noch einen anderen Grund, ſich ſo mit ganzem Herzen der Alchimie zu widmen.[2] Der große Reichtum hatte den Charakter der Apothekersfrau verwandelt. Ehe der Reichtum in ihr Leben kam, war ſie eine arbeitſame [3] Frau geweſen, die ihren Mann und ihre Kinder liebte und ſich ſonſt nicht um die große Welt außerhalb [4] ihres kleinen Häuschens kümmerte.[5] Jetzt aber wollte ſie eine vornehme [6] Dame ſein und der großen Welt angehören.[7] Sie trug die teuerſten Kleider und Juwelen, die zu haben waren. Das große Haus, das ihr Mann in einem Park in der Nähe der Stadt als Sommerhaus [8] für ſie hatte bauen laſſen, war der Schauplatz [9] großer Tänze und Feſteſſen.[10] Da war ein ſtändiges [11] Kommen und Gehen und Dutzende von Dienern [12] mußten für das Haus und die Gäſte ſorgen.

Das Stadthaus hatte einer alten Augsburger Patrizierfamilie [13] gehört, und Bertram hatte es auf den Wunſch ſeiner Frau gekauft, trotzdem er ſich in der Stadt damit keine Freunde machte, denn die Patrizier pflegten gegen Emporkömmlinge [14] nicht ſehr freundlich zu ſein.

Das führte natürlich zu vielen unangenehmen Situationen, und der Streit und die dauernden Kämpfe mit den alten Familien der Stadt verbitterten die reiche Frau immer mehr. Am meiſten litt unter all dem ihr Mann, der ein ſtiller und beſcheidener [15] Menſch war. Da ſeine Frau ihn zwingen wollte, das Leben eines reichen Patriziers zu führen, fühlte er ſich ſogar im Frieden ſeines Laboratoriums geſtört, und ſo begann der arme Bertram, um ſeiner Frau und ihren ſtändigen Wünſchen und Klagen zu entfliehen,[16] längere Reiſen zu machen. Er reiſte in Frankreich, Italien und Spanien, beſuchte überall die Alchimiſten und genoß [17] ſo ſein Leben, bis er wieder nach Hauſe zurückkehrte.

Einmal blieb er beſonders lange fort. Ein Jahr war vergangen, und ſeine Frau verlangte in ihren Briefen, daß er ſofort zurückkommen ſolle. Er antwortete ihr, daß er in Rom den Alchimiſten D'Alberto getroffen hätte, den größten Alchimiſten dieſer Zeit, und daß er ſehr viel von dieſem Manne lerne. Er werde erſt ein halbes Jahr ſpäter zurückkommen können.

Frau Bertram war außer ſich. Anderthalb [18] Jahre wollte ihr Mann wegbleiben, bloß [19] wegen der elenden ſchwarzen Kunſt. Je länger ſie darüber nachdachte, deſto [20] wütender wurde ſie. In ihrem Haß auf die Alchimie ließ ſie das alte

[1] umbauen, *rebuild.* [2] widmen, *devote.* *[3] arbeitſam, *hardworking.* *[4] außerhalb, *outside of.* *[5] ſich ſonſt nicht um die Welt kümmerte, *otherwise paid no attention to the world.* *[6] vornehm, *distinguished.* *[7] angehören, *belong to.* [8] das Sommerhaus, –es, ¨er, *summer-residence.* [9] der Schauplatz, –es, ¨e, *scene.* [10] das Feſteſſen, –s, —, *banquet.* [11] ſtändig, *constant.* *[12] der Diener, –s, —, *servant.* [13] die Patrizierfamilie, —, –n, *patrician family.* [14] der Emporkömmling, –s, –e, *upstart.* [15] beſcheiden, *modest.* [16] entfliehen, o, o (iſt), *escape.* *[17] genießen, o, o, *enjoy.* [18] anderthalb, *one and a half.* *[19] bloß, *merely.* *[20] je . . . deſto, *the . . . the.*

Häuschen ſofort niederreißen,[1] in dem ihres Mannes alchimiſtiſche Küche war, das alte Häuschen, in dem ſie außerdem die erſten glücklichen Jahre ihrer Ehe [2] verlebt [3] hatte. Sie dachte nicht daran. An Stelle des alten Häuschens wollte ſie ein größeres und ſchöneres Haus bauen [4] laſſen, für diejenigen [5] ihrer Gäſte, die im Stadthaus nicht untergebracht [6] werden konnten.

So wurde denn das Haus niedergeriſſen und Bertrams alchimiſtiſche Küche zerſtört.[7] Als ſeine Frau kam, um nachzuſehen, ob die Arbeit Fortſchritte [8] mache, hatten die Arbeiter gerade begonnen, das Fundament zu erweitern,[9] denn das neue Haus ſollte viel größer werden als das alte. Zwei Arbeiter ruhten ſich gerade ein wenig aus,[10] als von oben [11] die ſcharfe Stimme der reichen Frau kam. „Ihr Faulenzer“ [12] ſchrie ſie, „werdet ihr dafür bezahlt, daß ihr euch auf eure Schaufeln [13] lehnt und träumt? Arbeitet, ſage ich euch, oder ich werde dafür ſorgen,[14] daß ihr dieſe Woche keinen Lohn [15] bekommt.“

Die beiden Arbeiter griffen [16] wieder zu ihren Schaufeln, brummten [17] etwas vor ſich hin [18] und begannen wieder zu graben. Plötzlich ſtießen ſie auf etwas Hartes, und bald hatten ſie einen Holzkaſten ans Licht gebracht.

Die Frau war wieder gegangen, und ſo unterſuchten ſie den ausgegrabenen Kaſten, während die anderen Arbeiter neugierig herbeiliefen.[19] Der Deckel war eingeroſtet,[20] und ſie mußten ihn mit ihren Schaufeln aufbrechen.[21] Enttäuſcht [22] ſahen ſie, daß der Kaſten leer war. Plötzlich rief einer der Arbeiter: „Was iſt das?“ Er zeigte auf ein kleines, ſilbernes Schildchen, auf dem der Name „Grimaldi“ ſtand. „Das war das Haus des Apothekers Bertram,“ ſagte er nachdenklich. „Wie kommt [23] ein Kaſten mit Grimaldis Namen in Bertrams Keller? Der alte Grimaldi war ſehr reich. Ihr jungen Leute werdet euch nicht mehr an den alten Wucherer erinnern, aber wir älteren Leute wiſſen ganz gut, daß alles, was Grimaldi hinterließ, an die Stadt Augsburg kam.“ Er pfiff durch die Zähne. „Ich glaube, hier haben wir etwas, was der Dame, die hier eben ſo geſchimpft hat, das Schimpfen [24] abgewöhnen [25] kann.“ Noch am gleichen Tag brachten die Arbeiter, die den Kaſten gefunden hatten, denſelben zum Magiſtrat der Stadt. Der Magiſtrat beſtand aus Patriziern, von denen einige die Familie Bertram grimmig [26] haßten. Sie ruhten nicht, bis der ganze Fall öffentlich bekannt und eine Unterſuchung nötig wurde.

Umſonſt [27] verſuchte Bertram dem Gericht [28] von Augsburg alles zu erklären.

[1] niederreißen, i, i, *tear down.* [2] die Ehe, —, –n, *marriage, married life.* *[3] verleben, *spend.* *[4] bauen, *build.* *[5] diejenigen, *those.* [6] unterbringen, brachte unter, untergebracht, *accommodate.* *[7] zerſtören, *destroy.* *[8] der Fortſchritt, –es, –e, *progress.* [9] erweitern, *enlarge.* *[10] ſich ausruhen, *rest.* *[11] oben, *above.* [12] der Faulenzer, –s, —, *lazy fellow.* [13] die Schaufel, —, –n, *shovel.* *[14] ich werde dafür ſorgen, *I'll see to it.* [15] der Lohn, –es, ⸗e, *pay, wages.* [16] greifen, i, i zu, *pick up.* [17] brummen, *mutter.* *[18] vor ſich hin, *to themselves.* [19] herbeilaufen, ie, au (iſt), *come running.* [20] eingeroſtet, *rusted shut.* [21] aufbrechen, a, o, *break open.* *[22] enttäuſcht, *disappointed.* *[23] Wie kommt ein Kaſten in Bertrams Keller? *How does a box happen to be in Bertram's cellar?* [24] das Schimpfen, –s, *scolding, using abusive language.* [25] abgewöhnen, *make someone give up.* [26] grimmig, *furiously, violently.* *[27] umſonſt, *in vain.* [28] das Gericht, –s, –e, *court of justice.*

Man glaubte ihm nicht. Seine Frau hatte die Geschichte ganz anders erzählt. Das war schon sehr verdächtig.[1] Wahrscheinlich logen sie alle beide.[2] Der Alte war wohl gar nicht am Schlag gestorben. Der Apotheker mochte [3] ihn erwürgt oder vielleicht auch vergiftet [4] haben. Ja, so war es wohl gewesen. Der Kaufmann, den Grimaldi besucht hatte, hatte ausgesagt,[5] daß der Wucherer sich schlecht gefühlt hatte. Auf dem Nachhauseweg hatte er dann wohl Licht im Hause des Apothekers gesehen und ihn um Medizin gebeten. Der Apotheker konnte ihn dann leicht in seiner Apotheke vergiftet und den Toten auf die Straße getragen haben. Das war möglich. Aber vielleicht war es doch so, wie er es behauptete. In dem Fall war er nur ein Dieb und kein Mörder, und die Strafe konnte milder sein. Nun,[6] auf der Folterbank [7] würde der reiche Alchimist wohl die Wahrheit sagen.

Der reiche Alchimist hatte die Wahrheit gesagt und er sagte sie noch einmal, aber nicht auf der Folterbank, die er nicht hätte aushalten können, sondern in einem Brief, den man im Kerker [8] fand, wo er sich während der Nacht erhängt hatte. In dem Brief bat er um Gnade [9] für seine Frau und seine Kinder. Er sei an allem schuld.[10] Man solle besonders die Kinder, die an dem Verbrechen [11] des Vaters unschuldig wären, nicht zu Bettlern [12] machen. Das Augsburger Gericht erfüllte [13] dem Toten diese Bitte.[14] Seine Besitztümer [15] wurden von der Stadt konfisziert, aber eine gewisse Summe wurde der Frau und den Kindern gegeben unter der Bedingung, Augsburg zu verlassen und nie wieder zurückzukehren.

A. Practice Sentences:

1. Der Alte hatte recht; der Alchimist und seine Frau waren alle beide daran schuld.
2. Es war schade, daß Bertrams Frau nichts von seinen alchimistischen Experimenten hielt.
3. Hin und wieder hatte er größere Mengen Silber nötig.
4. Schließlich ist er den schweren Kasten losgeworden.
5. Sie tat, als ob sie sich um so etwas gar nicht kümmerte.
6. Bertram wollte gerade zu Bett gehen, als heftig an die Tür geklopft wurde.
7. Wie kommt es, daß Grimaldis Name auf dem silbernen Schildchen steht?
8. Laß dir die Geschichte von dem armen Apotheker erzählen, der zu einem reichen Herrn wurde!
9. Der Kasten, den die Arbeiter im Keller fanden, mochte wohl dem alten Grimaldi gehört haben.
10. Je reicher Frau Bertram wurde, desto unfreundlicher wurde sie.

[1] verdächtig, *suspicious.* *[2] alle beide, *both.* Alle cannot be translated; it adds emphasis. [3] mochte ihn erwürgt haben, *probably strangled him.* The imperfect tense of mögen is often used to express probability. [4] vergiften, *poison.* [5] aussagen, *testify.* *[6] nun, *well.* When nun is separated from the rest of the sentence by a comma or commas, it is used as an expletive; otherwise it means *now.* [7] die Folterbank, —, ⸗e, *rack.* [8] der Kerker, -s, —, *prison cell.* [9] die Gnade, *clemency, mercy.* [10] an allem schuld sein, *to be blamed for everything.* [11] das Verbrechen, -s, —, *crime.* [12] der Bettler, -s, —, *beggar.* [13] erfüllen, *fulfill.* *[14] die Bitte, —, -n, *request.* [15] das Besitztum, -s, ⸗er, *possession.*

11. Er machte eine Geschäftsreise nach Rom und zu gleicher Zeit besuchte er den großen Alchimisten D'Alberto.
12. Als der Apotheker seinen Freunden die Silberbarren zeigte, lächelte er vor sich hin.
13. Kollmann versuchte, den Glaskasten zu öffnen. Der Deckel hob sich.
14. Er galt als einer der besten Chemiker seiner Zeit.
15. Es ist ihm nie gelungen, künstliches Silber zu produzieren.

B. Securing the Vocabulary:

1. fern
   die Ferne
   entfernt
   die Entfernung
2. ziehen
   der Zug
   die Zugbrücke
   sich anziehen
   der Anzug
   abziehen
   vorziehen
   der Vorzug
   die Beziehung
3. der Freund
   die Freundin
   freundlich
   die Freundschaft
4. leiden
   das Leid
   es tut mir leid
   leider
   das Mitleid
   mitleidig
5. nehmen
   annehmen
   mitnehmen
   zurücknehmen
   abnehmen
   die Aufnahme
6. schließen
   schließlich
   der Schluß
   der Schlüsselring
   aufschließen
   zuschließen
   beschließen
   verschließen
7. arbeiten
   die Arbeit
   arbeitsam
   der Arbeiter
   der Arbeitslose
   die Arbeitslosenunterstützung
   die Arbeitslosigkeit
8. zahlen
   die Zahl
   zahlreich
   bezahlen
   einzahlen
   die Abzahlung
9. geben
   das Ergebnis
   aufgeben
   die Aufgabe
   angeben
   ausgeben
10. jeder
    jedermann
    jederzeit
    jedenfalls
    jedesmal

Neunundzwanzigste Aufgabe

* * * \

Glas Wein aus dem alten Zinnkrug,[1] rauchte ſeine Pfeife und blickte nachdenklich vor ſich hin.[2]

Die kartenſpielenden Bauern hatten ihr Bier ausgetrunken und zahlten Karl, der wieder ins Zimmer getreten war. Der Junge ging an den Tiſch, an dem Herr Huber ſaß, um abzuräumen.[3] Da faßte der ihn plötzlich am Arm und ſagte: „Karl, ich brauche einen geſchickten[4] und intelligenten Burſchen[5] wie dich auf meinem Bauernhof. Wenn du Luſt haſt, komm 'rüber,[6] du biſt willkommen." Karl lächelte: „Und am zweiten Tage käme mein Vater und holte mich mit der Hundepeitſche[7] zurück. — Ich danke Ihnen,[8] Herr Huber. Ich weiß, wie Sie es meinen, aber das wird nicht gehen."[9]

Huber nickte nachdenklich mit dem Kopf, dann ſagte er laut: „Bring mir die Rechnung, Karl, ich will zahlen!" Karl ging und brachte ein Stück Papier, das Huber ſorgfältig nachprüfte.[10] „Deine Mutter hat ſich geirrt, Karl," ſagte er endlich, „das war Schweizer Landwein, den ich da[11] getrunken habe und kein feuriger Italiener." Karl wurde rot und ging in die Küche zurück. Man hörte eine ſcheltende[12] Frauenſtimme, und dann kam Karls Mutter, ihre Hände an der Schürze[13] trocknend,[14] aus der Küche. „So," ſchrie ſie den Bauern an,[15] „du biſt ein Weinkenner. Du biſt kein Bauer, du biſt ein großer Herr, der einen ganzen Keller voll feiner Weine hat und genau weiß, wo ein Wein herkommt[16] und wie alt er iſt." „O, es iſt ſchon gut[17]; hier iſt das Geld, ich gehe," brummte der Dicke. „Glücklicherweiſe iſt Euer Wirtshaus nicht das einzige in der Schweiz." Ärgerlich ging er zur Tür hinaus,[18] gefolgt von Karl, der ihm half, ſein Pferd vor den Wagen zu ſpannen.[19]

Am Abend dieſes Tages, als der Wirt und ſeine Frau die kleine Summe Geld zählten, die die Gäſte im Wirtshaus am Berge — ſo nannten es die Leute — ausgegeben hatten, ſetzte ſich Karl zu ſeinen Eltern. „Was willſt du hier?" brummte ſein Vater. „Geh zu Bett, damit du morgen nicht ſo faul biſt, wie du heute warſt. Zwei Stunden hat es gedauert, bis du die Kornſäcke auf den Wagen geladen haſt. Man ſollte denken,[20] du wäreſt ein Mädchen und kein Junge." „Vater, wenn ich ſo ſchlechte Arbeit tue, wäre es dann nicht beſſer, Ihr nähmet Euch einen Knecht,[21] und ich ginge, mir Arbeit zu ſuchen? Ich könnte Euch mit meinem Lohn helfen, für den Knecht zu zahlen." Sprachlos vor Erſtaunen ſtarrten der Mann und die Frau ihren

[1] der Zinnkrug, –es, ⸗e, *pewter pitcher*. *[2] blickte vor ſich hin, *looked into space*. [3] abräumen, *clear (it) off*. *[4] geſchickt, *clever*. [5] der Burſche, –n, –n, *fellow*. [6] 'rüber, short for herüber, *over*. [7] die Hundepeitſche, —, –n, *dog whip*. [8] ich danke Ihnen, *thank you but I can't accept*. Danken is used to decline with thanks; acceptance is expressed by bitte. [9] das wird nicht gehen, *that won't be possible*. Gehen is often used in the sense of *to be possible* or *to work out*. [10] nachprüfen, *check*. [11] den ich da getrunken habe. The word da is not used here in its usual full significance of *there*, *here*, or *then* but has only very weak demonstrative force; it should not be translated. [12] ſchelten, *scold*. [13] die Schürze, —, –n, *apron*. [14] trocknen, *dry*. [15] anſchreien, ie, ie, *scream at*. [16] herkommen, a, o (iſt), *come from*. *[17] ſchon gut, *all right*. [18] zur Tür hinaus, *out of the door*. [19] ſpannen, *hitch*. [20] Man ſollte denken, *one might think*. [21] Wäre es dann nicht beſſer, Ihr nähmet Euch einen Knecht? *Wouldn't it be better then if you hired a man?* This is paratactic order, that is, the idea which is logically subordinate is syntactically coordinate.

Sohn an. Dann brach ein Sturm von Flüchen [1] und Schimpfnamen [2] über den armen Jungen her, und schließlich schlug ihm der Vater ins Gesicht und warf ihn aus dem Zimmer.

Beschämt [3] und zitternd vor Wut [4] ging Karl in seine Schlafkammer auf dem Boden. Lange stand er an dem kleinen Dachfenster und blickte auf die Berge, die im Mondlicht ungeheuer [5] und geheimnisvoll [6] aussahen. Was für Menschen mochten hinter diesen Bergen wohnen? Er wußte, daß weit, weit im Norden mächtige Flüsse flossen,[7] und ebenes [8] Land war. Dort lebten die Menschen in reichen, großen Städten, und wenn man immer weiter nach Norden wanderte, kam man ans Meer. Es war nicht das erste Mal, daß er hier am Fenster im Mondlicht stand und von fernen Ländern träumte; es war aber das erste Mal, daß er ernstlich daran dachte, von Hause fortzulaufen. Schließlich legte er sich, von Müdigkeit [9] übermannt,[10] auf sein Bett, aber nur zu kurzer Rast. Noch vor Sonnenaufgang [11] suchte er im Dunkeln die paar Sachen, die ihm gehörten, nahm aus einem Versteck in der Mauer [12] eine kleine Geldsumme, die er sich im Laufe der letzten Jahre durch Trinkgelder [13] erspart [14] hatte, und packte alles in ein Bündel.

Er war reisefertig. Lange lauschte [15] er an der Tür, aber nichts regte sich,[16] alle lagen noch im tiefen Schlaf. Mit klopfendem Herzen schlich er die alte Holztreppe [17] hinunter [18] und öffnete leise die Haustür. Die Hunde draußen sprangen hoch, aber Karl rief ihnen etwas Beruhigendes [19] zu, und winselnd [20] ließen sie sich von ihm streicheln.

Ohne sich umzusehen, lief er über den dunklen Hof und ging mit schnellem Schritt die Landstraße [21] hinauf, immer in Furcht, er könnte die grobe Stimme seines Vaters hinter sich hören. Der Weg ging bergauf,[22] und nach etwa zwei Stunden war Karl auf dem Gipfel [23] des Berges angekommen. Jetzt erst hielt er es für sicher auszuruhen. Er setzte sich auf einen Meilenstein und blickte auf das tief unter ihm liegende Heimatdörfchen zurück.

Er sah das Wirtshaus, die Scheune und auf dem Hof konnte er den Wagen mit dem zerbrochenen Rad erkennen, das er heute reparieren sollte. Das winzige [24] Häuschen mit dem roten Dach war das Hühnerhaus,[25] die weißen Pünktchen, die sich da unten bewegten, waren die Hühner.

Er dachte daran, wie er als kleiner Junge seiner Mutter beim Einsammeln [26] der Eier geholfen hatte, und wie sie ihm das Haar streichelte, wenn er ein verstecktes Ei gefunden hatte. Ja, damals waren die Eltern auf ihn stolz [27] gewesen. Als der

[1] der Fluch, –es, ⸗e, *curse.* [2] der Schimpfname, –ns, –n, *abusive name.* [3] beschämt, *humiliated.* *[4] die Wut, *rage.* *[5] ungeheuer, *enormous.* *[6] geheimnisvoll, *mysterious.* *[7] fließen, o, o (ist), *flow.* *[8] eben, *flat.* *[9] die Müdigkeit, *fatigue.* [10] übermannen, *overcome.* [11] Noch vor Sonnenaufgang, *even before sunrise.* *[12] die Mauer, —, –n, *wall.* [13] das Trinkgeld, –es, –er, *tip.* [14] ersparen, *save.* *[15] lauschen, *listen.* [16] sich regen, *stir.* [17] die Holztreppe, —, –n, *wooden staircase.* [18] hinunterschleichen, i, i (ist), *sneak down.* [19] etwas Beruhigendes, *something quieting, some quieting words.* [20] winseln, *whine.* *[21] die Landstraße, —, –n, *highway.* *[22] bergauf, *up-hill.* *[23] der Gipfel, –s, —, *top.* *[24] winzig, *tiny.* [25] das Hühnerhaus, –es, ⸗er, *hen-house.* [26] beim Einsammeln, *gathering.* *[27] stolz, *proud.*

Pfarrer[1] ihn lesen gelehrt hatte, und er dem Vater eines Abends nach dem Abendessen einen Psalm vorlas, da war der vom Tisch aufgesprungen, hatte ihn auf den Arm genommen und ihm, was er sonst nie tat,[2] einen Kuß gegeben. Damals sprachen die Eltern sogar davon, ihn einst zur Universität zu schicken.

Die Tränen[3] kamen ihm in die Augen, die Erinnerung[4] machte ihn weich, und fast bereute[5] er, was er getan hatte. Und wenn er jetzt umkehrte,[6] nach Hause ginge und seinem Vater gestände[7]: „Ich wollte fortlaufen aber ich konnte mich nicht von Euch trennen;[8] hier bin ich". — Die Hundepeitsche würde er von der Wand holen und ihn schlagen, bis er den Arm nicht mehr heben konnte.

Nein, seine Eltern liebten ihn nicht mehr. Die dachten an nichts weiter als an ihr Unglück und wie sie wieder zu Geld kommen könnten, seit sie in dem Unglücksjahr 1752 durch Mißernte[9] und durch ein Feuer im Wirtshaus fast alles verloren hatten. Nun, wenn er nichts weiter[10] war, als ein billiger[11] Knecht, dann konnte ja jeder[12] andere seine Arbeit genau so gut, vielleicht sogar noch besser tun.

Trotzig[13] drehte er sich um und ging weiter. Die Straße ging bergab, ein Dorf kam. Er kannte es, es war Bertendorf. Ein paar Mal im Jahr mußte er mit dem Vater nach Bertendorf, wenn sie Vieh,[14] Handwerkszeug[15] und dergleichen kauften. In Bertendorf wohnte auch der Pfarrer, der ihn getauft,[16] und bei dem er lesen gelernt hatte. Mit einem plötzlichen Entschluß ging er die enge[17] Dorfstraße hinab, die zum Pfarrhause[18] führte. Der Pfarrer war schon auf und war dabei,[19] ein paar Rosen zu pflücken, als Karl in den Garten trat.

„Karl, was für eine Überraschung!" sagte er und schüttelte ihm herzlich die Hand. „Was machst du so früh bei uns?" „Ich habe Geschäfte beim Huber in Langental," sagte Karl. Er plante jedoch, in der entgegengesetzten[20] Richtung weiterzugehen. „Ich wollte dem Herrn Pastor nur Guten Tag sagen." Der Pastor wunderte sich ein bißchen, aber da er kurzsichtig[21] war und seine Brille[22] im Hause gelassen hatte, konnte er nicht sehen, wie blaß und unglücklich Karl aussah. So sagte er nur: „Nun, wenn du keine Zeit hast, dich bei uns ein wenig zu erfrischen, so geh nur, und Gott segne[23] dich, mein Sohn!" Karl küßte dem Pfarrer die Hand und verließ den Garten. Der sah ihm noch eine Weile kopfschüttelnd nach. „Da stimmt etwas nicht,"[24] sagte er sich, aber dabei blieb es auch.[25]

[1] der Pfarrer, –s, —, *parson.* [2] was er sonst nie tat, *something which he usually never did.* The relative pronoun was is used with the thought of an entire clause as its antecedent. *[3] die Träne, —, –n, *tear.* *[4] die Erinnerung, —, –en, *memory.* [5] bereuen, *regret.* [6] umkehren, *turn around.* *[7] gestehen, gestand, gestanden, *confess.* *[8] sich trennen, *separate.* [9] die Mißernte, —, –n, *bad harvest, crop failure.* *[10] nichts weiter, *no more.* *[11] billig, *cheap.* *[12] jeder, *every.* [13] trotzig, *defiantly.* [14] das Vieh, –s, *cattle.* [15] das Handwerkszeug, –s, *tools.* [16] taufen, *baptize.* *[17] eng, *narrow.* [18] das Pfarrhaus, –es, ¨er, *parsonage.* *[19] Der Pfarrer war dabei, ein paar Rosen zu pflücken. *The pastor was busy picking some roses.* The particle da in the compound dabei anticipates the following phrase. [20] entgegengesetzt, *opposite.* *[21] kurzsichtig, *near-sighted.* *[22] die Brille, —, –n, *glasses.* [23] segnen, *bless.* *[24] Da stimmt etwas nicht. *There is something wrong there.* [25] dabei blieb es auch, *and he let it go at that.* Es bleibt dabei, literally: *it remains at that,* is an expression used to signify that no change will be made in the existing situation or agreement.

Karl war wieder auf der Landſtraße und er hatte Glück. Der Poſtwagen [1] nach Bern hielt gerade vor dem Dorfwirtshaus. Der Platz neben dem Kutſcher [2] war noch frei, und ſo kam er ſchneller nach Bern, als er erwartet hatte.

Die Eile [3] war nicht nötig. Als ſein Vater ihn fluchend und ſchimpfend im ganzen Hauſe geſucht und nicht gefunden hatte, ahnte [4] er ſofort das Richtige. Er hatte plötzlich Angſt, einen billigen Knecht zu verlieren. Er vermutete,[5] daß Karl über die Grenze nach Italien entflohen war. Als ſchließlich der Pfarrer, der ſich wegen des Jungen Sorgen zu machen begann, nach Karl fragen ließ, erfuhr man die allgemeine [6] Richtung, in der er verſchwunden war, aber zur Verfolgung [7] war es zu ſpät.

Eine Zeit lang warteten Karls Eltern und das ganze Dorf auf ſeine Rückkehr.[8] Schließlich aber gewöhnte [9] man ſich an den Gedanken, daß Karl gegangen war, und mit Seufzen und Stöhnen mietete [10] ſich der Wirt einen Knecht, der ihn zweimal ſoviel Geld wie Karl koſtete und nicht halb ſoviel arbeitete.

Karls geſpartes Geld war bald ausgegeben, und er mußte ſich nach Arbeit umſehen. Da er leſen und ſchreiben konnte und außerdem ein intelligenter Junge war, fiel es ihm nicht ſchwer,[11] bei vornehmen Familien Arbeit zu finden.

Ein Dutzend Jahre waren ſo vergangen, als es Karl gelang, bei einem reichen, alten Edelmann,[12] eine Stellung als Sekretär zu bekommen. Der alte Herr verließ ſich bald in faſt allen ſeinen Geſchäften auf Karl, den er mehr wie einen Freund als wie einen Diener behandelte. Da ſeine Tage gezählt waren, und er keine Kinder hatte, machte er ſein Teſtament,[13] in dem er Karl zum faſt alleinigen [14] Erben [15] machte. Kurz darauf ſtarb er, und Karl kam in den Beſitz eines großen Vermögens. So war aus dem armen Bauernjungen,[16] der vor Jahren mit ein paar Pfennig in der Taſche und einem Bündel über der Schulter von zu Hauſe fortgelaufen war, ein reicher Herr geworden.

Oft hatte Karl an ſeine Eltern und an ſein Heimatdorf gedacht, doch es war ihm immer unmöglich geweſen, ſeine Eltern zu beſuchen. Schon längſt [17] hatte er alles Böſe vergeſſen, und nun war endlich die Gelegenheit gekommen, zu ihnen zurückzukehren. Karl beſchloß, ſie zu ſich in ſein Landhaus [18] in Bayern zu nehmen, wo ſie ihre alten Tage ſorgenfrei und glücklich verleben ſollten.

Er machte ſich, von einigen Dienern begleitet, auf den Weg [19] und kam nach wenigen Tagereiſen nach der Schweiz. Immer wieder war ihm unterwegs [20] die quälende [21] Sorge gekommen, ob ſeine Eltern noch lebten, denn er hatte nicht den Mut gefunden, ihnen oder einem ſeiner Verwandten während der langen Jahre ſeiner Abweſen-

[1] der Poſtwagen, –s, —, *stage-coach.* *[2] der Kutſcher, –s, —, *driver.* *[3] die Eile, *haste, hurry.* *[4] ahnen, *suspect.* *[5] vermuten, *suspect.* *[6] allgemein, *general.* [7] die Verfolgung, —, –en, *pursuit.* *[8] die Rückkehr, —, *return.* *[9] ſich gewöhnen an, *get accustomed to.* [10] mieten, *hire.* *[11] es fiel ihm nicht ſchwer, *it was not hard for him.* [12] der Edelmann, –es, ...leute, *nobleman.* [13] das Teſtament, –es, –e, *testament, will.* [14] alleinig, *sole.* [15] der Erbe, –n, –n, *heir.* [16] der Bauernjunge, –n, –n, *farm-boy.* *[17] ſchon längſt, *long ago.* [18] das Landhaus, –es, ¨er, *villa.* *[19] er machte ſich auf den Weg, *he started out.* *[20] unterwegs, *on the way.* [21] quälen, *torture, torment.*

heit [1] zu ſchreiben. Möglich war es auch, daß die Armut [2] und die harte Arbeit ihr Leben verkürzt [3] hatten. Zwanzig Jahre waren ſeit ſeiner Flucht von zu Hauſe vergangen. Falls ſie noch lebten, würden ſie ihn wahrſcheinlich nicht einmal wiedererkennen. Mit ſolchen Gedanken war er bis Bertendorf gekommen, wo er ſeine Diener im Gaſthof [4] des Ortes zurückließ.[5]

Bevor er aber ſeine Eltern wiederſah, wollte er den Pfarrer beſuchen, der ihm einen Segen [6] mit auf den Weg [7] gegeben hatte, der ſo reichlich in Erfüllung gegangen war. Zu ſeiner Freude erfuhr er, daß der alte Mann noch lebte, und ſo ſaß er denn dem Greis [8] gegenüber, der ihn verwundert anſtarrte und es nicht glauben wollte, daß er Karl vom Wirtshaus am Berge war, der arme Karl, der vor vielen Jahren in die weite Welt gegangen war. Karl, in deſſen Erinnerung der Trennungstag [9] ſtets weiterlebte, beſchrieb dem alten Herrn genau, wie er damals im Garten die Roſen gepflückt hatte und daß er ſeine Brille im Hauſe hatte liegen laſſen. Der Paſtor nickte halb nachdenklich, halb ungläubig.[10] Dann holte er das Kirchenbuch [11] her und verglich die Daten der Geburt und Taufe ſowie [12] die Namen der Taufpaten [13] mit dem, was Karl ihm erzählt hatte. Nun konnte er nicht mehr zweifeln. Er zog Karl ans Fenſter und ſah ihm ins Geſicht, als wolle er dort das Kindergeſicht wiederentdecken, das er vor Jahren gekannt hatte. Erſt jetzt wagte Karl nach ſeinen Eltern zu fragen, denn er ſchämte ſich, nicht einmal zu wiſſen,[14] ob ſie lebten oder tot wären. Da erfuhr er denn, daß ſie noch lebten, daß ſie aber ſehr arm ſeien. „Warte einen Augenblick, wir können gleich in meinem Wagen zu ihnen fahren. Die Freude, wenn ſie ihren Karl als einen erwachſenen Mann wiederſehen, der ein vornehmer Herr geworden iſt, die Freude möchte ich mit anſehen.“ [15] Karl ſagte ernſt: „Ehrwürdiger [16] Vater, gerne täte ich Euch den Gefallen, aber einmal [17] fürchte ich, daß die plötzliche Freude den Alten ſchaden könnte, und dann möchte ich gerne eine Nacht unerkannt unter ihrem Dache ſchlafen. Alles wird ſich dann leichter und natürlicher ſagen laſſen.“ Der Pfarrer ſah das ein,[18] und ſo ritt [19] Karl dann bei einbrechender Nacht [20] auf ſeinem Pferd den ſteinigen Bergweg hinab, der zum Wirtshaus am Berge führte.

Die Freude nahm ihm faſt die Stimme, als er in dem weißhaarigen Greiſe, der auf ſein Klopfen an der Tür erſchien, ſeinen Vater wiedererkannte. Mühſam [21] beherrſchte [22] er ſich und fragte: „Kann ich hier Unterkunft für mich und mein Pferd

*1 die Abweſenheit, —, -en, *absence*. *2 die Armut, *poverty*. 3 verkürzen, *shorten*. *4 der Gaſthof, -es, ⸗e, *inn*. *5 zurücklaſſen, ie, a, *leave behind*. 6 der Segen, -s, *blessing*. 7 mit auf den Weg, *for his journey*. 8 der Greis, -es, -e, *old man*. 9 der Trennungstag, *day of separation*. 10 ungläubig, *unbelieving, sceptical*. 11 das Kirchenbuch, *parochial register*. *12 ſowie, *as well as*. 13 der Taufpate, -n, -n, *godfather*, pl. *godparents*. 14 er ſchämte ſich, nicht einmal zu wiſſen, *he was ashamed of not even knowing*. 15 die Freude möchte ich mit anſehen, *I would like to see that happiness too*. Here the word mit gives to the sentence the meaning that the speaker would like to be one of those who see that happiness. A common use of mit. 16 ehrwürdig, *venerable*. *17 einmal, *for one thing*. *18 einſehen, a, e, *understand*. *19 reiten, i, i (iſt), *ride, go on horseback*. 20 bei einbrechender Nacht, *at nightfall*. *21 mühſam, *with difficulty*. *22 ſich beherrſchen, *control oneself*.

finden?" „Freilich," [1] antwortete der Alte. „Tretet ins Gastzimmer und macht es Euch bequem,[2] ich werde gleich für Euer Pferd sorgen." Karl trat ins Gastzimmer, wo er im schwachen Licht zweier Kerzen [3] die alten Stühle und Bänke wiedererkannte. Er setzte sich an einen der Tische, und da kam auch schon seine Mutter herein und brachte eine Lampe, die sie vor ihn auf den Tisch stellte. „Frau Wirtin," sagte er und senkte den Kopf, als ob sie ihn wiedererkennen könnte, „falls es Euch nicht zu viel Mühe [4] macht, möchte ich gern etwas zu essen haben!"

Die alte gebückte Frau ging schweigend in die Küche und kehrte bald mit Brot, Butter, Schinken [5] und einem Kruge [6] Milch zurück. Es war derselbe Zinnkrug, in dem er manchmal einem Gaste Wein gebracht hatte.

„Ist kein feuriger Italiener in dem Krug?" fragte er scherzend,[7] aber die alte Frau starrte ihn nur verständnislos [8] an. „Das ist alles, was wir im Hause haben, Herr," sagte sie unfreundlich. „Es ist gut," sagte Karl. „Morgen könnt Ihr Wein im Dorfe kaufen."

„Kommt, Herr Wirt, setzt Euch zu uns! Ich möchte nicht alleine essen!" rief er dem Alten zu, der wieder ins Zimmer getreten war. Schweigend saßen die beiden alten Leute an Karls Tische und sahen vor sich hin. Vorsichtig begann Karl, auf den Zinnkrug zeigend: „Als ich ein Kind war, habe ich genau so einen Krug gesehen. Der Griff endete in einen Schlangenkopf. Als Kind habe ich oft meine Freude daran gehabt."[9] Er nahm die Lampe und rückte [10] sie nah an den Krug heran. „Das ist doch seltsam, dies ist derselbe Krug, an den ich mich erinnere." „Es wird wohl mehr Krüge dieser Art in der Welt geben," sagte der Alte, indem er in das dunkle Gastzimmer starrte.

Karl schwieg eine Weile, dann fragte er: „Lebt Ihr hier ganz alleine? Habt Ihr keine Kinder, keinen Sohn, der Euch helfen könnte?" Der Wirt blickte auf: „Wir hatten einen Sohn, einen faulen Taugenichts,[11] der weder im Hause noch auf dem Felde zu gebrauchen war. Eines Tages ist er uns davongelaufen, und wir haben nie wieder von ihm gehört. Wahrscheinlich haben sie ihn schon längst gehängt." „Glaubt Ihr das auch?" wandte [12] sich Karl an die Alte. „Ich weiß nicht, was aus ihm geworden ist. Es kümmert mich auch nicht." Karl aß schweigend den Rest seines Abendbrotes. „Zeigt mir die Kammer," [13] sagte er dann, „ich möchte zu Bett gehen." „Erst müßt Ihr zahlen, Herr," sagte der Alte unfreundlich. „Ich habe keinen Kredit im Dorf, außerdem sind wir alt und schwach, und wenn ihr morgen früh fortreitet, ohne zu zahlen, können wir es nicht hindern." [14]

Karl stand auf, nahm seinen Geldbeutel aus der Tasche und legte ein Goldstück [15] auf den Tisch. „Das ist für die Mahlzeit." „Dank, o Dank Herr," stammelte [16]

*1 freilich, *certainly.* *2 bequem, *comfortable.* [3] die Kerze, —, –n, *candle.* *4 die Mühe, *trouble.* [5] der Schinken, –s, —, *ham.* [6] der Krug, –es, ⸗e, *pitcher.* [7] scherzend, *jovially.* [8] verständnislos, *uncomprehending.* [9] ich habe oft meine Freude daran gehabt, *I have often taken pleasure in it.* [10] rücken, *move.* [11] der Taugenichts, *good-for-nothing.* *12 sich wenden, wandte, gewandt, *turn.* [13] die Kammer, —, –n, *room.* *14 hindern, *prevent.* [15] das Goldstück, –es, –e, *gold coin.* [16] stammeln, *stammer.*

der Alte und ſteckte das Goldſtück ſchnell in die Taſche. „Seid ſo gütig [1] und folgt mir!“ Er führte ihn in die Bodenkammer,[2] in der Karl als Junge geſchlafen hatte. Es war der einzige Raum, der für Gäſte hergerichtet [3] war. Mit tiefen Verbeugungen [4] verließ ihn der Wirt und wünſchte ihm eine gute Nacht.

Karl war zu traurig, um ſchlafen zu können. Seine Eltern waren dieſelben geblieben und hatten in all den Jahren nur mit Bitterkeit [5] an ihn gedacht. Er hätte ebenſogut [6] tot ſein können.

Er legte ſich in ſeinen Kleidern aufs Bett und dachte über ſeine Jugend [7] und ſein ſeltſames Leben nach.

Auch die Alten konnten nicht ſchlafen. Aufgeregt beſahen [8] ſie das Goldſtück und rieten, wer der reiche Fremde ſein möge und wo er herkomme. „Offenbar will er nicht erkannt werden,“ flüſterte der Alte. „Würde er ſonſt ohne Diener reiſen? Würde er in einem ärmlichen [9] Wirtshaus wie dem unſeren übernachten,[10] wenn er ein reines [11] Gewiſſen [12] hätte?“ „Er ſieht nicht danach aus,[13] als ob er das Geld geſtohlen hätte,“ flüſterte die Alte zurück, „aber ein Jammer [14] iſt es doch. Wir haben in unſerem Leben nichts als [15] Mühe und Arbeit gekannt, und ſo ein reicher Herr kann in der Welt herumreiſen, für ein paar Schinkenbrote,[16] ein Glas Milch und eine Nachtherberge [17] ein Goldſtück ausgeben und ſich für die Abenteuer [18] des kommenden Tages ausſchlafen.[19] Nein, es gibt keine Gerechtigkeit [20] in der Welt!“ Sie ſchwieg. Ihre Augen leuchteten [21] ſeltſam im Licht der Kerzen. „Woran denkſt du, Frau?“ fragte der Alte. „An die Ungerechtigkeit in der Welt. Der eine muß für jeden Pfennig arbeiten, der andere kann Goldſtücke wegwerfen.“ — „Ja,“ ſagte der Alte, „du ſollteſt ſein Pferd ſehen! Das iſt unter Brüdern hundert Taler wert!“ Die Frau legte ihm plötzlich die Hand auf den Mund. „Du ſprichſt zu laut,“ flüſterte ſie. „Der Herr muß ſich vom Nichtstun [22] ausruhen.“ Sie rückte näher an ihren Mann heran und wiſperte: „Der weiß ja gar nicht, wieviel Geld er bei ſich hat. Auf ein paar Goldſtücke mehr oder weniger kommt es ſo einem Reichen nicht an.[23] Jetzt wo er ſchläft, ſollte es doch leicht ſein. Wacht er auf, ſo kannſt du ſagen: Gnädiger Herr,[24] ich wollte nachſehen, ob Ihr warm genug ſeid. Ja, ſo kannſt du es machen. Geh mit der Wolldecke [25] in ſein Zimmer, der Beutel wird ſicher auf ſeinen Kleidern liegen.“

Dem Alten ſchien alles nicht ſo einfach zu ſein wie ſeiner Frau; er brummte etwas von Diebſtahl, und wenn der Herr ihn faßte und dem Gerichte überlieferte, dann

*1 gütig, *kind.* 2 die Bodenkammer, —, -n, *attic room.* 3 herrichten, *prepare.* 4 die Verbeugung, —, -en, *bow.* 5 die Bitterkeit, *bitterness.* *6 ebenſogut, *just as well.* *7 die Jugend, —, *youth.* *8 beſehen, a, e, *look at, examine.* 9 ärmlich, *poor, miserable.* 10 übernachten, *spend the night.* *11 rein, *clear.* *12 das Gewiſſen, -s, *conscience.* *13 Er ſieht nicht danach aus, *he doesn't look it.* 14 der Jammer, -s, *pity.* *15 nichts als, *nothing but.* 16 das Schinkenbrot, -es, -e, *ham sandwich.* 17 die Nachtherberge, *night's lodging.* *18 das Abenteuer, -s, —, *adventure.* 19 ſich ausſchlafen, ie, a, *sleep one's fill.* *20 die Gerechtigkeit, *justice.* 21 leuchten, *glisten.* 22 das Nichtstun, *doing nothing.* 23 auf ein paar Goldſtücke kommt es nicht an, *a few gold coins are of no consequence.* 24 Gnädiger Herr, *Sir.* Gnädig means *gracious;* it is not translated when used with Herr, Frau, or Fräulein. 25 die Wolldecke, —, -n, *blanket.*

könnte es ihm ſchlimm gehen. Aber ſeine Frau redete ihm zu,[1] und als ſie ſchließlich ſagte, wenn er ſo ein elender Feigling wäre, dann wollte ſie es ſelber tun, beſchloß er, es zu wagen.

So ſchlich er denn mit einer Decke in der einen und einer Laterne in der anderen Hand die Treppe hinauf. Lange lauſchte er an der Tür der Schlafkammer, aber drinnen [2] war alles ſtill. Jetzt öffnete er die unverſchloſſene Tür und wartete wieder. Er hörte die tiefen regelmäßigen [3] Atemzüge des Mannes auf dem Bette. Karl hatte ihn kommen hören und, auf das Schlimmſte gefaßt,[4] die Hand am Dolch, tat er, als ob er ſchliefe.

Der Alte wartete ſehr lange, dann leuchtete [5] er vorſichtig mit der Laterne in die Kammer. Der Gaſt lag auf dem Rücken, ſeine Bruſt hob und ſenkte ſich, ſein Mund war etwas geöffnet. Auf einem Stuhl neben dem Bett lagen der Mantel und der Hut des Fremden und daneben der Geldbeutel.

Der Alte hatte genug geſehen. Er ſtellte die Laterne draußen vor die Tür. Dann trat er in die Schlafkammer und machte die Tür hinter ſich halb zu. Wieder wartete er, aber nichts regte ſich. Langſam legte er ſich auf den Boden [6] und kroch dann, auf dem Bauche [7] liegend, auf den Stuhl zu. Vorſichtig fühlte er mit der Hand am Stuhl entlang [8] über die Kleider, bis er den Beutel fand.

Er öffnete die Schnur [9] und griff hinein.[10] Lautlos [11] nahm er einige Goldſtücke heraus, legte ſie auf die Decke, die er vor ſich liegen hatte, und machte wieder einen Knoten [12] in die Schnur. Dann kroch er, die Goldſtücke in der einen, die Decke in der anderen Hand, vorſichtig zur Tür zurück. Da ſprang Karl vom Bett, war mit einem Satz [13] an der Tür und hielt dem zu Tode erſchrockenen Alten die Laterne ins Geſicht. Der ſaß halb aufgerichtet auf dem Boden und hielt beide Hände flehend [14] ausgeſtreckt.[15] Sein zahnloſer Mund zitterte, als er kaum verſtändlich wimmerte [16]: „Gnade, Herr, Gnade! Hier iſt das Geld, das ich aus Eurem Beutel genommen habe. Nie in meinem Leben habe ich Gäſte beſtohlen.[17] Wenn meine Frau nicht — "

„Schon gut, Alter," fiel ihm Karl ins Wort, „ich bin auch zum Teil [18] ſchuld daran.[19] Ich hätte Euch den vollen Geldbeutel nicht zeigen und Euch dadurch nicht in Verſuchung führen ſollen. Geht, es iſt ſchon ſpät, und ich bin todmüde. Damit Ihr Euch von eurem Schrecken [20] erholt, nehmt den ganzen Beutel mit, der Euch ſo verblendet [21] hat."

Mit dieſen Worten drückte [22] er dem Greiſe den Beutel in die Hand und ſchob ihn zur Tür hinaus. Draußen gab er ihm auch noch die Laterne und ſagte: „Vorſicht, die Treppe iſt ſteil," [23] und Eure Knie [24] zittern! Sattelt [25] morgen früh mein Pferd,

[1] zureden, *urge.* *[2] drinnen, *inside.* *[3] regelmäßig, *regular.* [4] gefaßt ſein, *be prepared.* [5] leuchten, *light.* *[6] der Boden, –s, ¨, *floor.* [7] der Bauch, –es, ¨e, *belly.* [8] entlang, *along.* [9] die Schnur, —, –en, *string, cord.* [10] hineingreifen, i, i, *reach inside.* [11] lautlos, *silent, without making a sound.* [12] der Knoten, –s, —, *knot.* [13] der Satz, –es, ¨e, *leap.* *[14] flehend, *imploring.* [15] ausſtrecken, *stretch out.* [16] wimmern, *whimper.* [17] beſtehlen, a, o, *rob.* *[18] zum Teil, *in part.* *[19] ſchuld ſein an, *be guilty.* *[20] der Schrecken, –s, *fright.* [21] verblenden, *blind.* *[22] drücken, *press.* *[23] ſteil, *steep.* *[24] das Knie, –s, —, *knee.* [25] ſatteln, *saddle.*

ich werde ſchon ſehr früh weiterreiten." Er ſchloß die Tür und horchte. Der Alte ſtand eine Weile ſchwer atmend an der Treppe, dann ging er langſam und laut ſchluchzend die Stufen hinab.

Karl legte ſich wieder auf das Bett, er verſuchte über alles nachzudenken, was eben geſchehen war, aber er war zu müde. Seine Gedanken verwirrten ſich,[1] und bald war er eingeſchlafen.

Er ſchlief lange und tief. Als er aufwachte, ſtand die Sonne ſchon hoch am Himmel. Schnell ſprang er auf, warf ſeinen Mantel über, ſetzte ſich den Hut auf [2] und ging leiſe die Treppe hinab. Draußen im Hof ſah er ſein Pferd geſattelt und reiſefertig. Er band das Tier los [3] und ſtieg auf.[4] Die Alten kamen aus der Haustür gelaufen und riefen etwas. Er hörte es nicht. Er hatte ſeinem Pferd ſcharf die Sporen [5] gegeben, daß es ſich wild aufbäumte [6] und fortgaloppierte. Er erreichte bald den Gipfel des Berges. Ohne ſich umzuſehen, gab er dem Pferd wieder die Sporen und im Galopp ritt er die Landſtraße nach Bertendorf entlang. Vor dem Gaſthof empfingen ihn ſeine Diener mit freudigen Geſichtern. Er blieb ernſt. „Macht Euch fertig, wir reiſen nach Bayern zurück!" Das war alles, was er ihnen zu ſagen hatte. Er ging auf ſein Zimmer, und die Draußenſtehenden hörten ihn ſeufzend auf und ab gehen. Bald darauf kam er aus dem Hauſe. In der Hand trug er einen gefüllten Geldbeutel. Niemand wagte eine Frage an ihn zu richten,[7] denn er ſah blaß und bekümmert [8] aus.

Statt in den Wagen zu ſteigen, ging er zum Pfarrhaus. Dort ſagte man ihm, daß der Herr Pfarrer gerade nach dem Wirtshaus am Berge abgefahren wäre. Falls der Herr ihm nachreite,[9] werde er ihn leicht einholen.[10] „Das iſt nicht nötig," antwortete Karl. „Der Beſuch, den der Herr Pfarrer machen will, iſt wichtiger als alles, was ich ihm zu ſagen habe. Gebt ihm dies Geld für ſeine Kirche [11] und ſagt ihm, ich dankte ihm für alles." Er grüßte [12] und ging langſam die enge Dorfſtraße hinauf, an deren Ende der Wagen auf ihn wartete.

A. Practice Sentences:

1. Als ſie eintrat, waren die Arbeiter dabei, einen alten Kaſten auszugraben.
2. Der Knecht kam nun gelaufen und wollte alles mit anſehen.
3. Seine größte Freude hatte er an ſeinen Roſen.
4. Es ſieht danach aus, als ob in ſeiner Abweſenheit jemand in dem Haus gewohnt hätte.
5. Das Leſen fiel ihm ſchwer.
6. Er iſt ſchon längſt hier.
7. Es bleibt dabei: Du machſt dich auf den Weg nach Bubikon, und ich bleibe zu Hauſe.

[1] ſich verwirren, *become confused.* [2] aufſetzen, *put on.* [3] losbinden, a, u, *untie.* [4] aufſteigen, ie, ie (iſt), *mount.* [5] der Sporn, –s, Sporen, *spur.* [6] aufbäumen, *rear up.* *[7] richten, *direct;* eine Frage richten, *ask a question.* *[8] bekümmert, *grieved.* [9] nachreiten, i, i (iſt), *ride after, follow.* [10] einholen, *catch up with.* *[11] die Kirche, —, –n, *church.* *[12] grüßen, *greet.*

8. „Das Mädchen macht mir nichts als Sorgen," sagte Frau Schneider und seufzte tief.
9. Gestern früh ist sie um fünf Uhr aufgestanden, was sie sonst nie tut.
10. Man sollte denken, es stimmt da etwas nicht.
11. Es kommt mir nicht darauf an, ob du dableibst oder weggehst.
12. Vor Gericht tat er, als ob er nichts davon wüßte.
13. Kümmern Sie sich gefälligst nicht um meine Angelegenheiten!
14. Schon gut! Ich weiß ganz genau, was ich tun und lassen soll.
15. Er ließ die Kornsäcke auf den Wagen laden und in die Scheune fahren.

B. Securing the Vocabulary:

1. so
   sobald
   sodaß
   sofort
   sogar
   sogleich
   solange
   soviel . . . wie
   sowie
   sowieso
2. die Decke
   der Deckel
   die Deckung
   bedecken
   entdecken
   die Entdeckung
3. bauen
   der Bauer
   der Bauernhof
   der Bauernjunge
   das Bauernpferd
   die Baukosten (pl.)
   das Gebäude
   einbauen
4. sitzen
   der Sitz
   die Sitzung
   besitzen
   der Besitz
   der Besitzer
   das Besitztum
5. sehen
   das Gesicht
   der Gesichtspunkt
   sichtbar
   die Vorsicht
   vorsichtig
   aussehen
   die Aussicht
   (sich) ansehen
   einsehen
   besehen
6. suchen
   besuchen
   der Besuch
   der Besucher
   versuchen
   der Versuch
   die Versuchung
   sich aussuchen
7. der Tag
   täglich
   der Mittag
   der Nachmittag
   tagelang
   die Tagereise
8. stehen
   stehenbleiben
   aufstehen
   bestehen
   gestehen
   verstehen
   verständlich
   das Verständnis
   verständnislos
   anständig
9. sorgen
   sorgfältig
   sorgenfrei
   sorgenvoll
   besorgt
10. sich fürchten
    die Furcht
    furchtbar

Dreißigste Aufgabe

* * * \

ein Opfer nach dem anderen überfällt.[1] Nicht einmal den Namen des Ermordeten [2] wissen Sie, Lafalle! Zum Teufel,[3] was kann ich tun, wenn ich so unfähige [4] Helfer habe! — Hier ist ein Bericht, der morgen an den König geschickt werden soll. Ich muß ihn sogleich verbessern [5] und seiner Majestät berichten, daß vom Januar bis zum Oktober des Jahres 1680 siebzehn junge Kavaliere auf dieselbe Weise [6] ermordet worden sind, und zwar drei im Monat Oktober. — Wie oft habe ich Ihnen, meine Herren, befohlen,[7] Spione herumzuschicken, um ausfindig zu machen, wann junge Kavaliere nachts mit Schmuckstücken zu ihrem Rendezvous gehen, ihnen zu folgen und jeden Verdächtigen zu verhaften,[8] der sich spät abends auf der Straße herumtreibt!" [9]

„Aber alle Ihre Befehle [10] sind genau ausgeführt [11] worden, Herr Präsident! Darf ich Sie daran erinnern, daß ich selbst einmal dem Mörder oder einem seiner Helfer auf der Spur [12] war? Nicht dreißig Schritte von mir entfernt, entfloh er durch die Gassen des linken Seineufers.[13] Ich hätte ihn erwischt,[14] wenn er nicht plötzlich im Nebel [15] verschwunden wäre, als ob die Erde ihn verschlungen hätte."

„O ja, ich erinnere mich an Ihre Heldentat,[16] Lafalle. Ganz Paris sang mit den Straßensängern die hübsche Ballade von der tapferen [17] Polizei und ihrer Jagd auf Nachtgespenster,[18] die in die Erde versinken oder durch Mauern verschwinden können. Wenn ich mich nicht irre, kostete Sie diese Gespensterjagd Ihre Beförderung,[19] nicht wahr, Herr Lafalle?"

Der junge Offizier wurde rot, aber ehe er etwas antworten konnte, fuhr Desgrais fort: „Und nun, mein lieber Lafalle, werden wir den Rest der Nacht damit zubringen,[20] dieses neue Verbrechen richtig zu untersuchen und vor allem [21] festzustellen, wer der Ermordete ist. Vielleicht lernen selbst [22] Sie auf diese Weise ein paar elementare Regeln [23] Ihres Berufes."

Desgrais hatte nicht geprahlt.[24] Noch vor Tagesanbruch [25] gelang es ihm, den Namen des ermordeten Kavaliers ausfindig zu machen, so daß er ihn in den Bericht an den König einverleiben [26] konnte.

König Ludwig war in schlechter Stimmung, als er den Bericht seines höchsten Polizeibeamten [27] erhielt, denn es war ihm schon ein anderes Dokument überreicht [28] worden, das ihn in sehr liebenswürdiger Weise darauf aufmerksam machte,[29] wie hilflos seine Pariser Polizei gegen diese dauernden Raubmorde war.

[1] überfallen, ie, a, *attack.* [2] der Ermordete, –n, –n, *murdered person.* [3] Zum Teufel! *The deuce!* *[4] unfähig, *incapable, incompetent.* *[5] verbessern, *improve, amend.* *[6] die Weise, *way, manner.* *[7] befehlen, a, o, *order, command.* [8] verhaften, *arrest.* [9] sich herumtreiben, ie, ie, *loiter about.* *[10] der Befehl, –s, –e, *order.* *[11] ausführen, *carry out.* *[12] die Spur, —, –en, *track.* [13] das Seineufer, –s, —, *bank of the river Seine.* [14] erwischen, *catch.* *[15] der Nebel, –s, —, *fog.* [16] die Heldentat, —, –en, *heroic deed.* *[17] tapfer, *brave.* [18] das Nachtgespenst, –es, –er, *phantom of the night.* [19] die Beförderung, —, –en, *promotion.* *[20] zubringen, brachte zu, zugebracht, *spend.* *[21] vor allem, *above all.* *[22] selbst, *even; himself.* Observe position and meaning of selbst: selbst Sie, *even you;* Sie selbst, *you yourself.* *[23] die Regel, —, –n, *rule.* [24] prahlen, *boast.* [25] der Tagesanbruch, –s, ⸗e, *daybreak.* [26] einverleiben, *incorporate.* [27] der Polizeibeamte, –n, –n, *police official.* [28] überreichen, *hand.* [29] das ihn darauf aufmerksam machte, *which called his attention to the fact.*

Dieſes Dokument war eine in Verſen und durchaus nicht ohne Witz [1] geſchriebene Bittſchrift,[2] in der ſich die berühmteſten Kavaliere ſeines Hofes darüber beſchwerten, daß des Königs ſchöne Hauptſtadt [3] für ſie zu einer Räuberhöhle [4] geworden ſei. Ein Kavalier, der der Dame ſeines Herzens zu ſpäter Stunde einen Beſuch machen wolle, begebe ſich dabei in Lebensgefahr,[5] falls er ein Schmuckſtück bei ſich hätte. Nun ſei es zwar eine Ehre [6] und ein Vergnügen [7] für den großen König ſein Leben zu opfern,[8] aber niemand könne von einem Kavalier erwarten, daß er ſich bei jedem nächtlichen [9] Spaziergang [10] der Gefahr ausſetze,[11] das nächſte Opfer dieſer Mörderbande zu werden, deren Gier [12] nach Juwelen ebenſogroß zu ſein ſcheine wie ihr Haß auf Kavaliere. Da ſelbſt Desgrais vollkommen verſagt [13] hätte, bäten die Kavaliere den König, ſie zu ſchützen [14] und, falls nötig, Truppen nach Paris zu ſchicken.

Ludwig XIV. war ein Liebhaber [15] der Dichtkunſt,[16] und dieſe witzige [17] Bittſchrift hatte Eindruck auf ihn gemacht. Er las ſie dem Kreiſe der Damen und Herren vor, die an dieſem Nachmittag anweſend [18] waren, und bat um Vorſchläge,[19] was in dieſem ſonderbaren Fall getan werden könnte. Alle ſchwiegen, denn alles, was ſich zum Schutze der bedrohten Kavaliere hätte tun laſſen,[20] war von Desgrais ſchon längſt verſucht worden.

Der König blickte über die Gruppe der vornehmen Damen und Herren und entdeckte das alte Fräulein von Scudery, die in der Nähe des Kamines [21] ſaß und ſtill vor ſich hin lächelte. Das Fräulein war eine literariſche Berühmtheit,[22] was [23] im Paris dieſer Zeit viel bedeutete.

Dem König war ſie beſonders lieb [24] wegen ihres feinen Witzes, mit dem ſie die Hofgeſellſchaft ſchon oft unterhalten [25] hatte. Er trat vor ſie hin und fragte: „Nun, mein Fräulein, was halten Sie von dieſer dichteriſchen [26] Bittſchrift?"

Das alte Fräulein ſtand reſpektvoll auf, und nach einem Augenblick ſchweigenden Nachdenkens ſagte ſie ſich verneigend [27]:

„Ein Liebender, der Diebe fürchtet,
Verdient das Glück der Liebe nicht."

Der König war erſtaunt über den ritterlichen [28] Geiſt [29] dieſer wenigen Worte, die das ganze Gedicht [30] der Kavaliere mit ſeinen langen Tiraden zu Boden ſchlugen, und rief mit blitzenden [31] Augen: „Sie haben recht, Fräulein. Wir werden die Ängſt-

*1 der Witz, -es, *wit, esprit.* 2 die Bittſchrift, —, -en, *petition.* *3 die Hauptſtadt, —, ¨-e, *capital.* 4 die Räuberhöhle, —, -n, *den of robbers.* 5 begebe ſich dabei in Lebensgefahr, *runs the risk of losing his life.* *6 die Ehre, —, -n, *honor.* *7 das Vergnügen, -s, *pleasure.* *8 opfern, *sacrifice.* *9 nächtlich, *nightly.* *10 der Spaziergang, -es, ¨-e, *walk.* 11 ſich ausſetzen, *expose oneself.* 12 die Gier, —, *greediness.* 13 verſagen, *fail.* *14 ſchützen, *protect.* 15 der Liebhaber, -s, —, *lover.* *16 die Dichtkunſt, —, *poetry.* 17 witzig, *witty.* *18 anweſend, *present.* *19 der Vorſchlag, -es, ¨-e, *suggestion.* *20 was ſich hätte tun laſſen, *that could have been done.* 21 der Kamin, -es, -e, *fireplace.* *22 die Berühmtheit, —, -en, *celebrity.* *23 was, *something which.* 24 Dem König war ſie beſonders lieb. *The king was especially fond of her.* *25 unterhalten, ie, a, *entertain.* *26 dichteriſch, *poetic.* *27 ſich verneigen, *bow.* 28 ritterlich, *knightly, chivalrous.* *29 der Geiſt, -es, -er, *spirit.* *30 das Gedicht, -es, -e, *poem.* 31 blitzend, *flashing.*

lichen [1] nicht schützen. Desgrais' Schutz muß genug für sie sein, wenn sie sich nicht selber verteidigen [2] können."

Einige Tage waren seit dieser kleinen Episode im Versailler Schloß vergangen. Es war tief in der Nacht; das Fräulein von Scudery hatte gerade mit der Arbeit an einem Romanmanuskript aufgehört und wollte zu Bett gehen, als sie heftiges Klopfen an ihrer Haustür hörte. Nun war gerade in dieser Nacht nur ihre alte Dienerin Mathilde bei ihr, denn Theophile, ihr Diener, hatte Urlaub, um bei der Hochzeit [3] seiner Schwester anwesend sein zu können. Das alte Fräulein konnte sich nicht denken,[4] wer der späte Besucher sein möchte, schickte aber dennoch [5] ihre Dienerin ans Fenster.

Als Mathilde das Fenster öffnete, hörte das Fräulein die Stimme eines jungen Mannes unten auf der Straße: „Um aller Heiligen willen,[6] laß mich ins Haus, Alte, es handelt sich um Leben und Tod.[7] Ich muß unbedingt deine Herrin [8] noch heute nacht [9] sprechen. Meinen Namen kann ich ihr leider noch nicht sagen."

Mathilde kam blaß vor Angst zu ihrer Herrin zurück. „Es ist ein junger Mensch in einem grauen Mantel," berichtete sie.

Das Klopfen begann wieder, diesmal lauter als vorher. Ehe die Scudery etwas sagen konnte, lief Mathilde ins Haus und rief: „Theophile, Pierre, Claude, steht auf und seht, wer der Taugenichts ist, der sich so viel Mühe gibt,[10] unsere Tür einzuschlagen! [11]

Der junge Mann rief hinauf: „Alte Mathilde, ich weiß ja, daß du mit deiner Herrin allein bist. Hab keine Angst, ich habe nichts Schlimmes vor! [12] Falls du aber die Tür nicht aufmachen willst, muß ich . . ." Der Jüngling [13] brach mitten im Satz ab und lauschte in die Dunkelheit. Jetzt hörte auch die Dienerin etwas. In der Ferne klapperten [14] Pferdehufe [15] über das Pflaster.[16] Desgrais' Leute machten ihre nächtliche Runde. „Hilfe, Hilfe! Räuber, Mörder! Hilfe, Hilfe!" schrie Mathilde so laut sie mit ihrer alten schwachen Stimme schreien konnte. Ihr Rufen verhallte [17] ungehört. Das Geräusch der Pferde entfernte [18] sich. Dem jungen Mann schien die Sache aber zu gefährlich zu werden. Mit einem grimmigen Fluch nahm er ein Kästchen,[19] das er unter dem Mantel verborgen [20] gehalten hatte, heraus und stieß es durch ein kleines Fensterchen neben der Tür, daß das zerbrochene Glas im Flur [21] auf den Boden klirrte.[22] „Gib das Kästchen deiner Herrin, es enthält Juwelen!" rief er, sprang mit großer Gewandtheit [23] über eine Mauer, hinter der ein leerer Bauplatz lag, und war in der Dunkelheit verschwunden.

Das Fräulein war neben ihre Dienerin getreten und hatte die Flucht des selt-

[1] der Ängstliche, –n, –n, *timid person.* *[2] sich verteidigen, *defend oneself.* [3] die Hochzeit, —, –en, *wedding.* *[4] sich denken, *imagine.* *[5] dennoch, *nevertheless.* [6] Um aller Heiligen willen! *By all that's holy!* *[7] es handelt sich um Leben und Tod, *it's a matter of life and death.* [8] die Herrin, —, –nen, *mistress.* *[9] heute nacht, *tonight.* [10] sich Mühe geben, a, e, *take pains, try hard.* [11] einschlagen, u, a, *break down.* [12] ich habe nichts Schlimmes vor, *I have no evil intentions.* [13] der Jüngling, –s, –e, *young man.* [14] klappern, *clatter.* [15] der Pferdehuf, –es, –e, *horse's hoof.* [16] das Pflaster, –s, —, *pavement.* [17] verhallen, *die away.* *[18] sich entfernen, *disappear.* [19] das Kästchen, –s, —, *small box, case.* *[20] verbergen, a, o, *hide.* [21] der Flur, –es, –e, *hall.* [22] klirren, *crash, clatter.* [23] die Gewandtheit, *agility.*

ſamen Fremden beobachtet. „Geh hinunter und hole das Käſtchen herauf!“ [1] befahl ſie. „Es möchte uns ſonſt vielleicht geſtohlen werden. Morgen können wir es dann in Ruhe unterſuchen.“ Sie ſah ihre Dienerin an und bemerkte, wie blaß und aufgeregt ſie war. „Nun,“ fügte ſie hinzu,[2] „vielleicht iſt es beſſer, wir ſehen uns den Inhalt [3] des Käſtchens gleich jetzt [4] an, ſonſt könnten uns Angſt und Neugier [5] am Einſchlafen hindern.“

Während Mathilde mit zitternder Hand die Lampe trug, brachte die Scudery das Käſtchen in ihr Schlafzimmer und öffnete es mit einem kleinen Schlüſſel, der mit einem Band an das Käſtchen gebunden war. Ein goldenes, reich mit Juwelen beſetztes [6] Armband,[7] ein Halsband und Ohrringe funkelten [8] im Lampenlicht. Das alte Fräulein nahm die Schmuckſtücke mit Ausrufen [9] der Bewunderung in die Hand und zeigte ſie der vor Erſtaunen ſprachloſen Mathilde. Auf dem Boden des Käſtchens lag ein Brief mit der Anſchrift „Dem Fräulein von Scudery.“ Haſtig öffnete die alte Dame den Umſchlag [10] und las den wenige Zeilen enthaltenden Inhalt. Sie wurde ſchwach und mußte ſich auf den Tiſch lehnen. „Was iſt Ihnen, gnädiges Fräulein?“ rief Mathilde erſchrocken. Mit zitternden Lippen las das Fräulein vor:

Ein Liebender, der Diebe fürchtet,
Verdient das Glück der Liebe nicht.

Empfangen Sie dieſe Schmuckſachen, liebes Fräulein, zum Zeichen, daß wir Ihnen für Ihren Schutz dankbar ſind.

Ein Bewunderer

Sie warf den Brief auf den Tiſch und weinte. „Warum habe ich es verdient, daß Räuber und Mörder mich verhöhnen [11] oder mich zu ihresgleichen rechnen?“ [12] Das Lampenlicht, das auf die Edelſteine ſchien, gab ihnen ein rotes Feuer, ſo daß ſie wie Blutstropfen [13] ausſahen. Das Fräulein warf die Juwelen in das Käſtchen zurück und ſchickte Mathilde zu Bett.

Sie ſelbſt blieb die ganze Nacht auf,[14] und als am nächſten Morgen die Zeit für Beſuche herankam, ſchickte ſie Theophile nach einem Tragſeſſel [15] aus und ließ ſich zu ihrer Freundin, der Marquiſe de Maintenon, bringen.

Die Marquiſe war überraſcht und beſorgt, als ſie ihre ſonſt ſo würdevolle [16] Freundin aufgeregt und blaß ins Zimmer kommen ſah. Das Fräulein atmete ſchwer und war kaum imſtande [17] ihrer Freundin zu erzählen, wie ſehr ſie die Frechheit der Räuber erſchüttert hätte, und klagte darüber, daß ſie für den kleinen Scherz,[18] mit dem ſie die Bittſchrift der Kavaliere beantwortet hatte, ſchwer beſtraft [19] würde.

[1] heraufholen, *bring upstairs.* [2] hinzufügen, *add.* *[3] der Inhalt, –es, *contents.* *[4] gleich jetzt, *right now.* *[5] die Neugier, *curiosity.* [6] beſetzt, *studded.* [7] das Armband, –es, ⸗er, *bracelet.* [8] funkeln, *sparkle.* [9] der Ausruf, –es, –e, *exclamation.* [10] der Umſchlag, –es, ⸗e, *envelope.* [11] verhöhnen, *mock, deride.* [12] mich zu ihresgleichen rechnen, *class me as one of their kind.* [13] der Blutstropfen, –s, —, *drop of blood.* [14] aufbleiben, ie, ie, (iſt), *stay up.* [15] der Tragſeſſel, –s, —, *sedan chair.* [16] würdevoll, *dignified.* *[17] imſtande ſein, *be capable (of).* *[18] der Scherz, –es, –e, *joke, jest.* *[19] beſtrafen, *punish.*

Die Marquiſe war eine welterfahrene [1] Dame und ſchien wenig geneigt,[2] die ernſten Beſorgniſſe [3] des Fräuleins zu teilen.[4] Sie tröſtete ihre Freundin und ſagte ſcherzhaft,[5] daß ſie vielleicht trotz ihres vorgerückten [6] Alters [7] einen Bewunderer gefunden hätte, der ſeine Anonymität allerdings mit wenig Geſchmack verkleide,[8] und verlangte ſchließlich, die Juwelen zu ſehen. Mit einem lauten Ausruf der Bewunderung nahm ſie die Juwelen aus dem Käſtchen und trat ans Fenſter, um bald [9] die Edelſteine in der Sonne glitzern [10] zu laſſen, bald die feine Arbeit nahe vor die Augen zu halten.

Plötzlich drehte ſie ſich um und rief dem Fräulein zu: „Wiſſen Sie, daß niemand anders [11] in Paris ſo ein Schmuckſtück anfertigen [12] kann als René Cardillac, der als der beſte Goldſchmied im ganzen Königreich gilt? Kein Zweifel, der Meiſter wird uns ſagen können, an wen er dieſen Schmuck verkauft hat.“ Sie klatſchte [13] in die Hände, ein Diener erſchien. „Robert, geh ſofort zur Werkſtatt [14] des Meiſters Cardillac — Pierre kennt die genaue Adreſſe — und ſag ihm, ich bäte ihn, auf einen Augenblick zu mir zu kommen, um einige Juwelen zu beurteilen.“ [15]

Nach kurzer Zeit trat Meiſter Cardillac ins Zimmer und verbeugte [16] ſich mit Zeichen ſichtbaren Erſtaunens vor dem Fräulein von Scudery, die ihn gar nicht gerufen hatte und die außerdem nicht die Dame des Hauſes war.

Das Fräulein betrachtete den Schmied erſtaunt, denn ſie hatte ihn noch nie [17] geſehen und konnte ſich ſein ſonderbares Benehmen [18] nicht erklären. Meiſter Cardillac war ein Mann in den Fünfzigern,[19] nicht groß, aber breitſchultrig und ſtark gebaut, deſſen blitzende Augen und friſche Geſichtsfarbe [20] ungewöhnliche geiſtige und körperliche [21] Energie verrieten.

Die Marquiſe, die er nun endlich begrüßte, zeigte ihm den Goldſchmuck [22] und fragte ihn, ob das eine Arbeit aus ſeiner Werkſtatt ſei. Der Meiſter warf nur einen flüchtigen [23] Blick auf das Geſchmeide [24] und ſagte mit ſtolzem Lächeln: „Ich glaube nicht, daß es noch einen anderen Meiſter in Frankreich gibt, der ſo eine Arbeit machen könnte. Ja, ich habe dieſe Sachen vor einiger Zeit zu meiner eigenen Freude angefertigt. Sie verſchwanden aber auf unbegreifliche [25] Weiſe aus meiner Werkſtatt.“

Nun konnte das Fräulein nicht länger ſchweigen, und ſie erzählte dem Meiſter die Umſtände, unter denen die Juwelen in ihre Hände geraten,[26] oder beſſer, ihr aufgezwungen [27] worden waren. Cardillac hörte alles ſchweigend an, während er mit den Fingern wie liebkoſend [28] über die goldenen Ketten [29] des vor ihm liegenden Hals-

[1] welterfahren, *experienced in the (ways of the) world, worldly-wise.* *[2] geneigt ſein, *be inclined.* [3] das Beſorgnis, . . .niſſes, . . .niſſe, *anxiety, apprehension.* *[4] teilen, *share.* [5] ſcherzhaft, *joking(ly).* [6] vorrücken (iſt), *advance.* [7] das Alter, –s, *age.* [8] verkleiden, *disguise.* *[9] bald . . . bald, *now . . . now.* [10] glitzern, *glisten.* *[11] niemand anders, *nobody else.* [12] anfertigen, *make.* [13] klatſchen, *clap.* [14] die Werkſtatt, —, ¨-e, *workshop.* [15] beurteilen, *evaluate.* [16] ſich verbeugen, *bow.* *[17] noch nie, *never (yet).* [18] das Benehmen, –s, *behavior.* [19] in den Fünfzigern, *in his fifties.* [20] die Geſichtsfarbe, —, *complexion.* [21] körperlich, *bodily, physical.* [22] der Goldſchmuck, –es, *golden ornament.* [23] flüchtig, *fleeting, casual.* [24] das Geſchmeide, –s, *set of jewelry, jewels.* [25] unbegreiflich, *inexplicable.* *[26] geraten, ie, a (iſt), *get* or *fall into.* [27] aufzwingen, a, u, *force upon.* [28] wie liebkoſend, *as though caressing them.* [29] die Kette, —, –n, *chain.*

bandes glitt.[1] Als das Fräulein geendet hatte, ſtand er auf, verneigte ſich und ſagte: „Das Schickſal [2] will offenbar, daß Sie die Juwelen behalten [3] ſollen. Tun Sie es, wenn ſie auch[4] durch böſe Hände gegangen ſind.“

Bei dieſen Worten war er aufgeſtanden, verbeugte ſich nochmals [5] und ging verwirrt, an Tiſche und Stühle ſtoßend, wieder aus dem Zimmer.

Die Scudery blickte dem ſonderbaren Mann erſchrocken und verwundert nach, aber die Marquiſe lachte. „Machen Sie ſich keine Sorgen wegen dieſes Menſchen, er iſt ein Künſtler,[6] und Sie wiſſen, wie wunderlich [7] die Künſtler in der Regel [8] ſind.“

So blieb das Schmuckkäſtchen im Beſitz des Fräuleins, die ſich nicht recht über dieſen Beſitz freuen konnte. Der Gedanke, daß es einſt in den blutigen Händen der Verbrecher geweſen war, und auch das ſonderbare Benehmen Meiſter Cardillacs machten es ihr unmöglich, die Juwelen zu tragen oder auch ſie zu verkaufen und ſo ihre beſcheidene Penſion beträchtlich [9] zu vermehren.[10] Es war [11] ihr immer, als ob das Käſtchen noch einmal zur Auflöſung [12] eines blutigen Geheimniſſes dienen [13] ſollte, und ſie es deshalb behalten müßte.

Mehrere Monate waren ſeit dieſer ſonderbaren Begegnung [14] mit Meiſter Cardillac vergangen, als Fräulein Scudery in der Glaskutſche [15] der Herzogin von Montaſier eine Spazierfahrt machte.[16] Glaskutſchen waren zu dieſer Zeit noch ziemlich unbekannt, und ſo wurde denn die Kutſche [17] überall von den Leuten angeſtaunt,[18] und mehr als einmal mußte der Kutſcher langſam fahren, wenn in einer der engeren Straßen die gaffenden [19] Fußgänger den Weg verſperrten. Beſonders ſchlimm wurde es aber, als ſie auf den Pont-Neuf kamen. Es war kurz vor Mittag, und im Nu [20] war eine ſo gewaltige [21] Menſchenmenge zuſammengeſtrömt, daß es dem Kutſcher unmöglich wurde weiterzufahren. Während er noch ſchimpfend und mit der Peitſche [22] knallend [23] verſuchte, ſeinen Pferden Raum zu machen, drängte [24] ſich ein junger Menſch ganz dicht an die Kutſche heran, riß die Tür auf und warf der Scudery einen Zettel in den Schoß.[25] Ehe das Fräulein ſich von ihrem Schrecken erholen konnte, hatte ſich der ſtattliche kräftige Jüngling einen Weg durch die Menge gebahnt [26] und war verſchwunden. Dieſer Zwiſchenfall [27] und das drohende [28] Peitſchengeknall des Kutſchers brachten Bewegung in die Menge. Die Pferde bäumten ſich und drängten vorwärts, und endlich konnte der Wagen weiterfahren.

Die alte Mathilde erzählte nun dem Fräulein, daß der junge Menſch, der den Zettel in den Wagen geworfen hatte, derſelbe geweſen ſei, der das Juwelenkäſtchen gebracht hatte. „Um Himmels willen, was hat dieſer fürchterliche [29] Menſch vor, was will er von Ihnen?“

[1] gleiten, i, i, (iſt), *glide.* *[2] das Schickſal, –s, –e, *fate.* *[3] behalten, ie, a, *keep.* *[4] wenn auch, *even if.* *[5] nochmals, *once more.* *[6] der Künſtler, –s, —, *artist.* *[7] wunderlich, *strange, eccentric.* *[8] in der Regel, *as a rule.* *[9] beträchtlich, *considerably.* *[10] vermehren, *increase.* *[11] es war ihr, als ob, *it seemed to her as if.* [12] die Auflöſung, —, –en, *solution.* *[13] dienen, *serve.* *[14] die Begegnung, —, –en, *meeting.* [15] die Glaskutſche, —, –n, *glass-enclosed carriage.* [16] eine Spazierfahrt machen, *be out driving.* *[17] die Kutſche, —, –n, *carriage.* [18] anſtaunen, *gaze at, stare at.* [19] gaffen, *gape, stare.* *[20] im Nu, *in no time.* [21] gewaltig, *vast.* [22] die Peitſche, —, –n, *whip.* [23] knallen, *crack.* [24] ſich drängen, *force one's way.* [25] der Schoß, –es, *lap.* [26] ſich bahnen, *make oneself (a path).* *[27] der Zwiſchenfall, –s, ⸗e, *incident.* *[28] drohen, *threaten, menace.* *[29] fürchterlich, *horrible.*

Jetzt erſt erinnerte ſich die Scudery an den Zettel; ſie entfaltete [1] ihn und las: Ich bitte Sie mit verzweifelndem [2] Herzen, ich bitte Sie wie ein Sohn die Mutter bittet, mißtrauen [3] Sie mir nicht! Geben Sie Meiſter René Cardillac die Juwelen, die ich in Ihr Haus brachte! Sagen Sie, er ſolle ſie umarbeiten,[4] ſagen Sie irgendetwas, nur bringen Sie ihm den Schmuck! Ihr Leben hängt davon ab.[5] Wenn Sie die Juwelen nicht zu Meiſter Cardillac bringen, ſtürzen Sie nicht nur ſich ſondern auch andere unſchuldige Menſchen ins Verderben.[6]

Das Fräulein ließ den Zettel in den Schoß fallen und ſaß lange ſchweigend da. Das Geſicht des jungen Menſchen hatte einen ſeltſamen Eindruck auf ſie gemacht. Es kam ihr bekannt vor, und doch konnte ſie ſich nicht daran erinnern, wann ſie es geſehen haben könnte. Schließlich ſeufzte ſie tief und ſagte, ſich zu ihrer Dienerin wendend: „Beruhige dich, Mathilde, der junge Menſch kann unmöglich zu einer Räuberbande gehören. Offenbar will er mich vor einer Gefahr ſchützen, an die ich ſelber zu glauben anfange, obwohl es mir ein Rätſel [7] iſt, von welcher Seite mir eine Gefahr drohen könne. Es ſcheint mir faſt, ich habe den jungen Mann ſchon einmal geſehen, aber das iſt ſchon lange her,[8] und es kann deshalb nicht dieſelbe Perſon ſein, denn dieſer Jüngling iſt ungefähr fünfundzwanzig Jahre alt. Ich wünſchte nun faſt, wir hätten ihn in jener [9] Nacht in unſer Haus gelaſſen. Vielleicht wäre dann das ganze Geheimnis ſchon jetzt aufgeklärt.[10] — Was es auch ſei, das dieſen jungen Menſchen zwingt, ſo ſeltſam zu handeln,[11] ich werde das Käſtchen ſchon morgen zu Meiſter Cardillac bringen."

Der nächſte Tag kam heran, aber Beſuche, die ſie empfangen und Beſuche, die ſie machen mußte, verhinderten das Fräulein daran, zu Cardillac zu gehen. Sie verſchob [12] deshalb den Beſuch auf den folgenden Tag. In der Nacht konnte ſie vor innerer Unruhe kaum ſchlafen. Immer wieder ſah ſie das bleiche [13] Geſicht des Jünglings vor ſich, der ſie ſo verzweifelt [14] um Hilfe gebeten hatte. Vielleicht war es ſchon zu ſpät!

Schon am frühen Morgen fuhr ſie, das Schmuckkäſtchen unter dem Arm, zum Goldſchmied Cardillac. Als ſie in die Nähe ſeines Hauſes kam, mußte der Wagen langſam fahren, denn eine aufgeregte Menſchenmenge drängte ſich in der engen Straße. Von ihrem Wagen aus ſah die Scudery, wie die Tür zur Goldſchmiedewerkſtatt plötzlich geöffnet wurde, und zwei Soldaten einen blutenden jungen Menſchen herausſchleppten, den die wütende Menge mit Fauſtſchlägen [15] und Fußtritten [16] mißhandelte [17] und den ſie erſchlagen hätte, wenn die Soldaten die Angreifer [18] nicht zurückgetrieben [19] hätten.

Obgleich [20] das Geſicht des Unglücklichen blutüberſtrömt war, erkannte die Scudery

[1] entfalten, *unfold.* *[2] verzweifeln, *despair.* *[3] mißtrauen, *mistrust.* [4] umarbeiten, *rework.* *[5] abhängen, i, a, *depend.* [6] ins Verderben ſtürzen, *plunge into destruction.* *[7] das Rätſel, –s, —, *riddle; puzzle.* *[8] es iſt ſchon lange her, *that was long ago.* *[9] jener, –e, –es, *that.* [10] aufklären, *clear up.* *[11] handeln, *act.* *[12] verſchieben, o, o, *postpone.* *[13] bleich, *pale.* *[14] verzweifelt, *desperately.* [15] der Fauſtſchlag, –es, ⸗e, *blow (with the fist).* [16] der Fußtritt, –es, –e, *kick.* *[17] mißhandeln, *abuse.* [18] der Angreifer, –s, —, *attacker.* [19] zurücktreiben, ie, ie, *drive back.* *[20] obgleich, *although.*

ihn wieder. Es war der Jüngling, der ihr den Zettel in den Wagen geworfen hatte.

Jetzt ſah ſie auch, daß Desgrais anweſend war. Neben ſeinem Pferd ſtehend, gab er den Soldaten Befehle und wollte gerade aufſteigen, als ſich ein junges Mädchen von einem Soldaten losriß [1] und Desgrais zu Füßen fiel. Sie umklammerte [2] die Knie des Polizeipräſidenten, der ärgerlich auf ſie niederſah, und wimmerte: „Er iſt unſchuldig, Exzellenz, ich ſchwöre es, er iſt unſchuldig! Ich weiß es doch, ich . . .“ Sie konnte vor Schluchzen [3] nicht weiterreden.

Desgrais winkte [4] einem großen Soldaten, der das Mädchen bei den Armen packte und ſie mit ſolcher Gewalt hochriß,[5] daß ſie gegen die Hauswand geſchleudert [6] wurde und ohnmächtig [7] zuſammenbrach.

Das konnte die Scudery nicht ertragen, ſie ſtieg aus ihrer Kutſche und ſchritt [8] durch die Menge, die der weißhaarigen Dame reſpektvoll Platz machte. Schon von weitem rief ſie: „Desgrais, warten Sie bitte! — Was iſt geſchehen? Erklären Sie mir dieſe rohe [9] Szene!“

Desgrais lächelte kalt und erklärte: „In dieſem Hauſe liegt René Cardillac tot, durch einen Dolchſtoß ermordet. Sein Geſelle, Olivier Bruſſon, der junge Burſche, deſſen Verhaftung Sie eben mitangeſehen [10] haben, iſt unter Verdacht. Wir haben ihn mit blutigen Kleidern bei der Leiche [11] Cardillacs gefunden; außerdem lag in ſeinem Zimmer der Dolch, deſſen Griff den Buchſtaben [12] „O“ trägt. Der Dolch war blutig und paßte genau in die Todeswunde.[13] Das weinende Mädchen, das offenbar Ihr Mitleid erweckt [14] hat, iſt Madelon, die Tochter des Ermordeten. Sie behauptet, der Geſelle Olivier Bruſſon ſei unſchuldig. Nun, wir werden das bald wiſſen.“

Das Fräulein bückte ſich zu Madelon, die mit dem Kopf im Schoß einer mitleidigen Nachbarin lag. Das feine Geſicht und die Schönheit [15] des Mädchens rührten [16] die Scudery. Sie blickte auf und ſah, wie der Jüngling abgeführt [17] wurde. Wenn ſie nur wüßte, warum er ihr ſo bekannt ſchien! Mit einem plötzlichen Entſchluß wandte ſie ſich zu Desgrais: „Exzellenz, laſſen Sie das Mädchen mit mir gehen! Ich übernehme volle Verantwortung [18] für ſie.“ Desgrais blickte die alte Dame erſtaunt an und antwortete nicht ſogleich. Der Vorſchlag gefiel ihm nicht,[19] aber er wußte, in wie hoher Gunſt [20] das Fräulein beim König ſtand; ſo ritt er mit einem kalten: „Wenn Sie es ſo wünſchen, mein Fräulein,“ davon.

So kam Madelon Cardillac in das Haus des Fräuleins von Scudery, wo ſie ſich in wenigen Tagen von der rohen Behandlung [21] durch Desgrais' Soldaten erholte.

[1] ſich losreißen, i, i, *break away.* [2] umklammern, *clasp.* [3] das Schluchzen, –s, *sobbing.* *[4] winken, *beckon; signal.* [5] hochreißen, i, i, *pull up, grasp.* [6] ſchleudern, *throw.* *[7] ohnmächtig, *unconscious.* *[8] ſchreiten, i, i (iſt), *step.* [9] roh, *brutal.* [10] mitanſehen, *witness.* [11] die Leiche, —, –n, *corpse.* *[12] der Buchſtabe, –n, –n, *letter (written character).* [13] die Todeswunde, —, –n, *mortal wound.* [14] erwecken, *awaken, arouse.* *[15] die Schönheit, *beauty.* [16] rühren, *move.* [17] abführen, *lead away.* *[18] die Verantwortung, *responsibility.* *[19] Der Vorſchlag gefiel ihm nicht. *He did not like the proposal.* [20] die Gunſt, *favor, good graces.* *[21] die Behandlung, —, –en, *treatment.*

Das Fräulein, das Madelon ſelber gepflegt hatte, wartete, bis ihr Schützling [1] von ſelber [2] ſprechen wollte. Sie brauchte nicht lange zu warten. Am vierten Tage erlaubte der Arzt Madelon, das Bett zu verlaſſen, und als ſie von Mathilde geführt in den Salon [3] des Fräuleins trat, waren ihre erſten Worte: „Bitte, verehrtes [4] Fräulein, hören Sie von mir, was ſich in der furchtbaren Nacht ereignet [5] hatte. Ich könnte den Gedanken nicht ertragen, wenn Sie glauben müßten, eine Unwürdige [6] in Ihr Haus genommen zu haben."

Das Fräulein ſetzte ſich neben ſie auf das Sofa und verſicherte [7] dem Mädchen, daß ſie unerſchütterliches [8] Vertrauen [9] zu ihr hätte, und Madelon begann zu erzählen:

„Mein Vater pflegte früh zu Bett zu gehen, aber manchmal, wenn er eine dringende [10] Arbeit fertigzuſtellen [11] hatte, blieb er bis in die frühen Morgenſtunden auf. Am Abend ſeines Todes ſagte er, ich ſolle zu Bett gehen, er habe noch an einer wichtigen Beſtellung [12] zu arbeiten und werde vielleicht die ganze Nacht aufbleiben müſſen. Kurz nach Mitternacht wachte ich davon auf, daß Olivier an meine Tür klopfte und mir zurief, ich ſolle mich ſchnell anziehen und in meines Vaters Schlafzimmer kommen, mein Vater liege im Sterben." [13] Tränen kamen in Madelons Augen, und trotz aller Troſtworte [14] des Fräuleins dauerte es eine Weile, bis ſie ſich ſo weit gefaßt [15] hatte, daß ſie weiterreden konnte.

„Als ich in das Schlafzimmer kam, ſah ich meinen Vater auf dem Bett liegen. Er war totenblaß,[16] und Blut tropfte aus einer Bruſtwunde, das Olivier vergeblich [17] zurückzuhalten [18] verſuchte. Ich ſchrie vor Entſetzen,[19] aber Olivier bat mich, ſtille zu ſein, damit die Nachbarn uns nicht hörten. Mein Vater war noch bei Bewußtſein. Als ich mich über ihn beugte, um ihn zu küſſen, lächelte er und faßte meine Hand. Dann nahm er Oliviers Hand und ſegnete uns mit ſchwacher Stimme. Kurz darauf ſtarb er in Oliviers Armen."

„Ich war außer mir vor Schmerz und verlangte zu erfahren, wer der Mörder wäre. Olivier ſagte, ein Fremder habe meinen Vater ſpät nachts auf der Straße überfallen. Aber was wollte mein Vater ſpät nachts auf der Straße? Keine Antwort! Olivier ſah mich mit dem Ausdruck tiefſten Leidens [20] an und bat mich, nicht nach den Einzelheiten [21] zu fragen. Ein furchtbares Geheimnis verſchließe ihm den Mund. Er ſchwor bei ſeiner Liebe zu mir, daß er alles getan habe, um meinen Vater zu retten,[22] aber es ſei unmöglich geweſen. Ich weiß nicht, warum Olivier nicht ſofort die Polizei zu Hilfe rief, aber ich weiß eines,[23] Olivier iſt genau ſo unſchuldig am Tode meines Vaters wie ich."

[1] der Schützling, –s, –e, *protegee.* [2] von ſelber, *of her own accord.* [3] der Salon, –s, –s, *drawing-room.* [4] verehrtes Fräulein, *my dear lady, Madam.* *[5] ſich ereignen, *happen.* [6] die Unwürdige, –n, –n, *unworthy* or *undeserving person.* *[7] verſichern, *assure.* [8] unerſchütterlich, *unshakable.* *[9] das Vertrauen, –s, *confidence.* *[10] dringend, *urgent, pressing.* [11] fertigſtellen, *finish.* [12] die Beſtellung, —, –en, *order.* [13] im Sterben liegen, a, e, *be dying.* [14] das Troſtwort, –es, –e, *word of comfort.* [15] ſich faſſen, *compose oneself.* [16] totenblaß, *deadly pale.* *[17] vergeblich, *in vain.* [18] zurückhalten, ie, a, *stop.* *[19] vor Entſetzen, *horrified.* [20] das Leiden, –s, —, *suffering.* *[21] die Einzelheit, —, –en, *detail.* *[22] retten, *save.* *[23] eines, *one thing.*

Wieder kamen Madelon Tränen in die Augen, aber ſie erzählte weiter: „Die Nachbarn kamen früh am Morgen, denn unſer lautes Weinen hatte ſie geweckt, und fanden uns am Bette meines Vaters knien.[1] Erſt zeigten ſie großes Mitleid mit uns beiden,[2] als aber die alte Liſette, die Frau unſeres Nachbars, zu ſchreien anfing, Olivier habe meinen Vater ermordet, glaubten es bald alle! Sie holten die Polizei und klagten Olivier des Mordes an.[3] Umſonſt war alles, was ich ſagte, niemand hörte auf mich, niemand. Olivier wurde mißhandelt und fortgeſchleppt und an das, was ſpäter geſchah, kann ich mich kaum erinnern. Sie haben es ja aber ſelber geſehen, als Sie wie ein Engel des Himmels zu meiner Rettung [4] erſchienen." Madelon war auf die Knie gefallen und küßte dem Fräulein die Hände.

Hatte die Scudery auch [5] vorher kaum glauben können, daß der unglückliche Jüngling, der ſo ſtürmiſch [6] in ihr ruhiges Leben eingebrochen war, ein Verbrecher ſei, ſo war ſie jetzt von Oliviers Unſchuld [7] überzeugt. Sie erkundigte ſich aber trotzdem bei Madelons Nachbarn und fand, daß das Mädchen in allem die Wahrheit geſagt hatte. Sie wollte aber auch von anderer Seite etwas über Olivier erfahren, den ſie nur durch die Beſchreibungen der verliebten [8] Madelon kannte. Trotz der ſonderbaren Umſtände,[9] unter denen ſie mit Olivier in Berührung [10] gekommen war, fühlte ſie, daß Olivier ein edel [11] denkender Jüngling war, der keinen Mord begehen [12] könnte. Die Nachbarn, die ihre Willigkeit,[13] den Jüngling zu verdächtigen, bereuten, lobten [14] ſeinen Fleiß,[15] ſein freundliches Betragen [16] gegen jedermann und erwähnten, wie oft der Meiſter davon geſprochen habe, daß ſeine Madelon bald ſeinen Geſellen heiraten ſolle. Selbſtverſtändlich [17] hätte Madelon als einziges Kind das ganze Vermögen ihres Vaters geerbt.[18]

So erzählten die Nachbarn, und das Fräulein war mehr als je[19] von Oliviers Unſchuld überzeugt, denn was für einen Beweggrund [20] hätte der Jüngling haben können? So ging ſie denn guten Mutes [21] zum Polizeipräſidenten Desgrais und berichtete ihm alles, was ſie über den Fall Cardillac gehört hatte und fragte ihn, wie er den armen Jüngling mit ruhigem Gewiſſen im Kerker laſſen könne. Es ſei doch wirklich kaum möglich, ernſthaft an ſeine Schuld [22] zu glauben.

Desgrais hörte dem Fräulein mit Reſpekt zu, dann aber lächelte er ſein kaltes Lächeln, hinter dem die Scudery die ganze Grauſamkeit [23] und Brutalität ſpürte,[24] für die er bekannt und gefürchtet war. „Sehr intereſſant, verehrtes Fräulein," ſagte er, mit einem Dolch ſpielend, der vor ihm auf dem Schreibtiſch lag, „ſehr intereſſant. Ich muß Ihnen wirklich ein Kompliment machen für Ihre Nachforſchungen,[25] die mit den unſeren genau übereinſtimmen,[26] aber in unſerem Beruf als

*1 knien, *kneel*. *2 mit uns beiden, *with both of us*. 3 anklagen, *accuse*. *4 die Rettung, —, -en, *rescue*. *5 auch, inverted word order plus auch is translated by *even if*. 6 ſtürmiſch, *boisterously*. *7 die Unſchuld, *innocence*. 8 verliebt, *enamored, in love*. 9 der Umſtand, -es, ⸗e, *circumstance*. 10 die Berührung, —, *contact*. *11 edel, *noble*. 12 begehen, beging, begangen, *commit*. 13 die Willigkeit, —, *willingness*. *14 loben, *praise*. *15 der Fleiß, -es, *industry*. 16 das Betragen, -s, *behavior, conduct*. *17 ſelbſtverſtändlich, *of course*. 18 erben, *inherit*. *19 je, *ever*. 20 der Beweggrund, -es, ⸗e, *motive*. 21 guten Mutes, *with confidence*. *22 die Schuld, —, *guilt*. 23 die Grauſamkeit, —, -en, *cruelty*. 24 ſpüren, *notice, perceive*. 25 die Nachforſchung, —, -en, *inquiry, investigation*. 26 übereinſtimmen, *agree*.

Beſchützer [1] und Rächer [2] der Untertanen [3] unſeres großen Königs denken wir anders als Sie in Ihrem Beruf als Schriftſtellerin.[4] Mangel [5] an Beweiſen bedeutet für Sie, mein Fräulein, Unſchuld des Angeklagten. Wir ziehen aber den Schluß daraus, daß der Verbrecher ſchlau [6] iſt und keine Spuren zu hinterlaſſen verſteht. Wir kennen die Übeltäter [7] aus dem täglichen Kampf mit dem Verbrechen, Sie kennen ſie aus der Lektüre [8] von Romanen." Er machte eine Pauſe, während der er die Spitze [9] des Dolches anſah, dann fuhr er fort: „Es iſt Ihres edlen Herzens würdig, daß Sie an Unſchuld und Reinheit glauben, wir aber müſſen vorſichtiger ſein. Wir dürfen uns nicht von den Tränen eines verliebten Mädchens überzeugen laſſen, ſondern nur von Tatſachen.[10] — Es gibt da noch einige Punkte, verehrtes Fräulein von Scudery, um die Sie ſich nicht genug oder überhaupt [11] nicht gekümmert haben. Wie ſollen wir es erklären, daß Olivier angeblich [12] ſpät nachts mit ſeinem Meiſter in Paris umherläuft,[13] ohne [14] uns ſagen zu können oder zu wollen, was der Zweck [15] dieſes nächtlichen Spazierganges war? Auch Sie haben ohne Zweifel gehört, daß Meiſter Cardillac abends faſt nie ausging und nur hin und wieder bis ſpät nachts aufblieb."

„Wir haben ſeinen Hausknecht [16] genau verhört.[17] In der Mordnacht hatte der Mann an ſeiner Gicht [18] zu leiden und hat die ganze Nacht kein Auge zugetan.[19] Außerdem quietſcht die ſchwere Eingangstür im Hauſe des Goldſchmiedes ſo laut, daß ſie den Hausknecht gewöhnlich aus tiefem Schlaf aufweckt, wenn ſie nachts geöffnet wird. Kein Menſch hat das Haus nach acht Uhr abends verlaſſen, ſagt er. Madelon iſt um zehn Uhr abends zu Bett gegangen und hat noch um dieſe Zeit mit ihrem Vater geſprochen. Das haben Sie mir eben geſagt, und ich ſehe keinen Grund, dieſe Angabe [20] zu bezweifeln." [21]

„Und ſchließlich," Desgrais ſtand auf, trat auf das Fräulein zu und hielt den Dolch vor ſie hin, „iſt dies die Mordwaffe. Wir fanden ſie in Oliviers Zimmer. Hier iſt der Anfangsbuchſtabe ſeines Namens „O". Sie, verehrtes Fräulein, ſagen Olivier könne keinen Grund gehabt haben, ſeinen Meiſter zu ermorden! Madelons Hand und das Vermögen des Alten wären ihm ſicher geweſen. Ich ſtimme nicht mit Ihnen überein, ich kann mir ſehr gut einen Grund denken. Meiner Meinung nach [22] iſt Olivier der Mörder unſerer Kavaliere. Durch irgendeinen Zufall [23] hat Meiſter Cardillac die Verbrechen ſeines Geſellen entdeckt. Olivier will leugnen,[24] der Meiſter bringt Beweiſe für die Richtigkeit ſeiner Anklage, Olivier in furchtbarer Angſt, alles zu verlieren, erſticht den Meiſter. Was der ſterbende Mann gemurmelt oder getan hat, wiſſen wir nicht. Es kann ſchon ſein, daß Madelon glaubt, er habe

[1] der Beſchützer, –s, —, *protector*. [2] der Rächer, –s, —, *avenger*. [3] der Untertan, –en, –en, *subject*. [4] die Schriftſtellerin, —, –nen, *authoress*. *[5] der Mangel, –s, ⸗, *want, lack*. *[6] ſchlau, *clever*. [7] der Übeltäter, –s, —, *evil-doer, criminal*. [8] die Lektüre, *reading*. *[9] die Spitze, —, –n, *sharp point*. *[10] die Tatſache, —, –n, *fact*. *[11] überhaupt, *at all*. [12] angeblich, *allegedly*. [13] umherlaufen, ie, au (iſt), *run around*. *[14] ohne . . . zu, *without* plus verb in *–ing*. *[15] der Zweck, –s, –e, *purpose*. [16] der Hausknecht, –es, –e, (*house*) *servant*. [17] verhören, *question*. [18] die Gicht, —, *gout*. [19] zutun, tat zu, zugetan, *close*. [20] die Angabe, —, –n, *statement*. *[21] bezweifeln, *doubt*. *[22] meiner Meinung nach, *in my opinion*. *[23] der Zufall, –s, ⸗e, *coincidence*. [24] leugnen, *deny*.

ſterbend ihre Hand in Oliviers Hand gelegt. Es iſt auch möglich, daß das verliebte Mädchen den Mörder ihres Vaters ſchützen will."

„Nun, bald werden wir wiſſen, wer recht hat, Sie oder wir, denn in wenigen Tagen werden wir mit der Folter [1] beginnen, und unſere Poliziſten, Fräulein, ſind wahre Künſtler, wenn es gilt,[2] einen Sünder [3] dazu zu bringen, ein Geſtändnis [4] zu machen."

„Doch ich ängſtige [5] Sie mit Dingen, die nicht in Ihre klare, reine Welt gehören. Vergeben Sie mir!" Er küßte dem Fräulein galant [6] die Hand und begleitete [7] ſie zur Tür.

Die Scudery verließ den Polizeipräſidenten verwirrt und beinah davon überzeugt, Olivier müſſe Cardillac ermordet haben, wenn auch ihr Herz dem widerſprach.

Um ſo [8] erſtaunter war ſie, als am Abend dieſes Tages Desgrais perſönlich bei ihr erſchien und ihr mitteilte,[9] daß Olivier ihn gebeten habe, dem Fräulein ein volles Geſtändnis ablegen [10] zu dürfen. Dies Geſtändnis ſolle aber nur dem Fräulein bekannt werden, die es unter keinen Umſtänden verraten dürfe. Desgrais fügte hinzu, er habe ſeine Erlaubnis dazu gegeben, nicht um Olivier, den er für den Schuldigen [11] hielte, einen Gefallen zu tun, ſondern um dem Fräulein von Scudery, die ganz Paris, ja Frankreich, hochſchätze,[12] ſeinen guten Willen zu zeigen. Er müſſe allerdings verlangen, daß Olivier nur mit ihr und niemand anderem — ganz beſonders nicht mit Madelon — ſpreche. Das Fräulein verſprach es, und am nächſten Abend wurde Olivier in ihr Haus gebracht. Während die Polizei vor dem Hauſe Wache hielt,[13] ſaßen ſich der Goldſchmiedegeſelle und das alte Fräulein im Salon derſelben gegenüber.

Das Fräulein konnte kaum ihr Mitleid verbergen und je länger ſie den Jüngling betrachtete, der beſcheiden auf ihre erſte Frage wartete, deſto ſicherer wurde ſie, ihn ſchon vor Jahren geſehen zu haben.

„Olivier," ſagte ſie mit gütiger Stimme, „Sie müſſen mir vertrauen,[14] wenn ich Ihnen helfen ſoll. Antworten Sie mir bitte auf alle meine Fragen! Ich werde von Ihren Antworten nur dann Gebrauch [15] machen, wenn Sie es geſtatten. Das verſpreche ich Ihnen."

„Zunächſt: Warum wollten Sie mich ſo dringend ſprechen in jener Nacht, in der Sie das Käſtchen in mein Haus brachten?"

Der Jüngling blickte zu ihr auf und lächelte: „Erinnern Sie ſich noch an den kleinen Robert?" Das Fräulein ſah ihn erſtaunt an; dann legte ſie die Hand auf ſeinen Arm. „Iſt es möglich? Sind Sie Robert, Robert der Sohn meiner geliebten Anna? Nun bin ich vollkommen verwirrt. Aber natürlich, jetzt ſehe ich das Geſichtchen des kleinen Robert wieder ganz deutlich vor mir. Deshalb alſo kamen

[1] die Folter, —, –n, *torture.* [2] gelten, a, o, *mean.* [3] der Sünder, –s, —, *sinner; culprit.* *[4] das Geſtändnis, ...niſſes, ...niſſe, *confession.* [5] ängſtigen, *frighten.* [6] galant, *courteously.* *[7] begleiten, *accompany.* *[8] um ſo erſtaunter, *all the more astonished.* *[9] mitteilen, *inform.* [10] ablegen, *make.* [11] der Schuldige, –n, –n, *guilty person.* [12] hochſchätzen, *hold in high esteem.* [13] Wache halten, ie, a, *keep watch.* *[14] vertrauen, *trust* or *confide in.* *[15] der Gebrauch, –s, ¨e, *use.*

Sie mir so bekannt vor. Warum sind Sie nicht gleich zu mir gekommen? Warum haben Sie Ihren Namen geändert? O Robert, ich kann es nicht von Ihnen glauben, daß Sie — Sie geben mir Rätsel auf,[1] anstatt sie zu lösen." [2]

„Warum heißen Sie jetzt Olivier? Wo ist Ihre Mutter, meine kleine Anna? Warum habe ich nicht mehr von ihr gehört, seit sie mich verließ und mit Ihnen und Ihrem Vater nach Bordeaux ging?"

Olivier Brusson schwieg einen Augenblick, dann sagte er: „Meine Eltern sind beide tot. Sie wissen, daß mein Vater viel philosophierte und seine eigenen Gedanken über Gott und die Welt hatte, sodaß er bald als Ketzer [3] galt. Auf einer Reise geriet [4] er mit einigen unbekannten Männern in einem Wirtshaus in Streit und wurde totgeschlagen.[5] Meine Mutter hat ihn nicht lange überlebt.[6] Vergeben [7] Sie ihr, daß sie Ihnen nicht mehr schrieb! Alle Freunde unserer Familie standen im Verdacht, Ketzer zu sein, und meine Mutter fürchtete, die Verbindung [8] mit ihr könnte Ihnen gefährlich werden."

Der Jüngling schwieg und starrte an dem Fräulein vorbei ins Leere.[9] Sie streichelte seine Hand und sagte: „Sie kamen in mein Haus, um sich mir zu erkennen zu geben,[10] Sie waren in Not [11] und suchten meine Hilfe, und ich habe Ihnen meine Tür verschlossen. — Verzeihen [12] Sie mir!"

Olivier schüttelte den Kopf. „Ich weiß, Sie konnten nicht anders handeln, aber mir blieb auch kein anderer Weg offen in jener Nacht. Doch lassen Sie mich Ihnen meine Geschichte erzählen, und Sie werden alles verstehen."

„Nach dem Tode meiner Eltern nahm mich ein Verwandter, der Goldschmied war, in die Lehre.[13] Ich fühlte mich glücklich und liebte meine Arbeit, aber es konnte mir nicht verborgen bleiben, daß ihm mein Aufenthalt [14] in seinem Hause schadete. Die Leute von Bordeaux waren nicht gewillt, dem Sohn zu vergeben, daß der Vater ein Ketzer war. Ich schadete dem guten Mann in seinem Beruf und so ging ich nach Paris."

„Ich nannte mich jetzt Olivier Brusson, und mit diesem neuen Namen begann für mich ein neues Leben. Ein Brief meines früheren Meisters führte mich bei Cardillac ein,[15] ein Probestück,[16] das ich für ihn arbeitete, gefiel ihm, und so durfte ich zu meiner unbeschreiblichen [17] Freude bei ihm bleiben. Wie Sie wohl wissen, gnädiges Fräulein, galt Cardillac als der beste Goldschmied Frankreichs. Zwei Jahre lang arbeitete ich in seiner Werkstatt, und er lehrte mich manches Geheimnis seiner Kunst. Das Unglück wollte es, daß er ein sehr ehrgeiziger [18] Mann war, der für seine Tochter Madelon eine glänzende Zukunft erträumte.[19] Als er merkte, daß ich seine Tochter

[1] aufgeben, a, e, *propose.* [2] lösen, *solve.* [3] der Ketzer, –s, —, *heretic.* [4] in Streit geraten, ie, a, *become involved in a quarrel.* [5] totschlagen, u, a, *beat to death, kill.* [6] überleben, *survive.* *[7] vergeben, a, e, *forgive.* *[8] die Verbindung, —, –en, *connection.* *[9] ins Leere, *into space.* [10] sich zu erkennen geben, *make one's identity known.* *[11] die Not, —, ¨–e, *trouble.* *[12] verzeihen, ie, ie, *pardon, forgive.* [13] in die Lehre nehmen, nahm, genommen, *take as apprentice.* *[14] der Aufenthalt, –es, *stay.* *[15] einführen, *introduce.* [16] das Probestück, –s, –e, *sample.* *[17] unbeschreiblich, *indescribable.* *[18] ehrgeizig, *ambitious.* [19] erträumen, *dream of.*

liebte, und daß ſie dieſe Liebe erwiderte,[1] war er außer ſich vor Wut. Der Gedanke, daß ein Habenichts [2] wie ich ſeine Tochter zur Frau haben wollte, ſchien ihm eine ſchwere Beleidigung [3] ſeiner Ehre zu ſein, und er warf mich mit Verwünſchungen [4] aus dem Hauſe."

„Ich lebte eine Zeitlang von dem wenigen Geld, das ich mir erſpart hatte. Es war mir unmöglich, neue Arbeit zu ſuchen, der Gedanke an Madelon ließ mir keine Ruhe, und je länger die Trennung [5] von ihr dauerte, deſto unerträglicher wurde ſie mir."

„Oft ging ich zur Nachtzeit zu Cardillacs Haus, hoffend, ſie am Fenſter zu ſehen oder ihr irgendwie [6] eine Botſchaft [7] ſchicken zu können. Aber Cardillac, der wohl wußte, wie mir zumute war,[8] hielt ſeine Tochter wie eine Gefangene."[9]

„So ſtand ich eines Abends ſpät an eine Mauer gelehnt, die ſich an Cardillacs Haus anſchließt.[10] Die Mauer ſteht noch aus der Zeit, in der das Haus Teil eines Kloſters [11] war, und aus derſelben Zeit ſtammen [12] alte Steinbilder [13] in den Niſchen [14] der Mauern. Dicht bei einem ſolchen Steinbild ſtand ich, als ich plötzlich Licht in Cardillacs Werkſtatt ſah. Offenbar war der Meiſter noch einmal in ſeine Werkſtatt gegangen oder er wollte gegen ſeine Gewohnheit [15] zu ſpäter Stunde ausgehen. Von unklarer Hoffnung erfüllt, Madelon zu ſehen, drückte ich mich gegen eines der Steinbilder und blickte von Zeit zu Zeit über die Mauer nach den Fenſtern der Werkſtatt. Plötzlich war das Licht verſchwunden, und ich nahm an, Cardillac ſei wieder zu Bett gegangen. Dennoch wartete ich eine Weile. Plötzlich fühlte ich, daß ſich das Steinbild, gegen das ich mich lehnte, bewegte. Erſchrocken ſprang ich von der Stelle fort und verbarg mich im Dunkeln."

„Da ſah ich nun, wie ein Mann aus einer Öffnung in der Mauer hinter der Statue herausſchlüpfte.[16] An der Geſtalt und den Bewegungen [17] erkannte ich Cardillac."

„Er drehte die Statue wieder in ihre alte Stellung zurück und ging dann, ſich immer im Dunkeln haltend, die Straße hinab. Ich folgte ihm in einiger Entfernung und verſuchte zu begreifen,[18] was mein Meiſter zu nächtlicher Stunde auf dieſem ſonderbaren Spaziergang durch die Seitengäßchen [19] von Paris vorhatte. Eine dunkle Ahnung [20] ſagte mir, daß er nichts Gutes plante, und bald ſollte ich ſehen, daß ich mich nicht geirrt hatte."

„Nach einiger Zeit vernahm [21] ich das Singen und Pfeifen eines Mannes, der uns auf der dunklen Straße entgegenkam. Cardillac ſchlüpfte [22] geſchwind [23] in einen

*1 erwidern, *return, reciprocate.* 2 der Habenichts, —, -e, *penniless fellow.* 3 die Beleidigung, —, -en, *insult.* 4 die Verwünſchung, —, -en, *curse.* 5 die Trennung, —, -en, *separation.* *6 irgendwie, *somehow.* 7 die Botſchaft, —, -en, *message.* *8 zumute ſein, war, geweſen (iſt), *feel.* *9 die Gefangene, -n, -n, (*woman*) *prisoner.* *10 ſich anſchließen, o, o, *join.* 11 das Kloſter, -s, ¨, *monastery.* 12 ſtammen aus, *date from.* 13 das Steinbild, -es, -er, *statue.* 14 die Niſche, —, -n, *niche.* *15 die Gewohnheit, —, -en, *custom.* 16 herausſchlüpfen, *slip out.* *17 die Bewegung, —, -en, *movement, motion.* *18 begreifen, i, i, *understand.* 19 das Seitengäßchen, -s, —, *side-street.* *20 die Ahnung, —, -en, *suspicion.* *21 vernehmen, a, o, *notice, hear.* 22 ſchlüpfen, *slip.* *23 geſchwind, *quickly.*

Hauseingang [1] und stürzte sich auf den nächtlichen Wanderer, als er bei ihm vorüberging. Der fiel, ohne einen Laut [2] von sich zu geben, auf die Straße hin."

„Ich war entsetzt.[3] Ohne an die sonderbare Lage zu denken, in der ich mich befand, lief ich auf Cardillac zu mit dem Rufe: ‚Meister, was bedeutet dies?'"

„Cardillac sprang auf und erwartete mich, einen Dolch in der Hand haltend. Er sah wie ein Rasender [4] aus, seine Augen blickten wild, und das Haar hing ihm in die Stirn."

„Ich beugte mich über den Mann, der eben noch gesungen und gepfiffen hatte. Es war ein junger Kavalier, der da tot in seinem Blute lag. Cardillac stieß mich zur Seite und durchsuchte mit roher Hand die Taschen des Toten, bis er ein goldenes Halsband fand, das er einsteckte." [5]

„Jetzt schien er ruhiger zu werden und meinen Arm mit eisernem Griff [6] packend, flüsterte er: ‚Falls du ein Wort von dem sagst, was du hier gesehen hast, siehst du Madelon nie wieder. Schweigst du aber, so sollst du sie heiraten dürfen und zwar bald. Komm mit, ich nehme dich wieder als Gesellen in mein Haus.'"

„Ich war wie betäubt [7] von alledem und ließ mich fortziehen.[8] Ich schlüpfte mit ihm durch das Loch in der Mauer, das in einen engen unterirdischen [9] Gang [10] führte. Jetzt erst wurde mir klar, in welcher Gefahr ich mich befand. Welche Gelegenheit für den Mörder, den Augenzeugen [11] seiner Tat [12] umzubringen! Ich beschloß, mein Leben so teuer wie möglich zu verkaufen und erwartete mit klopfendem Herzen seinen Angriff. Cardillac, der in dem engen Tunnel vor mir ging, mußte meine Gedanken ahnen. Mit leiser und seltsam sanfter Stimme sagte er: ‚Fürchte nichts, Olivier! Dir droht keine Gefahr. Verurteile [13] mich nicht, bis ich dir alles erklärt habe!' Ich folgte ihm schweigend in ein kleines Zimmer, in das der enge Tunnel führte. Der Meister öffnete eine Truhe,[14] die voller Schmucksachen war, nahm das Halsband aus der Tasche, besah es von allen Seiten und legte es dann zu den anderen Schmucksachen. Er schloß die Truhe und öffnete ein kleines, verborgenes Türchen in der Wand, das sich als die Rückwand eines Kleiderschrankes [15] herausstellte.[16] Wir zwängten [17] uns durch die enge Öffnung und standen in seinem Schlafzimmer."

„Cardillac, dessen sonst so frisches Gesicht blaß wie der Tod war, holte eine Flasche Wein und zwei Gläser, bat mich zu trinken und begann zu sprechen, als ob er mit sich selber spräche und ich gar nicht in dem Zimmer wäre. ‚Du tust mir ein großes Unrecht,[18] wenn du denkst, daß ich diesen Kavalier überfallen habe, um ihm wie ein gemeiner [19] Straßenräuber dies Halsband zu rauben. Du weißt, dies ist nicht der

[1] der Hauseingang, –s, ⸗e, *entrance (to a house)*. *[2] der Laut, –es, –e, *sound*. [3] entsetzt, *horrified*. [4] ein Rasender, *madman, maniac*. *[5] einstecken, *put in one's pocket*. [6] der Griff, –es, –e, *grip*. [7] betäubt, *stunned*. [8] fortziehen, o, o, *draw away, pull away*. [9] unterirdisch, *subterranean*. *[10] der Gang, –es, ⸗e, *passage, corridor*. [11] der Augenzeuge, –n, –n, *eyewitness*. *[12] die Tat, —, –en, *deed, action*. *[13] verurteilen, *condemn*. [14] die Truhe, —, –n, *trunk, chest*. [15] der Kleiderschrank, –es, ⸗e, *wardrobe*. [16] sich herausstellen als, *turn out to be*. [17] sich zwängen, *squeeze*. *[18] das Unrecht, –es, *injustice*. [19] gemein, *common, ordinary*.

einzige Mann, den ich erſchlagen habe. Du haſt von den nächtlichen Raubmorden gehört, denen ſo viele Kavaliere zum Opfer gefallen ſind. Ich habe ſie alle ermordet, alle die jungen Herren. — Ja, da machſt du den Mund auf und ſtarrſt mich an, als ob ich der Teufel ſelbſt wäre. Das verſtehſt du nicht und doch ſollteſt du — aber hör mich erſt zu Ende!‘“

„Er ſchwieg und ſeufzte, dann fuhr er langſam fort, als ob er die richtigen Worte nicht finden könnte, die mir ſeine furchtbaren Taten erklären ſollten. ‚Mein Vater erzählte mir, daß meine Mutter, ehe ich geboren wurde, bei einem Hoffeſt [1] im Trianon, dem ſie zuſchaute,[2] einen Kavalier erblickte,[3] der eine funkelnde Diamantenkette um den Hals trug. Meine Mutter wurde von einem ſtarken Verlangen [4] gepackt, dieſe Kette zu beſitzen. Plötzlich ging ſie auf den Kavalier zu und faßte nach dem Schmuck. Jeder glaubte, ſie ſei wahnſinnig [5] geworden. Nach Hauſe zurückgekehrt, wurde ſie ſchwer krank. In ihren Fieberträumen [6] ſprach ſie von nichts als von dieſer Diamantenkette. Sie ſtarb, als ich geboren wurde.‘

‚Schon als Kind hatte ich ein unbezwingbares [7] Verlangen nach Juwelen. Ich verſuchte, ſie zu ſtehlen, und wurde von meinem Vater ſo grauſam [8] geſchlagen, daß ich mich aus Furcht beherrſchte. Um Juwelen um mich haben zu können, wurde ich Goldſchmied. Nun brach das Verlangen, das ich ſo lange unterdrückt [9] hatte, mit doppelter Gewalt hervor.[10] Jedesmal, wenn ich einen ſchönen Schmuck angefertigt habe, kann ich mich nicht von ihm trennen. Habe ich ihn an ſeinen Beſitzer abgeliefert,[11] ſo quält mich das Verlangen, ihn wieder zu beſitzen. Jahrelang [12] habe ich dagegen angekämpft,[13] aber es wurde immer ſchlimmer. Eine Stimme flüſterte mir ins Ohr: ‚Nimm die Juwelen zurück, ſie gehören dir.‘

‚Vor einiger Zeit kaufte ich dies Haus und der frühere Beſitzer zeigte mir den geheimen Eingang. Die Hölle [14] muß es ſo gewollt haben, denn jetzt hatte ich eine Möglichkeit, ungeſehen das Haus zu verlaſſen und zurückzukehren.‘

‚Noch eins! Du liebſt Madelon. Ich liebte Madelons Mutter von ganzem Herzen, aber ein Kavalier ſtahl ſie mir. Wenn ich nun für die edlen Herren arbeitete, und mein wildes Verlangen mich packte, ſo war es leicht für mich, ſie nachts zu überfallen und den Verhaßten [15] die Juwelen wieder abzunehmen.‘[16]

‚Madelon weiß nichts von alledem. Du weißt, wie ſie mich liebt. Erführe ſie, was du weißt, es würde ihr das Herz brechen.‘

Olivier ſchwieg und ſah auf den Boden. „Ich weiß, was Sie jetzt ſagen werden. Ich hätte den Meiſter verlaſſen ſollen. Ich wollte es tun, aber der Gedanke, Madelon auf immer zu verlieren, machte es mir unmöglich. Cardillac ſchien, ſeit ich um ſein Geheimnis wußte, ſeiner Leidenſchaft [17] mehr nachzugeben [18] als bevor. Da erfuhr er

[1] das Hoffeſt, –es, –e, *court-festival.* [2] zuſchauen, *watch.* *[3] erblicken, *see, notice.* [4] das Verlangen, –s, —, *desire, craving.* [5] wahnſinnig, *insane.* [6] der Fiebertraum, –es, ¨–e, *feverish dream.* [7] unbezwingbar, *uncontrollable.* *[8] grauſam, *cruel, terrible.* [9] unterdrücken, *suppress.* [10] hervorbrechen, a, o, (iſt), *burst forth.* [11] abliefern, *deliver.* *[12] jahrelang, *for years.* [13] ankämpfen, *fight.* [14] die Hölle, —, *hell.* [15] der Verhaßte, –n, –n, *hated person.* [16] abnehmen, a, o, *take away.* *[17] die Leidenſchaft, —, –en, *passion, rage.* [18] nachgeben, a, e, *yield, give in.*

von der Bittschrift der Kavaliere und Ihrer Antwort. Er gab mir den Auftrag,[1] Ihnen das Juwelenkästchen zu bringen, und in meiner großen Not dachte ich, das beste wäre, wenn ich Ihnen alles erzählte. Ihre Dienerin ließ mich in jener Nacht nicht in Ihr Haus."

„Nach einer Weile begann der Meister von den Juwelen zu sprechen, die er Ihnen geschenkt [2] hatte, und ich glaubte, dieselben Zeichen der Unruhe an ihm zu entdecken, die gewöhnlich auftraten,[3] wenn er eine seiner Mordtaten plante. In tödlicher [4] Angst um Ihr Leben, versuchte ich, Sie auf dem Pont-Neuf zu warnen, als ich den Zettel in Ihre Kutsche warf. Als der Meister wieder ausging, folgte ich ihm, entschlossen,[5] Sie mit meinem eigenen Leben zu beschützen.[6] Doch bald sah ich, daß ich mich geirrt hatte. Er ging in eine andere Straße, wo ich bald sein Opfer, einen Offizier der königlichen Garde, kommen sah. Er überfiel den Offizier, der aber offenbar den Überfall erwartete. Nicht er, sondern Cardillac empfing den Todesstoß." [7]

„Als ich meinen Meister zusammenbrechen sah, lief ich zu ihm, trotzdem der Offizier sofort den Degen [8] zog. Es wäre mir in diesem Augenblick am liebsten gewesen,[9] wenn er mich getötet hätte, denn ich sah sofort, daß mein Fall hoffnungslos war. Gelang es mir auch, den Meister ungesehen nach Hause zu tragen, so konnte ich doch [10] nicht erklären, was wirklich geschehen war. Der Offizier ging langsam fort, und, ohne zu wissen, was ich tat, hob ich seinen Dolch auf und steckte ihn ein. Es ist derselbe Dolch, der jetzt der meinige [11] sein soll, und dessen Besitz mich in den Augen meiner Ankläger schwerer verdächtig macht als irgendetwas anderes."

Olivier schwieg und schloß die Augen. Das Fräulein betrachtete ihn mit tiefem Mitleid. Leise stand sie auf und trat zu ihm. „Sie dürfen nicht verzweifeln, Olivier," sagte sie sanft und streichelte ihm das Haar. „Ich werde alles tun, was ich kann, um Sie zu retten, denn Sie sind unschuldig."

Der Jüngling öffnete die Augen weit und starrte sie entsetzt an. „Nein, verehrtes Fräulein, Sie haben unrecht.[12] Ich bin so schuldig, als ob ich das Blut der Ermordeten an meinen eigenen Händen hätte. Denken Sie an all die Menschen, die heute noch lebten, hätte ich Cardillac in jener Schreckensnacht [13] angezeigt,[14] statt ihm in sein Haus zu folgen! Ich konnte mich nicht dazu überreden. Ich konnte Cardillac ebensowenig [15] anzeigen wie ich mich nach meiner Verhaftung verteidigen konnte. Madelon hätte die Wahrheit über ihren Vater nicht ertragen können. — Nein, Fräulein von Scudery, ich kann nicht gerettet werden. Um eins [16] aber bitte ich Sie: Sie werden mein Geheimnis auch nach meinem Tode nicht verraten!"

„Aber Olivier," erwiderte das Fräulein, „bedenken [17] Sie doch, was Ihr Tod für

[1] der Auftrag, –es, ⸗e, *order, instruction.* *[2] schenken, *give (as a present).* *[3] auftreten, a, e (ist), *appear.* [4] tödlich, *deadly, mortal.* *[5] sich entschließen, o, o, *decide, determine.* *[6] beschützen, *protect.* [7] der Todesstoß, —es, *death-thrust.* [8] der Degen, –s, —, *sword.* [9] es wäre mir am liebsten gewesen, *I would have liked it best.* *[10] doch, *even so.* [11] der meinige, *my own.* *[12] Sie haben unrecht, *you are wrong.* [13] die Schreckensnacht, —, ⸗e, *terrible night.* [14] anzeigen, *report.* [15] ebensowenig . . . wie, *just as little . . . as.* [16] um eins, *for one thing.* [17] bedenken, bedachte, bedacht, *consider.*

Madelon bedeutet! Soll ſie nach dem Vater auch noch den Geliebten [1] verlieren? Vielleicht kann ſie das auch nicht ertragen!"

Olivier nickte ſchwach mit dem Kopfe, er konnte nicht ſprechen. Endlich flüſterte er: „Ich habe es mir alles im Kerker überlegt. Es iſt beſſer, daß Madelon einen unſchuldigen Vater und einen unſchuldigen Geliebten beweint,[2] als daß ſie einen blutigen Verbrecher verfluchen muß. Bitte, Fräulein, erfüllen Sie meinen Wunſch; es iſt der Wunſch eines Sterbenden. Verzeihung, wenn ich . . ." Er fiel in den Seſſel [3] zurück und murmelte unverſtändliche Worte.

Das Fräulein läutete [4] erſchrocken das kleine Glöckchen,[5] das die alte Mathilde herbeirufen ſollte, aber ſtatt ihrer kam Desgrais ins Zimmer. „Geſtatten Sie, Fräulein, daß ich die Gelegenheit ergreife,[6] meinen Gefangenen abzuholen." Er winkte zwei Soldaten herbei, die den Halbohnmächtigen bei den Armen packten und wegführten. Desgrais verbeugte ſich noch einmal tief und folgte dann ſeinem Gefangenen.

Als Mathilde hereintrat, fand ſie ihre Herrin wie betäubt auf dem Sofa ſitzen. Sie wußte, welchen Anteil [7] ſie an dem Schickſal Bruſſons nahm und ſo ſagte ſie nichts ſondern ging ſtillſchweigend hinaus, um ihr eine Taſſe Schokolade zu bereiten.[8] Als ſie mit der dampfenden [9] Schokolade zurückkam, blickte das Fräulein auf.

„Ich danke dir, Mathilde, du errätſt meine Gedanken. Hol dir auch eine Taſſe und trink mit mir." Die alte Dienerin wußte, daß ihre Herrin ſich wieder einmal ausſprechen [10] wollte, und wenn ſie auch nicht immer verſtand, was das Fräulein ſagte, ſo wußte ſie doch, daß ſie ihr einen großen Dienſt erwies,[11] wenn ſie zuhörte. Schweigend brachte ſie ihre Taſſe und ſetzte ſich auf einen Stuhl neben dem Sofa, wo ſie zu ſitzen pflegte, wenn ſie der Scudery Geſellſchaft leiſtete.[12]

Da das Fräulein nichts ſagte, ſondern nur von Zeit zu Zeit ſeufzte, begann Mathilde: „Es war recht dumm von mir, daß ich damals Herrn Bruſſon nicht ins Haus ließ, nicht wahr, gnädiges Fräulein?" „Nein, Mathilde," widerſprach die Scudery freundlich. „Weder du, noch ſonſt jemand [13] in der Welt hätte damals ahnen können, was dieſer Beſuch bedeutete, und du haſt recht gehandelt, einen fremden Menſchen zu ſo ſpäter Stunde nicht ins Haus zu laſſen. — Ja, ja, Mathilde, man ſoll nicht Schickſal ſpielen wollen, das habe ich auf meine alten Tage noch lernen müſſen."

„Können Sie denn nicht Ihren Einfluß [14] bei Hofe gebrauchen, gnädiges Fräulein? Man ſagt, es gäbe keine Dame in der ganzen Hofgeſellſchaft,[15] der der König ſo viel Achtung [16] erzeige,[17] wie Ihnen."

„Das iſt ein gewagtes [18] Unternehmen,[19] Mathilde. Der König iſt mein Trumpf.[20]

*1 der Geliebte, –n, –n, *sweetheart.* 2 beweinen, *mourn, weep over the loss of a person.* 3 der Seſſel, –s, —, *arm-chair.* 4 läuten, *ring.* 5 das Glöckchen, –s, —, *small bell.* *6 ergreifen, i, i, *seize.* 7 der Anteil, –s, –e, *interest.* *8 bereiten, *prepare, make.* 9 dampfen, *steam.* 10 ſich ausſprechen, a, o, *relieve one's mind.* 11 erweiſen, ie, ie, *do (a service).* 12 Geſellſchaft leiſten, *keep company.* *13 ſonſt jemand, *anyone else.* *14 der Einfluß, –es, ⸗e, *influence.* 15 die Hofgeſellſchaft, —, –en, *court-society.* 16 die Achtung, —, *respect.* 17 erzeigen, *show.* 18 gewagt, *daring.* *19 das Unternehmen, –s, —, *undertaking.* 20 der Trumpf, —, ⸗e, *trump.*

Habe ich den verspielt,[1] so ist das Spiel verloren. Nein, ein Gesuch [2] beim König ist das letzte Mittel, das ich versuchen kann. Du weißt nicht, wie zornig [3] der König über diese schrecklichen Mordtaten war, die seiner schönen Hauptstadt leicht einen schlechten Namen hätten geben können. Die große Schwierigkeit, die mich hindert, ist nicht Desgrais oder der König, es ist etwas, was ich weder dir noch sonst irgendjemand sagen darf. Ach Mathilde, ich fürchte, nichts wird den armen Olivier vom Galgen [4] retten. Wenn ich nur . . ." In diesem Augenblick schrie Mathilde laut auf. Der schwere Vorhang,[5] der das Schlafzimmer des Fräuleins vom Salon trennte, bewegte sich, und Madelon trat hervor. Sie kniete vor ihrer Beschützerin nieder, die ärgerlich zu ihr sprach: „Wie soll ich das verstehen, Madelon? Weißt du nicht, daß ich Desgrais versprechen mußte, du würdest nicht im Hause sein, wenn Olivier hierher käme?"

„Ich weiß, ich verdiene Ihren Zorn,[6] aber ich konnte der Versuchung nicht widerstehen, Olivier noch einmal zu sehen. Ich habe alles gehört. Strafen Sie mich, wie Sie wollen, übergeben [7] Sie mich dem Präsidenten Desgrais! O liebes Fräulein, nichts kann mich mehr schmerzen,[8] denn ich weiß, jetzt kann Olivier gerettet werden. Nichts kann mich mehr schmerzen, nicht einmal die Entdeckung, wie mein Vater lebte und starb! Ich will ihn beweinen und für seine arme Seele beten."

Trotz aller Sorge und dem Ärger über Madelons Betragen, fühlte sich das Fräulein plötzlich glücklich, denn Madelons Worte hatten ihr eine Last von der Seele genommen. Sie hob das knieende Mädchen auf, küßte es und besprach noch einmal alles mit ihr im Lichte von Oliviers Geständnis, das sie ja nun nicht mehr geheim zu halten brauchte.

Oliviers Lage konnte durch einen genauen Bericht an die Polizei sofort gebessert [9] werden. War er auch noch nicht gerettet, so bedeutete die offenbare Schuld des toten Cardillacs doch wenigstens neue Untersuchungen, die dem Fräulein mehr Zeit gaben, um für Olivier etwas zu tun. Selbstverständlich kam die Folter nicht mehr in Frage,[10] denn der unterirdische Gang aus der Werkstatt des Meisters war Beweis genug sogar für Desgrais, daß Cardillac der Mörder war. Da war allerdings das Schweigen Oliviers; das genügte, ihm den Kopf zu kosten. Es war nicht von Desgrais zu erwarten, daß er die Gewissensnot [11] des jungen Olivier, die aus seiner Liebe zu Madelon entsprang,[12] als mildernden Umstand [13] würde gelten lassen.

Außerdem bestand die Möglichkeit, daß Desgrais aus Ärger darüber, die ganze Lage falsch verstanden zu haben, neue Schwierigkeiten erfinden [14] würde, nur um nicht zugeben [15] zu müssen, daß er sich geirrt habe.

Das Fräulein sah ein, daß sie ohne die Hilfe eines Advokaten nicht sehr weit kom-

[1] verspielen, *lose.* [2] das Gesuch, –es, –e, *petition.* *[3] zornig, *angry.* [4] der Galgen, –s, —, *gallows.* *[5] der Vorhang, –s, ¨–e, *curtain.* *[6] der Zorn, –es, *anger, indignation.* [7] übergeben, a, e, *hand over.* [8] schmerzen, *pain, hurt.* [9] bessern, *improve.* *[10] kam die Folter nicht mehr in Frage, *torture was out of the question now.* [11] die Gewissensnot, —, ¨–e, *qualms of conscience.* [12] entspringen, a, u (ist), *originate.* [13] mildernder Umstand, *extenuating circumstance.* *[14] erfinden, a, u, *invent.* *[15] zugeben, a, e, *admit.*

men werde,[1] und ſo beſchloß ſie denn, Pierre D'Andilly für den Fall zu intereſſieren.

D'Andilly, der außerdem auch ein begeiſteter Leſer von Romanen war und die Romane der Scudery beſonders gern las, übernahm die Verteidigung [2] Oliviers mit Freuden,[3] teils [4] um dem Fräulein einen Gefallen zu tun, teils um Desgrais, den er grimmig haßte, ein Opfer entreißen [5] zu können.

Es kam, wie das Fräulein es erwartet hatte. Zwar ſah ſich der Polizeipräſident gezwungen, neue Unterſuchungen zu unternehmen und das Beſtehen des unterirdiſchen Ganges und der Geheimkammer, in denen die Juwelen der Ermordeten gefunden wurden, als Beweis für die Schuld des Schmiedes anzuſehen, er beſtand [6] aber immer noch darauf, daß Olivier — vielleicht im Streit über die Beute — den Cardillac erſtochen habe.

Es blieb dem Fräulein nichts anderes übrig,[7] als noch einmal zu Desgrais zu gehen und die neue Lage der Dinge mit ihm zu beſprechen. Als ſie in Desgrais Haus trat, ſagten ihr die Diener, der Präſident ſei plötzlich zum König nach Verſailles gerufen worden.

Das Fräulein kehrte mit der unbeſtimmten [8] Ahnung nach Hauſe zurück, daß der Befehl des Königs in irgendeinem Zuſammenhang mit dem Fall Bruſſon ſtehen müſſe. Sie ſollte bald genug erfahren, daß ſie wieder einmal mit ihren Ahnungen recht gehabt hatte, denn vor ihrem Hauſe ſtand ein reiſefertiger Wagen mit dem königlichen Wappen,[9] und im Hauſe empfing ſie die aufregende Nachricht, daß ſie mit Madelon ſofort zum König kommen ſolle. Auf die angſtvollen Fragen Madelons, was dies alles bedeute, konnte die Scudery nur antworten, daß der König eine Entſcheidung getroffen [10] hätte, denn der König habe es ſonſt immer vermieden,[11] mit ihr über den Fall Bruſſon zu ſprechen, obwohl es ihm bekannt war, welche Rolle ſie in dieſer ſchwierigen Angelegenheit ſpielte.

Viel zu langſam für die Ungeduld der alten Dame und des jungen Mädchens brachte ſie der Wagen des Königs nach Verſailles, wo die beiden ſofort in einen Saal geführt wurden, in dem Desgrais bereits [12] wartete. Sein Lächeln, noch kälter und höflicher als ſonſt, verriet nichts davon, daß er ſchon wußte, daß der König ſich für Bruſſon entſchieden [13] hatte, und daß Desgrais deswegen [14] äußerſt wütend war.

Gefolgt von einem jungen Offizier, trat der König bald in den Saal, begrüßte die Damen und Desgrais, ſtellte dann den jungen Offizier, einen Grafen Oldain, vor und ſagte: „Bitte, Graf Oldain, erzählen Sie unſerem Polizeipräſidenten, was Sie mir geſtern erzählt haben."

Graf Oldain wandte ſich zu Desgrais, der ihn mit unbeweglicher [15] Miene [16] anſah.

[1] ſie werde nicht ſehr weit kommen, *she would not get far.* [2] die Verteidigung, —, *defense.* [3] mit Freuden, *with pleasure.* *[4] teils . . . teils, *partly . . . partly.* [5] entreißen, i, i, *tear away, snatch away.* [6] beſtehen auf, beſtand, beſtanden, *insist.* *[7] Es blieb dem Fräulein nichts anderes übrig, als . . ., *There was nothing left for the lady to do but . . .* [8] unbeſtimmt, *vague.* [9] das Wappen, –s, —, *coat of arms.* [10] eine Entſcheidung treffen, a o, *make a decision.* [11] vermeiden, ie, ie, *avoid.* *[12] bereits, *already.* [13] daß der König ſich für Bruſſon entſchieden hatte, *that the king had decided in favor of Brusson.* *[14] deswegen, *for that reason.* [15] unbeweglich, *fixed.* *[16] die Miene, —, –n, *expression.*

„Herr Präſident," begann er, „ich hätte ſchon vor langem zu Ihnen kommen ſollen. Verzeihen Sie bitte, daß ich es nicht tat und ſo ſpät, von meinem Gewiſſen getrieben,[1] dem König alles entdeckte. Ich bin der Mann, der den Goldſchmied Cardillac in der Nähe des Hauſes des Fräulein von Scudery getötet hat. Ich weiß ſelbſt nicht, wie es kam, daß ich einen Verdacht auf den Meiſter hatte, als er mir voll ſichtlicher[2] Unruhe einen Schmuck brachte, den ich bei ihm beſtellt[3] hatte, und mich fragte, für wen der Schmuck beſtimmt[4] ſei. Als ich dann erfuhr, daß er auf recht liſtige[5] Weiſe meinen Diener ausfragte,[6] wann ich eine gewiſſe Dame zu beſuchen pflegte, war ich ſicher, daß er der Mörder und Räuber ſei, der immer nur junge Kavaliere überfiel. Ich trug deshalb einen leichten Bruſtharniſch[7] unter der Weſte.[8] Es geſchah, wie ich es erwartet hatte. Cardillac fiel mich von hinten an,[9] aber ſein Dolchſtoß glitt an dem Eiſen[10] meines Panzers[11] ab.[12] Nun tötete ich ihn mit meinem Dolche, den ich in Bereitſchaft[13] hielt."

„Der Dolch hat auf dem Griff den Buchſtaben ‚O', und die Inſchrift: ‚Zieh mich nicht ohne Grund, ſteck mich nicht ohne Ehre in die Scheide.' Dieſen Dolch, Monſieur Desgrais, haben Sie bei Olivier gefunden. Als der Goldſchmied Cardillac tödlich verwundet zuſammenbrach, hörte ich jemand gelaufen kommen. Ich dachte, das wird der Helfer des Mörders ſein, warf den Dolch hin und zog meinen Degen, um mich beſſer verteidigen zu können. Im Mondlicht, nur einen Schritt von mir entfernt, beugte ſich ein junger Menſch über den verwundet am Boden Liegenden und verſuchte, ihn aufzuheben. Nun hielt ich es für das Beſte, mich zurückzuziehen, denn ich hoffte in dieſen Tagen auf eine Beförderung, und der Tod des Goldſchmiedes hätte mich in große Schwierigkeiten verwickelt.[14] Ich weiß nicht, wie ich Ihnen, Herr Präſident, hätte beweiſen können, daß der geachtete[15] Schmied Cardillac in Wirklichkeit ein Mörder war. Ich ſagte nichts von der Sache, und als ich hörte, man habe den Geſellen des Schmiedes gefangen und hielte ihn für den Mörder der Kavaliere, dachte ich mir: Auch gut! Iſt er nicht der Mörder des Schmiedes, ſo iſt er doch ſein Freund und Helfer und hat wahrſcheinlich das Leben manches Kavaliers auf dem Gewiſſen. Trotzdem ließ mir aber der Gedanke keine Ruhe, daß er vielleicht doch unſchuldig wäre. Ich hörte von dem Intereſſe, das das Fräulein von Scudery für dieſem Fall zeigte und ſagte mir, wenn dieſe würdige Dame an die Unſchuld des jungen Mannes glaubt, ſo dürfe ich nicht ſo ſicher ſein, daß er ein Mörder iſt. Meine Nachforſchungen ſchienen darauf hinzuweiſen,[16] daß Olivier nichts mit den nächtlichen Raubmorden des Schmiedes zu tun hatte. Schließlich hielt ich es nicht länger aus,[17] denn ich hörte, man werde in dieſen Tagen Olivier auf der Folterbank zu einem Geſtändnis zwingen. Ich geſtand Seiner Majeſtät dem König, daß ich den Schmied in der Notwehr[18] erſtochen hatte."

[1] treiben, ie, ie, *drive.* *[2] ſichtlich, *apparent, obvious.* [3] beſtellen, *order.* [4] beſtimmt ſein, war, geweſen (iſt), *be intended.* [5] liſtig, *sly.* [6] ausfragen, *question.* [7] der Bruſtharniſch, –s, –e, *breastplate.* [8] die Weſte, —, –n, *vest.* [9] anfallen, ie, a, *attack.* *[10] das Eiſen, –s, *iron.* [11] der Panzer, –s, —, *armour.* [12] abgleiten, i, i, *glance off.* [13] die Bereitſchaft, —, *readiness.* [14] verwickeln, *involve.* [15] geachtet, *respected.* [16] hinweiſen auf, ie, ie, *indicate.* [17] aushalten, ie, a, *bear, resist.* [18] die Notwehr, —, *self-defence.*

Graf Oldain ſchwieg, und der König winkte einem Diener, dem er einen geflüſterten Befehl gab. Der Diener entfernte ſich ſofort, und der König wandte ſich an Desgrais. „Sie ſehen nun, Desgrais, daß Cardillac nicht ermordet wurde, ſondern nur ſeinen gerechten [1] Lohn [2] empfing. Heute morgen war D'Andilly bei mir in Verſailles, und ich habe von ihm die ſeltſame und traurige Geſchichte Olivier Bruſſons erfahren. Die Gewiſſensqualen [3] des jungen Menſchen haben unſer tiefes Mitleid erregt. Die Gewiſſensnot und die Kerkerhaft [4] ſind Strafe genug für Olivier Bruſſon, dem hiermit die Gnade ſeines Königs die Freiheit wiedergibt. Desgrais, ſchicken Sie Olivier Bruſſon in das Haus des Fräuleins von Scudery! Sorgen [5] Sie dafür, daß er einen Reiſepaß [6] erhält, und geben Sie ihm all ſein konfiſziertes Eigentum [7] zurück!"

Bei dieſen Worten wollte Madelon vor dem König in die Knie fallen, aber der verhinderte es, und als er Tränen in den Augen des ſchönen Mädchens ſah, ſagte er lächelnd: „Nun iſt ja alles gut, und wie hätte es anders ſein können, denn wen die Liebe in Schutz nimmt, der hat den mächtigſten Helfer auf ſeiner Seite. Ich weiß, Sie haben ſchwer gelitten, Madelon, aber bedenken Sie auch dies: In meinem ganzen Königreich könnte ich keine beſſere mütterliche Freundin für Sie finden als unſer Fräulein von Scudery, und deren Liebe hat Ihnen der Himmel in Ihrer größten Not geſchenkt."

In dieſem Augenblick erſchien der Diener, den der König fortgeſchickt hatte, mit einem Schriftſtück.[8] König Ludwig unterzeichnete [9] es und gab es Madelon in die Hand. „Laſſen Sie ſich hierfür von meinem Schatzmeiſter [10] Ihre Mitgift [11] auszahlen,[12] heiraten Sie Ihren Olivier, aber dann verlaſſen Sie beide Paris! Das iſt mein Wille!"

Wenige Tage ſpäter wurde Madelons und Oliviers Hochzeit im Hauſe des Fräuleins von Scudery gefeiert,[13] und dann verließ das junge Paar die Hauptſtadt, um ſich in Avignon niederzulaſſen.[14] Wäre es auch nicht des Königs Wille geweſen, Bruſſon hätte doch nicht in Paris bleiben können, wo ihn alles an jene entſetzliche Zeit der Mordtaten Cardillacs erinnerte. Begabt [15] mit großer Geſchicklichkeit [16] in ſeinem Handwerk, wurde er bald ein angeſehener Meiſter in Avignon.

Ein Jahr nach der Abreiſe des jungen Paares erſchien eine öffentliche Bekanntmachung,[17] daß alle, die bis zum Jahre 1680 durch Überfall auf der Straße Schmuckſtücke verloren hätten, ſich bei der Polizei melden ſollten, wo man ihnen ihr Eigentum zurückgeben werde. Die Juwelen der Ermordeten, die von den Angehörigen [18] nicht abgeholt wurden, übergab der Staat der Kirche St. Euſtache. Unter dieſen Juwelen befand ſich auch das Juwelenkäſtchen des Fräuleins von Scudery.

*1 gerecht, *just.* 2 der Lohn, –es, *reward.* 3 die Gewiſſensqualen (pl.), *anguish of conscience.* 4 die Kerkerhaft, —, –en, *imprisonment.* 5 ſorgen für, *see to.* 6 der Reiſepaß, –es, ⸗e, *passport.* 7 das Eigentum, –s, ⸗er, *possessions, property.* 8 das Schriftſtück, –es, –e, *document.* 9 unterzeichnen, *sign.* 10 der Schatzmeiſter, –s, —, *treasurer.* 11 die Mitgift, —, *dowry.* 12 auszahlen, *pay out.* *13 feiern, *celebrate.* *14 ſich niederlaſſen, ie, a, *settle, establish oneself.* *15 begabt, *gifted, endowed.* *16 die Geſchicklichkeit, —, *skill.* *17 die Bekanntmachung, —, –en, *announcement.* *18 der Angehörige, –n, –n, *relative.*

A. Practice Sentences:

1. Im Nu hatte er den Degen gezogen und begann, mit uns beiden zu kämpfen, wie ich noch nie einen Mann habe kämpfen sehen.
2. Hatte er auch in der Regel wenig Geld, so war er doch immer gut angezogen und wurde zu vielen Gesellschaften eingeladen.
3. Es wäre mir am liebsten gewesen, wenn er uns gesagt hätte, worum es sich in diesem Fall handelt.
4. Darf ich Sie darauf aufmerksam machen, daß der Herr im grauen Mantel der König selbst ist?
5. Meiner Meinung nach können wir ihm helfen, ohne ihn wissen zu lassen, woher die Hilfe kommt.
6. Sie können sich nicht vorstellen, wie mir zumute war, als ich das hörte.
7. Der Vorschlag gefiel mir; ich sagte ihm aber, es würde wahrscheinlich niemand anders als Richard geneigt sein, uns das Geld zu geben.
8. Das Fräulein ist im Begriff auszugehen. Können Sie nicht später wiederkommen?
9. Jahrelang habe ich darauf gewartet, einmal nach Europa fahren zu können. Sie müssen wissen, ich bin in meinem Leben noch nie auf einem großen Dampfer gewesen und fremde Länder kenne ich nur aus Büchern und Filmen.
10. Wir brauchen eine intelligente Sekretärin: Fräulein Müller kann nicht stenographieren, Fräulein Klein ist nach dem ersten Interview nicht wiedergekommen, Fräulein Witkop kann nachmittags nicht arbeiten — haben Sie sonst jemand auf der Liste, der in Frage käme?

B. Securing the Vocabulary:

1. greifen
   der Griff
   begreifen
   der Begriff
   im Begriff sein
   ergreifen
   angreifen
   der Angreifer
   der Angriff
2. fließen
   der Fluß
   der Einfluß
3. irgendein
   irgendetwas
   irgendjemand
   irgendwie
   irgendwo
4. die Ehre
   ehrgeizig
   ehrlich
   ehrwürdig
   der Ehrentitel
   Geehrtes Fräulein
   verehren
5. dienen
   der Diener
   die Dienerin
   der Dienst
   verdienen
6. binden
   die Verbindung
   das Band
   die Bande
   das Bündel
7. teilen
   der Teil
   zum Teil
   teils . . . teils
   teilweise
   die Abteilung
   der Anteil
   aufteilen
   mitteilen
8. schlagen
   der Schlag
   der Schlaganfall
   der Vorschlag
   der Tennisschläger
   die Schlägerei
   einschlagen
   erschlagen
9. die Schuld
   die Schulden (pl.)
   schuld sein
   der Schuldige
   die Unschuld
   unschuldig

entschuldigen
die Entschuldigung
10. geben
das Ergebnis
angeben
die Angabe
angeblich

aufgeben
die Aufgabe
vergeben
vergeblich
ausgeben
nachgeben

übergeben
zugeben
zurückgeben
mitgeben
die Mitgift
begabt

APPENDIX

1. Pronunciation

The pronunciation of German sounds does not offer insuperable difficulties for the speaker of English. You will be able to acquire a good pronunciation quickly by observing and imitating carefully the pronunciation of your instructor, at the same time bearing in mind the following characteristic features of German pronunciation in general. 1) Your instructor uses his lips more freely; 2) he enunciates words more clearly and distinctly than you do in English; 3) German short sounds are really short, and long sounds lack the gliding sound found in such English words as *so*^{u}. 4) In speaking or reading a sentence the individual words appear as distinct units and are rarely run together as you do in *That'senough.* In the case of words beginning with a vowel, the air flow is stopped just long enough to prevent the final consonant of the preceding word to merge with the vowel of the following word. Observe what appear to be very short pauses between the words: **Hier / ist / er.**

German and English use the same letters of the alphabet, but these letters do not represent necessarily the same sounds in both languages. For the most part, then, you will have to identify the familiar letters with different sound values. But since German spelling is more nearly phonetic than English you will have to learn in most instances only one sound for each letter. Note that in English the letter *a* has various pronunciations such as *arm, map, care,* etc. This is not the case in German.

Vowels: Accented German vowels are either long or short. They are long when followed by one consonant or **h** (**gut, wahr**) and when doubled **ee** (**Tee**). The combination **ie** (**hier**) represents a long *i* sound as English *ee.* A number of common words, however, have a short vowel, even though only one consonant follows: **an, des, das, es, hat, in, man, mit, um, was.**

a symbolizes the sound of long *a* as in *far* or short *a* as in *artistic.*

e symbolizes the sound of long *a* as in *gate* without the off-glide or short *e* as in *net.*

In a final syllable and in the prefixes **be-, ge-** the **e** is very short as *a* in *about.*

i symbolizes the sound of long *i* as in *machine* or short *i* as in *it.*

o symbolizes the sound of long *o* as in *old* (but without the *u*-glide) or short *o* as in *Ford* if *o* is pronounced short.

u symbolizes the sound of long *oo* as in *moon* or short *oo* as in *book.*

Three vowel symbols are new to you; only two, however, represent sounds which do not occur in English.

ö Long **ö**: Pronounce *a* in *gate,* but without the off-glide; now round and protrude your lips keeping the tongue in the same position. Pronounce long ö in **schön.**

Short ö: Pronounce *e* in *get* with rounded lips (**öffnen**).

ü Long **ü**: Pronounce *ee* in *bee;* now round and protrude your lips keeping the tongue in the same position. Pronounce long **ü** in **natürlich.**
Short **ü**: Pronounce *i* in *fin* with rounded lips (**fünf**).

ä You will have no difficulty with the pronunciation of this vowel. The long **ä** symbolizes the *a*-sound in *bear* (**trägt**). The short **ä** sounds like *e* in *net* (**älter**).

The above three vowels are known as umlaut or modified vowels. The modified vowel is indicated by two dots or, rarely, by the original vowel and **e** (**Goethe**).

The vowel combinations **ei, au, äu** and **eu,** called diphthongs, roughly correspond in sound to the English diphthongs *ai, ou,* and *oi.*

ei is similar to *ai* in *aisle*
au is similar to *ou* in *house*
äu, eu are similar to *oi* in *oil* pronounced with rounded lips.

Incidentally, you may get mixed up in the pronunciation of **ei** and **ie.** Associate in your mind **ei** with English *height* and **ie** with English *field.* This will help you to distinguish between **ei** as *ai* in *aisle* and **ie** as *i* in *machine.*

Consonants

The consonants **f, h, k, m, n, p, t** are pronounced alike in English and in German: (Note: **h** is silent in German when it appears in medial or final position; in the ending **-tion, t** is pronounced **ts** — **Konversation**).

b, d and **g** at the beginning of a word or syllable are pronounced as in English; however at the end of a word or syllable and before **-s** or **-t, b** is pronounced like **p** (**halb, Herbst**), **d** like **t** (**gesund**), and **g** like **k** (**Tag**). (Note: **ng** is pronounced as *ng* in *singer,* not as in *finger:* **g** in the uninflected suffix **-ig** is pronounced as **ch** in **ich** (**wenig**).

There is a distinct difference between the pronunciation of the English and German **l.** Pronounce in succession *full* and *William.* The sound of *l* in *William* resembles very much the German **l**-sound where the tip of the tongue is pressed against the upper teeth (**Held, alt, lesen**). Can you pronounce the German word **hell,** meaning *bright,* without any resemblance to the *l*-sound in the English word which is spelled the same way?

German has two pronunciations for **r,** the uvular and the tongue-tip **r.** The latter is recommended because it is easy to acquire. It is produced by placing the tip of the tongue against the palate just above the front teeth and then causing it to vibrate. You will observe varying degrees of clarity of the **r**-sound depending on the position of the **r** in a word. It is most distinct when followed by a vowel. (**Richard, braun, fragen**). It is pronounced less distinctly if it is preceded by a vowel. This is especially the case when it is preceded by a *long* vowel and in the combination **er** in unaccented position when the **r** has a kind of a vowel sound (**wir, nur, natürlich, Geburtstag; aber, Vater, Mutter**).

s is pronounced like *z* in *zeal* when followed by a vowel (**sagen, sie, lesen**); like *s* in *hiss* at the end of a syllable, before a consonant or when double (**Hans,**

ist, Fuß). Observe the pronunciation of **s** in the following combinations: **sch** as *sh* in *shy* (**Schulter**); **sp** and **st** at the beginning of a word or syllable as **shp** (**sprechen**) and **sht** (**Student**) respectively.

There are a few letters which represent entirely different sounds in German and deserve your special attention:

j is similar to *y* in *yes* (**ja, Jahr**).

v indicates the sound of *f* as in *fine* (**von, Vater**).

w Whenever you see a **w** in German pronounce it as English *v* in *vain* (**wahr, was**).

z, tz have the same sound value as *ts* in *rats, nuts* (**Anzug, jetzt**).
Pay particular attention to the pronunciation of **z** in initial position (**zehn, zu, Zeit**).

ch Pronounce the *h* in *hew* with the tip of the tongue pressed against the lower teeth; at the same time raise your tongue and breathe out and pronounce **ich, nicht, sprechen, nächsten.**

The sound you have just practiced (the so-called **ich**-sound) is used in all positions except when preceded by **a, o, u,** and **au.** In the latter position the so-called **ach**-sound is used. It is produced farther back in the mouth with the back part of the tongue raised toward the middle of the soft palate. Now press the tip of your tongue against your lower front teeth, arch your tongue as if you were to say **k.** Then breathe out, allowing the air to pass through the narrow space between the tongue and the roof of the mouth and say: **ach, noch, auch.**

The Alphabet

You are now ready to pronounce and memorize the names of the letters of the alphabet:

a	ah	**h**	hah	**o**	oh*	**v**	fow
b	ba(y)*	**i**	ee	**p**	pa(y)*	**w**	va(y)*
c	tsa(y)*	**j**	yot	**q**	koo	**x**	iks
d	da(y)*	**k**	kah	**r**	er (as in errand)	**y**	ü'psilon
e	a(y)*	**l**	ell	**s**	ess	**z**	tset
f	eff	**m**	emm	**t**	ta(y)*		
g	ga(y)*	**n**	enn	**u**	oo		

2. German Print

The so-called Gothic type is used in most German books and newspapers.

a) Pay particular attention to the two confusing letters **f** (f) and **ſ** (s). Notice the **f** is crossed.

b) Observe the different symbols which the Gothic type employs for the Roman type **s.**

long **ſ** is used

1. at the beginning of words not capitalized (**ſeit**).

* There is no off-glide to **i** or **u.**

2. at the beginning of syllables (le=ſen).
3. in the combinations ſch, ſp, ſt (ſchon, ſpät, aufſtehen).

final ſ is used

1. at the end of words (etwas).
2. at the end of syllables where the ſ marks the end of the word (Aus=ſicht).

double ſſ is used between two vowels, the first of which is short (laſſen).

ß (called eß=tſet) is used in place of double ſſ

1. after a long vowel or diphthong (Straße, außerdem).
2. before t (mußte).
3. at the end of words (weiß).

THE ALPHABET IN GOTHIC AND ROMAN TYPE

𝔄	𝔞	A	a	𝔍	𝔧	J	j	𝔖	ſ s	S	s
𝔅	𝔟	B	b	𝔎	𝔨	K	k	𝔗	t	T	t
ℭ	𝔠	C	c	𝔏	𝔩	L	l	𝔘	u	U	u
𝔇	𝔡	D	d	𝔐	𝔪	M	m	𝔙	𝔳	V	v
𝔈	𝔢	E	e	𝔑	𝔫	N	n	𝔚	𝔴	W	w
𝔉	𝔣	F	f	𝔒	𝔬	O	o	𝔛	𝔵	X	x
𝔊	𝔤	G	g	𝔓	𝔭	P	p	𝔜	𝔶	Y	y
ℌ	𝔥	H	h	𝔔	𝔮	Q	q	𝔝	𝔷	Z	z
ℑ	𝔦	I	i	𝔎	𝔯	R	r				

3. Punctuation

Most marks of punctuation in German are used as in English. Notice, however, the following principal differences:

(1) The **Comma** is used:

(a) between two independent clauses, when the clauses have different subjects:

Richard bleibt zu Hause und schreibt einen Brief.
Anna besucht Richard, und Gretel macht Einkäufe.

(b) to set off all subordinated clauses (relative and dependent clauses):

Das Halsband, das Anna zu jedem Kleid trägt, ist Richards Geschenk.
Richard freut sich, daß Anna zum Galaball kommt.

(c) to set off infinitive phrases if the infinitive is modified:

Anna ist Verkäuferin, um sich ein bißchen Geld zu verdienen.

but:

Er versuchte zu lesen.

Notice that the comma is not used before **und** and **oder** when they connect the last two parts of a series of words:

Sie liest Richards Brief morgens, mittags und abends.
Kaufen Sie ihr ein Kleid, einen Schmuckartikel oder einen Pelzmantel?

The comma is not used with parenthetical words:

Robert ist aber nicht gekommen.

It is not used to set off adverbs and adverbial phrases of time and place at the beginning of a sentence:

Später werde ich den Brief beenden.

(2) The **Exclamation Point** must be used:

(a) after the salutation in a letter:

Lieber Vater!

(b) after commands and requests:

Kommen Sie bitte rechtzeitig!

(3) **Quotation Marks** are used as in English, with the exception that the first ones are placed below at the beginning of the quotation:

Der Fremde sagte: „Sind Sie Berufsspieler?"

(4) A double **Hyphen** (=) instead of the single hyphen (-) is used in German print.

4. Syllabification

Words at the end of a line are divided into syllables according to pronunciation.

(a) A single consonant between vowels belongs to the syllable with the second vowel:

le-sen, lau-fen, lie-ber, Va-ter

(b) If two or more consonants stand between vowels, only the last one is carried over:

Mut-ter, fal-len, sin-gen, wach-sen, Verwand-te, Kat-ze, wis-sen

But **ß, ch, ph, st** are never divided:

Stra-ße, la-chen, Fi-sche, Geogra-phie, Fen-ster

If, however, the **t** is part of the ending (past tense of weak verbs), the two are separated: **reis-te.**

ck is separated into **k-k: Zuk-ker.**

(c) Compound words are separated into various elements of which they are made up and according to the rules given above:

Haus-ein-gang, Be-weg-grund, her-auf-ge-holt

5. Normal Word Order (The subject is followed by the verb.)

(a) Sie (1) verkaufte (2) der alten Dame (3) einen Pelzmantel (4).

(b) Sie (1) hat (2) ihn (5) ihr (6) gestern (7) im Warenhaus (8) gezeigt (9).

1 2 5 3 9
(c) Sie hat ihn der alten Dame verkauft.

1 2 7 4 9 10
(d) Er stellt jetzt das Radio im Schlafzimmer an.

1 2 5 7 10 11
(e) Er kann es jetzt anstellen.

1 2 4 11 11
(f) Er hat das Radio anstellen wollen.

Note: Each of the numbers used above represents a part of the sentence.

1 — subject
2 — inflected part of the verb
3 — dative (noun) object
4 — accusative (noun) object
5 — accusative (pronoun) object
6 — dative (pronoun) object
7 — adverb of time
8 — adverbial expression of place
9 — past participle
10 — separable prefix
11 — infinitive (In the case of a double infinitive construction, the infinitive of the modal auxiliary stands last.)

General Rules for Position

Verb: The past participle and the infinitive, as well as the separable prefix, must stand in the last place in main clauses and infinitive clauses.

Object: Of two noun objects the dative object precedes the accusative object.

Of two pronoun objects the accusative object precedes the dative object.

Of one pronoun and one noun object the pronoun precedes the noun object.

Adverbs: An adverb of time precedes that of place.

An adverb of time immediately follows the inflected part of the verb; but if the dative or accusative object in the sentence is a pronoun, the latter precedes the adverb of time.

An adverbial expression of place, such as **in der Schule, zu Hause, im Zimmer,** stands as close to the end of the sentence as other rules permit.

6. Inverted Word Order (The finite verb precedes the subject.)

(1) It is used in questions and imperatives of the conventional form.

2 1
(a) Verkauft sie der Dame den Pelzmantel?

2 1
(b) Zeigen Sie ihn ihr!

(2) It is used when the subject does not begin the sentence.

2 1
(a) Der Dame verkaufte sie den Pelzmantel.

2 1
(b) Gestern hat sie ihn ihr verkauft.

(c) Im Schlafzimmer stellt er das Radio an.
2 1

(d) Das Radio hat er im Schlafzimmer anstellen wollen.
2 1

Ja and **Nein,** which may precede a sentence, do not change the word order.

Ja, er kann es jetzt anstellen.

(3) Often the dependent clause precedes the independent clause. In such cases, the inverted word order is used in the independent clause.

Als er seinen Freund sah, gab er ihm das Buch.

(4) **Wenn,** introducing a conditional clause, may be omitted. In such a case, the inverted word order must be employed.

Wenn ich das gewußt hätte, wäre ich nicht gegangen.
Hätte ich das gewußt, wäre ich nicht gegangen.

7. Transposed Word Order (The inflected part of the verb stands at the end of the dependent clause.)

(1) Transposed word order is used after subordinating conjunctions:

1. als — when (*referring to a single event in the past*)
2. bis — until, till
3. da — since (*causal*)
4. damit — in order that
5. daß — that
6. ehe, bevor — before
7. nachdem — after
8. ob — whether
9. obgleich, obwohl — although
10. seit — since (*temporal*)
11. trotzdem — in spite of the fact that
12. während — while (*temporal*)
13. weil — because, since (*causal*)
14. wenn — if, when, whenever
15. wie — how (*if used in indirect questions*)
16. wo — where (" ")
17. wann — when (" ")

als er eintrat.
während mein Bruder arbeitete.
Ich sprach nicht mit meinem Freund, weil er arbeiten mußte.
weil er hat arbeiten müssen.

Note: 1. In clauses with transposed word order separable prefixes are not separated (—, **als er eintrat**).

2. If the double infinitive construction is used, the inflected part of the verb stands in the third place from the end (—, **weil er hat arbeiten müssen**).

3. In an indirect statement the **daß** may be omitted. If this is the case, the normal word order is employed.

Er sagt, daß er mit seinem Freund gesprochen habe.
Er sagt, er habe mit seinem Freund gesprochen.

(2) Transposed word order is used in relative clauses:

Ich sprach mit meinem Freund, der das Buch mitgebracht hat.

(3) Transposed word order is used in indirect questions:

Wissen Sie, wie alt er ist?
Wissen Sie, wo er vor einem Jahr gewohnt hat?

8. Position of *nicht*

The position of **nicht** varies widely.

(a) If it is used to negate the entire sentence, it stands as close to the end of the sentence as rules permit.

(b) If **nicht** modifies a certain element of the sentence, it precedes this element.

Er hat es seinem Freund nicht gegeben.
Er geht heute nicht ins Kino.
Sie hat ihr nicht das Kleid, sondern den Pelzmantel verkauft.
Nicht Neumann, sondern Niemann war Berufsspieler in Florida.

9. Co-ordinating Conjunctions

After the co-ordinating conjunctions **aber** *but*, **allein** *however*, **denn** *for*, **entweder . . . oder** *either . . . or*, **oder** *or*, **sondern** *but* **und** *and*, **weder . . . noch** *neither . . . nor*, normal word order is employed.

Aber ich werde zu Hause bleiben, denn es regnet schon.
Sie weiß, daß er es nicht selbst getan hat, sondern daß wir ihm geholfen haben.

10. Adjectives

Adjectives are divided into (1) limiting and (2) descriptive adjectives.

Limiting adjectives limit an object or person in regard to gender, number, and case. The limiting adjectives are (a) the definite article (§11) and the **der**-words (§12), (b) the indefinite article (§13) and the **ein**-words (§14).

Ordinary adjectives such as **schön, alt,** and **groß** are called descriptive adjectives (§15) because they serve to indicate the quality or condition of an object or a person.

11. The Definite Article

	SINGULAR			PLURAL
	MASCULINE	FEMININE	NEUTER	ALL GENDERS
NOMINATIVE:	der	die	das	die
ACCUSATIVE:	den	die	das	die
DATIVE:	dem	der	dem	den
GENITIVE:	des	der	des	der

12. The *der*-Words

The **der**-words are declined like the definite article. In the following the forms of the nominative singular for the three genders are given:

dieser, diese, dieses	*this*
jener, jene, jenes	*that*
jeder, jede, jedes	*each, every*
welcher, welche, welches	*which, what*
solcher, solche, solches	*such a*
mancher, manche, manches	*many a*

	Singular			Plural
	MASCULINE	FEMININE	NEUTER	ALL GENDERS
Nominative:	dieser Bruder	diese Tür	dieses Haus	diese Brüder
Accusative:	diesen Bruder	diese Tür	dieses Haus	diese Brüder
Dative:	diesem Bruder	dieser Tür	diesem Haus	diesen Brüdern
Genitive:	dieses Bruders	dieser Tür	dieses Hauses	dieser Brüder

13. The Indefinite Article

	Singular			Plural
	MASCULINE	FEMININE	NEUTER	ALL GENDERS
Nominative:	ein	eine	ein	keine
Accusative:	einen	eine	ein	keine
Dative:	einem	einer	einem	keinen
Genitive:	eines	einer	eines	keiner

14. The *ein*-Words

The **ein**-words are declined like the indefinite article. In the following list the forms of the nominative singular for the three genders are given.

kein, keine, kein	*no, not any*
mein, meine, mein	*my*
dein, deine, dein	*your*
sein, seine, sein	*his*
ihr, ihre, ihr	*her*
sein, seine, sein	*its*
unser, unsere, unser	*our*
euer, euere, euer	*your*
ihr, ihre, ihr	*their*
Ihr, Ihre, Ihr	*your*

	Singular			Plural
	MASCULINE	FEMININE	NEUTER	ALL GENDERS
Nominative:	mein Bruder	keine Tür	Ihr Haus	meine Brüder
Accusative:	meinen Bruder	keine Tür	Ihr Haus	meine Brüder
Dative:	meinem Bruder	keiner Tür	Ihrem Haus	meinen Brüdern
Genitive:	meines Bruders	keiner Tür	Ihres Hauses	meiner Brüder

15. Descriptive Adjectives

For the sake of convenience the declension of the descriptive adjective is divided into three classes:

Class I: No limiting adjective precedes the descriptive adjective (**junger Mann**).

Class II: A limiting adjective, namely the definite article or one of the **der**-words, precedes the descriptive adjective (**der junge Mann, dieses schöne Haus**).

Class III: A limiting adjective, namely the indefinite article or one of the **ein**-words, precedes the descriptive adjective (**ein junger Mann, mein schönes Haus**).

Note 1: Every descriptive adjective when used attributively, *i.e.* preceding a noun, whether in the positive, comparative, or superlative, takes an ending.

Note 2: Descriptive adjectives may be used as nouns. They retain their adjective declension.

Class I: **Armer,** *poor man;* **Arme** (pl.) *poor people*
Class II: **der Arme,** *the poor man* (*boy*)
Class III: **ein Armer,** *a poor man*

16. Class I:

No limiting adjective precedes the descriptive adjective. The endings are those of the definite article with the exception of the genitive masculine and neuter.

	Singular			Plural
	MASCULINE	FEMININE	NEUTER	ALL GENDERS
NOMINATIVE:	reifer Apfel	rote Tinte	gutes Kind	reife Äpfel
ACCUSATIVE:	reifen Apfel	rote Tinte	gutes Kind	reife Äpfel
DATIVE:	reifem Apfel	roter Tinte	gutem Kind	reifen Äpfeln
GENITIVE:	reifen Apfels	roter Tinte	guten Kindes	reifer Äpfel

17. Class II:

The definite article or one of the **der**-words precedes the descriptive adjective.

	Singular		
	MASCULINE	FEMININE	NEUTER
NOMINATIVE:	der gute Bruder	jene kleine Tür	dieses schöne Haus
ACCUSATIVE:	den guten Bruder	jene kleine Tür	dieses schöne Haus
DATIVE:	dem guten Bruder	jener kleinen Tür	diesem schönen Haus
GENITIVE:	des guten Bruders	jener kleinen Tür	dieses schönen Hauses

	Plural
	ALL GENDERS
NOMINATIVE:	die guten Brüder
ACCUSATIVE:	die guten Brüder
DATIVE:	den guten Brüdern
GENITIVE:	der guten Brüder

18. Class III:

The indefinite article or one of the **ein**-words precedes the descriptive adjective.

SINGULAR

	MASCULINE	FEMININE	NEUTER
NOMINATIVE:	ein guter Bruder	keine kleine Tür	Ihr schönes Haus
ACCUSATIVE:	einen guten Bruder	keine kleine Tür	Ihr schönes Haus
DATIVE:	einem guten Bruder	keiner kleinen Tür	Ihrem schönen Haus
GENITIVE:	eines guten Bruders	keiner kleinen Tür	Ihres schönen Hauses

PLURAL

ALL GENDERS

NOMINATIVE:	meine guten Brüder
ACCUSATIVE:	meine guten Brüder
DATIVE:	meinen guten Brüdern
GENITIVE:	meiner guten Brüder

19. Numeral Adjectives

alle	*all*	etliche	*some*
andere	*other*	manche	*many*
beide	*both*	mehrere	*several*
einige	*a few, some*	viele	*many*
wenige	*few*		

These numeral adjectives are used mostly in the plural and take the endings of the descriptive adjective of Class I (*see above*).

NOMINATIVE:	einige Bücher
ACCUSATIVE:	einige Bücher
DATIVE:	einigen Büchern
GENITIVE:	einiger Bücher

If any of the above numeral adjectives, except **alle** (*see below*), is followed by a descriptive adjective, the latter may take the plural endings of either Class I or Class II in the nominative or accusative cases. Usage favors the endings of Class II after **beide** and **manche,** the endings of Class I after the others. In the genitive and dative cases the adjective takes the endings of Class II.

NOMINATIVE:	manche guten Bücher	viele gute Bücher
ACCUSATIVE:	manche guten Bücher	viele gute Bücher
DATIVE:	manchen guten Büchern	vielen guten Büchern
GENITIVE:	mancher guten Bücher	vieler guten Bücher

Exception: If **alle** is followed by a descriptive adjective, the latter takes the endings of Class II:

NOMINATIVE:	alle guten Bücher
ACCUSATIVE:	alle guten Bücher

DATIVE:	allen guten Büchern
GENITIVE:	aller guten Bücher

20. Comparison of Descriptive Adjectives

Formation of the comparative and superlative degrees:

(a) The comparative is formed by adding **–er**, the superlative by adding **–st** to the positive. Adjectives ending in **d** or **t** or a sibilant (**s, ß, tz, z**) add **–est** for the superlative.

POSITIVE:	klein	schlecht
COMPARATIVE:	kleiner	schlechter
SUPERLATIVE:	kleinst–	schlechtest–

(b) Adjectives ending in **–el, –en, –er** drop the **e** in the comparative, but retain it in the superlative.

POSITIVE:	dunkel
COMPARATIVE:	dunkler
SUPERLATIVE:	dunkelst–

(c) Many monosyllabic adjectives take on an umlaut in the comparative and superlative, *e.g.* **alt, älter, ältest–, am ältesten.**

(d) The following forms of comparison are irregular:

POSITIVE		COMPARATIVE	SUPERLATIVE
groß	*big*	größer	größt–
gut	*good*	besser	best–
hoch	*high*	höher	höchst–
nah	*near*	näher	nächst–
viel	*much*	mehr	meist–

21. The Adverb *gern*

The three degrees of **gern** are: **gern, lieber, am liebsten.**

Ich trinke Wasser gern.	*I like to drink water.*
Ich trinke Milch lieber.	*I prefer to drink milk.*
Ich trinke Tee am liebsten.	*I like to drink tea best of all.*

22. Declension of the Comparative and Superlative

When a descriptive adjective in the comparative or superlative is used as an attribute, *i.e.* preceding a noun, it takes the same endings as the adjective in the positive degree.

POSITIVE:	das alte Haus
COMPARATIVE:	das ältere Haus
SUPERLATIVE:	das älteste Haus

23. Predicate and Adverbial Forms of the Adjective

(a) in the positive and comparative degrees:

When a descriptive adjective in the positive or comparative is used as a predicate adjective or as an adverb, it is not inflected.

PREDICATE FORM: Die Universität ist alt.
Unsere Universität ist älter.
ADVERBIAL FORM: Paul läuft schnell.
Richard läuft schneller.

(b) in the superlative degree:

When a descriptive adjective is used as a predicate adjective or as an adverb, the superlative form consists of **am** + the superlative form with **–en** (**am ältesten, am schnellsten**).

PREDICATE FORM: Unsere Universität ist am ältesten.
ADVERBIAL FORM: Richard läuft am schnellsten.

24. Personal pronouns

SINGULAR

					MASCULINE	FEMININE	NEUTER
NOMINATIVE:	ich	*I*	du	Sie	er	sie	es
ACCUSATIVE:	mich	*me*	dich	Sie	ihn	sie	es
DATIVE:	mir	*(to) me*	dir	Ihnen	ihm	ihr	ihm
GENITIVE:	meiner	*of me*	deiner	Ihrer	seiner	ihrer	seiner

PLURAL

					ALL GENDERS
NOMINATIVE:	wir	*we*	ihr	Sie	sie
ACCUSATIVE:	uns	*us*	euch	Sie	sie
DATIVE:	uns	*(to) us*	euch	Ihnen	ihnen
GENITIVE:	unser	*of us*	euer	Ihrer	ihrer

Note: If a personal pronoun is governed by a preposition and refers to an inanimate thing, it is replaced by **da–** (**dar–** before a vowel) in both the singular and plural:

Wir haben eine Villa mit einer Terrasse davor.
Die Bühne; es sind ein paar Bänke darauf.

25. Prepositions with the Genitive

Among the common prepositions that govern the genitive are:

(an)statt	*instead of*	trotz	*in spite of*
außerhalb	*outside of*	oberhalb	*above*
diesseits	*this side*	unterhalb	*below*
innerhalb	*inside of*	während	*during*
jenseits	*beyond*	wegen	*on account of*

26. Prepositions with the Accusative

bis	*until, up to, as far as*	gegen	*towards, against*
durch	*through, by means of*	ohne	*without*
für	*for*	um	*around, about, at*
		wider	*against, in opposition to*

27. Prepositions with the Dative

aus	*out of, from*	nach	*after, to, toward, according to*
außer	*besides, except*	seit	*since*
bei	*at, near, with, at the home of*	von	*from, of, by*
mit	*with, together with, at*	zu	*to, at*

28. Prepositions with the Dative or Accusative

an	*at, to, on, near, by*	neben	*beside, close by*
auf	*on, upon, at, in, on top of*	über	*over, above, about, concerning*
hinter	*behind*	unter	*under, among*
in	*in, into, at, within*	vor	*before, in front of, ago*
		zwischen	*between*

29. Paradigm of *sein*, to be

Principal parts: sein, war, ich bin gewesen, er ist.

	INDICATIVE	SUBJUNCTIVE I	SUBJUNCTIVE II
PRESENT	*I am*, etc.		
	ich bin	sei	wäre
	du bist	seiest	wärest
	er ist	sei	wäre
	wir sind	seien	wären
	ihr seid	seiet	wäret
	sie sind	seien	wären
SIMPLE PAST	*I was*		
	ich war		
	du warst		
	er war		
	wir waren		
	ihr wart		
	sie waren		
PRESENT PERFECT	*I have been; I was*		
	ich bin gewesen	sei gewesen	wäre gewesen
	du bist gewesen	seiest gewesen	wärest gewesen
	er ist gewesen	sei gewesen	wäre gewesen
	wir sind gewesen	seien gewesen	wären gewesen
	ihr seid gewesen	seiet gewesen	wäret gewesen
	sie sind gewesen	seien gewesen	wären gewesen
PAST PERFECT	*I had been*		
	ich war gewesen		
	du warst gewesen		
	er war gewesen		

	wir waren gewesen		
	ihr wart gewesen		
	sie waren gewesen		
FUTURE	*I shall be*		
	ich werde sein	werde sein	würde sein
	du wirst sein	werdest sein	würdest sein
	er wird sein	werde sein	würde sein
	wir werden sein	werden sein	würden sein
	ihr werdet sein	werdet sein	würdet sein
	sie werden sein	werden sein	würden sein
FUTURE PERFECT	*I shall have been*		
	ich werde gewesen sein	werde gewesen sein	würde gewesen sein
	du wirst gewesen sein	werdest gewesen sein	würdest gewesen sein
	etc.	etc.	etc.

IMPERATIVES: FAMILIAR, SINGULAR: sei! *be*
PLURAL: seid!
CONVENTIONAL FORM OF ADDRESS: seien Sie!

30. Paradigm of *haben*, *to have*

Principal parts: haben, hatte, ich habe gehabt, er hat

	INDICATIVE	SUBJUNCTIVE I	SUBJUNCTIVE II
PRESENT	*I have*, etc.		
	ich habe	habe	hätte
	du hast	habest	hättest
	er hat	habe	hätte
	wir haben	haben	hätten
	ihr habt	habet	hättet
	sie haben	haben	hätten
SIMPLE PAST	*I had*		
	ich hatte		
	du hattest		
	er hatte		
	wir hatten		
	ihr hattet		
	sie hatten		
PRESENT PERFECT	*I have had, I had*		
	ich habe gehabt		
	du hast gehabt		
	er hat gehabt		

	wir haben gehabt		
	ihr habt gehabt		
	sie haben gehabt		
PAST	*I had had*		
PERFECT	ich hatte gehabt	habe gehabt	hätte gehabt
	du hattest gehabt	habest gehabt	hättest gehabt
	er hatte gehabt	habe gehabt	hätte gehabt
	wir hatten gehabt	haben gehabt	hätten gehabt
	ihr hattet gehabt	habet gehabt	hättet gehabt
	sie hatten gehabt	haben gehabt	hätten gehabt
FUTURE	*I shall have*		
	ich werde haben	werde haben	würde haben
	du wirst haben	werdest haben	würdest haben
	er wird haben	werde haben	würde haben
	wir werden haben	werden haben	würden haben
	ihr werdet haben	werdet haben	würdet haben
	sie werden haben	werden haben	würden haben
FUTURE	*I shall have had*		
PERFECT	ich werde gehabt haben	werde gehabt haben	würde gehabt haben
	du wirst gehabt haben	werdest gehabt haben	würdest gehabt haben
	etc.	etc.	etc.

IMPERATIVES: FAMILIAR, SINGULAR: habe! *have*
PLURAL: habt!

CONVENTIONAL FORM OF ADDRESS: haben Sie!

31. Paradigm of *werden,* to become

Principal parts: werden, wurde, ich bin geworden, er wird

	INDICATIVE	SUBJUNCTIVE I	SUBJUNCTIVE II
PRESENT	*I become,* etc.		
	ich werde	werde	würde
	du wirst	werdest	würdest
	er wird	werde	würde
	wir werden	werden	würden
	ihr werdet	werdet	würdet
	sie werden	werden	würden
SIMPLE PAST	*I became*		
	ich wurde		
	du wurdest		
	er wurde		

	wir wurden		
	ihr wurdet		
	sie wurden		
PRESENT	*I have become; I became*		
PERFECT	ich bin geworden	sei geworden	wäre geworden
	du bist geworden	seiest geworden	wärest geworden
	er ist geworden	sei geworden	wäre geworden
	wir sind geworden	seien geworden	wären geworden
	ihr seid geworden	seiet geworden	wäret geworden
	sie sind geworden	seien geworden	wären geworden
PAST	*I had become*		
PERFECT	ich war geworden		
	du warst geworden		
	er war geworden		
	wir waren geworden		
	ihr wart geworden		
	sie waren geworden		
FUTURE	*I shall become*		
	ich werde werden	werde werden	würde werden
	du wirst werden	werdest werden	würdest werden
	er wird werden	werde werden	würde werden
	wir werden werden	werden werden	würden werden
	ihr werdet werden	werdet werden	würdet werden
	sie werden werden	werden werden	würden werden
FUTURE	*I shall have become*		
PERFECT	ich werde geworden sein	werde geworden sein	würde geworden sein
	du wirst geworden sein	werdest geworden sein	würdest geworden sein
	etc.	etc.	etc.

IMPERATIVES: FAMILIAR, SINGULAR: werde! *become*
PLURAL: werdet!

CONVENTIONAL FORM OF ADDRESS: werden Sie!

32. Paradigm of *lernen*, *to learn* (weak verb)

Principal parts: lernen, lernte, ich habe gelernt, er lernt

	INDICATIVE	SUBJUNCTIVE I	SUBJUNCTIVE II
PRESENT	*I learn*, etc.		
	ich lerne	lerne	lernte
	du lernst	lernest	lerntest
	er lernt	lerne	lernte

	wir lernen	lernen	lernten
	ihr lernt	lernet	lerntet
	sie lernen	lernen	lernten

SIMPLE PAST	*I learned*		
	ich lernte		
	du lerntest		
	er lernte		
	wir lernten		
	ihr lerntet		
	sie lernten		
PRESENT PERFECT	*I have learned; I learned*		
	ich habe gelernt	habe gelernt	hätte gelernt
	du hast gelernt	habest gelernt	hättest gelernt
	er hat gelernt	habe gelernt	hätte gelernt
	wir haben gelernt	haben gelernt	hätten gelernt
	ihr habt gelernt	habet gelernt	hättet gelernt
	sie haben gelernt	haben gelernt	hätten gelernt
PAST PERFECT	*I had learned*		
	ich hatte gelernt		
	du hattest gelernt		
	er hatte gelernt		
	wir hatten gelernt		
	ihr hattet gelernt		
	sie hatten gelernt		
FUTURE	*I shall learn*		
	ich werde lernen	werde lernen	würde lernen
	du wirst lernen	werdest lernen	würdest lernen
	er wird lernen	werde lernen	würde lernen
	wir werden lernen	werden lernen	würden lernen
	ihr werdet lernen	werdet lernen	würdet lernen
	sie werden lernen	werden lernen	würden lernen
FUTURE PERFECT	*I shall have learned*		
	ich werde gelernt haben	werde gelernt haben	würde gelernt haben
	du wirst gelernt haben	werdest gelernt haben	würdest gelernt haben
	etc.	etc.	etc.

IMPERATIVES: FAMILIAR, SINGULAR: lern(e)! *learn* (in colloquial German without e)

PLURAL: lernt!

CONVENTIONAL FORM OF ADDRESS: lernen Sie!

33. Paradigm of *sprechen*, *to speak* (strong verb)

Principal parts: sprechen, sprach, ich habe gesprochen, er spricht

	INDICATIVE	SUBJUNCTIVE I	SUBJUNCTIVE II
PRESENT	*I speak*, etc.		
	ich spreche	spreche	spräche
	du sprichst	sprechest	sprächest
	er spricht	spreche	spräche
	wir sprechen	sprechen	sprächen
	ihr sprecht	sprechet	sprächet
	sie sprechen	sprechen	sprächen
SIMPLE PAST	*I spoke*		
	ich sprach		
	du sprachst		
	er sprach		
	wir sprachen		
	ihr spracht		
	sie sprachen		
PRESENT PERFECT	*I have spoken; I spoke*		
	ich habe gesprochen	habe gesprochen	hätte gesprochen
	du hast gesprochen	habest gesprochen	hättest gesprochen
	er hat gesprochen	habe gesprochen	hätte gesprochen
	wir haben gesprochen	haben gesprochen	hätten gesprochen
	ihr habt gesprochen	habet gesprochen	hättet gesprochen
	sie haben gesprochen	haben gesprochen	hätten gesprochen
PAST PERFECT	*I had spoken*		
	ich hatte gesprochen		
	du hattest gesprochen		
	er hatte gesprochen		
	wir hatten gesprochen		
	ihr hattet gesprochen		
	sie hatten gesprochen		
FUTURE	*I shall speak*		
	ich werde sprechen	werde sprechen	würde sprechen
	du wirst sprechen	werdest sprechen	würdest sprechen
	er wird sprechen	werde sprechen	würde sprechen
	wir werden sprechen	werden sprechen	würden sprechen
	ihr werdet sprechen	werdet sprechen	würdet sprechen
	sie werden sprechen	werden sprechen	würden sprechen

FUTURE	*I shall have spoken*		
PERFECT	ich werde gesprochen haben	werde gesprochen haben	würde gesprochen haben
	du wirst gesprochen haben	werdest gesprochen haben	würdest gesprochen haben
	etc.	etc.	etc.

IMPERATIVES: FAMILIAR, SINGULAR: sprich! *speak*
PLURAL: sprecht!

CONVENTIONAL FORM OF ADDRESS: sprechen Sie!

34. Paradigm of *fragen* in the passive voice

	INDICATIVE	SUBJUNCTIVE I	SUBJUNCTIVE II
PRESENT	*I am asked*, etc.		
	ich werde gefragt	werde gefragt	würde gefragt
	du wirst gefragt	werdest gefragt	würdest gefragt
	er wird gefragt	werde gefragt	würde gefragt
	wir werden gefragt	werden gefragt	würden gefragt
	ihr werdet gefragt	werdet gefragt	würdet gefragt
	sie werden gefragt	werden gefragt	würden gefragt
SIMPLE PAST	*I was asked*		
	ich wurde gefragt		
	du wurdest gefragt		
	er wurde gefragt		
	wir wurden gefragt		
	ihr wurdet gefragt		
	sie wurden gefragt		
PRESENT PERFECT	*I have been asked, I was asked*		
	ich bin gefragt worden	sei gefragt worden	wäre gefragt worden
	du bist gefragt worden	seiest gefragt worden	wärest gefragt worden
	er ist gefragt worden	sei gefragt worden	wäre gefragt worden
	wir sind gefragt worden	seien gefragt worden	wären gefragt worden
	ihr seid gefragt worden	seiet gefragt worden	wäret gefragt worden
	sie sind gefragt worden	seien gefragt worden	wären gefragt worden
PAST PERFECT	*I had been asked*		
	ich war gefragt worden		
	du warst gefragt worden		
	er war gefragt worden		

wir waren gefragt worden
ihr wart gefragt worden
sie waren gefragt worden

FUTURE	*I shall be asked*		
	ich werde gefragt werden	werde gefragt werden	würde gefragt werden
	du wirst gefragt werden	werdest gefragt werden	würdest gefragt werden
	er wird gefragt werden	werde gefragt werden	würde gefragt werden
	wir werden gefragt werden	werden gefragt werden	würden gefragt werden
	ihr werdet gefragt werden	werdet gefragt werden	würdet gefragt werden
	sie werden gefragt werden	werden gefragt werden	würden gefragt werden

FUTURE PERFECT *I shall have been asked*

ich werde gefragt worden sein — werde gefragt worden sein
du wirst gefragt worden sein — werdest gefragt worden sein
etc. — etc.

würde gefragt worden sein
würdest gefragt worden sein
etc.

35. The Seven Ablaut Classes

(1)	ei — i — i	beißen	biß	gebissen	*bite*
	ei — ie — ie	bleiben	blieb	ich bin geblieben	*stay*
(2)	ie — o — o	verlieren	verlor	verloren	*lose*
(3)	i — a — u	singen	sang	gesungen	*sing*
	i — a — o	beginnen	begann	begonnen	*begin*
(4)	e — a — o	sprechen	sprach	gesprochen	*speak*
(5)	e — a — e	sehen	sah	gesehen	*see*
(6)	a — u — a	waschen	wusch	gewaschen	*wash*
(7)	a — ie — a	fallen	fiel	ich bin gefallen	*fall*
	au — ie — au	laufen	lief	ich bin gelaufen	*run*
	ei — ie — ei	heißen	hieß	geheißen	*to be called*
	o — ie — o	stoßen	stieß	gestoßen	*thrust, push*
	u — ie — u	rufen	rief	gerufen	*call*

IRREGULAR STRONG VERBS

gehen	ging	ich bin gegangen	*go*
stehen	stand	gestanden	*stand*
tun	tat	getan	*do*

36. Use of the tenses

(1) The present tense:

(a) The present tense in German has the function of any one of the three English present tense forms:

Herr Schröder macht Gruppenaufnahmen	*Mr. Schröder takes (is taking, does take) group pictures*

(b) It is used with an expression of time to denote action begun in the past and continuing in the present:

Wir sind schon seit Mittwoch hier	*We have been here since Wednesday*

(c) It is used very frequently to express a future meaning:

Morgen abend gehe ich ins Kino	*I am going to the movies tomorrow evening*

(d) It is quite often used as the historical present where English would require the simple past:

Da fragt mich ein Herr: „Wie heißen Sie?"	*Then a gentleman asked me, "What's your name?"*

(2) The simple past tense:

(a) The simple past tense has the function of any one of the three simple past forms in English:

Herr Schröder machte Gruppenaufnahmen	*Mr. Schröder took group pictures* or *Mr. Schröder was taking group pictures* or *Mr. Schröder did take group pictures*

(b) It is regularly used in past narrative:

Die Angeln und Sachsen eroberten Britannien und gründeten dort ein neues Reich	*The Angles and Saxons conquered Britain and founded a new state there*

(c) It expresses continued or customary action:

Ich stand immer früh morgens auf	*I always used to get up early in the morning*

(3) The present perfect tense:

(a) The present perfect tense in German has the function of the perfect tense in English:

Ich habe das Buch schon gelesen	*I have already read the book*

(b) It is regularly used, especially in conversation, to denote past action that is not connected with a longer narrative. This is one of the chief differences from English in the use of tenses. Thus:

Ich bin gestern abend ins Kino gegangen	*I went to the movies last night*

(4) The past perfect tense:

The past perfect tense is used in German as in English:

Ich wollte mit ihm sprechen, aber er war schon nach Hause gegangen	*I wanted to talk with him, but he had already gone home*

(5) The future tense:

(a) The future tense in German has the same use as the English future:

In den nächsten vierzehn Aufgaben werden Sie seine Briefe lesen	*You will read his letters in the next fourteen lessons*

(b) It is used, generally with the adverb **wohl,** to express present probability:

Der Elefant wird wohl das stärkste Landtier sein	*The elephant is probably the strongest terrestrial animal*

(6) The future perfect tense:

(a) The future perfect tense in German has the same use as the English future perfect:

Bis zu der Zeit wird er die Fragen beantwortet haben	*He will have answered the questions by that time*

(b) It is used, generally with the adverb **wohl,** to express past probability:

Dieses Rennpferd wird wohl viel Geld gekostet haben	*This race-horse probably cost a lot of money*

Vocabulary

(Personal and possessive pronouns, numerals and a few words which are almost identical in English and German are omitted)

A

abbrechen, a, o break off
der **Abend, -s, -e** evening
das **Abendbrot, -s** supper
das **Abendessen, -s** dinner
die **Abendluft, —, ¨-e** evening air
abends in the evening
das **Abenteuer, -s, —** adventure
aber but, however
abfahren, u, a (ist) depart, leave
der **Abfall, -s, ¨-e** refuse
abführen lead away
abgewöhnen break, make someone give up
abgleiten, i, i (ist) glance off
abhängen, i, a depend
abholen call for
abkommen, a, o (ist) get away, deviate
ablegen (ein Geständnis) make (a confession)
abliefern deliver
abnehmen, a, o take away, take off
abräumen clear off
die **Abreise, —** departure
der **Absender, -s, —** sender
absorbieren absorb
die **Abstammung, —** descent
die **Abteilung, —, -en** department
der **Abteilungschef, -s, -s** department head, boss
die **Abwechslung, —** change
die **Abwesenheit, —** absence
die **Abzahlung, —,-en** instalment (plan)
abzeichnen sketch
abziehen, o, o deduct
achten auf pay attention to
die **Achtung, —** respect
die **Adresse, —, -n** address
adressiert (*p.p.*) self-addressed
der **Advokat, -en, -en** lawyer
ägyptisch Egyptian
ahnen suspect
ähnlich similar
die **Ahnung, —, -n** suspicion
akustisch acoustic
der **Alchimist, -en, -en** alchemist
alle all, everybody; **von alledem** by all of that; **vor allem** above all
alleinig sole
allerdings to be sure
allerlei all sorts of, sundry
alles everything
allgemein general
die **Allgemeinheit, —** general public
allwissend all knowing
als than; as; when; **als ob** as if
also well, so then
alt old
der **Alte, -n, -n** the old man
das **Alter, -s** age
altmodisch old-fashioned
der **Amateur, -s, -e** amateur
(das) **Amerika** America
amerikanisch American
amüsieren amuse
an at
anbellen bark at
anbetreffen, a, o concern
anbieten, o, o offer
ander other
ändern change
anders differently
anderthalb one and a half

andrerseits on the other hand
anfallen, ie, a attack
der **Anfang, -s, ⸗e** beginning
anfangen, i, a begin, do
anfangs at first
der **Anfangsbuchstabe, -n, -n** initial letter
anfertigen make
die **Angabe, —, -n** statement
angeben, a, e indicate
angeblich allegedly
angehören belong to
der **Angehörige, -n, -n** relative
der **Angeklagte, -n, -n** accused person
die **Angelegenheit, —, -en** affair
die **Angeln** (*pl.*) Angles
angenehm pleasant
der **Angreifer, -s, —** attacker
der **Angriff, -s, -e** attack
die **Angst, —** anxiety, fear; **Angst haben** be afraid
ängstigen frighten
der **Ängstliche, -n, -n** timid person
angstvoll frightened
anhaben have on, wear
anhalten, ie, a stop
ankämpfen fight
die **Anklage, —, -n** accusation
anklagen accuse
der **Ankläger, -s, —** accuser
die **Ankunft, —** arrival
annehmen, a, o accept, assume
anorganisch inorganic
anrufen, ie, u call up
der **Ansager, -s, —** announcer
die **Anschauung, —, -en** view
sich **anschließen, o, o** join
anschreien, ie, ie scream at
(sich) **ansehen, a, e** look at, consider
anständig decent
anstarren stare at
anstatt instead of
anstaunen gaze at, stare at
anstellen turn on
der **Anteil, -s, -e** interest, share
die **Antwort, —, -en** answer
antworten answer
anwesend present
anzeigen report
(sich) **anziehen, o, o** put on; get dressed
der **Anzug, -s, ⸗e** suit
anzünden light
der **Apfel, -s, ⸗** apple
die **Apotheke, —, -n** apothecary's shop
der **Apotheker, -s, —** apothecary, druggist
der **Apparat, -s, -e** apparatus
der **Appetit, -s** appetite
die **Arbeit, —, -en** work
arbeiten work
der **Arbeiter, -s, —** workman
arbeitsam hard-working
der **Arbeitslose, -n, -n** unemployed
die **Arbeitslosenunterstützung, —** unemployment compensation, dole
die **Arbeitslosigkeit, —** unemployment
der **Ärger, -s** vexation
ärgerlich angry, irritated
sich **ärgern** be angered
die **Arie, —, -n** aria
arm poor
der **Arm, -s, -e** arm
das **Armband, -es, ⸗er** bracelet
die **Armbanduhr, —, -en** wrist watch
ärmlich poor, miserable
die **Armut, —** poverty
die **Art, —, -en** kind
artig good
der **Artikel, -s, —** article
die **Arznei, —, -en** medicine
der **Arzt, -es, ⸗e** doctor, physician
der **Atem, -s** breath
atemlos breathless
der **Atemzug, -es, ⸗e** breath
atmen breathe
auch also, too, even; **wenn auch** even if
auf on, upon; **auf . . . zu** up to; **auf und ab** up and down
aufbäumen rear up
aufbleiben, ie, ie (ist) stay up
aufblicken look up

aufbrechen, a, o break open
der **Aufenthalt, –es** stay
auffallen, ie, a (ist) strike the attention
die **Aufgabe, —, –n** lesson
aufgeben, a, e give up; propose
aufgeregt excited
die **Aufgeregtheit, —** excitement
aufhaben have to do
aufheben, o, o pick up, raise
aufhören stop
aufklären clear up
sich **auflehnen** lean on
die **Auflösung, —, –en** solution
aufmachen open
aufmerksam attentively; **aufmerksam machen auf** call attention to
die **Aufnahme, —, –n** picture
aufpassen pay attention
aufregen excite; **aufregend** exciting
die **Aufregung, —** excitement
sich **aufrichten** straighten up
aufrufen, ie, u call on
der **Aufsatz, –es, ⸗e** article, essay, composition
aufschlagen, u, a open
aufschließen, o, o unlock, open
aufschreiben, ie, ie write down
aufschreien, ie, ie scream (out)
aufsetzen put on
aufspringen, a, u (ist) jump up
aufstehen, stand auf, aufgestanden (ist) stand up, get up
aufsteigen, ie, ie (ist) rise, mount
aufteilen divide
der **Auftrag, –es, ⸗e** order, instruction
auftreten, a, e (ist) appear
aufwachen (ist) wake up
aufwachsen, u, a (ist) grow up
aufwärts upward
aufwecken wake up, rouse
aufzwingen, a, u force upon
das **Auge, –s, –n** eye
der **Augenblick, –s, –e** moment
der **Augenzeuge, –n, –n** eyewitness
der **August, –s** August
aus out, out of, from
ausbilden to train
ausbrechen, a, o (ist) break out
sich **ausdenken, dachte aus, ausgedacht** think out, figure out
der **Ausdruck, –s, ⸗e** expression
ausfindig machen find out
ausfragen question
ausführen carry out
ausgeben, a, e spend
ausgehen, i, a (ist) go out
ausgewachsen (*p.p.*) full grown
ausgezeichnet excellent
ausgraben, u, a dig up, unearth
aushalten, ie, a bear, stand; resist
die **Auskunft, —, ⸗e** information
das **Ausland, –s** abroad
der **Ausländer, –s, —** foreigner
ausländisch foreign
ausleihen, ie, ie lend out
der **Ausruf, –es, –e** exclamation
sich **ausruhen** rest
aussagen testify
ausschlafen, ie, a sleep one's fill
aussehen, a, e look, appear
außer besides, outside of
außerdem besides, moreover
außerhalb outside of
äußerst extremely
sich **aussetzen** expose oneself
die **Aussicht, —, –en** view
sich **aussprechen, a, o** relieve one's mind
aussteigen, ie, ie (ist) get out, alight
ausstrecken stretch out
aussuchen select
austrinken, a, u drink up, finish
auszahlen pay out
das **Auto, –s, –s** car
die **Autobremse, —, –n** automobile brake
der **Autobus, –ses, –se** bus
die **Autohupe, —, –n** automobile horn
der **Autor, –s, –en** author
die **Autorität, —, –en** authority
die **Autostraße, —, –n** highway, road
der **Autounfall, –s, ⸗e** auto accident

B

die **Backe**, —, –n cheek
der **Bäckermeister**, –s, — (master) baker
die **Badewanne**, —, –n bath tub
die **Bahn**, —, –en train
sich **bahnen** make oneself a path
der **Bahnhof**, –s, ⸗e railroad station
bald soon; **bald . . . bald** now . . . now
baldig prompt, early
der **Balkan**, –e Balkan countries
die **Ballade**, —, –n ballad
das **Band**, –es, ⸗er ribbon, band
die **Bande**, —, –en gang
der **Bandit**, –en, –en bandit
die **Bank**, —, ⸗e bench
die **Bank**, —, –en bank
das **Bargeld**, –s cash
die **Barre**, —, –n bar
der **Bart**, –es, ⸗e beard
der **Bau**, –s construction
der **Bauch**, –es, ⸗e belly
bauen build
der **Bauer**, –s, –n farmer
der **Bauernhof**, –es, ⸗e farm
der **Bauernjunge**, –n, –n farmboy
der **Bauernpatient**, –en, –en farmer patient
das **Bauernpferd**, –es, –e farm horse
die **Baukosten** (*pl.*) construction costs
der **Baum**, –es, ⸗e tree
beantworten to answer
die **Beantwortung**, —, –en the answer-(ing)
bedecken cover
bedenken, bedachte, bedacht consider
bedeuten signify, mean
die **Bedeutung**, —, –en meaning
die **Bedingung**, —, –en condition
bedrohen threaten
beenden end
sich **befassen** concern oneself
der **Befehl**, –s, –e order
befehlen, a, o order, command
sich **befinden, a, u** find oneself, be
befördern promote
die **Beförderung**, —, –en promotion
begabt gifted, endowed
sich **begeben, a, e** betake; **sich in Lebensgefahr begeben** run the risk of losing one's life
begegnen (ist) meet
die **Begegnung**, —, –en meeting
begehen, i, a commit
begeistert enthusiastic
die **Begierde**, — desire
der **Beginn**, –s beginning
beginnen, a, o begin
begleiten accompany
der **Begleiter**, –s, — companion
der **Begriff**, –es, –e idea, conception; **im Begriff sein** be in the process of, be on the point of
begrüßen greet
behalten, ie, a keep
behandeln treat
die **Behandlung**, —, –en treatment
behaupten to claim, assert
sich **beherrschen** control oneself
bei with, at, near
beide both; **mit uns beiden** with both of us
beinah(e) almost
das **Bein**, –es, –e leg, foot
das **Beispiel**, –s, –e example
beißen, i, i bite
bejahen affirm
bekannt (well) known, familiar
die **Bekanntmachung** announcement
bekommen, a, o receive, get
bekümmert grieved
die **Beleidigung**, —, –en insult
belgisch Belgian
bellen bark
belohnen reward
bemerken notice
die **Bemerkung**, —, –en remark
bemitleiden pity
sich **bemühen** trouble oneself
das **Benehmen**, –s behavior

benutzen use
das **Benzin, –s** gasoline
beobachten watch, observe
bequem comfortable
berauben rob
bereiten prepare, make
bereits already
die **Bereitschaft, —** readiness
bereuen regret
der **Berg, –es, –e** mountain
bergab downhill
der **Bergweg, –es, –e** mountain road
der **Bericht, –s, –e** report
berichten report
der **Beruf, –s, –e** profession, vocation
der **Berufsspieler, –s, —** professional player
beruhigen quiet; **sich beruhigen** calm oneself
berühmt famous
die **Berühmtheit, —** celebrity
die **Berührung, —** touch
beschädigen damage
beschäftigt occupied, busy
beschämt ashamed
Bescheid wissen to be informed
bescheiden modest
beschließen, o, o decide
beschreiben, ie, ie describe
die **Beschreibung, —, –en** description
beschützen protect
der **Beschützer, –s, —** protector
sich **beschweren** complain
besehen, a, e look at, examine
besetzt studded
die **Besiedlung, —** population, colonization
besiegen defeat
der **Besitz, –es** possession
besitzen, besaß, besessen possess, own
der **Besitzer, –s, —** possessor, owner
das **Besitztum, –s, ⸗er** possession
besonders especially
die **Besorgnis, —, –se** anxiety, apprehension
besorgt worried
besprechen, a, o discuss
bessern improve
best best
zum besten haben fool
bestehen, bestand, bestanden consist of, exist; **bestehen auf** insist
bestehlen, a, o rob
bestellen order
die **Bestellung, —, –en** order
bestimmt definitely; **bestimmt sein** be intended
bestrafen punish
der **Besuch, –es, –e** visit
besuchen visit
der **Besucher, –s, —** visitor
betäubt stunned
betrachten look at, consider
beträchtlich considerable
das **Betragen, –s** behavior, conduct
betragen, u, a amount to
betreffen, a, o concern; **was . . . betrifft** as far as . . . is concerned
betrübt grieved, depressed
ein **Betrunkener** a drunk
das **Bett, –es, –en** bed
der **Bettler, –s, —** beggar
sich **beugen** bend
beurteilen evaluate
die **Beute, —** booty
bevor before
bewachen guard
bewandert sein be well-versed
(sich) **bewegen** move
der **Beweggrund, –es, ⸗e** motive
die **Bewegung, —, –en** movement, motion
beweinen mourn, weep over the loss of
der **Beweis, –es, –e** proof
beweisen, ie, ie prove
bewölkt cloudy
der **Bewunderer, –s, —** admirer
die **Bewunderung, —** admiration
das **Bewußtsein, –s** consciousness
bezahlen pay

bezeichnen designate
die **Beziehung**, —, **-en** relation(ship)
bezweifeln doubt
biegen, o, o turn, bend
die **Bierstube**, —, **-n** tavern
das **Bild**, **-es**, **-er** picture
bilden form
der **Bildungsroman**, **-s**, **-e** novel of personality development
billig cheap
binden, a, u bind, tie
biographisch biographical
bis until, to
bißchen: ein bißchen a bit, a little
bitte please
die **Bitte**, —, **-n** request
bitten, a, e beg, ask for
die **Bitterkeit**, — bitterness
die **Bittschrift**, —, **-en** petition
blaß pale
blau blue
blenden blind
blond blond
bleiben, ie, ie (ist) remain, stay
bleich pale
der **Bleistift**, **-s**, **-e** pencil
der **Blick**, **-es**, **-e** glance
blicken look
der **Blitz**, **-es**, **-e** lightning
blitzen lighten; **es blitzt** it is lightening
blitzend flashing
bloß merely
die **Blume**, —, **-n** flower
das **Blumengeschäft**, **-s**, **-e** flower shop
das **Blut**, **-es** blood
blutend bleeding
blutig bloody
der **Blutstropfen**, **-s**, — drop of blood
blutüberströmt covered with blood
der **Boden**, **-s**, ¨ bottom, floor; attic
die **Bodenkammer**, —, **-n** attic room
das **Bonbon**, **-s**, **-s** bonbon
die **Börse**, — stock exchange
böse evil, bad; **etwas Böses** something bad
die **Botschaft**, —, **-en** message
die **Bratkartoffeln** (*pl.*) fried potatoes
brauchen need
braun brown
brechen, a, o break
breit broad, wide
breitschultrig broad-shouldered
die **Bremse**, —, **-n** brake
brennen, brannte, gebrannt burn
der **Brennstoffbehälter**, **-s**, — fuel tank
das **Brett**, **-es**, **-er** board
der **Brief**, **-es**, **-e** letter
der **Briefkasten**, **-s**, ¨ mail box
der **Briefträger**, **-s**, — postman
der **Briefumschlag**, **-s**, ¨**e** envelope
die **Brille**, —, **-n** glasses
bringen, brachte, gebracht bring, take something somewhere
(das) **Britannien** Britain
das **Brot**, **-es**, **-e** bread
der **Bruder**, **-s**, ¨ brother
brüllen roar, bellow
brummen mutter
die **Brust**, —, ¨**e** breast, chest
der **Brustharnisch**, **-s** breast plate
die **Brustwunde**, —, **-n** chest wound
das **Buch**, **-es**, ¨**er** book
der **Buchstabe**, **-n**, **-n** letter (written character)
sich **bücken** bend
die **Bühne**, —, **-n** stage
das **Bühnenbild**, **-es**, **-er** scenery, staging
das **Bündel**, **-s**, — bundle
der **Bürger**, **-s**, — citizen
der **Bürgersteig**, **-es**, **-e** sidewalk
der **Burgunder**, **-s**, — Burgundian
das **Büro**, **-s**, **-s** office
der **Bursche**, **-n**, **-n** fellow
der **Busch**, **-es**, ¨**e** bush
die **Butter**, — butter

C

der **Cent**, **-s**, **-s** cent
der **Chef**, **-s**, **-s** chief, head

der **Chefingenieur**, –s, –e chief engineer
die **Chemie**, — chemistry

D

da there, then; since (*conj.*)
dabei in doing so, at the same time, moreover
das **Dach**, –es, ⸗er roof
das **Dachfenster**, –s, — dormer (*garret*) window
dafür for it
dagegen against it; on the other hand
dahin there (to); along; **bis dahin** up to that time
damalig of that time
damals at that time
die **Dame**, —, –n lady
damit with it; so that
der **Dampf**, –es, ⸗e steam
dampfen steam
der **Dampfer**, –s, — steamer
daneben next to it
der **Dank**, –es thanks
danken thank; **danke schön** thank you very much
dann then
darauf thereupon
darin in it
darüber over it, about it
das **Dasein**, –s existence
daß that
das **Datum**, –s, **Daten** date
dauern last, take
dauernd continuous
davon from it, about it; away
davonlaufen, ie, au (ist) run away
die **Decke**, —, –n ceiling; cover, blanket
der **Deckel**, –s, — lid, cover
die **Deckung**, — cover
definieren define
der **Degen**, –s, — sword
der **Dekan**, –s, –e dean
denken, dachte, gedacht think; **sich denken** imagine
denn for (*do not translate when used as particle in question*)
dennoch nevertheless
deretwegen because of which
dergleichen the like
derjenige that one, that
derselbe the same
deshalb for that reason, therefore
deswegen for that reason
der **Detektiv**, –s, –e detective
deutlich clearly
deutsch German
der **Deutsche**, –n, –n German
(das) **Deutschland**, –s Germany
der **Dezember**, –s December
die **Diamantenkette**, —, –n diamond chain
dicht close, dense
dichterisch poetic
die **Dichtkunst**, — poetry
dick big, fat
der **Dieb**, –es, –e thief
der **Diebstahl**, –s, ⸗e theft
dienen serve
der **Diener**, –s, — servant
die **Dienerin**, —, –nen (woman) servant
der **Dienst**, –es, –e duty
der **Dienstag**, –s, –e Tuesday
dieser this
diesmal this time
das **Ding**, –es, –e thing; (*pl.*) matters
doch yet, but, nevertheless, of course; in question: don't you? aren't you?
der **Doktor**, –s, –en doctor
der **Dolch**, –es, –e dagger
der **Dolchstoß**, –es, ⸗e thrust of a dagger
der **Dollar**, –s, — dollar
die **Donau**, — Danube
der **Donner**, –s thunder
donnern thunder
der **Donnerstag**, –s, –e Thursday
doppelt double, two-fold
das **Dorf**, –es, ⸗er village
die **Dorfstraße**, —, –n village street
das **Dorfwirtshaus**, –es, ⸗er village inn

dort there
der **Drache**, –n, –n dragon
dramatisch dramatic
dramatisieren dramatize
sich **drängen** force one's way
draußen outside
die **Draußenstehenden** those standing outside
drehen turn
dringend urgent, pressing
drinnen inside
dritt third
drohen threaten, menace
drüben yonder; **da drüben** over there
drücken press; **sich drücken** squeeze
das **Dschungelgeräusch**, –es, –e jungle noise
duften smell
dumm stupid
dumpf dull
dunkel dark
das **Dunkel**, –s dark(ness)
die **Dunkelheit**, — darkness
durch through
durchaus absolutely, by all means
der **Durchgang**, –s, ⸗e passage
durchlöchern perforate
das **Durchschnittsgewicht**, –es, –e average weight
durchsuchen search
dürfen, durfte, gedurft, darf to be permitted, may
das **Dutzend**, –s, –e dozen

E

eben (*adj.*) flat
eben (*adv.*) just
ebensogroß just as great
ebensogut just as well
ebensowenig . . . wie neither . . . nor
echt real, genuine
die **Ecke**, —, –n corner
edel noble
der **Edelmann**, –es, –leute nobleman
der **Edelstein**, –es, –e precious stone
die **Ehe**, —, –n marriage, married life
ehe before
ehemalig former
die **Ehre**, — honor
der **Ehrentitel**, –s, — honorary title
ehrgeizig ambitious
ehrlich honest, honorable
ehrwürdig venerable
das **Ei**, –s, –er egg
der **Eifer**, –s enthusiasm
eigen own
eigentlich really, as a matter of fact, by the way
das **Eigentum**, –s, ⸗er possessions, property
sich **eignen** be suitable
die **Eile**, — haste, hurry
eilen hurry
eilig haben be in a hurry
einbauen build in
sich **einbilden** imagine
die **Einbildungskraft**, — imagination
der **Einbruch**, –s, ⸗e burglary
der **Eindruck**, –es, ⸗e impression
einfach simple
einfangen, i, a, apprehend, capture
der **Einfluß**, –es, ⸗e influence
einführen introduce
der **Eingang**, –s, ⸗e entrance
die **Eingangstür**, —, –en entrance door
eingerostet rusted shut
einholen catch up with
einige some, a few
der **Einkauf**, –s, ⸗e purchase
einladen, u, a invite
die **Einladung**, —, –en invitation
einmal once; **auf einmal** suddenly; **nicht einmal** not even; **noch einmal** once more; **schon einmal** (in a question) ever
einsam lonesome
einsammeln gather
einschicken send in
einschlafen, ie, a (ist) fall asleep
einschlagen, u, a break down

einsehen, a, e understand, realize
einst once, one day
einstecken put in one's pocket
einstellen to tune in; focus
eintreten, a, e (ist) enter
der **Eintritt, –es** entrance
einverleiben incorporate
einzahlen pay in, deposit
die **Einzelheit, —, –en** detail
einzeln single, individual
das **Einzelspiel, –s, –e** singles
einzig single; only
das **Eisen, –s** iron
die **Eisenbahnbrücke, —, –n** railroad bridge
das **Eisenstück, –s, –e** piece of iron
eisern iron
die **Elbe, —** Elbe river
der **Elefant, –en, –en** elephant
elementar elementary
elend miserable
die **Eltern** (*pl.*) parents
empfangen, i, a receive
der **Emporkömmling, –s, –e** upstart
das **Ende, –s** end; **zu Ende sein** be over
enden end
endlich finally
endlos endless
die **Energie, —, –n** energy
energisch energetic
eng narrow
der **Engel, –s, —** angel
der **Engländer, –s, —** Englishman
(das) **Englisch** English (language)
entdecken discover; disclose, reveal
die **Entdeckung, —, –en** discovery
entfalten unfold
sich **entfernen** disappear
entfernt distant, away
die **Entfernung, —, –en** distance
entfliehen, o, o (ist) escape
entführen kidnap, abduct
entgegengesetzt opposite
entgegenkommen, a, o (ist) come toward
entgehen, entging, (ist) entgangen escape
enthalten, ie, a contain
entlang along
entmutigen discourage
entreißen, i, i tear away, snatch away
entrinnen, a, o (ist) escape
entscheiden, ie, ie decide
die **Entscheidung, —, –en** decision
sich **entschließen, o, o** decide, determine
der **Entschluß, –es, ¨e** decision
entschuldigen excuse
die **Entschuldigung, —, –en** excuse
das **Entsetzen, –s** horror
entsetzlich horrible
entsetzt horrified
entspringen, a, u (ist) originate
enttäuscht disappointed
entweder . . . oder either . . . or
(sich) **entwickeln** develop, evolve
der **Erbe, –n, –n** heir
erben inherit
erblicken see, notice
der **Erdball, –es** globe
die **Erde, —** earth, ground
erdrücken crush
sich **ereignen** happen
das **Ereignis, . . .nisse, . . .nisse** event
ereignisreich eventful
erfahren, u, a find out, hear
erfinden, a, u invent
die **Erfindung, —, –en** invention
der **Erfolg, –s, –e** success
erfolglos unsuccessful
erfrischen refresh
erfüllen fill; fulfill
die **Erfüllung, —** fulfillment
das **Ergebnis, . . .nisse, . . .nisse** result
ergreifen, i, i seize
erhalten, ie, a receive
sich **erhängen** hang
sich **erholen** recover
erinnern remind; **sich erinnern** remember
die **Erinnerung, —** memory, recollection
erkältet ill with a cold
erkennen, erkannte, erkannt recognize
erklären explain

die **Erklärung**, —, **-en** explanation
sich **erkundigen** inquire
erlauben permit
die **Erlaubnis**, — permission
erleben experience
erledigen finish
die **Erleichterung**, — relief
ermorden murder
der **Ermordete**, **-n**, **-n** murdered person
der **Ernst**, **-es** seriousness
ernst serious(ly)
ernsthaft seriously
der **Eroberer**, **-s**, — conqueror
erobern conquer
die **Eroberung**, —, **-en** conquest
erraten, **ie**, **a** guess
erregen arouse
erreichen reach
der **Ersatz**, **-es** substitute
die **Ersatzblume**, —, **-n** substitute for a flower
erscheinen, **ie**, **ie** (**ist**) appear
erschießen, **o**, **o** shoot
erschlagen, **u**, **a** slay, kill
erschrecken, **a**, **o** (**ist**) be startled, frightened
erschüttern be deeply moved
ersetzen replace, make up for
ersparen save
erst first; only, not until
das **Erstaunen**, **-s** astonishment
erstaunt astonished, in amazement
erstechen, **a**, **o** stab
erstklassig first class
ertragen, **u**, **a** endure, bear
erträumen dream of
erwähnen mention
erwarten wait for, expect
erwartungsvoll full of expectation
erwecken awaken, arouse
erweisen, **ie**, **ie** do (a service)
erweitern enlarge
erwidern return, reciprocate, reply
erwischen catch
erwürgen strangle
erzählen tell
erzeigen show
der **Esel**, **-s**, — donkey; **So ein Esel!** What a dope!
essen, **aß**, **gegessen** eat; **das Essen** eating, meal; **zum Essen** for dinner
etwa perhaps; approximately
etwas something, some; somewhat

F

die **Fabrik**, —, **-en** factory
der **Fachmann**, **-s**, **-leute** expert
die **Fähigkeit**, — ability
fahren, **u**, **a** (**ist**) travel, drive
der **Fahrer**, **-s**, — driver
der **Fahrstuhl**, **-s**, **-e** elevator
die **Fahrt**, —, **-en** trip
der **Fall**, **-es**, **-e** case
fallen, **ie**, **a** (**ist**) fall
falls in case
die **Falltür**, —, **-en** trapdoor
falsch false, wrong
die **Familie**, —, **-n** family
der **Familienname**, **-ns**, **-n** family name
der **Fang**, **-es**, **-e** catch
fangen, **i**, **a** catch
die **Farbe**, —, **-n** color
der **Farmer**, **-s**, — farmer
die **Fasanenfeder**, —, **-n** pheasant feather
fassen seize, grasp; **sich fassen** compose oneself; **gefaßt sein** be prepared
fast almost
faul lazy
der **Faulenzer**, **-s**, — lazy fellow
der **Faustschlag**, **-es**, **-e** blow (of the fist)
der **Februar**, **-s** February
die **Feder**, —, **-n** pen, spring
fegen sweep
fehlen be absent; **ihm fehlt etwas** something is wrong with him
der **Fehler**, **-s**, — mistake, error
die **Feier**, —, **-n** celebration
feiern celebrate

feig cowardly
fein fine
der **Feind**, –es, –e enemy
das **Feld**, –es, –er field
das **Fenster**, –s, — window
die **Ferien** (*pl.*) vacation
fern far
die **Ferne**, — distance
fertig finished, ready; **sich fertig machen** get ready
fertigstellen finish
fest firm
das **Festessen**, –s, — banquet
sich **festhalten, ie, a** hang on, cling to
festlich festive
feststellen determine
das **Feuer**, –s, — fire; light
feurig fiery
das **Fieber**, –s fever
der **Fiebertraum**, –es, ⸗e feverish dream, delirium
der **Film**, –s, –e film, motion picture
die **Filmschauspielerin**, —, –nen movie actress
finden, a, u find
der **Finger**, –s, — finger
finster dark, gloomy
der **Fisch**, –es, –e fish
der **Fleck**, –es, –e spot
flehend imploring
das **Fleisch**, –es flesh, meat
der **Fleiß**, –es industry
fleißig industrious
fliegen, o, o (ist) fly
fließen, o, o (ist) flow
die **Flotte**, —, –n fleet
der **Fluch**, –es, ⸗e curse
flüchtig fleeting, casual
der **Flug**, –es, ⸗e flight
der **Flughafen**, –s, ⸗ airport
der **Flur**, –es, –e hallway
der **Fluß**, –es, ⸗e river
flüstern whisper
die **Folge**, —, –n consequence
folgen follow
die **Folter**, —, –n torture
die **Folterbank**, —, ⸗e rack
die **Form**, —, –en form
die **Formel**, —, –n formula
fort away
fortbleiben, ie, ie (ist) stay away
fortfahren, u, a (ist) leave; continue
fortgaloppieren (ist) gallop away
fortgehen, ging fort, fortgegangen (ist) go away
fortlaufen, ie, au (ist) run away
fortreiten, i, i (ist) ride away
fortschicken send away
fortschleppen drag away
der **Fortschritt**, –es, –e progress
die **Fortsetzung**, —, –en continuation
fortziehen, o, o draw away, pull away
die **Frage**, —, –n question; **es kommt nicht in Frage** that is out of the question
fragen ask
frankiert (*p.p.*) stamped
(das) **Frankreich**, –s France
französisch French
die **Frau**, —, –en woman; wife; Mrs.
die **Frauenhand**, —, ⸗e woman's hand
die **Frauenkleider** (*pl.*) women's clothes
die **Frauenstimme**, —, –n woman's voice
das **Fräulein**, –s, — Miss, young lady
die **Frechheit**, —, –en impertinence
frei free, **im Freien** in the open, out-doors
die **Freiheit**, — freedom
freilich certainly
der **Freitag**, –s, –e Friday
die **Freitreppe**, —, –n outside staircase
der **Fremde**, –n, –n stranger
fressen, a, e eat (*used of animals*)
die **Freude**, —, –en joy
freudig joyous, cheerful
sich **freuen** be glad; **sich freuen auf** look forward to
der **Freund**, –es, –e friend
die **Freundin**, —, –nen girl friend
freundlich friendly, genial
die **Freundschaft**, — friendship

der **Friede**, –ns peace
friedlich peacefully
frisch fresh
früh early; **früher** former(ly)
der **Frühling**, –s spring
der **Frühlingstraum**, –s, ⸗e spring dream
das **Frühstück**, –s, –e breakfast
frühstücken eat breakfast
fühlen feel
führen lead, take
der **Führer**, –s, — leader
der **Führersitz**, –es, –e driver's seat
füllen fill
die **Füllfeder**, —, –n fountain pen
das **Fundament**, –es, –e foundation
funkeln sparkle
für for
die **Furcht**, — fear
furchtbar terrible
fürchten fear
fürchterlich horrible
der **Fuß**, –es, ⸗e foot; **zu Fuß** on foot
der **Fußboden**, –s, ⸗ floor
der **Fußgänger**, –s, — pedestrian
der **Fußsoldat**, –en, –en footsoldier
der **Fußtritt**, –es, –e kick
füttern feed

G

gaffen gape, stare
der **Galaball**, –es, ⸗e gala ball
galant courteous
der **Galgen**, –s, — gallows
der **Galopp**, –s gallop
galoppieren gallop
der **Gang**, –es, ⸗e passage, corridor
ganz whole, all, entirely; quite, very
gar: **gar kein no . . .** at all; **gar nicht** not at all
die **Garde**, — guard(s)
der **Garten**, –s, ⸗ garden
die **Gartenmauer**, —, –n garden wall
die **Gasse**, —, –n side street
der **Gast**, –es, ⸗e guest
der **Gasthof**, –es, ⸗e inn
die **Gaststube**, —, –n taproom
geachtet respected
das **Gebäude**, –s, — building
geben, a, e give; **es gibt** there is, there are, they have
das **Gebiet**, –es, –e field (of interest)
geboren werden be born
der **Gebrauch**, –s, ⸗e use
gebrauchen use, make use of; need
die **Geburt**, —, –en birth
der **Geburtsort**, –es, –e birth place
der **Geburtstag**, –es, –e birthday
das **Geburtstagsgeschenk**, –s, –e birthday present
der **Gedanke**, –ns, –n thought, idea
das **Gedicht**, –es, –e poem
die **Geduld**, — patience
geduldig patient
die **Gefahr**, —, –en danger
gefährlich dangerous
gefallen, ie, a please; **es gefällt ihm** he likes
der **Gefallen**, –s, — favor
gefälligst please be so good as to
der **Gefangene**, –n, –n prisoner
die **Gefangenschaft**, — captivity
gefaßt sein be prepared
das **Gefühl**, –s, –e feeling
gegen against, toward, close to, around
die **Gegenfrage**, —, –n counter question
gegenseitig reciprocal
das **Gegenteil**, –s opposite; **im Gegenteil** on the contrary
gegenüber opposite
gegenüberliegen, a, e lie opposite
der **Gegner**, –s, — opponent
geheim secret
die **Geheimkammer**, —, –n secret room
das **Geheimnis**, . . . **nisse**, . . . **nisses** secret, mystery
geheimnisvoll mysterious
gehen, ging, gegangen (ist) go; **es geht um** is at stake
gehören belong
das **Gehuste**, –s coughing

der **Geiſt**, –es, –er ghost, spirit
die **Geiſtererſcheinung**, —, –en apparition
geiſtig mental
der **Geizhals**, –es, ⸗e miser
das **Gelächter**, –s laughter
das **Geld**, –es money
der **Geldbeutel**, –s, — moneybag, purse
der **Geldſack**, –es, ⸗e moneybag
der **Geldſchrank**, –es, ⸗e safe
die **Geldſumme**, —, –n sum of money
die **Gelegenheit**, — opportunity
geliebt beloved, dear
der **Geliebte**, –n, –n sweetheart
gelingen, a, u (iſt) succeed
gelten, a, o be considered, mean
gemein common, ordinary
genau exact(ly); **genauer** closer
geneigt ſein be inclined
das **Genick**, –es, –e neck
genießen, o, o enjoy
der **Genoſſe**, –n, –n comrade
genug enough
genügen suffice; **genügend** sufficiently
gepflegt well-cared-for
gerade just
geraten, ie, a (iſt) get or fall into, become involved
das **Geräuſch**, –es, –e noise, sound effect
gerecht just
die **Gerechtigkeit**, — justice
das **Gericht**, –s court of justice
geringſt least, slightest
der **Germane**, –n, –n Teuton
der **Germanenſtamm**, –s, ⸗e Germanic tribe
gern(e) gladly; *with infinitive:* like to, be fond of
geſamt total
das **Geſamtgewicht**, –es total weight
das **Geſchäft**, –es, –e store, business
geſchäftlich business (-like)
der **Geſchäftsmann**, –es, –leute business man
geſchehen, a, e (iſt) happen
das **Geſchenk**, –s, –e present
die **Geſchichte**, —, –n history; story, tale, affair
der **Geſchichtsroman**, –s, –e historical novel
die **Geſchicklichkeit**, — skill
geſchickt clever, skillful
das **Geſchirr**, –s table utensils
der **Geſchmack**, –es taste
das **Geſchmeide**, –es set of jewelry, jewels
geſchwind quickly
die **Geſchwindigkeit**, — speed
der **Geſelle**, –n, –n helper, assistant
die **Geſellſchaft**, —, –en society, company; **Geſellſchaft leiſten** keep company
der **Geſellſchaftsraum**, –s, ⸗e social room
das **Geſicht**, –es, –er face
die **Geſichtsfarbe**, — complexion
der **Geſichtspunkt**, –es, –e point of view
die **Geſpenſterjagd**, —, –en ghost chase
das **Geſpräch**, –s, –e conversation
die **Geſtalt**, —, –en form, shape, stature
das **Geſtändnis**, . . .niſſes, . . .niſſe confession
geſtatten permit, allow
geſtehen, **geſtand**, **geſtanden** confess
geſtern yesterday; **geſtern abend** last night
das **Geſuch**, –es, –e petition
geſund healthy
geübt skilled
gewagt daring
die **Gewalt**, —, –en force, power
gewaltig vast
die **Gewandtheit**, — agility
gewillt ſein be willing
gewinnen, a, o win, produce
die **Gewinnung**, — production
gewiß certain, certainly
das **Gewiſſen**, –s conscience
die **Gewiſſensnot**, —, ⸗e qualms of conscience
die **Gewiſſensqualen** (*pl.*) anguish of conscience

das **Gewitter**, –s, — (thunder-) storm
sich **gewöhnen an** get accustomed to
die **Gewohnheit**, —, –en custom
die **Gewohnheitssache**, — matter of routine
gewöhnlich usually
die **Gicht**, — gout
die **Gier**, — greediness
giftig poisonous; angry
der **Gipfel**, –s, — top
der **Gipsverband**, –s plaster cast
glänzend shining, brilliant, splendid
das **Glas**, –es, ⸗er glass
der **Glasdeckel**, –s, — glasslid
der **Glaskasten**, –s, ⸗ showcase
die **Glaskutsche**, —, –n glass-enclosed carriage
die **Glasplatte**, —, –n glass top
glauben believe, think
gleich like, same, at once, immediately
gleichzeitig simultaneously
gleiten, i, i (ist) glide
glitzern glisten
das **Glöckchen**, –s, — small bell
das **Glück**, –s luck, happiness
glücklich happy, fortunate
glücklicherweise fortunately
die **Gnade**, — clemency, mercy
gnädig gracious; *not translated when used with* Herr, Frau, *or* Fräulein
das **Gold**, –es gold
golden golden
der **Goldfisch**, –es, –e goldfish
die **Goldgewinnung**,—production of gold
die **Goldmünze**, —, –n gold coin
der **Goldschmied**, –es, –e goldsmith
der **Goldschmuck**, –es golden ornament
das **Goldstück**, –es, –e gold coin
die **Gondel**, —, –n gondola
der **Gönner**, –s, — benefactor
der **Gorilla**, –s, –s gorilla
der **Gote**, –n, –n Goth
der **Gott**, –es, ⸗er god
das **Grab**, –es, ⸗er grave
der **Graben**, –s, ⸗ ditch
der **Graf**, –en, –en count
gratulieren congratulate
grau gray
grausam cruel, terrible
die **Grausamkeit**, — cruelty
greifen, i, i pick up
der **Greis**, –es, –e old man
die **Grenze**, —, –n boundary, border
der **Grieche**, –n, –n Greek
griechisch Greek
der **Griff**, –es, –e grip, handle, hilt
grimmig furious, violent
grob rude, rough, heavy
(das) **Grönland**, –s Greenland
groß great, big, tall
die **Größe**, —, –n size
die **Großstadt**, —, ⸗e metropolis
der **Großvater**, –s, ⸗e grandfather
der **Grund**, –es, ⸗e reason
gründen found
gründlich thorough
grunzen grunt
die **Gruppe**, —, –n group
die **Gruppenaufnahme**, —, –n group picture
der **Gruß**, –es, ⸗e greeting
grüßen greet
die **Gunst**, —, favor, good graces
günstig favorable
gut good; well
gütig kind
gutmütig good-natured

H

das **Haar**, –es, –e hair
haben, hatte, gehabt have
der **Habenichts**, —, –e penniless fellow
der **Hafen**, –s, ⸗ harbor
halb half, halfway
halbirisch half Irish
der **Halbohnmächtige**, –n, –n semi-conscious man
die **Hälfte**, —, –n half
hallo! hello!, o say!
der **Hals**, –es, ⸗e neck

halten, ie, a to hold; stop; keep; **halten für** consider; **halten von** think of
die **Hand, —, ⸗e** hand
handeln act; **es handelt sich um Leben und Tod** it is a matter of life and death
die **Handschrift, —** handwriting
der **Handschuh, -s, -e** glove
die **Handtasche, —, -n** handbag
das **Handwerk, -s, -e** trade
das **Handwerkzeug, -s** tools
hängen, i, a hang, dangle
harmlos harmless, innocent
hart hard
der **Haß, -es** hatred
hassen hate
der **Haufen, -s, —** pile
die **Hauptrolle, —, -n** leading rôle
hauptsächlich chiefly
Hauptstadt, —, ⸗e capital
die **Hauptstraße, —, -n** main street
das **Haus, -es, ⸗er** house; **nach Hause** home; **zu Hause** at home
die **Hausarbeit, —, -en** housework
der **Hauseingang, -s, ⸗e** entrance (to a house)
der **Hausflur, -s, -e** hall
die **Hausfrau, —, -en** housewife
der **Hausknecht, -es, -e** (house) servant
das **Hausmärchen, -s, —** fairytale for the home
die **Haustür, —, -en** front door
die **Hauswand, —, ⸗e** wall of the house
die **Hautkrem, —, -s** skin cream
heben, o, o raise; **es hebt sich** it can be raised
der **Hedonist, -en, -en** hedonist
heftig violent
das **Heim, -s, -e** home
die **Heimat, —** native-place, homeland
das **Heimatdörfchen, -s, —** native village
die **Heimatstadt, —, ⸗e** home town
die **Heimreise, —, -n** trip home
heimwärts homeward
heiraten marry
heiß hot
heißen, ie, ei be named, called; **wenn es heißt** if it says
der **Held, -en, -en** hero
die **Heldentat, —, -en** heroic deed
helfen, a, o help
der **Helfer, -s, —** helper
hellblau light blue
das **Hemd, -es, -en** shirt
der **Hengst, -es, -e** stallion
herab down; **von . . . herab** from
herankommen, a, o (ist) approach
heraufholen bring upstairs
heraus out
herausdestillieren distil (out)
herausfischen fish (out)
herausschleppen drag out
herausschlüpfen (ist) slip out
sich **herausstellen** turn out to be
herausziehen, o, o pull out
herbeilaufen, ie, au (ist) come running
herbeirufen, ie, u call in
der **Herbst, -es** fall
hereinkommen, a, o (ist) come in
hereintreten, a, e (ist) enter
herkommen, a, o (ist) come from
die **Herkunft, —** origin
der **Heroismus, —** heroism
der **Herr, -n, -en** Mr., gentleman, lord
herrichten prepare
die **Herrin, —, -nen** mistress
herrlich wonderful, splendid
herstellen produce
herumreisen (ist) travel all over
herumschicken send around
herumsuchen look around
sich **herumtreiben, ie, ie** loiter about
hervorbrechen, a, o (ist) burst forth
hervorbringen, brachte hervor, hervorgebracht produce
hervorspringen, a, u (ist) jump out
das **Herz, -ens, -en** heart
die **Herzensdame, —, -n** lady of one's heart

herzlich heartily
das **Heulen** howling
heute today; **heute abend** this evening; **heute morgen** this morning; **heute nacht** tonight
heutig present-day
hier here
hierher over here
hiermit herewith
die **Hilfe**, — help
der **Hilferuf**, –s, –e cry for help
hilflos helpless
der **Himmel**, –s sky, heaven; **Um Himmels willen!** For heaven's sake!
hin there; **hin und her** back and forth; **hin und wieder** now and then
hinabführen lead down
hinabsteigen, ie, ie (**ist**) climb down, descend
hinauf up
hinblicken look
hindern hinder, prevent
hineingreifen, i, i reach inside
hinfallen, ie, a (**ist**) fall down
hingehen, ging hin, hingegangen (**ist**) go (there)
sich **hinsetzen** sit down
hinten behind
hinter behind; **hinter . . . her** behind; **hinter . . . hervor** out from behind
hinterher afterwards
hinterlassen, ie, a leave behind
der **Hintersitz**, –es, –e back seat
hinunterschleichen, i, i (**ist**) sneak down
hinweisen ie, ie auf indicate
hinwerfen, a, o throw down
hinzufügen add
historisch historical
die **Hitze**, — heat
hoch high
die **Hochbahn**, —, –en elevated train
der **Hochgenuß**, –es rare delight
hochreißen, i, i pull up, grasp
hochschätzen admire
die **Höchstgeschwindigkeit**, — top speed
die **Hochzeit**, —, –en wedding
der **Hof**, –es, ⸗e court, yard
hoffen hope
hoffentlich I hope
das **Hoffest**, –es, –e court festival
die **Hoffnung**, —, –en hope
hoffnungslos hopeless
die **Hofgesellschaft**, —, –en court society
der **Höhepunkt**, –s, –e climax
höhnisch sarcastic
holen carry off, fetch, get
(das) **Holland**, –s Holland
die **Hölle**, — hell
das **Holz**, –es, ⸗er wood
der **Holzkasten**, –s, ⸗ wooden box
der **Holzrahmen**, –s, — wooden frame
die **Holztreppe**, —, –n wooden staircase
hörbar audible
horchen listen
hören hear, listen to
der **Hörer**, –s, — listener
die **Hosen** (*pl.*) trousers
die **Hosentasche**, —, –n trouser pocket
das **Hotel**, –s, –s hotel
hübsch pretty
das **Huhn**, –es, ⸗er chicken, hen
das **Hühnerhaus**, –es, ⸗er hen-house
die **Hülle**, —, –n cover
der **Humor**, –s humor
der **Hund**, –es, –e dog
die **Hundepeitsche**, —, –n dog whip
hungrig hungry
husten cough
das **Hustenbonbon**, –s, –s cough drop
der **Hut**, –es, ⸗e hat

I

die **Idee**, —, –n idea
die **Immatrikulation**, —, –en registration
immer always; **immer noch** still; **immer wieder** again and again
imponieren impress
imstande sein be capable (of)
in in, into

indem while (by *plus verbal noun*)
der **Induſtriebaron**, –s, –e industrial baron, tycoon of industry
der **Infanteriſt**, –en, –en infantryman
informieren inform
der **Ingenieur**, –s, –e engineer
das **Ingenieurweſen**, –s engineering
der **Inhalt**, –es contents
die **Innenſeite**, —, –n inside
inner inner
innig tenderly
die **Inſel**, —, –n island
intelligent intelligent, smart
intereſſant interesting
das **Intereſſe**, –s, –n interest
das **Intereſſengebiet**, –s, –e field of interest
ſich **intereſſieren für** be interested in
das **Interview**, –s, –s interview
interviewen interview
inzwiſchen meanwhile
der **Ire**, –n, –n Irishman
irgendein any
irgendetwas anything
irgendjemand someone
irgendwie somehow
irgendwo somewhere
ſich **irren** make a mistake, be mistaken
(das) **Island**, –s Iceland
der **Isländer**, –s, — Icelander
italieniſch Italian

J

ja yes, indeed
der **Jackenärmel**, –s, — coat sleeve
die **Jagd**, —, –en chase
jagen chase
der **Jäger**, –s, — hunter
das **Jahr**, –es, –e year
jahrelang for years
das **Jahrhundert**, –s, –e century
die **Jahrhundertfeier**, —, –n centennial celebration
der **Jammer**, –s pity
der **Januar**, –s January
jawohl indeed, yes
je ever; **je . . . deſto** the . . . the
jedenfalls in any case
jeder, –e, –es each, every
jedermann everyone, everybody
jederzeit any time
jedesmal each time
jeher: von jeher always
jemand somebody
jener, –e, –es that
jetzt now
der **Jubiläumsball**, –s, ⸗e anniversary ball
die **Jugend**, — youth
der **Juli**, –s July
jung young
der **Junge**, –n, –n boy, fellow
der **Jüngling**, –s, –e young man
der **Juni**, –s June
das **Juwel**, –s, –en jewel
das **Juwelenkäſtchen**, –s, — jewel-case
der **Juwelier**, –s, –e jeweller

K

der **Kaffee**, –s coffee
das **Kalbfleiſch**, –es veal
kalt cold
die **Kameradin**, —, –nen girl friend
der **Kamin**, –s, –e fireplace
die **Kammer**, —, –n room
der **Kampf**, –es, ⸗e struggle, fight
die **Kampfkraft**, — fighting strength
der **Kanarienvogel**, –s, ⸗ canary (-bird)
die **Kapelle**, —, –n orchestra
die **Karte**, —, –n card
die **Kartoffel**, —, –n potato
das **Käſtchen**, –s, — small box, case
der **Kaſten**, –s, ⸗ box; case
der **Kater**, –s, — tomcat
die **Katze**, —, –n cat
kaufen buy
der **Kaufmann**, –es, –leute merchant
kaum hardly, scarcely
der **Kavalier**, –s, –e cavalier, man of the world

kein no, not any
keinerlei no . . . whatsoever
der **Keller**, –s, — cellar
kennen, kannte, gekannt know, be acquainted with
kennenlernen become acquainted
der **Kenner**, –s, — connoisseur, expert
der **Kerker**, –s, — prison cell
die **Kerkerhaft**, — imprisonment
der **Kerl**, –s, –e fellow
das **Kerlchen**, –s, — little fellow
die **Kerze**, —, –n candle
die **Kette**, —, –n chain
der **Ketzer**, –s, — heretic
kichern giggle
das **Kind**, –es, –er child
das **Kindergesicht**, –es, –er child's face
kinderlos childless
das **Kindermärchen**, –s, — fairy-tale for children
die **Kinderpsychologie**, — child psychology
das **Kinn**, –es, –e chin
das **Kino**, –s, –s movies
der **Kinobesucher**, –s, — movie patron
die **Kirche**, —, –n church
das **Kirchenbuch**, –es, ⸗er parochial register
die **Kirschblüte**, —, –n cherry blossom
die **Kirschblütenseife**, — Cherry Blossom Soap
die **Kirschblütenseifenflocken** (*pl.*) Cherry Blossom Soap Flakes
die **Klage**, —, –n complaint
klagen complain
das **Klangbild**, –es, –er sound picture
klappern clatter
klar clear
die **Klasse**, —, –n class
der **Klassengenosse**, –n, –n classmate
das **Klassenzimmer**, –s, — classroom
klatschen clap
das **Kleid**, –es, –er dress; (*pl.*) clothes
kleiden clothe
der **Kleiderschrank**, –es, ⸗e wardrobe
klein small, little; **Kleiner** little boy, youngster
klettern climb
der **Klient**, –en, –en client
das **Klima**, –s climate
die **Klinge**, —, –n blade
klingeln ring, clang
klingen, a, u sound
klirren crash, clatter
klopfen knock, beat, pound
das **Klopfen**, –s knocking
das **Kloster**, –s, ⸗ monastery
klug clever, smart
der **Knabe**, –n, –n boy
der **Knall**, –s, –e bang
knallen burst, explode, crack (a whip)
der **Knecht**, –es, –e hired man
die **Kneipe**, —, –n beer joint
das **Knie**, –s, — knee
knien kneel
der **Knopf**, –es, ⸗e button
der **Knoten**, –s, — knot
kochen cook
der **Koffer**, –s, — suitcase
der **Kollege**, –n, –n colleague
kommen, a, o (ist) come; **wie kommt es** how does it happen; **zu sich kommen** regain consciousness
das **Komitee**, –s, –s committee
die **Kommode**, —, –n dresser
kompliziert complicated
konfiszieren confiscate
der **König**, –s, –e king
die **Königin**, —, –nen queen
königlich royal
das **Königreich**, –s, –e kingdom
können, konnte, gekonnt, kann be able, can; know
der **Kopf**, –es, ⸗e head
kopfschüttelnd shaking his head
der **Kornsack**, –es, ⸗e sack of grain
körperlich bodily, physical
kostbar valuable
kosten cost
die **Kosten** (*pl.*) expenses

das **Koſtüm**, –s, –e costume, costuming
die **Kraft**, —, ⸗e strength, might
kräftig strong, powerful
der **Kraftmenſch**, –en, –en "strong man"
krank sick
der **Kranke**, –n, –n sick person
die **Krankheit**, —, –n illness
kratzen scratch
das **Kratzen**, –s scratching
der **Kreditbrief**, –es, –e letter of credit
der **Kreis**, –es, –e circle
kriechen, o, o (iſt) creep
der **Krieg**, –es, –e war
kriegen get
der **Krieger**, –s, — warrior
der **Kriegsroman**, –s, –e war novel
der **Kriminalroman**, –s, –e crime novel
die **Kritik**, —, –en criticism
der **Krug**, –es, ⸗e pitcher
die **Küche**, —, –n kitchen
der **Küchentiſch**, –es, –e kitchen table
kühl cool
die **Kultur**, —, –en culture
ſich **kümmern um** concern oneself with
der **Kunde**, –n, –n customer
die **Kunſt**, —, ⸗e art; profession
der **Künſtler**, –s, — artist
künſtlich artificial
kurz short
kurzſichtig near-sighted
der **Kuß**, –es, ⸗e kiss
küſſen kiss
die **Küſte**, —, –n coast
die **Kutſche**, —, –n carriage
der **Kutſcher**, –s, — driver

L

das **Laboratorium**, –s, –ien laboratory
lächeln smile; das **Lächeln**, –s smile
lachen laugh
lächerlich ridiculous
laden, u, a load
der **Laden**, –s, ⸗ store
das **Ladenfräulein**, –s, — girl store clerk
der **Ladentiſch**, –s, –e counter
die **Lage**, –e location, situation
lähmen lame, paralyze
die **Lampe**, —, –n lamp
das **Lampenlicht**, –es lamp-light
das **Land**, –es, ⸗er land; **auf dem Lande** in the country
der **Landarzt**, –es, ⸗e country doctor
das **Landhaus**, –es, ⸗er villa
der **Landkauf**, –es, ⸗e land purchase
die **Landſtraße**, —, –n highway
das **Landtier**, –es, –e terrestrial animal
der **Landwein**, –s common wine (of the country)
lang(e) long; **ſeit langem** for a long time
langſam slowly, gradually
längſt long ago
die **Langweile**, — boredom
langweilen bore
langweilig boring, tedious
laſſen, ie, a let, allow
die **Laſt**, —, –en load
die **Laterne**, —, –n lantern, lamp post
der **Laternenpfahl**, –s, ⸗e lamp post
der **Lauf**, –es, ⸗e course, run
laufen, ie, au (iſt) run
die **Laufmaſche**, —, –n run (in stockings)
die **Laune**, — mood, humor
lauſchen listen
der **Laut**, –es, –e sound
laut loud
läuten ring
lautlos silent, without making a sound
leben live
das **Leben**, –s life
lebendig alive
die **Lebensgefahr**, — danger of life
die **Leber**, —, –n liver
der **Lebertran**, –s cod liver oil
das **Lebewesen**, –s, — living being
lebhaft energetic
das **Lederband**, –es, ⸗er leather cord
leer empty

das **Leere**, –n emptiness; **ins Leere** into space
leeren empty
legen lay, put; **sich legen** lie down
legieren alloy
die **Legierung**, —, –en alloy
lehnen lean
die **Lehre**, —, –n apprenticeship; **in die Lehre nehmen** take as apprentice
lehren teach
der **Lehrer**, –s, — teacher
die **Leiche**, —, –n corpse
leicht light; easy
das **Leid**, –es, –en sorrow
leid: es tut mir leid I am sorry; **er tut mir leid** I feel sorry for him
leiden, i, i suffer
das **Leiden**, –s, — suffering
die **Leidenschaft**, —, –en passion, rage
leider unfortunately
leihen, ie, ie lend, borrow
leise soft, quietly
sich leisten afford
die **Leistung**, —, –en achievement
die **Lektüre**, — reading
lesen, a, e read
der **Leser**, –s, — reader
letzt last
leuchten light, glisten
leugnen deny
die **Leute** (*pl.*) people
das **Licht**, –es, –er light
lieb dear; **dem König war sie lieb** the king was fond of her; **es ist mir lieb** I like
die **Liebe**, — love
lieben love
der **Liebende**, –n, –n lover
liebenswürdig kind, amiable
der **Liebesroman**, –s, –e novel of love
liebhaben love
der **Liebhaber**, –s, — lover
liebkosen caress
lieblich lovely, sweet
der **Liebling**, –s, –e darling
das **Lieblingsfenster**, –s, — favorite window
die **Lieblingsmarke**, —, –n favorite brand
das **Lied**, –es, –er song
liefern furnish
liegen, a, e lie
link- left; **links** left
die **Lippe**, —, –n lip
listig sly
literarisch literary
loben praise
das **Loch**, –es, ⸗er hole
der **Lohn**, –es, ⸗e pay, wages, reward
die **Lokomotive**, —, –n locomotive
lösen solve
losgehen, ging los, losgegangen (ist) commence, begin, start
loslassen, ie, a let loose
sich losreißen, i, i break away
losschießen, o, o fire away
lossein: Was ist denn los? What's the matter?
die **Lösung**, —, –en solution
loswerden, u, o (ist) get rid of
der **Löwe**, –n, –n lion
die **Luft**, —, ⸗e air; **Luft holen** inhale
die **Lüge**, —, –n lie
lügen, o, o lie, tell a lie
die **Lungenentzündung**, — pneumonia
die **Lust**, —, ⸗e pleasure, desire; **Lust haben** want, feel like
lustig gay, funny; **sich lustig machen über** make fun of
der **Luxusartikel**, –s, — luxury article

M

machen make, do
die **Macht**, —, ⸗e power
mächtig powerful, mighty
das **Mädchen**, –s, — girl; maid
der **Mädchenname**, –ns, –n maiden name
magisch magic
der **Magistrat**, –s magistrate, municipal council
die **Mahlzeit**, —, –en meal

der **Mai**, –s May
das **Mal**, –s time; **ein paar Mal** a few times
mal once
die **Mama**, —, –s mother
man one, they
mancher, –e, –es many (a)
manchmal sometimes
der **Mangel**, –s, ⸗ want, lack
die **Manieren** (*pl.*) manners
der **Mann**, –es, ⸗er man, husband
männlich male
die **Mannschaft**, —, –en team
der **Mantel**, –s, ⸗ topcoat
das **Märchen**, –s, — fairy-tale
die **Mark**, —, — mark (*unit of money*)
die **Marke**, —, –n brand
der **Marsch**, –es, ⸗e march
martern torture
der **März**, –es March
die **Masche**, —, –n stitch, mesh
die **Maske**, —, –n mask
maskieren disguise
das **Material**, –s, –ien material, drugs (*pl.*)
die **Mathematik**, — mathematics
die **Matratze**, —, –n mattress
die **Mauer**, —, –n wall
das **Maul**, –es, ⸗er mouth (of animals)
mäuschenstill absolutely quiet
der **Mechaniker**, –s, — mechanic
das **Meer**, –es, –e ocean, sea
mehr more; **nicht mehr** no longer; **um so mehr** all the more
mehrere several
der **Meilenstein**, –s, –e milestone
meinen mean, think
der **Meinige** my own
die **Meinung**, —, –en opinion
meist– most; **am meisten** most; **meistens** mostly
der **Meister**, –s, — master
die **Meisterschaft**, —, –en mastery, championship
der **Meisterschaftskampf**, –es, ⸗e championship contest
sich **melden** volunteer, report
die **Menge**, —, –n crowd; quantity
der **Mensch**, –en, –en human being; fellow, man
die **Menschenmenge**, —, –n crowd of people
merken notice
merkwürdig remarkable
das **Metall**, –s, –e metal
metallisch metallic
die **Miene**, —, –n expression
die **Miete**, —, –n rent
mieten hire
der **Mieter**, –s, — renter
die **Mikrobe**, —, –n microbe
das **Mikrophon**, –s, –e microphone
die **Milch**, — milk
mild mild, gentle; **mildernder Umstand** extenuating circumstance
das **Militär**, –s military, service
mindestens at least
die **Minute**, —, –n minute
sich **mischen in** interfere with
die **Mißernte**, —, –n bad harvest, crop failure
mißhandeln abuse
mißtrauen mistrust
mit with
mitansehen, a, e witness
mitbringen, brachte mit, mitgebracht bring along
der **Mitbürger**, –s, — fellow citizen
die **Mitgift**, — dowry
mithelfen, a, o cooperate, assist, help
mitkommen, a, o (ist) come along
das **Mitleid**, –es pity, sympathy
mitleidig compassionate, sympathetic
die **Mitmenschen** (*pl.*) fellow-men
mitnehmen, a, o take along
mitschicken send along
der **Mitspieler**, –s, — team mate
der **Mittag**, –s, –e noon; **zu Mittag essen** have lunch

die **Mitte**, — middle, center
mitteilen inform
das **Mittel**, –s, — means
mittelalterlich medieval
(das) **Mitteleuropa**, –s Central Europe
mittelgroß of medium size
das **Mittelmeer**, –s Mediterranean
mitten in the middle of
die **Mitternacht**, —, ⸗e midnight
der **Mittwoch**, –s Wednesday
das **Möbelgeschäft**, –es, –e furniture store
modern modern
mögen, mochte, gemocht, mag may, like
möglich possible
die **Möglichkeit**, —, –en possibility
der **Monat**, –s, –e month
der **Mond**, –es, –e moon
das **Mondlicht**, –es moonlight
die **Mondsichel**, —, –n crescent or sickle of the moon
der **Montag**, –s Monday
der **Mord**, –es, –e murder
der **Mörder**, –s, — murderer
die **Mörderbande**, —, –n gang of murderers
die **Mordnacht**, —, ⸗e night of murder
die **Mordtat**, —, –en murderous deed, murder
die **Mordwaffe**, —, –n murder-weapon
der **Morgen**, –s, — morning
morgen tomorrow; **morgens** in the morning; **morgen früh** tomorrow morning
die **Morgenstunde**, —, –n morning hour
das **Motiv**, –s, –e motif
die **Motorhaube**, —, –n motor hood
das **Motorrad**, –es, ⸗er motorcycle
müde tired
die **Müdigkeit**, — fatigue
die **Mühe**, — trouble; **sich Mühe geben** take pains, try hard
mühsam with difficulty
der **Mund**, –es, ⸗er mouth
das **Mundtuch**, –es, ⸗er napkin
die **Munition**, — ammunition
die **Münze**, —, –n coin
murmeln mumble, mutter
der **Museumsplatz**, –es Museum Square
die **Musik**, — music
der **Musiklehrer**, –s, — music teacher
die **Muskel**, —, –n muscle
müssen, mußte, gemußt, muß have to
der **Mut**, –es courage; **guten Mutes** in high spirits, confident
die **Mutter**, —, ⸗ mother
mütterlich motherly, maternal

N

na well
nach after, to; according to
der **Nachbar**, –s, –n neighbor
der **Nachbarkasten**, –s, ⸗ adjoining case
der **Nachbarsaal**, –es, –säle adjoining room
nachdem after
nachdenken, dachte nach, nachgedacht think about
nachdenklich reflecting, pensive
der **Nachdruck**, –s emphasis
die **Nachforschung**, —, –en inquiry, investigation
nachgeben, a, e yield, give in
der **Nachhauseweg**, –es way home
nachkommen, a, o (ist) follow after
nachmachen imitate
der **Nachmittag**, –s, –e afternoon
nachprüfen check
nachreiten, i, i (ist) ride after, follow
die **Nachricht**, —, –en news
nachsehen, a, e look, see, check
nächst– next; nearest
die **Nacht**, —, ⸗e night
das **Nachtgespenst**, –es, –er phantom
die **Nachtherberge**, —, –n night's lodging
nächtlich nightly
die **Nachtmusik**, — serenade
nachts at night

der **Nachtwächter**, –s, — night-watchman
die **Nachtzeit**, — night-time
nah near, close
die **Nähe**, — vicinity
der **Name**, –ns, –n name
nämlich namely, you see
der **Narr**, –en, –en fool
die **Nase**, —, –n nose
das **Nashorn**, –s, ⸗er rhinoceros
naß wet
die **Nation**, —, –en nation
die **Natur**, — nature
natürlich natural, naturally, of course
der **Nebel**, –s, — fog
neben next to, beside
der **Nebenberuf**, –s, –e secondary occupation
nehmen, nahm, genommen take
nennen, nannte, genannt name, mention
nervös nervous
nett nice
neu new
die **Neugier**, — curiosity
neugierig curious
der **Nibelungenhort**, –es Nibelung treasure
nichts nothing
das **Nichtstun**, –s doing nothing
nicken nod
nie never
der **Niederländer**, –s, — Netherlander
sich **niederlassen, ie, a** settle, establish oneself
niederreißen, i, i tear down
niedersehen, a, e look down
niedrig low
niemand no one, nobody; **niemand anders** nobody else
die **Nische**, —, –n niche
noch still; **noch ein** another; **noch eins** one thing more; **noch nie** never yet
nochmals once more
der **Norden**, –s North
der **Nordgermane**, –n, –n North Teuton
nördlich northerly, north
der **Nordmann**, –s, ⸗er Norseman
die **Nordsee**, — North Sea
die **Normandie**, — Normandy
das **Normannenreich**, –es Norman Kingdom
die **Not**, — trouble
die **Note**, —, –n note
nötig necessary; **nötig haben** need, have need of
die **Notwehr**, — self-defense
nu well; **im Nu** in no time
die **Null**, —, –en zero
die **Nummer**, —, –n number
nun now; well
nur only
nutzlos useless, unprofitable

O

ob if, whether
oben above; **da oben** up there
obgleich although
oder or
offen open
offenbar apparently
öffentlich public
öffnen open
die **Öffnung**, —, –en opening
oft often
ohne without; **ohne . . . zu** without *plus verbal noun*
ohnmächtig unconscious
das **Ohr**, –es, –en ear
der **Ohrring**, –es, –e ear-ring
der **Oktober**, –s October
der **Ölfleck**, –es, –e oil spot
der **Onkel**, –s, — uncle
die **Oper**, —, –n opera
der **Opernkomponist**, –en, –en opera composer
das **Opfer**, –s, — victim
opfern sacrifice
die **Orchidee**, —, –n orchid
die **Ordnung**, —, –en order
der **Organismus**, —, . . .smen organism

originell original
der **Ort**, –es, ⸗er place
der **Osten**, –s east
(das) **Österreich**, –s Austria
der **Ostgermane**, –n, –n East Teuton
ostgermanisch East Germanic
die **Ostsee**, — Baltic
die **Ouvertüre**, —, –n overture

P

das **Paar**, –es, –e pair, couple
paar few
das **Päckchen**, –s, — small package, pack
packen pack (up), grasp, seize
das **Packen**, –s packing
die **Packung**, —, –en wrapper
das **Paket**, –es, –e package
das **Palastkino**, –s Palace movie theatre
panamerikanisch Pan-american
das **Panorama**, –s, –s panorama
der **Panzer**, –s, — coat of mail, armour
der **Papa**, –s, –s daddy
der **Papagei**, –en, –en parrot
das **Papier**, –s, –e paper
parfümiert (*p. pl.*) perfumed
passen fit
die **Patrizierfamilie**, —, –n patrician family
die **Patrone**, —, –n cartridge
die **Pause**, —, –n pause
die **Peitsche**, —, –n whip
das **Peitschengeknall**, –s cracking of the whip
der **Pelzmantel**, –s, ⸗ fur coat
die **Person**, —, –en person
die **Personenaufnahme**, —, –n picture of a person or persons
persönlich personally
der **Pfarrer**, –s, — parson
das **Pfarrhaus**, –es, ⸗er parsonage
die **Pfeife**, —, –n pipe
pfeifen, i, i whistle
das **Pferd**, –es, –e horse
der **Pferdehuf**, –es, –e horse's hoof
das **Pferderennen**, –s, –n horse race
das **Pflaster**, –s, — pavement
pflegen take care of; *with* **zu** *plus the infinitive* be in the habit of
die **Pflicht**, —, –en duty
pflücken pick
das **Pfund**, –es, –e pound
die **Phantasie**, — imagination
der **Photograph**, –en, –en photographer
die **Photographie**, —, –n photograph
photographieren photograph, take pictures
die **Photographierstellung**, —, –en position for having a picture taken
der **Pirat**, –en, –en pirate
planen plan
der **Platz**, –es, ⸗e place, seat; room; square
plaudern chat
plötzlich sudden(ly)
politisch political
die **Polizei**, — police
der **Polizeibeamte**, –n, –n police official
der **Portraitphotograph**, –en, –en portrait photographer
die **Post**, — post office; mail
das **Postamt**, –es, ⸗er post office
postlagernd in care of general delivery
der **Postwagen**, –s, — stagecoach
prahlen boast
der **Präsident**, –en, –en president
der **Preis**, –es, –e price, prize
preiswert reasonable
pressen hold tightly
primitiv primitive
die **Probe**, —, –n sample
das **Probestück**, –s, –e sample
der **Professor**, –s, –en professor
das **Programm**, –s, –e program
prophezeien prophesy
die **Provinz**, —, –en province
das **Prozent**, –es, –e percent
der **Prozeß**, –es, –e law suit
die **Psychologie**, — psychology
das **Publikum**, –s audience
der **Punkt**, –es, –e point, dot; **Punkt**

sieben Uhr at seven o'clock sharp
die **Puppe**, —, –n doll

Q

quälen torture, torment
quietschen squeak

R

der **Rächer**, –s, — avenger
das **Rad**, –es, ⸗er wheel
das **Radio**, –s, –s radio
der **Radioapparat**, –es, –e radio
der **Radiointerviewer**, –s, — radio interviewer
rasch rapidly
ein **Rasender** madman, maniac
sich **rasieren** shave
die **Rast**, — rest
der **Rat**, –es advice
raten, ie, a guess
das **Rätsel**, –s, — riddle, puzzle
rattern rattle
rauben rob
der **Räuber**, –s, — robber
die **Räuberhöhle**, —, –n den of robbers
der **Raubmord**, –es, –e (robbery-) murder
der **Raubmörder**, –s, — (robbery-) murderer
rauchen smoke
der **Raum**, –es, ⸗e room
rauschen roar
rechnen count, class
die **Rechnung**, —, –en bill
das **Recht**, –es, –e right, law
recht right, really; **recht haben** be right
rechts to the right
rechtzeitig on time, punctually
die **Rede**, —, –n speech
reden talk
der **Redner**, –s, — speaker
die **Regel**, —, –n rule; **in der Regel** as a rule
regelmäßig regular
sich **regen** stir
der **Regen**, –s rain
der **Regenschirm**, –s, –e umbrella
die **Regierung**, —, –en government
reiben, ie, ie rub
reich rich
das **Reich**, –es, –e empire, realm
reichen be sufficient
reichlich abundantly
der **Reichtum**, –s, ⸗er riches, wealth
der **Reifen**, –s, — tire
die **Reihe**, —, –n series, line; **an der Reihe sein, an die Reihe kommen** to have one's turn
der **Reim**, –es, –e rhyme, jingle
rein clear, pure
reinigen clean
die **Reise**, —, –n journey, trip
reisefertig ready to start
die **Reisekosten** (*pl.*) travelling expenses
reisen (ist) travel
der **Reisepaß**, –es, ⸗e passport
reißen, i, i, tear
reiten, i, i, (ist) ride, go on horseback
die **Reitstiefel** (*pl.*) riding boots
reizend charming
die **Reklame**, — advertisement
die **Reklamefirma**, —, –firmen advertising company
rennen, rannte, (ist) **gerannt** run
das **Rennpferd**, –es, –e race horse
reparieren repair
der **Respekt**, –es respect
respektvoll respectfully
der **Rest**, –es, –e rest
das **Restaurant**, –s, –s restaurant
die **Restaurantrechnung**, —, –en restaurant check
das **Resultat**, –es, –e result
retten save
die **Rettung**, —, –en rescue
der **Revolver**, –s, — revolver
der **Revolverschuß**, –es, ⸗e revolver shot
das **Rezept**, –es, –e recipe
rezitieren recite, declaim
der **Rhein**, –s Rhine

die **Rheintochter**, —, ¨ daughter of the the Rhine
richten direct; **eine Frage richten** ask a question
der **Richter**, –s, — judge
richtig right, correct; real
die **Richtigkeit**, — correctness
die **Richtung**, —, –en direction
der **Rieſe**, –n, –n giant
die **Rieſenſchlange**, —, –n python
rieſig gigantic, huge
der **Ring**, –es, –e ring
ringen, a, u struggle; **nach Atem ringend** gasping for breath
das **Riſiko**, –s, –s risk
riskieren risk
der **Ritt**, –es, –e ride
ritterlich knightly, chivalrous
der **Rock**, –es, ¨e coat; skirt
roh brutal
die **Rolle**, —, –n roll; part
(das) **Rom**, –s Rome, Roman Empire
der **Roman**, –s, –e novel
romaniſch Romance
der **Römer**, –s, — Roman
römiſch Roman
die **Röntgenaufnahme**, —, –n X-ray photograph
die **Roſe**, —, –n rose
roſtig rusty
rot red
'rüber (*short for* **herüber**) over
der **Rücken**, –s, — back
rücken move
die **Rückwand**, —, ¨e backwall
die **Rückkehr**, — return
rückwärts backward
rudern row
der **Ruf**, –es, –e cry, reputation
rufen call; **das Rufen** calling
die **Ruhe**, — quiet, rest, peace
das **Ruhebett**, –es, –en couch
ruhen rest
ruhig quiet, calm
(ſich) **rühren** move
rund round
die **Runde**, —, –n round
'runter (*short for* **herunter**) down

S

der **Saal**, –es, Säle hall, room
die **Sache**, —, –n thing, matter
der **Sachſe**, –n, –n Saxon
ſagen say
der **Salon**, –s, –s drawing-room
das **Salz**, –es salt
der **Sammler**, –s, — collector
die **Sammlung**, —, –en collection
der **Samstag**, –s, –e Saturday
ſanft gently
ſarkaſtiſch sarcastic
ſatteln saddle
der **Satz**, –es, ¨e sentence; set; leap
die **Schachtel**, —, –n box
ſchade (too) bad
ſchaden harm, hurt, injure; **das ſchadet nichts** that does not matter
der **Schaden**, –s, ¨ damage
ſchälen peel
ſich **ſchämen** be ashamed
ſcharf sharp
der **Schatten**, –s, — shadow
der **Schatz**, –es, ¨e treasure; sweetheart
der **Schatzmeiſter**, –s, — treasurer
die **Schaufel**, —, –n shovel
das **Schaufenſter**, –s, — show window
der **Schauſpieler**, –s, — actor
ſchauſpieleriſch like an actor, acting (*adj.*)
der **Schauplatz**, –es, ¨e scene
der **Scheck**, –s, –s check
die **Scheide**, —, –n sheath
der **Schein**, –e shine, light; illusion; bill (money)
ſcheinen, ie, ie shine; seem
der **Scheinwerfer**, –s, — head light
ſchelten, a, o scold
ſchenken give (as a present)
der **Scherz**, –es, –e joke, jest
ſcherzend joking(ly)

ſcherzhaft joking(ly)
die **Scheune**, —, **–n** barn
ſchicken send
das **Schickſal**, **–s** fate
ſchieben, o, o shove, push
die **Schiene**, —, **–n** splint
ſchießen, o, o shoot
das **Schiff**, **–s**, **–e** ship
das **Schildchen**, **–s**, — small sign
ſchimpfen bawl out; scold
das **Schimpfen**, **–s** scolding, using abusive language
der **Schimpfname**, **–ns**, **–n** abusive name
der **Schinken**, **–s**, — ham
das **Schinkenbrot**, **–es**, **–e** ham sandwich
der **Schlaf**, **–es** sleep
ſchlafen, ie, a sleep
die **Schlafkammer**, —, **–n** (small) bedroom
das **Schlafzimmer**, **–s**, — bedroom
der **Schlag**, **–es**, **¨e** blow, slap, stroke
der **Schlaganfall**, **–es**, **¨e** stroke
ſchlagen, u, a strike, hit, beat
die **Schlägerei**, —, **–en** fight(ing)
die **Schlange**, —, **–n** snake
der **Schlangenkopf**, **–es**, **¨e** snake's head
ſchlank slender
ſchlau clever
ſchlecht bad
ſchleudern throw
ſchleppen drag
ſchließen, o, o close, lock
ſchließlich after all, finally
ſchlimm bad; **das Schlimmſte** worst
das **Schloß**, **–es**, **¨er** castle
das **Schluchzen**, **–s** sobbing
das **Schlummerlied**, **–es**, **–er** lullaby
ſchlüpfen slip
der **Schluß**, **–es**, **¨e** end, conclusion; **Schluß machen** stop
der **Schlüſſel**, **–s**, — key
der **Schlüſſelring**, **–es**, **–e** key ring
ſchmal narrow
der **Schmerz**, **–ens**, **–en** pain
ſchmerzen pain, hurt
ſchmerzend aching
der **Schmetterling**, **–s**, **–e** butterfly
der **Schmuck**, **–es** adornment, jewels
der **Schmuckartikel**, **–s**, — decorative article
die **Schmuckſachen** (*pl.*) jewels
das **Schmuckſtück**, **–s**, **–e** piece of jewelry
ſchmutzig soiled, dirty
der **Schnee**, **–s** snow
ſchneeweiß snow-white
das **Schneewittchen**, **–s** Snow White
ſchneiden, i, i cut, trim
ſchnell fast, quick; **ſchnellſtens** as quickly as possible
der **Schnupfen**, **–s**, — head cold
die **Schnur**, —, **¨e** string, cord
der **Schnurrbart**, **–es**, **¨e** mustache
die **Schokolade**, **–e** chocolate
ſchon already; **ſchon einmal** (in question) ever
ſchön beautiful, pretty
die **Schönheit**, — beauty
die **Schönheitscreme**, — beauty cream
der **Schoß**, **–es**, **¨e** lap
das **Schoßhündchen**, **–s**, — lap dog
der **Schotte**, **–n**, **–n** Scot, Scotsman
der **Schrank**, **–es**, **¨e** closet
die **Schrapnellkugel**, —, **–n** shrapnel bullet
der **Schrecken**, **–s** fright
die **Schreckensnacht**, —, **¨e** terrible night
ſchrecklich terrible, horrible
der **Schrei**, **–s**, **–e** scream
ſchreiben, ie, ie write
die **Schreibmaſchine**, —, **–n** typewriter
der **Schreibtiſch**, **–es**, **–e** writing desk
ſchreien, ie, ie scream
ſchreiten, i, i (**iſt**) step
die **Schrift** —, **–en** writing
die **Schriftſtellerin**, —, **–nen** authoress
das **Schriftſtück**, **–es**, **–e** document
der **Schritt**, **–es**, **–e** footstep, step
der **Schuh**, **–s**, **–e** the shoe
die **Schuld**, — fault; debt; guilt; **die Schulden** (*pl.*) debts

schuld sein be guilty
der **Schuldige**, –n, –n guilty person
die **Schule**, —, –n school
die **Schulkameradin**, —, –nen schoolmate
die **Schulter**, —, –n shoulder
die **Schürze**, —, –n apron
der **Schuß**, –es, ⸗e shot
schütteln shake
der **Schutz**, –es protection
schützen protect
der **Schützengraben**, –s, ⸗ trench
der **Schützling**, –s, –e protégé
der **Schutzmann**, –s, –leute policeman
schwach weak
der **Schwächeanfall**, –es, ⸗e spell of dizziness
schwächlich weakly, sickly
der **Schwager**, –s, ⸗ brother-in-law
schwänzen cut class
schwarz black
das **Schwarze Meer**, –s Black Sea
der **Schwarzkopf**, –es, ⸗e brunette
schweigen, ie, ie be silent
das **Schweigen**, –s silence
schweigend silent(ly)
das **Schweinefleisch**, –es pork
der **Schweinsfuß**, –es, ⸗e pig's foot
der **Schweiß**, –es perspiration, sweat
die **Schweiz**, — Switzerland
schwer heavy, difficult; serious
das **Schwert**, –es, –er sword
die **Schwester**, —, –n sister
schwierig difficult
die **Schwierigkeit**, —, –en difficulty
schwimmen, a, o (ist) swim
der **Schwimmer**, –s, — swimmer
schwitzen perspire
schwören, o, o swear
der **See**, –s, –n lake
der **Seehund**, –es, –e seal
die **Seele**, —, –n soul
der **Segen**, –s, — blessing
segnen bless
sehen, a, e see
sehr very
die **Seide**, — silk
der **Seidenstrumpf**, –es, ⸗e silk stocking
die **Seife**, —, –n soap
sein, war, (ist) gewesen, ist be
das **Seineufer**, –s, — bank of the river Seine
seit since; **seit langem** for a long time
die **Seite**, —, –n side
das **Seitengäßchen**, –s, — side street
der **Sekretär**, –s, –e secretary
die **Sekretärin**, —, –nen secretary
die **Sekunde**, —, –n second
selber myself, *etc.*; **von selber** of his own accord
selbst myself; even
selbstverständlich of course
selten seldom
seltsam odd, strange
die **Semantik** semantics (*science of meaning of words*)
semantisch semantic
senden, sendete (sandte), gesendet (gesandt) send
der **Sender**, –s, — transmitter, radio station
die **Sendestation**, —, –en broadcasting station
senken lower
der **Sessel**, –s, — arm-chair
setzen set; **sich setzen** sit down
seufzen sigh
der **Seufzer**, –s, — sigh
sicher safe, certain, sure; no doubt
sicherlich undoubtedly
sichtbar visible
sichtlich apparent, obvious
der **Sieg**, –es, –e victory
das **Silber**, –s silver
der **Silberdollar**, –s, — silver dollar
silberhaltig containing silver, argental
der **Silberlöwe**, –n, –n cougar
silbern of silver
der **Silbertaler**, –s, — silver taler
singen a, u sing; **das Singen** singing
sinken, a, u (ist) sink, drop

der **Sinn**, –es meaning
der **Sitz**, –es, –e seat
sitzen, saß, gesessen sit; to be in jail
die **Sitzung**, —, –en meeting
(das) **Skandinavien**, –s Scandinavia
der **Skandinavier**, –s, — Scandinavian
so so; **so ein** such a; **so . . . wie** as . . . as; **so viel . . . wie** as much . . . as
sobald as soon as
die **Socke**, —, –n sock
sodaß so that
das **Sofa**, –s, –s davenport
sofort at once
sogar even
sogleich at once
der **Sohn**, –es, ⸗e son
das **Söhnchen**, –s, — small son
solange as long as
solcher such
der **Soldat**, –en, –en soldier
sollen, sollte, gesollt, soll shall, have to, be supposed to
das **Sommerhaus**, –es, ⸗er summer residence
sonderbar strange, odd
sondern but
der **Sonnabend**, –s, –e Saturday
die **Sonne**, — sun
der **Sonnenaufgang**, –es, ⸗e sunrise
der **Sonntag**, –s, –e Sunday
sonst otherwise; **sonst jemand** anyone else
die **Sorge**, —, –n worry, care; **sich Sorgen machen** to worry
sorgen worry; care for, see to
sorgenfrei free of care
sorgenvoll worried
sorgfältig careful(ly)
soviel . . . wie as much as
sowie as well as
sowieso anyhow
das **Spanisch**, –en Spanish (language)
spannen hitch
sparen save
der **Spaß**, –es, ⸗e fun
spät late
spazieren gehen take a walk
die **Spazierfahrt**, —, –n drive
der **Spaziergang**, –es, ⸗e walk
der **Speck**, –es bacon
der **Speer**, –es, –e spear, lance
der **Speisesaal**, –es, –säle dining room
das **Spezialgebiet**, –es, –e special field
der **Spiegel**, –s, — looking glass
das **Spiegelbild**, –es reflection
sich spiegeln be reflected
das **Spiel**, –es, –e play, game
spielen play
der **Spieler**, –s, — player
der **Spion**, –es, –e spy
die **Spitze**, —, –n sharp point
der **Sporn**, –s, **Sporen** spur
der **Sport**, –es sport
der **Sportanzug**, –es, ⸗e sport suit
der **Spott**, –es mockery
die **Sprache**, —, –n language
sprachlos speechless
sprechen, a, o speak
springen, a, u (ist) jump
spritzen splash
spucken spit
spülen rinse
die **Spur**, —, –en trace, track; clue
spüren feel, notice, perceive; experience
der **Staat**, –es, –en state
die **Stadt**, —, ⸗e city
das **Städtchen**, –s, — small town
der **Stahl**, –s steel
der **Stamm**, –s, ⸗e tribe
stammeln stammer
stammen: stammen aus date from, come from
ständig constant
stark strong
die **Stärke**, — strength
starren stare
die **Station**, —, –en station
statt instead of
stattfinden, a, u take place
stattlich stately, sturdy

der **Staub**, –es dust
stecken stick, put; **stecken bleiben** stick fast; **stecken lassen** leave sticking
stehen, stand, gestanden stand; be written, occur; **es steht ihr gut** it is becoming to her; **wie steht es mit** what about
stehen bleiben, ie, ie (ist) remain standing; stop
steigen, ie, ie (ist) climb
steil steep
der **Stein**, –es, –e stone
das **Steinbild**, –es, –er statue
steinig stony
die **Stelle**, —, –n place, spot
stellen place, put; **eine Frage stellen** to ask a question; **sich stellen** stand
die **Stellung**, —, –en position
sterben, a, o (ist) die
das **Sterben: im Sterben liegen** be dying
das **Steuerrad**, –es, ⸗er steering wheel
still still, quiet
stillschweigend silently
stillstehen, stand still, stillgestanden (ist) stop
die **Stimme**, —, –n voice
stimmen be correct
die **Stimmung**, —, –en mood
die **Stirn**, —, –en forehead
der **Stock**, –es, ⸗e floor
der **Stoff**, –es, –e material
stöhnen groan
stolz proud
stören disturb
stoßen, ie, o hit, knock, push
die **Stoßstange**, —, –n bumper
die **Strafe**, —, –n punishment
strahlen beam
die **Straße**, —, –n street
die **Straßenbahn**, —, –en streetcar
der **Straßengraben**, –s, ⸗ ditch
der **Straßenköter**, –s, — street cur
der **Straßenlärm**, –s street noise
der **Straßenräuber**, –s, — street robber
der **Straßensänger**, –s, — street singer
die **Strecke**, —, –n stretch
streicheln stroke, pat
das **Streichholz**, –es, ⸗er match
der **Streit**, –es, –e quarrel
streiten, i, i quarrel
streng strict
strömen pour
der **Strumpf**, –es, ⸗e stocking
das **Stück**, –es, –e piece
der **Student**, –en, –en student
die **Studentin**, —, –nen girl student
studieren study
die **Stufe**, —, –n step
der **Stuhl**, –es, ⸗e chair
die **Stunde**, —, –n hour; class
der **Stundenplan**, –s, ⸗e class schedule
der **Sturm**, –es, ⸗e storm
stürmisch boisterous
stürzen (ist) rush, plunge
stützen support
suchen search, seek
(das) **Südamerika**, –s South America
der **Süden**, –s South
südländisch southern
südlich southern
der **Südstaat**, –es, –en southern state
der **Sünder**, –s, — sinner, culprit
süß sweet
die **Szene**, —, –n scene

T

das **Tablett**, –s, –e tray
die **Tafel**, —, –n board
der **Tag**, –es, –e day
tagelang for days
die **Tagereise**, —, –n day's journey
der **Tagesanbruch**, –s daybreak
täglich daily
das **Talent**, –es, –e talent, ability
tanken buy gasoline
der **Tanz**, –es, ⸗e dance
tanzen dance
die **Tänzerin**, —, –nen dancer (feminine)
die **Tanzkapelle**, —, –n dance band
die **Tanzmusik**, — dance music
tapfer brave

die **Taſche**, —, –n pocket
das **Taſchentuch**, –es, ⸗er handkerchief
die **Taſſe**, —, –n cup
taſten grope
die **Tat**, —, –en deed, action
die **Tatſache**, —, –n fact
die **Taufe**, —, –n baptism, christening
taufen baptize
der **Taufpate**, –n, –n godfather; *pl.* godparents
taugen be good *or* fit
der **Taugenichts**, — good-for-nothing
das **Taxi**, –s, –s taxi
der **Teddybär**, –en, –en Teddy Bear
der **Tee**, –s tea
der **Teil**, –s, –e part; **zum Teil** in part
teilen share
teils . . . teils partly . . . partly
teilweiſe partly
das **Telephon**, –s, –e telephone
das **Tennis**, — tennis
der **Tennislehrer**, –s, — tennis instructor
der **Tennismeiſter**, –s, — tennis champion
die **Tennismeiſterſchaft**, —, –en tennis championship
der **Tennisplatz**, –es, ⸗e tennis court
der **Tennisſchläger**, –s, — tennis raquet
der **Tennisſchuh**, –s, –e tennis shoe
der **Tennisſpieler**, –s, — tennis player
der **Tenor**, –s, ⸗e tenor
die **Terraſſe**, —, –n terrace
das **Teſtament**, –s, –e testament, will
die **Tetralogie**, —, –n tetralogy
teuer expensive
der **Teufel**, –s, — devil
das **Theater**, –s, — theatre
das **Theaterpublikum**, –s audience
der **Thron**, –es, –e throne
der **Thronſaal**, –s, –ſäle throne room
tief deep, sound
das **Tier**, –es, –e animal
der **Tierarzt**, –es, ⸗e veterinary
die **Tieraufnahme**, —, –n picture of an animal
die **Tierfabel**, —, –n animal fable
der **Tierfilm**, –s, –e animal film
der **Tierliebling**, –s, –e animal pet
der **Tiger**, –s, — tiger
der **Tiſch**, –es, –e table
der **Titel**, –s, — title
die **Tochter**, —, ⸗ daughter
der **Tod**, –es death
der **Todesſtoß**, –es, ⸗e death-thrust
die **Todeswunde**, —, –n mortal wound
tödlich deadly, mortal
todmüde dead tired
die **Tomate**, —, –n tomato
der **Torweg**, –es, –e gateway, archway
tot dead; **der Tote** dead man
töten kill
totenblaß deadly pale
totſchlagen, u, a beat to death, kill
tragen, u, a carry, wear
der **Träger**, –s, — wearer
der **Tragſeſſel**, –s, — sedan chair
trainieren train
der **Tran**, –s fish oil
die **Träne**, —, –n tear
der **Traum**, –s, ⸗e dream
träumen dream
die **Träumerei**, —, –en reverie
träumeriſch dreamy
traurig sad
treffen, a, o meet; hit
treiben, ie, ie drive, perform
ſich trennen separate
die **Trennung**, —, –en separation
der **Trennungstag**, –es, –e day of separation
die **Treppe**, —, –n stairs
treten, a, e (iſt) step; kick
treu faithful, loyal
trinken, a, u drink
das **Trinkgeld**, –es, –er tip
trocknen dry
trommeln drum, tap
der **Tropfen**, –s, — drop
tropfen drip
tröſten console

das **Troſtwort, –es, –e** word of comfort
der **Trotz, –es** defiance
trotz in spite of
trotzdem in spite of the fact that, nevertheless
trotzig defiantly
die **Truhe, —, –n** trunk, chest
der **Trumpf, –es, ⸗e** trump
die **Truppen** (*pl.*) troops
das **Tuch, –es, ⸗er** cloth
tun, tat, getan do
der **Tunichtgut, –es, –e** good-for-nothing
der **Tunnel, –s, —** tunnel, underground passage
die **Tür, —, –en** door
das **Türchen, –s, —** small door
die **Türöffnung, —, –en** doorway
typiſch typical

U

der **Übeltäter, –s, —** evil-doer, criminal
über over
überall everywhere
übereinſtimmen agree
der **Überfall, –s, ⸗e** attack
überfallen, ie, a attack
übergeben, a, e hand over
überhaupt at all
ſich **überlaſſen ſein** be left to oneself
überleben survive
ſich **überlegen** think about, figure out
überlegen ſein be superior to
die **Überlieferung, —, –en** tradition
übermannen overcome
übernachten spend the night
übernehmen, a, o take over, assume; accept
überraſchen surprise
die **Überraſchung, —, –en** surprise
überreden persuade
überreichen hand (over)
ſich **überſchlagen, u, a** somersault
übertreiben, ie, ie exaggerate
überzeugen convince
übrig left over, remaining
übrigens incidentally, by the way
das **Ufer, –s, —** shore
die **Uhr, —, –en** watch, clock, o'clock
um around; by; **um ſein** be up; **um ſo** all the; **um . . . zu** in order to
umarbeiten rework
umarmbar embraceable
umarmen to embrace
umbauen rebuild
umbringen, brachte um, umgebracht kill
ſich **umdrehen** turn around
umherlaufen, ie, au (**iſt**) run around
umherwandern (**iſt**) wander around
umkehren (**iſt**) turn around
umklammern clasp
umkommen, a, o (**iſt**) perish
der **Umſchlag, –es, ⸗e** envelope
ſich **umſehen, a, e** look around
umſonſt in vain
der **Umſtand, –es, ⸗e** circumstance
unangenehm unpleasant
unbeantwortbar unanswerable
unbedeutend insignificant
unbedingt absolutely
unbegreiflich inexplicable
unbeſchreiblich indescribable
unbeſiegbar invincible
unbeſtimmt vague
unbeweglich fixed
unbezwingbar uncontrollable
unerkannt unrecognized, incognito
unerſchütterlich unshakable, firm
unerträglich unbearable, intolerable
unfähig incapable, incompetent
unfreundlich unfriendly
der **Unfug, –es** mischief
die **Ungeduld, —** impatience
ungeduldig impatient
ungefähr about, approximately
ungeheuer enormous
ungehört unheard
die **Ungerechtigkeit, —, –en** injustice
ungern(e) unwillingly, do not like to
ungeſehen unseen, unnoticed
ungeſtört undisturbed

ungesund unhealthy, sickly
ungewöhnlich unusual
ungläubig unbelieving, skeptical
das **Unglück**, –s bad luck, misfortune
unglücklich unhappy, unfortunate
das **Unglücksjahr**, –es, –e unlucky year
die **Unglücksstelle**, —, –n place of the accident
die **Universität**, —, –en university
das **Universitätsjubiläum**, –s, . . .äen university anniversary
der **Universitätsprofessor**, –s, –en university professor
unklar unclear, obscure
die **Unkosten** (*pl.*) expenses
unmittelbar direct, immediate
unmöglich impossible
die **Unpünktlichkeit**, — unpunctuality
das **Unrecht**, –es injustice
unrecht haben be wrong
die **Unruhe**, — unrest
die **Unschuld**, — innocence
unschuldig innocent
unsicher uncertain
der **Unsinn**, –s nonsense
der **Unsterbliche**, –n, –n immortal
unten below, down
unter under
unterbrechen, a, o interrupt
unterbringen, accommodate
unterdrücken suppress
untergehen, ging unter, untergegangen (ist) submerge
die **Untergruppe**, —, –n subgroup
sich **unterhalten, ie, a** converse, entertain
die **Unterhaltung**, —, –en conversation
unterirdisch subterranean
die **Unterkunft**, —, ¨e lodging
der **Unteroffizier**, –s, –e corporal
unternehmen, a, o undertake
das **Unternehmen**, –s, — undertaking
der **Unterschied**, –es, –e difference
untersuchen examine
die **Untersuchung**, —, –en examination
der **Untertan**, –en, –en subject
unterwegs on the way
unterzeichnen sign
ununterbrochen uninterrupted
unverheiratet sein be single
unvernünftig unreasonable, senseless
unverschlossen unlocked
unverständlich unintelligible
unwichtig unimportant
unwiderstehlich irresistible
unwillig unwilling
der **Unwürdige**, –n, –n unworthy, undeserving person
der **Urlaub**, –s furlough, vacation
der **Ursprung**, –s, ¨e origin
das **Urteil**, –s, –e judgment
usw. and so on

V

der **Vandale**, –n, –n Vandal
der **Vater**, –s, ¨ father
der **Venezianer**, –s, — Venetian
die **Verabredung**, —, –en appointment
verantwortlich responsible
die **Verantwortung**, —, –en responsibility
verbergen, a, o hide
verbessern improve, amend
sich **verbeugen** bow
die **Verbeugung**, —, –en bow
die **Verbindung**, —, –en connection
verbittert grown bitter, embittered
verblenden blind
das **Verbrechen**, –s, — crime
der **Verbrecher**, –s, — criminal
die **Verbrecherlaufbahn**, — career of a criminal
verbrennen, verbrannte, verbrannt burn
der **Verdacht**, –es suspicion
verdächtig suspicious
der **Verdächtige**, –n, –n suspect, suspicious person
verdächtigen suspect
verdanken owe
das **Verderben**, –s destruction
verdienen earn, deserve

verdoppeln double
verehren worship; **Verehrtes Fräulein** my dear lady, madamoiselle
das **Verfahren**, –s, — process, method
der **Verfasser**, –s, — author
die **Verfilmung**, —, –en film version
verfliegen, o, o (ist) fly away, vanish
verfluchen curse
die **Verfolgung**, —, –en pursuit
vergeben, a, e forgive
vergeblich in vain
vergehen, **verging**, **vergangen** (ist) pass away
vergessen, a, e forget
vergiften poison
vergleichen, i, i compare
das **Vergnügen**, –s, — pleasure
vergraben, u, a hide in the ground, bury
verhaften arrest
die **Verhaftung**, —, –en arrest
verhallen (ist) die away
die **Verhältnisse** (*pl.*) conditions
verhängen cover with a curtain
der **Verhaßte**, –n, –n hated person
sich **verheiraten** get married; **verheiratet sein** be married
verhindern prevent
verhöhnen mock, deride
verhören question
verkaufen sell
der **Verkäufer**, –s, — salesman
die **Verkäuferin**, —, –nen salesgirl
der **Verkehr**, –s traffic
der **Verkehrsstrom**, –s, ¨e stream of traffic
verkleiden disguise
verkürzen shorten
verlangen demand
das **Verlangen**, –s desire, craving
verlassen, ie, a leave; **sich verlassen auf** depend upon
sich **verlaufen**, ie, au lose one's way
verleben spend
verlegen misplace
verlegen embarrassed
die **Verletzung**, —, –en injury
verliebt enamored, in love
verlieren, o, o lose
der **Verlobte**, –n, –n fiancé
vermehren increase
vermeiden, ie, ie avoid
das **Vermögen**, –s, — wealth, fortune
vermuten suspect
vernehmen, a, o notice, hear
sich **verneigen** bow
verraten, ie, a betray
verrichten perform, accomplish
verrückt crazy
der **Vers**, –es, –e verse
versagen fail
verschieben, o, o postpone
verschieden different, various
verschießen, o, o use up (ammunition)
verschließen, o, o lock, close
verschlingen, a, u swallow up
verschwinden, a, u (ist) disappear
versichern assure
die **Versicherung**, — insurance (company)
das **Versicherungsgeld**, –es, –er insurance money
versinken, a, u (ist) sink; **in Gedanken versunken** lost or absorbed in thoughts
sich **verspäten** come late
versperren block
verspielen lose
versprechen, a, o promise
verständlich intelligible
das **Verständnis**, ...nisses understanding
verständnislos uncomprehending
das **Versteck**, –es, –e hiding place
verstecken hide
verstehen, **verstand**, **verstanden** understand
verstorben (*p.p.*) deceased, late
der **Versuch**, –s, –e attempt; experiment
versuchen try, attempt, tempt
die **Versuchung**, —, –en temptation
sich **verteidigen** defend oneself

die **Verteidigung**, — defense
vertrauen trust, confide in
das **Vertrauen**, –s confidence
vertreiben, ie, ie banish
verurteilen condemn
verwandeln change, transform
verwandt related
der **Verwandte**, –n, –n relative
verwechseln confuse
verwickeln involve
sich **verwirren** become confused; **verwirrt** confused
verwunden wound; **schwer verwundet** seriously wounded
verwundert surprised
die **Verwünschung**, —, –en curse
verzeihen, ie, ie pardon, forgive
die **Verzeihung**, — pardon
verzweifeln despair; **verzweifelt** desperately
das **Vieh**, –s cattle
viel much, a great deal; **viele** many; **sehr viel** a great deal of
vieldeutig ambiguous
vielleicht perhaps
die **Vierdollarfrage**, —, –n four dollar question
das **Viertel**, –s, — quarter
die **Viertelstunde**, —, –n quarter of an hour
die **Villa**, —, **Villen** villa
die **Völkergruppe**, —, –n group of people
die **Völkerwanderungszeit**, — era of tribal migrations
die **Volkswirtschaft**, — economics
voll full; **voller** filled with
vollkommen entirely, completely
von of, from; by
vor in front of; **vor sich hin** to oneself
voraus ahead; **im voraus** in advance
vorbei past
vorbeidonnern thunder past
das **Vorderrad**, –es, ⸗er front wheel
der **Vorderreifen**, –s, — front tire
der **Vorfahr**, –en, –en ancestor
der **Vorfall**, –s, ⸗e incident
der **Vorgesetzte**, –n, –n superior
vorhaben have plans, intend
der **Vorhang**, –es, ⸗e curtain
vorher before (that), a short time ago
vorig previous, last
vorkommen occur, seem, appear
vorlesen, a, e read aloud
der **Vorname**, –ns, –n first name
vornehm distinguished
vorrücken (ist) advance
vorsagen prompt
der **Vorschlag**, –es, ⸗e suggestion, proposal
der **Vorschuß**, –es, ⸗e advance
Vorsicht! Careful!
vorsichtig carefully
vorstellen present, introduce; **sich vorstellen** imagine
der **Vortrag**, –s, ⸗e lecture; **einen Vortrag halten** deliver a lecture
vorüber past, over
vorübergehen, ging vorüber, vorübergegangen (ist) pass
das **Vorwort**, –es, –e foreword, preface
vorwärts forward, ahead
vorziehen, o, o prefer
der **Vorzug**, –es, ⸗e excellence

W

wach awake
die **Wache**, —, –n guard, watch; **Wache halten** keep watch
der **Wachtmeister**, –s, — sergeant, policeman
die **Waffe**, —, –n weapon *pl.* arms
der **Waffensaal**, –es, ...säle weapon room
der **Wagen**, –s, — wagon, car, carriage
wagen dare
wählen choose, elect
der **Wahnsinn**, –s insanity, madness
wahnsinnig insane
wahr true, real
während during; while
die **Wahrheit**, —, –en truth

wahrscheinlich probably, probable
der **Wald**, –es, ⸗er woods, forest
der **Walfisch**, –es, –e whale
der **Walzer**, –s, — waltz
die **Wand**, —, ⸗e wall
der **Wanderer**, –s, — wanderer
wandern (ist) migrate, wander
wann when; **dann und wann** now and then
das **Wappen**, –s, — coat of arms
das **Warenhaus**, –es, ⸗er department store
warm warm
die **Wärmehalle**, —, –n warming room
sich **wärmen** warm oneself, get warm
warnen warn
warten wait
der **Wärter**, –s, — keeper, guard
warum why
was what; **was für ein** what kind of
die **Wäsche**, — wash, laundry; lingerie, linen
waschen, u, a wash
das **Wäschepaket**, –es, –e laundry package, laundry box
das **Wasser** water
wechseln change, exchange
wecken wake, awaken
weder . . . noch neither . . . nor
der **Weg**, –es, –e way, path, road
weg gone, off
wegbleiben, ie, ie (ist) stay away
wegen because of
wegführen lead away
weggehen, ging weg, weggegangen (ist) go away
weglaufen, ie, au (ist) go away
wegstoßen, ie, o push away
wegwerfen, a, o throw away
wehen blow
weiblich feminine, female
weich soft
weichen, i, i (ist) give way
die **Weihnachten** (*pl.*) Christmas
die **Weihnachtsferien** (*pl.*) Christmas vacation
das **Weihnachtsgeschenk**, –s, –e Christmas present
der **Weihnachtsmann**, –es, ⸗er Santa Claus
weil because
die **Weile**, — while
der **Wein**, –es, –e wine
weinen cry; **das Weinen** crying
weinerlich weepy
die **Weise**, — way, manner
weiß white
weißhaarig white-haired
weit wide; far; **weiter** further; **und so weiter** and so on
weiterfahren u, a (ist) drive on
weiterfragen keep on asking
weitergehen, ging weiter, weitergegangen (ist) go on
weiterleben live on
weiterlesen, a, e read further
weiterreden talk on
weiterreiten, i, i (ist) ride on
welcher, –e, –es which, what
die **Welle**, —, –n wave; wave-length
die **Welt**, —, –en world
die **Weltanschauung**, —, –en view of the world, philosophy of life
welterfahren experienced in the (ways of the) world
der **Weltkrieg**, –es, –e World War
sich **wenden**, wendete (wandte), gewendet (gewandt) turn
wenig little, few
wenigstens at least
wenn when, if, whenever
wer who
werden, wurde, geworden (ist) become, get
werfen, a, o throw, put
das **Werk**, –es, –e work
die **Werkstatt**, —, ⸗e workshop
der **Wert**, –es, –e worth, value
wert worth

wertvoll valuable
das **Wesen**, –s, — being
die **Weste**, —, –n vest
der **Westen**, –s West
der **Westgermane**, –n, –n West Teuton
westgermanisch West Germanic
wetten bet
das **Wetter** weather
der **Wetterbericht**, –es, –e weather report
wichtig important
wickeln wrap
widersprechen, a, o contradict; **widersprechend** contradictory
der **Widerstand**, –es, ⸗e opposition
widerstehen, **widerstand**, **widerstanden** resist
widmen devote
wie as; how; like; as if
wieder again
wiederentdecken rediscover
wiedererkennen recognize
wiedergeben, a, e return, restore
wiederholen repeat
wiedersehen, a, e see again
das **Wiedersehen**, –s seeing again, reunion; **auf Wiedersehen** good-bye
wiegen, o, o weigh
das **Wien**, –s Vienna; **Wiener** (*adj.*) Viennese, Vienna
wieviel how much
der **Wikingerzug**, –es, ⸗e Viking expedition
wild wild
das **Wild**, –es game
die **Wildnis**, — wilderness
die **Wildtieraufnahme**, —, –n wild animal shot
der **Wille**, –ns will
die **Willigkeit**, — willingness
wimmern whimper
der **Wind**, –es, –e wind
der **Windstoß**, –es, ⸗e gust of wind
winken beckon, signal
der **Winter**, –s, — winter
der **Wintersturm**, –es, ⸗e winter-storm
winseln whine
winzig tiny
wirklich real, really
die **Wirklichkeit**, — reality
die **Wirkung**, —, –en effect
der **Wirt**, –es, –e innkeeper
die **Wirtin**, —, –nen landlady, wife of the innkeeper
das **Wirtshaus**, –es, ⸗er inn
wispern whisper
wissen, **wußte**, **gewußt**, **weiß** know
die **Wissenschaft**, —, –en science
der **Witz**, –es, –e wit, esprit; joke
witzig witty
wo where
die **Woche**, —, –n week
das **Wochenende**, –s, –n week-end
woher whence, from where
wohin where (to)
wohl probably, I suppose
das **Wohlergehen**, –s welfare
wohlverdient well-deserved
wohnen live, dwell
das **Wohnzimmer**, –s, — living room
die **Wolke**, —, –n cloud
die **Wolldecke**, —, –n blanket
wollen want to, wish, intend
der **Wonnemond**, –es, –e moon of bliss
das **Wort**, –es, –e or ⸗er word
die **Wortzusammensetzung**, —, –en word compound
der **Wucherer**, –s, — usurer
das **Wunder**, –s, — wonder
wunderbar wonderful
wunderlich strange, eccentric
sich wundern be surprised
der **Wunsch**, –es, ⸗e wish
wünschen wish
würdevoll dignified
würdig worthy
das **Würstchen**, –s, — sausage
die **Wut**, — rage
wütend furious, raging

Z

die Zahl, —, **–en** number; figure
zahlen pay
zählen count
zahlreich numerous
der Zahn, **–es**, **⸗e** tooth
zahnlos toothless
die Zahnſchmerzen (*pl.*) toothache
zärtlich tenderly
die Zauberflöte, — 'Magic Flute'
zauberhaft magic
die Zauberkraft, —, **⸗e** magic power
das Zeichen, **–s**, — sign, symptom
zeigen show, point
die Zeile, —, **–n** line
die Zeit, —, **–en** time; **zur Zeit** at the time
die Zeitung, —, **–en** newspaper
der Zeitungsverkäufer, **–s**, — newspaper vendor
die Zenſur, —, **–en** grade
zerbrechen, **a**, **o** break
zerſchmettern smash
zerſchneiden, **i**, **i** cut up
zerſtören destroy
zerſtreut absent minded
der Zettel, **–s**, — piece of paper
ziehen, **o**, **o** move, pull, draw
zielen aim
ziellos aimlessly
ziemlich rather, quite
die Zigarre, —, **–n** cigar
das Zimmer, **–s**, — room
der Zimmergenoſſe, **–n**, **–n** roommate
der Zinnkrug, **–es**, **⸗e** pewter pitcher
die Zinſen (*pl.*) interest
der Zirkuslöwe, **–n**, **–n** circus lion
ziſchen hiss
zittern tremble, shake
zoologiſch zoological
der Zorn, **–s** anger, indignation
zornig angry
zu at; to; too
zubringen, **brachte zu**, **zugebracht** spend
zuerſt first (of all)
der Zufall, **–s**, **⸗e** coincidence
zufrieden satisfied
der Zug, **–es**, **⸗e** train
die Zugbrücke, —, **–n** drawbridge
zugeben, **a**, **e** admit
zugleich at the same time
die Zugkraft, —, **⸗e** tractive power
zuhören listen to
zukommen auf, **a**, **o** (**iſt**) come up to
die Zukunft, — future
zukünftig future
der Zukunftstraum, **–s**, **⸗e** dream of the future
zuletzt last
zumachen close
zumute: ihm iſt . . . zumute he feels
zunächſt first of all
die Zunge, —, **–n** tongue
zureden urge
zurück back
zurückbringen, **brachte zurück**, **zurückgebracht** bring back
zurückfahren, **u**, **a** (**iſt**) drive back
zurückfallen, **ie**, **a** (**iſt**) fall back
zurückgeben, **a**, **e** return
zurückhalten, **ie**, **a** hold back, stop
zurückkehren (**iſt**) return
zurückkommen, **a**, **o** (**iſt**) come back, return
zurücklaſſen, **ie**, **a** leave behind
zurücknehmen, **a**, **o** take back
zurücktreiben, **ie**, **ie** drive back
zurücktreten, **a**, **e** (**iſt**) step back
ſich zurückziehen, **o**, **o** withdraw
zurufen, **ie**, **u** call to
zuſammen together
das Zuſammenbrechen, **–s** collapse
der Zuſammenhang, **–s**, **⸗e** context, connection
ſich zuſammennehmen, **a**, **o** pull oneself together
zuſammenſchieben, **o**, **o** push together
zuſammenſchmelzen, **o**, **o** melt (down)
zuſammenſtoßen, **ie**, **o** (**iſt**) clash, collide

zuſammenſtrömen (**iſt**) crowd together, throng
zuſchauen watch
der **Zuſchauer**, –s, — spectator
zuſchließen, o, o lock
zutun, tat zu, zugetan close
ſich **zwängen** squeeze
die **Zwanzigdollarfrage**, —, –n twenty-dollar question
zwar to be sure, of course
der **Zweck**, –s, –e purpose
der **Zweifel**, –s, — doubt
zweifeln doubt
zweimal twice
der **Zwerg**, –es, –e dwarf
zwingen, a, u force
zwiſchen between
zwiſchendurch in the intervals
der **Zwiſchenfall**, –es, ⸗e incident

Addenda

allein alone
angeſehen (*p.p.*) respected
die **Anſchrift**, —, –en address
aufreißen, i, i jerk open
aufſitzen, a, e sit up
austrinken, a, u drink up, finish
austrommeln tap away
bäumen rear
der **Bauplatz**, –es, ⸗e lot
das **Beſtehen** existence
der **Beutel**, –s, — bag
die **Blondine**, —, –n blond (girl)
brauchbar useable
die **Brücke**, —, –n bridge
das **Bücherpaket**, –es, –e bundle of books
das **Büchlein**, –s, — small book
dahinter behind it
dankbar grateful
daſtehen, ſtand da, dageſtanden stand there
das **Deckenlicht**, –es dome light
das **Denkproblem**, –s, –e philosophical problem
deprimieren depress
diskutieren discuss
Donnerwetter: Zum —! Confound you
einbrechen, a, o break in, disturb
das **Elternhaus**, –es, ⸗er home (of one's parents)
erwachſen (*p.p.*) grown up
etwas: ſo — such a thing
fallen: ins Wort — interrupt
der **Feigling**, –s, –e coward
das **Fenſterglas**, –es window-pane
die **Flaſche**, —, –n bottle
das **Flugzeug**, –es, –e airplane
die **Frage: eine — ſtellen** ask a question
der **Franzoſe**, –n, –n Frenchman
freuen: ſich — über be happy about
froh happy
das **Ganze** all, the entire amount
das **Garagendach**, –es, ⸗er garage roof
die **Geldſorge**, —, –n financial worry
gern haben like
gießen, o, o pour, cast
grün green, immature
das **Halsband**, –es, ⸗er necklace
haſtig hasty
der **Haupterportartikel**, –s, — chief article of export
das **Hausdach**, –es, ⸗er house roof
herausnehmen, a, o take out
heraustreten, a, e (**iſt**) step outside
hervortreten, a, e (**iſt**) step forward, emerge
die **Herzogin**, —, –nen duchess
hierfür for this
hinab down
hinaufſchleichen, i, i sneak up(stairs)
hinaus outside

hinausgehen (ist) go outside
hinein in(side)
hineinfahren, u, a (ist) drive into, run into
hinunterrufen, ie, u call down
höflich polite
hundertmal a hundred times
inmitten in the midst of
jedoch however
die **Kaiserin**, —, **-nen** empress
die **Kampffront**, —, **-en** line of scrimmage
die **Kenntnis** knowledge, understanding
die **Kugel**, —, **-n** bullet
das **Kupfer**, **-s** copper
der **Lärm**, **-s** noise
lassen: sein Leben — die
das **Literaturdenkmal**, **-s**, **¨er** literary monument
der **Maskenball**, **-s**, **¨e** masked ball
die **Menschheit**, — humanity, mankind
die **Mischung**, —, **-en** mixture
das **Museum**, **-s**, **Museen** museum
der **Museumsdiener**, **-s**, — museum guard
die **Nachtluft**, —, **¨e** night air
niederknien kneel down
noch: noch nicht not yet
das **Notizbuch**, **-es**, **¨er** notebook
obwohl although
der **Parkplatz**, **-es**, **¨e** parking lot
patrouillieren patrol
praktisch practical
rammen ram, run into
das **Regenwasser** rain water
regnen rain
die **Reinheit**, — purity
die **Reparatur**, —, **-en** repair
die **Sammetdecke**, —, **-n** velvet cover
der **Schmied**, **-es**, **-e** (gold)smith
die **Schularbeiten** (*pl.*) homework
die **Seitensprünge** (*pl.*) side stepping
siegen be victorious
sinnlos senseless, meaningless
sorglos without worries
soviel that much
das **Spielfeld**, **-es**, **-er** playing field
die **Spielfront**, —, **-en** line
stehlen, a, o steal
stets always, continually
strafen punish
die **Studien** (*pl.*) studies
der **Taler**, **-s**, — taler; old silver coin, originally worth three marks.
der **Teller**, **-s**, — plate
der **Ton**, **-es**, **¨e** tone, sound
das **Tor**, **-es**, **-e** goal (post)
überliefern turn over
der **übernächste** the one after that
die **Übertreibung**, —, **-en** exaggeration
die **Umsitzenden** (*pl.*) people sitting near him
die **Vaterstadt**, —, **¨e** native town, home town
vereinigt (*p.p.*) united
vollspritzen splash
vorbereiten prepare
der **Waffenfachmann**, **-es**, **-leute** expert of arms
das **Wägelchen**, **-s**, — little car
wesentlich essential
wischen wipe
eine **Zeitlang** for a time
zusammenbringen bring together, raise
der **Zusammenstoß**, **-es**, **¨e** collision
zweit- second

Index

(*Numbers refer to pages; § refers to sections in the appendix*)

ablaut classes, § 35
accusative
  after prepositions, 33
  direct object, 23, 33
  idiomatic uses, 33, 284
adjectives
  as adverbs, § 23
  as nouns, 218
  comparison, 265, § 20
  declension, 15, 74, § 16–18
  description, § 15–18
  limiting, § 11–14
  numeral, § 19
  possessive, 44
  predicate, 74, § 23
adverbs
  comparison, § 20
  position, § 5
am- phrases, § 23
article
  contraction, 97
  definite, 7, 23, § 11
  indefinite, 15, 23, § 13
attribute, the long, 206, 277
auxiliaries
  haben, sein, werden, § 29–31
  modal, 129, 233, 234
capital letters, 7, 32
cases
  accusative, 23, 33
  accusative of time, 33, 284
  dative, 23
  dative of possession, 291
  genitive, 107
classes of verbs, § 35
comparative, 265, § 20
comparison of adjectives, 265, § 20
compounds
  inseparable, 232
  separable, 54, 232
conditional, 141
conjugation; paradigm of
  sein, haben, lernen, sprechen, werden, § 29–33
conjunctions
  co-ordinating, § 9
  subordinating, 180, § 7
contractions, 97
da- compounds, 98
  introducing dependent clauses or infinitive clauses, 283, 307, 313, 319, 325
dates, 108
dative, 23
  after prepositions, 23, 97
  indirect object, 23
  of possession, 291
dative plural, 65
days of the week, 35
declension
  adjective, 74, § 16–18
  nouns, 23, 65, 107, 108
der- words, 24, § 12
direct object, 15
double infinitive, 234
ein- words, 44, § 14
erst, 284, 290, 304
future, 119
future perfect, 249
ge- omitted, 233
gender of nouns, 7
  rules for determining, 7, 206
genitive, 107
  after prepositions, 107
  idiomatic uses, 296
German print, § 2
gern, § 21
Gothic type, § 2
her, 309, 323
hin, 309
imperative
  conventional, 14
  familiar, 23
  formation, 192
  infinitive as, 205, 306
indem, 308
indirect statement, 266
indirect object, 23
infinitive
  as noun, 205
  double, 234
  for imperative, 205
  position, 86
  present, 119
  passive, 308

past, 233
interrogative pronouns, 152
intransitive verbs, 86
inverted word order, 7, 266, 299, 317, 343, § 6
lassen, 170, 286, 288, 316
long attribute, 206, 277
mixed verbs, 249
modal auxiliaries, 129, 233, 234, 294
months, 35
nouns
declension, 23, 65, 107, 108
formation of plural, 64
principal parts, 107
rules for determining gender, 206
rules for determining plural, 218
numerals, 56, 67
ohne zu, 286
omission of **'wenn',** 317, 343
participles
present, 170
past, 170, 233
passive voice, 108, 153, 219, 314, § 34
past infinitive, 233
past participle, 170
idiomatic use of, 233
past perfect, 85
past tense
strong verbs, 180
weak verbs, 169
personal pronouns, 33, 43, § 24
plural of nouns, 64
rules for determining, 218
possessive adjectives, 44
predicate adjective, 74
prefixes
inseparable, 232
separable, 54, 232
variable, 232
prepositions with
accusative, 33, 97, § 26
dative, 23, 97, § 27
genitive, 107, § 25
dative or accusative, 97, § 28
present participle, 170
present perfect, 85
present tense, 7, 14, 33
principal parts of nouns, 107
principal parts of verbs, 180
pronouns
demonstrative, § 12
interrogative, 152
personal, 33, 43
reflexive, 53
relative, 152, 325
pronunciation, § 1
punctuation § 3
questions, formation of, 7
reflexive pronouns, 53
relative pronouns, 152
schon, 304
selbst, 334
separable prefixes, 54
simple past of
strong verbs, 180
weak verbs, 169
subjunctive
I, 193
II, 129, 141
indirect statement, 266
subordinating conjunctions, 180
superlative, 265
syllabification, § 4
tense
future, 119
future perfect, 249
past perfect, 85
present, 7, 14, 33
present perfect, 85
simple past, 169, 180
use of tenses, § 36
transposed word order, 98
use of tenses, § 36
variable prefixes, 232
verbs
ablaut classes, § 35
classes of strong verbs, § 35
conjugation, 7, 14, 33, 85, 119, 169, 180, § 29–34
imperative, 14, 23, 192, 306
infinitive, 205
inseparable prefixes, 232
mixed verbs, 249
modal auxiliaries, 129, 233, 234, 294
passive voice, 219, 108, 153, § 34
present and part participles, 170
principal parts, 180
reflexive, 53
subjunctive, 129, 141, 193
vowel change, 14
wissen, 131
wo- compounds, 98, 152, 284
word order
inverted, 7, 142, 266, 299, 317, 343, § 6
normal, 7, § 5
position of infinitive, 86
nicht, § 8
past participle, 86
transposed, 98, 142, § 7